The Culture of the Case

The Culture of the Case
Madness, Crime, and Justice in Modern German Art

Frederic J. Schwartz

THE MIT PRESS
Cambridge, Massachusetts • London, England

In memoriam
Pauline W. Schwartz and Alvin D. Schwartz

Introduction: The Culture of the "Case" and the Problem of Publicness

The world is everything that is the case.
—Ludwig Wittgenstein[1]

We can start with a work of Weimar's avant-garde: *Denn sie wissen was sie tun: Ein deutscher Justiz-Roman* (For they know what they are doing: a novel of German justice), published in 1931 by the Communist Ernst Ottwalt, a critique of the Republic's judiciary. One of many works that sought to address the so-called "crisis of justice" of the young democracy, it incorporates real documents and invokes then-current legal cases in the contemporary mode of reportage, disposed around a fictional judge, an exhausted man with reactionary views, questionable legal expertise, and a bad conscience.[2] *Denn sie wissen was sie tun* was published by Wieland Herzfelde's Malik-Verlag, and the cover was designed by Herzfelde's brother, the photomontage artist John Heartfield. Between the front cover showing a judge overwhelmed by case files and a back cover showing one of these legal documents, Heartfield covered the spine with a very specific graphic sign that spoke volumes to contemporaries: the section mark that signaled a legal statute, in German a *Paragraphenzeichen*.

Bound into the volume was a bookmark showing a man caught in an over-lifesize paragraph mark, as if being strangled by a boa constrictor or a terrifying sea creature. The bookmark is based on a drawing from George Grosz's portfolio *Hintergrund* (Backdrop) of 1928, where it bore the title *Rechtsordnung* (Rule of law) and shows its victim pursued by many more statutes than the one that has

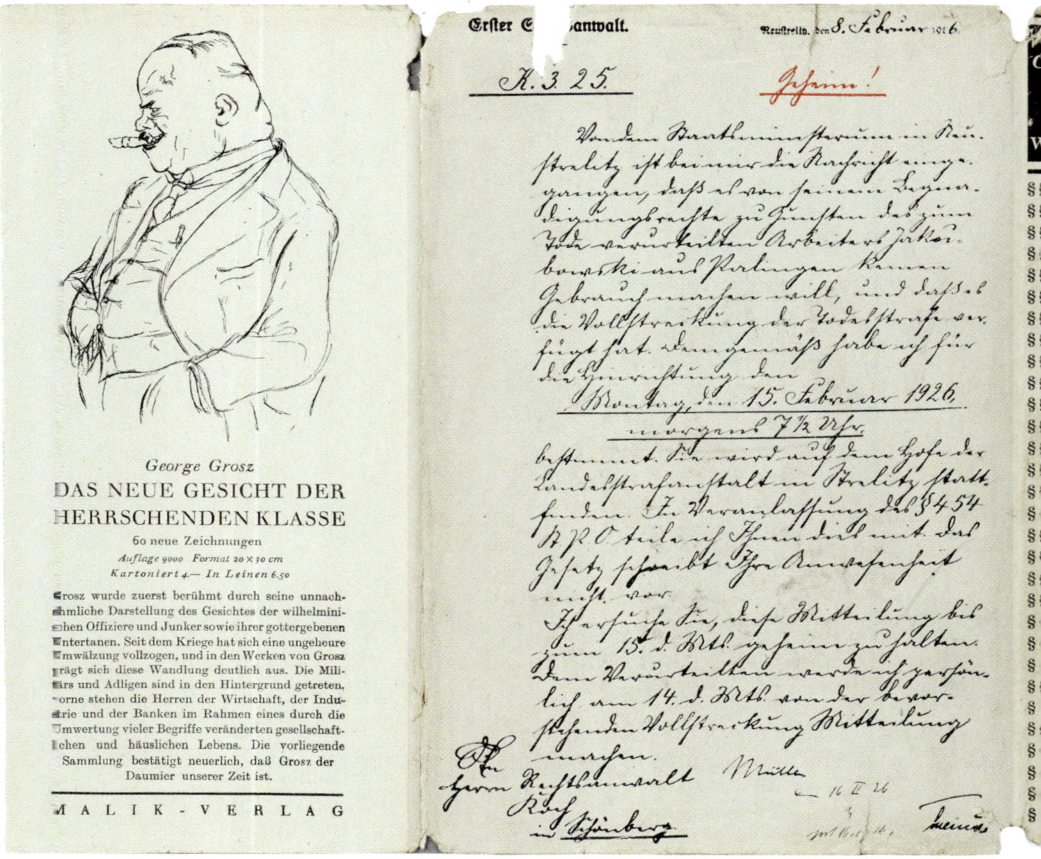

John Heartfield, book cover for Ernst Ottwalt, *Denn sie wissen was sie tun* (For they know what they are doing; Berlin: Malik-Verlag, 1931). Akademie der Künste, Berlin, Kunstsammlung, John Heartfield 70200/JH 3063. © The Heartfield Community of Heirs/DACS 2022.

caught him. *Hintergrund* contained two other sheets in which the graphic mark is presented as a character in a violent drama. In one, titled *Wir sind zum horchen geboren* (We are born to obey), the mark rises like a vision over the corpse of a soldier; in the other, *Der Lebensbaum* (The tree of life), it turns, like a Jugendstil ornament, into a tree from whose branches hang victims of justice.

Now Ottwalt had studied law, and Herzfelde, Heartfield, and Grosz all had bitter experience with the machinery of German justice. The last three appeared before the courts regularly, prosecuted for blasphemy and obscenity as well as for treasonous political subversion. I shall explore in detail some of those cases

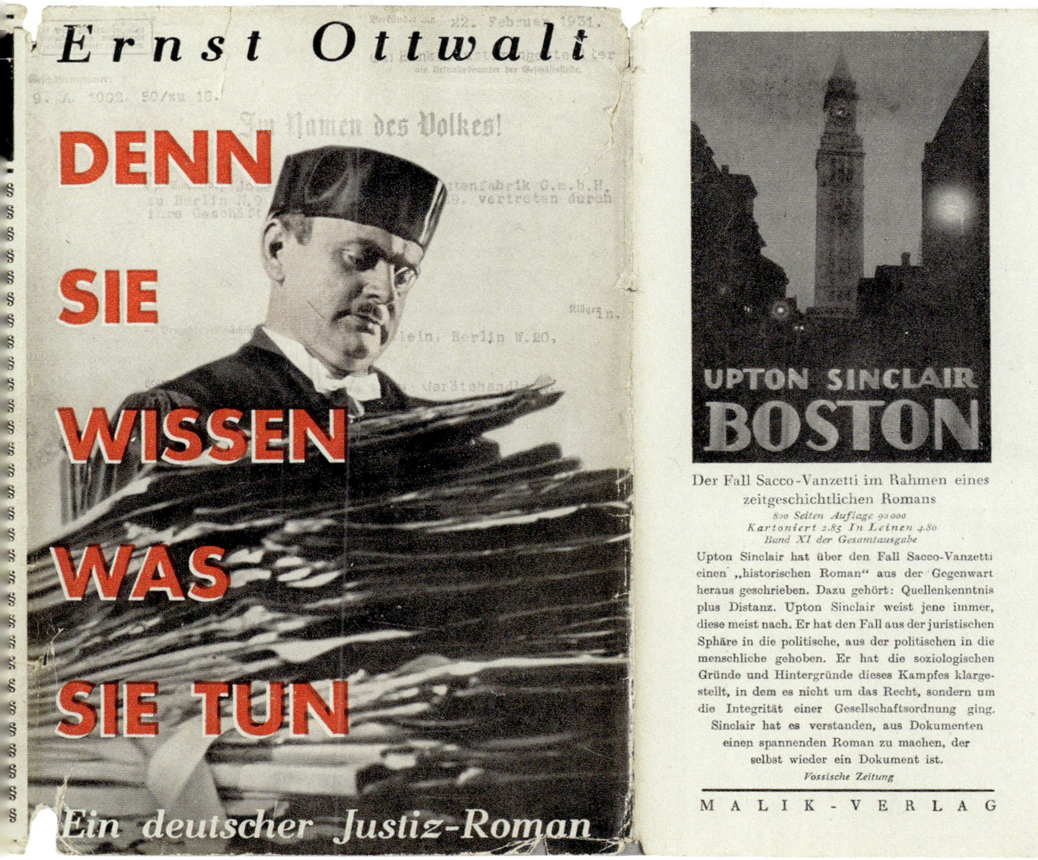

in the chapters that follow. But the curved mark of the legal statute was familiar far beyond the circles of the political left or the artistic avant-garde. Indeed, the ominous ornament insinuated itself into the everyday life and ordinary speech of the time. Certainly women knew chapter and verse of the law that made abortion illegal: the infamous §218 of the criminal code that denied safe termination to those who could not convince, or pay, a doctor to certify its medical necessity, a law which turned millions of women into criminals. In the year of a campaign against the abortion clause, Alice Lex-Nerlinger painted a monument to the toppling of the statute. And, as if it were a character in the story, the graphic mark snakes through Mela Hertwig's nightmarish novella of an immaculate conception and its legal consequences,

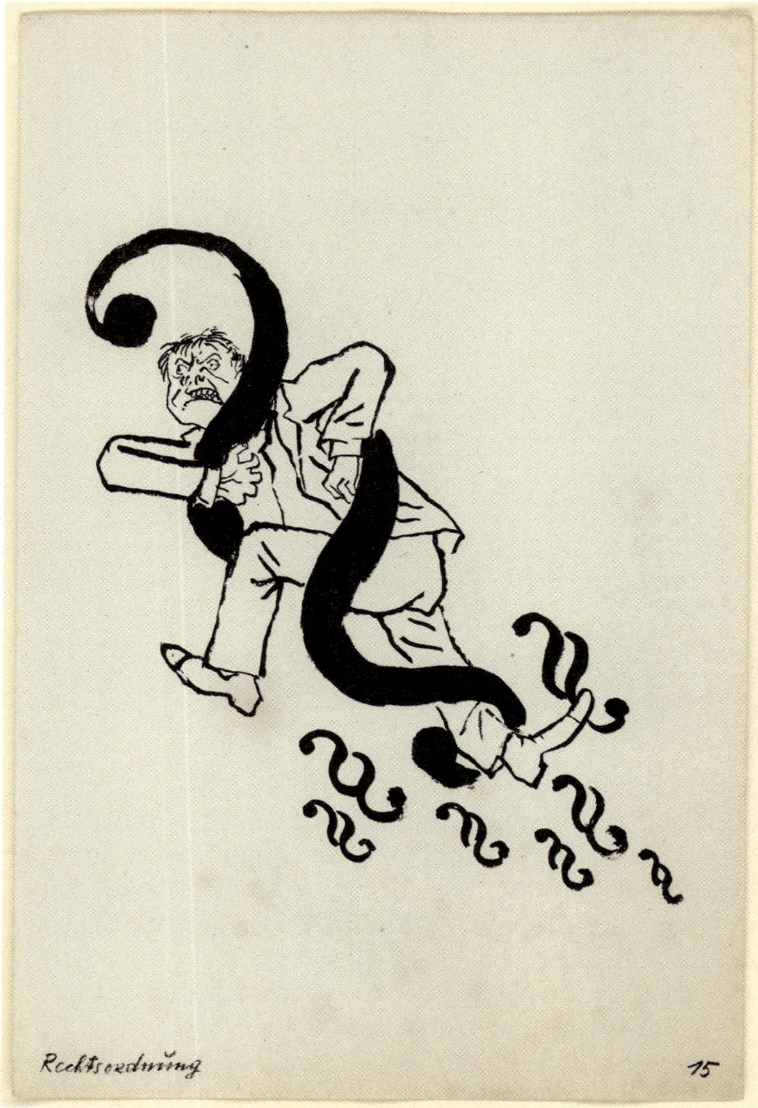

George Grosz, *Rechtsordnung* (Rule of law). From *Hintergrund* (Berlin: Malik-Verlag, 1928), no. 15. Photo © bpk/Kupferstichkabinett, SMB, Dietmar Katz. © Estate of George Grosz, Princeton, NJ/DACS 2022.

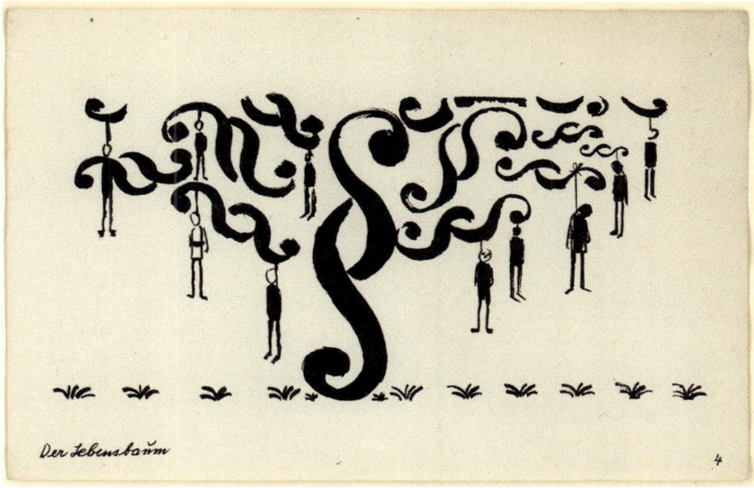

George Grosz, *Der Lebensbaum* (The tree of life). From *Hintergrund* (Berlin: Malik-Verlag, 1928), no. 4. Photo © bpk/Kupferstichkabinett, SMB, Dietmar Katz. © Estate of George Grosz, Princeton, NJ/DACS 2022.

"Der phantastische Paragraph" (The fantastical paragraph). Finally the symbol and the state prosecutor become one: "You are a Paragraph," the protagonist Sabine says contemptuously to her accuser, before she is returned to her prison cell.[3]

Contemporary court reporting reveals something surprising: the high level of legal expertise which a general public was exposed to, and clearly interested in. Indeed, an increasing number of citizens learned how to use the courts for their own purposes, producing an efflorescence of cases of slander or defamation. These cases often show an awareness of the statutes at play. Gabriele Tergit recounts an episode in which insults were traded in terms of the criminal code: "You're just a §51!" shouts one aggrieved neighbor to another in one of these cases, referring to the statute by which someone of unsound mind could not be convicted of a crime. The other party retorts: "Then you're a case of §175," invoking the statute against homosexual acts or bestiality.[4]

We see abundant evidence, in other words, of a fascination not only with crime—a perennial interest—but also with what constitutes crime in the changing legal codes of the time, with what the application of these legal codes reveals about society, with the complexities of justice and the tangible ways all these matters intersect with the everyday life of citizens. Consider two

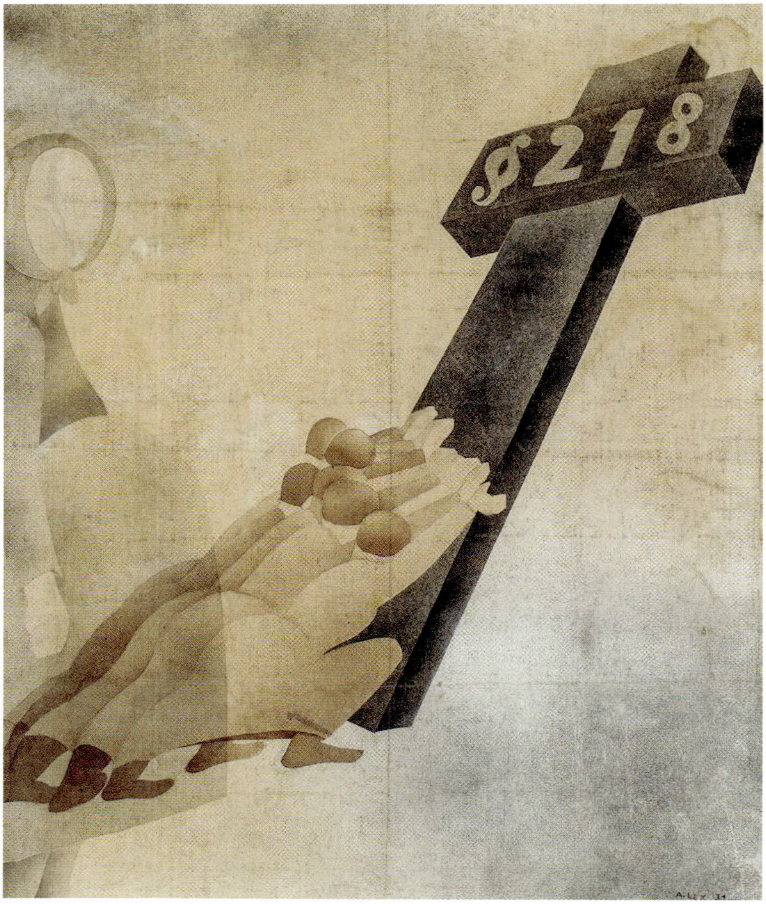

Alice Lex-Nerlinger, *Paragraph 218*, 1931. Pencil and airbrush on canvas, 95 × 76.5 cm.
© S. Nerlinger. Courtesy Stiftung Stadtmuseum Berlin, photograph Michael Setzpfandt.

bestselling German novels of the early twentieth century. Jakob Wassermann's *Der Fall Maurizius* concerns a man sentenced to life in prison—he was spared the death penalty—for the murder of his wife, a crime of which, we learn, he is innocent.[5] The book is one of many to look at judicial errors in a critique of the contemporary administration of justice. Ricarda Huch's equally successful *Der Fall Deruga* is a courtroom drama about the murder of the protagonist's ex-wife; the issue on which the plot ultimately turns is euthanasia.[6]

Of course there were miscarriages of justice—real and claimed. One inspiration for Wassermann's *Der Fall Maurizius* was probably the case of Carl Hau, a dashing young lawyer accused of killing his mother-in-law on purely circumstantial evidence in 1907. Till his death in 1926 he maintained his innocence. After serving seventeen years in prison—twelve of them in solitary confinement—Hau was released. The publicity surrounding the case was intense and the issues it raised were broad. Widespread public attention came to be focused on the use of evidence in court, the role of the judge and his instructions to the jury, investigative and courtroom procedure. After his release Hau published two extraordinarily popular accounts of his trial and incarceration.[7] These in turn prompted a new debate: should there be limits to convicted criminals' freedom of expression? If not, are they thus in a position to profit from publicizing their acts? The case came to be a lens through which a large and ever-expanding set of issues came into focus.

And then there were gruesome cases of serial murder. Perhaps the most famous today was that of Fritz Haarmann, the "werewolf of Hannover," executed in 1925 for the sexual murder of twenty-four boys and young men.[8] But just as widely discussed were others: Peter Kürten of Düsseldorf, who was convicted of nine counts of assault and murder and executed in 1931, and who had attempted to drink the blood of his victims; Carl Großmann, who took his life in prison awaiting execution for murder and cannibalism; or Fritz Angerstein, a quiet man who killed his wife and seven others with an axe and other improvised weapons in 1924.[9] There is no reason to dwell on the details; the reader can find them elsewhere. What is significant, though, is that these horrific crimes served as reference points for the public, which had for years been made aware of them through the development of the popular press, especially the growing tabloid press, as well as crime magazines, scientific and pseudo-scientific literature, films, and even songs.[10] These grisly events were, in other words, part of the spectacularization of news in general and of crime in particular. Even respected newspapers employed court reporters with regular columns and wide readerships.[11]

But I think the notion of "spectacularization" fails to do justice to the widespread discussions of crime, madness, justice, and their resonances. The Haarmann case occasioned a thoughtful and disturbing account by the philosopher Theodor Lessing, again a critique of law enforcement and the administration of justice, of the complicity of the police with the criminals they were meant to pursue, and the new and central role of psychiatric expertise in the courts.[12] Siegfried Kracauer wrote searching essays on the meaning of mass murder—his example was Fritz Angerstein, author of what Kracauer called a "crime without a criminal."[13] Kracauer was concerned with the strange disjunction between the modest, indeed mediocre, anonymity of modern middle-class life and the excessive acts of violence that lay just below its surface. And the court reporters themselves were crucial to developing attention to, and critiques of, the workings of justice. They took seriously their role of holding administered justice to the standards of both decency and sense. Popular court reporters such as Paul Schlesinger (who wrote under the pen-name "Sling"), Gabriele Tergit, Moritz Goldstein, and Kurt Tucholsky in fact mediated expertise: they discussed the different statutes that could be invoked in a case and the important distinctions between them; they gave insight into the role of expert witnesses, whether psychiatrists or forensic experts; they showed the way political crimes were dealt with in court; they followed in detail the numerous and often strange cases in which prominent figures were involved.[14]

In the history of art, we encounter a related phenomenon in some of the most disturbing works of the time: the so-called *Lustmord* images, graphic representations of sexual murder by artists such as George Grosz, Otto Dix, Rudolf Schlichter, and others.[15] Scholars have identified many of their visual sources and have situated the works in their social-historical context: in particular, scholarship rooted in feminist and psychoanalytical approaches has convincingly interpreted these images at the limits of madness in relation to threats to masculine identity in the wake of the First World War.[16] Such works raise fundamental concerns about both the widespread violence toward women then and now, and also about the role of these images as sources of (male) visual pleasure. Scholars have also pointed out that these images of sexual crime were widespread before the war and have explored the way they represented a highly developed set of tropes with complex meanings.[17] So how do they sit in the wider context of public concern with law, crime, and accountability, and what do they tell us about that culture? How do they relate to the many literary accounts of murder and violent male sexuality?

Though I shall start from the work of well-known artists, architects, and literary figures, ultimately the representation of and reflection upon crime and justice involves both extremes of what used to be called "high" and "low"—and in fact the distinction is probably not even remotely helpful. Robert Musil uses the case of a serial sex-killer, Moosbrugger, to explore both the conflicting emotions released into the public and the thorny legal issue of criminal responsibility: are the insane guilty of their crimes?[18] Where is the line of criminal responsibility drawn? The same matters were raised in newspapers, "serious" and mass-market, in novels and "penny dreadfuls"; they were simultaneously spectacular, mundane, and the object of highly specialized expert knowledge. They were discussed in different corners of culture, by publics of very different kinds and often for very different reasons. On the one hand, we can say that such a variety of representational contexts indicates that the uses to which these themes, concepts, and images were put were necessarily multiple and varied. On the other, we can say that they were shared points of reference across the wider public sphere.

It is not the purpose of this book to cover this field in any systematic or even summary way, but perhaps one final example is helpful for its familiarity: Fritz Lang's film *M—Eine Stadt sucht einen Mörder* (M—A city searches for a murderer).[19] It is a veritable inventory of these concerns of crime, justice, and madness. The film, about a serial killer of young children, is replete with references to real cases of serial sexual murder at the time: it opens with children singing a popular refrain making light of the Haarmann case of 1924,[20] and the investigating police refer to the cases of Haarmann and Carl Großmann.[21] The film points to knowledge identified as common and reveals how it moved through culture. Speaking of the case at hand, for example, one police official suddenly falters in his description of the victims, overcome by the brutality of the deeds: "Well ... we all know what state we found them in." This simple statement reveals two things. First, it alludes to a general familiarity with the reports. And second, it shows the sensitive limits of the various media through which such cases were discussed. For though the facts were known in detail through the press, they could not, legally, be shown or uttered in film. The cases, we see, took very different forms as they diffused through the developing mediascape of late nineteenth- and early twentieth-century Germany, and tracking these distinctions tells us much about the conditions of publicity at the time. *M* also foregrounds the handicraft of criminalistics, a familiar topic to contemporaries, as police detectives and others involved in law enforcement published memoirs of infamous and interesting cases, competing with fiction writers and revealing the real tools and tricks of the trade.[22] Forensic experts are shown in action—a dactylographer and a graphologist. The former shakes his head, showing the futility of the search for usable fingerprints on the taunting letter the murderer sends to a newspaper. The latter is unmasked as a quack: he finds signs of madness in the "broken, uneven writing" of the letter, but the viewer knows that the broken quality is merely the result of the letter having been written on the coarse wood of a worn windowsill. Finally, the film contains two trials—one a kangaroo court conducted by the criminals who are so eager to reduce the police presence in the city that they catch the murderer themselves; the other an official court, where the case centers on the question of whether Beckert—psychotic and probably traumatized by the First World War—should be put to death or institutionalized.[23] Specific statutes are invoked, in particular §51 of the criminal code, according to which the insane cannot be held criminally responsible. This is clearest as the charismatic safecracker Schränker, acting as "judge" for the criminals' improvised proceedings, refuses to turn Beckert over to the police and the proper courts, telling Beckert he would just "plead §51 ... and then spend your life cared for at state's expense. And then you break out, or there's some amnesty, and you, happy as a lark ... legally untouchable by reason of insanity, go after the little children again!" And the film makes light of the vernacular or demotic expertise in the law. Schränker, a criminal legend, gives ironic assurance to Beckert: "You'll get all your rights." He gestures toward the crowd of criminals. "Here everyone is a true expert in legal matters, from six weeks in Tegel to fifteen years in Brandenburg."[24] The dense set of cases, forms of knowledge, and experiences of modernity in *M* make it one of the richest examples of what I call in this book the "culture of the case"; such matters were of concern to a large variety of audiences and clearly so familiar that they were the material of irony, jokes, songs, and common sense.

My purpose here is to look at examples of this wide range of works from different angles, asking different questions, putting them into different genealogies that sit—sometimes uncomfortably—between disciplinary borders. My questions are those of an art historian, but the visual practices of the case, as

I shall argue, were so deeply imbricated with other, non-visual practices that my studies may not, in the end, look like art history at all. For the case as a cultural form was not tied to any single medium. To make sense of the images I have invoked above, we need to look at cultural practices that moved through many different forms of public address. I hope to show how images of violence and crime, verbal or visual, often functioned as tropes that circulated between different media and genres, often speedily, at times promiscuously, but often with a certain logic that can be followed. Moreover, making these representations was more than simply troping: they were also complex practices in their own right, meant to make things visible to different kinds of audiences for a variety of different purposes. And we need to look at a wider set of imagery (in various media and genres) and practices (legal, publicistic, political) to get a handle on the issues. The complex circulation of images, knowledges, and practices relating to crime, madness, and justice raise questions larger than any medium (such as "art" or "film"), larger than any single institution (for the concerns crossed over many), and larger than any single discourse or style. What larger issues were negotiated through such representations? Can representations in one medium be equated with those in another, or do they have different histories? Are we looking at something like a specific historical "imaginary," or, in Todd Herzog's felicitous formulation, a "criminalistic fantasy"?[25] If we accept that such crimes and controversies were not unique to the period, what particular work was being done by and through their public appearance in early twentieth-century German culture?

To do this, we must also ask the question of how spectacular crimes could be dealt with in public at all; how they worked in the space of public representations; in some cases how madness could be represented, and to what end; and even if the "mad" had the rights of public expression guaranteed to citizens at the time. The issue here is, in the end, that of the public sphere in general. What were the spaces and practices of representation? How broad was the range of the permissibly public? In asking these questions, my starting point has been that the images of crime "reflect" nothing straightforwardly but must instead be interrogated for the specific way they circulated between media at a time of technical innovations, the capitalization of mass media, and new conditions of representation as legal limitations on what could be made public were constantly revised. These images of violence, madness, and the workings of justice need to be questioned in terms of their functions in a public sphere whose shape and contours were in flux. The institutions through which such matters were negotiated—the press, the judiciary, the medical establishment—need also to be interrogated not only in terms of specific politics or general trends, but also in relation to their status as integral elements of the public sphere. But though this involves the work of thick description and careful contextualization, my hope is that it will also allow us to switch perspectives and draw larger conclusions about this specific (and changing) historical public sphere. In other words, these images of extreme states and actions, or simply their invocation, may help us map the very space of the representable.

My case studies are from the avant-gardes of the time: the architect Adolf Loos's notorious equation of ornament and crime; the *Lustmord* images of the 1910s and 1920s; the literary and legal valences of madness among the Expressionists; the censorship of visual and literary works deemed indecent, blasphemous, or treasonous; and Bertolt Brecht's obsession with legal proceedings, which led him to stage a lawsuit over intellectual property as a "sociological experiment," a way of exploring the modern conditions of justice more generally. These studies are informed by two hunches that prompted my research in this area many years ago. The first is that there is in fact something that can be called a "culture of the case." The dense web of references to crimes, to legal statutes and psychiatric practices was, I think, historically specific. People thought in terms of "cases," whether legal, medical, or scandalous. This informed a set of practices; it informed how subjects behaved in the spaces opened up between these institutions and discourses. People often sought to make their own cases, in the press or in the courts. Or they looked to such cases for purposes of different kinds, whether to gain insight into their world, find echoes of their own experiences, or even to negotiate their own subjectivities or sexualities.

The second hunch is that the culture of the case was a response to the conditions of the public sphere of the time. Perhaps the intense focus on "cases" of different forms was the result of a spectacularized public sphere that required an intervention to be extreme, if it was to be pushed across the threshold of the "public" at all. Or perhaps the extremes of crime and "deviance" were, for various reasons, privileged sites for knowledge of the world. The tendency to focus on cases, to produce them or follow them, has, I think, something to do with the fact that the public sphere was not, in the late nineteenth- and early twentieth-century German-speaking world, working in the classical, Habermasian fashion as a transparent arena of rational debate (leaving aside the question of whether it ever actually did so). "Cases" were a public form through which a certain kind of social work could be done when the institutions that otherwise sought to achieve knowledge, consensus, or justice—the courts, the sciences, the press—were not up to the job.

§

What is a "case"? It is Michel Foucault's notion of the case that has had the most resonance in the humanities in the past decades. For Foucault,

> *The examination, surrounded by all its documentary techniques, makes each individual a "case"*: a case which at one and the same time constitutes an object for a branch of knowledge and a hold for a branch of power. The case is no longer, as in casuistry or jurisprudence, a set of circumstances defining an act and capable of modifying the application of a rule; it is the individual as he may be described, judged, measured, compared with others, in his very individuality; and it is also the individual who has to be trained or corrected, classified, normalized, excluded, etc.[26]

The case was thus the form in which, since the late nineteenth century, power was brought to bear upon individuals by the institutions of medicine, education, and law, and later by psychiatry and criminology. These disciplinary authorities had their own discourses, sites, and practices, but they coalesced around the subject as an object of knowledge and control. "From the nineteenth century onwards," write Joy Damousi, Birgit Lang, and Katie Sutton, "cases constituted an increasingly prominent form of knowledge production and dissemination across a range of disciplinary milieus."[27]

Foucault's conception of the case has been extraordinarily productive, but it has been challenged in the various fields in which he was intervening. Scholars have shown how, even in the areas on which Foucault focused, cases could be more flexible and more varied than the assumption of their disciplinary nature—or the assumption of the success of that mode of disciplinary activity—would allow.[28] Scholars have also begun to cast the net more widely, looking at how knowledge and institutions intersected in other sorts of cases or in other contexts. They have identified other valences, uses, and potentials of the case as form of knowledge or practice. Introducing an important set of texts on the topic—two special issues of the journal *Critical Inquiry* titled together "On the Case"—Lauren Berlant describes this new, broader problematic:

> The case represents a problem-event that has animated some kind of judgment. Any enigma could do—a symptom, a crime, a causal variable, a situation, or any irritating obstacle to clarity. What matters is the idiom of the judgment. This varies tremendously across disciplines, professions, and ordinary life scenes.[29]

My own use of the notion of the case is situated in this wider field of inquiry. It starts from Foucault's, in that I am interested in the law, and often in its intersection with medical or psychiatric knowledge. And it is important to me that the judgments involved emerge in engagement with institutions of social and state control. But my use differs in that I add a third element to this intersection: that of the public sphere, of practices of publicity, of making things a matter of public concern.[30] Berlant captures this potential of the form of the case: it "organizes publics, however fleeting," she writes. "It expresses a relation of expertise to a desire for shared knowledge."[31]

Considered from the perspective of publicity, the case begins to look quite different. Though we might accept the disciplinary origins of many cases, the practices of making them public often *disrupted* the functions of social and state order. By making cases public, or by turning a state of affairs into a case to put before a public, the institutions of control could be thrown open. The case exposed them to public view, opened up the possibility that the roles could switch, making the very forms, institutions, and apparatuses of social discipline themselves subject to scrutiny. There is no doubt about the tendencies of knowledge and power, but the case allowed, perhaps, room for some agency, some appeal to the public; it allowed some things, when crossing from the "dossier" of the bureaucracies into the more public realms of the press, of film, of radio, to be made matters of public concern, to be debated by a public that might otherwise be silently or invisibly subject to the tendencies toward control that are put into view.[32] In other words, if the case originated in the centripetal, centralizing apparatuses of discipline, making them public could make them centrifugal and could challenge this authority. Cases were entropic, chaotic, and often confusing, almost always unpredictable, and as often as not inconclusive. But they ultimately resulted less in the exercise of power than in some sort of negotiation with it. I should add that this is not, necessarily, an entirely happy state of affairs. My point is that these cases could not otherwise become matters of public concern without intervention, spectacularization, or manipulation. As Berlant writes, rather than producing a stable and transparent public sphere they tended to create punctual moments of publicity, fleeting episodes in which reason could be used in public and consensus sought. For this reason, as my examples will show, practices of the case were often improvised and not always planned. In fact, I shall argue that the production of cases resulted more from a set of habits, reflexes, or instincts than the functioning of a well-oiled apparatus.

That, in any case, is my starting point. Questions remain. What could be a case? How could a case be made, and how could it work? What were the potentials and pitfalls? Is there a politics, or are there different politics, of the case? I shall try to propose some tentative answers in the studies that follow. I make no effort to be systematic: the material is far too complex and ramified. My point is not to develop a theory of the case, but instead to look at the specific form or forms of things called "cases" in a particular historical constellation, what work they did, what resistances they encountered, and what other phenomena they allow to come into view that might otherwise remain invisible.

§

And what is the "public sphere"? This too needs clarification. The term is the usual translation of the German word *Öffentlichkeit*, whose meanings are more fluid and varied than the English term. It is cognate with the English "openness." The adjective *öffentlich* can be reliably rendered as "public," but the substantive form has meanings that vary from "publicity" in general to *a* specific public, or *the* public, or indeed just "publicness." Thus politicians worry about what the *Öffentlichkeit* will think of a policy at the same time as the law enshrines the *Öffentlichkeitsprinzip*, the guarantee of public access to most legislative and legal proceedings. But as "publicity" it refers to the generation or manipulation of public attention, and *Öffentlichtkeitsarbeit* is the German term for "public relations." *Öffentlichkeit* is therefore a far more flexible and capacious concept than the English term "public sphere," which implies, unhelpfully and often misleadingly, a specific and contained social locus or zone, a pre-existing social site whose contours are clear. For this reason, I shall use different English words to capture specific nuances of publicness that are often absent from Anglophone discussions.

The widespread use of *Öffentlichkeit* as a term of historical analysis can be dated from Jürgen Habermas's habilitation, *The Structural Transformation of the Public Sphere* of 1962.[33] He defines it, most pithily, as "a realm of our social life in which something approaching public opinion can be formed," a space to which "access is guaranteed to all citizens."[34] There private individuals enter into discussion and relate, according to Habermas's ideal type, in a very specific way. When they gather as a public and exchange views, citizens are required to address concerns shared by all in this realm: the views expressed and conclusions drawn thus transcend individual interests and constitute legitimate views about the common good. Social status and rank are bracketed out: all members of the public are equal, and what is decisive is not the status of the speaker or writer but only the persuasiveness of the argument. The public sphere is thus the arena for the "public use of reason," as Immanuel Kant wrote in his short essay "What is Enlightenment?" of 1784.[35] The public sphere mediates between private citizens, with their individual interests and legally protected spaces, and the state; it allows for consensus about the commonweal that goes beyond the mere quest for private advantage and serves as an effective check on state power.

The public sphere that Habermas describes and whose fate he traces is the bourgeois or liberal one that emerged in late seventeenth- and eighteenth-century western Europe and continued, by and large, to function there, in slightly different forms, through the middle of the nineteenth century. It is an historical development—and achievement—which depended on the post-feudal distinction between private and public that developed in the absolutist period. Citizens were guaranteed the private realm of the οἶκος—the household based on family bonds and the economic activity originally centered upon it. The absolutist state that guaranteed public order (and demanded public obedience) also held a monopoly on public representation: its public sphere was a representative one displaying the power and prerogatives of those who ruled. Measures such as control of the press and public assembly prevented challenges to this monopoly. The public emerged, however, out of the development of bourgeois forms of sociability: Habermas's example is the press that grew out of the English "moral weeklies" and the coffee houses where they were read, in which literary and artistic judgments were debated by equals free to prevail by the better argument. As in Kant's third critique, judgments of taste created a model by which the personal or subjective might productively posit a negotiable claim for the universal. It is this "literary public sphere" that provided the form for, and evolved into, the various institutions of a public sphere as an effective political force: the press, clubs, voluntary associations, societies of all sorts.

The bourgeois public sphere emerged out of a transformation of the relation between the state and a developing social class, and it was itself subject to further transformation. For Habermas, mass politics and the commercialization of the press opened audiences beyond the bourgeoisie and led to a breakdown of the distinction between public and private on which the public sphere was predicated, and ultimately to its decline as an inclusive site for the public use of reason. The form taken by economic interests soon exceeded the model provided by the private household and assumed the status and forms of public bureaucracies. Instead of an essentially artisanal press that served as a largely transparent medium for the exchange of views, increasingly capitalized newspapers and publishers had their own interests that were represented by these publications. Similarly, political parties became public institutions: instead of sites of debate, they grew to be large, bureaucratic organizations that represented competing interest groups and overlapped with the state rather than confronting it. With the ascendancy of bourgeois political power, however uneven and halting, the personnel of the private realm—of industry, the press, the parties—became in principle indistinguishable from that of the state. Public discussion of interests no longer sought a common good but instead negotiated between interest groups. Institutions of democratic exchange—parliaments—were reduced to the announcement of private accommodations negotiated elsewhere. From the late nineteenth century, the state increasingly established forms of direct intervention into the private life of citizens as it assumed the role of guarantor of public welfare and simultaneously became the medium by which competing interests were brokered. Finally, with the development of mass literacy along with new printing technology and new media such as film, radio, and television, the culture-debating public around which the public sphere proper originally coalesced became a culture-consuming public, that now huge market for printed material of many kinds, for film, radio, and other cultural commodities.

Habermas's conceptualization and account of the public sphere has been the object of sustained criticism. The main immanent critique of Habermas's theory is that it confuses an historical category with a normative one.[36] More interesting, however, are critiques that take seriously the norm of inclusive and wide-ranging, reasoned and representative public debate but take issue with Habermas's history and idealization of the *bourgeois* public sphere. Nancy Fraser's 1989 essay "Rethinking the Public Sphere: A Contribution to the Critique of Actually Existing Democracy" is one of the most incisive and influential.[37] Fraser makes three main points. Her first is that access to the public sphere is never free. Differences of social status cannot be "bracketed": the protocols by which the public sphere operates (such as urbanity, articulate expression, markers of education and property) serve to limit access to a relatively homogenous group of (specifically) heterosexual men. Indeed, the lip-service paid to open access is particularly pernicious, implying that competing interests and basic inequalities can be transcended, as opposed to accepting them as fundamental problems. The public sphere in its liberal guise acts as a form of control and exclusion of the subaltern (women, the unpropertied, racial, ethnic, and sexual minorities); rather than a norm of rational debate, it is fundamentally ideological, justifying the hegemony of a group with specific interests. Second, Fraser argues that the desire for a single public sphere prevents the articulation of particular and legitimate voices; a variety of conflicting public spheres is indispensable for social inequalities to be articulated and addressed, and social identities formed and enacted. Finally, she challenges Habermas's distinction between private and public and his exclusion of private interests from the public sphere. Can a public sphere function for the "common good" when matters of domestic, personal, and sexual life are disqualified from mention as "private," as are employment conditions in private industry? Can social inequalities be addressed when issues of private property in a capitalist economy are not considered "public"?

These objections are well-founded. Yet Habermas's account is still enormously productive, and it has been fundamental to the studies collected here. For in the six decades since its formulation, I think, the conceptual achievement of Habermas's work on publics has been forgotten. A look at his footnotes reveals a quite extraordinary variety of sources and the ambitiously interdisciplinary nature of his enquiry. Habermas draws on political and constitutional history, legal theory, literary and art history, philosophy, the history of the press, and social history as well as the sociological and marketing research of his time. He attempts to define an object of study that eludes the grasp of scholars working within the parameters of any single discipline, for the public sphere is an entity that is not identical with any particular medium, institution (such as "the press"), class, or state form. Publicness happens *between* these traditional objects of historical research, and a public sphere of the kind Habermas elevates to a norm, one that is the site of the public use of reason, develops on an unstable and shifting terrain defined by a large variety of forces with seemingly separate histories. As a space between such forces and institutions, the public sphere is as much a process, or the conditions of possibility for it, as the fluid locations within which it takes place. Whether Habermas's account of the rise of the liberal public sphere is historically accurate or not is, to a certain extent, beside the point: the development of a model for mapping the social spaces of representation and effects in relation to institutions, media, social and economic developments with their own histories sets a complex and productive challenge to historiography (not to mention criticism, social theory, and political practice).

Fraser's stands here for many of the criticisms of Habermas's model, but most were anticipated in the most ambitious critique of Habermas's notion of the public sphere to date, one that comes from a Marxist perspective and takes up the challenge of *Structural Transformation* by attempting to rework it for the present. But the reception of this work—*Public Sphere and Experience* by Oskar Negt and Alexander Kluge (1972)—has been halting and incomplete.[38] This is not entirely surprising: the book's arguments emerge unevenly through the main text, footnotes, and a series of appendices; its terminology seems antiquated, reflecting a moment of the New Left and resisting moves that might label it post-Marxist; and its publication in English took more than twenty years (I am not aware of any other translations). Yet in its complexity, scope, and philosophical ambition, it remains extraordinarily fruitful, and in many ways it has guided my use of the slippery and unruly concept of publicness.

Negt and Kluge's first move is to reject any notion of a single public sphere, drawing a picture of multiple, sometimes overlapping, and occasionally mutually exclusive publics. They allow for the vestigial existence of the liberal-model bourgeois public sphere but argue that this has been taken over by what they term the "public sphere of production," which encompasses private and semi-public organs of news and information as well as what Horkheimer and Adorno called "culture industry," and also the public relations of large corporations, political parties, and bureaucratic organizations. (One could do worse than think here of Guy Debord's notion of "spectacle," a concept which has some roots in common with these formulations, namely Lukács's theory of reification from *History and Class Consciousness* of 1923.[39]) Finally, they posit the—or *a*—"proletarian public sphere," a realm of representations and communication that would serve non-bourgeois or non-hegemonic interests. Negt and Kluge are aware of the anachronistic flavor of the concept but clearly wish to preserve the sense of subaltern groups united by exploitation and exclusion; the term "proletarian" thus serves to combat, *avant la lettre*, the fragmentation of resistance to which identity politics can succumb. Elsewhere they refer to a "counterpublic sphere" or "counterpublicity" (*Gegenöffentlichkeit*).

Negt and Kluge also redefine what *happens* in the proletarian public sphere, their model of an effective public; they redefine its work. If for Habermas the public sphere was the site of rational debate and consensus, for Negt and Kluge "the public sphere possesses use-value when social experience organizes itself within it."[40] At issue is whether the public realm offers adequate information and context for a subject to make sense of her own situation, whether she can understand her position and the experiences it generates in the light of the social totality. What is striking is the move from *reason* to *experience*: Negt and Kluge specifically consider the subjective, the personal, and indeed the physical as the very stuff of the public sphere. They are explicit in opening their concerns to the realm of the hermeneutic: elsewhere they define a public sphere itself as a "horizon of experience," by which they mean the totality of information and experience through which a subject can piece together knowledge of the world. This necessarily does away with the traditional distinction between public and private: precisely the quotidian worlds of "childrearing, factory work, and watching television"[41] represent experiences whose nature and causes need explanation, but whose "contextualization" is systematically blocked by the public sphere of production and its programmatic obscuring of a large horizon of experience. Negt and Kluge thus resuscitate the emphatic notions of experience developed by Walter Benjamin and Adorno; they revive the notion of totality asserted by Marx and Lukács; and in line with the project of Critical Theory they reinvest culture with stakes that are cognitive: at issue is not consensus, but knowledge.

In interesting ways, Negt and Kluge also anticipate recent approaches to the politics of affect. Precisely emotions and physical experiences of pain, pleasure, and exhaustion are matters to be both explained and exploited in the public sphere. Like Ernst Bloch, they trawl history for heterodox moments of resistance; their account of the compensatory role of proletarian fantasy is particularly striking, as is their description of mass demonstrations as "sensuously tangible solidarity."[42] Indeed, the last words of the book (albeit in the final footnote) again reorient our sense of the materials to be considered as constituting this realm: "Proletarian public sphere is the name for a process of collective social production whose object is coherent human sensuousness."[43] And perhaps a visual turn can also be seen in *Public Sphere and Experience*: rejecting Habermas's circumscription of the public to discourse and reason, Negt and Kluge write of the public sphere as "an aggregate of appearances that have completely diverse characteristics and origins."[44] Negt and Kluge address these aspects of the visual, the somatic, and indeed the vitalistic in greater depth in their subsequent joint-authored project, *History and Obstinacy*.[45] *Public Sphere and Experience*, in any case, remains a monument, an idiosyncratic inventory of the historical and philosophical implications of the spaces of public representation.

It is Negt and Kluge's sense of the central importance of publicity, of publicness, that has informed this book. The public sphere as described here is less a matter of workable consensus about the "common good," and more about making sense of experience. Sometimes it is a space for the public production of knowledge, sometimes simply a space for exchanging information and experiences that others might use, for processing and understanding the concerns of shared aspects of life. And Negt and Kluge's description of the public sphere as "an aggregate of appearances that have completely diverse characteristics and origins" is central to the notion of publicness used in this book. For a view toward a homogeneous public sphere prevents us from seeing the way publics form, and even speaking of an official or hegemonic public sphere on the one side and a "proletarian," "subaltern," or "counter public sphere" on the other obscures the way publics work. People use their various public spheres and move between them; moreover, they move the contents of these public spheres at will. They use whatever can be represented from that "aggregate of appearances," or they misuse it, even abuse it. They take what they can from any source to do the work of making something public, or finding a public, opening up communication among those who share specific concerns and could benefit from information or perspectives to which they might not have easy access.

Thus at some level we can consider the public sphere in the most general sense as a flat field on which representations can be made and the sum total of all representations that are permissible. If there is anything constitutive for the work of publicity, it is the space and contents of the publicly representable, the sites and materials in and through which publics can form. And herein lies its potential. A public sphere as a set of institutions or infrastructures for specific conversations or constituencies is relatively easy to control and police; as a larger field in which such constituencies *find* sites for their own use, it is much less so.[46] Such sites are not simply "out there" but need to be invoked. Sometimes this happens on its own, accidentally and surprisingly; sometimes this happens by design and hard work, and against the odds. As sites of public appearance and attention, they are fragmentary and fleeting, temporary and mobile.

In the history of art, the notion of publicness has certainly had an impact. Indeed, a special issue of the *Art Journal* devoted to an exploration of the art-historical potential of Fredric Jameson's idea of a "political unconscious" contained as many references to Habermas and his model of publicity as to Jameson.[47] But most uses of the concept of the public draw primarily on Habermas's *historical* account and focus on an overlap of their objects of study with the spaces and projects of the liberal public sphere explored in the first half of *Structural Transformation*.[48] Few art historians have grappled with issues of the visual in the light of Habermas's historiographical innovations and the various projects of exploring the complexities of publicness by Negt and Kluge. Film and gender studies have offered more fertile ground for such work, perhaps because they demand a view beyond media and institutions of the male bourgeoisie. And the most ambitious and productive approaches have extended the enquiries and speculations of *Public Sphere and Experience*. I am indebted in particular to Miriam Bratu Hansen—perhaps the most important figure in the introduction of their work to an English-reading audience—on gender and silent cinema.[49] Her exploration of the way new and uncharted spaces were fleetingly thrown open by the emergence of a new medium, film, is exemplary. Hansen finds in early silent cinema a space in which new protocols of the representable were open for negotiation and the audiences, institutions, and spaces of cinema were in flux. And she gives sustained attention to precisely the issue of experience, the resolutely subjective, the incompletely conceptualized elements of life, as something that does not need to be transcended but can nonetheless be shared.[50] Even if the specific emphases of her work are not mine, the attention paid in this book to the shifting of media and genres owes much to her account of the possibilities of the public sphere as technical innovation intersects with, and stimulates the production of, new possibilities of unpredictable dialogue.

Identifying in "cases" a few of these moments of punctual publicity in the late nineteenth- and early twentieth-century German-speaking world, describing how they arose and the field out of which they were constituted as well as the attempts to control them, is the purpose of the studies that follow. For the issues here are in no way confined to the specific episodes I focus upon.

They concern a more widespread way that the law, diverse forms of power, and practices of publicity converge in modernity. The formation of publics around cases deserves our attention and resonates to this day. The details, the media, the specific matters negotiated will be different, but the challenges of publicity and the scale of resistances to it remain the same.

1 *Architecture and Crime: Adolf Loos and the Culture of the Case*

This is the "current" of public opinion that breaks through all barriers, but can also be driven on by important newspapers, even a single one. ... Often this current is already present, and when the press tests the weather it can decide, like Aeolus, to let out of the bag the wind that stirs up calm waters. It could be an ethical, a political, or an aesthetic wind, but the press must howl. ... More often, though, it happens that, excited by a particular event, a "scandal" or some "case," the great wind of public opinion rises without the news organs being involved beyond passing on the news.

—Ferdinand Tönnies[1]

To raise the issue of crime in the context of the Viennese architect Adolf Loos puts us in seemingly familiar territory. His polemic "Ornament and Crime" of 1909–1910 is, of course, a founding text of architectural modernism.[2] Here, in an attack on recent developments in Viennese Secessionism, the Wiener Werkstätte, and the Jugendstil, Loos unforgettably equates architectural ornament with tattoos, and tattoos with degeneration and crime. "There are prisons," Loos writes, "where eighty percent of the inmates bear tattoos. Those who are tattooed but are not imprisoned are latent criminals or degenerate aristocrats. If a tattooed person dies at liberty, it is only that he died a few years before he committed a murder."[3] Scholars have sought to make sense of this very strange essay by tracing the intellectual sources of Loos's mixture of criminology and the discourse of decadence, his treatment of the primitive, and his echoes of Gottfried Semper, Alois Riegl, and Sigmund Freud.[4] Yet there are other, more direct and literal ways of thinking about Loos and crime: the architect was himself involved in two widely reported criminal cases, in 1905 and 1928. These incidents are more than mere footnotes to a colorful career, and an examination of Loos's experiences with these trials and the press reports about them suggests that we should look beyond the issue of crime itself and focus on what I will call the culture of the "case."

The "case" will be defined in this book as a set of practices that involve the convergence of scientific inquiry, legal process, and the public sphere—a confluence that seems to have been particularly important in the late nineteenth and early twentieth centuries as providing a way for the public production of knowledge at a time when the classic public sphere was not serving this function (if, indeed, it ever did so). The case was a flexible form in which the individual, the private, was exposed: to scientific inquiry, to the public eye, to the power of the state. It was also a form in which these kinds of power could themselves be brought to light, discussed, and called to account. A close look at scandals and court proceedings can reveal how practices of the case cut through a variety of different media, how forms of knowledge intersected, how matters of public concern at a specific moment of modernity were negotiated.

§

Loos, Karl Kraus, and the Case of Theodor Beer

Let us start in 1905, when a question haunted Vienna. Do children speak the truth? Do they know the truth? Is children's knowledge true, and in what way? We know some of these children's names: Dora, Anna O, Irma. But even the names are fictions, masks behind which, occasionally, several patients are condensed. Freud changed his mind between the "Aetiology of Hysteria" in 1896[5] and the *Three Essays on the Theory of Sexuality* in 1905.[6] His negative answer—that reports of childhood sexual experiences were largely fantasy and not the memory of actual events—opened up an enormous and rich theoretical terrain for a different kind of truth, though it raises serious questions, since we know of the appalling incidence of child abuse at the time.[7] In 1905, the stakes of such cases in which the truth of children was questioned were epistemological and therapeutic, but also artistic, practical, and public, matters of the law, the press, the courts, and the police. We need to work outward from this question and this moment, giving equal weight to all these incommensurate orders of enunciation—from philosophy to gossip, from slander to science, from the poetic to the "obscene." These are the elements that coalesced into a sort of cultural form and a set of practices for the production of knowledge in the mixture of private and public that characterized the culture of fin-de-siècle Vienna. These practices converged on specific events, with the problems or questions disposed about a dizzying array of axes distinguishing true from false, normal from pathological, public from private. The goal here will be to try to cut across different discourses, media, and styles to identify a set of practices of publicity through which work of various kinds could be done. In that sense, the argument is more about the "case" than about Loos himself, and making it will involve putting the architect into contexts very different from those through which he is usually understood. Nevertheless, the case as form is particularly revealing about the work of Adolf Loos, and it helps shed light on his polemical recourse to matters of criminality while also raising intriguing questions about the way one of his most important theoretical statements was conceived and one of his most important buildings was designed.

It is 1905: Loos had been hard at work for over a year on his first major commission, the rebuilding of the Villa Karma on the banks of Lake Geneva. His patron was one Theodor Beer, a wealthy physician, naturalist, writer, amateur photographer, and man-about-town.[8] But soon the plans needed to be simplified, the materials made more modest, and then work ground to a halt.[9] Beer was on the run, fleeing through England to the United States for a year before returning to face arrest and trial.[10] He had been accused of showing two boys obscene photographs, taking indecent photographs of them, enlightening them about sexual matters, and molesting them. The case was a media event, a breathlessly reported scandal involving a prominent figure of the time. The trial, held on October 25 and 26, 1905—he was convicted, on scanty evidence, and immediately lodged an appeal—was accompanied in the major newspapers by reports and even, in the *Neue Freie Presse*, stenographic transcripts of the proceedings. Images of the convicted professor abounded in the press. Drawings from the newspaper *Illustrirte Kronen-Zeitung* and the satirical weekly *Der Floh* show how the physiognomy of Beer, a Jew, was adapted to current antisemitic stereotype, with his nose made hooked and prominent, his brow heavy and low, his lips thick and full. Even the arrest warrant (which implies, misleadingly, that Beer had already been convicted of criminal charges instead of being merely charged on suspicion) has a description that puts in bold type his putatively "long, prominent nose."[11]

The Beer trial is best known today because of the extraordinary coverage of Karl Kraus, the Viennese journalist and anti-journalist,

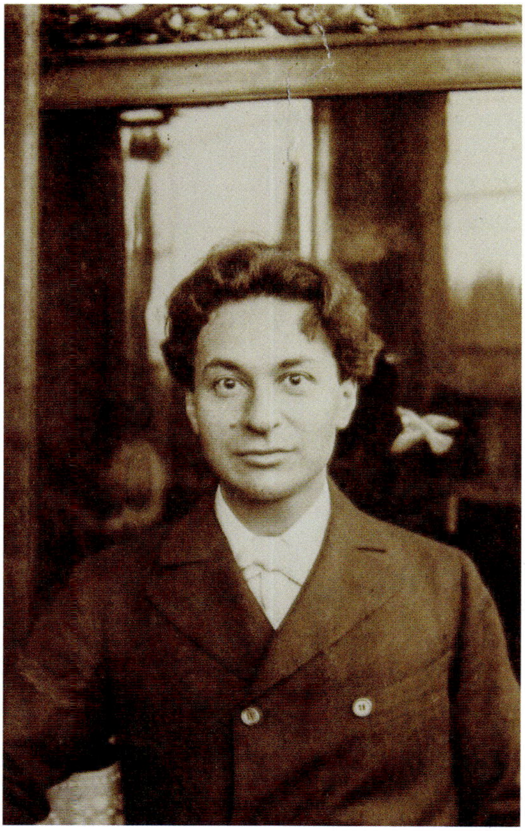

Theodor Beer, possibly a self-portrait, photograph, ca. 1900. Wiener Stadt- und Landesarchiv, Landesgericht für Strafsachen, A11: Vr 4586/1905.

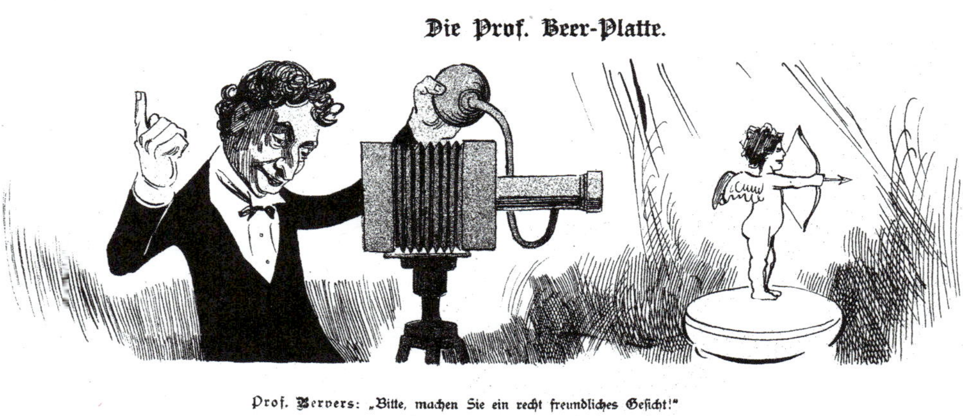

Anonymous satirical drawing of Theodor Beer: “Professor Beer Plates. Professor Perverse: ‘Make a friendly face, please!’” Published in *Der Floh*, October 29, 1905.

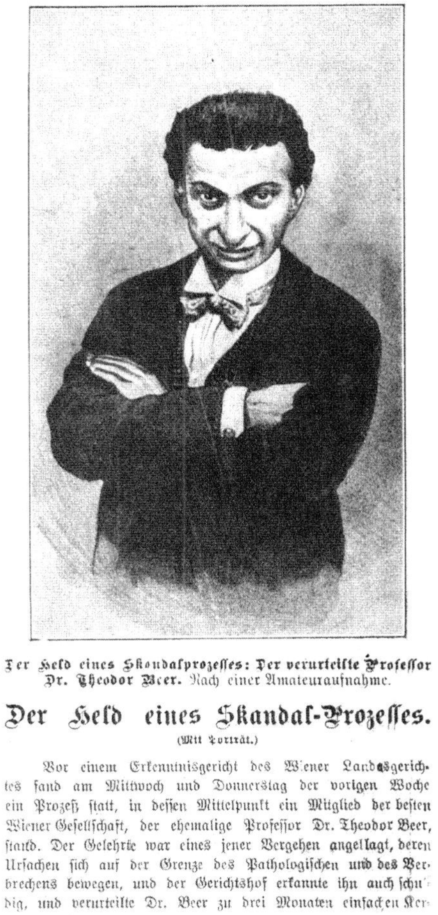

Der Held eines Skandalprozesses: Der verurteilte Professor Dr. Theodor Beer. Nach einer Amateuraufnahme.

Der Held eines Skandal-Prozesses.

(Mit Porträt.)

Vor einem Erkenntnisgericht des Wiener Landesgerichtes fand am Mittwoch und Donnerstag der vorigen Woche ein Prozeß statt, in dessen Mittelpunkt ein Mitglied der besten Wiener Gesellschaft, der ehemalige Professor Dr. Theodor Beer, stand. Der Gelehrte war eines jener Vergehen angeklagt, deren Ursachen sich auf der Grenze des Pathologischen und des Verbrechens bewegen, und der Gerichtshof erkannte ihn auch schuldig, und verurteilte Dr. Beer zu drei Monaten einfachen Ker-

Drawing of Theodor Beer, published in *Wiener Bilder*, November 1, 1905.

the publisher and usually sole author of the journal *Die Fackel* (The torch), and a close friend of Loos.[12] Indeed, Kraus's work can be taken as paradigmatic for the culture of the case. The case was the unit he worked in, and usually it was the legal one. The forensic mode of enquiry and style of thought were central to Kraus. *Die Fackel* can be considered a guide to the scandals and controversies in Vienna and Europe at the time. Kraus's material was precisely the reports that reached the public, the texts of the press. His working method consisted of the citation, juxtaposition, and commentary of publicly available discourse as a way of uncovering hypocrisy and cleaning up the arena of information and debate in a country whose publicity was filtered through a small number of newspapers working in collusion with the powers of government.[13] And one of his main focuses was the courtroom. He devoted extensive articles, and often entire issues, to criminal trials and civil litigation, the strategies of argumentation, and the press's involvement with them. As indicated by the title under which many of these reports were collected and republished—*Sittlichkeit und Kriminalität* (Morality and criminality)—he tried to pinpoint the difference between matters of the conscience and those of the police.[14] His project was a study of the distinction between public morals and legal statute, between public and private under conditions of a decaying, pathological public sphere, one in which the interests of the state were shot through with private interests and the organs of the press vested in the hands of private capital with a stake in government actions.[15] *Die Fackel* served to police the press, to make sure that this public forum worked transparently and was held to account. Thus, in the case of Theodor Beer, we read of the unreliability of the newspaper reports, of the press's hypocritical fascination with some scandals and their attempts to avert public attention from others, their enthusiasm to take on the role of prosecutor, and their blind eye to the excesses of the police.

The Beer trial takes pride of place in *Sittlichkeit und Kriminalität*. It is in the context of this case that Kraus developed his dictum about the prosecution of prostitution and other so-called "moral crimes": "A prosecution for moral crimes is the deliberate development of a private indecency into a public one, a murky background against which the demonstrable guilt of the accused stands out in shining relief."[16] Evidently, Kraus's journal also served to police the machinery of state justice, in particular the conveniently gray area between the police and the courts.[17] Readers learned of the relentless pursuit of evidence against Beer, of his conviction, the death of his ill father during the trial, and the suicide of his wife immediately afterwards, as an appeal—later denied—was pending. The complex distinction between public and private in this stage of modernity, in all its legal and political implications, formed the fulcrum of Kraus's work, as well as an important component of Loos's own architectural theory.[18] Like Kraus, Loos insisted on a radical and complete separation between inside and outside as a way of preserving the space for subjectivity in an alienated, urban modernity: the outside of a home should be mute and civil, revealing nothing of the occupant;

the inside could be whatever the occupant wants and needs—but as the haven of a unique soul and body, it should be resolutely private. "We should build in a way ... that shuts the house off from the outside world," wrote Loos in 1912. "The house should be discreet on the outside; its entire richness should be disclosed on the inside."[19] Let us consider, though, not Loos's purely architectural concerns but instead his involvement in the affair, one that reveals the complexities of the public production of knowledge through the press and institutions of state power and administration; it is an extraordinary tale, and Loos clearly learned important lessons from it.

First, Loos testified at the trial,[20] called as a character witness by the defense on the basis of his familiarity with the family.[21]

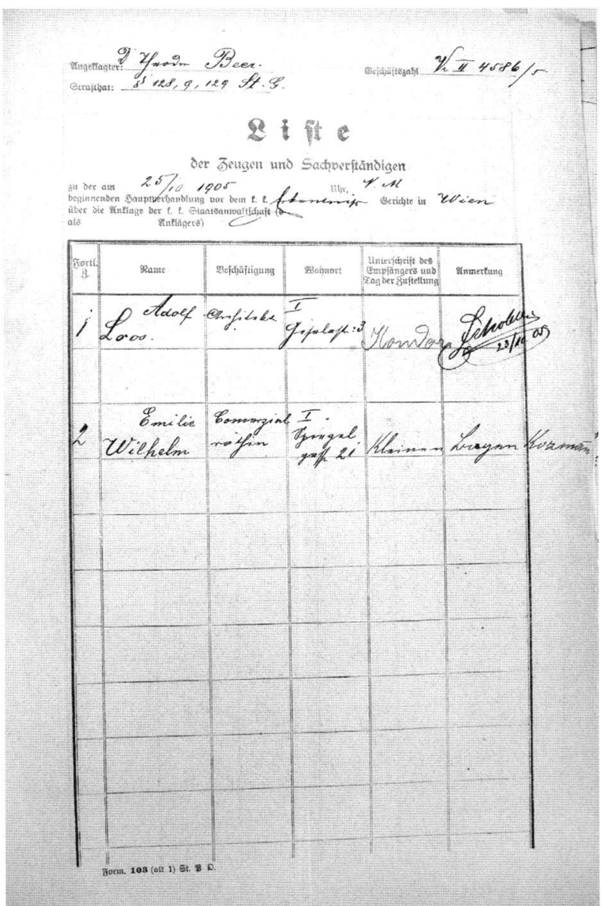

Angeklagter:

Strafsat:

Geschäftszahl

Liste

der Zeugen und Sachverständigen

zu der am 25/10 1905 Uhr, beginnenden Hauptverhandlung vor dem k. k. Gerichte in Wien über die Anklage der k. k. Staatsanwaltschaft (als Ankläger)

Fortl. Z.	Name	Beschäftigung	Wohnort	Unterschrift des Empfängers und Tag der Zustellung	Anmerkung
1	Adolf Loos				
2	Emilie Wilhelm				

Form. 103 (alt 1) St. P. O.

Entry for Adolf Loos on the court's list of witness and experts testifying on October 25, 1905. Wiener Stadt- und Landesarchiv, Landesgericht für Strafsachen, A11: Vr 4586/1905.

Loos and his then wife Lina were essentially a part of the Beer household during a difficult time of their disintegrating marriage (it was in the unfinished Villa Karma that Lina Loos heard of the suicide of her lover, Heinz Lang[22]), and Loos's extensive correspondence with Beer, his wife, and their friends discussed the prosecution of the case at great length.[23] (A theme that comes through is a shared sense of standing above the moral judgments of the bourgeois press, state, and public, coupled with the denial of any wrongdoing on Beer's side.)[24] In the event, Loos was questioned most closely as an expert on artistic matters, on the nature of the distinction between the poetic and the pornographic. He put Beer's own, often erotic, photography firmly in the area of the poetic, and he denied that his friend had any truck with photographs of completely naked bodies.[25] Indeed, the court archive's extensive file on the Beer case includes only three photographs, none of which, it seems, was presented in court. One of them recalls a photograph mentioned in the proceedings: young Oscar Freund's mother spoke of a picture of her son with an unclothed

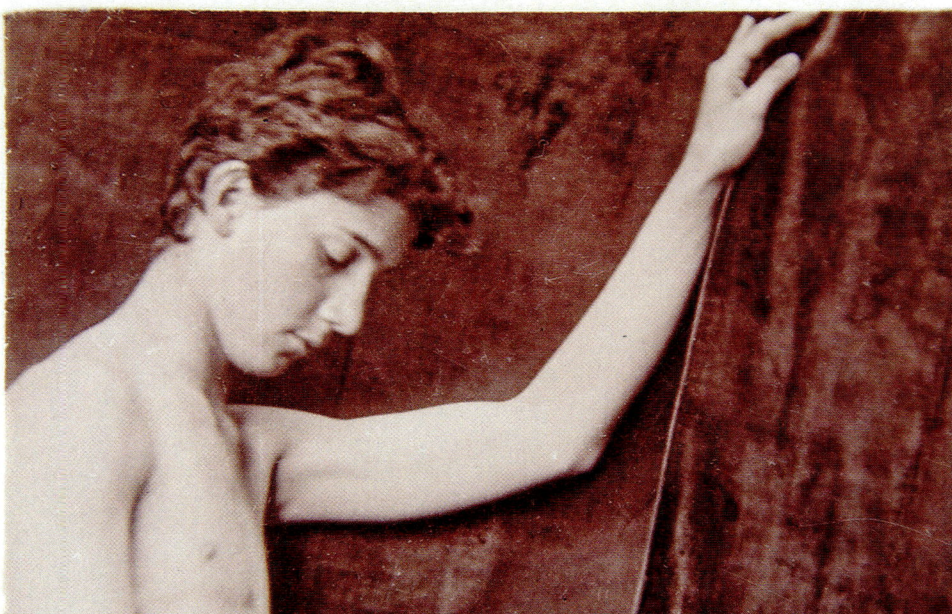

Photograph made from a negative in the court files of the Beer case, presumably Theodor Beer's photograph of Oscar Freund. Wiener Stadt- und Landesarchiv, Landesgericht für Strafsachen, A11: Vr 4586/1905.

upper body.[26] This photograph was the best that the prosecution could muster against Beer.

But in his involvement with the case of Theodor Beer, Loos himself crossed the line of the law. He tampered with evidence and, it seems, perjured himself. Beer owned a large collection of more obviously pornographic pictures of young children—whether he took them himself or not is unknown. Late in life, Elsie Altmann-Loos recalled that Loos had removed these photographs from Beer's rooms in his parents' Vienna home after Beer's arrest.[27] Her account of many matters is notoriously inaccurate,[28] but an undated letter from a correspondent signed "A.B." in the Villa Karma file of the Loos Archive in the Albertina perhaps confirms this.

> Esteemed Herr Loos,
>
> Tomorrow (Wednesday) morning I shall wait for you in a closed carriage in front of Wiedener Hauptstraße 20 between quarter- and half-past nine. We need to carry out the agreed action as quickly as possible. I am counting on your help.[29]

Loos would probably have waited in a coffee house—the Café Paulanerhof, then at that address at the corner of Wiedner Hauptstraße and Schleifmühlgasse.[30]

Back to the picture: a boy on the cusp of manhood, eyes closed in reverie, seen in profile with arm raised, mimicking an ancient relief. It is an extraordinarily complex image. Whether such pictures were indecent or poetic, whether pornography or art, was one matter debated in court and in the press. As a work of art, the photograph is chaste. The boy's upper body is bare, but to assume the model's nakedness beneath this exceeds the image. Such an extrapolation can happen only in the mind of the viewer and is thus not part of the work; the cropping establishes that with certainty. As the trace of the encounter involved in its production, however, the photograph testifies to the presence of an at least half-naked boy posed by an older man in a real space. We are shown an antique ideal, but also a real person between childhood and adulthood. From this perspective, the cropping, instead of determining chasteness, leaves this precisely open to question. The photograph hovers between an abstracted space without referents and the real studio, where the raised left hand rests on the edge of a curtain. Given the different directions in which the single image pointed, it could have been used by the prosecution or the defense. And thus the picture, the most compelling the case produced, the only one mentioned in the trial, the only trace left of the encounters in question, was not used as evidence. In a case that centered on images, it proved useless in court. It demonstrates how the relation between images and the case is so often shifting and unclear: as evidence, photographs needed to be interpreted and thus turned into discourse. If photographs could be used to document the scene of a crime, we see here their paradoxical tendency to dissolve as the *site* of a crime.[31]

Finally, the photograph points to but could not resolve another legal distinction drawn controversially in court: whether Beer was to be judged against §128 of the Austrian penal code—for sexual abuse of children—or §129—for homosexual acts.[32] Beer was charged with both crimes, and was convicted of the latter, homosexuality. In his letters to Loos when he was a refugee from justice, Beer denies being or having ever been a "sexual invert," but also argues against the legal persecution of homosexuality. (Beer, a physician, also offered Loos bibliographic advice on the topic, recommending in particular a work that had recently been published by Benedict Friedlaender.)[33] It is interesting to see how in the courtroom, the set of laws became elastic: instead of the truth of guilty or innocent, statutes could be tried on for size for a verdict that may have been readymade according to extralegal measures. On the one hand, the criminal charges exposed to debate the issue of what constitutes a crime; on the other, they allowed room for maneuver in a case in which a style of life rather than an event was really what was on public trial.

An interview with Sigmund Freud on the Beer case appeared in Hermann Bahr's weekly *Die Zeit* immediately after the conviction. Freud said in no uncertain terms that "homosexual persons are not suffering from an illness, and they do not belong before the courts."[34] With Loos's testimony, art confronts the law and inflects its application; here we see the outlines of a similar encounter of science and the law. In both cases, crucial distinctions for legal judgment were drawn—or redrawn—in public by experts. Freud's statement is interesting in showing the kind of authority he had. It derived not from his psychoanalytic theories but from his position as a prominent professor of psychiatry.

For psychiatry achieved its professional and academic status to a significant extent as a result of its forensic role—in particular, determining whether defendants could be held accountable for their actions. (Freud was in fact atypical at the time for basing his scholarship not on work in the asylums, university clinics, and courts but instead on results gained in private practice.)[35] Psychiatry itself was a product of the culture of the case, a form of professional knowledge that arose in the public area between the asylum or clinic, the courts, and, as issues about criminal accountability and involuntary commitment to mental institutions became controversial, the press.[36] Especially in cases of "moral crimes," of unreliable witnesses, of deeds emerging from the darker regions of the mind, professional expertise was the epistemological prerequisite of legal judgment, for determining the truth of guilt. Psychiatrists were regularly called in (though their contributions were, ultimately, judged by *legal* experts).[37] Interestingly, though, the opening of the legal system to the lay public by means of the jury was precluded in such cases; their subtlety required the unemotional and clear-headed legal expertise of professional judges.[38] Unfortunately for Beer, his proceedings were conducted by Johann Feigl, who readers of Kraus will know was infamous for losing his temper during a trial and sentencing a purse snatcher to life imprisonment with hard labor.[39] And in accordance with the reciprocal logic of the case, the workings of psychiatry were exposed precisely through its new and public forensic role. An early and widespread form of anti-psychiatry emerged out of the reports of medical assistance in stripping the (questionably) mentally ill of their legal rights, a controversial practice of prominent figures such as Richard von Krafft-Ebing and Freud himself, one discussed at length in *Sittlichkeit und Kriminalität*.[40]

Poetic or perverse, erotic liberty or abuse: we also find issues of true versus false in the testimony of child witnesses at the center of the Beer case. The case turned on the testimony of young Oscar Freund, described by his mother as a "fanatic of the truth."[41] But the alleged crimes had taken place three full years before the trial; they were reported by Freund and his friend Gustav Steger more than a year later; prosecution was pressed by the parents, Heinrich Steger and Arthur Freund, whom Kraus criticized for dragging their children through the quagmire of testimony and making their putative erotic education a very public affair. Initially vague, the claims of young Oscar grew more precise, elaborate, and certain over the years. Thus the question of the testimony of children in matters of sexual offences was not only a specific concern of Freud in the years leading to 1905, but to psychiatry in general in its function of servant to the court, as part of the machinery of the medico-forensic case.

An expert was called: an affidavit was requested by the defense from the prominent psychologist William Stern. Stern reviewed the testimony and came to the conclusion that Oscar Freund's accounts were inconsistent and unreliable, and that the young man in various ways "deviates from the norm."[42] The court's file on the Beer case, with a collection of carefully marked articles on these topics, confirms both that the investigating judges took this issue seriously as well, and that the issue was the subject of wide public discussion at the time.[43] The prosecution, however, quoted from a manual on legal investigation by the prominent criminologist Hans Gross (father of the renegade psychoanalyst Otto Gross), which claimed that young men are perhaps the most observant of witnesses (though Gross had long since abandoned this position).[44] Both young witnesses contradicted themselves and also failed to notice any irregularity in Beer's physique, though the latter presented to the court medical affidavits showing that he had recently had a large genital mole removed, one that would have been evident to the child to whom he had allegedly exposed himself.[45] They also made no mention of the fact that Beer usually had his pubic hair shaved, as the pre-trial investigation revealed (this information was used not against the witnesses but instead to establish the defendant's alleged homosexuality).[46] For the defense, the testimony was simply inadmissible, while the prosecution took it at face value. Neither the experts nor the court seemed able to acknowledge, let alone cope with, the expansive gray area between fact and fantasy in the psychic life of children to which Freud had drawn attention in these very years. The question of the truth of children could not be posed productively from the forensic realm, though it often originated there.

The final axis around which the case turns is that which separates public from private. Here, too, Loos was an active participant. For one, he apparently orchestrated one of the more comic elements of the case, helping Beer's wife, Laura, attack Heinrich Steger, the main force behind the persecution of Beer, on the street with a riding crop.[47] Loos's role, however, seems to have been more involved and important than that. There are letters in the Loos Archive begging the architect to help galvanize public support for Beer. And there is also a transcript of a letter from Laura Beer to her lawyer that shows that the latter had urged restraint and persuaded them to keep the matter out of the public eye:

> I am furious that ... public opinion, the public in general has not learned about the trivial basis on which he was arrested and sentenced. ... You have managed to keep my husband's prominent intellectual friends such as [Max] Burckhardt, or [Hermann] Bahr or [Josef] Popper or Kraus away from the proceedings. I won't hesitate to state my position—which, by the way, has long been shared by our closest friends—in public, if necessary with an act of violence ... *Our voice must be heard.*[48]

And so Beer's friends changed tactics. Laura Beer's letter outlines a strategy for publicizing their side of the case. The copy of the letter was part of it: it was sent by Theodor Beer to Loos. In his hand is written on the envelope to Loos: "Private. Not for publication. Please return ... Th.B."[49]

Two conclusions can be drawn from this: first, that Loos, recipient of this transcript with an outline of a publicity campaign, was perhaps the one to involve Kraus, who weighed in only after the conviction. Kraus himself put his reputation on the line with the assurance that he had no direct contact with Beer, and Loos's involvement would indicate how he might have become so well informed.[50] And second, that if this letter was not, then others *were* meant for publication. Whatever its uses, the press was not transparent but involved work of this kind, the work of disclosure. Paradoxically, the publication of private letters was often one of the means of policing the public realm. Freud suffered from this in the very same years, 1905–1906, when some of his private letters to Wilhelm Fliess were published, implicating him in a public scandal involving plagiarism and the priority of Fliess's theories about bisexuality. Freud had apparently shared Fliess's ideas with Otto Weininger, who published them first in *Geschlecht und Charakter* in 1903.[51]

Kraus's strategy—so complex in its literary tools, its typographical virtuosity, and legal reasoning—was essentially to make public matters of general importance that hid behind the rigid facades of official pronouncements, events, and the murky workings of the press, which pursued its own political and occasionally literary agendas. In this, he famously used the tools of satire and caricature, but also simply the transcripts of private letters, documents, and public court proceedings. He named and shamed.

> The "father of the first boy" and the "father of the second boy," the "father of the boy who just testified," the "father of the boy who testified first." ... The genteel press simply named the man who photographed the children naked, but not the names of those friends of children who exposed them naked to the public. Their names are Steger and Freund.[52]

He published letters verbatim, in particular the letter from young Oscar's former teacher Professor Duchinsky, who, horrified that a man had been convicted on the word of a student he had found to be unreliable, unbalanced, and a compulsive liar, wrote a long letter to the judge.[53] Somehow Kraus gained access to documents that exist, as far as I know, only in the secret court files.[54] He also revealed that Steger and Freund were pursuing a private vendetta: rumor had it, wrote Kraus, that both were insulted because they expected their daughters to be married to Beer, who had courted them. Indeed, the earliest document contained in the court file is the offended letter of Frau Steger to Beer's mother, demanding an explanation for the sudden marriage to Laura Beer. Kraus knew everything, all the sordid details on both sides, not just what reached the public from the press. And he allowed his public to see what otherwise lay hidden.

There are two sides to Kraus's work in this respect. First, in response to the official press, he established a smaller counterpress, one known to cognoscenti, that responded to scandal. It dealt with innuendo, rumor, and textual traces of private enunciation, but with the purpose of laying bare the workings of an often opaque and corrupt system. The press was itself, in any case, laying bare intimate secrets. Though the trial was conducted behind closed doors, "with the strictest exclusion of the public," the proceedings were published verbatim, with only slight protection for the protagonists' identities. Thus Kraus's caustic comment about a trial conducted "with the strictest exclusion of secrecy."[55] Yet there is a deep ambivalence here. Though using scandal as a foil to allow injustice or untruth to emerge in relief,

Kraus used the same tools as his opponents: the selective disclosure of private information. He does so here so that the invasion into the private life of Beer is not allowed to send him to jail for a crime that perhaps should not be a crime, or a crime it seemed hard to establish had even been committed. But in the process, in addition to policing the news, he mimicked its worst practices. He exposed and ridiculed the same children he claimed needed protection. He fought mud with mud. And in doing so, he set himself up as prosecution, defense, or judge tactically, as he saw fit, and often simultaneously. There is no doubt that he often acted in the spirit of public enlightenment, and that many of his enemies were corrupt. Nevertheless, while his distinction between public and private, between morals and the criminal code, is clear and compelling, a matter of the fundamental rights of citizens in a democracy, it does not take into account the distinctions that cross this axis, those that say that matters that concern the *state* do not necessarily concern the *public*, or that private matters and interests might legitimately be of interest to other citizens. These permutations complicate the early Kraus's legal positivism in ways that he smoothed over with his extraordinary prose.[56] Though Kraus positioned himself as one speaking from the moral high ground, it is in this murky and ambivalent area of the case that he worked.

The development of Kraus's project after the First World War reveals much about these complexities and about the use of the public side of the legal system and its interface with the press. After the war, Kraus increasingly became what could be called an *activist* of the case in a way that clashes with his earlier legal positivism, which sought to separate moral right from legal code, and insisted on minimal judicial discretion in pursuit of justice. He began to use the intersection of the courts and the press not defensively but offensively; as a legal activist, not a positivist. By the 1920s, the courtroom was one of the main sites of his work. Instead of simply covering cases, he used them to generate the text of *Die Fackel*, in which he published the results, and even the full transcripts, of the cases he *instigated*.[57] Not unusually, he responded to every misrepresentation of his own position or person by legal means. More ambitiously, however, he made a habit of issuing insulting or potentially libelous statements with the intention of provoking prosecution or litigation from those he had insulted. He chose the sites of his insults carefully, according to the precise laws that obtained. The technique was to force the discussion of the actions of prominent people into the public—problematically public—zone of the courts and their coverage in the press. He did not just intervene in scandals; he created them, provoking over two hundred cases. In 1927 he travelled especially to Berlin to call one of his favorite targets, the theatre critic Alfred Kerr, "the biggest crook in the country," forcing Kerr to defend various aspects of his behavior over two decades before the courts and the public.[58] In Germany, Kraus could not be accused of slander or defamation if he could prove a factual basis for his claims.[59] It is in this context that Walter Benjamin wrote of the "demonic" aspect of Kraus:

> Nothing is understood about this man until it has been perceived that ... everything—language and fact—falls for him within the sphere of justice. All his fire-eating ... philology in the newspapers pursues justice just as much as language. It is to misunderstand his theory of language to see it as other than a contribution to the linguistic rules of court [and] the word of someone else in his mouth as other than a corpus delicti.[60]

And Bertolt Brecht described Kraus's strategy as "the construction of a space in which everything becomes a procedure in court (*Gerichtsvorgang*)."[61]

Kraus may still be on the side of justice, but the developments in his practice are indicative of changes within the public sphere of the time. We see the disappearance of some of the conditions in which the courts and the press could be brought together, tactically and indeed messily, in ways that allowed for the public production of knowledge under conditions of a less than successful public sphere in the classic sense. We can see this precisely in the further experiences of Adolf Loos with the strategies of the case. Compared to Kraus, Loos was a dilettante, and he was certainly less successful; but these episodes are revealing about the architectural possibilities of the cultural constellation that has been described here. They clarify the cultural conditions under which architectural work could become a public concern, and they even cast light on Loos's built work.

§

Ornament and Crime, Papuans and Chinamen

Consider again the lecture "Ornament and Crime." It was a carefully staged event.[62] As a statement about architecture, however, its importance has perhaps been exaggerated. As Burkhardt Rukschcio has argued, it appeared more than ten years after Loos had begun to espouse his views on ornament publicly.[63] While the position developed in the lecture can be plotted and the sources identified with precision, recent commentators have admitted that there is really no logical and coherent argument in "Ornament and Crime." To explain its oddness as the result of its form of "satire" and "polemic" misses the point that it makes more sense as practice, a publicistic strategy that tries to achieve a public profile under the conditions of the culture of the case.[64] What Loos does is to draw the weft of a discussion of architecture through the warp of elements that readers would know from the boulevard press: crime, passion, and psychology.

> The urge to ornament one's face, and everything within one's reach is the origin of fine art. It is the babble of painting. All art is erotic. The first ornament that came into being, the cross, had an erotic origin. ... A horizontal line: the reclining woman. A vertical line: the man who penetrates her. The man who created it felt the same urge as Beethoven, he experienced the same joy that Beethoven felt when he created the Ninth Symphony. ... But the man of our time who daubs the walls with erotic symbols to satisfy an inner urge is a criminal or a degenerate.[65]

Loos makes architecture a matter of sex and crime.

Look at a front cover of the popular *Kronen-Zeitung* from June 1909. It shows the same elements used as a sensationalist strategy: the story of the murder of a young woman New York's Chinatown similarly mixes sex, decadence, the primitive, and crime. The murder of the nineteen-year-old Elsie Siegel by a Chinese immigrant was one of the major sensations of the year in Austria-Hungary, something that remained in the public eye during the months before Loos first gave his lecture on November 11, 1909. The badly decomposed body of Siegel, the granddaughter of an Austrian army officer who became a hero of the Union Army during the American Civil War, was found in a trunk, strangled, on June 17, 1909.[66] The apartment where she was found belonged

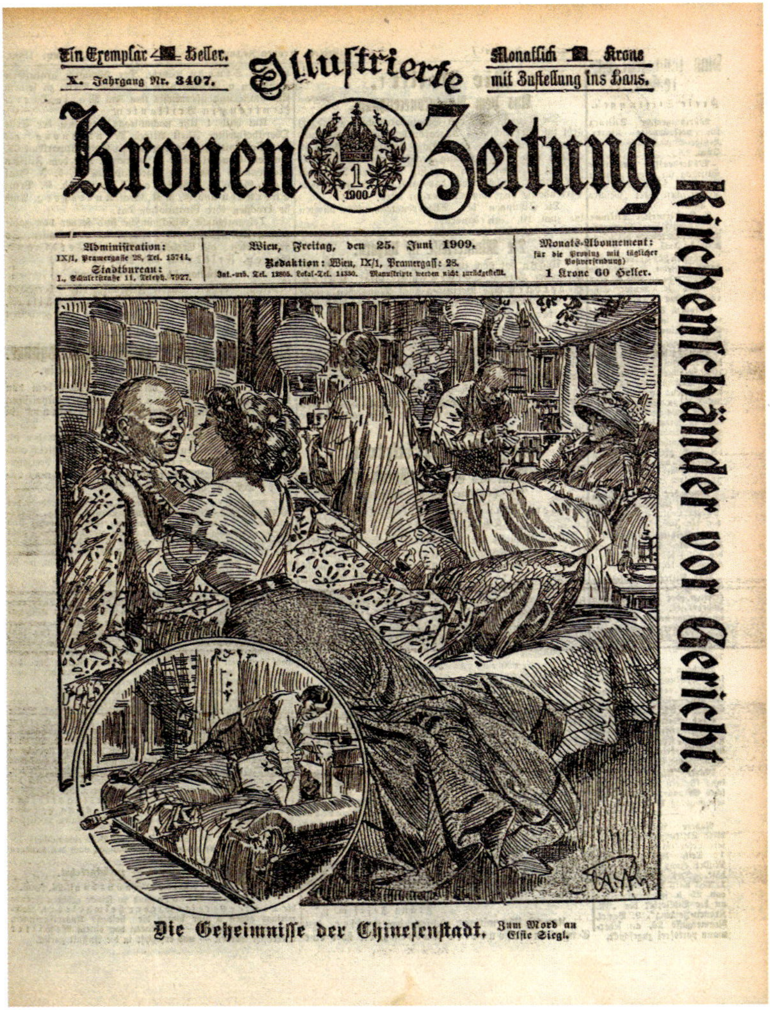
Ein Exemplar 4 Heller.
X. Jahrgang Nr. 3407.

Illustrierte
Kronen Zeitung

Monatlich Krone
mit Zustellung ins Haus.

Administration:
IX/1, Pramergasse 28, Tel. 15744.
Stadtbureau:
I., Schulerstraße 11, Teleph. 7927.

Wien, Freitag, den 25. Juni 1909.
Redaktion: Wien, IX/1, Pramergasse 28.
Int.-urb. Tel. 12805. Lokal-Tel. 14330. Manuskripte werden nicht zurückgestellt.

Monats-Abonnement:
für die Provinz mit täglicher Postversendung)
1 Krone 60 Heller.

Kirchenschänder vor Gericht.

Die Geheimnisse der Chinesenstadt. Zum Mord an Elsie Siegl.

Cover of the *Illustrierte Kronen-Zeitung*, June 25, 1909: "The Secrets of Chinatown," referring to the murder of Elsie Siegel.

to the presumed murderer, Leon Ling, who worked as a waiter in a Chinese restaurant. He had met the young Elsie during her work as a missionary, endeavoring to convert immigrants to Christianity, and became her lover. The motive was presumably jealousy, and the culprit never caught. In the lower left-hand corner, the illustration shows the murder scene as imagined by the artist; the rest of the image is an opium den, with one politely dressed western woman lounging languidly, another in an intimate pose with a Chinese man, seemingly cutting his pigtail. It was a story of seduction, of the allure of the exotic and the primitive, of the presence of immigrant criminal subcultures in the modern western city. Did the murderer have a tattoo? The reports do not say. Ling was, in any case, what would have been called "degenerate," known as a smooth-skinned cross-dresser who in fact escaped detection by wearing women's clothes.[67] The tattoo, however, is what held Loos's conceit together, allowing him to link architecture with degeneracy, sex, and crime, and to conflate the higher discourse of culture with the lower practices of the boulevard press (which were hardly worse than those of the "serious" press).

Loos's "Ornament and Crime" cannot be read simply as architectural theory; to read it so is to flatten out important aspects of its nature as a cultural intervention, one that raises interesting issues concerning how discussions about architecture were conducted at the time. For to juxtapose the discourse of architecture with lurid accounts of degeneracy and crime made a certain sense in the context of the Viennese cultural field, and it was not exactly novel. Debates over architecture took place across the same plane, indeed, the same page, as reports about crime in the press. One example, almost certainly known to Loos, makes this point clearly. In the *Illustrirtes Wiener Extrablatt* of June 26, 1909, we see an article on the recent competition for the design of the new Technical Museum to be erected near the Schönbrunn Palace. According to the article, the decision had not yet been announced, but it seemed that the design by Hans Schneider had been chosen. Loos had entered the competition with a project designed together with his cousin, Victor Loos; their entry (number 22) is described by the author as follows: "Absolutely practical locomotive shed. Not without monumentality."[68] An inch or two below the mention of Loos's entry, the paper's latest report on the Chinatown murder appears.[69] Architecture and murder on the same page: in a way, to discuss architecture in public, Loos had to compete with crime, and he apparently chose to meet it on its own ground.

The Chinatown murder would have captured Loos's attention; he used its tropes, perhaps, to bring attention to his architectural ideas. But beyond a perfectly sensible, if crude, publicistic strategy, there are indications that the case provided both a set of terms and rhetorical moves by which to do so as well. Let us look again to Karl Kraus, who devoted one of his greatest tirades to the case; he called it "The Great Wall of China" and used it as the lead essay in another of his collections (for which Loos designed the dust jacket).[70] This is one of the texts Kraus featured in his public readings; it was also published in a 1914 edition with eight lithographs by Kraus's and Loos's friend Oskar Kokoschka, one of which shows a violent sexual murder.[71]

For Kraus, what gave the crime its *frisson*, its place on the front page, was not only the fact that Elsie Siegel was the daughter of a prominent Austrian émigré. The scandal was that the economy of lust and violence, the power of erotic transgression, had an untoward, disconcerting element. A sex crime committed by the Chinese waiter would have fit into all the patterns, but this case challenged fundamental assumptions of civilization versus degeneration, Christian chastity versus pagan license. For besides the trunk with its decaying corpse in Ling's apartment, police found thirty-five letters from Elsie. They were love letters. This was the cause of the outrage, the confusion, the ambivalent

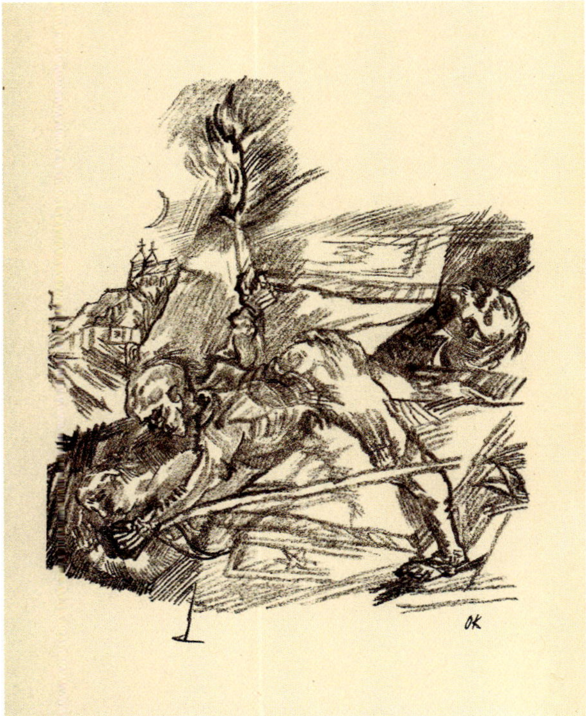

Oskar Kokoschka, *Der Mord* (The murder), 1913, lithograph illustration for Karl Kraus, *Die chinesische Mauer* (The Great Wall of China; Leipzig: Kurt Wolff Verlag), 38.4 × 49.1 cm, Museum of Modern Art, New York, Purchase Fund acc. no. 334.1947. Digital image © 2022 The Museum of Modern Art/Scala, Florence. © Fondation Oskar Kokoschka/ DACS 2022.

and uncomfortable fascination: the vision of a mix of races, of the primitive awakening of a fatal excess of desire in the white woman. For some, this made Ling a demon, preying on the innocent European. For others, it became a tale of what happens when a woman of proper society forgets her place, her culture, her religion, her morals. For Kraus, it simply pointed out the inability of western culture to cope with the fact of female desire, its tendency to lock women in the shackles of Christian morality that granted men the monopoly on pleasure. Elsie Siegel's parents, like Brabantio and his wife in Shakespeare's *Othello*,

> have had their white skins stuffed with lies, and were it not for the murder, they would never have found out the complexion of their dearest daughter's taste. The serious side of life, that ridiculous accountant of their intellectual inventory, only let them enjoy their conjugal pleasures if they were properly declared as "duty." So it takes some pretty strong stimulation to direct their gaze to a side of life in which dear things are exchanged more quietly, but no less urgently, than in business. The corpse in the trunk is just the sort of sensation without which such lessons cannot be learned in this noisy age.[72]

For Kraus this was a case precisely as we have defined it: a crime, a scandal, that brings issues of importance to light, one that moves the press, usually so murky, to open matters of public concern. At the same time, the production of the case is predicated on hypocrisy, prurience, and false moral outrage, and as such can be read against its creators, revealing much about them.

Kraus's argument about the primitive and crime is not so far from Loos's. For Kraus, the larger crime, beyond the murder, was the west's hypocritical subjugation of female desire behind the fig leaf of Christian morals. The Chinese is not degenerate; it is the west that is so for its utter inability to deal with sexual desire, for its attempts to legislate, control, and dominate it.

> The Chinaman commits no sin when he commits one. He has no need for the scruples of conscience in order to find pleasure in pleasure. He is backwards in that he has not had to get to grips with the stores of knowledge that have accumulated over the last millennia. He can face the

> future and survive the injuries that in our world are cobbled together by botched medicine and technology. He has no nerves, no fear of bacteria, and he is safe even when he dies. ... He does the work of a dozen white men and has the pleasures of a hundred. He separates pleasure and ethics, and thus saves both from ruin. After what we would call debauchery, he can return to everyday life with body and soul unchanged, interrupted perhaps to serve a white-skinned lady. He is not sentimental and does not suffer from the flaw of the soul that we call "morals."[73]

"The Chinaman commits no sin": the echo of this line of thought is hard to overlook in "Ornament and Crime." "The Papuan slaughters his enemies and devours them. He is no criminal. If, however, the modern man slaughters and devours somebody, he is a criminal or a degenerate."[74] For Kraus and Loos, the acceptance of natural drives is innocent. What is degenerate for Loos is the primitive pleasure that considers itself culture (and that, immorally, leads to the waste of labor power). More in line with Friedrich Nietzsche's critique of modernity, Kraus considers degeneration in terms of the disingenuous morality that insists on female innocence but must enforce it as domination. Interesting here is that he describes this form of degeneration, precisely like Loos, as a kind of ornament: "Is this the end of a morality that wears its chains as decoration (*Schmuck*)?"[75] Just a few months before Loos, Kraus had already brought together decoration and crime in a critique of western culture.

§

The Goldman & Salatsch Building on the Michaelerplatz

Loos's publicistic moves in the scandal surrounding his Michaelerplatz building for Goldman & Salatsch clothiers can also be considered in light of Kraus's strategies of the case. The story of the planning of the building and the controversy it engendered is a complicated one, and it can only be summarized here.[76] In the elevations approved in early March 1910 by the Viennese building authorities, the upper floors display a conventional but simple treatment of window surrounds and courses, with the understanding that decisions about details would be made on site in response to the final appearance of the lower floors.[77] Loos explained this as follows:

> I requested that they [the authorities] not insist on [drawings for] my final treatment of the four stories [above]. I did not yet know what material would be available to me, as I still needed to locate it in Greece. The project architect [*Baumeister*], [Ernst] Epstein, had in the meantime drawn a simple façade for the four stories. I knew that I would choose Cippolino marble [for the lower stories]. But each block has different veining, and I did not yet know the specific stone. So I delayed the final solution for the upper four floors.[78]

The next set of elevations, submitted in late July, left this area blank, in other words uncompleted. They were approved on the assumption that they *would* be completed with a form of

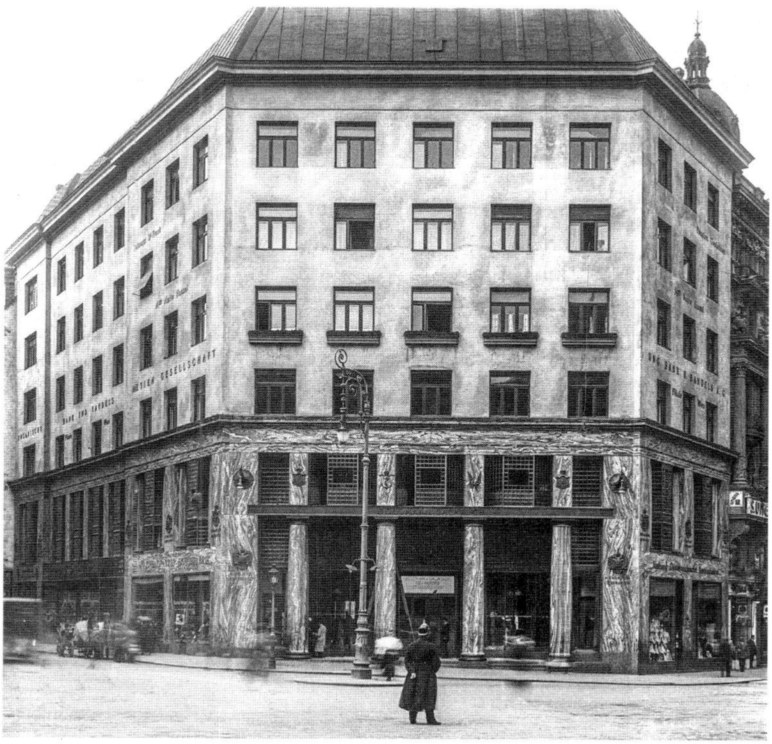

Adolf Loos, Goldman & Salatsch Building, 1910/11, Michaelerplatz, Vienna.
© Bildarchiv Foto Marburg.

rectilinear pattern in stucco; Loos also submitted a photographic copy of the elevation showing the upper floors decorated with a meander pattern.[79] At the end of September 1910, the scaffolding was removed to reveal the controversial bare stucco façade. Whether Loos considered the façade complete at this point has never been determined; in any case, the city building authorities became nervous and ordered a stop to the construction work, leading to the controversy.

Concluding, correctly or not, that Loos intended the façade to be bare, some newspapers then defended the building as it stood,[80] while the architect himself stated publicly that it was still his intention to complete it in the way assumed by the building office.[81] Whether Loos's statements at this point were disingenuous or not, the scandal took on its own energy. The building authorities apparently accepted Loos's assurances, but the matter was taken up in the city council. In a flurry of articles, statements, and a public lecture, Loos defended his right to determine the final appearance of the building. The question was what should happen to the façade, and it was, from this point on, debated in public. It is far from clear that Loos originally intended the façade to be devoid of ornament, and he never would have been able to achieve this within the closed circle of negotiation between architect, client, and building authorities. That it might remain bare had now become a possibility due to the opening of a case into a public sphere of debate. Loos's position was strengthened by various attempts to impose a new façade without his approval; in particular, one drawn by the city councilor Hans Schneider, an architect, with Epstein, and approved by the council in December became a bone of contention. Loos seems to have accepted the fact that this design might be executed,[82] but the scandal was revived by the decision of Goldman and Salatsch to stage a competition for a new façade, launching another round of defenses of Loos's authorship of the building. Loos then suggested a "compromise": the mounting of bronze flower boxes beneath five of the windows; he had these manufactured and installed at his own expense and without the approval of the city (in fact the city officials ordered them to be removed, which Loos did not do). To a full house of 2,700 listeners at the prestigious Sophiensaal on December 11, 1911, Loos gave a widely reported lecture presenting his account of the controversy. Finally, in March 1912, the city council decided to let the matter rest.

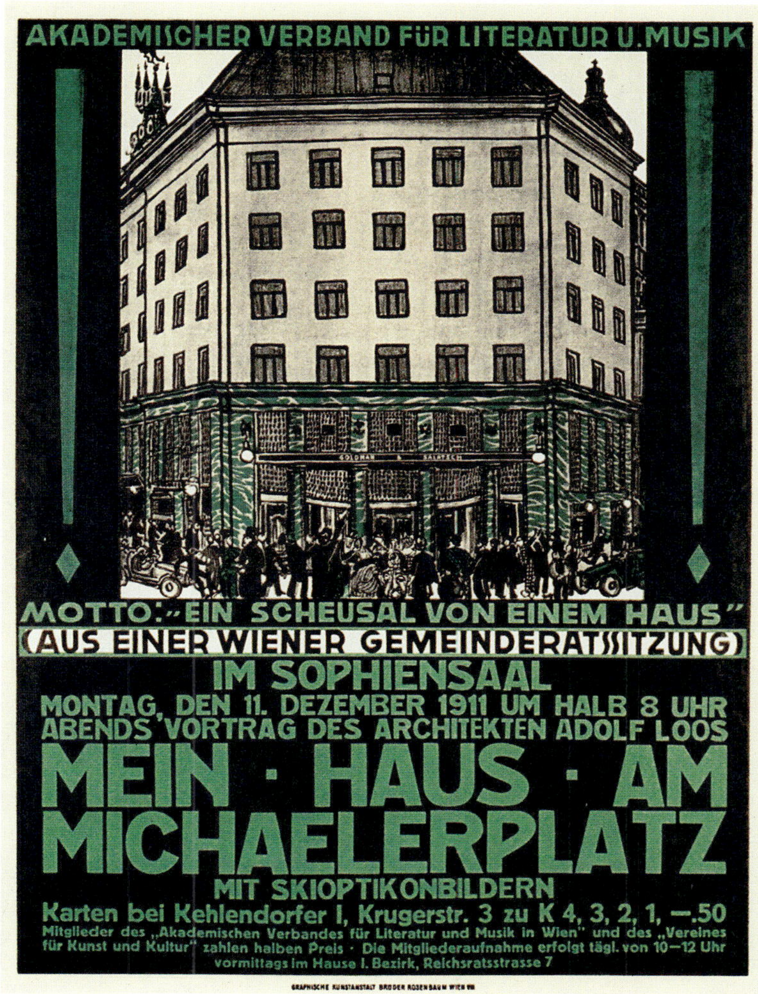

Urban Janke, *Mein Haus am Michaelerplatz*, 1911, color lithograph poster for Adolf Loos's lecture at the Sophiensaal, Vienna, December 11, 1911, 84 × 62 cm. Courtesy Österreichische Nationalbibliothek, Vienna.

Two points can be made here. The first concerns how Loos handled the matter. He went to the public. His lecture in the Sophiensaal seems to have been the turning point, and it is instructive. Here, and in correspondence with newspapers afterward, he named names. "A city councilor notified the mayor, asking how he could tolerate such a monstrosity of a building. The councilor's name is Ryckl."[83] He showed slide reproductions of a personal letter of support from Hans Berger, an architect who later attacked the building in the *Neue Freie Presse*, suggesting that the change of mind was due to personal grudge.[84] He quoted from the protocols of meetings; he disclosed the precise role of various inexperienced and self-serving city officials. For example, writing to a newspaper concerning the role of the official who had sketched an alternative façade: "The magistrate consulted Councilor Schneider for artistic advice on the decision between my façade and his own. The Councilor announced the result on the third of August. He seems to have concealed the fact that the design he approved was the one that *he himself* had submitted."[85] To humiliate Schneider further, Loos read the judgments of two prominent German architects damning Schneider's most recent major building (the Technical Museum in Vienna, the competition for which Loos had entered with his cousin Victor).[86] One is usually powerless against the anonymous and slow forces of municipal authority; aware that the only leverage he had was support from the public, Loos brought the usually invisible decisions of civil servants into the public eye on his own terms, by means of the case or scandal. Though couched in the rhetoric of honesty and transparency, however, his defense can hardly be considered a rational debate over architectural matters. He revealed matters of public concern, but he was simultaneously settling scores. Like Kraus, Loos was operating in a space that was densely woven by the warp of the properly public and the weft of the private. The result was the none-too-clean fabric of politics.

The second point concerns the reciprocal effect of the controversy—the press reports, the public events, the leaked documents—on the architecture itself. Did these practices of the case perhaps affect the design? Loos's skillful handling of the press has often been noted. Most often it is simply assumed that his plan had always been to present to Vienna the bare façade revealed in September 1910, that his assurances about the stucco decorations were decoys to ensure approval, and that the controversy was a battle to achieve his vision of an architecture without ornament. It is, of course, possible that this is the story of "Loos's tactical gambits to push through his ideas."[87] But even those who largely follow this line of thought recognize that such an interpretation is far from certain. Referring to the classic account of Loos's Michaelerplatz building by Hermann Czech and Wolfgang

Mistelbauer, the most careful recent discussion of the case notes the following:

> Should this interpretation of Loos's strategy in fact be correct, then Loos would be not only an ingenious architect, but an even more ingenious tactician, one who long in advance knew how his opponents would react. Friend and foe of the Loos building would have been merely submissive tools of his careful calculations. Now Loos was certainly a great demagogue and polemicist, but such cool cunning is hardly to be ascribed to a man who has gone down in the history of art as a sensitive artist.[88]

In any case, the idea of Loos the modernist as Loos the tactician is based on quite specific presuppositions. The first is a remarkably traditional notion of artistic intention. And the second is a corollary: a somewhat otherworldly notion of how buildings are made. Changes of plans, on-site decisions, retrospective approvals, and continuing negotiations with clients, suppliers, and planning officials are par for the course. An architect uncertain about how the final elevations would be developed is more than plausible. This means that one must at least entertain the possibility that Loos's account of the building plans can be taken at face value; and that the Viennese authorities' halting of construction was a mistake. Should that be the case, and had the officials not misjudged the situation, the most famous building of the architect would probably have had a much more conventional façade. In this scenario, Loos grasped the opportunity provided by the error of a bureaucrat who thought that the façade was meant to be plain to make his own architectural design considerably more radical. Sensing support, he felt empowered in his breach of decorum. In this scenario, the design emerged from the scandal considerably changed.

Or it might be the case that the final building, apart from the flower boxes on the window, those fig leaves covering nothing, corresponds to the architect's original intention. In this case, Loos was still aware that the architect's work happens in public and is negotiated there. Not surprisingly, Karl Kraus knew this too. With an irony that alludes to, but ultimately equates, both possibilities—that the Michaelerplatz building was meant to be bare, or that it only emerged so out of give-and-take between artist and city dweller, bureaucracy and press, statute and opinion—Kraus described the public nature of the architectural process:

> "Never show a fool an unfinished building" an old proverb tells us. ... The work of the architect happens on the street. It cannot defend itself from prying eyes by claiming some sort of "workshop secret." The painter, the sculptor may reveal what is being formed to a confidant or an initiate; the crowd will only ever stand before the finished work. But the work of architecture grows, so to speak, under the public control of the passers-by. The criticism starts already with the foundation ... and the first story is hardly finished before the chorus of acrimony and griping is let loose.

Kraus published these lines at the end of October 1911, seven days after the installation of the flower boxes.[89] Typically for Kraus, the passage is just a lengthy quote to which he adds a short commentary, a montage technique that turns another writer's text into a grave dug with his or her own words. Here he is quoting another critic: Berta Zuckerkandl, a supporter of and propagandist for the Wiener Werkstätte, writing about a work by Loos's archenemy Josef Hoffmann. She and Hoffmann are paid back. At the end of the long quotation, Kraus writes: "And whom is she writing about? Adolf Loos? But no: Josef Hoffmann! Whose expert opinion she had invoked when she dismissed the unfinished building on the Michaelerplatz."[90]

Unfinished? Because the marble had not yet arrived for Loos to decide how to proceed? Because construction was halted, freezing an image of an evolving building in a way that gave it—once the proposition was mooted that the architect meant to leave it thus—an unexpected form that could suddenly be defended? Again, the image of Loos's building that faced the public and appeared in the press late September 1910 tells us little. It showed the bare building for all to see, but precisely what state of affairs it revealed could not be established. As the case proceeded with a momentum that seemed to surprise everybody, no one even tried.

Or is Kraus too being disingenuous? We will presumably never know this either. What is clear, however, is that scandal, whether carefully orchestrated or manipulated opportunistically, was, for Loos, part of the process. The practices of the case allowed for the design process to be opened to public debate, allowed for the always already public nature of building to be incorporated into the design. Architecture happens in public, and like a building, a case has many authors. Knowing this, and knowing how a case and a public might work, gave Loos possibilities to make an actual edifice match his public statements against ornament in ways he had perhaps not even planned, gave him the means to break through the usual practices of compromise and bureaucratic control. In other words, the case, the impure form by which matters could be made public in fin-de-siècle Vienna, had effects; as the site of architectural discussion, it had its own dynamic that played a part in design decisions. One could say that Loos found the Aeolus bag containing the "aesthetic wind" of public opinion to which Tönnies refers in his *Kritik der öffentlichen Meinung* (Critique of public opinion) and knew how and where to open it up.[91] Planned or not, the façade of the Goldman and Salatsch building looks the way it does because its design was negotiated in public, and it bears the marks of its mediation.

§

The Loos Case

The last of the Loos cases is a sad dénouement, but it is revealing of the change in the structure of the public sphere in the 1920s, of the new relations between the state and the press. Loos was arrested on the morning of September 4, 1928, and charged with the sexual molestation of three girls, aged between eight and ten, and illicit sexual solicitation of minors.[92] Loos had encountered the girls at the Prater amusement park, offered to include them in an exchange program he claimed to be organizing to send children to France, and encouraged them to earn their pocket money with fees for posing nude for him, unsupervised, in his flat. And so the sordid details of the Loos case appeared in the newspaper headlines at the same time as post office workers announced a work-to-rule action, as nineteen people were killed in a catastrophic accident at the auto race in Monza, as a spectacular murder in a Prague courtroom was reported, and a ban on the export of animal feed was announced.

One of the main items of evidence was a box of pornographic photographs of young girls, from the age of five years old through adolescence, 2,271 in all.[93] According to Elsie Altmann-Loos, they were the photos Loos had removed from Theodor Beer's studio

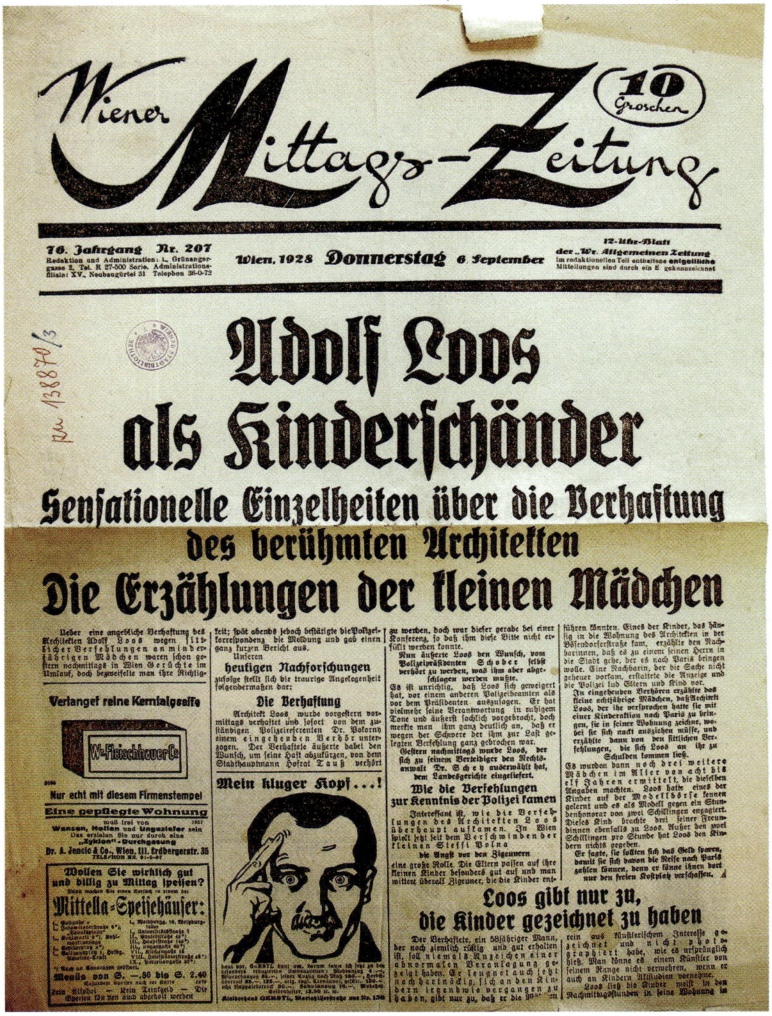

Wiener Mittags-Zeitung

10 Groschen

76. Jahrgang Nr. 207
Redaktion und Administration: I., Grünangergasse 2, Tel. R 27-500 Serie. Administrationsfiliale: XV., Neubaugürtel 31 Telephon 36-0-72

Wien, 1928 Donnerstag 6. September

12-Uhr-Blatt der „Wr. Allgemeinen Zeitung"
Im redaktionellen Teil enthaltene entgeltliche Mitteilungen sind durch ein E gekennzeichnet

Adolf Loos als Kinderschänder

Sensationelle Einzelheiten über die Verhaftung des berühmten Architekten

Die Erzählungen der kleinen Mädchen

Ueber eine angebliche Verhaftung des Architekten Adolf Loos wegen sittlicher Verfehlungen an minderjährigen Mädchen waren schon gestern nachmittags in Wien Gerüchte im Umlauf, doch bezweifelte man ihre Richtigkeit; spät abends jedoch bestätigte die Polizeikorrespondenz die Meldung und gab einen ganz kurzen Bericht aus.

Unseren

heutigen Nachforschungen

zufolge stellt sich die traurige Angelegenheit folgendermaßen dar:

Die Verhaftung

Architekt Loos wurde vorgestern vormittags verhaftet und sofort von dem zuständigen Polizeireferenten Dr. Pokorny einem eingehenden Verhör unterzogen. Der Verhaftete äußerte dabei den Wunsch, um seine Haft abzukürzen, von dem Stadthauptmann Hofrat Tauß verhört zu werden, doch war dieser gerade bei einer Konferenz, so daß ihm diese Bitte nicht erfüllt werden konnte.

Nun äußerte Loos den Wunsch, vom Polizeipräsidenten Schober selbst verhört zu werden, was ihm aber abgeschlagen werden mußte.

Es ist unrichtig, daß Loos sich geweigert hat, vor einem anderen Polizeibeamten als vor dem Präsidenten auszusagen. Er hat vielmehr seine Verantwortung in ruhigem Tone und äußerst sachlich vorgebracht, doch merkte man ihm ganz deutlich an, daß er wegen der Schwere der ihm zur Last gelegten Verfehlung ganz gebrochen war.

Gestern nachmittags wurde Loos, der sich zu seinem Verteidiger den Rechtsanwalt Dr. Schey auserwählt hat, dem Landesgerichte eingeliefert.

Wie die Verfehlungen zur Kenntnis der Polizei kamen

Interessant ist, wie die Verfehlungen des Architekten Loos überhaupt aufkamen. In Wien spielt jetzt seit dem Verschwinden der kleinen Steffi Polna

die Angst vor den Zigeunern

eine große Rolle. Die Eltern passen auf ihre kleinen Kinder besonders gut auf und man wittert überall Zigeuner, die die Kinder entführen könnten. Eines der Kinder, das häufig in die Wohnung des Architekten in der Bösendorferstraße kam, erzählte den Nachbarinnen, daß es zu einem feinen Herrn in die Stadt gehe, der es nach Paris bringen wolle. Eine Nachbarin, der die Sache nicht geheuer vorkam, erstattete die Anzeige und die Polizei lud Eltern und Kind vor.

In eingehenden Verhören erzählte das kleine achtjährige Mädchen, daß Architekt Loos, der ihr versprochen hatte sie mit einer Kinderaktion nach Paris zu bringen, sie in seiner Wohnung zeichne, wobei sie sich nackt ausziehen müsse, und erzählte dann von den sittlichen Verfehlungen, die sich Loos an ihr zu Schulden kommen ließ.

Es wurden dann noch drei weitere Mädchen im Alter von acht bis elf Jahren ermittelt, die dieselben Angaben machten. Loos hatte eines der Kinder auf der Modellbörse kennen gelernt und es als Modell gegen ein Stundenhonorar von zwei Schillingen engagiert. Dieses Kind brachte drei seiner Freundinnen ebenfalls zu Loos. Außer den zwei Schillingen pro Stunde hat Loos den Kindern nichts gegeben.

Er sagte, sie sollten sich das Geld sparen, damit sie sich davon die Reise nach Paris zahlen können, denn er könne ihnen dort nur den freien Kostplatz verschaffen.

Loos gibt nur zu, die Kinder gezeichnet zu haben

Der Verhaftete, ein 58jähriger Mann, der noch ziemlich rüstig und gut erhalten ist, soll niemals Anzeichen einer abnormalen Veranlagung gezeigt haben. Er leugnet auch jetzt noch hartnäckig, sich an den Kindern irgendwie vergangen zu haben, gibt nur zu, daß er die [illegible] rein aus künstlerischem Interesse gezeichnet und nicht photographiert habe, wie es ursprünglich hieß. Man könne es einem Künstler von seinem Range nicht verwehren, wenn er auch an Kindern Aktstudien vornehme.

Loos ließ die Kinder meist in den Nachmittagsstunden in seine Wohnung in

Mein kluger Kopf . . . !

"Adolf Loos as Child Molester. Sensational Details on the Arrest of the Famous Architect. The Reports of the Little Girls." Cover of the *Wiener Mittags-Zeitung*, September 6, 1928. Wienbibliothek im Rathaus, Vienna, Handschriftensammlung, H.I.N. 138.870/3, Teilnachlass Karl Kraus.

twenty-three years earlier (Beer had, in the meantime, taken his own life, destitute, in 1919).[94] This is perfectly plausible. Loos himself said only that they were given to him by a writer fifteen years earlier. More he would not say, except to deny explicitly that they had belonged to his friend Peter Altenberg.[95]

Did the children speak the truth? The judges—both professional and lay—were not certain. It is interesting to see here that words and images functioned in ways that precisely reverse their use in the Beer case. Loos did indeed sketch the girls, producing pictures in a medium that put the product in the orbit of art. But they served here as evidence as well. They showed children in positions the court decided were chosen to reveal their sex, and since the girls' testimony about their poses corresponded to the images, they were used to establish details about the nature of the encounter between the older man and the unclothed children. Faced with this evidence, the judges convicted Loos of solicitation and indecency.[96] Now, however, it seems that at least the questions raised by Freud's account of the fantasized erotic life of children had found their way into the courts. This time the court accepted the expert opinion of a child psychiatrist who concluded that the witnesses' testimony was not reliable. They therefore exonerated Loos of the charge of child abuse, of the more serious acts that were discussed in court and are outlined in the decision.[97]

The roles played by the courts, the press, and the state were also different in this last Loos case. The architect was sentenced to four months in jail, but the sentence was suspended for a three-year probationary period. The press noted the mildness of the judges.[98] Unlike Theodor Beer, Loos spent no time in prison after his conviction, and he was stripped of no rights or privileges. Not the result of mere lenience, it had to do with changes in the criminal code and the rules of criminal proceedings. For the system was no longer the older, liberal judiciary, with all its problems. It was now open to politics and activism. Sometimes it served the politics of a radical right, especially in the disproportionate prosecution of the crimes of the political left. Here, though, we see the effects of the paternalistic, socially minded politics of the First Austrian Republic. The suspended sentence was made possible by legislation such as new probation law of 1920.[99] The notification of the sentence sent to Loos is a model of a state served by benevolently offered social services, outlining the conditions of the probation and the supervision order for social support.[100] And as the state assumed this new role, the courts could more effectively shield the children from public view. Again, the proceedings were held behind closed doors, but this time, reporters, the conduit to a reading public, were banned as well.

The press was different, too.[101] The *Neue Freie Presse* still tried to raise larger issues. Writing under the headline "The Loos Case: The Tragic Fall of a Great Talent," it presented the affair as a replay of the Beer case, referring to the parallels of a great intellect brought low by claiming to stand above prevailing morals.[102] It also printed defenses of Loos, written anonymously by friends of the architect.[103] Again, a prominent psychologist—this time, Karl Bühler—wrote at length about the problems of child witnesses in court; he does not mention Loos but does refer to the work of the psychologist William Stern, who had, like Loos twenty-three years earlier, sought the acquittal of Theodor Beer.[104] And the paper also published an account of the exploitation of children as models, again without specific reference to Loos but in obvious relation to the case.[105] But the *Neue Freie Presse* was no longer the newspaper of record, or one that even mattered. The tone was set by the new, more obviously politicized mass-market papers that now put an ordinary criminal proceeding on the front page, with the kind of headline formerly reserved for important acts of state such as the declaration of war. Though it was unable to reveal the details of the courtroom action or imply the identity of the victims, the coverage was far more sensationalist than that under the monarchy, not merely, in its ambivalent way, exposing the private to public view. The politics were cruder. Newspapers no longer maintained even the semblance of objectivity; one referred erroneously to "the Jewish architect Loos," echoing this later with an account of "his three Jewish lawyers."[106] There were, as far as I know, no repercussions for this inaccuracy and its antisemitic tone. Only the Communist *Rote Fahne* was pursued, for its suggestion that Loos was convicted because of his closeness to Karl Kraus, who had waged one of his many press campaigns against Johannes Schober, the head of the Austrian state police.[107]

There was, in other words, little debate. Perhaps the facts of the case simply did not leave space for the public debate about morals and the nature of public discussion. But the shape of the space for debate and disclosure had also changed dramatically. The press had once been murky, but in ways that made possible the tactics that led to the final appearance of the building on Michaelerplatz, and might even have led to the completion of the Villa Karma. Now, the colors in which a picture for the public was painted were more lurid and glaring. The space in which the culture of the case could develop—the room opened up between scientific expertise, the judiciary, and the press—was changing its shape and losing its elasticity as a site for the public production of knowledge. Instead of debate there were headlines, and even games. The same week as Loos's sentence was announced, for example, we see in the *Illustrierte Wochenpost* a competition testing readers' prowess in criminal psychology. It is a sign of the continued interest in the police and the courts, but interests now turned from a public matter to a private game.

Even though Kraus responded to these broader changes, using them to his own ends and indulging in the questionable power of the headline, he clearly saw nothing to be gained in the last of the Loos cases. This time, he stayed silent (though he was probably active behind the scenes, and he accompanied his friend to the sentencing).[108] Nonetheless, it is significant that, in

Fünf Minuten Kriminalpsychologie

Eine kriminalistische Denkaufgabe von Otto Schwerin.

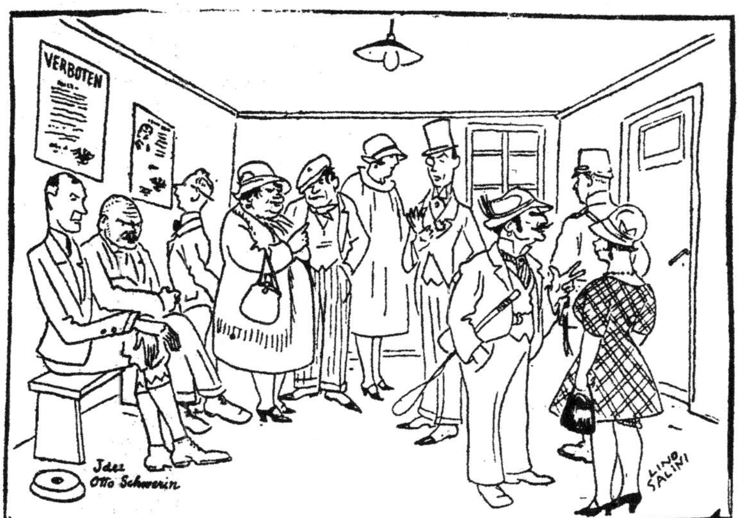

Aufgabe:

Auf der Wachstube im Polizeipräsidium sind neun verhaftete Individuen eingeliefert worden. Jedem der Verhafteten wird ein anderes Verbrechen zur Last gelegt. Es sind folgende Verbrechen und Vergehen vorhanden: Ladendiebstahl, Totschlag, Meineid, Zuhäl-

Auflösung: 1. Zollhalle einer kleineren Grenzstation (Wenige Reisende und Beamte.) 2. An der ungarisch-rumänischen Grenze. (Der uniformierte Beamte links, der militärisch grüßt, ist ein Ungar, der Zollraum, an den Anschriften und dem Wappen erkennbar, bereits rumänisch.) 3. Am 27. 4. Nicht ein-

Otto Schwerin, "Five Minutes of Criminal Psychology: A Criminalistic Brain-Teaser." Published in the *Illustrierte Wochenpost*, December 7, 1928.

a reversion to older patterns, Loos himself fought strenuously for a public trial.[109] It would hardly have been enlightening and, as the court judgment shows, would have been damaging indeed to Loos's reputation. This turn to the public was clearly a reflex born at a time when the courts could allow the law itself to be put on trial, and issues of what constituted art could be debated in the press through the case. It did not happen this time: for better and for worse, the shape of the public space for debate and disclosure, the conditions Loos had for decades known as a culture of the case, had changed.

Vienna's Culture of the Case

Conclusions are hard to draw, especially if questions are posed in terms of art history's traditional objects of knowledge—in this instance, the writings and buildings of Adolf Loos. However, my purpose here is a different one: to shed light on the spaces of public discussion and the means by which access was gained to them at a certain moment of modernity. It is also to establish that Loos worked in a cultural field where tactics of publicity were an important part of many practices, and that these were the precondition of all architectural, all cultural work that was ambitious and public. In other words, that the medico-forensic question of whether a child speaks the truth could be central to an architect's endeavors, that it might have been reasonable to believe that invoking crime was a good way to make a point about architecture, that scandal could be a productive and constitutive part of the design process. And that the practices forming around "scandals" and "cases" could inflect, in central and sometimes surprising ways, Loos's work. The point has been to insert Loos into another history that intersects the history of architecture as it is usually conceived: the history of the case. Here the "case" is not merely an epistemological paradigm, as Carlo Ginzburg has convincingly described in the context of art history and medicine, or the unit of juridical or medical knowledge and power, as in Foucault's influential work.[110] Nor is it a matter of setting up a "case study" as a form of inquiry. Instead of constructing a case, we often find "cases," readymade, in history.

What was, here, the "case"? It was a way in which actions and individuals were isolated so that certain forces could be brought to bear: not only forms of disciplinary knowledge and state power, but also the power of public scrutiny and debate. But not everything that was scandalous, that would bring to light something socially significant, or that, for a society to work properly, needed to be known, was a case. Much could remain in the dark. The case—here and elsewhere—needs to be seen as the cultural form and the set of practices by which such matters were, or could be, brought to the public. Further, the phenomenon of historical cases reveals something crucial: that the "public" is not simply "out there." For if an ideal public exists in a transparent space of rational debate, then we certainly have seen nothing of the sort here. The example of Loos and Vienna demonstrates that the space for public discussion, the space through which the winds of public opinion blew, including the aesthetic winds of architecture, has its own complex history. The tactics of the case elaborated here need to be seen as the attempt to create or call forth a public, episodically, punctually, by the means available at specific points in time. The public addressed in these fin-de-siècle Viennese examples was one sought but also shunned, alternately feared and desired; but whether it even existed in any straightforward way is doubtful. It was an "interpellated" public, one the figures here sometimes sought to call into being, but coyly, indirectly, rudely, or on the sly. The matter of public interest—legitimate concerns of political subjects—was compelling in its necessity but obscure in its form. And in the Loos-Kraus circle it was unfortunately crossed with an impure politics of sexual freedom. The goal of rendering transparent the realm of public information and protecting the private realm of desire, of bringing desire and its legitimate demands to the fore but leaving them out of public view, led to contradictions. The twin aspects of the Kraus-Loos project could not be united so neatly as they thought, and their project left their own interests and actions in the dark.[111] The intense reciprocal calculus of the protection of the private sphere and the appeals to a public show repeatedly the problematic side of the practices of the case surveyed here.

As a form of public knowledge, the case will also inevitably have a politics. One of the few attempts to turn Kraus himself into a "case" is enlightening about how the phantom public was conceived, and thus of the politics that could be pursued through it. In 1910, the young doctor Fritz Wittels, at various times a confidante of both Kraus and Freud, delivered a paper to the Vienna Psychoanalytical Society. Called "The *Fackel*-Neurosis," it was a crude attempt to psychoanalyze Kraus.[112] Writing in the same year as the lecture "Ornament and Crime" and the Michaelerplatz controversy, Wittels saw Kraus's skewering of the press as the enactment of an Oedipal scenario based on the elision of the satirist's father with Moriz Benedikt, the powerful editor of the *Neue Freie Presse* and the target of the most sustained attacks in *Die Fackel.* Rather than locating Kraus's interventions within a society of classes and institutions requiring transparency and modernization, Wittels presented them as a family drama. The circle around Kraus was blind to some of the most straightforward forms of class and gender domination; they lacked the self-consciousness to see that the frame was not (or should not be) the family, but rather society. This undermined the political potential of the case. Loos's attack on Councilors Rykl and Schneider, his description of the imagined Papuan, even Kraus's writings on the unfortunate Elsie Siegel did not lead to the public production of knowledge but remained, as often as not, at the level of the private, that area of sexual desire or personal vendetta that was not the proper object of public discussion.[113]

In the cases of Adolf Loos, we have not really dealt with issues of style or medium-specific technique. Nor have we been considering discourses or, alternatively, ideologies. Something else is at stake. It has more to do with the way culture in a broad sense *worked*, with the public conditions of many kinds of practices. In other words, there was a specificity to the folding of the true and the false, the public and the private, one that was common to many projects of the time. There are other practices of the case, but in Vienna at the time (and certainly elsewhere) there is something that unites the moves, gambits, discoveries, and defenses of the figures addressed here. True and false, right and wrong, art and life folded together in extraordinary complex ways. In the newspapers, the poles were separated by the *Strich*, the black line that supposedly divided news from feuilleton but often failed to distinguish between fact and fantasy; in the courtroom, the issue was the space between art or science and pornography. The medical profession accepted the poles of the normal and the pathological, but also had to navigate the extremes of the generalization of the case in terms of psychic laws, on the one hand, and the specificity of the case in terms of the right of the defendant before another kind of law on the other. Practices of the case consistently crossed boundaries into realms where the stakes were very different, but people at the time seemed to grasp at them repeatedly and even indiscriminately. The results were unpredictable and often unexpected, but the sense that a case could make or break an individual was a constant. Perhaps we should think of it as an uncodified practice of everyday life, the instinctive tactics of which Michel de Certeau describes in this way: "These practitioners make use of spaces that cannot be seen; their knowledge of them is as blind as that of lovers in each other's arms. The paths that correspond in this intertwining, unrecognized poems in which each body is an element signed by many others, elude legibility."[114] Though the practices of the case certainly had other potentials, Adolf Loos's habits of publicity and engagement with the law show a play of hiding and revealing, denial and disclosure, tenderness and violence, ornament and nudity that describe not a logic, but instead an ambivalent and sometimes brutal *erotics* of the case.

2 *Madness, Expressionism, and the Public Sphere: From Oskar Panizza to George Grosz*

Grosz—Panizza

George Grosz's *Widmung an Oskar Panizza* (Dedicated to Oskar Panizza, 1917/18) is a modern metropolitan *danse macabre*.[1] "*Heute Tanz*" (Dance today) the building on the left announces over its portal, invoking the traditional *Totentanz*. At the center of the painting a coffin has opened, releasing a rotting corpse as a contemporary man of bones, as death personified. The pandemonium around him blurs the distinction between the living on earth—"a seething mass of possessed human-animals," Grosz wrote—and the dead in hell.[2] The skeleton with decomposing flesh sits atop the coffin, drinking a dark fluid, no doubt liquor from one of the nearby bars. Around it we see the elements of the artist's apocalyptic images of the modern city: an urban vista by night, with sharply receding space and buildings threatening to topple, their interiors lit up and offering a view into the private spaces whose eerie glow seems to be both the light of incandescent electric bulbs and that of an underworld inferno. The interior lighting renders the outside architecture schematic, reducing the buildings to gridlike structures with seemingly identical spaces inside, differentiated only by the mysterious but threatening figures and events behind the glass.

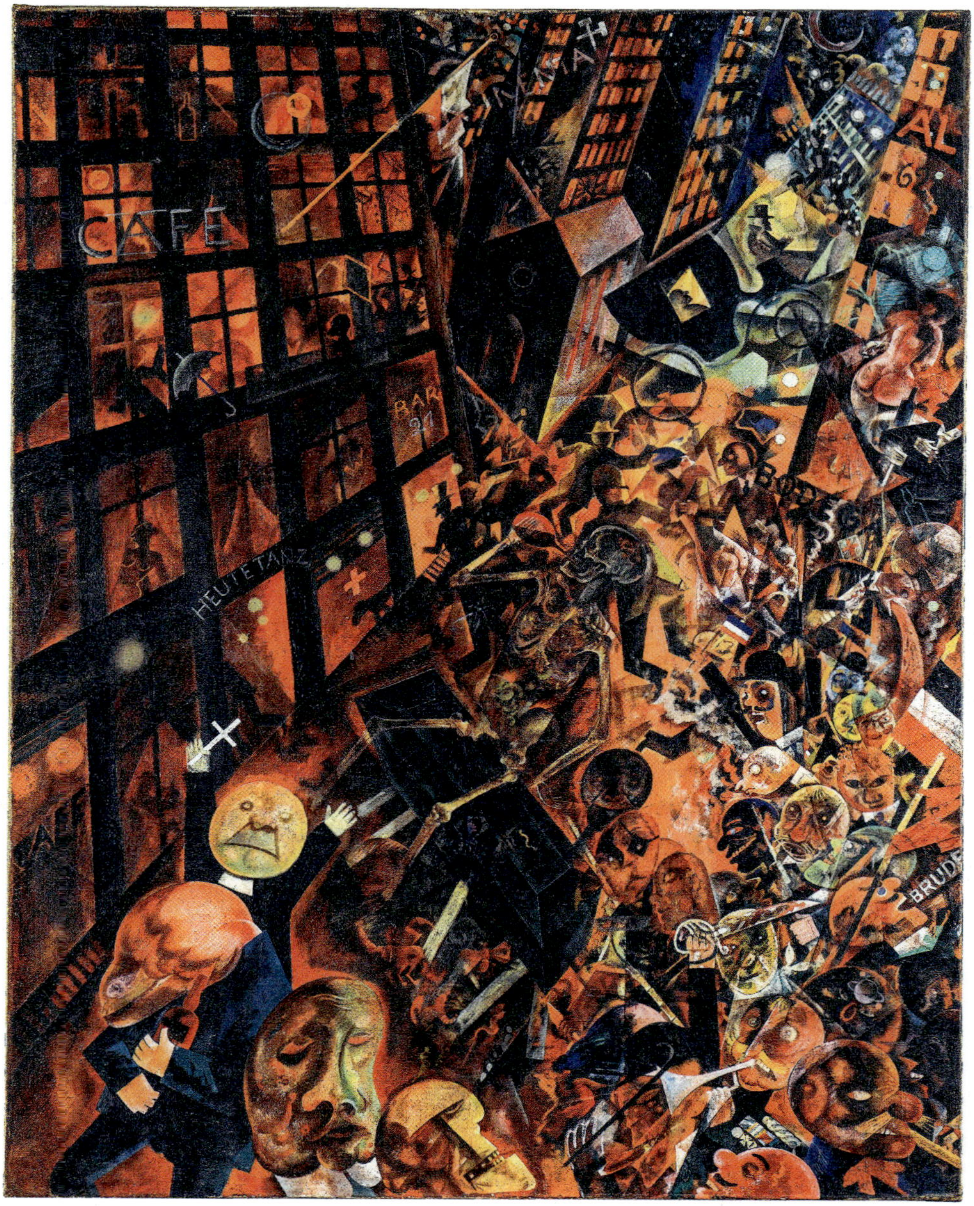

George Grosz, *Widmung an Oskar Panizza* (Dedicated to Oskar Panizza), 1917/18. Oil on canvas, 140 × 110 cm. Staatsgalerie Stuttgart. © Photo Scala, Florence/bpk Berlin. © Estate of George Grosz, Princeton, NJ/DACS 2022.

Grosz described the work in terms of the tradition of religious painting: "The picture was related to my ancestors, the medieval masters, Bosch and Breughel."[3] Yet this is an explicitly modern vision of damnation. Instead of the *Totentanz*'s melancholy reminder of the vanity of earthly success, we see a hellish vision of metropolitan debauchery. Instead of the temptations of the flesh as a path to damnation, we see a more contemporary constellation of the Fall: at the bottom left of the canvas, Grosz has painted "faces representing Alcohol, Syphilis, Pestilence ... Against Mankind gone mad, I painted this protest."[4] "That this epoch is sinking in destruction—I'm adamant in this view—our besmirched Paradise":[5] the staccato phrases of Grosz's letter to his friend Otto Schmalhausen describing the painting seem to speak the traditional language of the apocalypse foretold in the Book of Revelation, but the artist calls into question the religious import. For Grosz shows a priest as helpless, arms raised in surrender before the onslaught, the cross ineffectual and seeming to slip from his grasp. What, then, is the nature of this updated Last Judgment, no longer framed in traditional religious terms, but as a modern form of madness and guilt?

Perhaps an answer lies in the dedication of this ambitious painting to the writer Panizza, at the time living in a mental asylum near Bayreuth, where he would die less than four years later. Grosz referred often to Panizza over the course of his life: letters from the 1920s through the 1950s show a thorough and admiring familiarity with both the writer's work and his fate. "How I love the poor, utterly unknown Oskar Panizza," he wrote to his friend Mark Neven DuMont in the late 1920s.

> If he should be considered in terms of great literature I can't say—he was a man of interesting fragments (12 years' insane asylum)—just pieces—a few marvelous, highly artistic novellas glowing with secrets—an ingenious play—blasphemously great (unfailingly banned, *Liebeskonzil*, even today), an unhappy man, marked by fate, but a great writer. Just read his *Visionen der Dämmerung* sometime: that's something not many could do besides E. T. A. Hoffmann and Villiers de l'Isle-Adam and Poe. All honor to his ashes![6]

In 1944, Grosz recalled specifically the short story "Der Korsettenfritz" (Corset-Fritz), a comic tale of sexual awakening gone

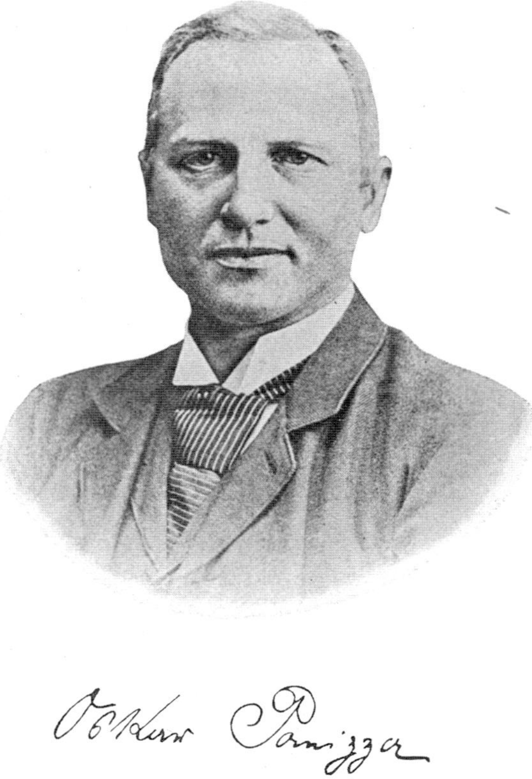

Oskar Panizza, photograph.

awry, leading to the asylum and the protagonist's development stalled at the object choice of a most trivial fetish. "*Corsettenfelix*," he wrote, misremembering the title, "was, by the way, a nice little novella, written long, long before the First World War by that remarkable man from Munich, Oscar [*sic*] Panizza. I tried to awaken some interest with a large picture dedicated to him."[7]

Who was Oskar Panizza, and why, beyond sharing a taste for the grotesque, was Grosz so intrigued by him? Though not concerned only with Grosz and Panizza, this chapter will attempt to answer that question. Panizza, in any case, was hardly unknown among circles of writers and artists at the time, and remains of interest in the history of literature.[8] Born in 1853 in Bad Kissingen to a Catholic father and a Pietist mother, Panizza studied medicine in Munich and Paris, but with an independent income turned to writing. Well-known in the circles of literary Naturalism in 1890s Munich, he is most notorious for being convicted of blasphemy in 1895 for his drama *Das Liebeskonzil* (The council of love) and spending a year in prison. He was, however, infamous before this, having been the subject of litigation between the Catholic Church and his mother over his religious upbringing after the death of his father. And even though he lived a relatively peaceful life after his release from prison, his complex relations with the law in several countries continued. In a way, his life was a series of cases between the court and the asylum, the public prosecutor and the psychiatrist.

Panizza's life and work were emblematic not only for Grosz. The scandal surrounding *Das Liebeskonzil* launched the career of one of Germany's foremost publicists of the early twentieth century, Theodor Lessing;[9] an as yet unknown Kurt Tucholsky sought in vain to publish Panizza's collected works before the First World War;[10] after it, Grosz's fellow Dadaist Walter Mehring tried unsuccessfully to visit Panizza in his asylum.[11] Karl Kraus admired him;[12] Freud recalls Panizza's "strongly revolutionary literary drama" in *The Interpretation of Dreams*;[13] Walter Benjamin discussed his work in a radio broadcast;[14] Alfred Kubin illustrated his work;[15] André Breton championed him in France.[16] Panizza was a reference point for figures of this generation, I shall suggest, not only for his themes of religion, sexuality, and insanity, but for the way he explored in public an artistic space between the asylum and the courtroom, between "madness" and the law. This site came to be an important one for artists at the time: it was the ground for certain kinds of politics that are the subject of this chapter. This politics of the case is different from the one we saw in chapter 1. For Kraus and Loos, cases involved a simpler form of publicity whose tone was set by an emerging but nonetheless circumscribed mass press. Their cases were unpredictable, but productively so, and they impacted on media beyond those of public and published scandal. Others at the time, however, sought to mobilize the forms of publicness differently, for more urgent and often more ambitious reasons. They were not always successful, but their milieu—the German avant-garde between Expressionism and Dada, in which Grosz found his feet as an artist—will be reconsidered here in terms of a series of emblematic cases that cast further light on the practices of politics and publicity of the time.

§

Oskar Panizza

Panizza's first career was as a psychiatrist, and indeed one with a particularly impressive pedigree. After receiving his doctorate and medical license in Munich and continuing his studies for six months in Paris, Panizza became an assistant to Bernhard von Gudden at the Upper Bavarian Insane Asylum in 1882.[17] Gudden was one of the most prominent psychiatrists of his day, notable for innovations in the humane treatment of patients and the avoidance of physical restraint. He had been first director of the famous Burghölzli psychiatric hospital in Zurich, later headed by Auguste Forel and Eugen Bleuler and institutional home to Carl Jung and the young Ludwig Binswanger. Emil Kraepelin served as Gudden's assistant at the same time as Panizza. Panizza, in other words, worked at the very heart of the developing field of psychiatry. In 1884, however, he abruptly resigned his post, having noticed alarming signs of mental illness in himself.[18] Friends and acquaintances had already witnessed disturbing behavior, but psychotic episodes became more frequent from this point on.

Panizza had long wished to pursue a literary career and began to do this from the following year. He published a series of poems and grotesque tales which received favorable critical attention but did not bring him the fame he sought. In 1890, he met Otto Julius Bierbaum, Detlev von Liliencron, and other figures of literary modernism in Munich, including Michael Georg Conrad, publisher of the journal *Die Gesellschaft* from 1885 and in 1890 founder of the Gesellschaft für modernes Leben. This put him at the center of the Naturalist avant-garde. Panizza was active in the organization, and, though he soon left its governing body, he remained a regular contributor to Conrad's *Gesellschaft* and to the organization's journal *Moderne Blätter*, its events, and its other publications.

Though he published on a wide range of topics in Munich, Panizza's stories and dramas were the works that would have been best known to Grosz and others.[19] These focus on religion and sexuality as complex legal, artistic, and social problems. Sexual repression is a major theme, and it leads inevitably, in his fictions, to madness. The stories also led to an intense cat-and-mouse game with the courts over charges of indecency and blasphemy. His first encounter with the law occurred in 1891, when an anthology of the Munich moderns was confiscated and five of its authors prosecuted for their contributions to it. Panizza's text was "Das Verbrechen in Tavistock-Square" (The crime in Tavistock Square), an accomplished satire of public morals and hypocrisy in which a chaste police recruit loses his psychological equilibrium when confronted with the open and sultry sexuality of roses and magnolias in the squares of London's Bloomsbury and fails to come to terms with his simultaneous erotic fascination and horror as they are projected onto the natural realm.[20] It is a clever play on the themes of literary Decadence and Jugendstil in the visual arts, one that shows a psychiatrist's fascination with the logic of fetishism. The court dismissed the case, but the affair ignited an interest in provocation, a delight in causing offence combined with a commitment to exposing the real damage of patriarchal and religious repression, the pathologies they both concealed and produced.

A crucial part of Panizza's project in the early 1890s was in fact the exploration of the space of public representation in terms of the legally representable. He identified two partially overlapping fronts in the battle to expand the limits of public address: first, the area of sexual morals as it was policed by the law; and second,

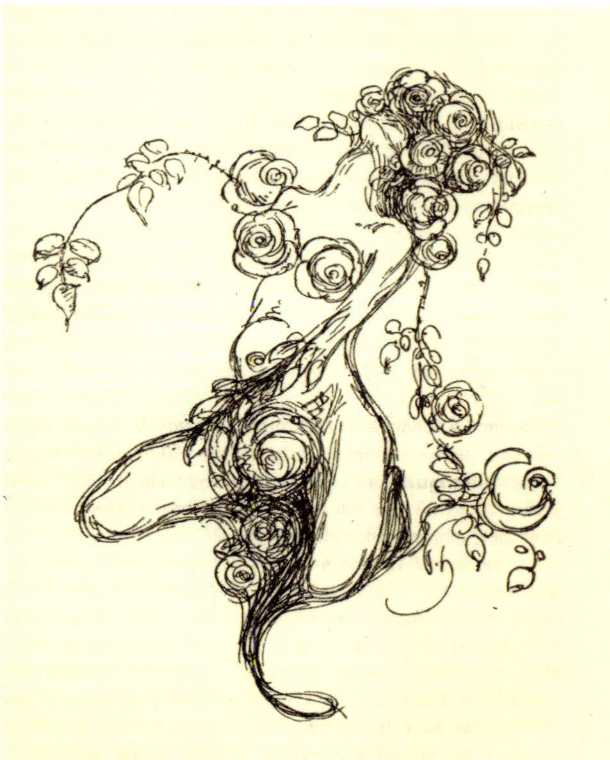

Paul Haase, illustration for "Das Verbrechen im Tavistock-Square," in Panizza, *Visionen der Dämmerung* (Munich: Georg Müller, 1914).

the power of the Church to circumscribe free expression. He did this by a precise mapping of the permissible as it filtered through specific zones opened up by and between media and genres.

The legal background to this is formed by the controversies that raged in Germany over politics and public morals in the final decade of the nineteenth century. These first centered on an attempt to amend existing legislation in order to combat a perceived rise in moral corruption. The bill, the so-called Lex Heinze, was named after a petty criminal and pimp whose Berlin murder trial in 1891 served as a "case" in the sense I am using the term in this book: as the nucleus around which public discussion crystallized.[21] Kaiser Wilhelm II initiated the moves by calling for new laws, a project then hijacked by the Bavarian Catholic Center Party. Over the course of nine years, increasingly draconian measures were proposed. The age of consent was to be raised to eighteen (§182); the code concerning pornography was widened to include writings or pictures which "without being obscene, tend to cause annoyance by grossly offending feelings of modesty and morality"[22] (§184a); and the law concerning indecent behavior (§183) was to be adapted to include stage performances, and to make actors, directors, and producers liable for causing offence, with absurdly wide discretion given to judges over what might offend modesty. This latter "Theatre Paragraph" (§184b) would have overlaid existing stage censorship (in general, scripts were submitted to censors for approval; rehearsals and performances were monitored by police) with new statutory offences, creating a *mise en abyme* of restrictive measures that risked hollowing out the theatrical canon.[23] The debates continued with varying intensity until 1900, when a relatively anodyne version of the law was passed without paragraphs 184a and b. The second controversy began in 1894, when Wilhelm II introduced the *Umsturzvorlage*, or "Subversion Bill."[24] This proposed tighter restrictions on the Social Democratic Party and widened the definition of acts construed as threats to the political and social order, including measures circumscribing press and academic freedom. Again the Center Party sought to intensify the bill by including attacks on religion and the Church, though there was already a *Gotteslästerungparagraph*, or statute against blasphemy, in the criminal code (§166). The bill was rejected by the Reichstag within a year. The parliamentary victories did not, however, defuse the very real threats to freedom of public expression. Under Wilhelm II, existing laws were interpreted by the judiciary with increased severity.[25] This was especially the case in Bavaria, where journals such as *Jugend* and *Simplicissimus* and writers from Ibsen to Frank Wedekind found their publications regularly confiscated by the police.[26]

As the artists and writers of Munich mobilized against the Lex Heinze, Panizza wrote a parody of the proposals in 1894: *Der heilige Staats-Anwalt* (The holy state prosecutor), a "moral comedy" in five scenes.[27] Allegorical figures of Morals, the Eternally Good, True, and Beautiful are called upon by the prosecution in the trial of Sensuality, who had been apprehended

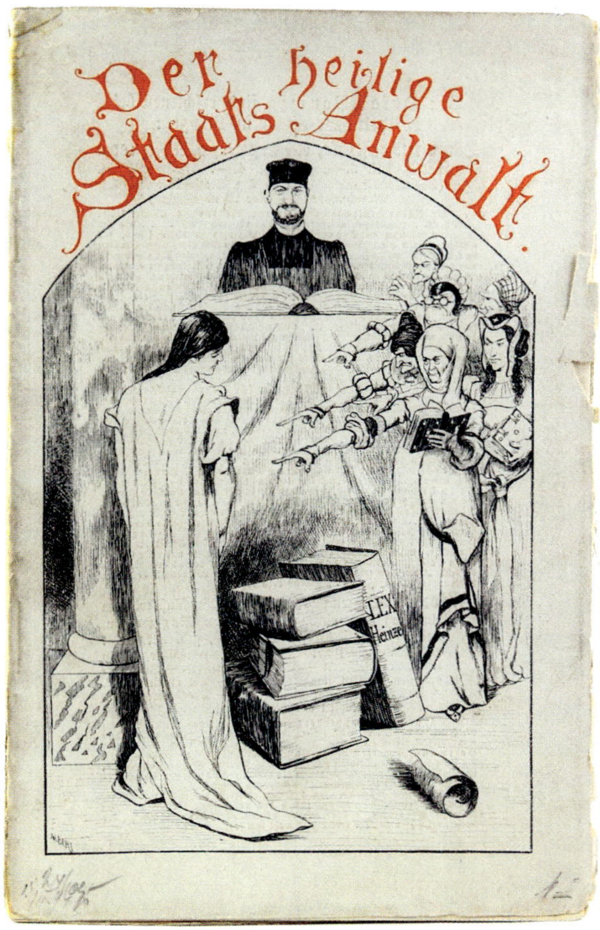

Cover, *Der heilige Staats-Anwalt* (The holy state prosecutor; Leipzig: Wilhelm Friedrich, 1894). Private collection.

> in a white feather hat and mustard yellow coat, proceeding down the street at a dilatory and prohibited pace, and addressing an elegant gentleman against his will. They conversed for an extended period and remained standing in a forbidden way.[28]

The proceedings move toward conviction but are stopped by the miraculous appearance of Martin Luther, who defends human instincts against exaggerated Catholic and bourgeois morals; his intervention, in the earthy form of his famous *Tischreden*, dominates the final scene. The legal statues are invoked precisely in the somewhat clumsy farce, leavened only by the strange and comic translation of everyday life into the criminal code by moral zealots wielding abstract concepts. However Panizza's deliberate conflation of issues of morals and of confession, of judge and Catholic priest, adds a further polemical barb, one particularly sharp in the Bavarian context. It also anticipates Karl Kraus's project of separating morality from criminality.

The play was never performed and so not submitted to the censor; indeed, it was published in Leipzig to avoid legal exposure in Bavaria. Since the courts held the spoken or performed word to more stringent standards of "decency" than those printed on paper,[29] Panizza remained unprosecuted. Such geographical and medial subtleties were part of the delicate weave of the plane of public representation. But the careful, prudent measures they prompted tended in fact to rob such works of their resonance. For the Damoclean sword of confiscation and prosecution was double-edged: invoking the wrath of the censors was a way of ensuring press coverage beyond Bavaria, connecting the local avant-garde with public opinion in the larger German-speaking world (most of which was more tolerant) and with a larger artistic confraternity increasingly mobilized by the Lex Heinze debates. And Panizza seems to have tired of the limited public sphere of a local subculture, and of the relatively polite alternative forms of meetings and lectures before the Gesellschaft für modernes Leben, whose audience was mainly the like-minded intelligentsia (and police observers, whose reports survive in the archives).[30] For those with strong nerves, public prosecution was both a badge of honor and an effective form of publicity. Panizza wrote disparagingly of colleagues who feared conflict, and colleagues would greet him by asking if he had written "anything confiscatable" recently.[31]

And this—writing something to be confiscated—he had certainly done. Panizza's account of Tavistock Square's vegetal erotics had been brought to court, but the case was dismissed. Two other works, however, were banned: his 1893 mock-scholarly rebuttal of the Pius IX's papal bull of 1854 making the doctrine of the Immaculate Conception Church dogma, and his equally anti-Catholic *Der teutsche Michel und der römische Papst* (The German Michel and the Roman Pope) of early 1894.[32] Yet though they were confiscated and banned by courts beyond Bavaria, Panizza was not charged with a crime.

There can be no doubt that the publication of Panizza's final work of this series, *Das Liebeskonzil* of late 1894, was intended to goad the authorities into action. The ensuing trial, strangely symbiotic and mutually sought, took so long to happen because the "authorities" were not of one piece. The Wittelsbach administration in Munich was traditionally liberal, Protestant, and north Bavarian. Its functionaries had no qualms about Bismarck's earlier anti-Catholic *Kulturkampf* and were generally tolerant; since the eighteenth century, the Bavarian monarchy had a largely antagonistic relation to the Catholic Church. But the Catholic Center kept the pressure on the administration, and to placate this large and vocal constituency, senior authorities occasionally left the police and the public prosecutor to their own devices in cases that usually saw popular opinion side with the conservative forces.[33] And here, at last, Panizza was thrown to the wolves, accepted as collateral damage in the stand-off between a liberal, educated administration and populist forces. In other words, the space of public representation was not policed in a uniform way; its shape was constantly negotiated anew on the basis of local concerns and tactics in complex and intersecting battles.

Das Liebeskonzil was, in any case, a virtuoso work of provocation. It explains the emergence of syphilis in late fifteenth-century Italy as a result of the corruption of the papacy. God the Father is presented as senile and ineffectual, Christ as decrepit and sickly, and—in a direct attack on the Catholic cult of the Virgin and its new doctrinal form—Mary as a seductive coquette. Scandalized by the moral degeneracy of the Borgia pope, Alexander VI, but unable to counter it, the three enter into a pact with the Devil, who creates the "great pox" to punish a dissolute humanity for its pursuit of pleasure. The historical complexity and doctrinal intricacy of the play are impressive, and its literary quality underestimated.[34]

The play was published in Zurich. It was never meant to be performed, and should be considered part of the tradition of the *Lesedrama*, works written without performance in mind (a form the Munich modernists were in fact reviving).[35] It received a positive review in the Social Democratic *Münchner Post* in January 1895, which attracted the attention of the police. Within three days, a confiscation order was issued and the matter turned over to the public prosecutor. Yet the police could not find any copies of the book to impound—only thirty, it seems, were sold—or anyone who felt insulted in his or her religious feelings. This should have prevented prosecution, but it was not an insurmountable problem. A policeman in Leipzig agreed to testify to finding the text objectionable, and Panizza was charged with ninety counts of an "offence against religion, carried out in printed form"[36] according to §166 of the criminal code.

The police now had their case against a recurrent nuisance. Panizza's lawyer accepted the mandate as he had an excellent defense: the play had been published in Switzerland, and an offence committed in a foreign country in which the act was not illegal could not be indicted in Germany.[37] But Panizza wanted a tribune. In the course of the trial, he confirmed that he had wanted the play to be read in Germany, and used his court statement for a lengthy lecture on the history of art and literature, placing his own work in a satiric and anticlerical tradition. He cited and read examples from German and French literature, and even brought illustrations from the work of Hogarth, which were circulated in the courtroom.[38] But cultural history was not found to be relevant to the legal case: he failed to convince the lay judges and was given the unusually harsh, indeed unprecedented, sentence of a full year of prison in solitary confinement.[39] He was arrested immediately but released on posting a very high bond due to the perceived risk of flight. Forced then to serve his entire sentence, he emerged a physically and psychologically broken man.

Panizza would be seen as a martyr in artistic circles for several decades. In many ways, his interventions into the public sphere tell us little new: they were relatively straightforward and simply went wrong. But Panizza's fate deserves our attention,

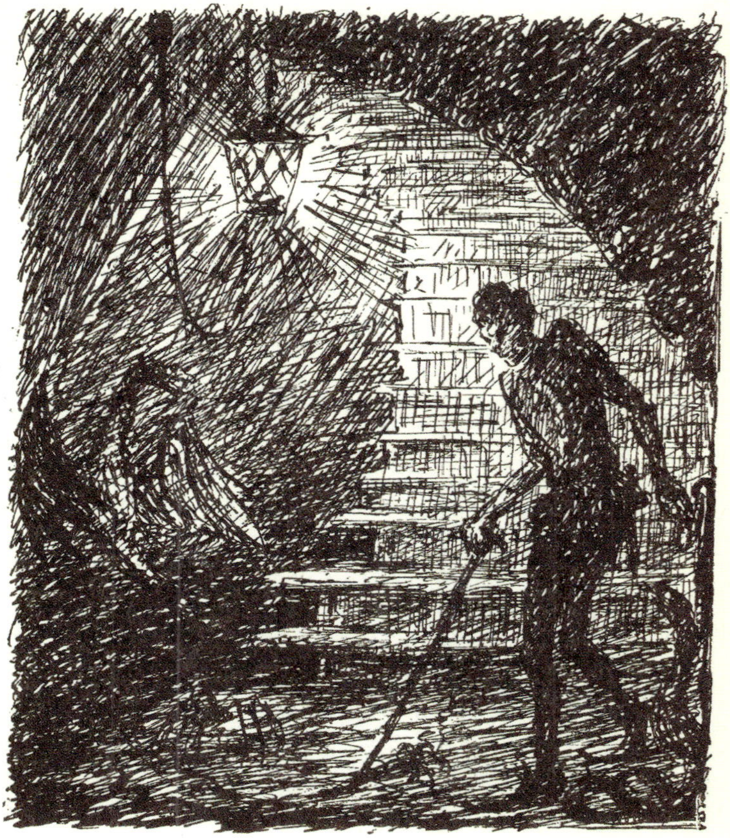

Alfred Kubin, illustration for *Das Liebeskonzil: Eine Himmelstragödie in fünf Aufzügen von Oskar Panizza* (Munich: Gesellschaft der Münchner Bibliophilen, 1913). © Eberhard Spangenberg, München/DACS 2022.

for his commitment to artistic freedom was an existential one. Consider the figure of the Devil in *Das Liebeskonzil*: he has, as did the writer himself, a crooked leg. The reward he has chosen for his assistance is also particularly revealing: first, free access to audiences with God; and second, "He must allow my books to be freely published and given the widest circulation in Heaven and Earth."[40] For "when someone thinks but may not express his thoughts to others—that is the most awful of all tortures."[41] And lurking behind the issue of the representable and its limits in the area of religion and morality as a political matter was something else: madness and its relation to these same freedoms. Over the years Panizza's mental health would deteriorate, and as it did so he shifted his attention from *sexuality* and *religion* to *madness* as a complex legal, artistic, and social problem. Here he picked up the threads of his career as a psychiatrist and engaged in another sort of mapping, now of madness as a political problem, the relation of the psychiatrist to the law, and the relation of madness to the spaces of public representation, all explored through the various media of the case.

It was the psychiatrist's insight into mental instability crossed with a satirist's irreverence and *schadenfreude* in exposing hypocrisy that struck a chord in the 1890s. Panizza's work had little to do with Naturalism in its literary form (though it shared some of the themes); instead it is the sophisticated literary garb of Romantic fantasy, Gothic horror, and the grotesque that continued his appeal to a later generation responsive to the Expressionist and

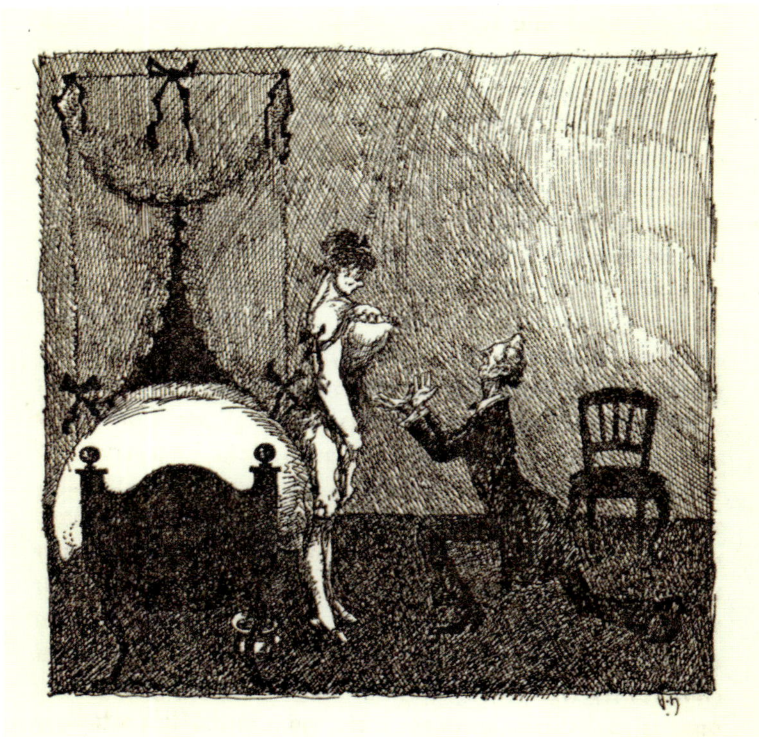

Paul Haase, illustration for "Der Korsetten-Fritz," in Panizza, *Visionen der Dämmerung* (Munich: Georg Müller, 1914).

the absurd. And it is crucial that many of his stories take the form of the case. The "Crime of Tavistock Square" is a police case, taking place in the mind of a constable whose sexual repression causes his insanity. "Korsettenfritz," perhaps the most famous—and the one recalled by Grosz—is a psychiatric case.[42] It follows the path of the son of a Protestant priest, shielded from worldly knowledge but expected to have absorbed it, who seeks to extrapolate the nature of human pleasure and desire from a single view into the display window of a corset-shop. The story is the report of the man himself, after a final breakdown caused by an inability to comprehend his own displaced desire: "Six weeks later I was brought into a building of which it is said, it is an insane asylum. And it is from here that I write these lines, my life story, at the request of the Director."[43] His symptoms are clearly paranoia and what came to be called at the time "sejunction," a splitting of identity as mental associations are blocked and diverted, a condition later absorbed in Bleuler's system of schizophrenia.[44] The text presents itself as an autobiographical case history of the kind written by patients for various reasons—a medical anamnesis for doctors, a reckoning for posterity, or an apologia meant for publication. (Panizza himself would write one in 1904 as he entered an asylum for the last time, as a patient.[45]) Panizza's "Ein skandalöser Fall" (A scandalous case, translated into English as "A Scandal at the Convent") is the fictionalization of one such autobiographical text: it was a famous medical case of hermaphroditism, and parts of the subject's diaries were published by Auguste Tardieu, the most prominent forensic medical doctor in France at the time, less than a decade before the young Dr. Panizza was in Paris.[46] In 1978 Michel Foucault published the full memoir; his introduction discusses Panizza's short story, which is included in the English edition, and notes the transformation from a patient's text into a self-consciously literary narrative (though Panizza does include a fictional physician's case report).[47] Panizza moves between the textual genres of the case, exploring an intergeneric space of writing in which case studies could be confession, medical casuistry, or literature.

In an extraordinary book of 1898 Panizza engaged directly with another genre of the case: the medico-forensic texts produced by doctors for use in the courts, usually in determining whether a person was to be considered legally insane and therefore unfit to manage his own affairs, or, if a crime had been committed, whether the accused was mentally ill and therefore not legally responsible for his actions. One of the most famous of these is Richard von Krafft-Ebing's *Psychopathia Sexualis*, first published in 1886, an authoritative compendium that sought to define and classify sexual deviance for the medical and judicial spheres. This was Panizza's starting point.

Compare the lengthy titles of Krafft-Ebing's classic and Panizza's self-consciously paranoid satire of psychiatry:

> Psychopathia Sexualis
> with particular reference to
> contrary sexual instinct.
> A medico-forensic study
> for doctors and lawyers
> by
> Dr. R. v. Krafft-Ebing[48]

> Psichopatia Criminalis
> A manual
> scientifically investigating and defining
> mental illnesses deemed relevant for courts of law.
> For doctors, laypeople, lawyers,
> legal guardians, administrative officials, ministers, etc.
> by
> Oskar Panizza[49]

But beyond its easy echo of the medico-forensic manual, Panizza's text is subtle and complex: it recasts Krafft-Ebing's typical disciplinary classification of desire by medicine and law into a discussion of state political repression as policed by psychiatry. He also shifts ground, from the mapping of public morals by the Lex Heinze to the mapping of politics by the *Umsturzvorlage* or "Subversion Bill."

Psichopatia Criminalis makes the point that psychiatry is a fundamentally political matter, for it was complicit in the creation within society of a class of subjects devoid of legal, and often human, rights. The later nineteenth century saw the emergence of countless scandals concerning the issue of *Entmündigung* or legal incapacitation, the suspension of rights ranging from the mere declaration of an individual as legally insane and thus unable to discharge his or her own affairs to enforced mental hospitalization. These cases showed dramatically how, in an instant, the legal or authoritative medical declaration of insanity created a personal zone in which all actions or utterances could be logically construed as nothing but the symptoms of psychosis. The time was rife with accounts of people whose declarations that they were *not* mentally ill were rendered *a priori* false as they were forced into asylums. The declaration of legal insanity was in essence an administrative step, one that could be initiated by families or local authorities. And it certainly happened that the motivation for such steps was pecuniary on the part of relatives or expediency on the part of authorities. The laws governing such procedures varied from state to state, but the path to legal insanity was pursued by administrative means on the basis of documents, largely witness statements and evaluations by experts, by doctors. A legal hearing might take place in the absence of those who contested the step. These procedures could be prevented or reversed only in high-profile episodes, and the likes of Karl Kraus pursued the making public of such cases.[50] The suspicion and scandal surrounding instances of legal incapacitation constituted one of the pangs of psychiatry's birth as a profession, long before the politicization of mental health by Foucault and the anti-psychiatrists of the later twentieth century.[51] As Panizza put it in *Psichopatia Criminalis*, speaking from his former position as a professional, "anything that we [psychiatrists] determine is pathological, is so, whatever else it may be, even if it led to the Reformation or the invention of the steam engine ... or 'human rights,' whether the person in question is named Luther or Lafayette, Lincoln or Lucian."[52]

Having identified a very real tautology at the intersection of psychiatry and the courts, Panizza pursues the point in a deeply but darkly comic vein. In many ways it is a one-line joke to point to the inherent contradiction of the medico-forensic nexus, but it allowed the practitioner familiar with the protocols endless opportunities for satire. In his account, any political demands or assertions of rights are *a priori* dangerous to the state and thus politically criminal. But the authority of the psychiatrist, writes Panizza, allows for a new expedient: instead of crime, politics is considered under the rubric of psychopathology. Suffering from a belief in political rights, those who demand them are thus not responsible for their own actions. The importance of the point is its efficiency: those who demand rights can be called before the courts, but the criminal nature of their action need not be proven; the law allows for involuntary psychiatric commitment by proving insanity instead of seeking conviction in a criminal case, where the burden of proof weighs heavier. Panizza invokes the treatments and sedative measures of the time:

> A moderately sized asylum between the Neckar and Rhine, about the size of the Rhineland-Palatinate ... would have overnight, in just a few weeks, nipped the criminal movement, I mean the epidemic of psychosis, in the bud. The cure is surprisingly speedy. Gentle handling, properly tempered water baths, peace and seclusion, birdsong beyond the iron bars, the benevolent tone of the doctor—a bit of hyoscyamine, and a bit of bromide—and the political understanding of all the inmates would be immensely improved.[53]

Echoing the nosological debates in contemporary psychiatry, Panizza describes this as a newly identified psychopathological condition, but one that can be traced back in history:

> The *psychopathia criminalis* runs through all revolutionary movements like a red thread, whether in Antiquity or the present ... If the Romans had had our present-day form-filling forensic physicians, or a Latin edition of one of the excellent psychiatric textbooks available today, they would simply have filled out an arrest warrant for the elder Gracchus, and with the help of a second form certifying "public danger due to an incurable mental illness," his transfer to a state mental asylum would have been brought to perfection.[54]

Transposing politics onto sex, §175 of the criminal code (outlawing homosexual acts) onto the "Subversion Bill," he describes democratic sentiments as "political inversion," love of one's own rights instead of subjection to superiors.[55]

It is an extraordinarily learned satire. Panizza refers, largely accurately, to contemporary psychiatric texts; he faithfully describes symptoms of what was called at the time dissociation and "*oxy- and par-ästhesian*," drawing from the discussions of *dementia praecox*.[56] Over the course of the book, however, the voice of the forensic expert becomes cynical, deranged, and abusive:

Frequent changes of mood and weepiness, the tendency to cry even over trivial matters, is recognized by experts ... as an early symptom of cerebral paralysis. ... But why are you crying, anyway? Why is your brain so weak? When your thoughts begin to raise themselves to the heights of individuality and the rights of individuals, and your soul flies like an eagle, why do you cry, when you stand before the State and should confess? ... Do you think *Brutus* cried? Or did *Mirabeau* shed tears? Do historians write of the sobs of *Danton*?

Well, if you *cry*, you make it easy for the state, and the court doctor will always be able to claim conditional grounds for referral to the asylum. ...[57]

Well, who wouldn't bloody cry?! Why? Because they have to pay taxes. Because they have to squeeze their last drop of blood to pay for incessant wars. Because their families are at the mercy of a brutal bunch of marauding soldiers. Because they're at the mercy of a blindly ambitious and corrupt judiciary. Because they can no longer speak, no longer publish their cries for help. ...

What do you want, you weepy people? Why are you so soft?[58]

Slowly the narrative voice goes mad. The footnotes remain calm, but the references break down: "the title escapes me."[59] The case studies too are those of a forgetful and distracted observer. In the main text, the psychiatrist rants. He is desperate, brutal, and insane but still in charge, still setting the terms. In his tirade the psychiatrist slips into the role of unhinged interrogator, drill sergeant, or prison guard. It is bravura comedy, but deeply dark—a perfect iteration of the genre of the medico-forensic psychiatric study, references erudite and correct, but showing its bloodthirsty underside and authoritarian core. Displaying the symptoms of his patients, the psychiatrist reveals the irrationality of political, judiciary, and disciplinary power.

§

Panizza did, in fact, become a patient. A few words on his later fate. Released from prison, he fled to Zurich but continued publishing his and others' texts (they included *Psichopatia Criminalis*, but also works of important modernist writers and figures of the contemporary reform movement) in his press Zürcher Diskussionen, until he was declared an undesirable alien and forced to leave in 1898; an underage prostitute and nude photos ("for medical purposes") were involved.[60] Yet since he had committed no felony, the measure was inappropriate. Panizza detected the hand of the German emperor, Wilhelm II, behind the deportation. Unable to return to Munich—he had renounced his Bavarian citizenship—Panizza moved to Paris. He published a book of verses defaming Wilhelm—*Parisjana*—which was banned; he was charged with insulting the monarch in 1900, and his German assets were frozen.[61] He had no choice but to return to Munich and face arrest. After his conviction and five months of prison, he was transferred to an asylum, where the doctors found him mentally unsound and not responsible for his actions, prompting his release. Though he returned to Paris, his symptoms were now so severe that he was unable to continue his existence. He began to hear constant singing and whistling sounds that were his tormentors' weapon, suffered from olfactory hallucinations, feared to eat lest he be poisoned, became convinced of his persecutors' power as he noted that the sounds could follow him to any country in Europe. It was, in his own world, the work of the kaiser. Recently a psychiatrist and historian has considered the Panizza case in great detail and found what would have been called "'paranoia,' '*dementia praecox*,' 'schizophrenia,' or 'paraphrenia,' depending on which diagnostic system is used."[62] Panizza himself denied the existence of "insanity": a subject's construction of reality was the only reality there is, and no single such construction can reliably be labelled "normal" by political or epistemological fiat.[63] But plagued by hallucinations and constant noises, locked in a delusional system, he returned to Germany and sought admission into the state asylum. He was refused, so he prompted his own psychiatric commitment. On September 9, 1904, Panizza twice attacked passers-by whom he mistakenly took for his tormentors, shouting abuse and throwing stones. On October 19—he was fifty years old at the time—he walked down a Munich street clad only in a shirt, was arrested, gave a false name, and acted erratically. Within two months he was declared legally insane and sent to the asylum in which he died seventeen years later. For years, Panizza had been the author of the many public cases he created; with his voluntary withdrawal from the public, he became merely the anonymized Case 59 ("systematic paraphrenia") in his former colleague Emil Kraepelin's *Einführung in die psychiatrische Klinik*.[64]

Panizza operated in the space between the public realm of debate and the institutionalized and circumscribed space of the asylum. He moved in and out of the roles of psychiatrist, forensic expert, defendant, and patient. He knew both the pain of mental illness and the power of those who sought to relieve it at the same time as they sought to protect others and serve an apparatus that disciplined public behavior and discourse. He saw in himself both the subject and the object of psychiatric knowledge and power, and attempted to make public his insights. But after he chose his role as patient in an asylum (or "a refuge of the mind," as he had called the asylum in an early poem, showing his ambivalence[65]), his works disappeared from the space of public representation. In the decades following his final hospitalization, many writers sought to publish his collected works; most were denied permission by a family who now controlled Panizza's written works and wished them to disappear. ("For my mother," he wrote in a letter of 1900 to his friend, the psychiatrist Paul Ostermaier, "is the police, or state power (*Staatsgewalt*)."[66]) Only Hanns Heinz Ewers was allowed to publish an edited version of fourteen short stories; all requests to republish any of the other writings were refused.

Though Panizza spent his life both inside and outside the asylum, he argued that there was no real "outside." But psychiatrists did not want to even imply the possibility of such a state of affairs. Indeed, Kraepelin identifies Panizza in his psychiatric textbook not as a former psychiatrist, or even a doctor, but as "a fifty-one-year-old writer." For Panizza, all were equally mad, but "when insanity becomes epidemic, it is called sanity."[67] Reason was the sleep of madness. But in the newly developing field of medicine, such a blurring of distinctions was to be fought as hard as the custodians of legal order policed the realm of public representations. At issue was control over the representation of madness and desire. Panizza tried to represent these as social issues that rendered distinctions between patients and doctors problematic. He tried to show that people in whom psychiatrists saw symptoms (of madness, of desire) were really public subjects whose access to the space of representations was at stake. Panizza did so by opening the zones between art, medicine, and the law as a space of articulation. He mixed the media of the written word and the public trial, and he mixed the genres of the case study, the anamnesis, the literary text, and the medico-forensic treatise that gave the legal map of licit and illicit action and desire. He showed that there were various gradations of publicity—that of the reading public, the public of the performance, the legal institution in a specific political context, with its lay judges—and showed ways of moving through them (often by moving too far). In the end, his question was whether the person labelled "insane" had access to the public. The answer was no: no more than the man who insults a God in whom he does not believe, or the man who writes about the willful blindness of moral repression. Living through scandal, as scandal, Panizza succeeded in limning the contours of the public sphere at a particular moment in history. Navigating with expert instincts and professional knowledge between the converging fronts of religion, politics, and science, Panizza made himself into a perfect storm.

Panizza's flight into the privacy of the asylum was a choice. He was no innocent victim, and rumors among writers and artists that he was held against his will by a family eager to protect its fortune, though understandable in the context of the time, are false. His compulsive attempt to map the contours of the publicly representable, his constant testing of these borders, his attempts to open up the space between institutions, discourses, and genres to provide a space for expression at the same time as demonstrating publicly the limits imposed—all these show the signs of a set of planned campaigns that was simultaneously heroic, astute, and foolhardy. Yet it is certain that he was, as the doctors wrote in their reports, genetically predisposed to mental illness.[68] Equally certain is that his encounters with the disciplinary institutions of the Church, the court, and the asylum exacerbated any congenital instability. And he pushed back against the institutions that in a very real way robbed him of rights, of liberty. He was not allowed to write, publish, or speak as he wished. As he wrote in *Das Liebeskonzil*, when he was midway between the poles of psychiatrist and patient, to think but not be allowed to communicate one's thoughts was "the most awful of all tortures." Panizza knew as well as anyone else that, for the patient as well as the public, there were practical reasons why such liberties must always be conditional, but he could find no rigorously logical principles for limiting them and knew the abuse that this situation engendered.

Panizza negotiated his life and his subjectivity, his beliefs and his literary identity, in the spaces of the case, the zone between the court and the asylum. If Karl Kraus had called court psychiatry "the latest parlor game" of "the tarot players of justice,"[69] Panizza showed that the space across which it was played was not marginal or one found only at the extremes of social life; instead it was a space central to the definition of both the public sphere and the subject who could act there. He showed that a citizen might be free in his thoughts, his political and religious beliefs, and his expression, but making use of that freedom could be seen as crossing the line into illegality and insanity. And he showed that the very institutions of power that policed that line, both to discipline and to relieve suffering, displayed the same rigidity, obsessive behavior, and distance from reality that they had to deal with in certain of their wayward and unfortunate subjects. It was of course not just a matter of inadequate medical knowledge, improper judicature or legislation, but of a more complex field in which the changing roles of art, politics, and science could be negotiated, and had to be..

§

Otto Gross

On May 23, 1917, four weeks after his release from psychiatric observation at the mental asylum in Görden, Brandenburg, and three days before his official discharge from the military, declared unfit for service, George Grosz appeared at the seventh *Neue Jugend* evening in Berlin.[70] The event was a series of performances marking the launch of the first weekly edition of the redesigned, newspaper-sized Dada journal. Grosz read a text by his Dada friend Franz Jung, *Der Fall Grosz* (The Grosz case). "Apparently the fanciful novel of his own life as an adventurer in America," reported the *Berliner Börsen-Kurier*. "A tall tale of scant depth."[71]

The reporter's ambiguity—was it a novel of George Grosz's own experiences, or those of Franz Jung?—is typical of the many confusions surrounding this text. The authorship is uncontested: it was written by Jung, a university-trained economist, writer, *bohémien*, and veteran of the Munich anarchist *Tat* group who had become a key figure of the Berlin Expressionist avant-garde after relocating to the capital in 1913. Yet neither George Grosz nor Franz Jung had been to America. This is in fact the story of another Grosz, Anton Wenzel Groß, a schizophrenic at an insane asylum in Troppau, Silesia, who had spent many years in the United States. Jung had met the patient when visiting his friend Otto Gross, a psychiatrist and psychoanalyst. And though Otto Gross might have been treating Anton Groß, the psychiatrist was himself a patient at the asylum: like Oskar Panizza, in his life and work Otto Gross straddled the publicly problematic line that separated the subjects and objects of medical knowledge.

In exploring the cultural form of the case in the early twentieth-century avant-garde, it is well worth tracing the convoluted relations between George Grosz, Otto Gross, and Anton Groß as mediated—indeed orchestrated—by Franz Jung. The confusion of identities is central to the constellation and to the way the dramatis personae experienced and explored the issues of madness and modernity that occupied such an important place in the public sphere of the time. Indeed, the characters of the drama were joined by other similar and famous names: the prominent Austrian criminologist Hans Gross, the young Carl Gustav Jung, and his early mentor Sigmund Freud, to mention just a few. This is an extended episode in which George Grosz collaborated

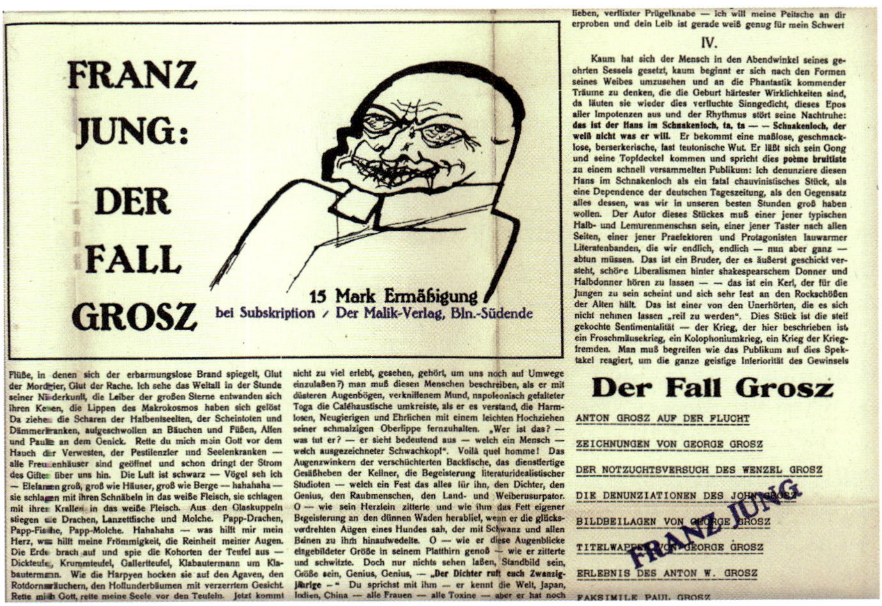

FRANZ JUNG: DER FALL GROSZ

15 Mark Ermäßigung
bei Subskription / Der Malik-Verlag, Bln.-Südende

Flüße, in denen sich der erbarmungslose Brand spiegelt, Glut der Mordgier, Glut der Rache. Ich sehe das Weltall in der Stunde seiner Niederkunft, die Leiber der großen Sterne entwanden sich ihren Kernen, die Lippen des Makrokosmos haben sich gelöst Da ziehen die Scharen der Halbentseelten, der Scheintoten und Dämmerkranken, aufgeschwollen an Bäuchen und Füßen, Affen und Pauken an dem Genick. Rette du mich mein Gott vor dem Hauch der Verwesten, der Pestilenzler und Seelenkranken — alle Freudenhäuser sind geöffnet und schon dringt der Strom des Giftes über uns hin. Die Luft ist schwarz — Vögel seh ich — Elefanten groß, groß wie Häuser, groß wie Berge — hahahaha — sie schlagen mit ihren Schnäbeln in das weiße Fleisch, sie schlagen mit ihren Krallen in das weiße Fleisch. Aus den Glaskuppeln stiegen die Drachen, Lanzettfische und Molche. Papp-Drachen, Papp-Fische, Papp-Molche. Hahahaha — was hilft mir mein Herz, was hilft meine Frömmigkeit, die Reinheit meiner Augen. Die Erde brach auf und spie die Kohorten der Teufel aus — Dickteufel, Krummteufel, Gallertteufel, Klabautermann um Klabautermann. Wie die Harpyen hocken sie auf den Agaven, den Rotdornsträuchern, den Hollunderbäumen mit verzerrtem Gesicht. Rette mich Gott, rette meine Seele vor den Teufeln. Jetzt kommt

nicht zu viel erlebt, gesehen, gehört, um uns noch auf Umwege einzulaßen?) man muß diesen Menschen beschreiben, als er mit düsteren Augenbögen, verkniffenem Mund, napoleonisch gefalteter Toga die Caféhaustische umkreiste, als er es verstand, die Harmlosen, Neugierigen und Ehrlichen mit einem leichten Hochziehen seiner schmalzigen Oberlippe fernzuhalten. „Wer ist das? — was tut er? — er sieht bedeutend aus — welch ein Mensch — welch ausgezeichneter Schwachkopf". Voilà quel homme! Das Augenzwinkern der verschüchterten Backfische, das dienstfertige Gesäßheben der Kellner, die Begeisterung literaturidealistischer Studioten — welch ein Fest das alles für ihn, den Dichter, den Genius, den Raubmenschen, den Land- und Weiberusurpator. O — wie sein Herzlein zitterte und wie ihm das Fett eigener Begeisterung an den dünnen Waden herablief, wenn er die glücksverdrehten Augen eines Hundes sah, der mit Schwanz und allen Beinen zu ihm hinaufwedelte. O — wie er diese Augenblicke eingebildeter Größe in seinem Platthirn genoß — wie er zitterte und schwitzte. Doch nur nichts sehen laßen, Standbild sein, Größe sein, Genius, Genius, — **„Der Dichter ruft euch Zwanzigjährige —"** Du sprichst mit ihm — er kennt die Welt, Japan, Indien, China — alle Frauen — alle Toxine — aber er hat noch

lieben, verflixter Prügelknabe — ich will meine Peitsche an dir erproben und dein Leib ist gerade weiß genug für mein Schwert

IV.

Kaum hat sich der Mensch in den Abendwinkel seines geohrten Sessels gesetzt, kaum beginnt er sich nach den Formen seines Weibes umzusehen und an die Phantastik kommender Träume zu denken, die die Geburt härtester Wirklichkeiten sind, da läuten sie wieder dies verfluchte Sinngedicht, dieses Epos aller Impotenzen aus und der Rhythmus stört seine Nachtruhe: **das ist der Hans im Schnakenloch, ta, ta — — Schnakenloch, der weiß nicht was er will.** Er bekommt eine maßlose, geschmacklose, berserkerische, fast teutonische Wut. Er läßt sich sein Gong und seine Topfdeckel kommen und spricht dies **poème bruitiste** zu einem schnell versammelten Publikum: Ich denunziere diesen Hans im Schnakenloch als ein fatal chauvinistisches Stück, als eine Dependence der deutschen Tageszeitung, als den Gegensatz alles dessen, was wir in unseren besten Stunden groß haben wollen. Der Autor dieses Stückes muß einer jener typischen Halb- und Lemurenmenschsn sein, einer jener Taster nach allen Seiten, einer jener Praefektoren und Protagonisten lauwarmer Literatenbanden, die wir endlich, endlich — nun aber ganz — abtun müssen. Das ist ein Bruder, der es äußerst geschickt versteht, schöre Liberalismen hinter shakespearschem Donner und Halbdonner hören zu lassen — — das ist ein Kerl, der für die Jungen zu sein scheint und sich sehr fest an den Rockschößen der Alten hält. Das ist einer von den Unerhörten, die es sich nicht nehmen lassen „reif zu werden". Dies Stück ist die steif gekochte Sentimentalität — der Krieg, der hier beschrieben ist, ein Froschmäusekrieg, ein Kolophoniumkrieg, ein Krieg der Kriegfremden. Man muß begreifen wie das Publikum auf dies Spektakel reagiert, um die ganze geistige Inferiorität des Gewinsels

Der Fall Grosz

ANTON GROSZ AUF DER FLUCHT

ZEICHNUNGEN VON GEORGE GROSZ

DER NOTZUCHTSVERSUCH DES WENZEL GROSZ

DIE DENUNZIATIONEN DES JOHN GROSZ

BILDBEILAGEN VON GEORGE GROSZ

TITELWAPPEN VON GEORGE GROSZ

ERLEBNIS DES ANTON W. GROSZ

FAKSIMILE PAUL GROSZ

FRANZ JUNG

George Grosz, announcement for Franz Jung, *Der Fall Grosz*, in *Neue Jugend* (June 1917). © Estate of George Grosz, Princeton, NJ/DACS 2022.

with Franz Jung, providing illustrations for a planned publication by Wieland Herzfelde's Malik-Verlag. The joint edition never appeared, though Jung's writings on Anton Groß were indeed published; we shall consider them later in this chapter. In the course of this work, Grosz produced a set of drawings that are closely related to some of his most problematic and controversial works of the time, works to which we shall also return. Franz Jung himself was a major, if embattled, force in Berlin Expressionism and Dada. And the psychiatrist Otto Gross is central to the history of these two overlapping tendencies as well.

Both Oskar Panizza and Otto Gross are examples of what would, by the 1920s, be a popular trope: the mad psychiatrist. And each was at the center of the avant-garde of his generation. Panizza, we have seen, came to be a sort of reference point for two generations of German writers and artists. It is easy to see why: he could stand for rebellion against the institutions and authorities of social control, whose martyr he became. More importantly, as I have argued, he came to stand for the problem of madness not as a medical but as a social and political problem. Through his life and work we see how organized religion, the law, and science acted together, if awkwardly and in an ad hoc way, to generate the limits of the normal and to mark the excesses that became, by definition, insanity or crime. Finally, Panizza was exemplary for the way his person and oeuvre served to map the public sphere, demonstrating by tactical interventions (and errors) some of the intricate medial and generic parameters of what was publicly representable. He showed how art and science worked in a larger social field; and he provided a model for what might happen when their respective protocols were mixed and reshuffled. Otto Gross can be seen to serve many of the same functions two decades later. He too took as his life's work the exploration of psychopathology as a social and political matter, and, in his own way, drew consequences as radical as Panizza's. But he did so for the generation of Expressionism, not Naturalism, for the generation of nascent psychoanalysis, and not professional psychiatry. Though central to milieus of Expressionism and Dada, Gross, crucially, appears in their historiography only at the margins. The excavation of his role has begun (and shows no signs of ceasing), but his near invisibility till recent years is itself an historical fact that is revealing of the shifting, unstable, but compelling relations between sex, madness, politics, and art, and how these could be represented publicly.

§

Born in 1877 in Styria, Austria, Otto Gross was of the cohort that followed Panizza's generation, students of Emil Kraepelin, Eugen Bleuler, and others of the highly professionalized asylum and forensic psychiatrists of the turn of the century.[72] (Carl Jung was also of this cohort, born in 1875.) Gross studied medicine in Graz, Munich, and Strasbourg, and from 1901 he published regularly on psychiatric and general medical topics. He had contact with Bleuler and Carl Jung at the Burghölzli clinic in Zurich from 1902, and with Freud from about 1904; he briefly served in Munich as assistant to Kraepelin (with whom Panizza was assistant to Gudden). In 1906 he was appointed *Privatdozent* in psychopathology at the University of Graz, and in the following year participated in the International Congress for Neuropsychiatry, where he spoke prominently in defense of Freud's work; in 1908 he attended the first Psychoanalytic Congress in Salzburg. By this time, he was also prominent in the anarchist and bohemian circles of Munich and Ascona.

These bare bones of an intellectual biography—of Gross's personal life-path more will be said later—reflect the development of his ideas. His psychiatric principles were solidly traditional—materialist and associationist—but he developed them with considerable ambition and subtlety.[73] He focused on situating the range of psychopathologies in the so-called "secondary functions"—not simple associations but the complex relations between association, affect, and attention. With Bleuler, Freud, and Jung, he took a psychological approach, paying particular attention to the contents of mental processes and not merely their resulting symptoms in isolation. Gross's 1902 book *Die cerebrale Sekundärfunktion* (The cerebral secondary function) had a lasting influence, for example, on Carl Jung. And Gross used his insights here to intervene actively in the most urgent discussions of the day, on the psychosis *dementia praecox*, controversially renamed "schizophrenia" by Bleuler. Developing his own sense of the complexities of secondary functions informed by Freud's notion of the workings of the unconscious, he contributed important articles on the psychological disintegration of ideas and of consciousness.

Along with Carl Jung (and to a certain extent Bleuler), Gross was one of the first psychiatrists to take up Freud's ideas, and as such offered Freud an invaluable route from his isolation in private practice to a voice in mainstream university and asylum psychiatry. The results, published in *Das Freud'sche Ideogenitätsmoment und seine Bedeutung im manisch-depressiven Irresein Kraepelin's* (Freud's ideogenic factor and its meaning in Kraepelin's manic depression, 1907)[74] and *Über psychopathische Minderwertigkeiten* (On inferiority complexes, 1909),[75] impressively explore the extrapolation of Freud's insights into hysteria and neurosis onto other pathologies and psychotic states. At this time, Gross stood only after Carl Jung in Freud's estimation.[76]

Gross did not, however, merely help assimilate the new developments of psychoanalysis to school psychiatry: he proved an able analyst and made important contributions to the new approach. Ironically, for someone whose life came to signify free love and the irreconcilable opposition of fathers and sons, his starting point was a partial rejection of Freud's insistence on the primacy of the sexual drive. He considered the latter, and the attendant Oedipus scenario, a special case of a larger conflict of instincts, that between the "own/self" and the "foreign/other" (*das Eigene* and *das Fremde*). The self includes the erotic drive, emerging from the need for contact, but includes the self-preservation instinct and assertion of will. Through conventionalized social (that is, patriarchal) norms, all of these are undermined: the child suppresses its own desires out of fear of abandonment, loneliness, and rejection. It is the internalization of the conflict between the self and the other that he defines as masochism: "the attempt of the child to identify with the passive situation he faces and through subordination to it achieve a certain amount of contact."[77] At this point, he reconfigures slightly the Freudian account by postulating the division as one of masochism (subordination to the other) and sadism (assertion of the self). Heterosexual men assume the attitude of sadism, while women accept the state of masochism. The socially sanctioned relation between the sexes becomes ruled by the principle of domination. Male homosexuality results from the adoption of the submissive role, essentially out of the refusal to rape; while female homosexuality results from the natural instinct of self-preservation of the woman. Yet male accession to sadism comes out of a masochistic root: the subordination to the patriarchal order and to its institutions such as the state.

The seeds of the inevitable conflict with Freud were not, however, sown on the terrain of theoretical differences but rather due to the radical conclusions drawn by Gross: that no psychological healing was possible without changing the patriarchal order and its corruption of natural drives. The fundamental root of psychopathology lay, according to Gross, in society itself, and a fundamental cure could only proceed on the basis of the release of legitimate desires and a return to what Gross saw as the original, paradisiacal form of society: matriarchy. The liberation of female desire would also liberate the male subject, and free love was a fundamental tenet of any society not based on repression. Whatever the details of Gross's vision of freedom, at stake was the raison d'être of the new direction taken by psychiatry. Anticipating the anti-psychiatrists of the mid-twentieth century, Gross rejected the limited form of therapeutic psychoanalysis in its Freudian form, which he felt could lead only to adaptation and conformity. His conclusion appeared in a manifesto of 1913:

> The psychology of the unconscious is the philosophy of revolution; that is, it is ordained for it as the ferment of revolt in the psyche, as the liberation of the individuality fettered by one's own unconscious. It is called upon to inwardly create capacity for freedom, invoked as the *groundwork* of revolution.[78]

Freud had rejected the politicization of his own ideas many years earlier, replying to Gross simply: "We are doctors and will remain doctors."[79]

Gross's ideas were significant and influential. It was through his life and actions, however, that he became a series of scandals, of cases in the press, the courts, and the asylum. His father Hans (or Hanns) was a public figure in Austria and beyond: starting as a state prosecutor, he turned to criminalistics and is to be credited with establishing both the academic field and police procedures of forensic science. In practical terms, his influence far exceeds that of criminal anthropologists such as Cesare Lombroso; his standard work *Handbuch für Untersuchungsrichter* remained in print for nearly a century; the *Archiv für Kriminal-Anthropologie und Kriminalistik*, which he founded in 1898, is still published (as *Archiv für Kriminologie*). Hans Gross was also, by all accounts, an authoritarian figure who was in permanent conflict with his son. While a ship's doctor in 1901, Otto became addicted to morphine and cocaine and remained so for the rest of his life. Indeed, it was as a private patient at Burghölzli, receiving treatment for his addiction, that he met Bleuler and Carl Jung. Gross's second cure at Burghölzli involved an intense mutual analysis with Jung. Their conversations had a profound influence on Jung, until Gross escaped the asylum and went underground; Jung subsequently diagnosed Gross with *dementia praecox* (and slowly removed all indications of Gross's influence from his own writings).[80] In Munich and Ascona, Gross analyzed many members of the anarchist circles and entered into affairs with his female patients, two of whom took their own lives with drugs he had provided. In 1913, Hans Gross, finally realizing that his hopes of a university career for his son were dashed—Otto was, after all, sought by the Swiss police for his roles in these deaths—lost his patience and reacted in a typically heavy-handed way. Using his international connections, he had Otto, then staying with Franz Jung in Berlin and part of the circle around Franz Pfemfert's journal *Die Aktion*, arrested, deported as an undesirable alien, and brought to the border, where he was met by Austrian authorities and delivered to a private asylum at Tulln, near Vienna. In the wake of an international press campaign launched by Franz Jung, Gross was moved to a secure institution in Silesia, while in the courts, his father, supported by medical affidavits (supplied by, amongst others, Freud and Carl Jung), succeeded in having his son declared legally insane. Though in and out of institutions afterwards, functioning as both physician and patient, Gross lived without complete legal rights until his death in Berlin in 1920: homeless, penniless, and unable to secure his drugs, he succumbed to pneumonia complicated by malnutrition. His father Hans had died a bitter man in 1915.

§

Gross's complex oeuvre and turbulent life touched many people deeply. It was a life that connected the worlds of psychiatry in its forensic forms to the circles of artists and bohemians, and moreover one that unfolded as public scandal in and beyond them. Following its traces and its impacts allows us to explore the form of the case as it is inscribed in various works of the Berlin Expressionists and Dadaists, and moreover to track the way these circles engaged with, and worked through, the public sphere of the time.

Certainly the press campaign to free Otto Gross has entered into the mythology of Expressionism as a key intervention in the public sphere, a successful attempt to turn a police and medical case into a press affair, countering the behind-the-scenes machinations that put him in an asylum against his will and had him declared legally incapacitated with the public exposure of prominent figures and their questionable and possibly illegal actions. Led by Franz Jung, Gross's friends and supporters mobilized the overlapping circles of the Expressionist and anarchist press, a set of small journals published mainly in Berlin and Munich. Within two weeks, one of the most important of these—Franz Pfemfert's *Die Aktion*, to which Gross was closely linked—reported on the matter. *Die Aktion* was the key journal of Berlin's independent left radicals who maintained a distance from the institutionalized and bureaucratized Social Democratic Party; it was also the most important venue for the Expressionist writing of Jakob van Hoddis, Alfred Lichtenstein, Carl Einstein, Else Lasker-Schüler, Gottfried Benn, Ludwig Rubiner, and Franz Jung himself.[81] In the visual arts, *Die Aktion* was the site at which the Expressionism of the *Brücke* artists and those inspired by them was most widely circulated. The journal was vocal in support of the Berlin Neue Sezession, with which the *Brücke* artists were associated since their moves to Berlin in the years after 1911; and in turn the artists' harsh woodcut aesthetic came to give *Die Aktion* its visual profile. (In this, it can be contrasted to its rival, Herwarth Walden's *Der Sturm*, which publicized instead Munich and Vienna Expressionists as well as international developments in Cubism and Futurism.[82]) As a publication defining the intersection of the avant-gardes in literature and the visual arts with the politics of the independent left in the 1910s, the importance of *Die Aktion* cannot be overstated. "There was hardly a poet or painter in Berlin of the 1920s," wrote the Socialist writer Henry Jacoby, "who did not get his start in *Die Aktion*."[83]

On November 22, 1913, in a brief introduction to the fourth text Gross published in the journal in that year, Pfemfert reported on Gross's abduction:

> Around midday on Sunday November 9, the important scientist Dr. Otto Groß was visited in his Wilmersdorf flat

> by three burly men who apparently identified themselves as police officers and held him there against his will until evening. Staff from *Die Aktion*, sent by me to collect manuscripts, were not allowed access to the "prisoner." That evening, Groß (who was not active politically but was writing a new scholarly book) was secretly removed from the flat ... and most likely incarcerated in an Austrian insane asylum.[84]

Two weeks later, the Expressionist writer and critic Ludwig Rubiner raised the matter again, and another of Gross's articles, along with an editorial reminder of his fate, was published. Pfemfert dedicated the December 20 issue to Gross. On the title page, under the headline "To Professor Hans Gross (Graz)," he made public his attempts to communicate with the elder Gross and to determine Otto's whereabouts; and Ludwig Rubiner published a fulminant "Call to Writers" to pursue justice for the renegade psychiatrist. For months the case was a fixture in the pages of *Die Aktion*. With the help of Johannes R. Becher, Franz Jung also oversaw a special issue of the short-lived Munich journal *Revolution* devoted to Otto Gross, with a manifesto by Jung addressed to Hans Gross and statements by Rubiner, Blaise Cendrars, Erich Mühsam, Becher, and others. Jung claims to have secretly distributed over one thousand copies of the issue in Hans Gross's hometown of Graz. The affair was raised in the small journals *Kain*, *Wiecker Bote*, and the *Schaubühne*.

The alliance of Jung, Pfemfert, and others then sought to bring news of the affair to a wider public. Articles appeared in local newspapers such as the *Wilmersdorfer Zeitung*, as well as larger-circulation cultural journals such as *März* and the international press. The *Prager Tageblatt* and the *Neues Wiener Journal* reported under the headline "Involuntary detention in a mental asylum: Prof. Dr. Hans Groß against his son"; the *Neues Wiener Abendblatt* carried two notices; even Guillaume Apollinaire wrote on the abduction in the *Mercure de France*.[85] In *Die Zukunft*, Maximilian Harden published a letter from Otto Gross himself, an attempt to prevent his father, who had already become Otto's legal guardian with his legal incapacitation of January 9, from taking custody of his daughter from Gross's wife Frieda, then living with another man, the painter Ernst Frick, in the anarchist colony on Monte Verità in Ascona. Gross used the opportunity to assert his political position in terms echoing Panizza's *Psicopatia Criminalis* but in a tone more pathetic:

> And one thing is held against me: that I am not satisfied with the prevailing social order. Whether one considers this proof of a mental defect depends on what one takes as the norm of mental health. If one takes conformity to the status quo as normal, then dissatisfaction with it can be understood as a sign of mental deficiency. If one takes the highest development of all possibilities innate to man as the norm and knows, intuitively and from experience, that the existing social order renders impossible the highest development of the individual and mankind as a whole, then he recognizes satisfaction with the status quo as a form of inferiority.[86]

For Franz Jung and others, this politics of publicity came to be emblematic of the concentration of intellectuals' efforts, the effectiveness of concerted public action, and the strength of the younger generation. In his autobiography Jung writes of their success:

> As the campaign was taken up in the Austrian public sphere ... the old man caved in. It was just a misunderstanding, he let it be known. Otto Gross had admitted himself into the asylum voluntarily in order to undergo treatment for his addiction; he could be released at any time. I was invited by telegram to come to the facility in Troppau. I went there and took him away. I was treated like an inspecting minister from the government in Vienna. In the meantime, Otto Gross had already been taken out of the category of the incurably insane and had advanced to the position of assistant clinical doctor.[87]

For the Expressionist generation, the Gross case came to stand for an effective union of literature and politics, an example of what Ludwig Rubiner had called for in the pages of *Die Aktion* in his essays "Writers Intervene in Politics" and, expanding on the theme, "Painters Build Barricades," about Expressionist artists such as Karl Schmidt-Rottluff.[88] It is a Krausian scenario: through concerted action, a public could be reached, truth told, authorities held to account, and the world of injustices rendered transparent. If a few backroom machinations were required, then that went with the territory.

But what does the case of Otto Gross really tell us about how the space of publicity in the German-speaking world before the First World War worked? We can say, I think, three things. First, no such realm of transparent and rational debate was created at all.[89] Hans Gross was indeed forced to respond in print to his son's letter in the prominent *Zukunft*, but not because the Expressionists had succeeded, in Franz Jung's words, in presenting "Professor Gross ... as a type of person who needed psychiatric treatment far more urgently in the interest of public safety than his son."[90] Hans's reply was reasoned, detailed, and spoke to a father's pain at his son's illness. It was convincing, or at least convincing *enough* to level the playing field, pitting the word of the father against that of the son and friends. The latter could not prove anything in the press nor demand any mechanism by which the truth could be determined in public. And in the absence of a clear "smoking gun" or a public procedure to be triggered, the press, as a surface on which to make public representations, showed itself to be quite flat, tending to equalize the valences of what was projected onto it. Recent research has shown that communications flowed back and forth within the Austrian Ministry of Internal Affairs, which, responsibly enough, wanted to investigate the allegations, and moreover to preserve the public image of mechanisms of the state. Bureaucrats were soon convinced that no law had been broken and that the reputation and image of the state would not suffer. The only thing that the press campaign ultimately achieved was the transfer of Otto Gross from the public asylum in Tulln to a secure asylum in Austrian Silesia, to prevent any violent attempt to free him.[91] When he was released on July 8, 1914, it was not the result of real or perceived pressure from the public as mediated through the press, but rather because Gross had accepted in writing that he was ill and agreed to the conditions of his father's custodianship. Otto was indeed ill—though there is little reason to accept Carl Jung's diagnosis of *dementia praecox*, or incurable schizophrenia.[92] Whether Gross's acquiescence to the diagnosis was sincere or a tactical move to regain a limited freedom we shall never know. But a relatively few bureaucratic documents—the doctors' affidavits, the court's decision, the ministry's assent, and the patient's submission—proved enough to withstand the assault of parts of the press and the concerned publics, whether motivated by conviction, principle, or sensationalism.

My point is not to debunk a myth—a myth that was important to the self-understanding of certain subcultures, to the terms of discourses we can consider avant-garde, and that had a real value precisely *as* myth. Instead it is to use the episode to see what can be said about historical possibilities of publicity. And this leads us to the second point that can be made. The example of the Gross case shows that there are different kinds of publics, and different kinds of public spheres. The publicity generated by the small magazines, in close contact with specific social circles and their habitus, with specific subcultures, could respond quickly and move its subjects. Gross—in person, through his reputation or his writings—would already have been familiar to many of the readers of *Die Aktion*—or they would immediately have been prompted to find out more. The discursive framing of the appeals—specifically that of a generational conflict between authoritarian father and rebellious son—coded the matter politically and raised shared concerns where distinctions between right and wrong, urgency or not, would be prejudged. And this limited publicity had a certain depth, with its relevance to the specific concerns, life experiences, and convictions of a particular group, a subculture. The attempt to move to what could be called a mass public sphere, however, involved inserting the project into a space whose fundamental logics, discursive protocols, and material practices worked by very different rules. It would be an impossible task to determine precisely those intricate and overdetermined logics: suffice it to say they would concern editors' choices about reader interest, choices about the relative importance of competing stories, choices about political tendencies and the way they would inflect the possible meanings of the stories. In fact, the ability of the press campaign to cross from a partial to a mass public sphere was extremely limited: there were interventions in two or three important places (*Die Zukunft*, *März*, *Mercure de France*) but only small notices in a limited number of mass-circulation newspapers of the kind that Kraus dealt with. Franz Pfemfert's letters show how the line could not effectively be crossed. He had written urgently to the art editor of the Viennese Social Democrat *Arbeiter-Zeitung* about the need to publicize the events.[93] Nothing appeared, no doubt because the overall editor, Friedrich Austerlitz, had made a decision about the relevance of the matter to a specifically proletarian public, or a sector of the mass public that sought to represent proletarian interests as general ones. (The *Arbeiter-Zeitung* was in turn trying to establish itself on the same plane of publicity as the bourgeois and boulevard newspapers.) This complex jump—representing the Gross case as relevant to the concerns and experiences of a broader public—failed.

The third point we can make concerns Jung's and Pfemfert's limited success in reaching a broad public and, conversely, how this could be achieved. The Gross scandal in fact conforms to a type: it is one of countless cases of controversial *Entmündigung* or legal incapacitation that accompanied the rise of psychiatry in its simultaneously professional and forensic form.[94] This suspension of rights was the target of many of Karl Kraus's diatribes, the subject of numerous pamphlets, and the impetus for the founding of an organization and journal to lobby for legal reform. It was a scandal with a number of generic possibilities and plot options. The court declaration could be made in the absence of the subject, based on medical affidavits (as in Otto Gross's case); it could take the auto-anamnetic form of the patient's medical history, as it did monumentally in the case of Judge Schreber; it could involve family finances or honor. Panizza had identified the logical core of *Entmündigung*: "Anything that we [psychiatrists] determine is pathological, is so, whatever else it may be." By the time of the Gross case, this was something of a commonplace, and not only amongst those who fed off the spectacular fruits of the ripe gardens of injustice and iniquity (as arguably Kraus did). Indeed, in the satirical journal *Der Zwiebelfisch*, Hans von Weber alludes to the nascent anti-psychiatric feeling in a way that shows how familiar it was: "The insane asylum as a substitute for the no longer so serviceable *lettres de cachet* has been discussed often recently: apparently power and capital are trying to use the same means as were used before the Revolution in the eighteenth century to suppress the mind [*um den Geist zu knebeln*]." He then took sides: "But the mind will now, as then, only be strengthened in its explosive power."[95] That was, perhaps, local solidarity: *Der Zwiebelfisch* was a Munich journal, part of the scene of literary modernism and café culture, if somewhat distant from anarchist and Expressionist circles. But such partisanships were precarious. When we recognize the sort of readymade scandal, the generic nature of the case, we can see why Friedrich Austerlitz might have decided that it was not worth devoting column inches in the Viennese *Arbeiter-Zeitung* to a renegade psychoanalyst with an overbearing and influential father. (Franz Pfemfert's and Otto Gross's distance from organized Social Democracy would also have played a role.)

A simple injustice might not be enough to break into the large press, but if it was going to, the scandal of *Entmündigung* or incapacitation provided an established genre and set of narratives by which it could do so. This was the sort of case that formed a public, a pre-existing condensation nucleus around which publicity precipitated. We thus get a sense of how the public sphere worked, and did not work, a feel for the texture of editorial decisions and public visibility, an indication of the challenges of moving from a small, partial public sphere rooted in specific interests and experiences into a broader, flatter mass public sphere, one with more coverage but which hovered less connectedly over more diverse demographics. We see that the press was not the arbiter, not the place of formation of public opinion, discussion, decision, and resolution, but instead one of many instances and institutions that could be mobilized to achieve not some mythic form of social transparency but at most a punctual visibility, offering the chance of an outcry, a recognition, some concern or passion, one that could start a discussion or hunger for information that would feed back into the complex institutions and machineries of representation. Whether such opinions or themes,[96] or as I would argue *cases*, could turn into sites of the public production of knowledge and opinion was highly contingent and always unpredictable.

That the case of Otto Gross failed to create a site of effective publicity, a punctual public sphere, is hardly all that can be said about Gross's intersection with the multimedial set of appearances that came to be called Expressionism. It can in fact provide a case study into how a certain kind of Expressionism, a certain set of interventions into art, literature, and politics, sat in the public sphere of the time, in the space of social representation. But to study this we need to explore why this intersection happened in the first place. For Gross's involvement with the likes of Franz Pfemfert and Franz Jung, and George Grosz's interest in illustrating the case of a paranoid schizophrenic held in the asylum in Troppau, Austrian Silesia, is neither a complete accident nor something self-evident. We need to consider Gross's work in relation to its interactions with social institutions, discursive venues, and specific professional and artistic cultures. For though his oeuvre is relatively small and even straightforward in its evolution, it is remarkably rich in shifts and turns of vehicle and audience.

§

Expressionism and Publicity

Gross's first two publications, both in 1901, are those of a medical clinician. His doctoral thesis was a pharmacotherapeutic compendium, and his second published work an essay on cardiorenal theories; they appeared in a specifically medical literature. He then published two articles in his father's *Archiv*, broad and somewhat speculative discussions of social behavior that were framed as criminal anthropology. It is interesting, but biographically logical, that he engaged with this field that so closely conformed to the socially disciplinary side of the medicine of the time. From 1902, his work moved into the area of mainstream psychiatry. Between 1902 and 1909, in nine articles and three books, Gross engaged in the discussions around *dementia praecox* and a psychological approach to psychotic states, drawing imaginatively on Freud's perspectives and findings.

These publications appeared in the most respected journals and presses of the time; they brought him considerable prominence at a young age and foretold a promising career.[97] Yet around 1907, it became clear to Gross that he no longer wished his interventions to be seen simply as psychiatry: his work had always struck a socially critical undertone, and this is what he wished to pursue. He made a number of attempts to redirect his psychiatric work in a speculative or political direction. First, he engaged with the "psychoanalytic movement" as Freud understood it. But over the course of 1908 he quickly burned his bridges there. The First Psychoanalytic Congress in Salzburg, when Freud realized that Gross's efforts were directed in an extra-therapeutic direction that was anathema to his own attempts to have psychoanalysis recognized as a medical science; Gross's escape from Burghölzli and his obvious addictions; Gross's relinquishment of his university position—all made Gross more a liability to Freud's "cause" than an asset.

Already in 1907 Gross had sought to place an essay in Max Weber and Edgar Jaffé's *Archiv für Sozialwissenschaften und Sozialpolitik*, a journal of reformist politics and the organ of emergent

German sociology.[98] This was no shot in the dark: Gross had met Weber and his wife Marianne, who both found him sympathetic; he was also having an affair with Jaffé's wife, Else, whom he knew through his own wife, Frieda. Weber rejected the text: echoing Freud's objections to Gross's psychoanalytic positions, he found that it crossed the line from science to ethical and political norms based on value judgments.[99] Gross had tried to publish in the Munich anarchist circle around Erich Mühsam and Gustav Landauer. He and Mühsam (whom he had analyzed) planned from 1907 to bring out a journal titled *Zeitschrift für psychologische Gesellschaftskritik*.[100] Landauer refused—he disapproved harshly of Gross's views on matriarchy, marriage, and homosexuality—effectively blacklisting Gross from the Munich anarchist press.

So, after rejecting criminology and school psychiatry, by 1913, Gross found himself also effectively barred from the discourses and venues of sociology, psychoanalysis, and Landauer's influential political project.[101] He had failed in the attempt to find a broad public for his work; there were no venues open to him. So when he was welcomed into the pages of *Die Aktion* by Franz Jung and Franz Pfemfert, he had little choice; he published there *faute de mieux*. Yet in his second contribution to the journal, he presents his disciplinary migration from science to art as a logical and necessary move: "Clearly it has been art that has hitherto alone illuminated unconscious psychological relationships, and it will depend on the power of the artist to drive forward new paths of knowledge."[102] From then on, Gross's works appeared mainly in the small magazines: *Die Aktion*, his and Franz Jung's *Die freie Straße*, and the short-lived revolutionary journals *Sowjet*, *Die Erde*, and *Räte-Zeitung*. Only posthumously, with his study *Drei Aufsätze über den inneren Konflikt*, did a major work appear again, this time in a series on sexual science, presumably placed by Wilhelm Stekel.

Indeed, the strange fact of Gross's written traces is that they were usually second-hand. He was far more often an object of representation than its subject. This is how he seemed to have made his mark, blossoming in a bewildering variety of generic contexts of the kind we recognize from Panizza's nearly parasitic presence in the media of art, law, and psychiatry.[103] In addition to his own writings, and reaching far beyond them in scope, Otto Gross appeared 1) to a very limited extent in the scholarly apparatuses of others in his fields, for example in a few references by

Carl Jung (which were partially suppressed in later editions); in 2) the press of the time as an item of *news*; and, as the recent and energetic Gross research has discovered, in 3) a huge number of legal and medical documents involved with lawsuits against him, his father's attempt to gain custody of his grandchild, and with his own case, in which his legal majority was suspended. Overlapping with this, we find 4) his medical anamneses, his own accounts of his illness—a medical case history and evidence of pathology—that were the objects of medical science and not communicative on his own terms. Because diagnoses of Gross were extremely controversial, we find few 5) accounts of Gross as a case history in the broader psychiatric literature, but he does appear, anonymized as "M.K.," as case number 37 in Stekel's *Sadismus und Masochismus: Für Ärzte und Kriminologen dargestellt* (Sadism and masochism: presented for doctors and criminologists)—precisely the disciplinary literature of medico-forensic science (here in its psychoanalytic form) that Gross rejected so strongly.[104]

Finally, Gross appears in an astounding number of 6) novels and memoirs of those who met him: as Dr. Weber in Leonhard Frank's *Traumgefährten* (Dreammates, 1936), as Dr. Hoch in Johannes R. Becher's *Abschied* (Farewell, 1940), as Dr. Askonas in Max Brod's *Das große Wagnis* (The great gamble, 1918), as Hans Termaden in Curt Corrinth's *Potsdamer Platz oder die Nächte des neuen Messias* (Potsdamer Platz, or the nights of the new Messiah, 1919), as Othmar in Karl Otten's *Wurzeln* (Roots, 1963); Franz Werfel also cast him as Chaim Leib Beschitzer in *Nicht der Mörder, der Ermordete ist schuldig* (Not the murderer—the one murdered is guilty, 1920), as Ottokar Grund in the play *Schweiger* (Schweiger, 1922), and as Dr. Gebhart in *Barbara, oder die Frömmigkeit* (Barbara, or devotion, 1929). Some of these are biographical, others more novelistic; nonetheless, Gross and his ideas are clearly identifiable. He appears in the memoirs of Franz Jung, Emil Szittya, and others, and as Jennifer Michaels has traced, his ideas informed plots and characters in other works of most of these authors.[105]

There are, for the most part, two kinds of representation here. The first is as a *case*: scandalous or controversial news, involvement in legal action and medical scrutiny, treatment, and narration. But unlike Panizza, or indeed Loos and Kraus, Otto Gross was the object of cases, not their subject. He was unable to set the terms for his own appearance in public or to mobilize the media and genres of the case for his own ends. However, the second kind of representation—as a *character*—is evidence of a public that nonetheless formed around him: he was a catalyst, a charismatic figure whose compelling ideas, personality, and example commanded attention and provoked discussion of matters of concern to a set of subcultures. He was a key figure of certain bohemian circles.

La bohème, die Boheme, bohemia: it is a loose term. Some scholars, such as Mary Gluck, define it as a "discursive configuration."[106] For others, it is a "symbolic space." In his monumental work on the topic, Helmut Kreuzer sees it as a real social space with a specific set of actors, relatively constant over a specific period, and with "a consistency of attitudes and effects."[107] Perhaps most productively, Rolf Schwendter considers bohemia to be simply one of several subcultures, or groups with values, norms, needs, institutions, and manifestations that differ fundamentally from those of a prevailing society.[108] In such fluid groups, a persona or mode of life can have powerful effects, as did Otto Gross's. Schwendter has mapped Gross's relation to bohemia as well as to other, smaller subcultures (Expressionism, Monte Verita, the homosexual subculture as well as that of addicts).[109] And "social movements" can encompass several subcultures or move through them. Psychoanalysis is a case in point: the subcultures of Freudian theory and bohemia regularly crossed, and, as we have seen, that was something that exercised Freud considerably. He was at pains to represent his "movement" as scientific and not artistic, as respectable and not libertine, as theory and therapy but not social practice beyond this. Thus his severing of ties with so many of his followers: Fritz Wittels, Otto Gross, Wilhelm Reich, and others. His goal was for psychoanalysis to be a recognized part of establishment culture.

Subcultural groups can be traced, but it is important to separate them from the sort of publicness that occupies me here. Instead of fluid groups, I am interested in looking at spaces of representation and how their shape can change, at what can be seen, and said, both from within these groups but also from beyond them. Consider it a screen, broadly visible, on which images can be presented and ideas articulated. Even if these images have specific currency for some social groups, public representations can create new groups that do not even meet, that have little material social structure. They can provide points of identification and solidarity, but also provide meanings and associations for opponents to reject, distort, combat. And while such publicness can provide meanings for small groups, it follows not so much a logic of personal bonds but one of representation and circulation, even if that logic is every bit as material. One could, with Jürgen Gerhards and Friedhelm Neidhardt, talk of a small or "encounter" public sphere, but that would be to miss the point.[110] In that kind of public sphere, Gross had a public persona and his habitus made meaning. However he failed to go beyond that and develop his ideas in a way that allowed him to be the subject in control of their representation; he failed to work within what one could call the dispositive of public representation, with its fairly well-defined discourses, genres, venues, and types of authors. Thus, for all his very real importance for a number of important groups and his very solid engagements with movements from anarchism to psychoanalysis to the progressive sociologists and economists of Heidelberg, for all the discursive traces he left, for all the texts that take him as their object, his own interventions—as thinker, writer, clinician, citizen claiming his rights—remained largely under the threshold of public view.

§

Precisely because of his extraordinary variety of engagements, Otto Gross remains endlessly revealing. His very presence in *Die Aktion* gives us some interesting indications about how the public for art and politics was negotiated in the Expressionist years—not only what could be public but what could not, and how their permutations could make meaning in surprising ways.

Die Aktion was one of two pre-eminent Expressionist journals in Berlin in the 1910s. Its origins were as a political weekly; the editor, Franz Pfemfert, had worked with two anarchist magazines before founding his own in 1911. But soon it started to include literature—novellas, poetry, and criticism—specifically that of the young generation around Georg Heym, Kurt Hiller, Jakob van Hoddis, and others who came to be considered Expressionist. This increased its circulation considerably and served to distinguish it from purely political journals, and also from one of its main competitors, *Der Sturm*, whose cultural coverage began to seem somewhat narrow. The inclusion, from 1913, of regular title illustrations by prominent artists and the increasing coverage of the visual arts not only widened its scope but gave it its immediately recognizable visual profile.

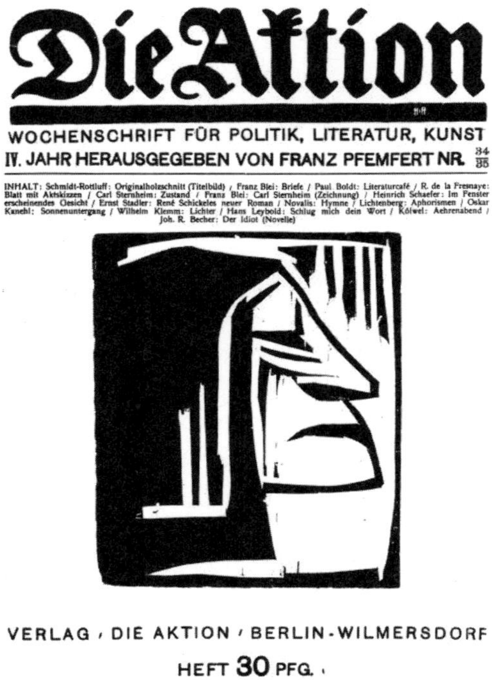
Die Aktion

WOCHENSCHRIFT FÜR POLITIK, LITERATUR, KUNST

IV. JAHR HERAUSGEGEBEN VON FRANZ PFEMFERT NR. 34/35

INHALT: Schmidt-Rottluff: Originalholzschnitt (Titelbild) / Franz Blei: Briefe / Paul Boldt: Literaturcafé / R. de la Fresnaye: Blatt mit Aktskizzen / Carl Sternheim: Zustand / Franz Blei: Carl Sternheim (Zeichnung) / Heinrich Schaefer: Im Fenster erscheinendes Gesicht / Ernst Stadler: René Schickeles neuer Roman / Novalis: Hymne / Lichtenberg: Aphorismen / Oskar Kanehl: Sonnenuntergang / Wilhelm Klemm: Lichter / Hans Leybold: Schlug mich dein Wort / Kölwel: Aehrenabend / Joh. R. Becher: Der Idiot (Novelle)

VERLAG / DIE AKTION / BERLIN-WILMERSDORF

HEFT 30 PFG.

Cover for *Die Aktion* 4, no. 34/35 (September 12, 1914).

This specific balance proved to be an advantage after the outbreak of the First World War. A notice appeared in the first issue after the start of hostilities: "*Die Aktion* will, in the next weeks, concern itself with only literature and art."[111] Though the hiatus lasted more than four years, the journal was uniquely positioned simply to shift emphasis and continue publishing. Pfemfert handled this with considerable skill and delicacy. Politics appeared at the back, à la Karl Kraus: Pfemfert simply reproduced items appearing elsewhere in the press that showed the cynicism and irrationality of the war, juxtaposing them with items showing its horror. Of this time of war he wrote:

> I had my answers before they [the times] posed their questions. Today my silence must speak for me—and the times themselves must speak. The folder in which I save these times has already become quite thick and ungainly; I want to clear it out and have begun to clip out the times, in order to show their countenance ... My scissors squeak; I clip

out the times [*ich schneide die Zeit aus*]; they shall speak in my *Aktion*; for themselves and for me.[112]

A clear and critical editorial line was established not only by the reuse of already published—and thus already permitted—material. Pfemfert's handling of what remained permissible—artistic content and criticism—helped to clarify the journal's pacifist position. It did so first by default: poetry, short stories, images, and the discussions of them spoke, explicitly, his *political* silence. And second, carefully but not without risk, Pfemfert used such content allusively to condemn the Central Powers' prosecution of the war. The poetry that appeared in *Die Aktion* longed for peace, but it was not specifically anti-German. German, French, Italian, and British writers and artists were still published: even in the first days of war works by Roger de La Fresnaye, Honoré Daumier, Henri Matisse, and Paul Cézanne were reproduced. Artists and writers associated with the journal who were killed in the war were honored—even those who had fought for the Allied powers. Remarkably, there were themed issues on the art and writing of England, France, Belgium, and Italy.[113] They were kept apolitical, but they were a constant reminder of the unity of the arts, and this was framed as a proxy for the unity of the left, of the Socialist movement. These silences could speak: they held specific places open and allowed one kind of content to stand for other matters, when those other matters did not speak for themselves. So when in the issue of August 29, 1914, a harrowing Expressionist short story of madness and persecution by Franz Jung ("Die Telepathen," which we shall discuss below) appeared next to an Expressionist drawing by Heinrich Richter-Berlin and drawings by Daumier, a constellation was created: in the main venue of Expressionist work in Germany, Expressionism was identified with an anti-war position—one readers knew to associate with *Die Aktion* and could recognize in the work of a French artist—and the cause of the story's madness, the nature of the persecution, could be equated with the war. Thus the restrictions of content—not to oppose the war by criticizing it overtly or siding politically with the enemy—were counterbalanced by the areas that remained open, those of art and literature. And the material that met with less resistance—art and literature—was coded as anti-militaristic. The mechanisms of this delicate balance gave shape to the space of public representation and reveal the way a public sphere and its rules were defined. Within this space, meanings were made less by open discussion and rational debate than by shifts of meaning and its vehicles, by metonymy and synecdoche.

But it was not just the First World War that produced such conditions of signification. While it made these matters more obvious, the same logic applied earlier. Its workings were even more complex. Consider the topics and themes of the contributions to *Die Aktion* in the years before the hostilities. Censorship was one. A series of articles about "Secret Theatre" explored the possibilities of organizing performances at a large scale but as private events, to evade the censorship requirements for public performances. There were reports of overenthusiastic state attorneys confiscating postcards of Old Master paintings as pornographic. An issue of *Die Aktion* was in turn confiscated in 1914. But Pfemfert had trouble determining which contributions had caused offence. Was it due, for example, to his account of Rosa Luxemburg's incarceration for, as he put it, "optimism"—for stating her hopes that the working classes of Germany and France would refuse to fight each other in an upcoming war? In the end, it turned out that a translation of two medieval Provencal love songs had been found to violate §183 of the criminal code. There was a lengthy series following a complex court case involving a contributor's negative review of a play in another journal and the lawsuits that surrounded it.[114] Then there were articles on madness: Wieland Herzfelde's essay "Die Ethik der Geisteskranken" (The ethics of the mentally ill) and, in another issue, a short story by his father, Franz Held (actually Herzfeld), an anarchist and old ally of Oskar Panizza who was similarly charged with blasphemy, and who also died in an asylum, in 1908.[115] There was a poem by Max Herrmann-Neiße with the title "Das Sittlichkeitsdelikt" (The sexual offence); among other contributions on legal matters an essay on §218, the law criminalizing abortion; and reports on sexual sciences, including Magnus Hirschfeld's publication of a fictional story as the author's actual sexual case history or anamnesis. And there were accounts of legal incapacitation and forced institutionalization for mental illness. A year before the Otto Gross affair, Pfemfert wrote about an up-and-coming poet under the title "Gewaltsam ins Irrenhaus" (By force into the insane asylum):

> About five weeks ago, after a long editorial conference with me, Jakob van Hoddis was seized in his flat by a doctor and two assistants, rendered docile by an injection and locked into an asylum near Nikolassee [-Berlin]. The internment was instigated by members of his own family, with whom he was involved in an inheritance dispute ... Jakob van Hoddis ceased to exist until he escaped, deciding that the risk of a fall to his death was less than the risk of intellectual death among incurable madmen.[116]

By the time he wrote about Gross, Pfemfert clearly had practice in describing such events.

So in addition to Expressionist writing and art in *Die Aktion*, we find attention to politics, censorship, court cases, scandal, sex, and madness. It is a curiously familiar constellation. Oskar Panizza's project anticipated the mix of media, genres, and themes of the Expressionist avant-garde. If Panizza was seen as an eccentric loner in the 1890s, by 1914 he would have looked strangely prescient. An isolated *cause célèbre* in 1894, he was soon emblematic of a set of issues that many intellectuals were grappling with immediately before the war.

All this gives us a handle on the thorny issue of the politics of Expressionism. Surely the Expressionist texts and images were, most often, not explicitly political, nor can one attribute a politics to them simply on the basis of their appearance in a political, specifically anarchist, journal. But the specific mix of contributions in *Die Aktion* says something about the politics of culture at the time. The Expressionists can hardly be considered an avant-garde in Peter Bürger's sense of politics: they did not seek to reintegrate art into the praxis of life (as if they were ever truly apart), or better, they did not seek to alter political reality so that art would not need to mark a distance from it (though some Expressionist artists did seek to take over the art institutions of the state as their part of a postwar revolution).[117] One could adduce a politics from the thematics of the works ("anti-bourgeois"). One could call their skirting the line of the legal a form of politics. But it is hard to call them political on those grounds. Contemporaries were well aware of this. Consider the first issue of the Munich journal, *Revolution*—Becher, Leybold, and Bachmair's attempt to mimic Pfemfert—which had a woodcut by Richard Seewald, Expressionist texts (by Becher, Hugo Ball, and Else Lasker-Schüler), reviews, and a contribution by Erich Mühsam on revolutionary politics. There were complaints that publishing poems and artworks simply had nothing to do with revolution. In Hugo Ball's account:

> Someone in Berlin said, "What sort of a revolution are you making there in Munich! There's not a word of politics in it!" "Correct," said Leybold, "There's not a word of politics in it. What should one do?"[118]

All the same, the journal was confiscated for having published indecent material. And at first, they had no idea which contribution was seen as breaching the laws governing the press. Suspicion naturally fell on Leonhard Frank's short story "Der Erotomane und diese Jungfrau" (The sex maniac and this virgin). But they later learned that it was instead Ball's poem "Der Henker" (The hangman) that had crossed the line. Bachmair, as publisher, was prosecuted, but the court threw out the case with the delightful logic that the poem could not be considered indecent as it was utterly incomprehensible.[119] (The state attorney appealed, but the Reichsgericht upheld the ruling.) And thus the journal continued to publish, using the confiscation as effective advertising.

"Not a word of politics": and yet, Ball, Frank, Seewald, and the others soon found that their insufficient efforts had nonetheless made them criminals. They cannot be credited with radical politics for such work, and their involvement in the same milieu and same venues as political writers and agitators is not a convincing argument. But they found a politics when they were seen as criminal. They found their politics in the reflection of the broken mirror of state policing, in the interdiction from making certain kinds of public statements. They both provoked and thematized the precise issues around which the limits of the representable were drawn and enforced.

We can put it this way: the journals mixed a set of topics and styles that existed side by side, without a clear connection—as parataxis. But the parataxis turned, in the eyes of the police charged with guarding the morals and behavior of the populace, into a form of metonymy. From existing side by side, incomprehensible poems, discussions of sexual deviance, critiques of the law, political comment, and Expressionist woodcuts began to share their meanings; each began to mean the others.

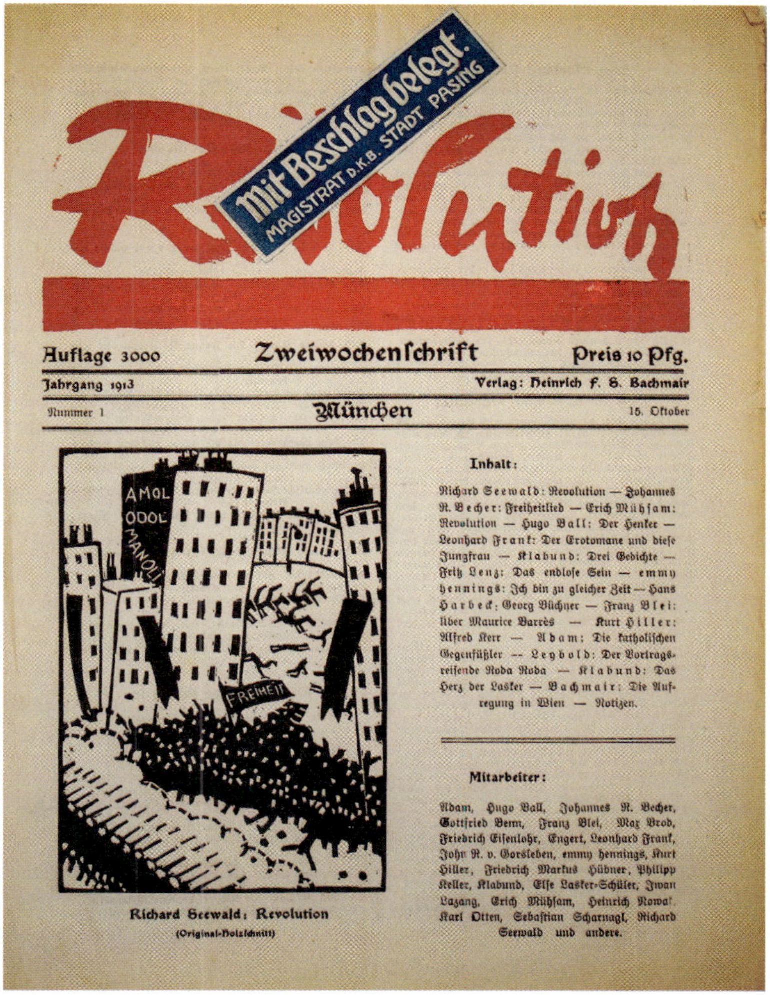
Revolution

mit Beschlag belegt.
MAGISTRAT D.K.B. STADT PASING

Auflage 3000 | Zweiwochenschrift | Preis 10 Pfg.

Jahrgang 1913 | Verlag: Heinrich F. S. Bachmair

Nummer 1 | München | 15. Oktober

Richard Seewald: Revolution
(Original-Holzschnitt)

Inhalt:

Richard Seewald: Revolution — Johannes R. Becher: Freiheitlied — Erich Mühsam: Revolution — Hugo Ball: Der Henker — Leonhard Frank: Der Erotomane und diese Jungfrau — Klabund: Drei Gedichte — Fritz Lenz: Das endlose Sein — emmy hennings: Ich bin zu gleicher Zeit — Hans Harbeck: Georg Büchner — Franz Blei: über Maurice Barrès — Kurt Hiller: Alfred Kerr — Adam: Die katholischen Gegenfüßler — Leybold: Der Vortragsreisende Roda Roda — Klabund: Das Herz der Lasker — Bachmair: Die Aufregung in Wien — Notizen.

Mitarbeiter:

Adam, Hugo Ball, Johannes R. Becher, Gottfried Benn, Franz Blei, Max Brod, Friedrich Eisenlohr, Engert, Leonhard Frank, John R. v. Gorsleben, emmy hennings, Kurt Hiller, Friedrich Markus Hübner, Philipp Keller, Klabund, Else Lasker-Schüler, Iwan Lazang, Erich Mühsam, Heinrich Nowak, Karl Otten, Sebastian Scharnagl, Richard Seewald und andere.

Revolution, no. 1 (1913), with a label noting that the issue had been confiscated. Private collection. Photo Hans L. Merkle.

The situation was confusing: such a mix clearly bewildered the police and the judiciary, who were forced into actions that could be dismissed as irrational; and it confused the publishers, who could not predict which of these topics or modes would land them in court. Thus the political valence that accrued to all of these modes and topics was not an essential fact of them, but it *was* an historical fact of their reception. The manifestations of the culture of the case—the thematizing of legal and medical matters and the production of responses to them—were *de facto* political.

If the individual works cannot be considered radical in their politics, did the culture of the case in which they participated represent a political project? Here we are on firmer ground. These works—by Otto Gross, Franz Jung, accounts of disappearances and suspensions of legal rights, Expressionist woodcuts and poems—appeared in a context in which the conditions of public representation were ambitiously discussed, the rights of those deviating from social norms constantly asserted, the bounds of the acceptable crossed and analyzed. The Expressionists followed the example of Panizza, who had explored these limits through the themes of sexuality and religion, psychiatry, and politics. The mapping of the public sphere was part of the project: the attempt to determine and demonstrate what could be represented and what could not. Those were its politics.

§

Gross—Jung—Groß

In the example of the case of Otto Gross, we can see how madness and sexuality came together as matters of common concern, matters that were political in their own right and came also to resonate more broadly in a larger politics of publicity. What brought them together was the attempt of a counter-cultural intelligentsia to represent them in public; they found their politics defined for them in the push-back from the forces of the state that could deprive a person of liberty or deny them the opportunity of public utterance, issues identified so urgently by Panizza. Deviance or indecency could be policed by disciplinary forms of the case, while this discipline itself could be challenged by the case in its publicistic form. This interface served to map the surfaces of public representation, to limn the shape of the public sphere; and this very project must be seen as political at a time when forms of active politics were being discussed but were also severely curtailed—by the police and courts in a traditionally restrictive society whose norms often clashed with its constitutional existence as a *Rechtsstaat*, and then by the military at a time of war. The episodes of Oskar Panizza and Otto Gross did not bring about these conditions or serve to change them; instead they were examples of how discipline and freedom could be negotiated through the form of the case. We can call them meta-cases. The conditions of both politics and representation would become quite different after the First World War, with a new set of social conditions and a new constitution that provided the legal basis for their articulation. Before turning to later forms of the case, however, it is worth looking at how the controversial ideas of Otto Gross were represented in the literary and visual arts in ways that were separate from the case itself. For the case of Otto Gross lurks beneath the surface of a surprising number of works of the time, and some of them are revealing, not so much about the possibility of representation, but about their possibilities of success in finding an audience and presenting the ideas as important ones.

The most sustained engagement with the work of Otto Gross is to be found in the early Expressionist fiction of Franz Jung. In a series of novellas and short stories that are clearly autobiographical, Jung obsessively rehearsed Gross's analysis of the relations between the sexes, governed by the complex dystopian psychic economy of sadism and masochism. From the stories in *Das Trottelbuch* (The book of the halfwit, 1912), first published in *Der Sturm* and *Die Aktion*, and *Saul* (1916) through the novels *Kamaraden ... !* (Comrades ... !, 1913), *Opferung* (Sacrifice, 1916), and *Der Sprung aus der Welt* (The leap out of the world, 1918), the set-up is always the same: a man is in love with a woman, who loves him only when he is humiliated, a man torn between his desire and his disgust for the woman, to whom he is alternately tender and violent.[120] (*Sophie: Kreuzweg der Demut* (Sophie: Crossroads of humility, 1915), focusses on the same psychological dynamic, but the relationship is Otto Gross's and leads to the suicide of his lover, the painter Sophie Benz.[121]) These are harrowing accounts of psychological warfare, domestic violence, infidelity, and occasionally death. Even a positive review of *Kamaraden ... !* sums up the reading experience as follows: "We want to cast aside this dreadful book, and keep reading, greedily devouring all the filth, this squalor, these martyrs."[122] In an early review, Robert Musil sums up the plot in a way that applies to most of the other stories: the autobiographical protagonist's

> recurring experience looks like this: someone moves through the company of others with his fists tightly clenched in his pockets. He feels a tenderly childish defiance that makes his lips tremble; but out of them comes abuse. He drinks;

> he's thrown out onto the street. He screams abuse; inside it means: don't you see that I'm saying something tender, difficult? No one understands it. Someone—a woman—perhaps understands. And every up and down of his life ends with him beating her.[123]

Other regular figures are the protagonist's manipulative parents and the woman's scheming mother; occasionally a male "friend" is included, with whom the woman is unfaithful (most interpreters identify the figure of the friend with Otto Gross).[124] Jung's literary means are spare and stark; if there is any interest left in these works, it is in the extraordinary concentration of the narrative and the allusiveness of the occasionally opaque exposition. *Das Trottelbuch* was well received at the time, as were others within Expressionist circles; but with their relentless repetition of the themes of rape, violence, cruelty, humiliation, hatred, jealousy, dependency, and the futile hopes of freedom and harmony, these texts are unyielding and unsatisfying today. Their closeness to the works and themes of Otto Gross is beyond question: even as Jung worked through the permutations of Gross's analysis of the impossibility of love and the destructive nature of desire in a patriarchal society, Gross himself drew upon the writer's work to illustrate his ideas.[125] It is another example of the imbrication of fiction, confession, and theory in the realm of psychoanalysis.

By 1921, Jung had exorcised the demon of Otto Gross, from whom he had slowly distanced himself during the war. He did so in two ways. First, he wrote a substantial account of his friend's life and theories, of Gross's attempt through deed and word to fuse the insights of psychoanalysis and the Marxist critique of bourgeois society. (This was meant to be the introduction to a two-volume edition of Gross's writings.) Second, he wrote—and rewrote—one of Otto Gross's psychiatric case studies of an asylum patient suffering from paranoia, but as fiction. Originally a short story with the title "Die Telepathen" (The telepaths, 1914), the novella it turned into was called, emblematically, *Der Fall Groß* (The Groß case, 1920/21).

Jung's essay "From Sexual Misery to Social Catastrophe" is a clear but subtle account of Gross's theories interwoven with biographical information and reflection on Jung's own role in his subject's story.[126] To this day, it is an essential introduction to the phenomenon of Otto Gross. It is the rewritten case study, however, that is of more interest here. The subject is one Anton Wenzel Groß, a German-speaking technical draughtsman from Bielitz-Biala in Austrian Silesia (now Bielsko-Biała, Poland) who had gone to New York to work. While there he began to suffer from hallucinations and develop symptoms of paranoia: "Whenever a crime was committed, he would hear voices denouncing him."[127] Specifically, he feared he was suspected of a series of sexual crimes that had occurred in the vicinity; once he was heckled by a crowd and kept "hearing of a John Groß [who had] raped and murdered prostitutes (*Lustmord an Prostituierten*)."[128] These crimes were the work, claimed Groß, of a criminal group around a family he had known in Silesia, the Seidels from Tarnow. Members of the family and their agents pursued Groß up and down the East Coast as he changed residence and jobs in his attempt to escape them; they also continued their crimes and their attempts to frame him. Fleeing America for home, Groß found that the Seidel band had maintained their surveillance of him on the ship. Groß got as far as Breslau. He checked into a small hotel, but when he heard them murdering a victim on the other side of his wall, he barricaded himself into his room. Armed with two pistols, he fired first at hotel staff and then at the police as they tried to enter. Groß was shot and seriously wounded in the exchange of gunfire but survived and was sent to the asylum at Troppau (where Otto Gross was held). There he identified the director as one of the criminal band. Celebrating black masses in the catacombs beneath the asylum, they continued to abduct, rape, and murder women. Groß could follow everything they did, said, thought, and felt by telepathy, even experiencing their sexual release in this way. Jung based his stories on the patient's own notes: before leaving the asylum at Troppau with Otto Gross, Anton Groß had "pressed a bundle of papers into my hands, manuscript pages filled every which way with his writing, sharp as if engraved, with drawings in between. There were diagrams and a constantly recurring portrait sketch—a round face with slightly protruding eyes and a probably pointed head that was, however, covered by a stiff hat with a narrow brim: the Seidel type."[129]

"Die Telepathen," Jung's first fictionalized version of Groß's plight, appeared in the pages of *Die Aktion* in 1914.[130] It stays close to Gross's case study, reporting the paranoid schizophrenic experiences as if fact, largely in third-person narration, though in the fourth and final section recounting Groß's life in the asylum

Jung places his subject's perceptions in quotation marks, making concrete the subtle movement across the fluid line separating the social world from the patient's delusions. The second version, *Der Fall Groß*, expands the account considerably, relying more on Groß's own notes justifying his actions, giving information about how the criminals could be caught, clarifying the horrible conspiracy that only he could see due to his familiarity with the perpetrators, his telepathic connection through which they continued to taunt him, and the tortuous pleasure in which the Seidels implicated him.[131] The narration is also much more complex. Jung places the action within the authorial frame of his own involvement, the way he had been entrusted with Anton Groß's papers and tasked with mediating between the patient's delusions and the truth of the world they nonetheless reflected. As David Bathrick has compellingly described, Jung's use of *erlebte Rede*, or free indirect speech, consistently and systematically undermines "the bounds separating narrator from narrated to recreate in *total* detail the complicated but absolutely logical and consistent web of occurrences in Anton's life."[132] Articulating "the gap between the individual victim of oppression and those who would help overcome it," Bathrick describes Jung's project of doing by literature what Otto Gross had sought to do by analysis: "to speak the other's silence."[133]

Jung's texts are, by their very nature, extraordinarily complex: like so many products of the culture of the case, they are accounts of individual experience that were repeatedly reinscribed in different discursive and institutional contexts. From the entropic and constantly regenerated media and genres of the case, we can identify two medical forms that are recombined into a work of fiction. The first is Otto Gross's clinical case study, soberly written and incorporated into his final work of psychiatry, the monograph *Drei Aufsätze über den inneren Konflikt*, published with Stekel's help in 1920.[134] The second is the patient's anamnesis, his own account of his symptoms, here taking the form of the apparently endless set of notes Anton Wenzel Groß wrote while in Troppau and which were entrusted to Jung—the details of his persecution and his persecutors, the explanation of his behavior, the evidence of the Seidels' crimes.

Before turning to this next iteration of the case, it is worth noting some important implications of Jung's final treatment of the work of Otto Gross. Both Jung and Gross had previously blurred the distinction between the discourses of science, politics, and art. We have seen the conditions under which this practice developed and had its specific expedience. Having tried to publish in the context of psychiatry and psychoanalysis, then of politics, Otto Gross found an audience for his work in the circles of bohemians and artists, a counterculture separate from political institutions but with political interests, interests tied with artistic ones that served best to take over the work of public address. *Revolution*, *Die Aktion* and similar journals are examples of the kind of mobility of themes and (incomplete) access to public representation that developed before the war. The strategy of presenting politics under the aegis of art was a response to the shape of the public sphere of the time and the way its borders were patrolled; and this strategy served as the model for publication during the war as well (as shown by *Die Aktion*'s surprising success in appearing continuously during the hostilities).[135] With the general lifting of censorship and overall confusion about what could be made public following the defeat in the war, with the collapse of the monarchy and the civil war surrounding the new Republic's founding, this strategy had to be reconsidered. Jung's literary ambitions disappeared with his direct involvement in revolutionary politics; the novels he wrote from then up to the 1930s were explicitly *Tendenzliteratur*, political literature. Franz Pfemfert too began to separate portfolios. With the struggles of early Weimar, he jettisoned his interest in Expressionism, and indeed any art, explicitly and harshly rejecting aesthetic concerns and with them the media and genres that had hitherto been his most reliable vehicle to the spaces of public representation.[136] (It is easy to see why, as the efflorescence of Expressionism at the end of the war saw the idiom appropriated by both Social Democracy and a problematic politics of the "spirit," as in the excesses of so-called *O Mensch!* Expressionism and Kurt Hiller's *Rat geistiger Arbeiter*.[137]) This was a reversal of allegiance to certain discourses and codes, and it represents a response to new conditions of public representation.

Jung's final text on Anton Groß is a powerful one. A deft account of paranoid terror, it carefully stages the slow emergence of madness, the reader's own confrontation of the split between levels of experience and his or her ultimate inability to identify the border between experience and world, the line that constitutes the relation of self to other. But it is well worth considering the material on which Franz Jung based his works, for Anton

Groß's own notes have been preserved (as blueprint copies with added text in pencil), and they reveal additional medial and discursive procedures that shed light on practices of the case that are of interest here.[138]

The extant notes exist as seven large sheets folded into smaller pages, including sketches and maps. They are numbered, but begin with folio 9:

> On 1 June 1910 I was given a position as draftsman at the Garrison Foundry, Southside in Pittsburgh. Since it was too far from East-Pittsburgh I moved to Knoxville near Southside on 1 July 1910 + stayed there till 5/12 1910. During this time there were 2 murders in Mont-Oliver in Southern-avenue near Pittsburgh + in Allentown a few severe attacks on young girls, which I did not do but was accused of by the criminals [*Thätern*]. It was always some of the aforementioned criminals that did that + had dressed themselves like me. ... Suspicion was directed toward me + as it says in the case history [*Krankengeschichte*] I suffered much from the people and children.
>
> I lived in Knoxville in Orchard Street No. 144 in the house of a Mr. Adolf Sleap ... in a room downstairs in which the blinds of the only window did not close properly + could be opened from outside + one could easily climb straight into my room in the summer. ... One of the murderers climbed into the room + poured typhus cultures into my distilled drinking water bought at the pharmacy for 10 cents, upon which I had repeated attacks of nausea + vomiting, diarrhea, nosebleeds + often severe chills. I knew that they were attacks of typhus but could not explain it; only here in Troppau where I had + have enough time, have I slowly come to the realization that makes so much sense that there can no longer be any doubt that my account is correct.[139]

The chronology that can be ascribed to these notes is that of their drafting by Groß in the asylum at Troppau; but despite the precise notation of geographical and temporal coordinates, we can begin reading the notes anywhere. They are written, in other words, as a sort of filmic loop, but one that constantly expands as the writer revisits the same events and adds detail, and also perpetually takes up other events, temporally separate, shifting between America and Silesia, that Groß feels need to be considered to understand the situation into which he is thrust.

> Near to me possibly in No. 209 Fall alley, but probably in the house next door, the worst murderer lived ... He was 167 cm to 168 cm tall and had a thin face, gray or gray-blue eyes, long pointed nose + was narrow shouldered + wore small soft hat + is perhaps a Seidel but definitely the same one who went through the yard of Mr. Sleap in Knoxville. The farmer Groß in Ośiek [Silesia] was perhaps the Seidels' man—should be followed up but is otherwise only my assumption. (I must mention that circa 1901 + at the time when the retired District Sergeant Schönherz still lived in the Jewish house-block in Lipnik [neighborhood of Bielitz-Biala] where Schubert had his restaurant ... there the murderers lived next to Schönherz's flat. They were then only young men in their 20s. ... The murderers have a great similarity to them + I think they could be them, since they were also narrow-shouldered, with long, pointed noses + gray (gray-blue) eyes. ... Tomatschek was probably poisoned by these people + died, so that they could control his 5 daughters. They have turned many from Bielitz-Biala into criminals and killed them. ...)[140]

There is neither start nor end point: the Seidels, the band who torment him, are everywhere and have always been. The logic of the narration shows other temporal tics, as the reverse logic of paranoia continually breaks into the account with retrospective conclusions, necessary assumptions, renewed speculation and dawning realizations. "Perhaps," "one will recall," "they must have ... ," and so on: "there can no longer be any doubt."

The temporality—prefiguring but centrifugally expanding the simple film loop with the vertiginous prehistory of every single moment—is that of the repetitive and vigilant surveying of a system of delusion, the constant repetition and confirmation of an intricately wrought state of affairs that requires flashbacks and encourages premonitions. It is the compulsive, motoric, and never-ending work of avoiding unbearable desires through which, as Freud wrote in 1910 of Judge Daniel Paul Schreber, "the paranoiac builds [his world] again, not more splendid, it is true, but at least so that he can once more live in it. He builds it up by the work of his delusions."[141] At every moment it requires corroboration, verification, and evidence, and will do so as long as Groß continues to engage with the world. The Seidels were always already there and always will be; thinking involves connecting the manifestations of their omnipresence. Unlike Jung's story, there is no overall narrative or plot, just a terrifying simultaneity of both persecution and inscription. The result is a text that turns the spatial axis of Borges's map, identical with the territory it describes, into the temporal one of paranoid case historiography in which every moment expands into the details of its infinite past.

Groß's notes also foreground the *media* of his case, something that remains beneath the surface of Jung's novella. His metrics, we have seen, are accompanied by sketches, his descriptions by maps. The latter in turn provide a new surface on which to narrate his persecution, a narration that fills any available space. On a map of the farm on which he worked from September 10 to 18, 1911, he marks the location where "around the same time as I worked as farmer for C. H. Dickerson on Shelter Island another murderer worked for another Dickerson over the river, for the third brother who had the same farm."[142] The thumbnail drawings of the murderers are simple and repetitive, but show the characteristics of the Seidel-type, which Groß can recognize through their many disguises, whether ship steward, foundry employee, or asylum doctor. Groß also makes cross-references to Otto Gross's medical paperwork ("as it says in my medical history"). And he draws attention to the importance of those medico-forensic texts, the contingencies of their notation, and the use that is made of them:

> The murderers also have doubles for Director Boeck of the Troppau district insane asylum for Dr. Stefan Felkl then Dr. Thum, Neumann, Heinz + the chief nurse Nitsche + for several nurses of the asylum ... They go into the pavilions on the men's side while the real doctors are on the women's side + write medical histories + send petitions from patients, who mostly soon die ... the files, medical histories are then taken by someone at the court + held there and perhaps exchanged.[143]

These texts can be falsified, but unfortunately can only be rectified in Groß's own parallel text: "The old man in the All Saints Hospital in Breslau who forged my medical history is perhaps

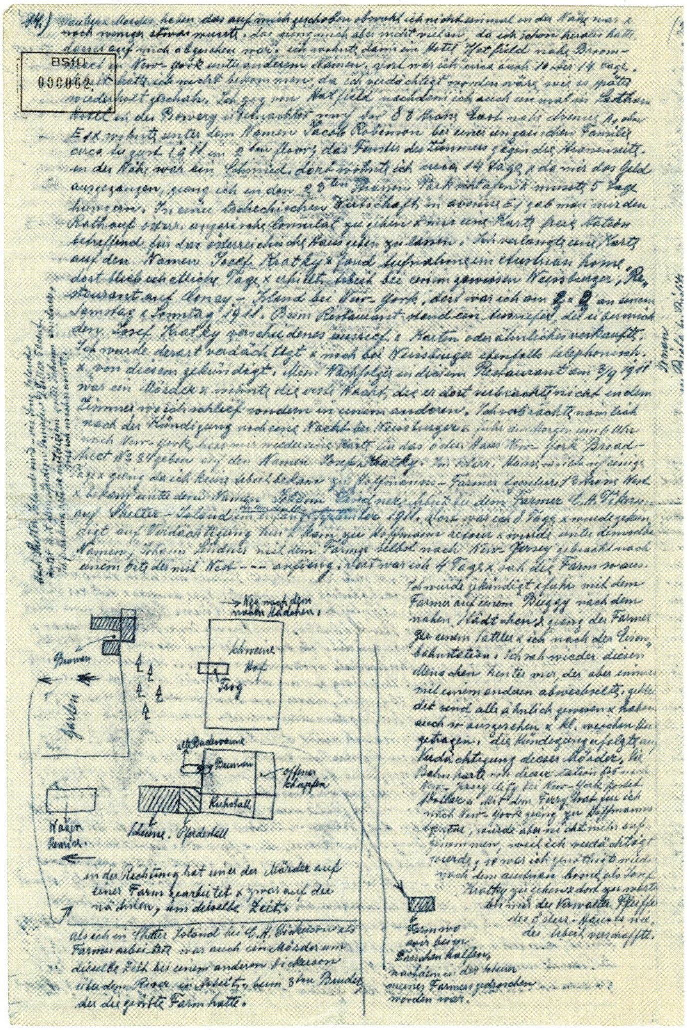

14.) [illegible] Mörder haben das auf mich geschoben obwohl ich nicht einmal in der Nähe war x noch weniger etwas wusste. das gieng mich aber nicht viel an, da ich schon heraus hatte, dass es auf mich abgesehen war. ich wohnte dann im Hotel Hatfield nahe Broomstreet in New-York unter anderem Namen. dort war ich circa auch 11 oder 14 Tage. [illegible] hatte ich nicht bekommen, da ich verdächtigt worden wäre, wie es später wiederholt geschah. Ich zog von Hatfield nachdem ich auch einmal im [illegible] in der Bowery übernachtet [illegible] 88 Strasse East nahe Avenue A, oder E[illegible] wohnte unter dem Namen Jacob Robinson bei einer ungarischen Familie circa August 1911 im 2ten floor, das Fenster des Zimmers gegen die Strassenseite. in der Nähe war ein Schmied. dort wohnte ich circa 14 Tage, x da mir das Geld ausgegangen, gieng ich in den 23ten Strassen Park [illegible] x musste 5 Tage hungern. In einer tschechischen Wirtschaft, in avenue E, gab man mir den Rath auf österr. ungarische Consulat zu gehen x mir eine Karte [illegible] betreffend für das österreichische Haus geben zu lassen. Ich verlangte eine Karte auf den Namen Josef Kratky x fand Aufnahme im Austrian home, dort blieb ich etliche Tage x erhielt Arbeit bei einem gewissen Weinsberger, Restaurant auf Coney-Island bei New-York. dort war ich am [illegible] an einem Samstag x Sonntag 1911. Beim Restaurant stand ein [illegible], der [illegible] dem Josef Kratky verschiedenes [illegible] x Karten oder ähnliches verkaufte. Ich wurde derart verdächtigt x noch bei Weinsberger ebenfalls telephonisch. x von diesem gekündigt. Mein Nachfolger in diesem Restaurant am 3/9 1911 war ein Mörder x wohnte die erste Nacht, die er dort verbrachte, nicht in dem Zimmer wo ich schlief sondern in einem anderen. Ich verbrachte nämlich nach der Kündigung noch eine Nacht bei Weinsberger x fuhr am Morgen um 6 Uhr nach New-York, liess mir wieder eine Karte für das österr. Haus New-York Broadstreet No 34 geben auf den Namen Josef Kratky. Im österr. Haus [illegible] einige Tage x gieng da ich keine Arbeit bekam zu Hoffmanns-Farmer Agentur [illegible] Street x bekam unter dem Namen Johann [illegible] Arbeit bei dem Farmer C. A. Dickerson auf Shelter-Island im Anfang September 1911. dort war ich 8 Tage x wurde gekündigt auf Verdächtigung hin x kam zu Hoffmann retour x wurde unter demselben Namen, Johann [illegible] mit dem Farmer selbst nach New-Jersey gebracht nach einem Orte der mit Wert--- anfieng. dort war ich 4 Tage x sah die Farm so aus.

Ich wurde gekündigt x fuhr mit dem Farmer auf einem Buggy nach dem nahen Städtchen x gieng der Farmer zu einem Sattler x ich nach der Eisenbahnstation. Ich sah wieder diesen Menschen hinter mir, der aber immer mit einem anderen abwechselte, gekleidet sind alle ähnlich gewesen x haben auch so ausgesehen x kl. weichen Hut getragen. die Kündigung erfolgte auf Verdächtigung dieser Mörder, die Bahnkarte von dieser Station bis nach New-Jersey City bei New-York kostet [illegible] Dollar. Mit dem Ferryboat fuhr ich nach New-York gieng zu Hoffmanns Agentur, wurde aber nicht mehr aufgenommen, weil ich verdächtigt wurde, so war ich gezwungen wieder nach dem austrian home als Josef Kratky zu gehen x dort zu warten bis mir der Verwalter Pfeiffer des österr. Hauses wieder Arbeit verschaffte.

Anton Wenzel Groß, from Troppau, 1913, showing map of farms on Shelter Island. Akademie der Künste, Berlin, Franz-Jung-Archiv, Jung 1260, Bl. 62.

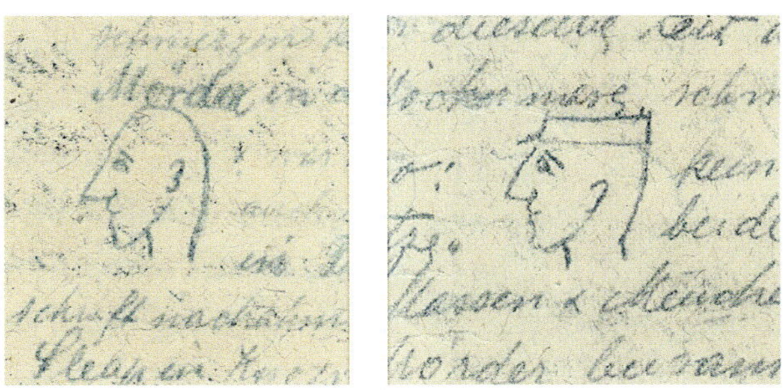

Anton Wenzel Groß, sketches of the "Seidel type" in notes from Troppau, 1913. Akademie der Künste, Berlin, Franz-Jung-Archiv, Jung 1260, Bl. 58, 72.

named Halbreich or Simachowicz in Andrychau, near Wadowice in Galicia."[144] Groß rehearses the problem of the untenable tautology, the a priori of medico-forensic authority: "In general it's a favorite method of the leaders of the band of murderers to take people they no longer need or who know too much and put them in awkward situations and stick them in an insane asylum; there they can say what they want and no one believes them and considers them delusional."[145] The antinomy at the heart of the naming of madness is rendered infinite by the medial detachability of identity, a constant theme in Groß's notes: "The murderers they have documents that are genuine but stolen + their former owners are either dead or sit locked up somewhere in America or under another name in an insane asylum."[146] And Groß himself, his actions, his place in the records, diagnoses, and so on, are all rendered unstable by this medial possibility of transposition:

> One of the bandits ... looked quite like me, so that I was mistaken for him by patients who have been here for several years, as his name is also Gross [*sic*] ... and they'll try to stir up laborers + farm people against me, because I look like the false Anton Gross, who in order to destroy me rode around with someone who looks like my father and made people drunk, hurt, cheated + attacked girls + said that his name is Anton Groß and was called the Garrison fellow in America. The scoundrel did this to stir people up against me + kill me, so he could play my role or just to get rid of me, since I'm too dangerous for the leaders of the murderers.[147]

Groß's never-ending text, with its cross-references to other texts and attention to the medical and legal institutions in which they function, gives a remarkable picture of the mediation of madness by texts, files, reports, commissions, and courts. And he rehearses the media practices and technologies: transcribing his own notes, only later to take a tack different from the original; copying the notes using blueprint techniques but then letting his pencil continue the account differently.[148] (If Friedrich Kittler has described Schreber in terms of the medial production of insanity in the "Discourse Network 1900," with Groß we see a Schreber for a slightly later age, one of technical knowledge.[149] Now the problematic desires and their satisfaction are mediated not by God but by the invisible communication channel of telepathy, just as the transcription develops into the blueprint copy.) In rewriting the Groß texts, Franz Jung weaves delusion and narrative into a self-contained *work*, which from the secure frame begins to reveal the fracture in experience until the distinction between internal and external collapses. For Groß himself, however, that distinction is entirely rejected for the simultaneity of notations of various and innumerable kinds. Jung created a work that, in Bathrick's terms, *can* speak the other's silence, while Groß gives the lie to that silence, which emerges as the flipside of endless chatter surrounding the visceral, compulsive, but highly intellectualized experience of modern madness. Franz Jung smooths out the narrative voice (only then to fragment it), but still tells the story of slow emergence of insanity instead of reproducing the schizophrenic mind perpetually narrating in full flow. Jung turns Groß's complete simultaneity of persecution into isolated temporal detours; he creates an uncertain relation of inside and outside instead of a constantly exteriorized medial surface; he shows a descent into madness and silence instead of the labor of constant reinscription. Jung, in other words, turns Groß's insanity into a closed text, for Bathrick a modernist one. Groß reveals instead something else: the very medial conditions of madness and the infinite repetition of the texts they create.

Anton Groß's fate is constant surveillance and narration, the vigilant observation of the world before him and its careful, precise, and tedious inscription into the a priori system of his mind. Yet his notes do not merely mimic, but fully replicate the way texts (reports, affidavits, case studies, theories, decisions, and marks of identity) circulate in the system of the courts and hospitals, the press and the minds of the agents of this dispositive, this apparatus. Both the madman's notes and the medical documents are equally repetitious, familiar, manipulable systems of the flattened-out paper currencies of sanity and madness, freedom and incarceration. If madness was managed in a system of writing and therefore appeared in the form of this system, Franz Jung found that the attempt to write his way out was, though cathartic, doomed to failure and thus the end of a project: "Anyone can be too much of a coward to destroy everything. There's no sense in spinning out the story of Anton Wenzel Groß any further."[150] It no longer paid to write a literary work recreating the experience of insanity; the society that created and controlled it needed to be destroyed, but that took more courage than any one person could muster. Otto Gross too failed to find a way out of the systematized forms of madness around the turn of the century: he moved errantly and aimlessly within the apparatus and its different forms of writing, never succeeding in articulating its politics to a large public. Anton Groß managed what Panizza had done before him. Instead of allowing madness to be controlled as an orderly set of transactions between texts and institutions, inscribing madness into law, Groß and Panizza folded the experience of madness back onto its mediations, its genres and discourses and institutions, exposing their complicity. Panizza had done this before a public; Anton Groß could not do so. It was the task of Franz Jung to bring Groß and his important, inside knowledge of the discontents of civilization before that public. It was part of his reckoning with Otto Gross, who had foundered on his messy mixture of life and text and oscillated ineffectively between institutions of control and their unstable knowledge. Jung sought to reassert control, as I have argued, by a split between a proper edition of Otto Gross's work on the one hand, and an intense, compact, and sophisticated literary text on the other.

§

Groß—Grosz

To bring the lessons of Gross and Groß before a public was George Grosz's project as well, in the various illustrations meant to accompany Jung's novella. But if Jung had tried to "speak the other's silence," in Bathrick's fine phrase, Grosz, I think, took a different tack: he sought to inscribe the other's endlessly repetitive chatter, to show that the delusion and suffering were not confined to the twilight zone of madness, an experience to which we have only indirect access, but were instead everywhere, in limitless variations of omnipresent notation.

Grosz knew Franz Jung's writings on Anton Groß well: "Die Telepathen" had appeared in *Die Aktion*, to which Grosz contributed at the time, and of course he read from a version of *Der Fall Groß* at the Neue Jugend evening in May 1917.[151] Four or five of Grosz's drawings can be directly related to his work illustrating Jung's text.[152] Three are reproduced in Grosz's collection *Ecco Homo* of 1923: *Franz Jung gewidmet* (Dedicated to Franz Jung, 1917), *Das Ende* (The end, 1917), and *Johannisnacht: Der Fall G* (Midsummer night: The G case, 1918). All are in the tense and barbed graphic idiom

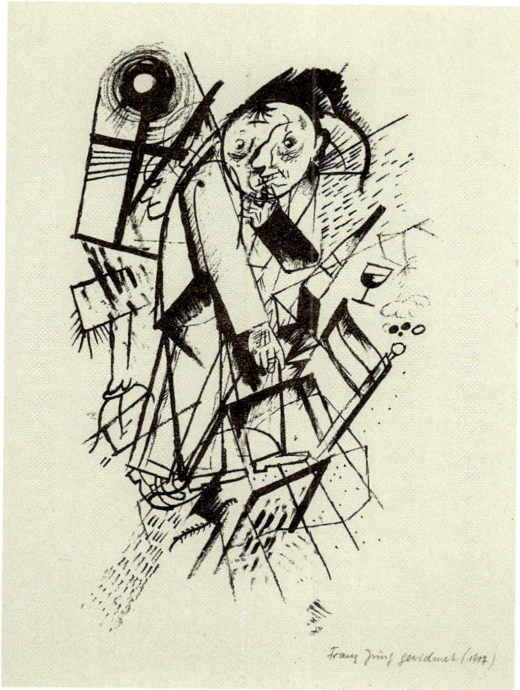

George Grosz, *Franz Jung gewidmet* (Dedicated to Franz Jung), 1917. From *Ecce Homo* (Berlin: Malik-Verlag, 1923), no. 46. Photo © bpk/SSK/Tom Gundelwein. © Estate of George Grosz, Princeton, NJ/DACS 2022.

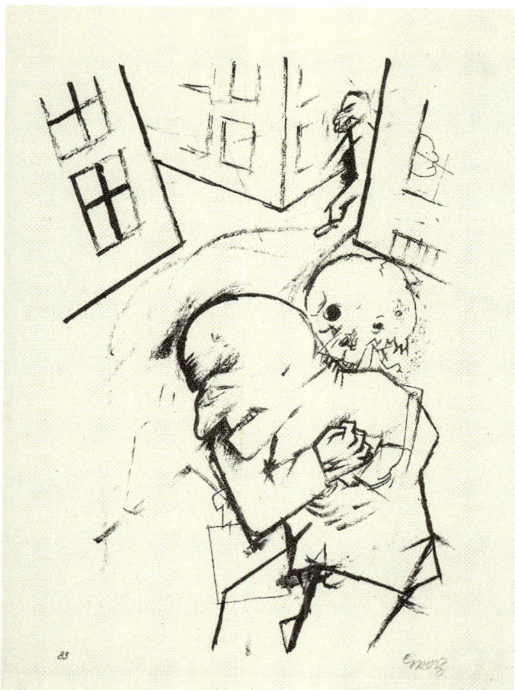

George Grosz, *Das Ende* (Fall Grosz II) (The end [Grosz case II]), 1917. From *Ecce Homo* (Berlin: Malik-Verlag, 1923), no. 83. Photo © bpk/Kupferstichkabinett, SMB / Wolfram Büttner. © Estate of George Grosz, Princeton, NJ/DACS 2022.

that had become, in the years since 1915, Grosz's trademark style, and all use Cubist fragmentation to produce a distinctly Expressionist skewing of perspective into vertiginous urban spaces in which the distinction between interior and exterior is often blurred. In *Franz Jung gewidmet*, we see a male figure in a state of extreme anxiety, drinking alone in a modest room (the chair is crude and the floorboards bare), with a threatening figure looking in through the window. Michael White has convincingly argued that this is the image that corresponds most closely to Jung's text, showing the window in Groß's room at Mr. Sleap's house, with blinds that do not reach the sill and leave both Groß and his possessions vulnerable to the omnipresent Seidels from Tarnow; this is where "one of the murderers climbed into the room + poured typhus cultures into my distilled drinking water bought at the pharmacy for 10 cents."[153] *Das Ende* seems to show Groß as he plunges a dagger into his own heart; a skeletal figure of Death stealthily embraces him from behind while a man emerges threateningly from around the narrow corner. Franz Jung's Groß had indeed tried to end his misery, though in *Der Fall Groß* he "opened the arteries of his right wrist."[154] In the watercolor and ink *Johannisnacht*, interior and exterior, day and night merge in a horrific scene of murder, as an unshaven man in a hat stabs and kills a man at the center of the composition; passers-by seem unconcerned or unaware, including a carefree man in front, flowers in hand and heart revealed on the outside of his chest showing hopes for a romantic encounter. Though identified as part of the "Fall Groß" works, this drawing does not correlate directly to a specific scene of the texts, but echoes the atmosphere of distress, confusion, desperation, and mortal threat at the hands of a band of murderers; it also figures the fateful intersection of desire and violence. A fourth drawing, *Fliehender Mann (Zum Fall Grosz von Franz Jung)* (Fleeing man [for the Grosz case by Franz Jung], 1917), remained unpublished and similarly relates to no particular scene in Jung's published texts. It shows a man running across an expanse at the edge of a town with signs of urban and industrial development in the background. This is the kind of environment in which Anton Groß lived, in the conurbations around Pittsburgh and the farms on the outskirts of New York City, and indeed the similarly mixed areas of industrial Silesia. Does he hold a knife in his right hand? It is not clear. Is he a soft-hatted bandit fleeing one of his countless crimes, "perhaps a Seidel but definitely the same one who went through the yard of Mr. Sleap in Knoxville"? Or is he Anton Groß on his seemingly endless flight from them? The distinction between victim and culprit is unclear. (A final, unpublished drawing labelled as part of the series was shown in an exhibition of 1962 but not reproduced in the catalog; it has proved impossible to locate.[155])

Yet it is not only the line between victim and culprit that fades, but also that between inside and outside of the texts. For these figures—Groß and the Seidels—appear everywhere in Grosz's oeuvre of the time. Some can be pegged to Jung's stories, for example the drawing reproduced in *Ecce Homo* titled *Apachen oder: Als alles vorbei war, spielten sie Karten* (Apaches, or when it was all over, they played cards, 1916). It shows a dark room, illuminated by a bare bulb and a high window, where three men relax after an orgy of violence. There is a bloody axe and an open razor, torn clothes

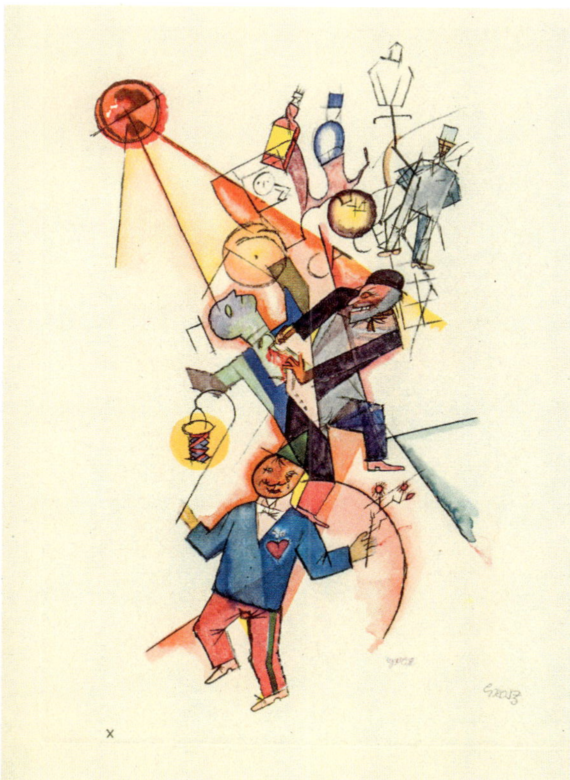

George Grosz, *Johannisnacht (Der Fall G)* (Midsummer night [The G case]), 1918. From *Ecce Homo* (Berlin: Malik-Verlag, 1923), pl. X. Photo © bpk/ Kupferstichkabinett, SMB/ Wolfram Büttner. © Estate of George Grosz, Princeton, NJ/ DACS 2022.

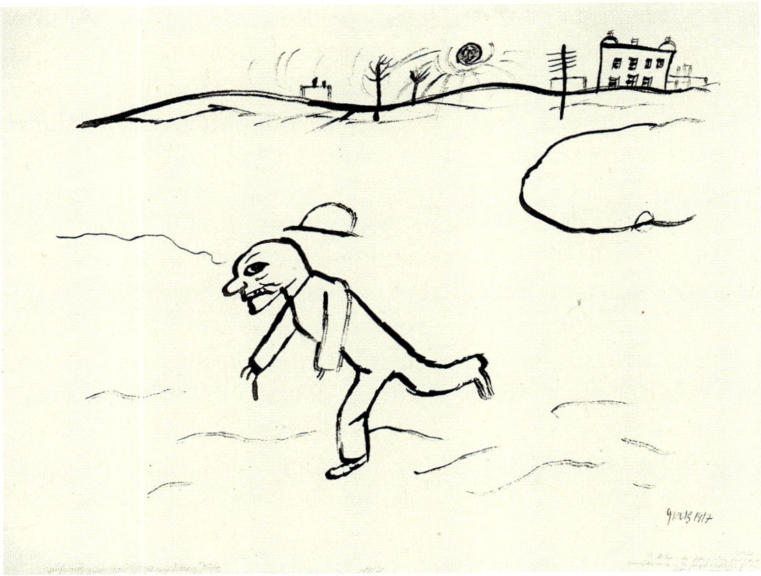

George Grosz, *Fliehender Mann (Zum Fall Grosz von Franz Jung)* (Fleeing man [for the Grosz case by Franz Jung]), 1917. Pen and ink on paper, 46 × 58.5 cm. Photo Galerie Nierendorf, Berlin. © Estate of George Grosz, Princeton, NJ/DACS 2022.

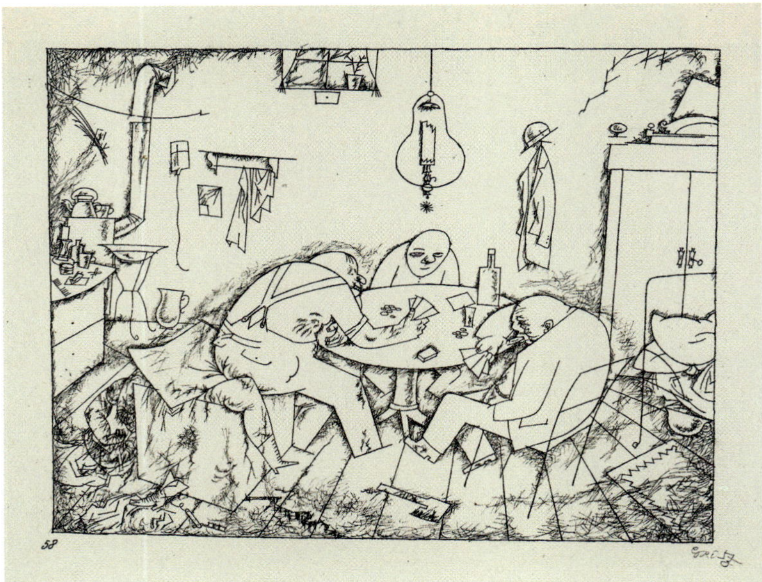

George Grosz, *Apachen oder: Als alles vorbei war, spielten sie Karten* (Apaches, or when it was all over, they played cards), 1916. From *Ecce Homo* (Berlin: Malik-Verlag, 1923), no. 58. Photo © bpk/Kupferstichkabinett, SMB/Wolfram Büttner. © Estate of George Grosz, Princeton, NJ/DACS 2022.

and perhaps blood on the floor, and a dead woman's booted leg emerges from a crate on which one of the card-players nonchalantly sits. This surely shows the fate of the women of whom Groß wrote: "Sales girls, women factory workers and so on are seduced, stuck into a brothel and after three years' work there murdered in the cellars."[156] Or perhaps these are the telepaths who run the insane asylum at Troppau: in his account of Anton Groß as a case study in *Drei Aufsätze über den inneren Konflikt*, Otto Gross reports:

> He believes he is in telepathic contact with a band of persecutors that he describes as "telepathists" who want to eliminate him—above all: want to render him harmless in the asylum because he knows their secrets. The asylum director was one of the leaders of the telepathists. He believes he has seen him in a different form before, in America.
>
> G. claims that the telepaths have built catacombs underneath the asylum where they carry out their work. He experiences by telepathy everything they do, say, think, and feel.
>
> The telepathists celebrate "black masses" in their catacombs; they drag women there, murder them, and "get off."[157]

And consider the rehearsal of the murders, almost identical. A man lies dead in the back court of a house at the industrial edge of the city while the criminal escapes. It happens in broad daylight and at night with a dog the only witness, or perhaps Anton in the window, in Knoxville, the Bronx, or Bielitz-Biala. We recognize the dog from "Der Fall Groß":

> Furthermore he sees a second man with a soft hat go around the house, accompanied by a collie. This dog—long-haired, light brown, with white patches around the mouth, belly, and on the feet—signals for Anton that he is surrounded. Later it turns up everywhere when Groß is at the end of his tether: in East Pittsburgh, New York, Cuxhaven, and Breslau.[158]

In Grosz's work of the time, the murders recur *ad infinitum*, the crimes are eternally reprised, the figures blandly repetitive, murderous or pursued, or both, showing indistinguishably Anton

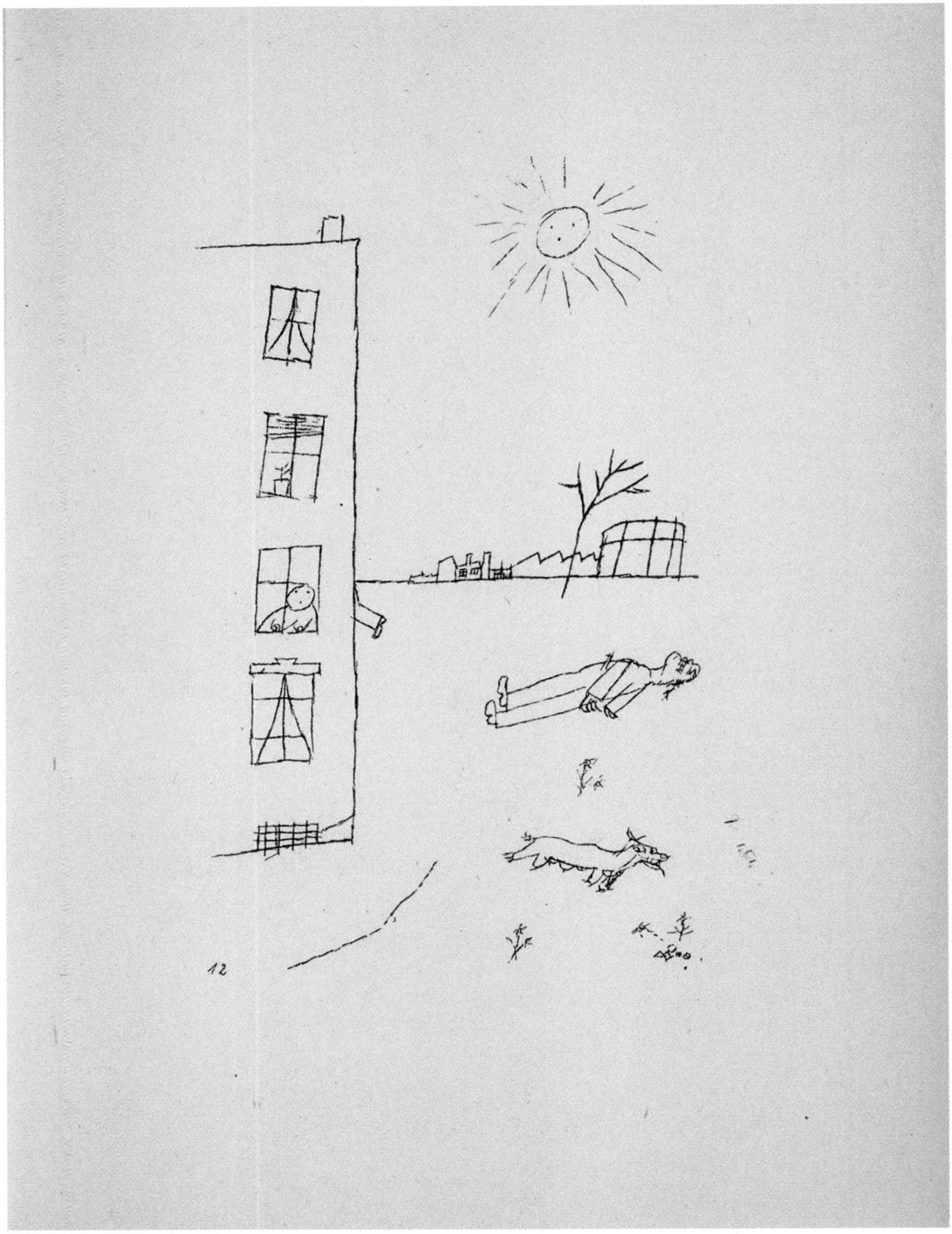

George Grosz, *Mord* (Murder), 1915/16. From *Ecce Homo* (Berlin: Malik-Verlag, 1923), no. 12. Photo © bpk/Kunstbibliothek, SMB/Atelier Petersen. © Estate of George Grosz, Princeton, NJ/DACS 2022.

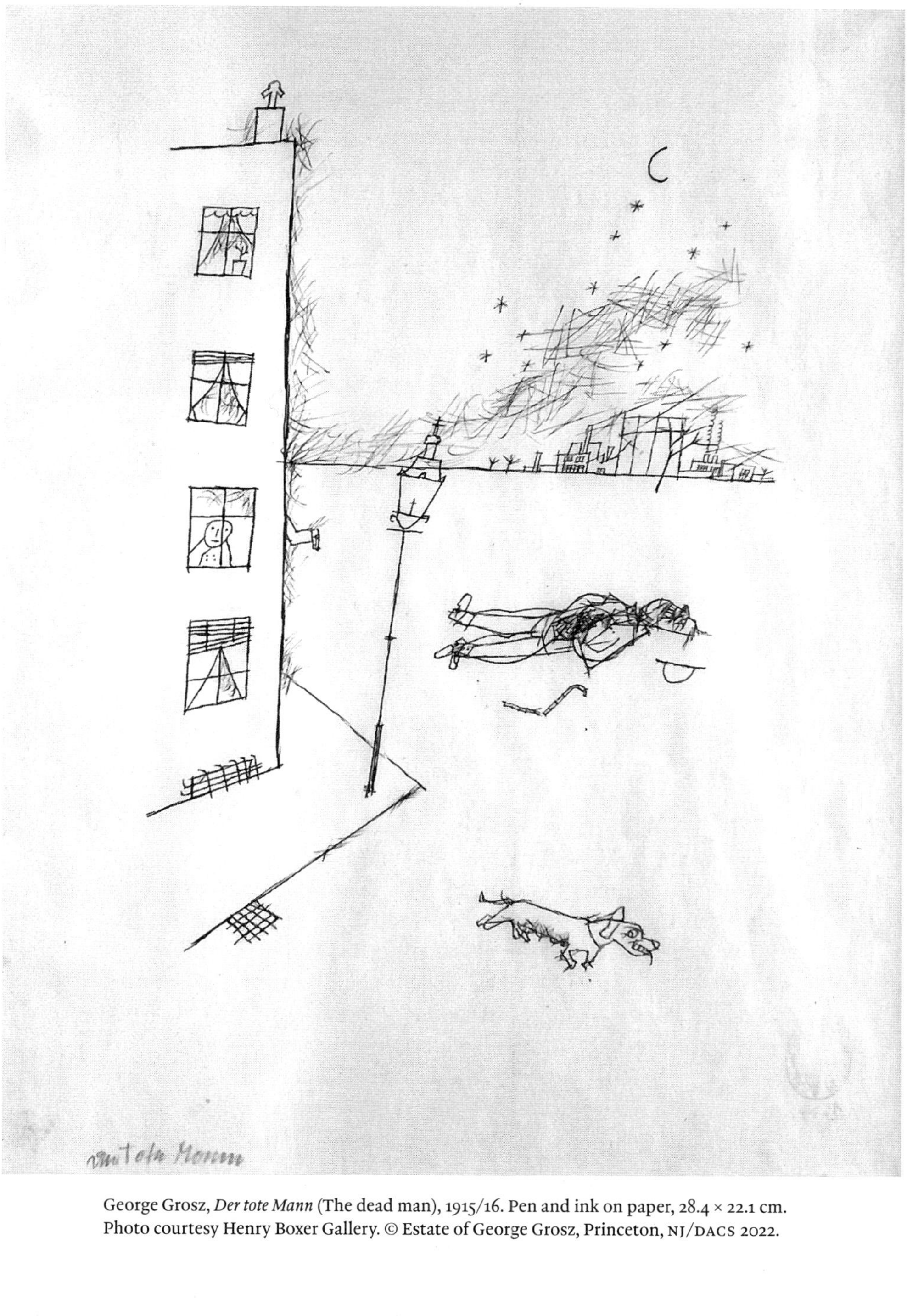

George Grosz, *Der tote Mann* (The dead man), 1915/16. Pen and ink on paper, 28.4 × 22.1 cm. Photo courtesy Henry Boxer Gallery. © Estate of George Grosz, Princeton, NJ/DACS 2022.

Groß or one of the bandits. The madness is omnipresent, the world mad. Grosz follows the recipe of Panizza from *Psichopatia Criminalis*: "Turn the madhouse out onto the street and you'll see something new every day."[159] But you see the same thing over and over. Grosz's drawings of the time rehearse the motoric repetition of murder, the eternal presence of the murderer confirmed ever anew, the film loop with new details added, madness and murder in all its variations. It is like Anton Groß's constant reinscription of the crimes and the criminals in his endless notes. Indeed the drawings *look* like Groß's own compulsively written manuscript, with its maps of the city and its outskirts, and its repeatedly scrawled notation of the Seidel type, 167 to 168 centimeters tall, narrow-shouldered, and with (presumably) blue or bluish-gray eyes. The only difference now is the ironic distance created by the awkwardly drawn and stiff, infantilized figures. Instead of tracing, like Franz Jung, the emergence of madness in the world, the inability to secure the borders of the self, we see a last, compulsive, potentially infinite reinscription of the account of Anton Groß, the omnipresence of murderers and the repetition of the same crime.

We can look too at Grosz's *Lustmord* paintings of the time in relation to the drawings of the Groß case. They are more ambitious and more complex: due to their slower and more expensive medium, and also to the conditions of their viewing, they must capture some of this complexity at once instead of being viewed serially (as in *Ecco Homo*). But they too are repeated: *John, der Frauenmörder* (John, the woman-killer, 1918), *Der kleine Frauenmörder* (The small woman-killer, 1918), *Man mit Messer, der eine Frau verfolgt* (Man with knife, pursuing a woman, 1917), and an image known variously as *Der kleine Frauenmörder* or *Die Menschen sind Engel* (Humans are angels, 1917).[160] Their resonances are somewhat different and broader than the Groß drawings; referring to both images and text, they are intermedial and intergeneric.

In *Der kleine Frauenmörder*, we see a man in a murderous rage and the gruesomely mutilated body of a largely unclothed woman in a simple furnished room. Her arms are hacked off, and we see wounds to the chest and abdomen; blood drips from the knife held in the murderer's stiff right arm and covers his white shirt. In *John, der Fraunmörder*, the male figure (with a soft hat, a long nose, and indeed blue eyes: a Seidel from Tarnow) sheepishly flees the scene of the murder; his victim behind and above him is naked, with one arm severed and throat crudely cut, the flowers of the

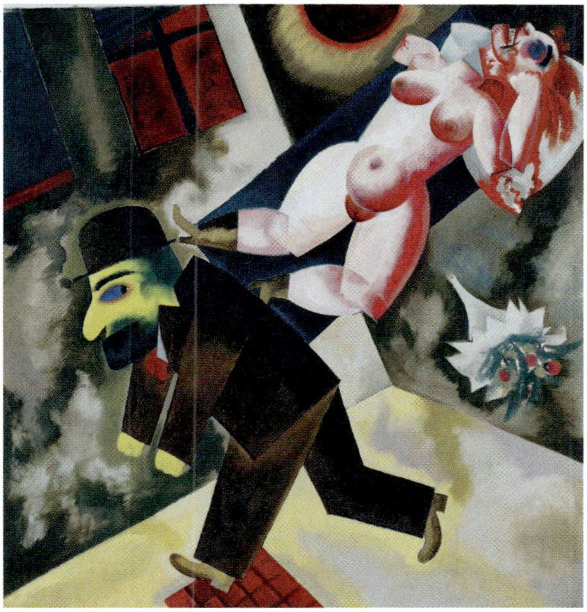

George Grosz, *John, der Frauenmörder* (John, the woman-killer), 1918. Oil on canvas, 86.5 × 81 cm. Photo © bpk/Hamburger Kunsthalle/Elke Walford. © Estate of George Grosz, Princeton, NJ/DACS 2022.

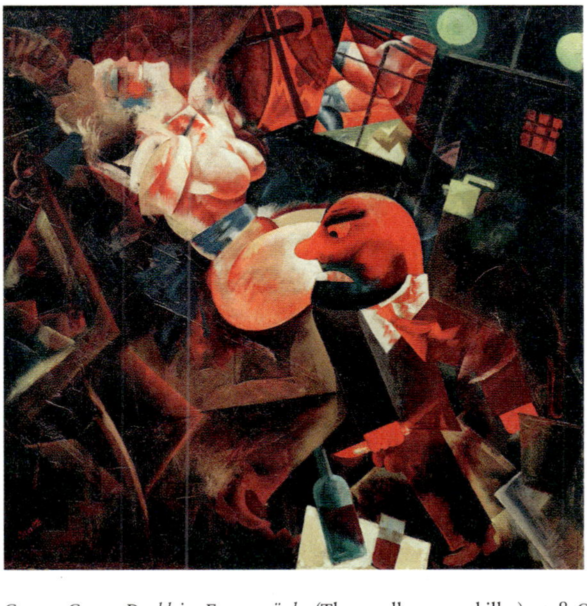

George Grosz, *Der kleine Frauenmörder* (The small woman-killer), 1918. Oil on canvas, 66 × 66 cm. Private collection. Photo © akg-images. © Estate of George Grosz, Princeton, NJ/DACS 2022.

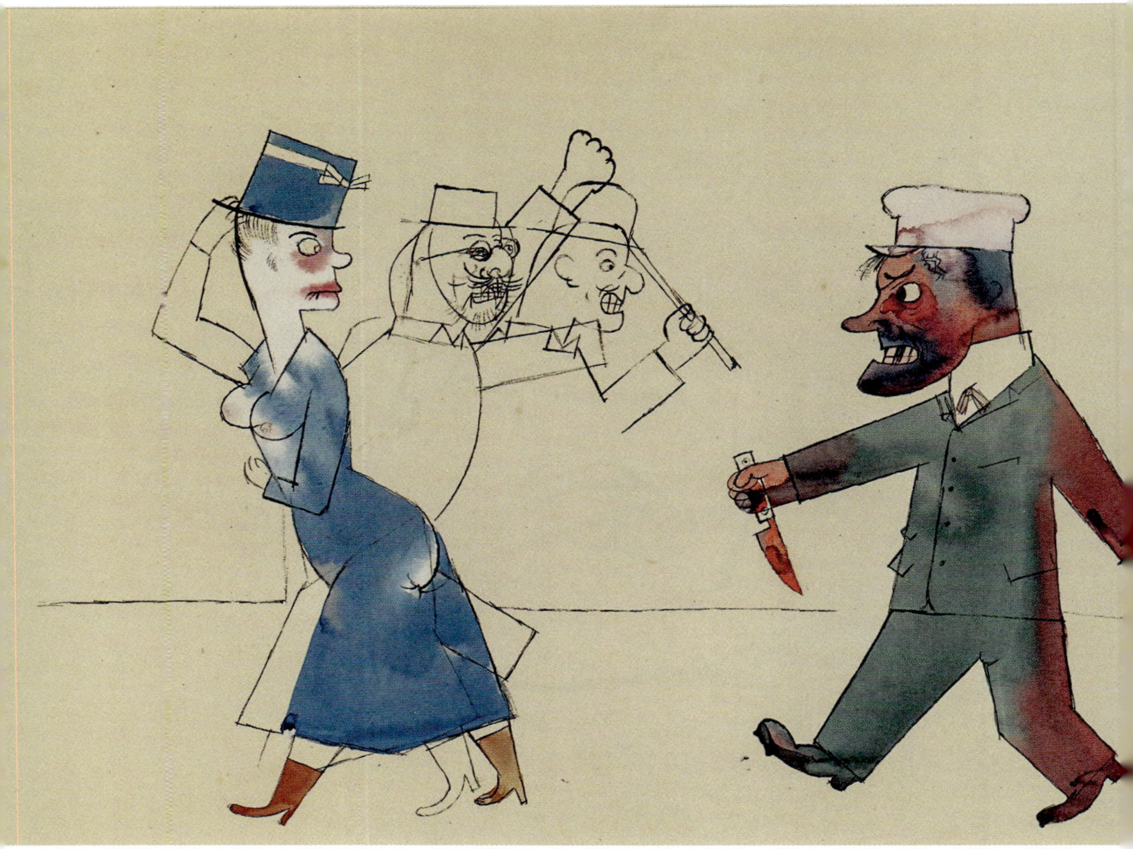

George Grosz, *Man mit Messer, der eine Frau verfolgt* (Man with knife, pursuing a woman), 1917. Watercolor, reed pen, pen and ink on paper, 36.5 × 51 cm. Private collection, photo courtesy Richard Nagy Ltd., London. © Estate of George Grosz, Princeton, NJ/DACS 2022.

earlier stages of their encounter cast aside. These horrific scenes have provoked serious questions about their relation to sexual violence toward women at the time.[161] But they aroused little comment when they were first produced, and one reason can be that images of brutal violence toward women were actually fairly familiar. An erudite audience would recall the tradition of the broadsides in the *Moritat* tradition, which showed woodcut depictions of the violence above a text narrating the crimes.[162] Surely their comically crude portrayals recall the caricatured murderers in Grosz's paintings; especially the childish John, with his sheepish grin, clenched fists, and jerky movements, looks like a modern

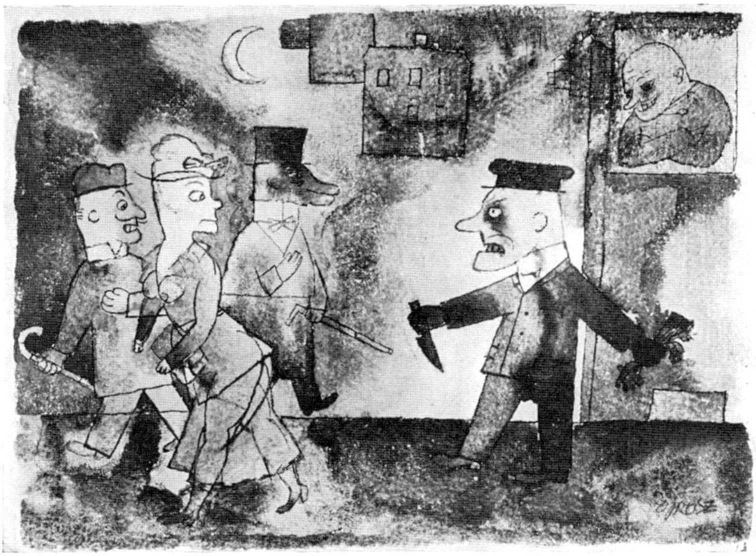

DER KLEINE FRAUENMÖRDER, 1917 Aquarell

George Grosz, *Der kleine Frauenmörder* or *Die Menschen sind Engel* (Humans are angels), 1917. Watercolor and ink on paper. Photo from Mynona [Salomo Friedlaender], *George Grosz* (Dresden: Rudolf Kaemmerer Verlag, 1922). Whereabouts unknown. © Estate of George Grosz, Princeton, NJ/DACS 2022.

version of trivially awkward figures of sixteenth- and seventeenth-century prints. Or we can look at the cover of a *Groschenroman* or penny dreadful that Grosz himself owned: *Jack, der geheimnissvolle Mädchenmörder* (Jack, the mysterious girl-killer), where Jack the Ripper stands, with bloodstained clothes and a dagger, above the bloodied corpse of his victim, lying as if on a stage before a proscenium arch.[163] Here the blood of the lithographic image ends up everywhere, as in Otto Dix's *Der Lustmörder (Selbstbildnis)* (The sexual murderer [self-portrait]) of 1920. Or perhaps the disturbingly comic disjunction between the savage murder and the burlesque cartoon murderer refers to a published account of an actual *Lustmord*, for example one near the beginning of Krafft-Ebing's widely read *Psychopathia Sexualis*:

> Case 16. Alton, a clerk in England, went for a walk out of town. He lured a child into a thicket. Afterwards at his office he made this entry into his note-book: "Killed to-day a young girl it was fine and hot." The child was missed, searched for, and found cut into pieces.[164]

Discussing this account, Gisela Steinlechner has noted several cases characterized by the "naïve, fully unrepentant, indeed cheerful speech of the murderer," words that describe John's body language quite well.[165]

We have a name for one of these murderers: he is John (and thus pointedly not "Jack"). Who is John? Recall the confusion to which Groß was subjected in New York, when in a case of mistaken identity he was identified as "John Groß," a sexual murderer. Indeed, the picture of the fleeing John raises the question of whether this was in fact mistaken identity. John could be, of course, John Heartfield; he looks not dissimilar to Grosz's rendering of his friend in in *"Der Sträfling": Monteur John Heartfield nach Franz Jungs Versuch ihn auf die Beine zu stellen* ("The convict": Monteur John Heartfield after Franz Jung's attempt to get him up on his feet, 1920). But the prisoner John Heartfield, after Franz Jung's assistance, also looks like Grosz himself:[166] we thus have another John Groß, again a hybrid of two people, one perhaps guilty while the other is innocent. Here John Groß is in prison, or an asylum, for one of these crimes. He certainly looks as much like a Seidel

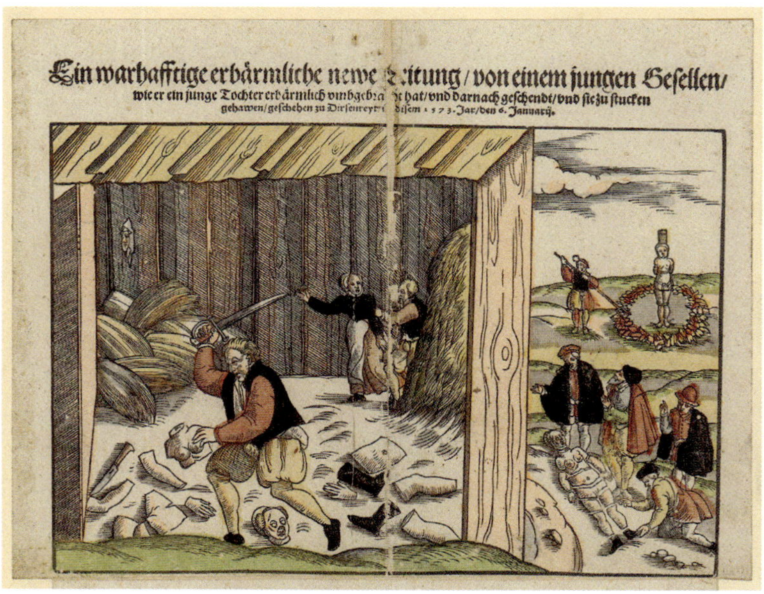

"Ein wahrhafftige erbärmliche newe Zeitung von einem jungen Gesellen." Broadside, woodcut and type on paper, detail. Augsburg: Hans Moser, 1573. Zentralbibliothek Zürich, Graphische Sammlung und Fotoarchiv, PAS II 13/23.

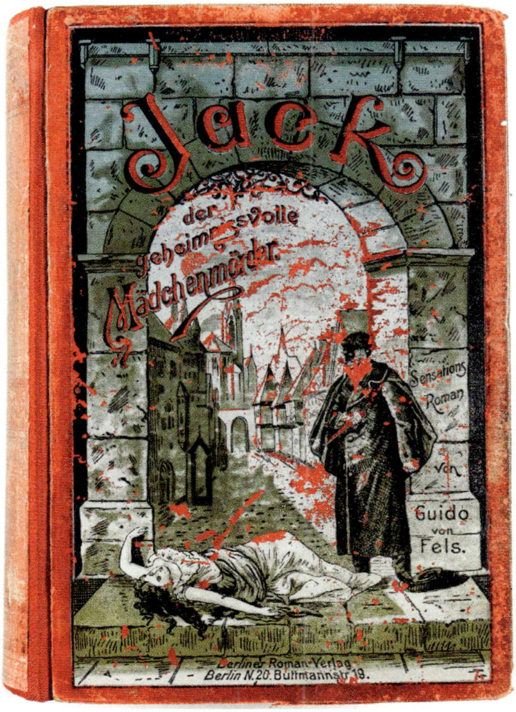

Cover of Guido von Fels, *Jack, der geheimnissvolle Mädchenmörder* (Berlin: Berliner Roman-Verlag, 1897). Photo DLA Marbach.

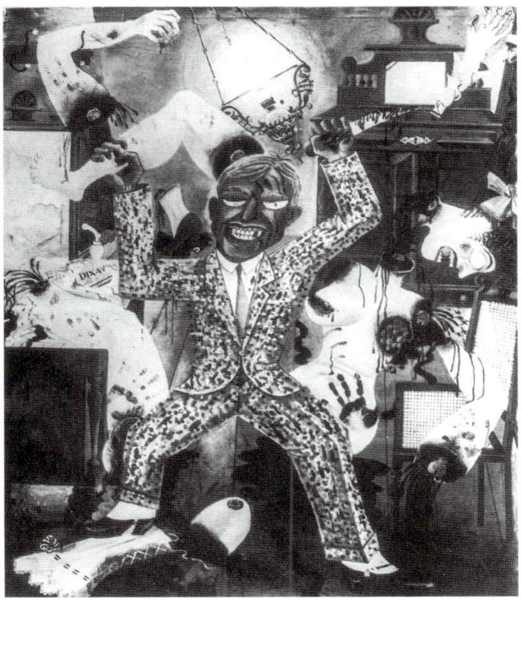

Otto Dix, *Der Lustmörder (Selbstbildnis)* (The sex murderer [self-portrait]), 1920. Oil on canvas, 170 × 120 cm. Whereabouts unknown. Photo © bpk. © DACS 2022.

as he does like Anton Groß at his end, plunging a knife into his own breast.

Scholars have noted this dizzying play of identity, but here I would like to point to a few specific frameworks for making sense of it. George and John changed names, of course, from Georg

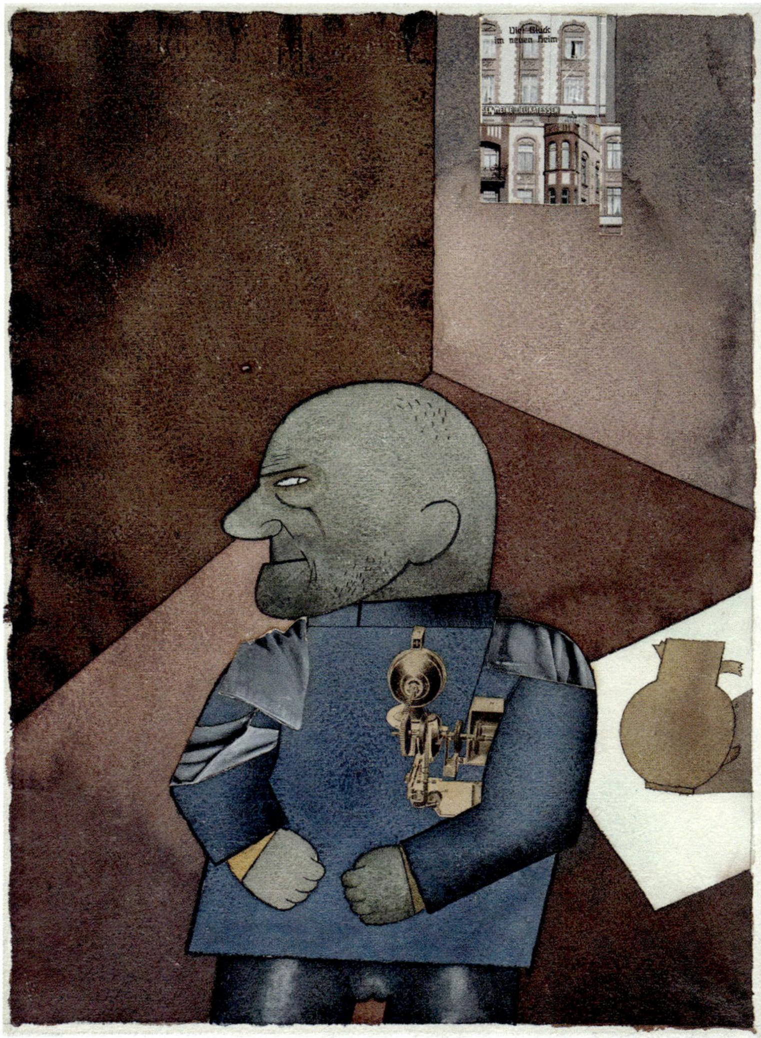

George Grosz, *"Der Sträfling": Monteur John Heartfield nach Franz Jungs Versuch ihn auf die Beine zu stellen* ("The convict": Monteur John Heartfield after Franz Jung's attempt to get him up on his feet), 1920. Watercolor, pencil, cut-and-pasted postcards and halftone relief on paper, 41.9 × 30.5 cm. Museum of Modern Art, New York. Gift of A Conger Goodyear, acc. No. 176.1952. Digital image © Museum of Modern Art/Scala, Florence 2022. © Estate of George Grosz, Princeton, NJ/DACS 2022.

Groß and Helmut Herzfeld, playfully but aggressively recoding themselves as American or English, in defiance of the general mobilization of all Germans for the war. But this was something rather different: it was a play on the commercial logic of the name during wartime. Every German would have been familiar with the lists appearing prominently in local newspapers at the beginning of the hostilities, as businesses changed their names to avoid association with the enemy. Columns showed old names and their new wartime versions: "Café Piccadilly" on Potsdamer Platz turned into "Vaterland Kaffeehaus," for example, and "Hotel Westminster" became "Der Lindenpalast." Always attuned to the commercial logic of word and image, Grosz and Heartfield simply reversed it. And as for uncertain identity, Franz Jung's texts on Anton Groß stage the identification and ultimate fusion of narrator and subject; we no longer know who is talking as the narrator moves between first and third person and ultimately affirms the truth of Groß's "delusions." Yet this is also something different from the mysterious murderer of Grosz's paintings: Jung slowly develops empathy for the madman and ultimately enters into the silent world of the other with a guilty, halting voice intact. In the paintings we see instead the state of affairs that is made clear in Anton Groß's notes: the medial detachability of identity as paper documents organize subjects, their histories, and their medico-legal status as sane or mad. Based on the patients or papers before them, doctors (and judges) would separate the sane from the insane. And their ultimate authority was tautologically based on their own title: Doctor. Of course, this untenable and illogical state of affairs had other, more subversive, possibilities. The Dadaist Dr. Walter Serner wrote a letter for Jung, attesting that the latter's absence from his regiment was due to illness (cardiac problems) and that he was on his way to treatment, thus giving Jung a chance to leave the country. Serner, however, was actually named Seligmann, and he was a doctor, not of medicine, but of jurisprudence. He too had to flee the country when he was pursued for fraud and accessory to desertion.[167] Similarly, Dr. Otto Gross wrote a psychiatric affidavit for Jung to protect him from the serious consequences of his desertion. But Otto Gross had been declared insane and legally incapacitated by this time; he had already crossed the line from doctor to patient.

Despite their disciplinary nature, the medico-forensic conditions of the case ultimately made it impossible to identify the madman—either as mad, or as man. An error could happen at any time and be rehearsed in perpetuity by the media involved and their fallible (or conniving) human agents. With this in mind, we have to ask if there is a mistake *in these paintings*, whether the John figures are mad, and indeed whether they have committed the crimes we see. For the paintings make us ask where to draw the line between delusion and reality, fantasy and fact. In *John, der Frauenmörder*, the victim lies on a white pillow and thus inside, while the murderer is clearly outside; there is a spatial and temporal sequence. But there is another spatial ambiguity: the presence of the mutilated woman above and nearly touching John's head. Is this a memory or a fantasy? Is it lived out or repressed? Is John fleeing from a deed or merely from a drive, a terrible instinct? Similarly, in *Der kleine Frauenmörder*, the woman in blue undergarments is doubled: we see her brutally mutilated in the foreground, while she appears through the window, cropped but seemingly unmolested, at a stage in a less violent transaction of commercial sex. And is not the man doubled too—silhouetted at the top center, next to the unmolested woman inside? Do we see a sequence of states, or a conflation of them in the "murderer's" mind?

Or perhaps we are seeing these terrible acts from the point of view of the criminally insane. In *Mann mit Messer*, the woman is under imminent threat. But as she looks back in shock and fear, the murderer sees not a woman but a man, in fact two men. One has a bowler hat, walking stick, and white collar; the other perhaps a trilby, glasses, and a mustache, and also a collar. They are bourgeois males of roughly the generation of the murderer's father. Is he, in his mind, really attacking them, and not the woman? In *Die Menschen sind Engel*, the males reappear, now looking more made of flesh and blood. But who is the voyeur at the upper right, and what is his relation to the attacker? Both images raise the question of the relation between patriarchal authority and violence toward women.

Otto Gross had, of course, an answer to this. In a patriarchal society, the man is forced into a stance of sadism toward women; resisting this produces neurosis, homosexuality, psychosis, or isolation. Male sadism, rape and destruction of the woman is the fate of both sides. Sometimes it will be lived out literally; other times it will be a metaphor for the relation; always there will be every stage in between. There is thus a structural logic to the ambiguities in these images. Importantly, however, these ambiguities do not exonerate the male figures, whether their instincts are slightly reined in or violently lived out. They accuse, they indict, they charge the figures with the crime that is endemic to this world.

This guilt, this gamut of male sadism, the acculturation of female masochism, the bloody war of the sexes and its collateral psychic trauma is the subject of Franz Jung's early work, from the Expressionist stories to the Groß texts. This is what appears in Grosz's *Frauenmörder* scenes. We see it too in *Fliehender Mann*, where we cannot distinguish between Anton Groß and the Seidels who pursue him, between criminal and victim. And precisely that is the secret of Anton Groß. In his study "Beitrag zum Problem des Wahnes" (Contribution to the problem of insanity), published in *Drei Aufsätze über den inneren Konflikt*, where the Silesian draughtsman appears in the professional literature of psychoanalysis, Otto Gross writes as follows about the patient's sexual release via the telepathic signals of the murderers in the basement:

> This is the key to his psychosis. G. is a sadist. He realizes through psychosis the complete fulfillment of his unconscious sadistic desires. In his psychosis, he is able to live out his sadistic perversion—one thinks of Stekel's expression "pleasure without guilt," for G. explains his own sexual satisfaction in the fantasy of sexual murder (*Lustmord*) as being achieved through "telepathy" ...
>
> If we look for antagonistic drive components juxtaposed on the basis of their content in this case, then we notice ... heterosexual sadism, the fear of this drive, the impossibility of escaping it, and finally the insane wish fulfillment: first, the moment of identification with the sexual murderer and his acts, and later the sexual satisfaction through the insane experience of hallucinated scenes of sexual murder.[168]

Anton Gross was guilty, at some level. His satisfaction came from cruelty; the violent deeds of the Seidels from Tarnow were an invention for his own pleasure. He had absorbed the inherent sadism of patriarchal society but nonetheless resisted, fleeing into madness.

It would be satisfying to give Otto Gross the last word here. But there are no last words, and there is no escape—except through repression and madness. We learn as much when we turn doctor into patient again and consult not Gross's own texts but the representation of him as a case. He appears, anonymized but transparently recognizable, as case number 37 in Wilhelm Stekel's *Sadism and Masochism*, in the chapter entitled "The Tragedy of an Analyst."

> The original attitude of this patient was sadistic toward woman and masochistic toward man. With the great reversal of all values which took place in him, this attitude ... was turned about, chiefly, however, to mask his relationship toward his father. I will now cite some of his dreams, which inform us of the true relationship and grant us a profound insight into this person's psyche ...[169]

The dreams reveal that the patient

> fears his sadistic attitude toward women. For he struggles with the impulse to stab a woman, stick a dagger into her abdomen, and become a lust murderer.
>
> He dares not be jealous, and he must assume a masochistic position of obedience toward a woman in order to escape this greatest danger ...
>
> [T]he disposition to lust murder was compensated through reversion to the opposite.[170]

So Otto Gross too was a sadist. As a child he jealously desired both mother and father, and flew into a murderous rage when he could not have complete possession. He came to fear his own violent love:

> It is characteristic of all parapathics that they always want that which they cannot have. This tendency is most strongly in evidence in masochism and sadism. One has entered into conflict with one's own ego and believes that one has come off conqueror. Thus our patient, too, considered his parapathy as a conclusion, as a world philosophy, as something finished, while it was only a transition, an artificial construction, a routine measure ...
>
> It was in a certain sense a struggle for freedom that the boy was carrying on. He wanted to free himself from his family, from his love to his parents ... He could not effect this liberation because it was built upon parapathic principles.

His differentiation was only a negative form of family slavery. Analysis, which put new weapons into the patient's hands, was especially dangerous for him. He analysed himself and had himself analysed by other physicians, who were themselves under analysis by him. This is naturally impossible. So important a man as he had it in his power to dupe all his physicians and make them believe that his attitude was the product of his philosophy. ...

He should not have attained his world philosophy until after the primary attitude had been revealed; then it would have been his own.[171]

Stekel tells us that Gross's extraordinary and still challenging insights into the social nature of psychological suffering could only come about through repression of typical and indeed banal sadism. Stekel does not accept Carl Jung's spiteful diagnosis of *dementia praecox*, nor does he describe the paranoia that Gross found beneath the dysfunctional vigilance of Anton Groß. For Gross the price was nonetheless addiction, neurosis, and personal tragedy, and he shared these, *nolens volens*, generously with those around him.

What George Grosz shows in the repetitive works from 1916 to 1920 is not simply the paranoid schizophrenia of a simple draughtsman, or the imbrication of lust and murder that emerged so disturbingly in the psychiatric literature, popular culture, and police reports of the late nineteenth century. It is the set of variations of patriarchal male sexuality as sadism and the myriad possibilities of acceptance or rejection, the madness of society or the madness of those who refuse its logic. As Panizza too asserted, there is no single, privileged viewpoint from which to make any sense of the situation. There is instead an intermedial and interdiscursive accumulation of narration, illustration, report, administrative notes, anamnesis, case study, maps of crime scenes, and sketches of criminal types and their victims. Everything depicted in these images is *reported*. A dead body could be a crime scene or a fantasy (and enjoyed, feared, or both); the infantilized murderers could be Lombrosian degenerates[172] or what became of Otto Gross's young boys who turn to sadism for patriarchal approval; the attacks are fragmented into crime reports, case studies, male fantasies, fears, or delusions. Grosz gives us the visual equivalent of Franz Jung's *erlebte Rede* or free indirect speech: it is always—or can be—someone else talking, confessing, dreaming. Who is never clear, nor does anyone really own these thoughts, fantasies, desires, and culpabilities. Grosz shows the subjects who committed these crimes, who have been accused of them, who give in to sadism or masochistically refuse but nonetheless experience, tortuously and vicariously, that sexual pleasure as their own desire. He shows crimes, and the etiology of the social disease of which they are the symptoms. And he rehearses visually the genres and discourses of murder and its psychiatric inscription. These are the patients and the doctors and the judges, the subjects and objects of the case. They are all guilty, and they are all mad.

§

George Grosz's work between 1916 and 1920 shows one way in which the ideas developed by and around Otto Gross could be represented publicly. They might not have been associated with the bohemian psychoanalyst, prophet, and patient, but the very fact that these scenes of rape and murder, madness and the city seem to have raised no eyebrows, but were instead accepted as a coherent vision of modern urban life, testifies to the fact that they were somehow comprehensible, somehow adequate to the conditions of representation at the time. We can see this by looking at one example of a representation of Otto Gross and his ideas that was patently *not* adequate.

Consider Curt Corrinth's expressionist novel *Potsdamer Platz, oder die Nächte des neuen Messias: Ekstatische Visionen* (Potsdamer Platz, or the nights of the new Messiah: ecstatic visions, 1919). It is another version of Otto Gross's teachings, and it *did* raise eyebrows.[173] Its protagonist is one Hans Termaden from Barmen on the Wupper, a wealthy industrialist's son who arrives in Berlin to spread the emancipatory message of free love and *Mutterrecht*, or social and sexual matriarchy. Like Gross, young Termaden seeks to liberate women from their fate of miserable chastity or masochistic pleasure; like Gross, he attracts "disciples" of both sexes; like Gross, he sows the seeds of social conflict. The style is Expressionist, but rather than the dystopian variety we see in the work of Franz Jung, this is the ecstatic version, proclaiming the birth of a New Man out of the destruction of the failed Wilhelmine materialist patriarchy.

Corrinth's hero combines revolutionary violence with sexual freedom. In one scene, for example, where he conquers the repression of Berlin's finest families, the result is a clumsy combination of rape, humiliation, and redemption. The alliterative mixture of fairytale narrative and religious rhetoric can hardly be translated.

> The girl, soon gracefully displayed from the obligingly placed divan, filled the air with her bejeweled rights and beckoned with well-rehearsed pose:
> "You bold one. Do tell."
> "?"
> "Adventures and nights."
> "To turn a self-satisfying tool for your lonely and cowardly desires?"
> No lightning struck, it is true. But the best-bred composure sank into the abyss.
> "You—"
> "Play the prophet before you? Burn brightly before your dull flame, conjure smoldering before you visions that demand to be life?"
> Succumbs anew. Hands before face preparing horror. Saw, how never fulfilled body curves writhed beneath the soothing scourge of the whip of his voice.
> Before her, cries:
> "We flog your kind! Scum of the earth! Sophists of desire! Sinners against the Holy Spirit of the Flesh!"
> Pregnant pause, brooding deeds.
> Then, flexing forth, panting voice:
> "You—yes—strike—strike—" ...
> Alalà alalà â! thundered the triumph of boiling blood—— raised the fists, clenched, high——
> And strikes her down, in rage, fists over tiny breasts and doubled womb, effects and unfolds the mighty deed ...
> "You so strong—oh—oh oh you–" ...
> Ah ...
> Faint whimpering only ...
> But then, on her knees, crawls over to the mighty one, confused raptured prayer, shrill sobs
> "You—you——
> Messiah——
> I see–
> I acknowledge and avow——"[174]

This is taxing, and it taxed its readers. A Catholic reviewer was furious: "It is not even an attempt at art, just pornography in the un-German, easily aped language of the novelist [Carl] Sternheim. Before the collapse of the German state this would only have been furtively sold but now it appears in a luxurious edition in Georg Müller's series 'Bücher der Zeit.'"[175] The reviewer alludes here to the brief relaxation of the enforcement of §184 of the criminal code, against obscenity. Even the editor of the Expressionist journal *Die Erde* found little to like: Corrinth "writes not as the bird sings but as the steer thrusts." He preaches "the gospel of the flesh, the redemption ... of mankind through the marvelous organization of ... uncontrolled sexual desire."[176]

What these critics miss, of course, is Corrinth's irony; this can only make sense as satire.[177] In any case, Paul Klee, who had the unfortunate (but well-paid) task of illustrating *Potsdamer Platz*, interpreted it that way.[178] His drawing for the scene above shows the woman's eyes closed in rapture but the arms flailing comically. He does not show the violent Messiah but tries to describe a gently exaggerated bodily confusion and sensuous release in his naïve and childlike style of stick figures and crescent moons.[179] This is not a picture of a woman murdered and dismembered, but it is still one of a brutalized woman who has been sexually violated. Klee manages, perhaps, to find the ironic tone Corrinth seems to have missed. In the light of the questionable quality of the literary text, even to come close is quite an achievement. Corrinth's satire fell flat: it hardly seems to have been recognized as such. Certainly the complexities of the cultural form of the case from Panizza to Gross do not emerge here, and few readers, it seems, even recognized the references.

Satire failed, but George Grosz's works were not satire. We see some of the same relativizing strategies that Klee uses: the incongruous but unavoidable signs of innocence and infantilization amidst the violence; the spatial ambiguities signaling that a scene might be fantasy; the confusion between objective portrayal and the *erlebte Rede* of the psychotic subject of modernity. Satire or not, George Grosz's works of the period caused no alarm—but they were not, for that, discussed very much. Indeed, how should they be described, if they were neither satire nor niche pornography? Few attempted to analyze these works at the time. One attempt, however, is notable. In a sympathetic but not uncritical monograph on Grosz from 1922, Salomo Friedlaender—who

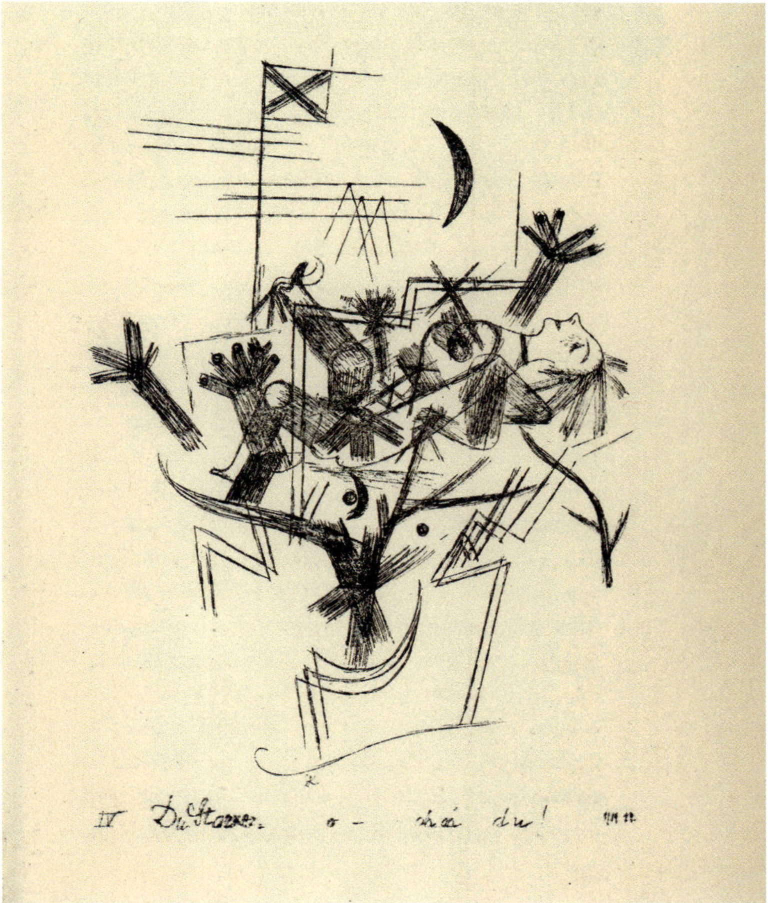

Paul Klee, *Du Starker; o—oh oh du!* (You so strong—oh—oh oh you), 1919, lithograph illustration for Curt Corrinth, *Potsdamer Platz oder die Nächte des neuen Messias. Ekstatische Visionen* (Munich: Georg Müller Verlag, 1919), 20.3 × 13.5 cm. Museum of Modern Art, New York, Abby Aldrich Rockefeller Fund, acc. No. 384.1951.4. Digital image © 2022 The Museum of Modern Art/Scala, Florence.

published in Expressionist and Dada circles under the pseudonym "Mynona"—writes in a way that is as confusing as it is resonant: "George Grosz himself is the most radical artistic legal tool [*Rechtsmittel*]. His pictures administer criminal justice [*sprechen Strafrecht*]. They operate on this sick age the way doctors do."[180] This impacted analysis is deeply obscure yet utterly compelling. It points to the issues of judgment and its impossibility, evidence and the problem of its interpretation, insight and its implication in the very pathology it illuminates, the normality of crime and the inevitability of guilt that surrounded the texts and images of the time focussing on the case.

§

Madness and Guilt

Franz Kafka mixed some of these seemingly incompatible but insistently connected elements too, though in a different way. And he knew the work of George Grosz well. Gustav Janouch recalls:

> We saw a collection of political drawings by George Grosz.
> "What hatred!" I said.
> Franz Kafka gave a strange smile.
> "Disappointed youth," he said. "It is a hatred which springs from the impossibility of love. The force of expression comes from a perfectly definite weakness. That is the source of the despair and violence in these drawings. What is more, in some annual I have seen poems by Grosz."
> Kafka pointed to the drawings.
> "They are literature in pictures."[181]

Young Gustav was no doubt in awe of Kafka's off-the-cuff but deeply thoughtful words about hatred and love, but the writer had been thinking about these matters for a long time. He knew Otto Gross, his writings, his travails, and the sad fate he had faced. Indeed, Kafka gives here a Grossian interpretation of George Grosz's drawings.

Kafka had studied law with Hans Gross, Otto's father, for three semesters in Prague, before Hans was called to a chair in Graz.[182] In the wake of Otto's arrest and deportation in 1913, Kafka would have noticed the scandal in which his former teacher was caught, a legally quite complex and opaque one. Kafka was, at the time, getting to grips with psychoanalysis, less by reading Freud than through the works by (then) followers such as Wilhelm Stekel and Theodor Reik, who published in journals read by the writer: the *Prager Tageblatt* and *Pan*, respectively.[183] His close friend and mentor Franz Werfel had known Otto Gross well from Munich; after a short time under his spell, Werfel reacted strongly against this charismatic figure.[184] Kafka finally met Gross in early July 1917, when they spent a long night in the corridor of a packed wartime train.[185] They met for a last time in the apartment of Max Brod a few weeks later, concocting plans to publish—what else?—a journal; it was to bear the title *Blätter zur Bekämpfung des Machtwillens* (Review for the fight against the will to power). On hearing of Gross's death three years later, Kafka wrote to Milena Jesenska of the experience. Gross had apparently talked incessantly to an increasingly dazed and tired Kafka, disappearing periodically to administer his injections.[186]

Kafka was also an avid reader of Pfemfert's *Die Aktion* in the 1910s and would have seen the important essays Gross published there in 1913 and 1914. Perhaps he read Franz Jung's "Die Telepathen" or the installments of the novel *Sophie: Kreuzweg der Demut*. He certainly noticed George Grosz's work there: it was in *Die Aktion* that the artist published his poem *Lied* (Song) in 1915. (Kafka does not mention Grosz's early drawing of a man murdering a woman a few issues earlier.[187])

Thus when Kafka wrote his *The Trial* in those very years around the outbreak of the First World War, he knew of Pfemfert's account:

> Around midday on Sunday November 9, the important scientist Dr. Otto Groß was visited in his Wilmersdorf flat by three burly men who apparently identified themselves as police officers and held him there against his will until evening ... That evening, Groß ... was secretly removed from the flat ... and most likely incarcerated in an Austrian insane asylum.[188]

He might well have had a shudder of recognition when he read how Jakob van Hoddis was involuntarily committed to an asylum:

> About five weeks ago ... Jakob van Hoddis was seized in his flat by a doctor and two assistants, rendered docile by an injection and locked into an asylum near Nikolassee [-Berlin]. The internment was instigated by members of his own family, with whom he was involved in an inheritance dispute ... Jakob van Hoddis ceased to exist until he escaped, deciding that the risk of a fall to his death was less than the risk of intellectual death among incurable madmen.[189]

And it is not far-fetched to imagine that the young jurist had noticed an article titled "Der 'verdächtige' Staatsbürger" (The "suspect" citizen):

> If one morning, say around 6.00 a.m. ... you are dragged from your warm bed and arrested, you can experience all sorts of things. Once you have been taken to an official building and its welcoming doors have been shut behind you, you are "provisionally" a free legal subject—or you *were*. You don't know what you are supposed to have done; you feel completely innocent and you think you have the right to be treated as a respectable human being, until a court should decide otherwise? That is a serious error.[190]

The author is Alfred Bader, a Hamburg anarchist who outlines the long period—several months—in which he was held under harsh conditions, including in chains, and moved from prison to prison in Germany before he was finally charged and his case immediately dismissed. "Finally, you—perhaps completely innocent—have been photographed sufficiently for the arrest warrant. The green van brings you back to the remand prison, where the investigating magistrate apprises you of your crime and the text of *your own* statute."[191] He shows the wide authority of magistrates who can suspend the rule of law as that very law goes about its slow machinations. The suspicion of crime, of insanity, of being a danger to society or being in danger—all provided a flexible sort of statutory black hole into which anyone could fall.

So when Kafka wrote the resonant opening sentence of *The Trial*—"Someone must have slandered Josef K., for one morning, without having done anything wrong, he was arrested"[192]—it was as much a rehearsal of many cases, real and hypothetical, as the beginning of something new. Of course, *The Trial* is not about Otto Gross: it is about Franz Kafka. But the scene was a familiar one at the time, and thoroughly overdetermined. The cases considered in this chapter—of crime, madness, and the suspension of the rights to live in freedom and address the public freely—show where the rationality of the modern rule of law ended, where persecution could become mysterious and resistance futile, where the tautologies of modern governmentality become evident, where the system of laws and rights could both be utterly opaque and make perfect sense. Like Panizza, and having witnessed the case of Otto Gross, Kafka chooses the suspension of rights as the paradigm of a highly bureaucratized and formalistic system and its dangers, showing what it looks like when it is not the subject but the system itself that has gone mad. Or rather, Kafka simply switches perspective, presenting the subject as rational and transparent, and the system as surrounded by mystery, syllogism, tautology—as paranoid, as producing crime and madness. From Panizza to Gross to Groß to Grosz, we know that both perspectives are always in play.

But it is not so much about the "system." It is about a specific kind of guilt: *a priori* guilt. Internalized, the crime, as Josef K. found out "In the Cathedral," is always committed against one's *own* personal statute. In painting a picture of a society in which everything one says necessarily establishes one's culpability, in which any statement is by definition proof of madness, Kafka paints a picture of society through the lens of the medico-forensic case. It is a fractured lens whose cracks are hidden by mirrors; the view is crisp and the regulations clear, but the logical gaps and seams are there. Oskar Panizza sought to draw attention to some of these aporias, and Otto Gross sought to explain others and find a way out of them. Both argued, but from within a context that prevailed over them. Grosz and Kafka, perhaps a bit blandly and repetitively, simply represented madness and guilt as the prevailing state of affairs, as a specific constellation of ambiguous legal and medical regimes. They invoked the experiences of the subject defined by them and worked through the possibilities of public representation these regimes enforced. That the subject of their work seems to be madness is not because it lies beyond the purview of these forces of discipline; instead, this work reveals the specific forms of madness this system produced through its apparatus—its laws, media, discourses, genres, and institutions.

There is a risk that this net of structures—psychic, discursive, institutional—beyond individual volition might seem overwhelming. Indeed, the logic of the medico-forensic case, its happy sanctioning of the tautological functioning of disciplinary institutions, its ever-inventive and flexible use of this logic, would suggest the futility of resistance. That would seem to be the message of Robert Wiene's *The Cabinet of Dr. Caligari*, where the mad psychiatrist is flanked by the sign of the legal statute, the paragraph mark, invoking the doctor's arbitrary and unchecked power over the paradoxical zone devoid of all rights written into the law. But

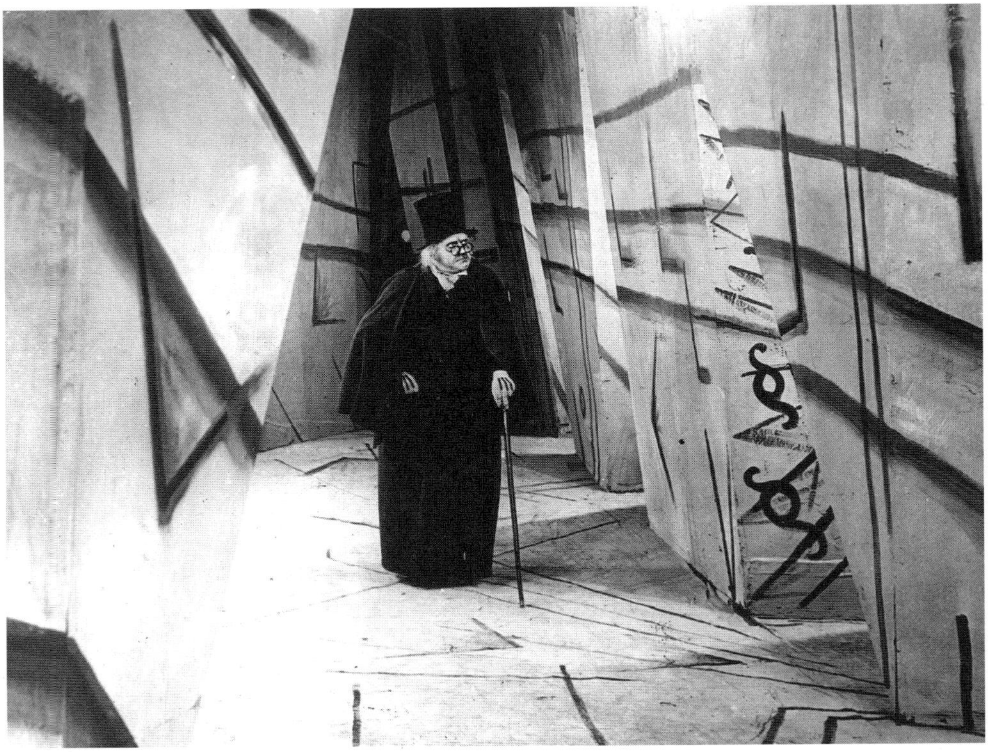

From *Das Cabinet des Dr. Caligari*, dir. Robert Wiene, 1920.

there was always a way out. The way out functioned too in the illogical and fleeting spaces between these institutions and their media. The way out involved expanding the medico-forensic case into a public one. There was, to hand, a set of tropes that could signal these issues, and a wealth of experience that said that such larger cases were a sore point, that the centripetal logic of the medical and legal case—the pressure to close it—could be made centrifugal and opened to a public, where the terms might be negotiated. Perhaps the instinct to make such cases lies behind the constant repetition, at the time, of newspaper reports of incapacitations, of fictional figures from Caligari to Mabuse. In the will to make such matters public, to use the media and genres of discipline against those very forces, lay a productive potential—or at least an irresistible instinct to trace the highly politicized line between the "mad" and the "sane."

3 Lustmord: *Mapping the Public Sphere*

We have encountered *Lustmord* images in the previous chapters. These works combine representations of two kinds: images of violent crime and images of an explicitly sexual nature. And in combining them, they potentiate the disconcerting aspects of both. Almost as shocking as the images themselves is the fact that it is only since the 1980s that questions have been asked in the art-historical literature about the disturbing nature of these images; until then, they seemed, in the words of Beth Irwin Lewis, "an expected manifestation of the nasty underworld of the metropolis."[1]

Lewis, one of the first scholars to explore these works in depth, notes the existence of *Lustmord* imagery in German popular culture from the late nineteenth century and situates this firmly in the context of shifting gender roles and the deep challenge to masculine identity in the wake of the women's movement. Drawing on the writings of George Grosz, Otto Dix, and others, she dates the efflorescence of *Lustmord* and other extreme forms of misogynistic imagery in painting to the period immediately after the First World War. The traumatic wartime experience of these artists accelerated and intensified their "heightened anxiety about sexuality" and "obsessive dread of woman."[2] Maria Tatar expands the scope of the inquiry into *Lustmord*, looking not only at the paintings of Dix and Grosz but also at literature (Alfred Döblin's *Berlin Alexanderplatz* and Robert Musil's *The Man Without Qualities*) and film (Fritz Lang's *M*, but also the postwar work of Hitchcock). The artists' work, she writes, "might be called a continuation of war by other means and with a very different adversary." The war "functioned as an event that released the creative energies of artists and legitimized the representation of brutal violence directed at the female enemy on the domestic front rather than the male adversary on the military battlefield."[3] As for Lewis, the war experience of violence against the male body intensified an already existing constellation, but it is one she goes on to consider in post-Freudian psychoanalytic terms:

> Depictions of *Lustmord* in the era following World War I frequently become implicated not only in issues of sex, violence, and gender but also in issues of maternity, mastery, and (pro)creating, with artists ... entering into competition with the reproductive powers of the maternal body or striving to contain the unruly sexuality of the female body.[4]

Tatar sees a larger context of perceived male victimhood, one in which violent retaliation in images creates a specifically artistic pleasure in *Lustmord* apart from the pathology of actual *Lustmord*, which itself only takes the structural violence toward women too far and too literally. Similarly, in her study of Weimar discourses of violent crime—literary and scientific—Hania Siebenpfeiffer shows how *Lustmord* is inscribed in complex ways in the constitution of modern masculinity, and indeed represents the vanishing point in the construction of this identity.[5]

Lewis and Tatar treat *Lustmord* motifs in the arts primarily as evidence of violence toward women in discourse, attitude, or act, and they do so convincingly. The work of Kathrin Hoffmann-Curtius, though equally informed by feminism, shows that there are other, specifically art-historical logics at work in these images. In several publications she has analyzed historical sources and themes, pointing to the self-reflexive play with the conventions of painting in the use of windows and the tropes of the pornographic gaze; the suggestion of modernist destruction of traditional art conveyed by, for example, the allusions to allegorical femininity; and an attempt to get to grips with the possibilities of film's combination of different views and moments of an evolving narrative.[6] For while today's viewers immediately see—and then cannot un-see—the violated female body being offered, apparently and disturbingly, for some sort of visual pleasure, Hoffmann-Curtius makes the point that the images as such cannot simply be equated with the acts depicted. If Lewis, Tatar, and Siebenpfeiffer give extensive (and in the case of Tatar, somewhat speculative) reference points by which to consider this violence, Hoffmann-Curtius embeds the works in multiple contexts, giving a sense of their position in other histories. They emerge as more complex and overdetermined, and analyzing these complexities gives a fuller picture of the representative modes by which femininity is constructed and the way it fits into other social practices.

This is not to relativize these images. Precisely Hoffmann-Curtius's point that even representations of "whole" female bodies still do them violence makes clear the fundamental imbalance of power and the forms of aggression at their core.[7] Violence against women was a fact, one from which the images cannot so easily be separated. They testify to the logic and naturalness of pleasure in the viewing of images of the violated female body, and to the relative ease with which one might move from this to other meanings. Even if the violated female body is a figure, an allegory for something else, it is impossible to ignore the fact that it so easily becomes perfectly acceptable collateral damage of a kind that naturalizes violence toward the socially marginalized, the othered part of any asymmetric power relation. And precisely these relations were under threat. The pleasure offered by such images testifies to the fact that for some viewers—and rather a broad range of cultural consumers—these images were not incompatible with, and to a certain extent represented, a world in order, one that made sense.

So there is a delicate balancing act to be struck between acknowledging the disturbing signs of violence and the forms of visual pleasure they evoked, on the one hand, and treating the existence of these images as an historical phenomenon that is also *about images*. As a male art historian, I am not terribly comfortable with this balancing act. But it is an approach that is nonetheless worthwhile. As Mark Seltzer has shown in his study of the representation of serial killers, the public is "convened" around scenes of violence, and the violence calling a public into being reveals how the public sphere itself is responding to pressures that distort and pervert it. It is not just the violence depicted that we must consider, but the "pathological public sphere" in which they appear.[8]

Expanding on the work of literary historians who have focused not only on the acts of *Lustmord* but their medialization in modernity, I shall be looking here precisely at the conditions under which these images were produced and circulated.[9] They did not move through the media and public of early twentieth-century Germany quite so smoothly as we might think. Precisely the frictions they aroused, however slight, tell us much. And they cannot be understood in isolation from the very space of representation in which they functioned. To grasp their variety and strangeness in any detail, we need to consider the complex medial systems in which they moved. For this was in fact a time of fundamental changes in many media, from increasing capitalization (for example, in film) to the increased speed of the circulation of images by means of developing print technology, and also changing conditions of representation as legal limitations on what could be made public were altered at the same time as relations between media and genres were renegotiated (one used to speak of a mixing of "high" and "low"). In this chapter I would like to take a few examples to work toward answers to the question of how images of sexual violence worked across and between media in roughly the third decade of the twentieth century, the way they sat in the public sphere of the time and were interwoven with complex practices of publicity. This does not deny the gender violence of which they were a part, but it does allow us to understand more fully why so many of these representations were made.

In exploring such questions, the first thing to bear in mind is that representations of sex (in its "deviant" forms), of criminal violence, and their merging in *Lustmord* had both a history and a wide medial presence already in the late nineteenth century. They were, in other words, nothing new irrupting in the work of Dix, Grosz, Schlichter et al. in the 1920s, or even in the drama of Frank Wedekind a few decades earlier. In the previous chapter, we have noted violent early modern broadsides and their embeddedness in the *Moritat* tradition of street ballads; also the extraordinarily widespread and graphic depictions in the penny dreadfuls or dime novels of the *colporteurs*.[10] And we have mentioned George Grosz's fascination with the book *Jack, der geheimnisvolle Mädchenmörder* (Jack, the mysterious girl-killer; see p. 147), its cover showing the bloodstained corpse of the victim of *Lustmord*. In his autobiography, Grosz also mentions his "little picture collection of beautiful, half-dressed women" that he had gathered from "the erotic crime magazine *Reporter*."[11] Such magazines left little to the literary or visual imagination: one cover of *Reporter: Illustriertes Welt-Blatt* from 1900 shows an attempted rape and murder with the caption "Ein Menschenfresser" (A cannibal).[12] A crazed man has thrown a woman, clothes torn revealing a bare breast, onto the floor and bends over her while she resists. Such crimes and their setting—a humble or squalid rented room by night—would reappear in the works of Grosz, Schlichter, and Dix; here, though, the woman is saved by the arrival of outraged neighbors. That same year—Grosz was about seven years old—another cover shows a similar bloody scene of a man bent over a woman he has murdered, a pistol on the ground beside her.[13] The scene is described breathlessly a few pages into the cheap magazine:

> The unfortunate woman fled, screaming horribly ... [T]he frenzied husband fired the revolver at close range to her neck. The woman collapsed, whimpering, dying a few moments later. The murderer tore open the wound with his hands and gorged himself on the warm, pulsing blood of his wife.[14]

Beyond the penny dreadfuls, representations of violent sexuality abounded in visual and literary pornography.[15] *Lustmord* was codified in the medico-forensic literature of psychiatry: the first sustained treatment of this class of criminal sexual pathology appeared in 1886, in the first edition of Richard von Krafft-Ebing's *Psychopathia Sexualis*.[16] Police crime-scene photographs captured such crimes in horrific detail. And there were works that occupied indeterminate positions between genres. Émile Laurent's *Sadismus und Masochismus* (Sadism and masochism), for example, gathers cases from psychiatrists' observations as well as literary texts, flattening the distinctions between the sources into a compendium of errant erotic practices.[17] And new genres emerged between erotica and enlightenment, for example the works of sexologists portraying the varieties and pathologies of sexual life in an encyclopedic way for a broader public (I discuss some of these below).

Yet the more disturbing images of *Lustmord* cannot simply be reduced to these prior representations. We still have to explain their sudden appearance and efflorescence specifically in the realm of the visual arts and literature. Did they really raise

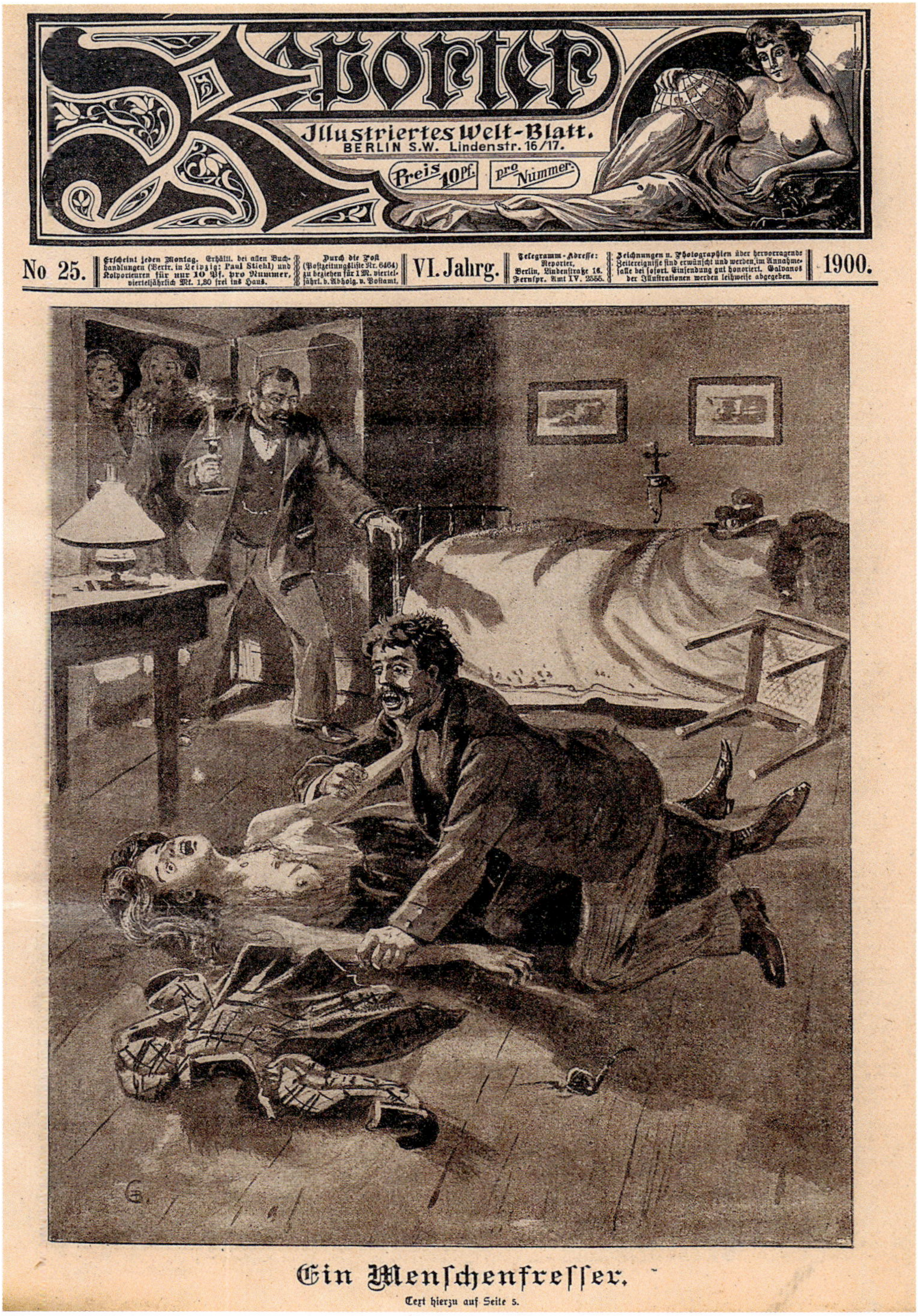

"Ein Menschenfresser" (A cannibal), cover of *Reporter*, vol. 6, no. 25 (1900). Photo Staatsbibliothek zu Berlin Preußischer Kulturbesitz.

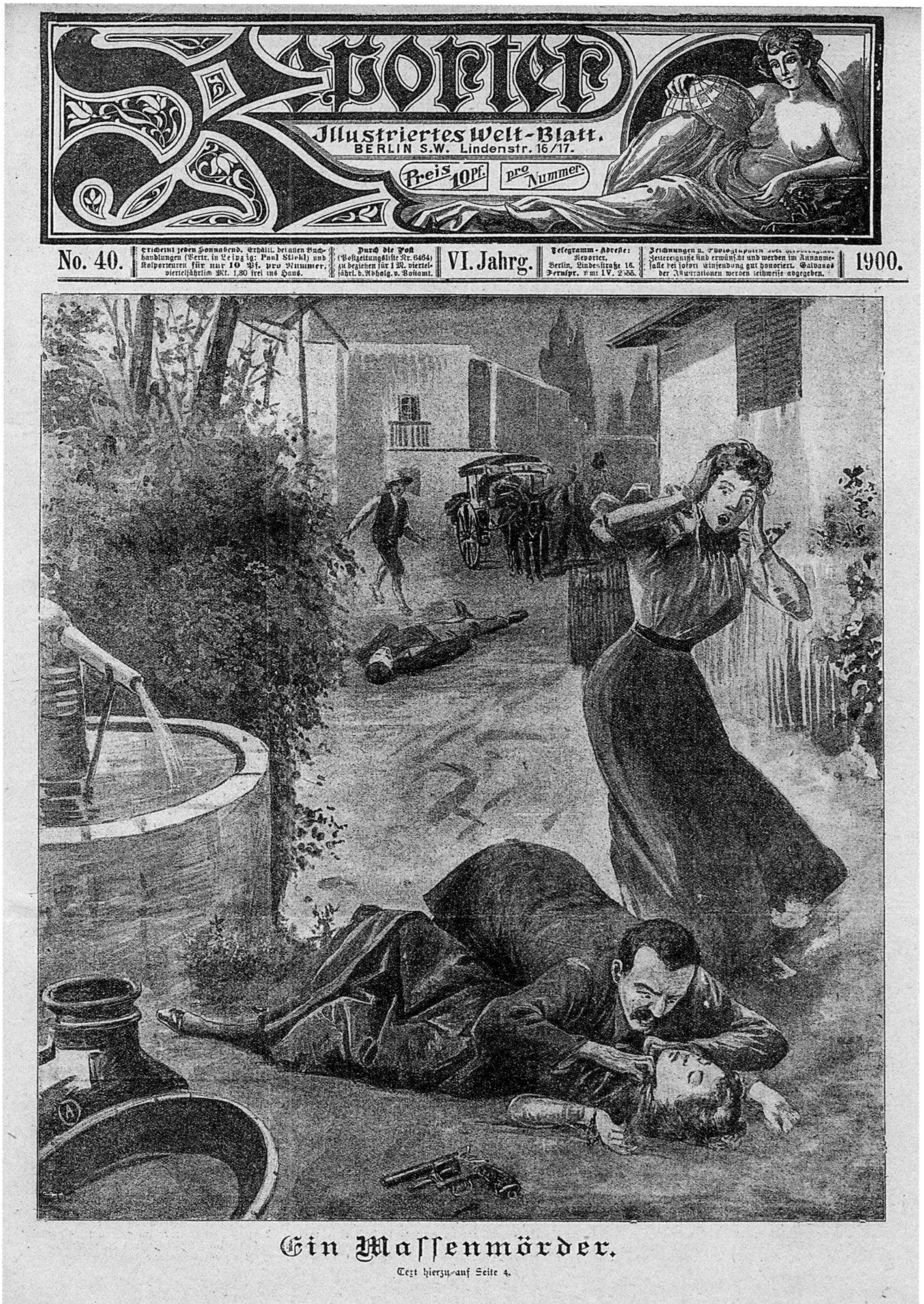
Reporter
Illustriertes Welt-Blatt.
BERLIN S.W. Lindenstr. 16/17.
Preis 10 Pf. pro Nummer.

No. 40. | Erscheint jeden Sonnabend. Erhältl. bei allen Buchhandlungen (Vertr. in Leipzig: Paul Stiehl) und Kolporteuren für nur 10 Pf. pro Nummer, vierteljährlich Mk. 1,80 frei ins Haus. | Durch die Post (Postzeitungsliste Nr. 6464) zu beziehen für 1 M. viertelljährl. b. Abholg. v. Postamt. | VI. Jahrg. | Telegramm-Adresse: Reporter, Berlin, Lindenstraße 16. Fernspr. Amt IV. 2355. | Zeichnungen u. Photographien über Zeitereignisse sind erwünscht und werden im Annahmefalle bei sofort. Einsendung gut honoriert. Galvanos der Illustrationen werden leihweise abgegeben. | 1900.

Ein Massenmörder.
Text hierzu auf Seite 4.

“Ein Massenmörder” (A mass murderer), cover of *Reporter*, vol. 6, no. 40 (1900). Photo Staatsbibliothek zu Berlin Preußischer Kulturbesitz.

no eyebrows? Were they simply accepted, in Beth Irwin Lewis's terms, "as an expected manifestation of the nasty underworld of the metropolis"? How could they appear in a society that was, in many ways, quite restrictive, and what functions might they have served? One thing is certain: if our starting point is that *Lustmord* images had a history, then what we are dealing with is not a sudden irruption but instead a movement of images within and around the visual culture, and more general culture, of the time. Thus we need to consider these images' migration from specific media and genres into different ones, from one zone of representation into others in the larger field of signs that could be produced, manipulated, seen, read, repeated, shared, and circulated. To do so, we can take these images as a case, availing ourselves of the reciprocal logic of the form. The crimes—perhaps fantasized or fictive ones, media creations, but nonetheless familiar and at some level accepted and understood—let us reverse our perspective and consider the context in which they assumed their meanings. Tracking the movements of these images tells us much about how that field—the field of representations—developed, in all its complex and unpredictable ways. Exploring the conditions that made possible the appearance of these violent images allows us to begin the work of mapping the space of representations under modernity, grasping and describing the shape of the public sphere and its transformations.

§

Policing the Public Sphere: Medium, Genre, and the Law

Let us consider, in the first half of this chapter, the legal parameters in which these—and indeed all—representations could be made public in these years. The new constitution of the German Reich—the *Weimarer Reichsverfassung*—that was signed into law on August 11, 1919, and took effect three days later, seemed to be unequivocal. Article 118 reads as follows: "Every German has the right, within the limits of the general laws, to express his opinion orally, in writing, in print, pictorially, or in any other way."[18] Furthermore, "No censorship shall be established." (Though this is immediately qualified: "but exceptional provisions may be made by law for cinematographs. Moreover, legal measures are permissible for the suppression of indecent and obscene literature (*Schmutz- und Schundliteratur*), as well as for the protection of youth at public plays and exhibitions."[19]) Article 142 goes further in the direction of permissiveness: "The arts, sciences, and their teaching are free. The state guarantees their protection and takes an active part in their cultivation."[20]

But the Weimar Constitution is a notoriously ambiguous and conflicted document. (Consider just the contradiction of its very first article: "The German Empire (*Reich*) is a republic."[21]) The seeming clarity of these principles is an illusion: they neither herald a complete lifting of restrictions nor a fundamental change in the conditions of publicity. First, few restrictions were abolished by these new guarantees of freedom of expression. For there had been no censorship of the press since 1874 in the sense of pre-publication scrutiny by government authorities.[22] Inspection of literary and scientific works had ceased long before. The only significant area of formal control of public statement before the Weimar Republic was in live performance: most German states and cities required all theatre scripts to be submitted to the police before their public staging. Though they rarely banned plays or revues outright, censors regularly required changes to specific passages, and police officials monitored performances to ensure that such instructions were followed, and also that the manner of staging did not alter the ostensible meaning of an approved text. The lifting of this system of theatre censorship was the only notable change in the conditions of public utterance ushered in by the new constitution.

Second, freedom was guaranteed only in traditional media and cultural forms. For the new media of film and, later, radio, the constitution in fact invited new and restrictive legislation. This took the traditional form of pre-censorship: boards would view films or read radio scripts before public screening or broadcast, and had the power to require deletions and alterations or to prohibit release. For the rising problem of literature no longer considered art but rather a mass-market commodity—so-called trash literature (*Schmutz- und Schundliteratur*)—the constitution also set the stage for restrictions, updating the possibility of controls under new technological and market conditions that altered and seemingly undermined the cultural status of the literary text. These matters were hotly debated and resulted in a new law controlling publications considered "sub-" or "under-cultural" (*untergeistig*).[23] The result of Article 118 was thus a net *increase* in official control of public representations and a shift of regulation toward the new media and mass-produced products of industries that were increasingly offering commercialized forms of leisure. George Grosz's fond memories of penny dreadfuls and erotic crime magazines were thus not only nostalgia for his youth but also for the pleasures of an "under-cultural" realm of representations that was increasingly under threat.

Finally, with the sole exception of theatre censorship, the new constitution abolished none of the existing legal restrictions on public representation. Freedom of expression was posited as a fundamental civil right, but only "within the limits of the general laws," few of which were repealed. The "general laws" were solidly established in the various legal codes that continued in full, unchanged force from the Kaiserreich. These laws were many, varied, and intricate, and though the interpretation of them continued to evolve under the new social and medial conditions of the early twentieth century, they remained the bread and butter of the judicature concerning the public sphere. In legal terms, we can characterize this situation in two ways. First, the constitution was seen to add *Rechtsgüter*—legally protected interests and rights—to those already existing; they represented merely principles for future legislation and additional legal interests that were to enter into the calculus of legal judgments. No such interests were abolished by it; the right of freedom of expression was to be weighed against existing rights which lost none of their force (these will be outlined below). Second, the Weimar Constitution staged a confrontation between, on the one hand, the *natural law* that informed the new principles of fundamental rights in the first German republic and, on the other, the *positive law* of the German legal code that remained the bedrock of the administration of justice, the logical, closed legal order to be applied impartially and impersonally.[24] The constitution established fundamental rights, but the practical work of the courts continued in its positivist mode. The conflicting theoretical bases of Weimar jurisprudence were never untangled: the political principles of the new state were ultimately undermined by their base in an existing legal and institutional structure. And indeed, *all* of these rights and interests could be superseded—and often were—by the notorious Article 48 of the constitution that allowed rights to be suspended under emergency decree. These decrees regularly took the form of restrictions on the public sphere, including the banning of specific publications and performances.

So it is to the existing, pre-Weimar legal structure that developed since 1871 that we need to look to understand the limits of the representable as defined by the law, and to the slow and uneven developments within it. There were other nonsimultaneities as well, as some laws and their enforcement came under the competence of the different *Länder*, the federal states comprising Germany. Local conditions, mores, and traditions determined many aspects of enforcement. Moreover, Bavaria regularly (and unconstitutionally) overruled Reich laws and suspended them; and other largely rural *Länder* were loath to cede control to the Reich and often subverted the legal mechanisms that required them to do so.

Such complexities inevitably resist summary, but roughly speaking we can plot the legally defined space of representation along three axes of limits or controls that remained by and large intact until 1933: a) the division of protected rights into the categories of religion, politics, morals, and personality; b) the different legal codes under which cases were considered; and c) specificities of medium and genre.

(a) Representations of *religion* were addressed in §166 of the criminal code (*Strafgesetzbuch* or *StGB*), which states that

> Whoever publicly causes a scandal by blaspheming God through irreverent, insulting remarks (*beschimpfende Äußerungen*) or who publicly reviles one of the Christian Churches or another of the legally incorporated and officially recognized religious associations within the federal domain or reviles their institutions or rituals ... shall be punished with up to three years' imprisonment.[25]

Though the statute was meant only to punish particularly crude or contemptuous statements or acts, the penalties were comparatively harsh.[26] And because the signs of Christendom were deeply inscribed in public discourse of all kinds, the potential for blasphemy was real: any critique of hegemonic morality that took ironic recourse to such symbols was at risk. Oskar Panizza, we saw, fell foul of these strictures (indeed, on ninety-three counts). Prosecutions in the Weimar period were rare but significant and high in profile. Carl Einstein's unperformed drama *Die schlimme Botschaft* (Ill tidings) of 1921, imagining the arrival of Christ in contemporary Germany, was banned; Einstein and his publisher were convicted of blasphemy and given heavy fines, while unsold copies of the book and the letterpress plates were destroyed.[27] More famously, George Grosz was brought to trial for his portfolio *Hintergrund* (Background) in 1928, in particular for the notorious tenth plate *"Maul halten und weiter dienen"* (Shut up and do your duty), commonly called *Christ with a Gasmask*.[28] The proceedings dragged over three years and were a *cause célèbre*; though ending with Grosz's acquittal, the Reichsgericht's overturning of a not-guilty decision in the second instance shows the direction the country's highest court sought to lead the Berlin judge.

The criminal code's constraints on the public expression of radical *political* views were numerous, encompassing the distribution of propaganda for illegal parties, insulting the constitution, the state, or its officials, as well as outright treason. The latter was of most concern for the press, as even factual reports of the right's illegal activity could be seen as "dangerous to the state" in the light of the Versailles treaty and its terms; simply reprinting such reports that had already been published could and did lead to prosecution. But these statutes were also widely used in the arts, as will be discussed in this and the next chapter. The actions of separatist movements, the betrayal of state secrets to other powers, and any attempt to alter the constitution by violent means were all considered treasonous. In the arts, the expression of radical political views could be pursued under §86, which stipulates the punishment of "[a]ny other actions in preparation of a treasonous enterprise with imprisonment of up to three years with hard labor (*Zuchthaus*) or fortress detention (*Festungshaft*)." This statute was used with disturbing frequency against artists of the left, even in the absence of any specific planned act. A general call to opposition or revolution often prompted prosecution. In the areas of fiction, drama, or poetry, such acts became known as "literary high treason" (*literarischer Hochverrat*). In 1926, for example, Johannes R. Becher's political novel *Levisite* was confiscated by authorities in Berlin and the author charged with this crime.[29] The book was a dystopian account of a civil war in Germany following the horrors of the First World War and took its title from the lethal chemical agent deployed in both the actual war and the fictional one. In the wake of a series of amnesties for political crimes and an ambitious publicity campaign, charges were, in the end, dropped.[30] The stakes were raised by the wide reach of the law regarding those who could be charged with preparation of treason in these cases: not only authors, artists, editors, and publishers but printers, typesetters, distributors, and retail sellers as well.[31] Moreover, the courts followed the expansive logic that, in the words of the Reichsgericht,

> Preparation of a treasonous enterprise is possible even in the case of the dissemination of publications that are not in themselves treasonous, in which an author pursued only artistic or scientific aims, if the works are objectively suitable for treasonous aims and the disseminator, because of these qualities, abuses them by distributing them for these purposes.[32]

The legal mainstay governing representations in terms of *morality* was §184 of the criminal code: "Whoever sells, distributes, or otherwise disseminates obscene (*unzüchtige*) publications (*Schriften*), illustrations (*Abbildungen*), or representations (*Darstellungen*), or who exhibits or displays these in public places, shall be punished with a fine of up to three hundred marks or imprisonment for up to six months."[33] The statute is vague, and the courts were required to develop guidelines for its use. In 1886 the Reichsgericht formulated the principles which long remained in effect: the law was meant to address "such threats to morality and the violation of the sense of modesty of normal persons (*normal angelegter Personen*) ... i.e. publications, illustrations, or representations that tend to seriously violate the sense of modesty and morality in a sexual sense."[34] The measure of the offence is thus the *effect* of the work in question, defined as the effect on the "normal" person. And as in all criminal offences, there are two questions to be answered (and often two separate proceedings): the *actus reus* (the objective element of the case, here whether the work itself violates the *Rechtsgut* of public morality and how it is to be dealt with—by redaction, cuts, withdrawal from distribution, or destruction), and the *mens rea* (the subjective element, whether the artist could be found guilty of the crime). An artist's intention was not considered in the determination of whether a work was to be considered obscene (or treasonous), though that could be considered in "subjective" proceedings.

The measure of whether a "normal person" could legitimately take offense at an image when faced with erotic or sexual subject matter, or whether the category of "art" was present (and thus a legal interest worthy of protection, even before its specification as such in the Weimar Constitution), was also defined more directly, if equally vaguely. Text or image could be considered "artistic" if, in the opinion of the court (informed by an increasing number of embattled expert advisory bodies) the subject matter was, in good Kantian fashion, rendered "intellectual" or "spiritual" (*durchgeistigt*), was "transfigured" (*verklärt*) to the extent that "for the natural aesthetic sensibility the sensuous feeling is contained and curtailed (*zurückgedrängt*) by the disinterested pleasure of the beautiful."[35] The legal claims of art had no inherent priority over other interests, which flattened the field of representations considerably, often undermining accepted cultural hierarchies and leaving relatively little protection for "art" in such matters.

Prosecutions for obscenity were legion in the arts. Most famously Otto Dix's *Mädchen vor dem Spiegel* (Girl in front of a mirror) of 1922 was among the works removed by authorities from the Berlin *Juryfreie Rundschau* exhibition. Three artists were charged with obscenity; two of them—Erich Godal [Goldbaum] and George Kobbe—were convicted, while Dix, in a separate trial, was acquitted due to the "moral tendency" of the work.[36] Just as prominently, George Grosz and his publishers Wieland Herzfelde and Julian Gumperz were brought to trial for the prints in the portfolio *Ecce Homo*.[37] On the basis of objections to thirty-four of the images, the state prosecutor demanded high fines and the withdrawal of the entire portfolio from sale. In the subjective aspect of the proceedings, the defendants were found guilty and fined; on the objective side the judge ordered the removal and destruction of seventeen black-and-white lithographs and five color lithograph reproductions. The printed prospectus and the plates for the images were destroyed too.

When prominent artists or writers were involved, these cases could attract wide attention. But policing the public presence of "immoral" or "obscene" works was a huge task that took place largely out of the public eye. The work of the public prosecutors and courts could not be streamlined, but it was crucial that duplicate prosecutions be avoided and that the police have up-to-date lists of indexed material. To this end, a "Central Police Office for the Control of Obscene Publications, Pictures, and Advertisements" (*Zentralpolizeistelle zur Bekämpfung unzüchtiger Schriften, Bilder und Inserate*) was established and came to be administered by the Berlin police department. Their efforts have given us the only reliable, if terse, record of the almost unbelievable activity of the administration of justice in this area. In 1920 and again in 1926 (with supplements in 1929 and 1930), the office issued its so-called *Polunbi* catalogs (named after the telegram address of the authority).[38] These listed not only every printed work found to be obscene, along with brief information about the objective outcome of the case, but also works brought to court—often by the office itself—but found not to be obscene, as well as cases considered but not brought by state and local prosecutors.[39] Court decisions are referenced but the legal grounds, for reasons of brevity, omitted; very few of these case records are preserved.[40] The *Polunbi* catalogs, however, provide the only summary of the tens of thousands of obscenity cases considered or brought and sometimes cursory information about the works involved.

Finally, the realm of *privacy* or *personality rights* (*Persönlichkeitsrecht*) contains within it limitations on public expression. The rights over the use of one's likeness (*Recht am eigenen Bild*) was protected to varying degrees. Artists were particularly well informed about this as it pertained to the practices of satire and caricature: the journal *Werkstatt der Kunst*, for example, ran a series of articles, a refresher course for artists as humor magazines—often political—became an increasingly important source of work and income.[41] Laws against defamation were also in principle limits on expression. Yet as the work of Karl Kraus shows, these laws could also be spectacularly *productive* of controversial discourse, as insults were issued precisely in order to air and establish them in the public space of the court and its reporting. Critics such as Kurt Tucholsky regularly lamented the drain on the justice system caused by these laws.[42]

(b) The legal statutes concerning permissible expression, and competence in enforcing them, were also various; this constitutes a second axis in our mapping of the public sphere as a legally regulated space. Most of the above examples were matters of the *criminal code*, but rights of other legal kinds traversed the space of public representation. Specifics are not terribly important here, but it is worth pointing out that important aspects of personal rights, for example, were governed by *civil law*, as was copyright. The activities of theatres and cinemas were governed by *commercial law* (the *Gewerbeordnung*); it is here that many aspects of censorship were inscribed and enforced. The new cinema law of 1920, which established review boards with censorship powers, came under the aegis of *administrative law* (*Verwaltungsrecht*); radio came under public law or *öffentliches Recht*. And administrative law was the rubric under which the police could act in almost any capacity at all in the name of preserving public order: banning film screenings, confiscating publications, forbidding performances. Constitutional law (*Verfassungsrecht*) established many fundamental rights (to vie with other legal protections). These differences needed to be negotiated in traversing the public sphere. And perhaps most importantly, under Article 48 of the constitution *all* laws could be suspended by the president of the Reich, who could then rule by emergency decree.

(c) Medium and genre represent the final axis to be considered here, perhaps the hardest to grasp but ultimately the most interesting in mapping the public sphere. Constitutional and criminal law, we have seen, tended to be written in broad terms of media and the human faculties they engaged: the constitution's blanket protection of expression "orally, in writing, in print, pictorially, or in any other way," the criminal code's closer scrutiny of publication (*Schrift*), image (*Bild*), and representation (*Darstellung*). Distinctions here were important. The human voice was subject to greater restriction than the written word:[43] political poems that were published without objection and freely available to read privately became treasonous when read aloud to an audience, even when the assembly was approved.[44] The specificities of media in the realm of the visual were also an area of fine distinction. Unclothed female bodies, for example, were the currency of the western tradition in art, and examples filled the museums. To print and sell postcards of these images, however, could be considered dealing in pornography. The reduction in format, the transposition from oil on canvas to ink on card, the duplication and sale in large numbers at very low prices were all seen to change the nature of the image fundamentally, desublimating the contents and rendering them lewd. The years immediately before the First World War saw numerous trials of this kind. One contemporary referred to state prosecutors pressing such charges as "dilettantes of vice"[45]—a wonderfully Krausian phrase—but they had the support of the Reichsgericht. Overturning the dismissal of such a case, it wrote that

> this concerns not the works themselves produced by the artists but the copies of them on postcards. That which

> applies to the products of art cannot simply be transferred to replications of them ... Furthermore, the question of whether a representation is obscene is not a question of whether their display has the goal of arousing sexual or sensual excitement. What is decisive is instead the objective content of the representations themselves, whether alone or in conjunction with the precise circumstances of their display.[46]

Determining the *objektiver Tatbestand*, the objective facts of the case, involved a close consideration of the object itself.

More consistent, perhaps, is the situation with the new media. Material appearing freely in novels or scientific work could not necessarily be transposed into the medium of film. One example: the administration of justice itself was under fire in the 1920s, the time of a widely perceived "crisis of confidence in the judiciary,"[47] and scenes of overworked, incompetent, reactionary, and even intoxicated judges were commonplaces in the literature of the time.[48] To suggest such criticism in film, however, was considered insulting to institutions of the Reich. Bertolt Brecht and Ernst Ottwalt's film *Kuhle Wampe* (1932) contains a courtroom scene that did not pass the censors.[49] A judge is shown giving three successive eviction orders to families of the unemployed; he is visibly bored and does this mechanically. Censors insisted on cuts to show at most one such courtroom judgment.[50] Peter Jelavich has written an exemplary account of the successive dilution of Alfred Döblin's *Berlin Alexanderplatz* from novel to radio play to film;[51] one can trace such dilution in more extreme form in the parallel emergence of Karl Plättner's factual account of the sexual privations of prison life based on experience and interviews in *Eros im Zuchthaus* (Eros in prison, 1929) to the feature film that emerged from the same circle of reformers: *Geschlecht in Fesseln* (Sex in chains, 1928).[52] The move from text read in private to moving image on a screen collectively viewed (and soon including the audible voice) traversed a complex legal and administrative space that determined the permissibility of representation; it was a space characterized by inconsistencies, surprises, comedy, and sudden and unpredictable points of resistance—and, as we shall see, zones of unexpected freedom—within the parameters of the permissibly public. Media and the "precise circumstances of their display" were subject to myriad forms of control, logical within their own purviews but often contradictory as a whole.

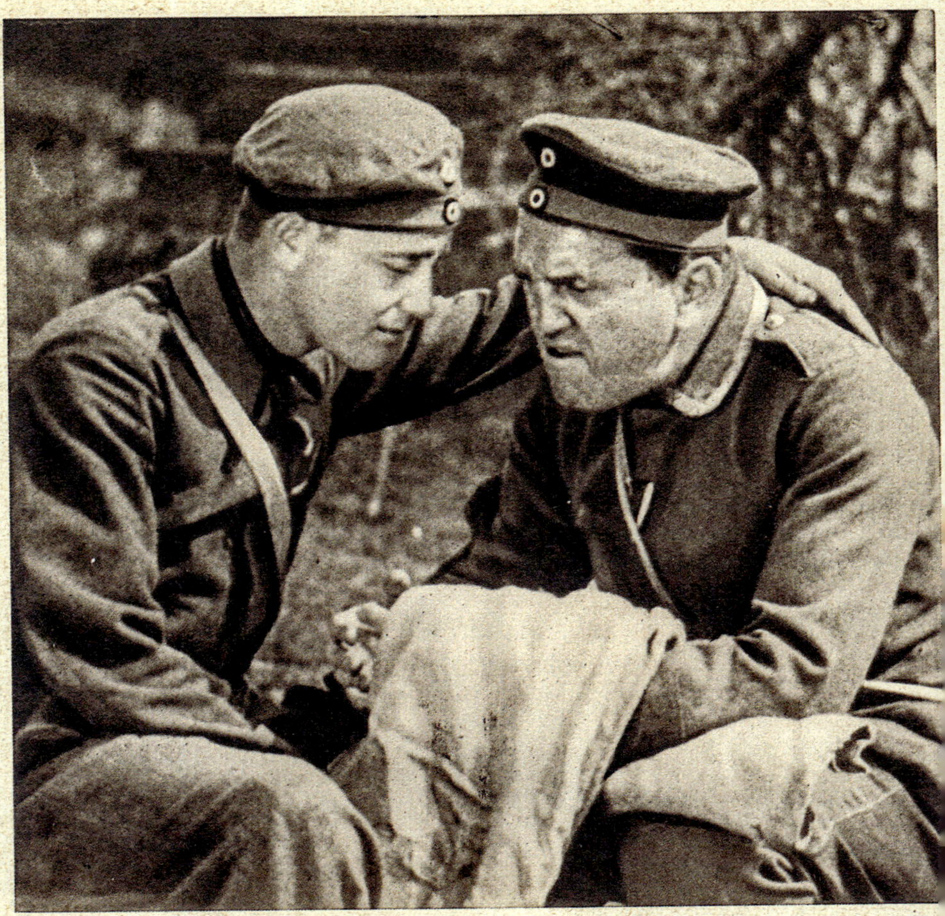

„Ich hätte nie nach Hause gehen sollen, Kat, es ist alles so anders“

116

From *Der Film Im Westen nichts Neues* (Berlin: Verlagsgesellschaft des Allgemeinen Deutschen Gewerkschaftsbundes/Ernst Rowohlt Verlag, 1931).

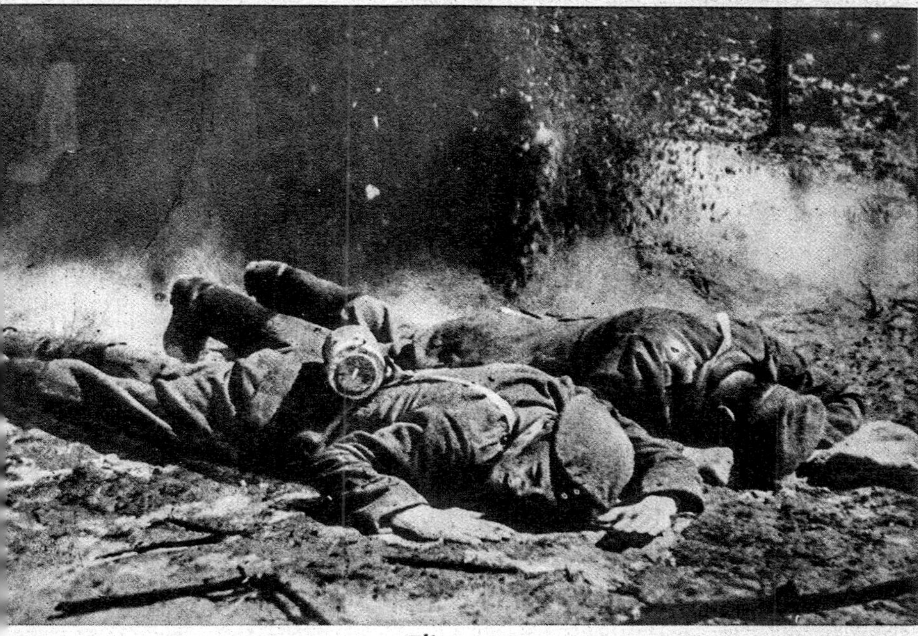

„Flieger!“

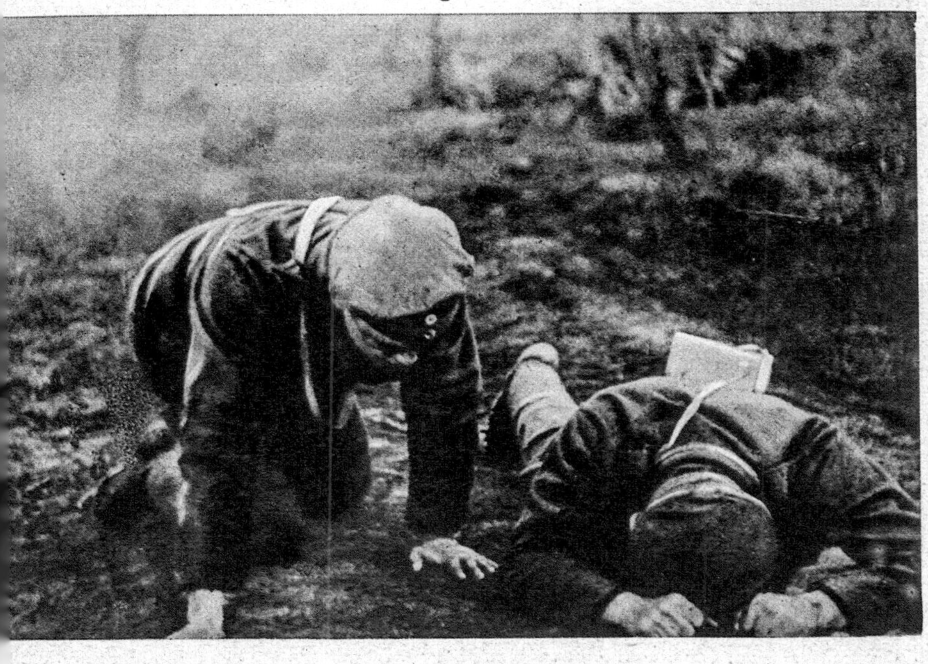

Kat ist getroffen

And indeed, these contradictions opened up room for maneuver, both for those trying to make representations and those trying to control them. The result was a certain tendency to range freely across media according to the expedient of the moment. When faced with the banning of the 1930 film of Erich Maria Remarque's novel *Im Westen nichts Neues* (All quiet on the western

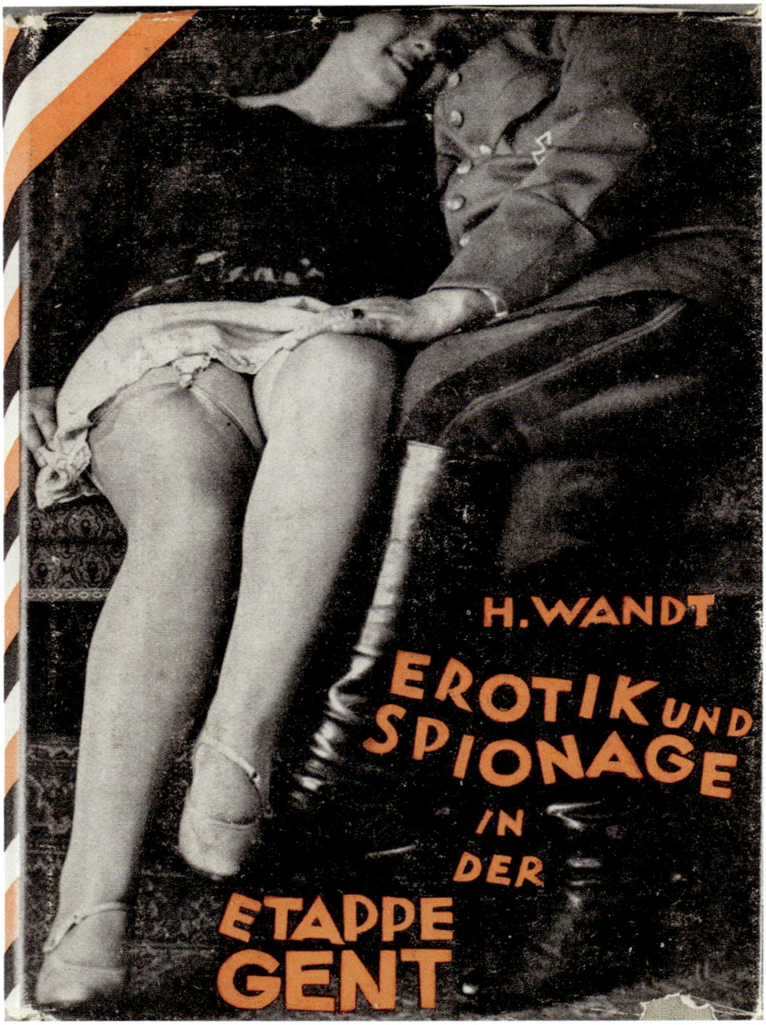

John Heartfield, first (censored) book cover for Heinrich Wandt, *Erotik und Spionage in der Etappe Gent* (Erotics and espionage in the Ghent command; Vienna: Agis Verlag, 1928). Akademie der Künste, Berlin, Kunstsammlung, John Heartfield 250400/JH 2680. © The Heartfield Community of Heirs/DACS 2022.

front, 1928/29), which turned out to be temporary, a trade union organization simply arranged for a cheap picture-book (in an edition of sixty thousand) of several hundred still images from the film to be published with captions; the film could be pieced together nearly seamlessly through a slightly more primitive reception of montage, in the reader's mind and not in a cinema, at a small scale on paper and not on a large screen of moving images.[53] On the side of authorities, when the state prosecutor opened proceedings for obscenity against Heinrich Wandt's book *Erotik und Spionage in der Etappe Gent* (Erotics and espionage in the Ghent command), an exposé of immoral behavior in the wake of the German occupation of Belgium in the First World War, they failed due to an expert's report (by Herbert Jhering, left-leaning critic and friend of Brecht) attesting to the thoroughly ethical tendency of the work.[54] They then tried shifting legal argumentation from text to image, specifically the cover by John Heartfield, a photomontage showing "a male person" (in an officer's uniform) with his hand on the thigh of "a girl with her clothes in a revealing state" (a prostitute with her skirt hiked above her stockings). Here they succeeded, though it was a pyrrhic victory as the book soon reappeared with a slightly altered cover.[55] (And since both author and publisher lived abroad, the authorities went after the artist and nearly found him. The case file reveals an attempt to summon Heartfield through his brother Wieland Herzfelde's Malik-Verlag. Herzfelde wrote back to the police as follows: "I return the enclosed letter for Herr Johann Herzfelde, sent to my address in error. To the best of my knowledge no such Herr Johann Herzfelde exists, and this person is not identical with Herr John Heartfield."[56] Showing little sense of humor, the police did not accept Herzfelde's back-handed help: the ensuing court proceedings list as the defendant "Unknown."[57])

The common denominator of these restrictions is, of course, the perceived or presumed audience for the works in question. Works of art in a museum or reproduced in art-historical literature were viewed by a self-selecting audience familiar with the protocols of high culture and its institutions, its spaces of visibility; cheap postcards hawked on the street were available to the underaged and those who could not be trusted to sublimate their pleasures into the disinterested contemplation of art. Similarly, the anatomical illustrations of a medical book could be entrusted to print, as the availability of medical literature and its recalcitrant text filled with Latin terms would resist prurient curiosity and pleasure, while such images freely available and in the absence of text would invite the wrong sort of attention and thus cried out for control. In the political realm, the works of Marx and Engels were freely available, but when these ideas were put in a form considered "propaganda" by the courts, they could be seen as preparation of high treason.[58] (Interestingly, even if "propaganda," the organs and publications of legally permitted political parties were free from prosecution, while the exact same text or image could be subject to control in the absence of this protection.)

Legislation of the new technologies of film and radio was proactively restrictive. But the older media of the word and the image in print had ramified due to new markets and printing techniques to such an extent that medium was no longer a reliable indicator of the extent of sublimation of base desires, the potential for danger to the constitutional order, the possibility of injury, insult, or offence. Such matters were often a function of the particular audience or public interpellated by the works, and the mechanism of such reciprocal construction of work and audience was, of course, the genre.[59] Thus, while overarching legislation was couched in the language of media, judicature tended inevitably and predictably toward distinctions of genre or form. And thus the laws of the public sphere produced shifts not only between media but also between genres, producing overlapping and hybrid forms that would allow representations to slip through the mesh of the law and its executors and to reach audiences unable or unwilling to seek out information and images in places that were straightforwardly sanctioned by necessity, tradition, and the law.

Emblematic of such mixed and overlapped genres is the work of Erich Wulffen, a distinguished lawyer, state prosecutor, and criminologist who published important works on the psychology of crime before the First World War.[60] His encyclopedic book *Der Sexualverbrecher* (The sexual criminal) of 1910 was the standard work for doctors and lawyers confronting such crimes.[61] As scholars have pointed out, his extensive chapter on *Lustmord* was the source for many of the images of Otto Dix and Rudolf Schlichter.[62] For the book contains not only case studies culled from his own experience, notorious crimes (including the murder of Elsie Siegel of interest to Adolf Loos and Karl Kraus), and the sexological literature of Krafft-Ebing and others; there are also thirty-two police photographs reproduced in fairly large format in the *Lustmord* section alone, including many harrowing crime-scene photos that can be traced through the art of the time.[63] The book—though scientific—was clearly in wide circulation among those interested in crime, including artists, and went through eleven editions by 1928. There can be no doubt that it served a sort of recreational readership and came to be a general cultural reference point among the educated. The writer Ernst von Salomon, for example—a friend of Schlichter and Brecht—notes in his memoirs that when he worked as an assistant in the administrative library of a prison during the early 1920s, "No one came in ... aside from the occasional official who was interested in Wulffen's *Sexual-Verbrechen*."[64] And in the pages of *Die neue Bücherschau*, a critic reduces the dramas of Arnolt Bronnen, a member of the same group, to the following formula: "Wulffen—*Sexualverbrecher*—turned into drama plus [Alfred] Hugenberg editorials turned into dialogue."[65]

Indeed, Wulffen cultivated wide audiences in an attempt to popularize knowledge of crime, psychology, and the law in a set of works that cross genre boundaries. *Der Sexualverbrecher* was clearly meant for use by medical, police, and court specialists, as were his books *Das Weib als Sexualverbrecherin* (Woman as sexual criminal) and *Psychologie des Giftmordes* (Psychology of murder by poisoning).[66] But they fed the market for sex and crime as well, as their subsequent histories show: the former was later published in abridged form as erotica and was translated into English as a cheap paperback with an alluring cover.[67] The latter went through many editions, becoming famous when it turned out that a domestic accused of poisoning her employers in a high-profile murder trial had borrowed the book from the library.[68] Wulffen also wrote a series of books on the treatment of criminality in literature (Shakespeare, Ibsen, and Schiller) as well as popular accounts of famous criminals and swindlers. He had great success with criminal novels and also contributed to the growing literature on sex and crime seen in cultural perspective: his *Sexualspiegel von Kunst und Verbrechen* (Art and crime as the mirror of sex) is a sumptuous illustrated volume, an erudite and critically astute tour through the western canon and recent developments in art and literature of the overlapping areas of sex and crime.[69] *Irrwege des Eros* (Eros astray) treated female sexuality in a sober and expert manner, but in a popular format with an alluring title.[70] Wulffen published extensively on sex and crime in the popular press and was a regular contributor to the so-called *Sittengeschichten* or moral histories, which similarly combined word and image, straying between historical scholarship and erotic content. Magnus Hirschfeld, whose scholarly credentials were beyond question, wrote such works, as did Curt Moreck (Konrad Haemmerling), who ranged from erotic-cultural history to a famous guidebook to the areas of erotic interest in Berlin.[71] Such books were trying for the justice system, which devoted considerable resources to determining their legality.[72] They are well represented in the *Polunbi* catalogs, which in fact reveal that few were censored before 1933. The scholarly aspect of these books regularly allowed their images to appear; and the images in and surrounding them attracted audiences beyond the "cultural" or scientific readership for which they, in generic terms, were written.

§

Lustmord in the Public Sphere

So: could *Lustmord* be represented? And if so, how? There are, in fact, relatively few cases of such images prompting attempts to forbid them, but though details are scant and indirect, they are worth considering for the light they cast upon the conditions of public representation.

George Grosz's *Frauenmörder* paintings were rarely exhibited and rarely reproduced, but they were not invisible. *John, der Frauenmörder*, for example, spent most of its time in private collections or in the possession of dealers. The painting was held by the dealer Hans Goltz before being bought by the Hannover collector Herbert von Garvens-Garvensburg, who owned it until about 1927. (Garvens also owned *Der kleine Frauenmörder* at the time and displayed it in his bedroom, which was decorated in black.)[73] It was exhibited twice in these years: first, in April and May 1920 in Goltz's gallery in Munich, and then in Gustav Friedrich Hartlaub's landmark 1925 *Neue Sachlichkeit* exhibition in Mannheim.[74] As noted in the literature, neither event provoked any documented protest. Looking at the *publication* of the image, however, yields a slightly different story. It appeared in the catalog for Goltz's exhibition, published as a special issue of his art journal *Der Ararat*. A year later, it was reproduced as a black-and-white plate in Willi Wolfradt's short monograph on the artist to the series *Junge Kunst*, which prompted the *Polunbi* office to attempt to have the book confiscated, withdrawn, and destroyed.[75] In the end, the state prosecutor decided not to pursue the case, but it is worth noting that the image prompted a reaction, and that before the prosecutor's decision, it was briefly confiscated by the Dresden police.[76] Other, albeit less graphic, images from the series were occasionally published without problem.[77]

This suggests that exhibitions were somehow less "public" than book publications. But this is inconclusive, and certainly the devil lies in the detail. For exhibitions were brief, requiring the authorities to move quickly. And, as Peter Jelavich notes, authorities "were generally loath to prosecute writers and artists. They did so only when important pressure groups, such as the churches or the more vociferous members of the conservative parties, forced the issue" (though as we have seen, this did happen).[78] The Goltz exhibition in Munich also took place in 1920, during a brief postwar lull in censorship; and the catalog was printed in small numbers for a limited audience of journal subscribers and exhibition visitors. Wolfradt's more popular monograph was published in 1921, but it was late 1924 before the Dresden police temporarily confiscated it. Perhaps their sensitivities to Grosz's work were aroused by the *Ecco Homo* trial of that year? We shall never know. In any case, matters of publics, venues, and timing were certainly at play in deciding whether images would prompt a negative reaction from authorities.

Two other cases suggest that it was in the unstable legal spaces opened up between genres and media that *Lustmord* could be represented visually in a public forum. Consider the *Ecce Homo* trial, which is well documented, the court records preserved and analyzed by Wolfgang Hütt and Rosamunde Neugebauer.[79] The records contain careful descriptions of the offending plates, but the image of *Lustmord* in the portfolio is not among those brought to the attention of the court. And *Lustmord in der Ackerstraße* (Sex murder in the Ackerstraße), ignored by the state prosecutor, is a disturbing image indeed. It shows the aftermath of a murder in a rented room, probably that of the sex worker killed. Before a screen, the corpse lies uncovered on the bed next to the axe used. The upper body is bare, the head missing, the stump of the torso bleeding profusely. Behind the screen is the murderer washing his hands, rendered in a caricatured way: his shirt loose over his ample belly, braces dragging around his bottom, with a childish and sheepish look on his face. He is neither crazed nor enraged but instead strangely comic in his bashful look back at the dismembered victim of his horrific crime.

The image was seen as acceptable, I would argue, simply because it was old hat. The reference is quite clear. Ackerstraße, running between the proletarian districts of Mitte and Wedding in north Berlin, was famous for a particular case of *Lustmord*: the June 1904 murder of nine-year-old Lucie Berlin by the local pimp Theodor Berger, whose lover Johanna Liebetruth lived along the same corridor as the Berlin family. The young girl had disappeared, and over the following week the dismembered parts of the corpse were fished out of rivers and canals around the city, variously loose, wrapped in newspaper, and in a wicker basket. It was one of the most sensationalized cases of the time, due to the grisly nature of the crime, the youth of the unfortunate victim, the initial lack of conclusive evidence against the accused and, finally, the first use in a courtroom of a new procedure in forensic science which allowed human blood to be distinguished chemically from animal blood, and which led to the conviction.[80]

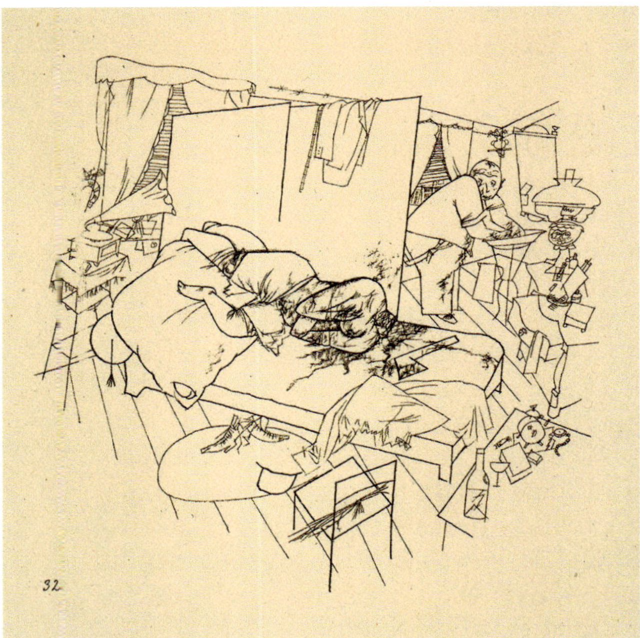

George Grosz, *Lustmord in der Ackerstraße* (Sex murder in the Ackerstraße), 1916/17. From *Ecce Homo* (Berlin: Malik-Verlag, 1923), no. 32. Photo © bpk/Kunstbibliothek, SMB/Atelier Petersen. © Estate of George Grosz, Princeton, NJ/DACS 2022.

But more important than the familiarity of the case, I suspect, is the fact that Grosz's print represents a sort of illustration to a specific, well-known text that circulated legally and was clearly recognized. The text was from a popular "harlot's song" about the case of Lucie Berlin:

Tief in der Ackerstraß' Da ist ein Mord passiert Die Lucie Berlin verführt	Deep in the Ackerstrasse There was a murder there Lucie Berlin was seduced
Die war die Liebetrut, Die war dem Berger gut. Sie war erst 15 Jahr, Als er ihr Lude war.	Then there was Liebetrut To Berger she was good She was just 15 years old When he became her pimp.

The song itself could not be removed from the world; what is sung in the streets is not subject to such measures. It had, in fact, been printed, in a popular collection of *Lieder aus dem Rinnstein* (Songs from the gutter) published by the pioneering urban ethnographer of Berlin Hans Ostwald,[81] an example of the humorous attempts to document the Berlin working class and underworld, much like the contemporary work of Heinrich Zille.[82] Similarly, it explains the disturbing irony of Grosz's image combining violence with cartoon-like caricature: the performer would have rendered the song of *Mordlust* with black humor as a grotesque. We cannot reconstruct any performance, but Ostwald tells us all we need to know, noting that the text was sung to the rousing and cheery tune of "Tief im Böhmerwald," a *Heimat*-song popular to this day.[83]

This bawdy black humor is not mere background to the image but is interior to it, part of its very fabric. The image contained within it, and commented upon, a gutter song; the song itself made light of the dangers of the city while ridiculing patriotic *Heimat* music. The image is also a song and a poem, or two performed songs, with their overlapping confrontation of country and city, *Volk* and *Lumpenproletariat*—subversive enough, but contained by its scholarly inscription in the new genre of urban ethnography. It is an utterly intermedial and intergeneric work, and in the space within this complex fabric is found a strange and violent motif that was nonetheless deemed permissible.

Lustmord and other perversions could clearly be represented in song, and examples are not rare. Frank Wedekind wrote and performed a *Moritat* about a man who kills his girlfriend, but seemingly for the money: "Ich habe meine Tante geschlachtet" (I've slaughtered my old girl).[84] In the *Threepenny Opera*, Bertolt Brecht borrowed a title from a chapter of Krafft-Ebing's *Psychopathia Sexualis*: "Die Ballade von der sexuellen Hörigkeit" (The ballad of sexual dependency).[85] There was, however, another case in which *Lustmord* figures in the context of song, but this time images serving as illustrations crossed the line of the permissible. It is instructive to see where exactly the lines were drawn within the medial architecture of the complex work. This was in a book of 1924 by the poet and cabaret artist Paul Althaus called *Jack der Aufschlitzer* (Jack the Ripper), subtitled "a few dozen songs (*Lieder*)."[86] Rudolf Schlichter provided the illustrations. In fact, these were poems: no indications are given as to how they were to be sung, and the loose verse seems to resist any popular songs or ballad tunes. The author was no doubt using the *Moritat* tradition as an alibi, and we see again the gusto and bloodthirsty irony with which the lower side of urban life was held up to the forms of high or folk culture. One poem is titled "Fatum? Fatum?" (Fate? Fate?):

> With Lina—her last name I know not
> I really had no good reason
> For that they can drag me to court
> Her face was full of spots
> And clammy she was too
> And smelled like she lived in manure
> And stank for other reasons too.
> Well, in the cold light of day
> She really couldn't in this world stay.
> No—that's not the reason for Lina.
> I'd just had enough, at the end of the day.
> For that they can drag me to court.[87]

The poems themselves are ambiguous, but the reference to Jack the Ripper, a touchstone for *Lustmord*, is clear enough. It is the explicitness of Schlichter's images that identify precisely the nature of the crime, though one press report refers merely—and flippantly?—to his "mildly sadistic drawings."[88] His illustration to "Fatum? Fatum?" rehearses Grosz's *Ackerstraße* scene almost verbatim, a clothed man washing his hands, looking back upon his female victim, upper body exposed and with blood dripping from her brutally slit throat. But he does so without the irony of Grosz, or of the texts; or he relies on the juxtaposition of image and text to generate this distance from the acts presented, thus bearing the brunt of the complex and calculated work of flirting with obscenity and the discourses of deviance.

A second poem is illustrated with an image copied almost directly from Wulffen's *Der Sexualverbrecher*, merely turning the corpse from supine to prone. The image shares much of the cold detail of its source, a poem telling of fleeting attraction and sudden murder with the title "Die Lotosblume ängstigt sich" (The lotus flower takes fright), which reads like a verse version of a particularly grim case study from Wulffen or Krafft-Ebing—but was clearly meant as humor:

> Mimi was a waitress at the slaughterhouse inn
> In the back room.
> The girl was built like a cow.
> Last winter I would always go there
> And just had to stare.
> She couldn't take my ogling,
> One hand in my pocket fiddling ...
> She nearly went mad,
> Such a fright she had.
> But of the silly cow I soon had enough.
> Pity, the girl was pretty and tough,
> But in the end I'm only human
> Forgive me, keeper of the slaughterhouse inn.[89]

The poem performed the work of slipping into the role of Jack the Ripper, playing with what one critic called the "uncanny mixture of manly tenderness and criminal brutality."[90]

A third poem shows sexual delight in murder by hanging, fantasies and acts well-documented in Krafft-Ebing.[91] Here too the suggestion is extreme, but it is the image that completes the suggestion. Schlichter shows a dead or dying woman dangling from a noose, breasts bared, negligee transparent, and clad in high-heeled boots. A well-dressed man sits in a comfortable chair, near the stool he has kicked from beneath the victim, and politely contemplates the scene, smoking a cigar—again a playful, if

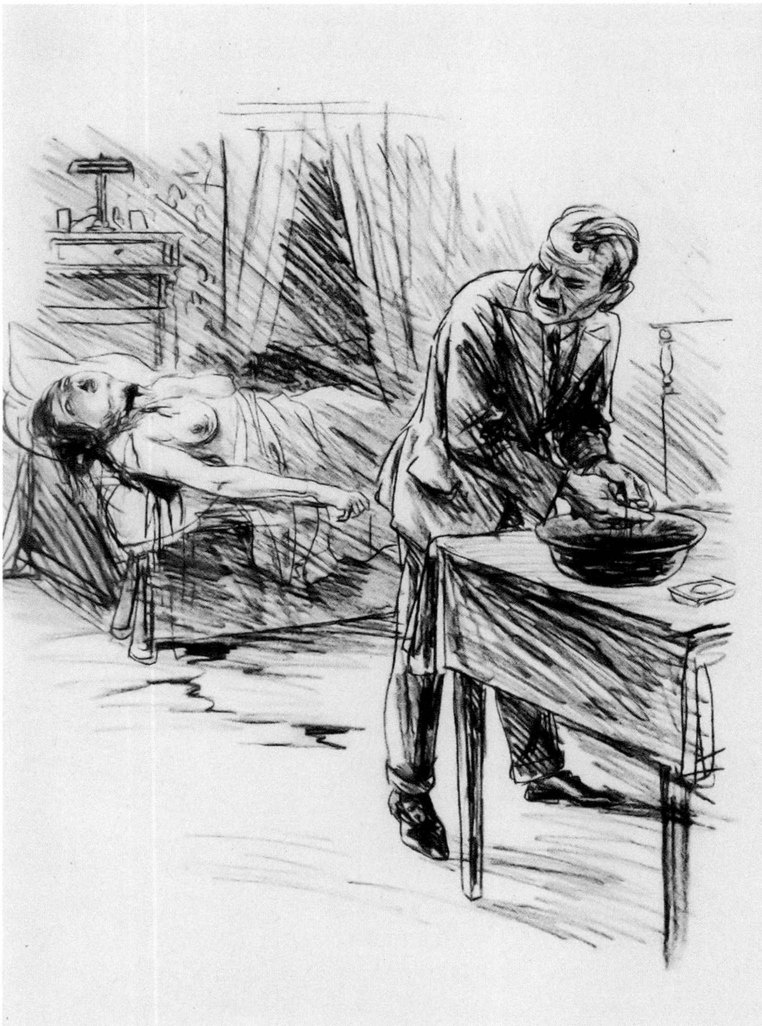

Rudolf Schlichter, illustration in Peter Paul Althaus, *Jack der Aufschlitzer* (Berlin: Elena Gottschalk, 1924). Private collection. © Viola Roehr v. Alvensleben, München.

gruesome, mixture of bourgeois correctness and deviant violence. It replicates and completes the allusive irony of the poem, which does not detail the crime but merely ends, primly, "A gentleman does not kiss and tell" (*Der richtige Kavalier genießt und schweigt*).

The edition (a mere two thousand) was confiscated in April 1925, and the state prosecutor brought the case before the

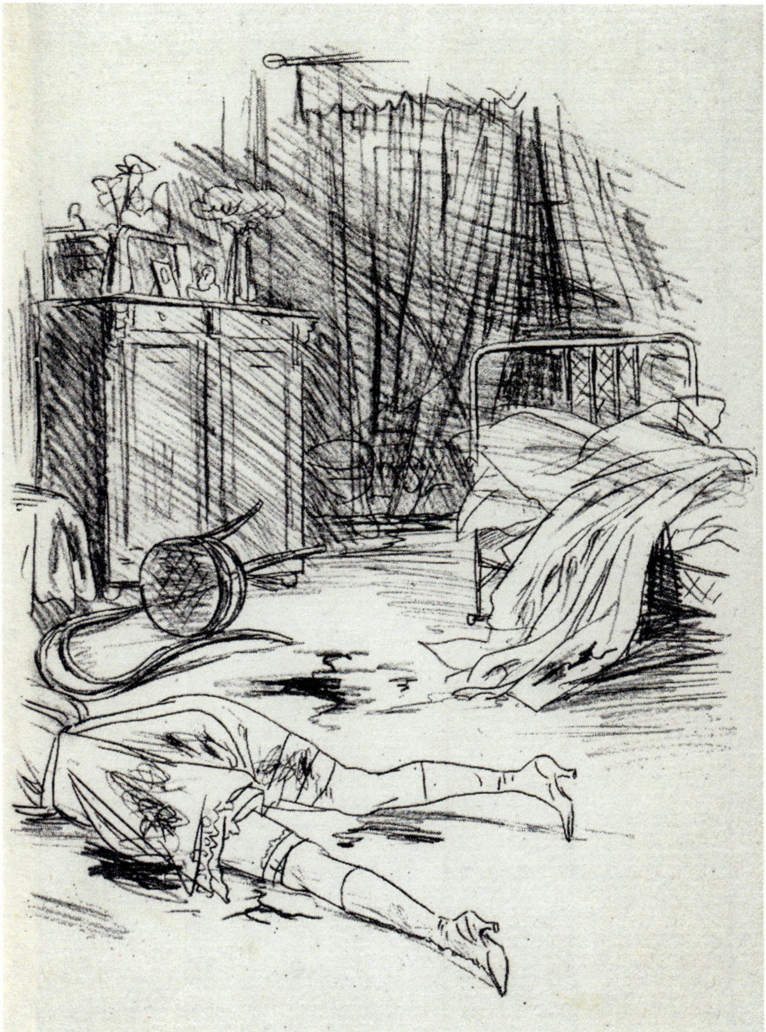

Rudolf Schlichter, illustration in Peter Paul Althaus, *Jack der Aufschlitzer* (Berlin: Elena Gottschalk, 1924). Private collection. © Viola Roehr v. Alvensleben, München.

magistrates' court in Moabit in October. The court records are lost, but surviving press reports make clear that the *texts* themselves were not found indecent. The public was excluded from the proceedings "due to the danger to public morals," and members of the press were allowed in only "after careful inspection of their credentials."[92] The court's expert witness, critic

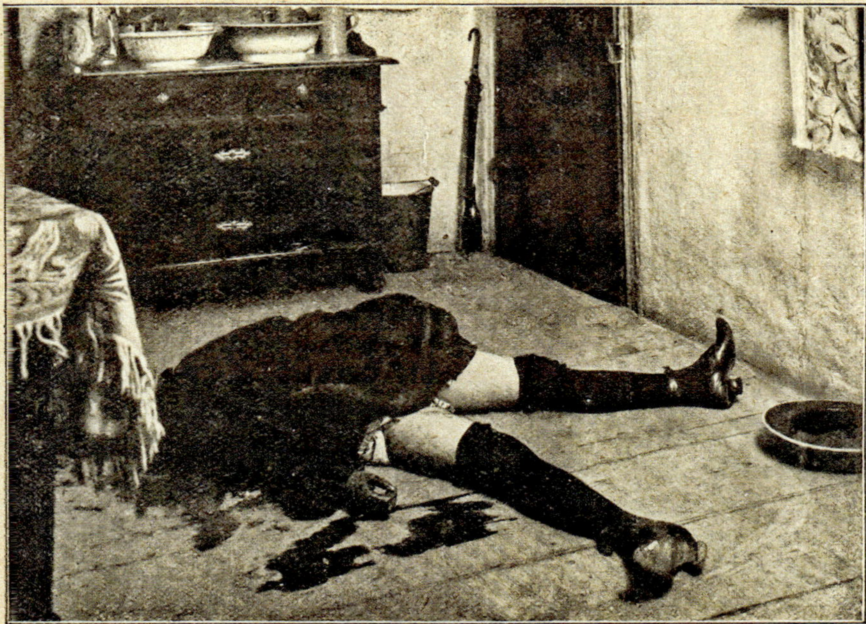

Abbildung 13. Lustmord an der Prostituierten B. L., September 1906. Täter nicht ermittelt. Erkennungsdienst München.

From Erich Wulffen, *Der Sexualverbrecher* (Berlin: Langenscheidt, 1910).

Max Osborn, argued for the artistic importance of Schlichter's drawings, while finding Althaus's poems unsuccessful. But the court would have nothing of it.[93] Only the editor of the press and Schlichter were found guilty of crimes against §184 and fined two hundred marks. Though the newspaper reports are less than clear, it seems that Althaus was never pursued.[94] And though the court ordered all the typeset plates for the book to be destroyed,[95] the *Polunbi* catalog notes only the order for their partial destruction.[96] Gerhart Pohl, the editor representing the publisher, reported in *Die neue Bücherschau* simply that "Rudolf Schlichter, the illustrator of Paul Althaus's 'Jack der Aufschlitzer' (E. Gottschalk, Berlin) was convicted of the 'production (*Anfertigung)* of indecent images' simply because his drawings were artistic variations on the theme of *Lustmord*."[97]

Whatever the details of the court's decision or any possible appeal, it is easy to see why Schlichter's drawings were found

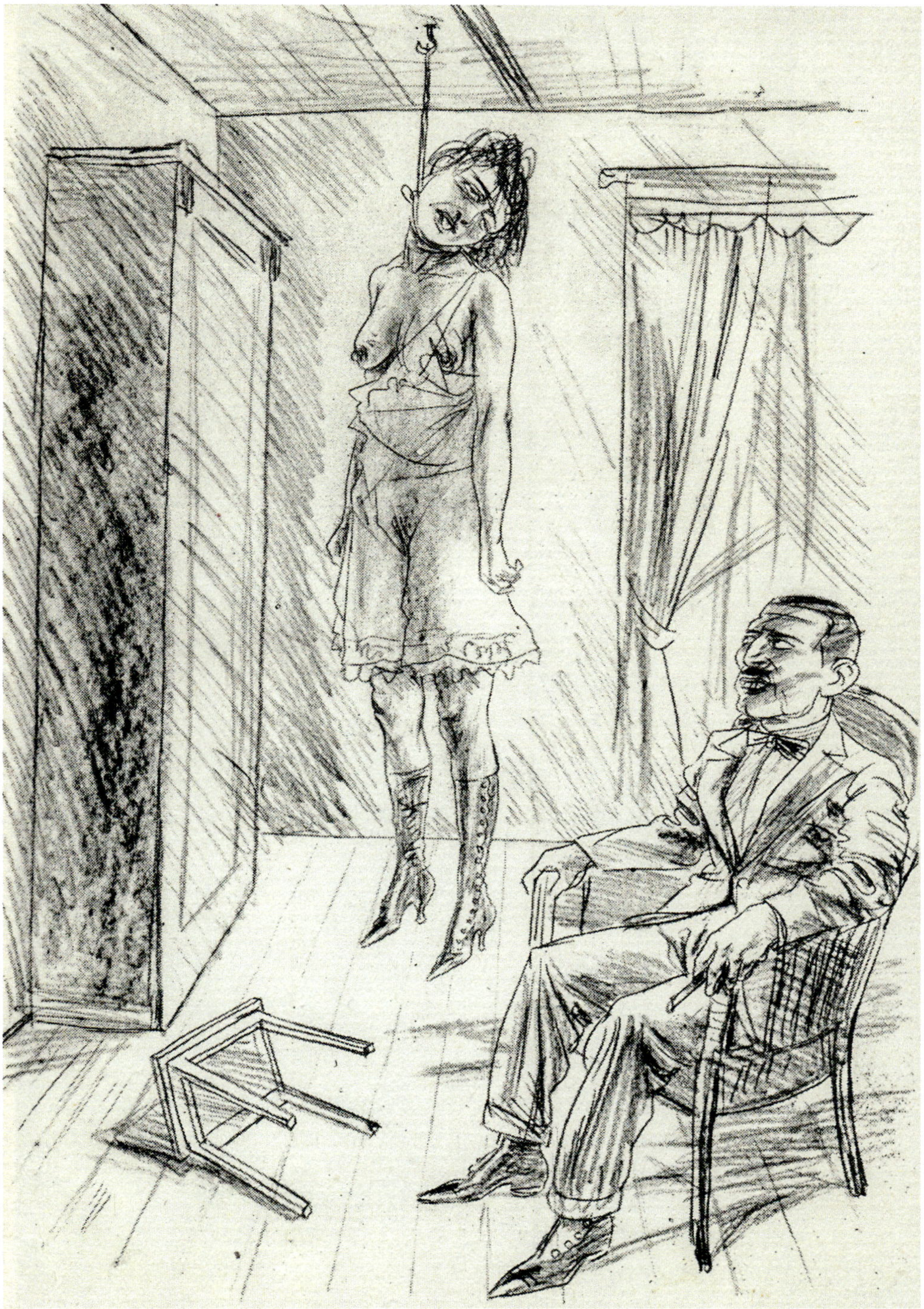

Rudolf Schlichter, illustration in Peter Paul Althaus, *Jack der Aufschlitzer* (Berlin: Elena Gottschalk, 1924). Private collection. © Viola Roehr v. Alvensleben, München.

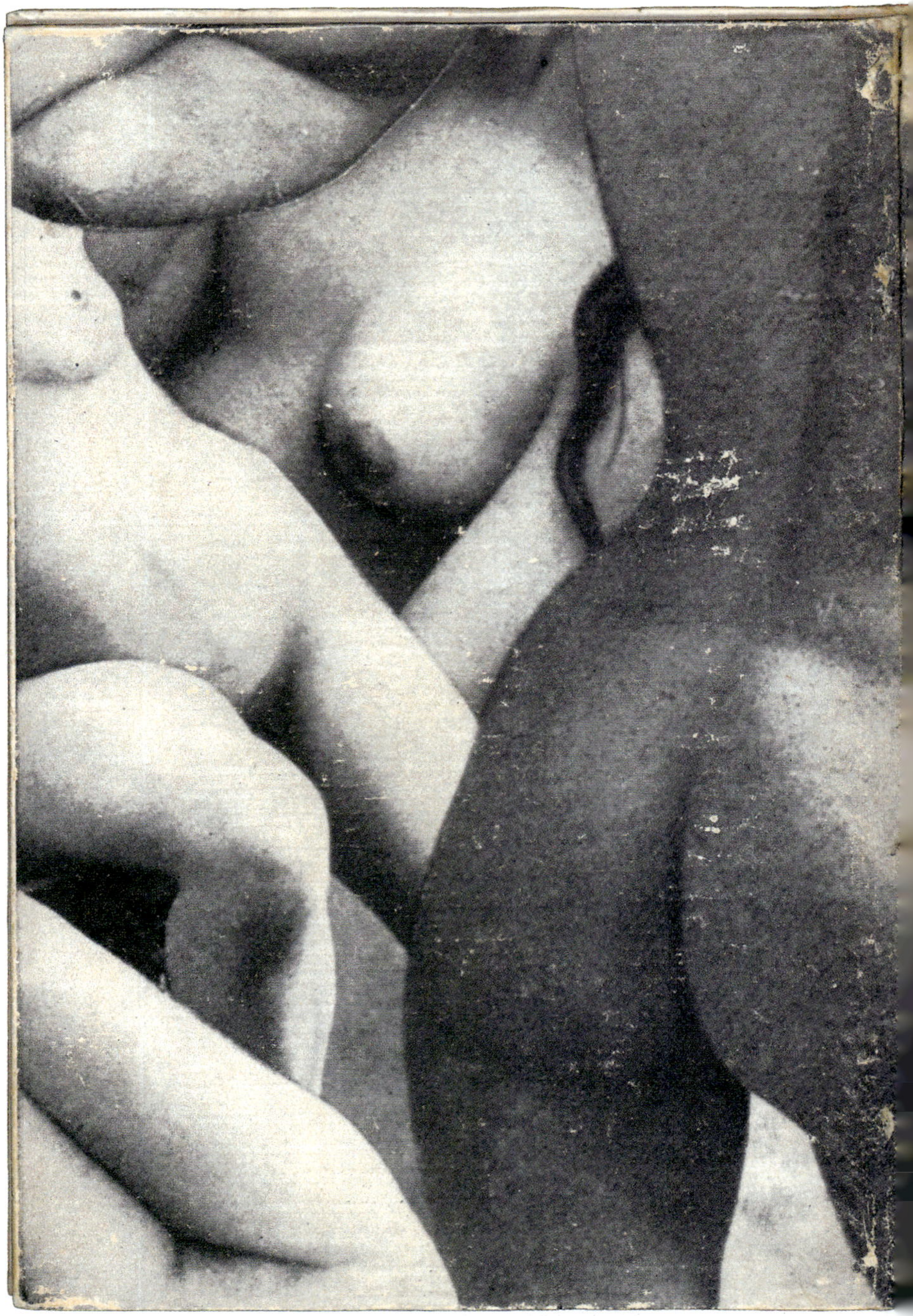

Hans Bellmer, cover for Peter Paul Althaus, *Jack der Aufschlitzer* (Berlin: Elena Gottschalk, 1924). Private collection. © ADAGP, Paris and DACS, London 2022.

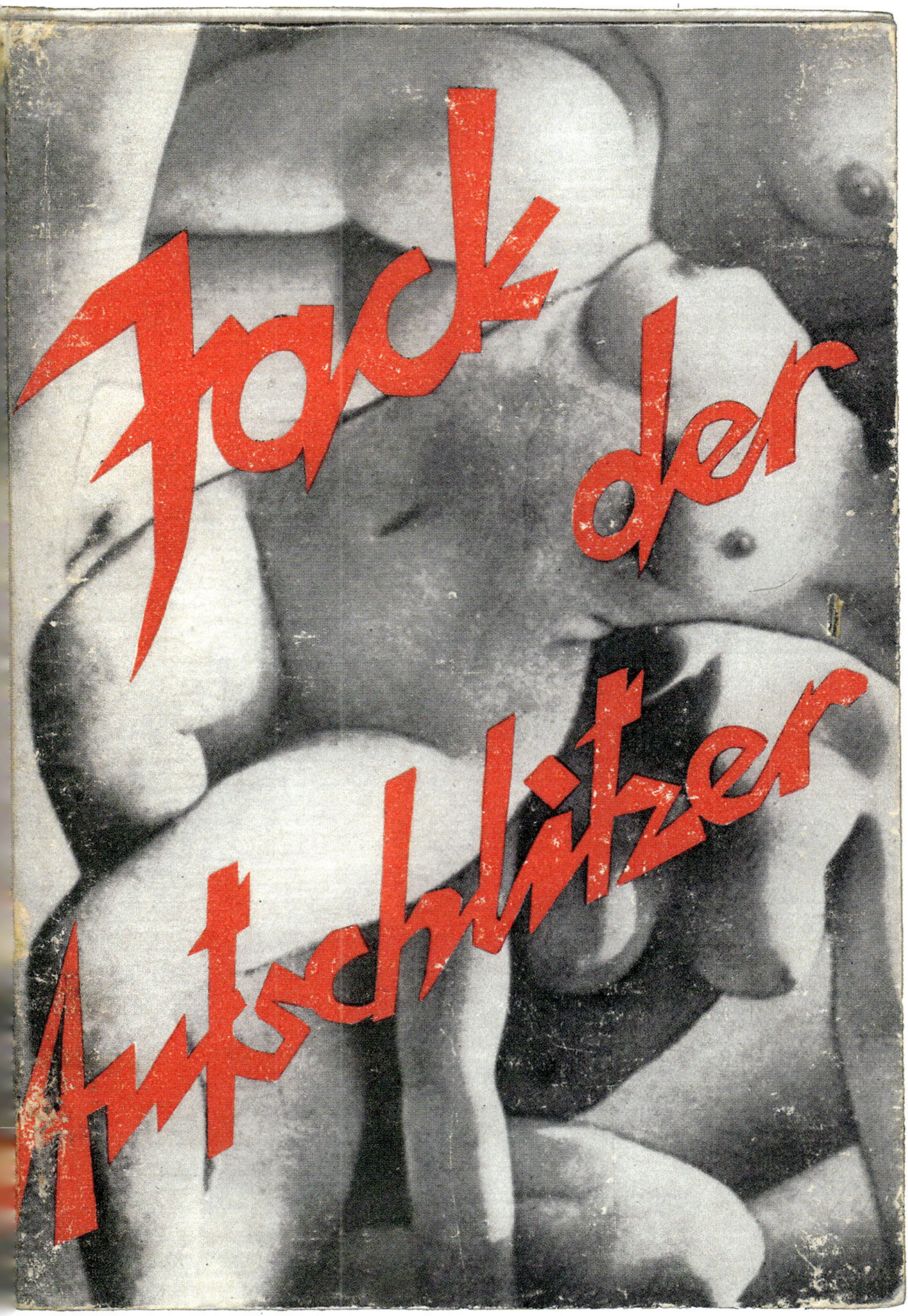
Jack der Aufschlitzer

indecent while the text slipped through the complex, multidimensional net of statutes and protected rights. The verses were mostly clear enough about the murder but less so about the specific varieties of *Lustmord*, allowing the texts to be subsumed under the *Moritat* tradition, which was popular, documented, and anyway hard to pursue. The images, however, were clear, cool, and precise. Their status as "art" was shaky: they were not autonomous works but illustrations, a subordinate form. And in their invocation of crime-scene photos, they entered an area that the court clearly felt must be separated from "art." There was no tradition of the play of meanings borrowing from the forensic genre of the crime-scene photo. Though they only completed the joke, provided the punchline after the seemingly artless and naïve voice of Jack the Ripper, the images alone were censored. The irony arose between the images and the text, not within the images themselves.

Finally, the book engages with images in another way that unsettles the relation of medium and meaning. The cover is an extraordinary photomontage of female body parts by Hans Bellmer that comments on the deeds described and depicted within. The title appears in rough text, not scrawled but, like the images of the female body, seemingly cut or hacked, both in paper and its referent flesh. The female body is partitioned into breasts, arms, and buttocks by a gaze that neatly separates and fetishizes; at the same time, it alludes to an embodied male subject who wounds, penetrates, and dismembers. Bellmer's cover bears comparison with, for example, the painterly and photographically isolated and repeated images of dancers' legs in late nineteenth-century France,[98] but the visual violence here is more obviously conflated with the brutal contents of the book. One could also compare the cover to Hannah Höch's montage treatment of female body parts, but Bellmer shows no heads or faces, reducing the women to their body parts, and none of the irony of Höch's recombinations of gender attributes and roles.[99] In the space between signifier and referent that Bellmer both collapses and opens up, there is implied an intimate equivalence of the violence toward both. And this fetishistic exercise, with the alibi of the innocent, abstracted signifier before the violation of referents, seems to have confused the prosecutor and judge. Bellmer's "astonishing murder idea"[100] was accepted as "artistic" and had already been excluded from the charges before the trial.[101] Whether they were impressed by the clever image, clothed in the metaphors of media, or they were assuaged by the lack of anatomical detail or literal violence, or they simply did not understand the joke, they left the space between the overlapping media and references as one still free for play. If Wedekind, wrote the critic W. Zadek in the *Berliner Tageblatt*, was "the pornographer of our fathers, he is an altar-boy for the sons," and the sons found their forbidden pleasures in a later set of medial conditions.[102]

But the very images that moved the court to confiscate books and destroy plates could still be seen, albeit within different generic contexts. Take the ambitious publishing enterprise whose four volumes (and nearly four thousand pages) bore the title *Bilder-Lexikon der Erotik* (Illustrated lexicon of the erotic). Issued by the Institut für Sexualforschung in Vienna, it sought to cover sexuality in all its aspects, as signaled by its subtitle: "Reference work for all areas of medical, legal, sociological, literary-historical, art-historical, and cultural-scientific sexual research (*Nachschlagewerk für alle Gebiete medizinischer, juridischer, soziologischer, literaturhistorischer, kunstgeschichtlicher und kulturwissenschaftlicher Sexualforschung*)."[103] It ranges over a huge, multifarious terrain of knowledge, leaving no aspect of its subject undiscussed or unillustrated. It is, of course, one of the recognizable genre-bending works in this area. The scholarly level is high and the aims encyclopedic, but instead of a set of handbooks for "sexual science," it uses in its main title the term "the erotic," signaling a very different kind of readership and use. The volumes were sumptuously produced, with many color plates and the spines bound in suede, delighting the touch. Scenes from the censored illustrations in *Jack der Aufschlitzer* appear, opposite illustrations from Wulffen's *Sexualverbrecher*;[104] in general, reproductions of crime-scene photographs are placed in the same context as drawings, prints, and paintings of gallant courtship or medical illustrations, as well as diagrams of sex toys, illegal forms of contraception, and tools for the termination of pregnancy, portrayals of sex and occasionally violence in fact and fiction. Reproductions of images from many censored books appear freely. The volumes themselves were never censored before 1933, though they were considered by the courts. Masochism, sadism, and fetishism are dealt with in depth, and Schlichter's images are used in these discussions, extending to a long article on sexual satisfaction in strangulation, one of his recurring motifs.[105] *Lustmord* is dealt with extensively—in accounts of historical cases, literary examples, and artistic motifs as well as material from the medico-forensic handbooks for experts. There are even separate sections on *Lustmord* and the *Lustmord*-motif in the supplement of 1931.[106] In this one sanctioned publishing project, nothing was censored, and the uses of it range from scientific to artistic and polite, or impolite, prurience. The entire complex legal space of representations, seen from the moral side, is flattened out and systematically displayed. Of course the audiences for this book would be self-selecting and not without means, but the volumes were available. Library catalogs today give eloquent testimony about the uses to which they could be put: in the British Library, they can be consulted only in a restricted area of the Rare Books room, while the Staatsbibliothek in Berlin allows them to be freely viewed and borrowed—and more than half are missing.

§

In looking at *Lustmord* in the light of complexities of the legal conditions of publicity, one more point needs to be made: not all representations are, in the eyes of the law, public. Many of the images studied by scholars were neither reproduced nor exhibited, and thus fell outside of the area covered by, for example, §184 of the criminal code, which applies only to word or image to the extent that they are sold, reproduced, distributed, or displayed publicly. Or they were not reproduced *widely* or exhibited *prominently* or for a substantial period of time. Painters, of course, could paint what they wished, and most of the oil paintings or drawings portraying *Lustmord*, and many prints, simply disappeared into private collections. They were, however, seen and discussed, and these contexts represent a sort of publicity, for subcultures are public too, even if they can remain relatively invisible to the law. Artists' memoirs mention having seen the images in the studios in which they were made.[107] Private *images* were in fact more protected than *texts*: privately published works of literature (even when circulated as typescripts) were regularly confiscated. Thus the realm of the visual arts in its traditional form was relatively protected (though not due to constitutional change). In private collections, small galleries or brief exhibitions, painting, drawing, and hand-printing ended up, to a certain extent, in a sort of safe haven of representation, in a space in which there are different degrees of publicness. It is a form of nonsimultaneity: painting and drawing (like unpublished words, for example in correspondence) served an important function by cultivating the value of the unique original, the conditions of which tended to keep them beyond the reach of the law. They were, however, seen and discussed nonetheless.

§

I have been discussing the legal *space* of public representations as the precise position, measured along the axes of protected interests, legal code, and medium or genre, that determined the limits placed on the representations that could appear. But when considering that public sphere—those signs that had passed unscathed through that legal space—I think the notion of a *plane* is ultimately more useful. The field of representations was a flat one. There were, for artists and publics, no real hierarchies, only edges or borders. The artists and their publics, the writers and experts, ranged across this field according to the possibilities of publication (to make their views known, to show their interest and delight, and to make a living) that obtained at specific and local places on this plane. Statements could be made as politics that were not allowed as art. If not as art, they could be recuperated as science. Cultural zones from the folkloric to the artistic could accommodate works, images, and sounds that might be banned from other zones. And once representations appeared, even under the controlled conditions that prevailed (and even as these conditions were changing), they were *available*. I have been describing publicness less in terms of the mechanisms of audiences and the kinds of consensus that could develop, and more as the sum total of representations available for manipulation. Laws, institutions, technologies, and overlapping audiences gave this flat field fluid borders. What lay within these borders—wherever it was, in whatever form, sanctioned for whatever purposes—was public.

The rules and other factors that governed publicity were thus not limits but instead must be seen in their positivity: they constructed and gave contours to the space of representations and left subjects to find them, to use them as they wished. While the censor's pencil can be seen to produce the parameters of the representable by showing its crude borders—a shadow here could render an image, in some contexts, permissible, while its lack would render it obscene—the rules and conditions were far more productive and presented a field of public utterance that could be traversed in innumerable ways. These conditions encouraged shifts in genre and medium, dealing with representations that were themselves intermedial and intergeneric. It was not really chaos: the intricacies mapped a positive field that could be tested, worked on from the edges, that was unpredictable but often quite negotiable. The field of the public was constantly mapped and surveyed, used and perhaps abused, traversed and entered into through a bewildering variety of different routes. When artists did so, it was not only a matter of play or provocation. Though the gestures often took such forms, forms that can be deeply offensive and arouse our ire, the matter was more serious than that. The ability to make representations was a matter of a livelihood, of what could be represented and to whom. Access to a public, however sought, was a political matter. Exploring the edges of the field of representations was an existential matter, and a task that never ended.

The *Lustmord* images and similar representations of sexual violence that appeared in the work of artists in the wake of the First World War had long circulated before, and artists (like everyone else) knew where to find them. These works did not emerge solely out of an increase in resentment toward women, nor were they due only to the economic tribulations of the time, or the brutalization brought about by the war.[108] They were not the result of the theories of, say, Otto Weininger or Sigmund Freud, nor of discussions of criminality or degeneration. Nor can they be seen to correspond in any clear way to a statistical increase in the kind of violence they depict.[109] This violence was a very real fact—and many of the representations of it attest to this disturbing and utterly gendered state of affairs. But we cannot take the presence of these works just as evidence of the violence they show; representations, of course, do not simply reflect the events represented but are phenomena with their own complex logics and histories. Works thematizing *Lustmord* also emerged as part of a long-term pattern of shifts and displacements, as movement across and around a field; they emerged as they did because of the changing shape of the public sphere as it opened up new spaces to occupy while closing off others. The public sphere generated constantly new hybrid forms and genres to serve old and new audiences, moving them around the space of representations; audiences formed and re-formed around the signs deemed permissibly public wherever they appeared. At the same time, new media—or, better, new medial constellations—consistently opened up room for maneuver. Sexual violence toward women was, and remains, a real social problem with its own histories, something to which the forensic works discussed here attest. The works by George Grosz, Otto Dix, Rudolf Schlichter, and others discussed here cannot be separated from that, but their efflorescence and their complexities also show them to be a particular mutation of the protean public sphere in which they briefly and spectacularly appeared.

§

Lustmord as Image

The legal conditions of representation defined a field of permissible publicity, but there were other logics of representation at play as well. A close look at images of violence of the time and the way they situate themselves between media and genres reveals more about how they functioned and the kind of cultural work they could be called upon to perform.

Consider a drawing from 1923/24 entitled *Liebestod in der Jägerstraße* (Crime of passion in Jägerstrasse) in the light of a text from the period:

> Through the open window to the street came the echoing sound of shots nearby. ... [Josef] left the apartment. Over the heads of the people around him he saw an apparently dead body lying on the pavement. It was right in front of a corset shop. The corpse was swimming, as the common man is wont to say, in its own blood. The rainy sky and the frivolous appearance of the lingerie store heightened the impression of gloomy depravity. ... He was about to walk on when the corpse stirred. ... Clearly it was still alive.
>
> The not quite dead corpse, that of a woman, was left untouched. And soon she stirred no more. ... Josef saw—it was a particularly distasteful detail—that the skirt of the apparently young woman who lay in the middle of the street, in an unnaturally twisted and unseemly position—that the skirt had been pushed up and both her slip and a bit of bare skin were visible. ...
>
> [Then] an incompletely dressed man ran out of one of the nearby buildings and threw himself on the corpse. ... [T]he crazed man, clothed only in shirt, trousers, and yellow brogues, seemed beside himself.[110]

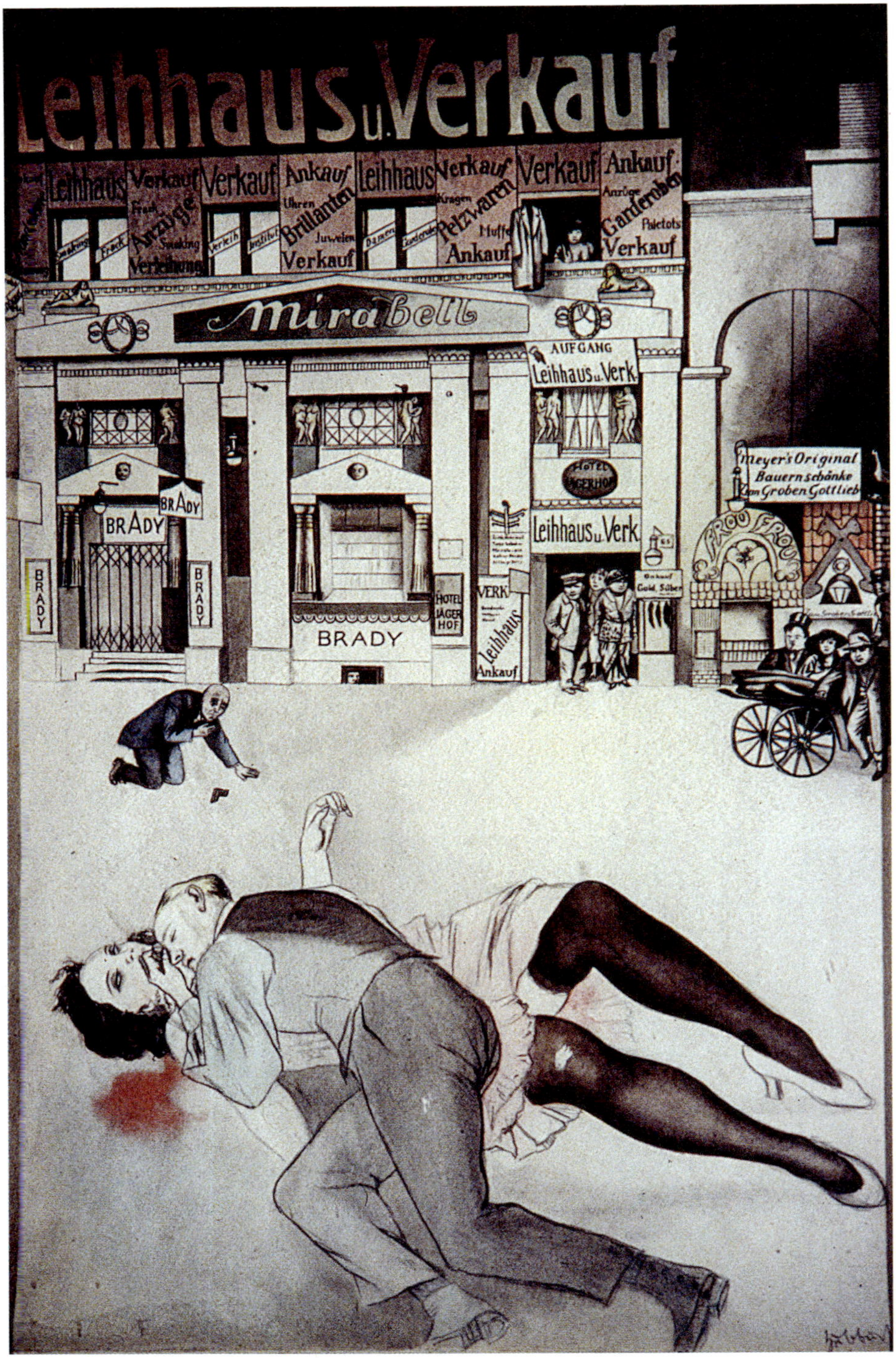

Karl Hubbuch, *Liebestod in der Jägerstraße* (Crime of passion in the Jägerstrasse), 1923/24. Pencil and watercolor on paper, 41 × 27 cm. Formerly Robert Lebeck Collection, Berlin. © Karl Hubbuch Stiftung/Städtische Galerie Karlsruhe.

In Hubbuch's drawing, we see exactly such a scene: the urban setting, the woman with hitched-up skirt in a pool of blood, the distraught man, not dressed for the street, cradling her corpse. In fact, Hubbuch's drawing with watercolor—to which he devoted great care, including preparatory sketches[111]—is not an illustration of this text, a fictional murder scene from Hermann Kesten's novel *Ein ausschweifender Mensch* (A dissolute man) of 1929. But I think the notion of illustration fits nevertheless here to some extent: at any rate, we see how a text could fill out the detail of the episode depicted visually. The image implies a narrative, but for all its detail, that narrative remains sketchy, the frozen climax of a story without the story itself. It is strangely incomplete, contingent, fragmentary, with the specificities and details not quite adding up to a narrative on its own. A text seems to complete it—even one that had nothing to do with it. Hubbuch seems to be

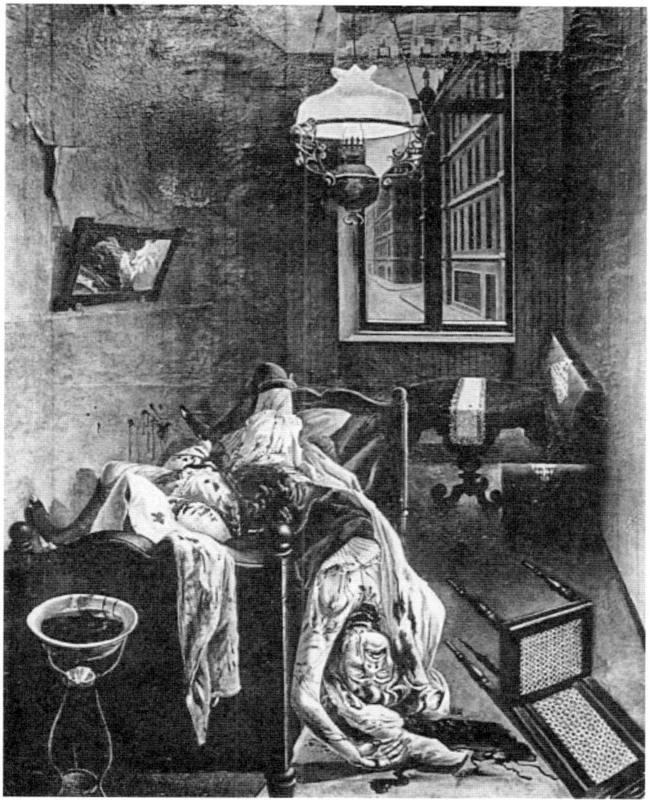

Otto Dix, *Lustmord* (Sex murder), 1922. Oil on canvas, 165 × 135 cm. Whereabouts unknown, presumed destroyed. © DACS 2022.

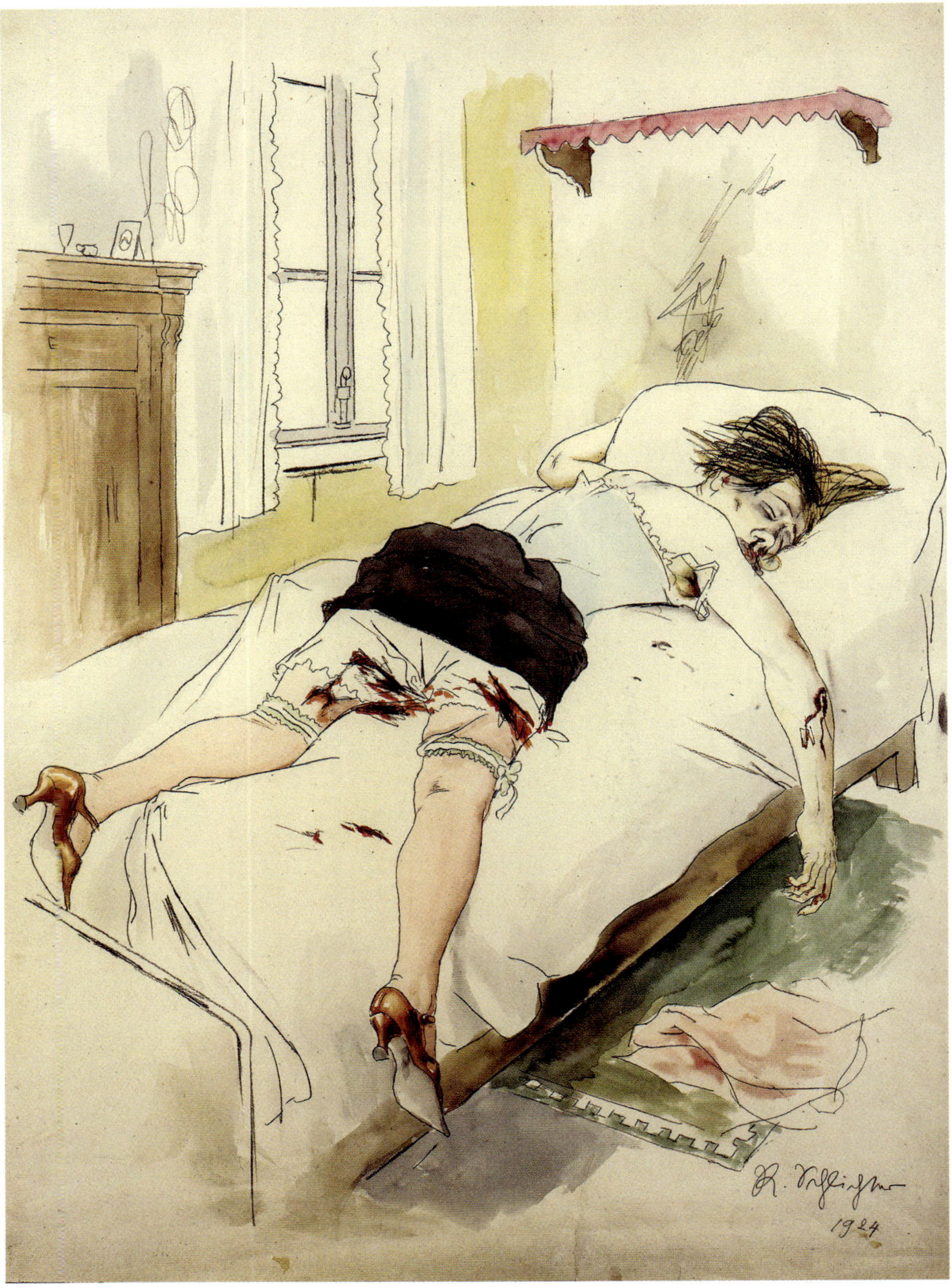

Rudolf Schlichter, *Lustmord* (Sex murder), 1924. Watercolor, 69 × 53 cm. Private collection.
© Viola Roehr v. Alvensleben, München.

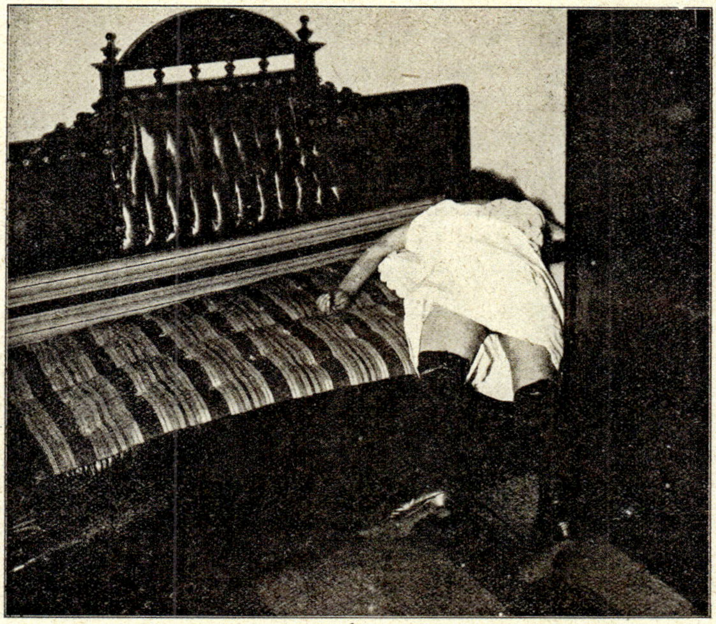

Abbildung 19. Raubmord. Tötung einer Prostituierten in Wien. Der Täter hat die Prostituierte nach dem Geschlechtsakt erstochen.

Erkennungsdienst Wien.

From Erich Wulffen, *Der Sexualverbrecher* (Berlin: Langenscheidt, 1910).

working in the mode of illustration here and elsewhere—a mode that has not been explored much as a topic in its own right[112]—but the text is missing. To borrow a concept from history painting, Hubbuch shows a "pregnant moment" in the sense of Gotthold Ephraim Lessing's analysis of painting in his *Laokoon*, yet the picture does not quite give birth to a narrative on its own.[113] The picture is an illustration without a text to illustrate, a supplement without a work to complete or enhance.

We can compare this image to other ways of depicting similar material. Dix and Schlichter, of course, worked from crime-scene photographs found in the medico-forensic literature of the time. As images, they are fragments (albeit carefully constructed and controlled) of the visual world and are characterized by temporal stasis: they are part of the material gathered in the course of *establishing* a virtual narrative that is pieced together out of heterogeneous elements and indices. In the absence of a perpetrator, Dix's

Lustmord of 1922 or Schlichter's *Lustmord* two years later resemble such documents in their temporal stasis; they depict no action in themselves, invoking not the illustration but instead the criminalistic document. Only with the addition of other figures, as in many of Schlichter's drawings for *Jack der Aufschlitzer*, do these works engage more directly with narrative.[114]

At the other end of the spectrum, we can look at history paintings. There are two classic examples.[115] Both have a narrative richness and complexity foreign to the more narrowly defined illustration, and which the Hubbuch drawing makes no attempt to invoke. Pierre Paul Prud'hon's *Justice and Divine Vengeance Pursuing Crime* (1808) has an Albertian *istoria*, a narrative, references, and a larger allegorical meaning. A man has just murdered and robbed another, whose corpse lies in the right foreground; we see the murderer fleeing the scene, casting a final glance at his victim. He is pursued by allegorical figures of justice and vengeance. It is Lessing's "pregnant moment," but in fact it goes beyond a single one. Different narrative moments are telescoped: the murder in

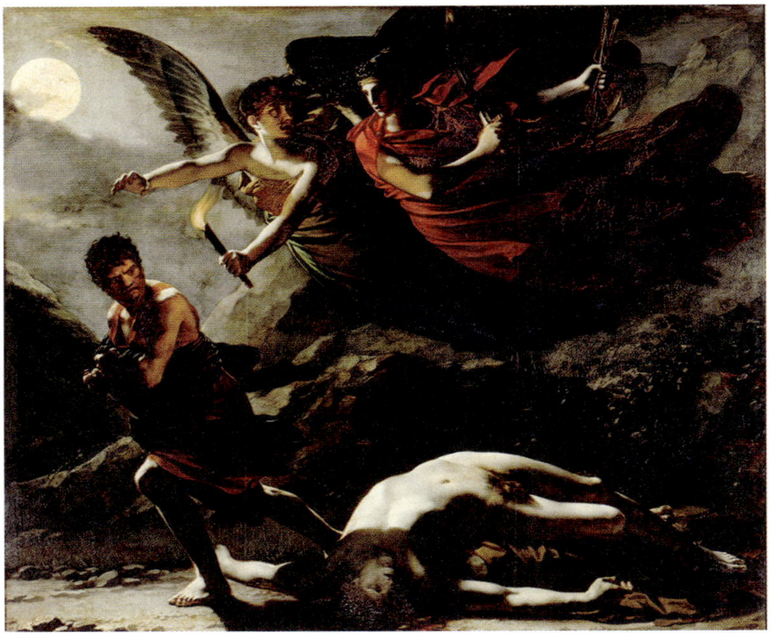

Pierre Paul Prud'hon, *Justice and Divine Vengeance Pursuing Crime*, 1808. Oil on canvas, 244 × 294 cm. Louvre, Paris. Inv.: INV7340. Photographer: Jean-Gilles Berizzi © 2022 RMN-Grand Palais/Dist. Photo Scala, Florence.

the immediate past, the present of flight combined with memory of the event, and the future, with the inevitable capture of the murderer by the forces of justice. Instead of implying a prior text or event, an outside reference to complete the image, Prud'hon constructs his own narrative within the image (though relying on a western viewer's allegorical habits of viewing and range of reference). A painting by Léon Gérôme works differently, as Wolfgang Kemp has explored in his essay on constitutive blanks.[116] Even if its title, *The Death of Marshal Ney (December 7, 1815, 9 o'clock in the Morning)*, serves as an anchoring caption, referring to a specific event, it has a narrative resonance and complexity carefully constructed by visual means. Marshal Michel Ney, who had betrayed the Bourbon king Louis XVIII for Napoleon, has been executed by loyalist soldiers. We see four narrative moments unfolding in a complex but orderly way: stray bullet holes in the wall show the rifle shots, the prone figure shows where the victim has fallen after the fatal volley, the backs of the soldiers show them moving away in formation, and the commanding officer (like Prud'hon's criminal) looks back one last time at the corpse left in dishonor.

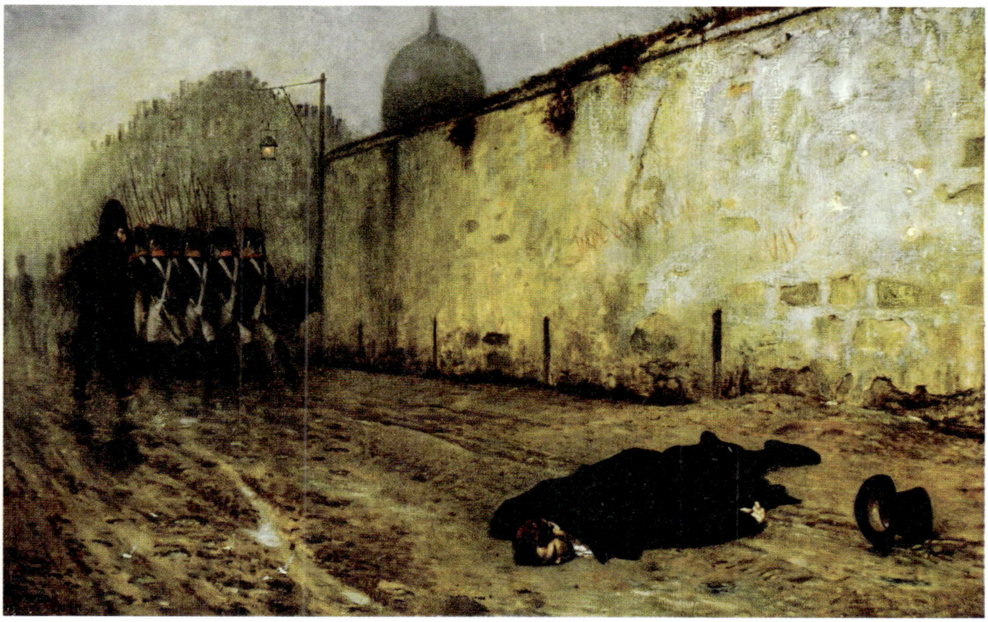

Jean-Léon Gérôme, *The Death of Marshal Ney (December 7, 1815, 9 o'clock in the Morning)*, 1867. Oil on canvas, 65 × 104 cm. City Art Gallery, Sheffield.

For Lessing and Denis Diderot, a painting generates narrative by carefully constructing an apparent moment that actually allows for the merging of several distinct moments into a plausible image, and by leaving room for the viewer's imagination to supply a logical and meaningful sequence of actions and consequences.[117] Both of these paintings do this. Prud'hon's constructs its own narrative, however, with a little help from the title, while the blanks in Gérôme's contemporary history painting leave larger gaps to fill in. Hence the longer text of the title, explaining or calling to memory a story with which the viewer is meant to be familiar and which helps make sure the moments are grasped in their proper order. There is here a greater degree of deferral to a text beyond the work itself, which becomes internal to the image.

Illustrations work rather like history paintings, especially of the latter, deferring kind, with blanks that can be filled in by non-visual means. A cover from *Reporter* titled "Ein Frauenmord in Wien" (Murder of a woman in Vienna) gives a good sense of what is happening—a woman killed in a stairway, another woman in fright, and the culprit descending the stairs at speed—and any blanks or doubts can be filled in easily when reading the accompanying article or the additional information in the vignettes. Like a history painting, we see motion and emotion, action and reaction, but with the sense and significance of the event contained in an external text. Of course all history paintings are tied to their subject matter, but the sophisticated visual means, the presumed familiarity of the references, and the artist's work in thematizing aspects of the story—heroism, redemption, doubt, rage, regret—lend these images a greater autonomy. In the light of this, the text drops out of the equation, or the image becomes an independent commentary on it. The illustration on the other hand—and particularly the workaday kind in the lower-market journal—usually requires a specific text for a full and satisfying experience of it.

As with most illustrations (of course this is an ideal type) the nature of the event in Hubbuch's *Liebestod in der Jägerstraße* is relatively clear but the work of diegesis seems deferred to an outside text. There is little room left for the imagination; indeed the grotesque, dreamlike detail of the setting and the incidental viewers—*neusachliche* caricatures rendered in a style that contrasts with the fluid but spare, workaday naturalism of the foreground figures—works against this, freezing the action and distracting the viewer from it, as does the copious text on the building in

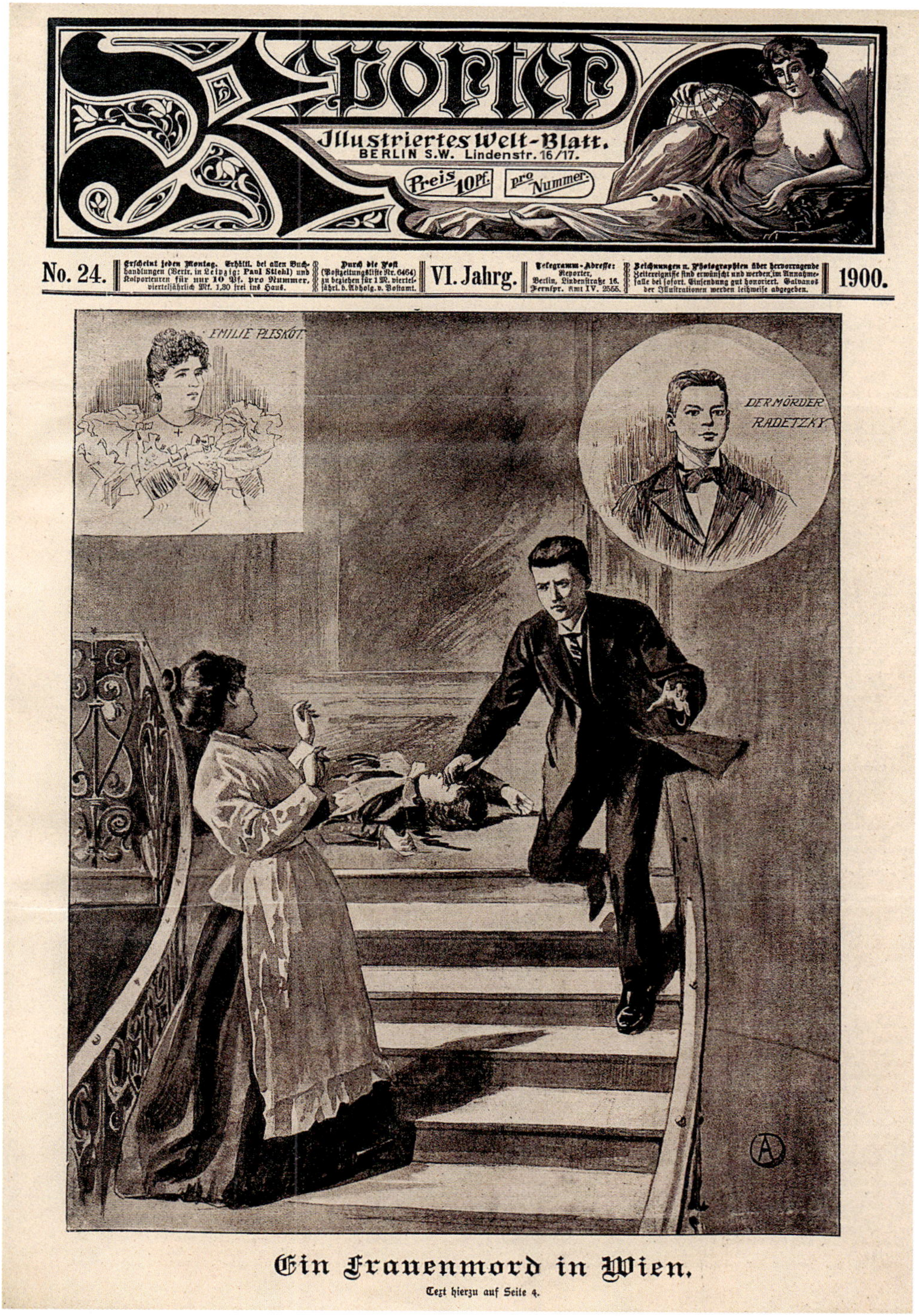

“Ein Frauenmord in Wien” (Murder of a woman in Vienna), cover of *Reporter*, vol. 6, no. 24 (1900). Photo Staatsbibliothek zu Berlin Preußischer Kulturbesitz.

the background, which demands to be read but tells the viewer very little of relevance to the event. There are plenty of blanks in the image, spatial and stylistic, but they resist imagination and cannot be filled. The image seems reliant on something else to resonate and make a meaningful narrative, but it lacks a text, or information, or reference to do this. There are signs of narrativity, but no narrative that might explain the precision of background or the distance and detached curiosity of the onlookers. Something is missing.

A look at our textual example puts this problematic of incompletion in a larger and perhaps surprising perspective. The passage in Kesten's text, one of a kind that might just have served to anchor an image like Hubbuch's, is itself similarly unanchored. We never find out who the murderer or his victim are, the cause or the effect of the action. The incident has no function in the novel except to cause the protagonist, named Josef Bar, to take a more or less unrelated action. With no larger meaning or significance, it is strangely intransitive. It represents the moment of another story intersecting with that of Josef Bar, erupting suddenly but then left untracked, its trajectory ignored. It is a free-floating fragment of narrative, which, like the illustration without a text to illustrate, flaunts its own diegetic inadequacy or irrelevance. In fact, the illustration from *Reporter* shows something similar. The text to which the reader is referred in the caption—on page four—is surprisingly brief and uncomplex. The crime was simply a failed robbery. Here too the short text is more an alibi for the image and something to be completed by it than vice versa. The relation between image and text is loosening up and becoming uncertain; such images were tending to stand alone, to float more freely from a textual anchor. It is the logic of a move from illustration to motif. But the pretense of the relation to another medium, whether one consults the text or not, is an adequate alibi, and the relation that obtains in illustration seems to be maintained.

Hubbuch was interested in the genre of the detective or criminal story and its relation to the image. His lithograph *Flucht über Dächer* (Escape across the roofs, 1924), for example, does so without irony. It captures a precise moment of a quickly moving narrative, much like the illustration to a mass-market crime story. Here the event is evoked without complexity and the image holds together without temporal gaps implied by spatial and stylistic dislocations. One could so easily imagine the words that their

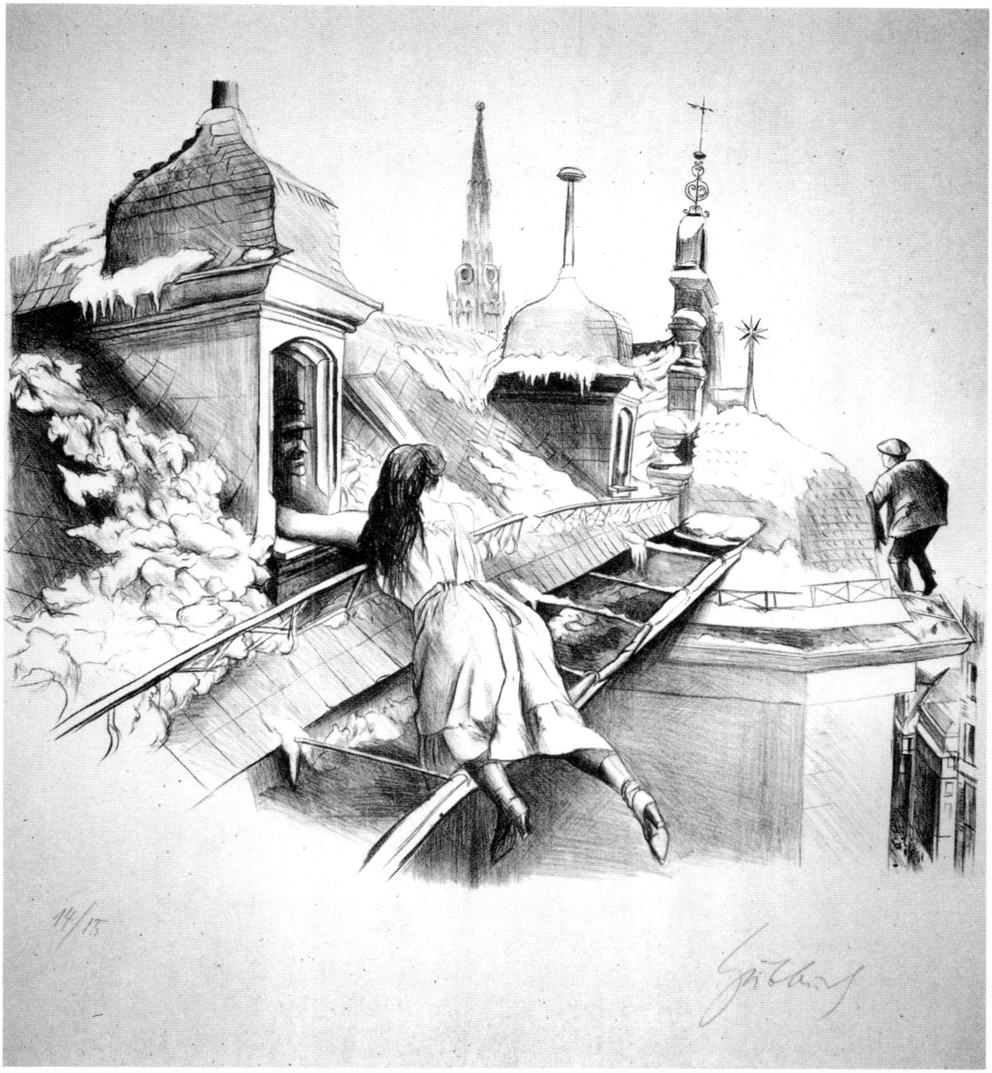

Karl Hubbuch, *Flucht über Dächer* (Escape across the roofs), 1924. Lithograph, 29 × 34 cm. Private collection. © Karl Hubbuch Stiftung/Städtische Galerie Karlsruhe.

lack seems incidental: it is an image meant to defer to a text, not one that falls apart across the gaps and joints that fragment the spatio-temporal unity of an image like *Liebestod in der Jägerstraße*.

But the simple illustration as unproblematic supplement to text, existing or implied, does not seem to have interested Hubbuch much. He seems drawn to the more problematic play of the

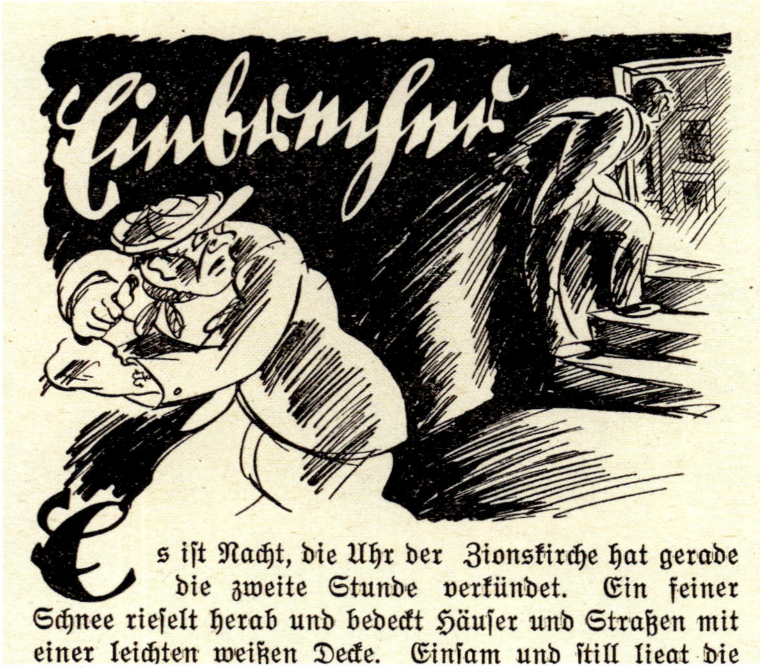

Conny (Conrad Neubauer), *Einbruch* (Break-in), illustration in Ernst Engelbrecht and Leo Heller, *Berliner Razzien* (Police raids in Berlin; Neu-Finkenkrug bei Berlin: Hermann Paetel, 1924).

image as Derridean supplement or *parergon*, the image that does not simply complete the text but undermines its very possibility of completion.[118] Consider the allusion to the detective story in *Leichter Krimi* (Crime thriller), a drawing from the same year. It is every bit as strange as *Liebestod in der Jägerstraße*. The title raises the issue of narrative, but the drawing frustrates even more any attempt to grasp one. A man reads from a cheap dime novel, seeming to play a role from the story as he reads. His hat has fallen, his shoe is threadbare. The woman beside him in this harbor scene looks confused, alarmed, or frightened. A moment has been caught with great detail—the fifty million mark note in the man's vest pocket puts the scene at the time of the Weimar Republic's hyperinflation—but with the disturbing incoherence of a random photograph of a complex event, one that necessarily lacks a painter's various means of constructing a meaningful visual narrative, the usual indications of temporal unfolding, of cause and effect. There is an obvious erotic tension—the woman's disheveled state, the phallic forms near the man's open trousers—but this complicates rather than clarifies the whole scene. Like a detective story or crime novel, it presents a sort of puzzle. With one difference: while we could imagine an account that would render the image coherent, we hardly have the sense that it would render the action significant or interesting, only *explicable*. Rather than a message, "content," or plot, it seems that any answer would complete the narrative but not render it satisfying in the way that, for example, Max Klinger's *Dramen* prints suggest a rich narrative, one that seems self-sufficient without the text they might simply seem to supplement.[119] Here the "constitutive blanks" provide a resonant space that, though impossible to fill with precision, nonetheless invites speculation and reflection. The viewer is inserted into positions that allow for the active and productive work of filling in the gaps, and where diegetic clues are lacking, a prevailing unity of atmosphere, of *Stimmung*, evokes a plenitude that helps fill in missing information. In Hubbuch's work, the blanks are often simply a void, part of a picture with missing parts: the image could be explained, but not filled with meaning. The viewer neither understands the action depicted nor why it was depicted at all. As in Kesten's murder, the viewer or reader is left without a position from which to knit together an event and a relation to it: there is no mystery, no solution, and no real need for one, though the scenes remain incomplete in a nagging way.

Techniques of visual narrative—diegetic markers such as the gazes within a scene that tell a viewer where to look next, multiple figures showing a single action in its temporal sequence, the equation of time with movement across the picture plane—are highly developed and complex in western art, though competence in their use decreased in importance over the twentieth century. Yet the artists of the Neue Sachlichkeit worked in this tradition, one which was still very much of their own time. They did not, however, simply rehearse it. Ambitious artists committed to figurative work found ways to focus on and explore the medium that did not involve abstraction. Instead of liberating purely visual elements, releasing them from reference, they took the visual elements of highly textualized and narrativized practices and used them to liberate narrative itself, now floating freely from any coherent ground that might give it meaning. If one cares about such modernist terms, it is an exploration of the mechanisms of the medium, but the medium is not simply the

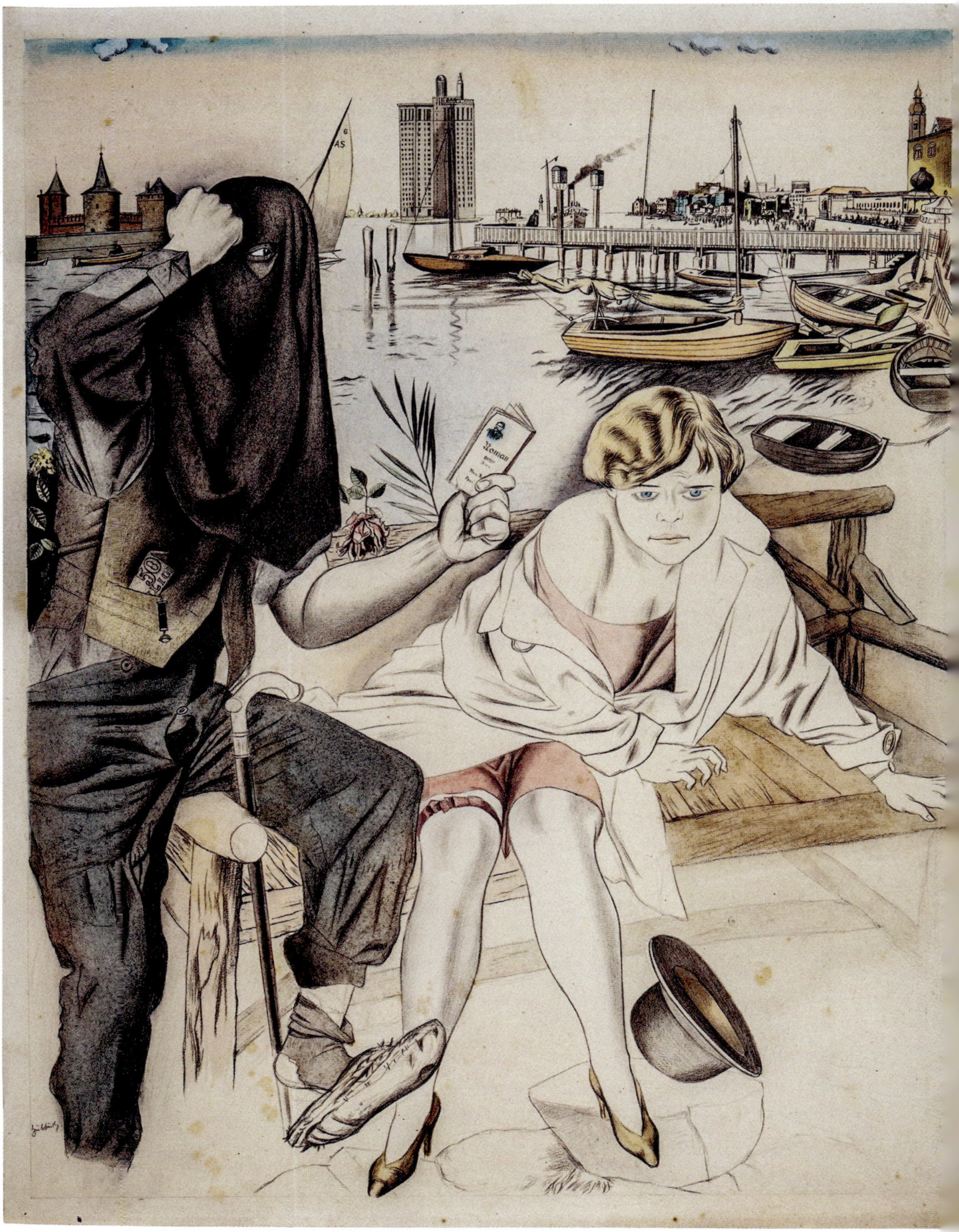

Karl Hubbuch, *Leichter Krimi* (Crime thriller), 1924/25. Pencil and watercolor on paper, 54 × 42 cm. Merrill C. Berman Collection. © Karl Hubbuch Stiftung/Städtische Galerie Karlsruhe.

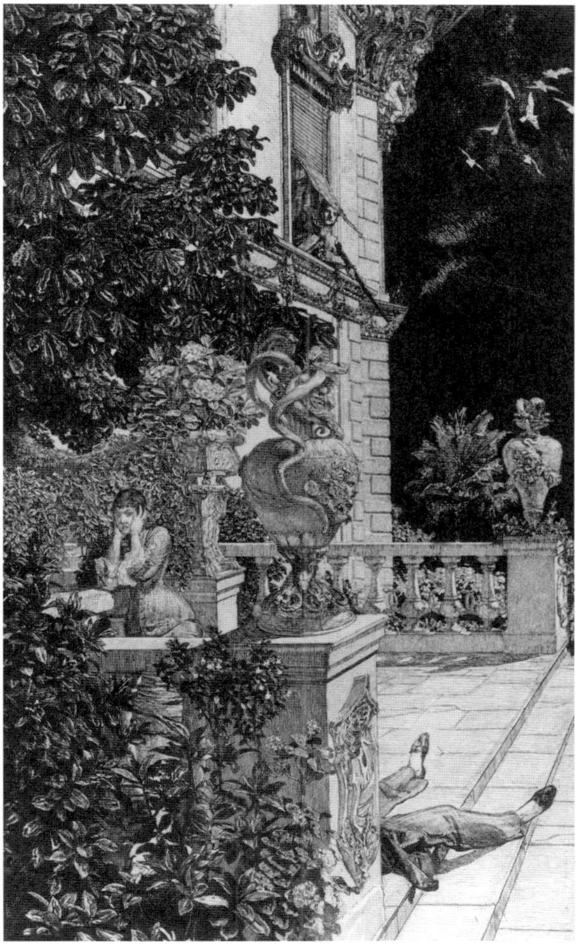

Max Klinger, *In Flagranti*, from *Dramen*, Opus IX, 1883. Etching, 46 × 32 cm. Photo © akg-images.

optical one, but rather its narrative conventions, often invoking the form of the illustration and its lower-cultural operations. It is thus an investigation not of the purity of the medium, but of its impurity, its messiness, its supplementarity, its inadequate and occasionally crude relation to other cultural products under modern medial conditions. Other media or genres are implied—fiction, true crime, song, or film—but the stress is on the strange and uncertain spaces between them, the very same intermedial and intergeneric spaces through which writers, artists, and other producers of public representations moved for reasons of many kinds.

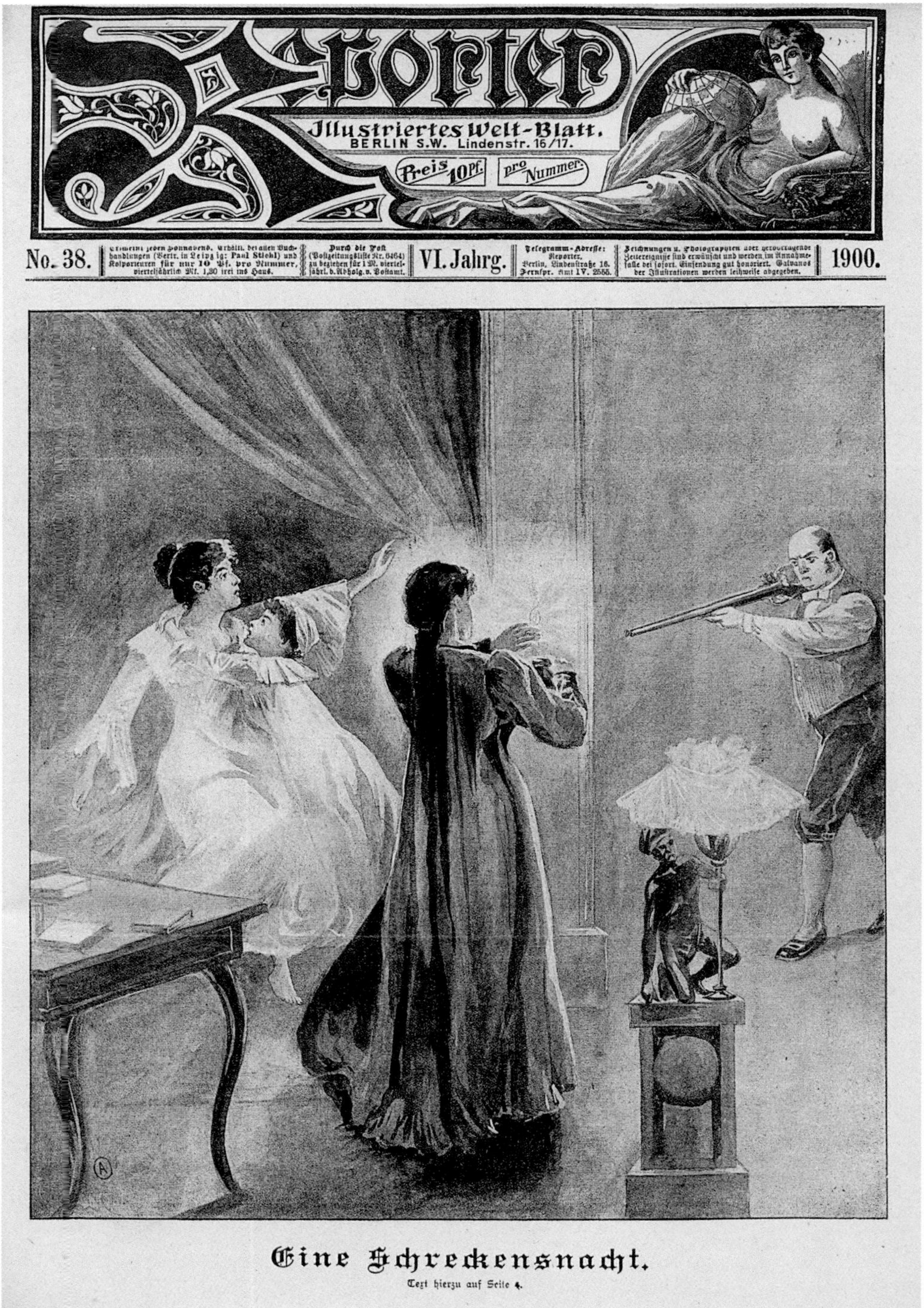

"Eine Schreckensnacht" (A night of terror), cover of *Reporter*, vol. 6, no. 38 (1900). Photo Staatsbibliothek zu Berlin Preußischer Kulturbesitz.

Hubbuch plays here with the adequacy of the illustrative image and its possible relations to an implied or existing narrative, raising the possibility of both a plenitude of meaning or of its absence. To grasp what is at issue here, we can look to Siegfried Kracauer's extraordinary writings on crime and crime fiction to see if they offer any sort of conceptual purchase on the representation of violence, and also to see if these representations themselves might shed any light on the adequacy of Kracauer's concepts. In his manuscript *Der Detektiv-Roman: Ein philosophischer Traktat* (The detective novel: a philosophical treatise) of 1925, Kracauer discusses the crime novel in terms of a Kierkegaardian typology of "spheres": highest is the sphere defined theologically as that of transcendent meaning, one inaccessible to the intellect; lowest, the sphere of thoroughly rationalized modernity devoid of meaning beyond an empty and unreflexive logic.[120] The highest sphere is occupied by God; the lowest Kracauer identifies with the police, the merely lawful. The detective, a heroic figure for Kracauer, mediates between the spheres, keeping open the possibility of meaning through his freedom and ability to survey beyond the facts of a case. But he is only a vestige of autonomy and transcendence in a world essentially devoid of larger purpose or sense.

The spheres allow one to derive a sort of typology: behind the mystery in higher spheres lies something transcendent, a truth. Behind the mystery in the lower sphere lies only a solution, an adequate explanation. In higher spheres, knowledge is transcendent; in lower spheres it exhausts itself in immanence. In the disenchanted world of modernity, the solution just explains a mere chain of events and yields an answer that is of a low order of knowledge. Each is merely an isolated, intransitive case in which instrumental knowledge's sense of causality can be confirmed. The contrast is between the revelation of truth and mere explanation, filling in the gaps without any larger stakes.

Such binary distinctions might seem simplistic, but in fact they serve as a frame on which Kracauer can plot the various literary elements of the detective story in a remarkably complex and dynamic way, and also grasp the aesthetic potentials of a disenchanted, rationalized modernity. This binary does not, however, describe the works of Neue Sachlichkeit invoked here: the novels Kracauer analyzes have, in fact, a satisfying narrative, if one severely restricted in scope; and the narratives have a sort of closure that serves to reaffirm the power of instrumental reason,

reason of a lower order. But drawing a distinction between lower-order solution (*Lösung*) and higher-order meaning (*Sinn*) is helpful in two ways. First, it gives terms by which to understand how narrative works in these images, opening up an uncomfortable distinction between solution and significance. And second, it points up the fact that in the detective novel, crimes—usually murders—are not presented as violations of a divine order, but rather as simple facts that need to be dealt with for a disenchanted society to continue to operate by its abstract logic of function without higher purpose, its self-perpetuating mode of the empty, mechanical functioning of a society for its own sake. Such crimes are disturbances in the realm of mere "legality," not matters to be addressed at the higher level of *Gott* (God), existential *Gefahr* (danger) and *Geheimnis* (secret). Kracauer points here to the challenge of thinking about crime in the context of disenchantment. More specifically, he shows that these narrative forms do not require that the violation of human law be violent or gruesome: only a disturbance of order is required. And this leads to a crucial point: whether these crimes are violent or not, they often function in narrative essentially as *tropes* of disturbance, as *figures* of disruption.

It is on this tropic aspect of the images of murder that I would like to focus. It could take two forms. Works of Otto Dix, for example, and some of Schlichter, resist the tendency toward the simple motif: they confront the viewer with scenes of such horror and crimes of such brutality that they seem to insist that they be looked at and no longer simply classified (and we have seen how these typologies permeated culture and their utter familiarity to many). But the tropic aspect reveals itself in their repetition, in the never-ending spiral of shock and blunted affect that replicates the domestication of the concept, the classification. But something else is going on in other *Lustmord* images. Just as the title *Leichter Krimi* serves to trivialize the ominous and incoherent events of Hubbuch's drawing, so too do some, indeed many, of these images work to trivialize, ambivalently, their own disturbing subject matter. We have seen how Grosz's *Lustmord in der Ackerstraße* blunts the brutality of the scene by embedding it into a tradition of the *Moritat*, and how it gains its specificity, indeed humor, in the confrontation of urban cynicism and the commercialized *Heimat* song. Schlichter's illustrations for *Jack der*

Aufschlitzer similarly work between media and genres, providing a sort of second, visual punchline to the cabaret song-like text. There were other techniques of trivialization. Consider the mannerist relegation of a *Lustmord* to the margins of Heinrich Maria Davringhausen's *Der Träumer II* (The dreamer II) of 1919, with the absurd contrast of the dead body and the contemplative murderer's dream of togetherness on an idyllic desert island, again the contrast of the grisly and kitsch. As in Grosz's *Frauenmörder* scenes, there is a typical, if now strange, mixture of the gruesome and the burlesque signaled by the disturbingly comic infantilization of the murderer. The grotesque aspect of the onlookers and the caricature of the rueful murderer in Hubbuch's *Liebestod* are similar. So too is the disjunctive mix of styles or modes in this drawing: the stereotyped figures and attention to fashion details mark the foreground group as something out of a jobbing artist's illustration; the simplified form of the murderer (identified by the pistol on the ground before him) and his circular eyes seem to be in the mode of caricature; and the background has the exaggerated detail of work of contemporary Magic Realism as one sees in the work of Georg Scholz, a fellow graduate, with Hubbuch, of the Karlsruhe Academy. This stylistic pastiche signals the fundamental irony of the treatment of crime in this drawing.

Indeed, in the literature and art of the time in Germany, one aspect of surprisingly many of these scenes is their irony, their status as cliché, commonplace—and, implicitly, that of *Lustmord* as commonplace. Mynona, alias Salomo Friedlaender, plays incongruously with the topic in a grotesque of 1925 titled "Ist Verbrechen denn Liebe?" (Is crime therefore love?), an inversion of the slogan protesting the laws against homosexuality.[121] An elegant spoof centered on a fictional *Lustmörder*, it challenges the psychiatrists' argument for a sexual root of crime by reversing the logic. Or there is the practical joke in Hanns Heinz Ewers's short story of the same year, "Der Lustmord einer Schildkröte" (Sexual murder of a turtle). Accusations of the crime prompt energetic police action, which then just as suddenly ceases: "Some clever state prosecutor must have thrown the police file opened on Eckener and his accomplices into the bin."[122] One could also point to the jokey equation of photomontage and sex crime, which was clearly not unfamiliar at the time. Consider again Hans Bellmer's cover design for Althaus's *Jack der Aufschlitzer* in relation to a

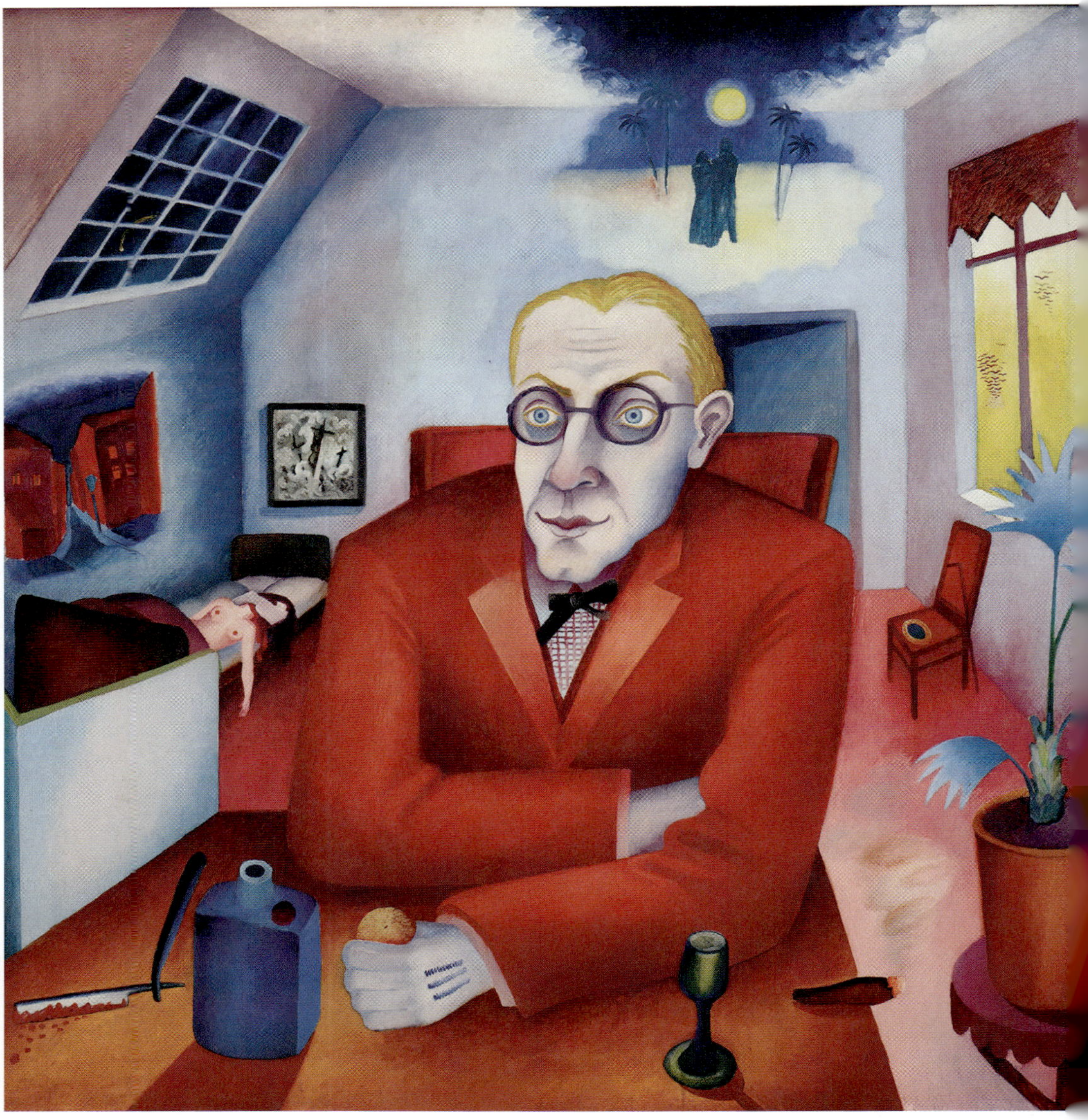

Heinrich Maria Davringhausen, *Der Träumer* (The dreamer), 1919. Oil on canvas, 120 × 120.8 cm. Hessisches Landesmuseum, Darmstadt, Inv. No. Gk 764. © Foto: Wolfgang Fuhrmannek, Hessisches Landesmuseum Darmstadt. © Renata Davringhausen c/o Dr. Eimert.

passage from Ernst Weiss's novel *Georg Letham: Arzt und Mörder* of 1931. Here the protagonist Letham finally understands the reason for a fellow convict's incarceration:

> He asks me for his suitcase, and from the bottom of it he brings out scraps of illustrated magazines. Photos of naked and half-clothed young women, in candy-cane colors, posing provocatively. He turns the pages with his pencil-thin, tobacco-stained fingers, and suddenly he begins to cut the figures out with his nail scissors, laying them out on the grubby blanket in front of him ... So this is a harmless person, someone who arrived on this convicts' ship just because of a moment of recklessness? ... Look at the depravity in his pathologically glowing blue eyes as he carefully, precisely, dismembers the paper figurines with the scissors as though they were living, suffering flesh. Off comes the left foot, extended in a toe dance, then the right foot, then the delicate, supple left forearm ... Now he hesitates: should he first cut the paper head off straight across, or slice the slender lingerie-clad midriff top to bottom? Pure evil at play is an exciting thing to see up close.[123]

Whether we like it or not, there was something banal about the topic of murder at the time. When murder becomes a trope, the specific horror is emptied out and is often filled in with humor or signs of the trivial.

Kracauer too sought to get to grips with the banality of violent crime at the time in its more literal form in a series of articles on the trial of the mass murderer Fritz Angerstein, which he covered for the *Frankfurter Zeitung* in 1925.[124] As in his work on the detective novel, his discussion focusses on an inability to fit the murderer's deed into a larger narrative, one that might give it meaning. Angerstein, a small businessman in a small town in Hesse, western Germany, had killed his wife and seven others with an axe and other improvised weapons in an orgy of violence the year before. At the trial, Kracauer was exercised by the mediocrity of the criminal, or "pseudo-criminal" (*Pseudo-Täter*), as he called him.[125] The "small, subaltern man with modest manners"[126] simply did not live up to the horror of his deeds: he had committed what Kracauer called "a crime without a criminal."[127] He was not a proper murderer, could only explain his acts in terms of small details that did not add up to a proper story, could give no sense of any origin of the terrible act. In terms from history painting, he was not a great man, a protagonist or antagonist; his act could not be part of a proper *istoria*. The narrative resisted recasting in the mode of the epic or the novel. Kracauer distinguishes this crime both from the disenchantment of the detective story and from the "great" crimes of the past that were the stuff of legends and passed down in the tradition of the *Pitaval*, a genre in which crimes are given social significance.

Kracauer reaches, somewhat half-heartedly, to psychoanalysis, as did one of the experts asked to prepare an expert opinion for the defense. While conceding that depth psychology and an investigation of the unconscious might yield certain truths and explanations, he insists they cannot "solve the riddle" of the event.[128] Indeed, as in his study of the detective novel, Kracauer finds no logic or significance in the banality of violence in a rationalized world, one which cannot frame crime in terms of sin, greatness, or the violation of the divine. In his "philosophical treatise," it was the pursuit and capture of the criminal that give a crime meaning, but the Angerstein case could not be so neatly analyzed, nor do the horrific details allow for the emptying of specific violence from the acts and their use as mere narrative device. The articles on Angerstein thus provide a reality check and a corrective to his account of crime as an arid violation of legality in a rationalized world, and give us a broader sense of another problematic within which these images function.

To name the problematic, I would point to a detail in Kracauer's account of Angerstein. The murderer's wife (and victim) was a devout Methodist.[129] On the one hand, this subordinated their life to a regimented existence that is described much as Max Weber characterized the methodical style of life that led to the instrumental rationality of capitalism in his *The Protestant Ethic and the Spirit of Capitalism*.[130] On the other, adherence to this Christian sect led to a constant fear for the state of their souls, something that also resonates with Weber's account of the contradictory emergence of a rationalized modernity out of religious faith. What Kracauer points to, in other words, is a coexistence of danger and disenchantment, something that characterizes the detective novel, in Kracauer's account, and also the subverted, lower-order narrative indeterminacies and puzzles of some of the work we have considered, not to mention the simultaneity of horrific crime and nonchalant black humor in so many of the *Lustmord* images.

Danger and disenchantment: at issue are fundamental questions about the very nature of modernity. The descriptions of a thoroughly rationalized world and the emancipation of reason developed in Kracauer's *Der Detektiv-Roman* are of a piece with the critique of instrumental rationality that finds its strongest expression in the work of the early German sociologists, Weber and Georg Simmel in particular, and their progeny in Georg Lukács and the Frankfurt School. Weber recast the trajectory of modernization from one of Enlightenment, a value-laden term, to that of a more neutral, value-free "rationalization." The instrumental reason cut loose from values that Weber finds in modern capitalism—the result of the fateful intersection of value-rationality and instrumental rationality in the Puritan sects—leads to the emancipation of the natural sciences, the rational forms of law, bureaucracy, and production, the alienated forms of what Simmel called "objective culture" and which produced, for Lukács, the larger problem of reification.[131] Weber called this *Entzauberung*, a modern form of alienation caused by the overwhelming weight of impersonal forces. Though Max Horkheimer and Theodor W. Adorno went on to explore a dialectic of enlightenment that found the seeds of irrationality and domination within instrumental reason itself,[132] the world described as dominated by means-end rationality is one that is predictable, known by objective and nonhuman terms, in which the subjective figures, as Lukács writes, as a mere source of error.[133] Thus Kracauer's recasting of crime from violation of divine order to mere disturbance of the predictable unfolding of the impersonal mechanisms of a society—a flaw or abnormality that needs to be, and always can be, corrected. The detective's ability to identify and eliminate such sources of error by means of autonomous reason is thus ultimately affirmative of this emancipation of rationality, whose transcendent or, in Kierkegaard's terms, existential content has been evacuated. The empty stares of passers-by, the irrational irruption and swift disappearance of crime, and the dismissive irony we see in certain works of art and literature are also lower-order symptoms of a disenchanted modernity.

But still, the violence, fear, brutality, and blood of the murder images we have been considering are hard to dismiss and suggest the limits and one-sidedness of notions of disenchantment, a fact recognized both on the left and on the right.[134] In his writings of the late 1920s and early 1930s, Ernst Jünger, among others, elaborated a different vision. He saw reason and calculability as belonging to a bourgeois era of the *past*, and the twentieth century as one dominated by danger. The "violation of order" that characterizes the soldier and the criminal (and, he writes, the artist) is what he sees as capturing the truth of modernity; their violence as the rule of the twentieth century, not the exception.[135] And while this answer to the question as to the nature of modernity, one based on an epistemology of the extreme, was a forerunner of the Fascist glorification of violence, it was also central to the theological politics and revolutionary epistemology of Walter Benjamin.

In other words, the dangerous moment—crime, war, catastrophe—was suspended ambivalently between exception and rule, accident and essence. And the complex relation of danger and disenchantment was one that had to be negotiated by artists too, in various ways that were open to misinterpretation and confusion. For they could look quite similar. In 1920 George Grosz, Raoul Hausmann, and Rudolf Schlichter all began producing watercolor and pencil drawings in a similar style.[136] These clearly fall on the side of disenchantment: streets are empty and lifeless, figures dehumanized, capable only of expression through automatically uttered, readymade statements, drained and indistinguishable from machines. Even the signature is mechanically stamped instead of revealing the touch of the creator, completing a critique of bourgeois subjectivity and its expression. Yet these drawings were immediately equated with the *Pittura Metafisica*, which used similar means but to opposite ends. Instead of the event reduced to meaningless mechanics, the works of Carrà and Giorgio de Chirico suggest mystery, combining objects by a logic that seems compelling but remains obscure. They are, to use the terms developed above, scenes of mystery rather than puzzles to be solved. Empty squares seem to be waiting for a momentous event, with the contrast between dark sky and bright light in the middle ground, itself traversed by deep shadows, all traditional visual markers of suspense. Grosz was moved to write about these new pictures, lest his images of emptiness be interpreted as omens: "The effort to create a clear, simple style," he wrote, "brings one involuntarily close to Carra. Nevertheless, I remain worlds apart from him. He meant to be appreciated on a metaphysical level, and his whole approach is bourgeois."[137] But his

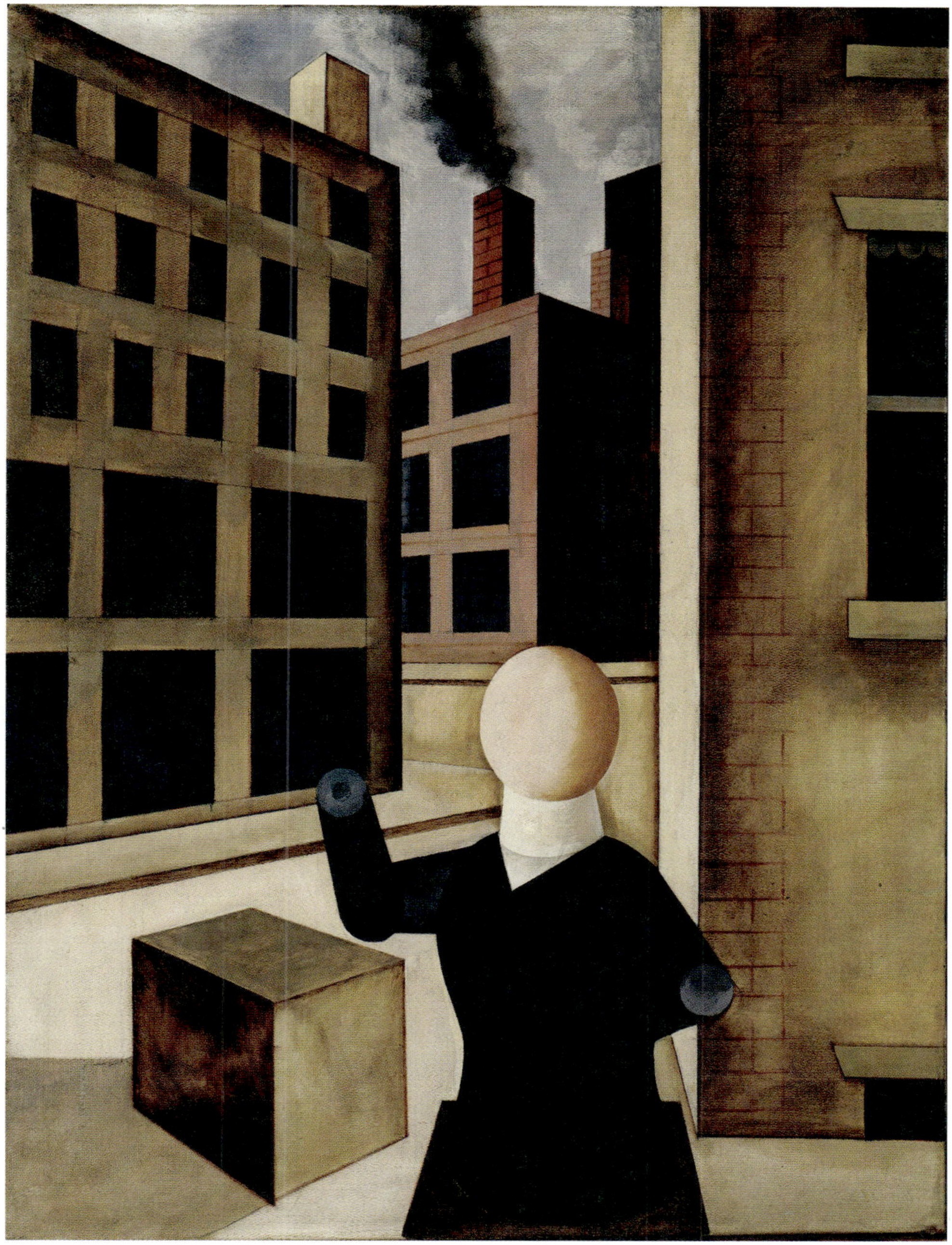

George Grosz, *Konstruktion (ohne Titel)* (Construction [Untitled]), 1920. Oil on canvas, 81 × 61 cm. Kunstsammlung Nordrhein-Westfalen, Düsseldorf. Photo © Scala, Florence/ bpk Bildagentur für Kunst, Kultur und Geschichte, Berlin 2022. © Estate of George Grosz, Princeton, NJ/DACS 2022.

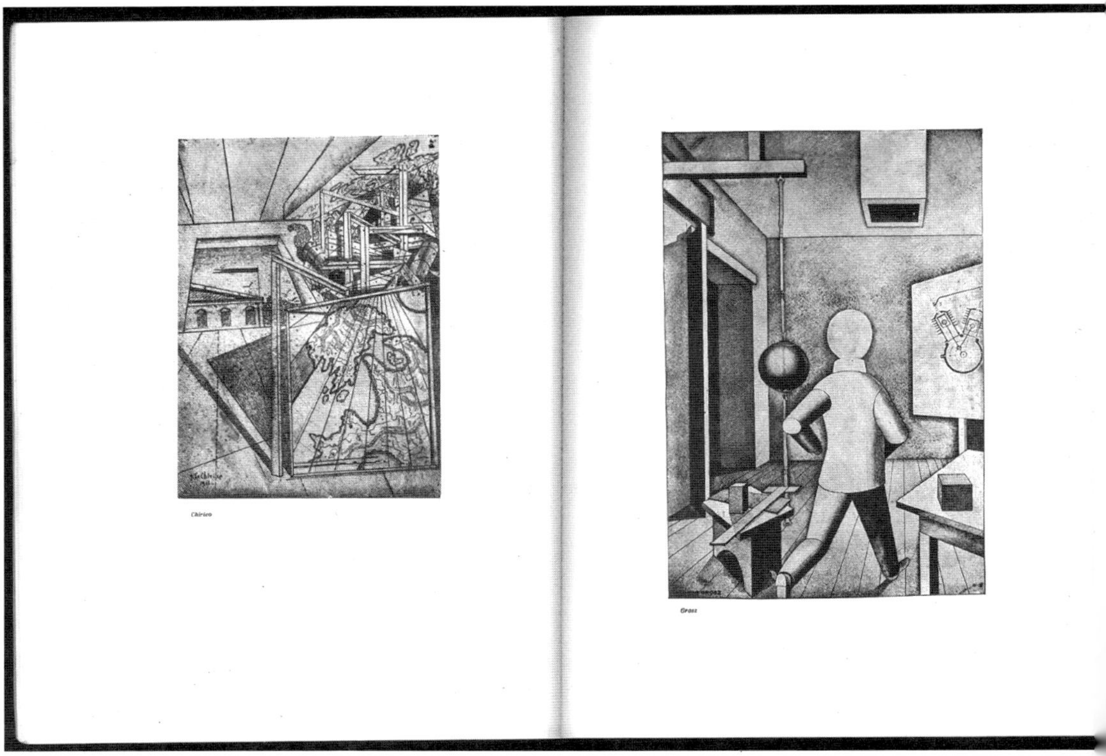

From Ludwig [Lajos] Kassàk and Ladislaus [László] Moholy-Nagy, *Buch neuer Künstler* (Vienna: Buch- und Steindruckerei Elbermühl, 1922).

efforts to avoid misunderstandings did not prevent the wordless juxtaposition of such works, for example in the *Buch neuer Künstler* of 1922, an instinct or reflex that led, I suspect, to the swift abandonment of this mode.[138]

Other works, however, sought to hold danger and disenchantment in a more programmatic tension. Fritz Lang's *M—Eine Stadt sucht einen Mörder* (M—A city searches for a murderer) of 1931 is one of the richest examples of such a tendency. As part of the moment when critical theory sought to get to grips with the challenge of thinkers like Jünger and Carl Schmitt, Anton Kaes offered a compelling interpretation of *M* as a "mobilization" film in which an entire city rallies, as if in war, in the face of a danger that threatens mass hysteria;[139] a whole society operates with military precision to isolate and neutralize a serial killer of young children. Yet the film falls just as neatly into the scheme of the detective novel as Kracauer described it, as an exploration of the workings of an autonomous rationality in the suppression of disorder. The crime is more a disturbance than a violation; the goal is not justice but "*geordnete Verhältnisse*," order and normality—a goal pursued, ironically, as ruthlessly by the criminal underworld as by the state-sanctioned forces of order. The criminal is caught not by heroic action on the field of battle but by the deployment of a net of rational and bureaucratic measures, by the inexorable intersection of the systematic, overlapping procedures of mapping the city, accumulating information, and methodically drawing on the files and records of rationalized institutions. The court's judgment is withheld from the viewer, which turns the narrative into one merely of the elimination of aberration; no higher order is asserted or affirmed. Issues of right and wrong, madness and responsibility, are raised, but a bland and indeterminate legality is the only result. The capture of the criminal does not change the inability to find larger meaning either in the crime or its punishment.

Film such as *M* and the countless examples of what Todd Herzog has called the "criminalistic fantasy" of the Weimar years[140] were able to hold in suspension two opposing interpretations, and indeed experiences, of modernity; they worked by a sort of mythic structure in the sense of Claude Lévi-Strauss and Roland Barthes. This is one aspect of the paradox of the images of *Lustmord*, images that appeared in such numbers and had the ability simultaneously to disturb and to amuse, to shock and *not* to shock. The *Lustmord* trope was thus at one level a myth, a picture of modernity in which the horrific and the banal are held in tension, in which the dangers of the modern city are both addressed and dismissed. The song about the murder of Lucie Berlin in the Ackerstraße does the same thing in its ironic commentary on the metropolis as a new and violent sort of *Heimat*.

Representations of violence such as *Lustmord* were, in other words, figures through which the perceived social and political crises of modernity were negotiated, and through which citizens sought to make sense of their experiences.[141] And social historians have shown how profound the experiences of violence were, and how representations of it were mediated though the public sphere in complex and consequential ways.[142] But that is not the subject of this chapter, nor are the larger historical processes and

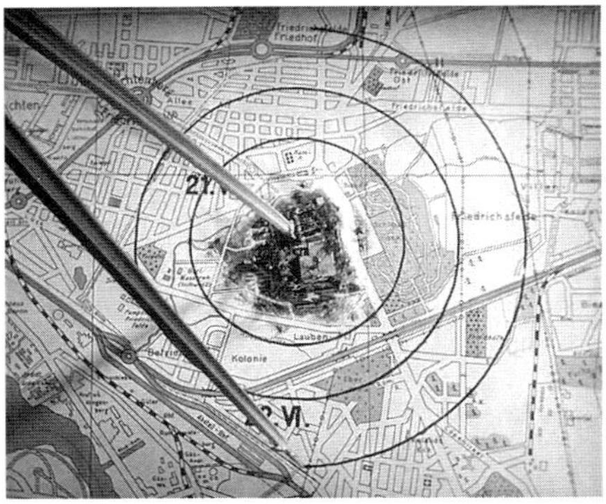

From *M: Die Stadt sucht einen Mörder*, dir. Fritz Lang, 1931.

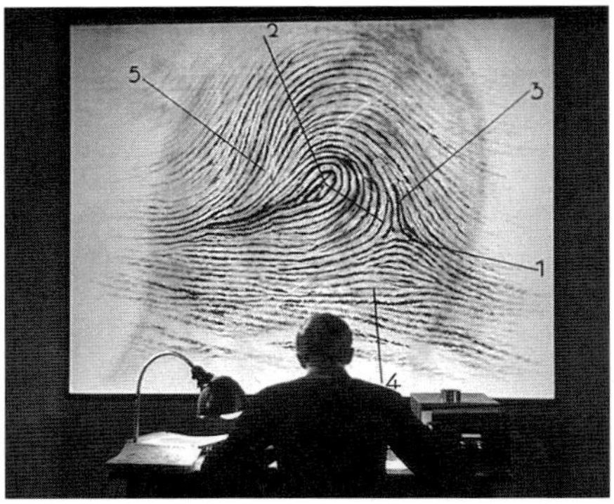

From *M: Die Stadt sucht einen Mörder*, dir. Fritz Lang, 1931.

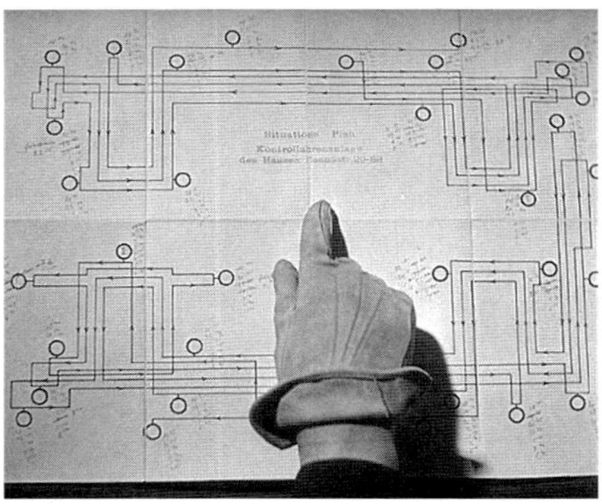

From *M: Die Stadt sucht einen Mörder*, dir. Fritz Lang, 1931.

pressures that motivated the brutal acts we find depicted. At issue is an archaeological level beneath, the possibility of representing this, and the dynamics to which the representations themselves were subject. For the experiences of violence are, I think, less at play in the *Lustmord* imagery of the artists of the early twentieth century. To treat these works simply as tropes of modernity would be to say both too much and too little. In any case, these works cannot be completely subsumed under the experiences of modernity but must, as I have argued, be considered in the specificity of their production and circulation. For the complex shifting between different sites in the field of representations is a phenomenon somewhat separate from the one described by historians who have traced the cultural work discourses on violence were asked to perform. My concerns are, in a way, much smaller than the public work through which the larger problems of modernity were managed: I am interested instead in the processes and shape of the field of representations for artists and writers.

About these processes we can say a few things, things that help us move toward an understanding of their irruption in more general culture, beyond the intricacies of medium and genre. First, the ability—or tendency—to hold competing notions in precarious balance is very much of the moment. The circulation of images and texts across a wide range of media, discourses, and contexts, "high" and "low," made these sorts of representations possible. Indeed, Barthes's *Mythologies* are predicated on these conditions of mass culture, on the way images could be introduced into the flat field of mass media visibility, emptied of specifics, and then filled with new meanings or with "myths," his term for the functioning of ideology under modern medial conditions.[143] The new conditions of visibility and textuality encouraged this process and increased its velocity. The same circumstances enabled the contradictory mix of modes in *Liebestod in der Jägerstraße* and the simultaneous sexuality and triviality, menace and low-order mystery of *Leichter Krimi*. They are the precondition for the promiscuous use of images of violence across such a range of registers, intersecting with discourses from the forensic and the psychiatric to the pacifistic, from comedy to *Kulturkritik*. The wide span of contexts—the disturbing and chaotic variety of ways in which physical violence was represented visually—has certainly as much to do with this saturation of media and the shifts it encouraged as it does with other unavoidable historical facts, such as the World War and political violence of the era. It was a situation that was met with irony, a mix of modes, and a tendency to trope.

It is, in other words, a matter of the relation of crime to the spectacular conditions of early twentieth-century culture, the conditions of visuality and textuality. This tropic mobility of meanings, the mixing and matching of text and image, was, of course, the bread and butter of wartime propaganda and, in reverse, of Dada, but it characterized the field of culture as a whole, from advertising to painting, literature, theatre, and music, from painting to illustrations to caricature. For these conditions of representation—timeless in their possibility, but historically specific in their appearance—were also the conditions of any public representation, of the *Öffentlichkeit*, of the period. These conditions came into focus, and indeed became figured, in the spectacularization and simultaneous trivialization of murder and violence between roughly 1890 and 1933. Whatever else they might have meant specifically, whatever forces might have determined their particular medial or generic appearance, it seems that under these circumstances images of murder came to represent the limits to which the contours of the public sphere could be stretched. In a world where the media of public representation and debate tended toward the saturated and the opaque, sexual murder became a trope for the pathological limit of the representable.

Two final examples, both literary, suggest what is at issue here. One is from a popular potboiler: Hugo Bettauer's novel *Der Frauenmörder* (The lady-killer) of 1922.[144] The set-up is rather standard. Five unattached young women have disappeared under similar and highly suspicious circumstances, after being courted by a man of the same description; this sends Berlin into a panic. A detective tracks down the man, but the *corpus delicti*, bodies or reliable and verifiable missing person reports, are lacking. The twist in this story is that the murders are a ruse by an unrecognized author to draw the breathless attention of the public to his work. The hoax is successful, but in line with a Kracauerian assertion of reason, it is discovered by the detective before being revealed by the culprits. Literature, law, and publicity intersect over the site of *Frauenmord*, the killing of women; but that site is, tellingly, empty. It is an ironic equation of murder with the public sphere, the space of publicity itself.

The second has more literary merit and is certainly more familiar, but it juggles the same elements: Robert Musil's *The Man without Qualities*.[145] It is a book often invoked in discussions of *Lustmord*, but without consideration of the way *Lustmord* functions in the novel in relation to publicity. Two topics dominate the space of public discussion in Vienna before the First World

War as Musil describes it. One is Graf Leinsdorf's so-called *Parallelaktion*, meant to celebrate the seventieth jubilee of Franz Joseph's monarchy. A project designed only to occupy the public sphere, it turns into an empty vessel, impossible to fill, without real content or qualities. The other, of course, is the figure of a rapist and murderer, one based on a real case.[146] The mad murderer Moosbrugger turns out to fascinate the public, occupying the space of public representation as a case—a crime, a psychiatric riddle, a scandal, an event. The space of public discussion is stretched between the murder trial, all-encompassing but comet-like, and a protracted, long-term, and ultimately empty attempt to celebrate the nation. Through the novel, the *Parallelaktion* comes to be intertwined with, compared to, and distracted by Moosbrugger's heinous crime and courtroom antics, unable to shake them off. Politics and murder define the poles of a pathologized public sphere, one side reasoned and planned but empty, the other side trivial, spontaneous, gruesome, and total—and figured as *Lustmord*.

§

Lustmord and the Case

The spectacularization of murder, and specifically sexual murder, had its own logic and, paradoxically and uncomfortably, its uses. While these images have much to do with endemic violence in a society where gender relations were both asymmetrical and under severe stress, they cannot be reduced to those relations and their own histories, however much those histories intersect with the history of representation. Images of *Lustmord* and violence also served to define an important contour of the space of publicity in Germany at the time, and specifically its limits. The appearance of this motif, often shocking in its brutality, was a matter of the shape of a changing, contradictory, and problematic public sphere, and the baffling frequency of its use can be seen as a result of the fact that the motif was called upon, in turn, to figure that very space of representations.

Taking *Lustmord* as a case study shows us that the limits of the public sphere—whether in the oppressive form of censorship and legal prosecution, or the protocols of specific genres and discourses—must not be seen as a negative force, as boundaries of an otherwise free zone that should, in its ideal type, be free.

Instead the limits should be seen in their positivity, in their active production of a real but constantly changing space of public representation. This production can be seen in the zones of confusion. The rules—always contested and changing—tried to define possibilities and interdictions first on the criteria of media. But media (photography, printed texts, street and cabaret songs, the visual arts) had their many genres; texts could sit in different discourses (or straddle them); images, concepts, or even tunes could circulate between them. To complicate matters further, we have not only the objects (text, film, image, radio broadcast) or discourses (scientific literature, legal codes, titillating stories, ambitious fiction, journalism) but also different institutions or dispositives whose practices were determined and developed in multifarious ways. Science and law required the ability to represent certain things (attitudes, practices, instincts, etc.) in order to classify and discipline them, while these same representations were to be held under tight control in other dispositives (publishing with its calculated balance of idealism and commerce, its organization of production and distribution). Producing representations often depended on shifting from one area of culture to another. The very same subject matter could be represented in some, but not others: that some hypothetical "content" could be uttered or pictured might depend on shifting from one zone to a different one. In the end, however, most matters of concern or interest could be represented in one form or another. The possibility of representation, in other words, often developed and moved *between* these media and genres. The movement of images of *Lustmord* around the complex field of publicity reveals this with a certain grim clarity.

The example of *Lustmord* also tells us much about the nature of the case itself. These representations came out of documented cases, and they became cases themselves. The motif emerged between media and styles and was not endemic to any one of them. And this is the very nature of the case, which as a cultural form emerged between media, styles, ideologies, and institutions. As a cultural form, the case was in itself invisible, inaudible, and illegible, but it might have recourse to any of the existing forms of visual production, text, or performance. It was a form in which cultural subjects sought to call attention to specific problems but found the existing institutions of representation and discussion inadequate, requiring interventions to draw attention and prompt debate, interventions we can call spectacular. It did so as a response to the very problems of the spectacularization of culture, the conditions of representations, the problems of the public sphere. The practitioners of the case found solutions to these problems in the contradictions of the social space of representations itself. It was the work of *Lustmord*, as a sort of rogue or deviant topos, to figure this complex state of affairs.

4 *Politics and "Perversion": The Cases of Rudolf Schlichter*

In the 1920s, George Grosz represented his friend Rudolf Schlichter repeatedly as a deviant, a pervert, and a prisoner. A lithograph of around 1920 shows Schlichter as a shoe fetishist. Unshaven and introspective, Schlichter stands in his studio surrounded by a set of attributes. Below the paintbrush in his left hand, his ankle is secured by a ball and chain, signaling the entrapment in his pathological sexuality. Schlichter is wearing women's high-heeled button boots (as was, we shall see, his wont); grasped in his right hand is another women's boot, its twin on the floor. Beside the boots, a book with the title *Sadismus und Masochismus* by "Dr. Dühren" gives further perspective to Schlichter's aberrant erotics. Now, no such book existed, but "Eugen Dühren" was in fact the pseudonym of the prominent medical doctor and sexologist Dr. Iwan Bloch, used for publications that were less scientific and more popular, a way of exploiting a broad market for information about sex without mortgaging his professional capital.[1] Yet there were two popular books with this title containing extensive case studies and analyses of the topic, one by the French doctor Émile Laurent, the other by the German sex expert Albert Eulenburg.[2] Indeed, confusing one sexologist with another merely indicates a broader degree of familiarity with this growing literature, whether Grosz's or Schlichter's is not important. And below the wrinkled shirt, Grosz shows Schlichter with his trousers open, exposing his penis. Beyond showing the object of Schlichter's desire and the nature of his sexual self, Grosz thus also alludes to the fundamentally solitary form of sex to which the fetishist is condemned.[3] Grosz published the lithograph as number 42 of his 1923 portfolio *Ecce Homo*, for which the artist was brought to trial for indecency. This image was one of thirty-four images found obscene (*grob unzüchtig*) by the court and removed from circulation; Grosz was found guilty of the criminal offence and fined five hundred marks, while his publishers Wieland Herzfelde and Julian Gumperz were fined one thousand marks each.[4]

Around 1929, Grosz drew his friend again. This time Schlichter appears in a jail cell, standing at his easel. He is painting from the model, but it is not the traditional nude. Instead Schlichter stands before a larger-than-life female leg, clad in the button shoes of his predilection, which he reproduces faithfully on the vertical canvas. Behind him and beneath the barred window, Grosz shows three pairs of women's shoes. This was a symptom of the pathology of the obsessional sexual surrogate, which Wilhelm Stekel described in 1923 as follows: "This collecting of the symbolic objects is what I have called the harem cult of the fetishist. It is never absent in any case of genuine fetishism ... Instead of collecting women ... [the fetishist] collects fetishes."[5]

At the same time, Grosz finished a large painting of Schlichter as prisoner and deviant, though a preparatory drawing shows considerably more detail. Schlichter is again in a jail cell, but the implication here is that it is for his Communist activities. Once more, we see an easel painting and its model showing Schlichter's attributes: here, though, it is the hammer, sickle, and clenched fist of the German Communist Party. For good measure, the model hammer is labelled "Marx," but the painting within the drawing is signed by "Rudolf Karger," an allusion to a medical publisher; and a thermometer mounted on the canvas reveals Schlichter's cooling ardor toward the party, reading "four degrees below zero." For Schlichter, again wearing women's high-heeled button boots, is distracted and turns his back on his political commitments. He prays on his knees before the torso and legs of a woman, nude but for her boots, hovering above him; whether she is a picture or a phantasm is not clear. But the airborne women were a fact. "In order to satisfy his passions," Grosz recounted to his son Marty, Schlichter had "installed in his studio a sort of harness. He coaxed prostitutes into allowing themselves to be strapped into it. The

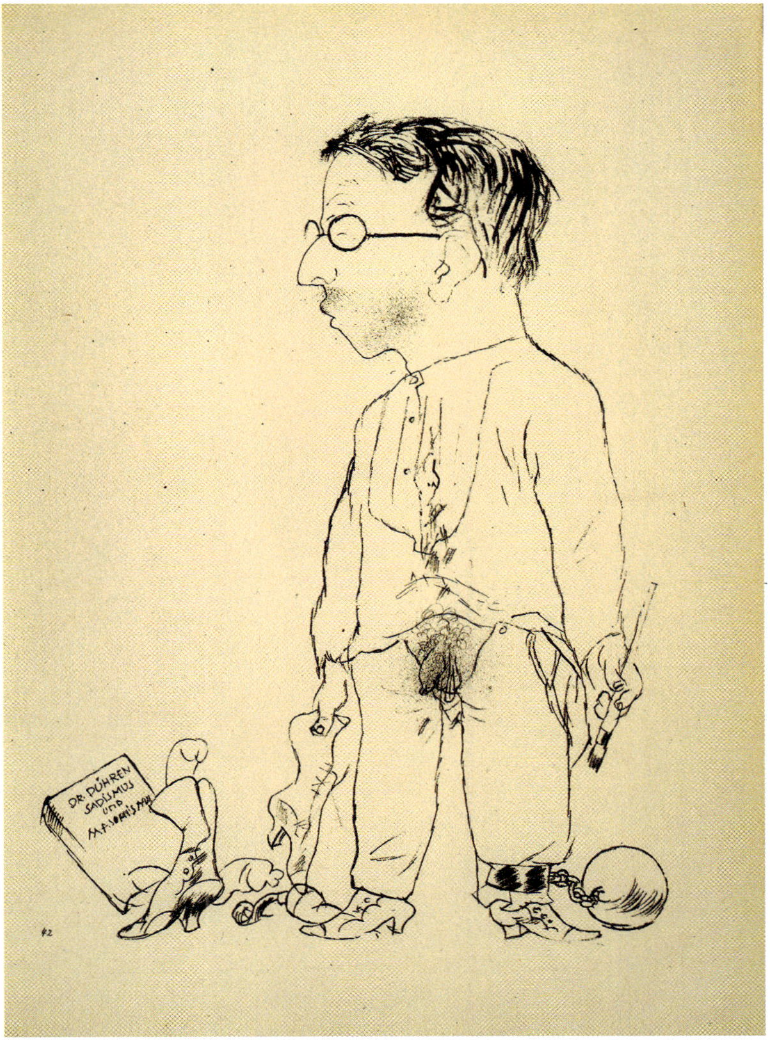

George Grosz, *Rudi S.*, 1921. From *Ecce Homo* (Berlin: Malik-Verlag, 1923), no. 42. Photo © bpk/Kunstbibliothek, SMB/Atelier Petersen. © Estate of George Grosz, Princeton, NJ/DACS 2022.

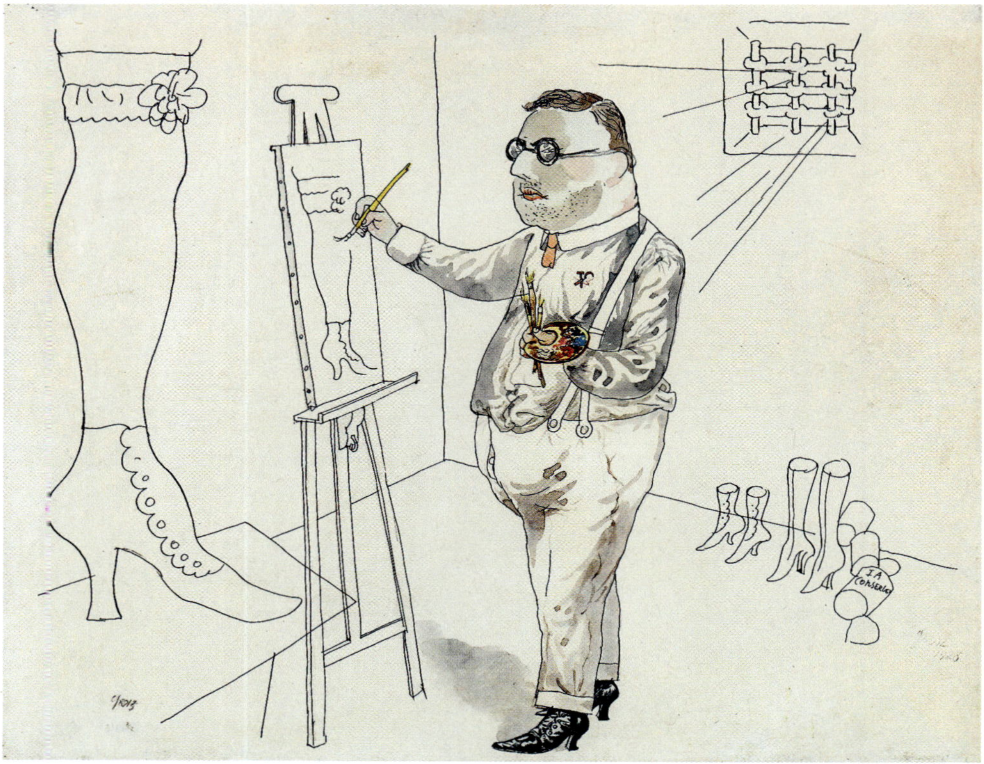

George Grosz, *Der Maler (Rudolf Schlichter)* (The Painter [Rudolf Schlichter]), 1928. Pen and ink and watercolor on paper, 46 × 59.9 cm. Photo © Ketterer Kunst GmbH und Co. KG. © Estate of George Grosz, Princeton, NJ/DACS 2022.

prostitute was then hitched up in it, drawn up to the ceiling, and then slowly lowered again. During the descent Schlichter could indulge in his veneration of the Virgin."[6] But this time Schlichter—now with Nietzsche in his pocket instead of a book on sex or revolution—is distinctly plump, and we see why. He is surrounded by open tins of fine food ("Prima Konserven"). Indeed, Schlichter suffered from what he called *Fresssucht*, the eating disorder hyperphagia or chronic overeating.[7] Schlichter's passions had taken over, but they were always shifting between the political and the psychiatric, between the desire for revolution and consuming personal appetites and obsessions.

Grosz's drawings are, however, affectionate, and in these allusions to incarceration and erotic eccentricity he was simply elaborating on his friend's own self-characterizations. Indeed,

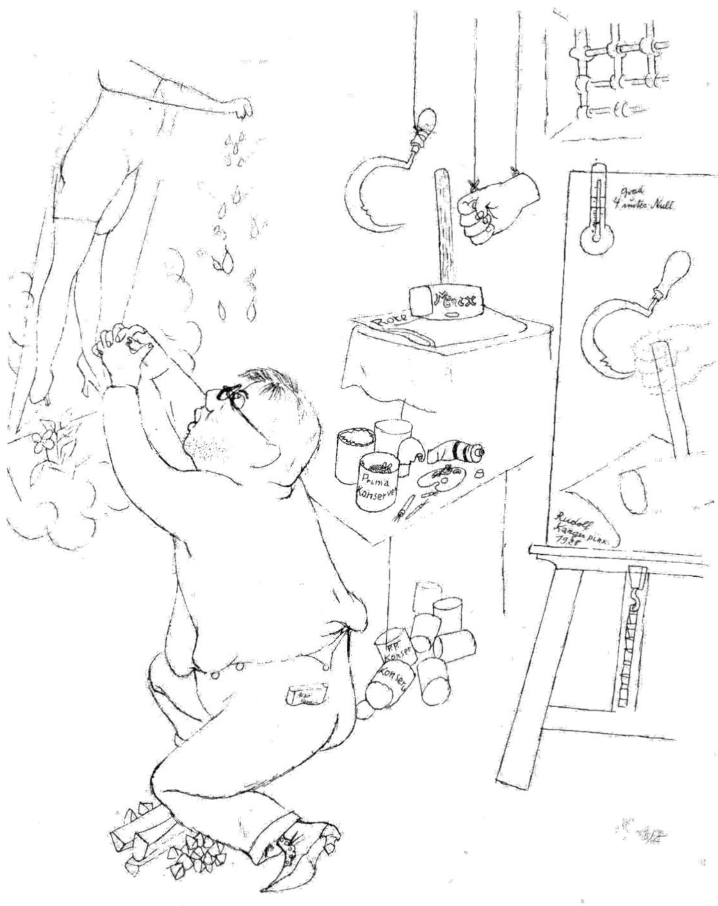

George Grosz, *Rudolf Schlichter in seinem Atelier* (Rudolf Schlichter in his studio), 1928–1929, pen and ink, 34.5 × 24.9 cm. Private collection. © Estate of George Grosz, Princeton, NJ/ DACS 2022.

Schlichter actively and compulsively surrounded himself with the signs of deviance and dissent. He used them about himself, and others used them about him. From a young age, Schlichter cultivated the persona of an outsider. Along with his dandyish tendencies and attraction to the underworld, his radical politics and fascination with the erotic and "deviant" have been subsumed by scholars under the rubric of "anti-bourgeois self-fashioning."[8] This is no doubt correct but represents, I think, a somewhat reductive common denominator that tends to trivialize the radical nature of Schlichter's life and career.[9] Self-stylization or not, Schlichter was pursued by the police and other governmental law-enforcement agencies as a result of his actions concerning both sex and the state, and of the evidence of these actions that he gave so freely in both word and image. In this chapter I shall argue that Schlichter *inhabited* (I can think of no better word) the spaces and discourses of dissent and deviance, repeatedly either producing himself as or finding himself a case for medicine, the police, the courts, and the bureaucracies of power. Like Oskar Panizza, I shall argue, he lived his life through a set of cases, using them in shifting ways that intertwined publicity and subjectivity. This chapter is an attempt to explore precisely what he did in the various spaces of the case. What were its politics for this difficult artist? What sort of leverage did the forms of the case give him in his various projects—political, artistic, literary, and personal?

§

Images of sexual deviance occupy a prominent position in Schlichter's artistic oeuvre. Already as a student before the First World War, Schlichter supported himself by satisfying a local market for erotic drawings and prints, and he favored sadistic scenes. The lithograph *Die Polin* (The Polish woman) shows in cool and precise lines a fully dressed woman, in high-heeled boots with spurs, before another woman suspended from a contraption not unlike Schlichter's; she is naked but for boots and is being hoisted by another figure similarly undressed. The Polish woman is a *piqueuse*: she holds a rapier in her left hand while carefully inserting smaller knives into the suspended victim with her right.[10] Other lithographs from the time include a delicately drawn scene of flagellation and an explicit, *japoniste* image of lesbian love. In the early 1920s, Schlichter again created a short series of six erotic works, this time etchings. His *Liebesvariationen* (Erotic variations) are brothel scenes, more gallant than sordid, but include flagellation and a depiction of a man being fellated while suspended in a harness and strangled by a noose.

Such works served a lucrative market, but in his autobiographical writings Schlichter takes a distance from them. He describes the early lithographs and drawings as merely

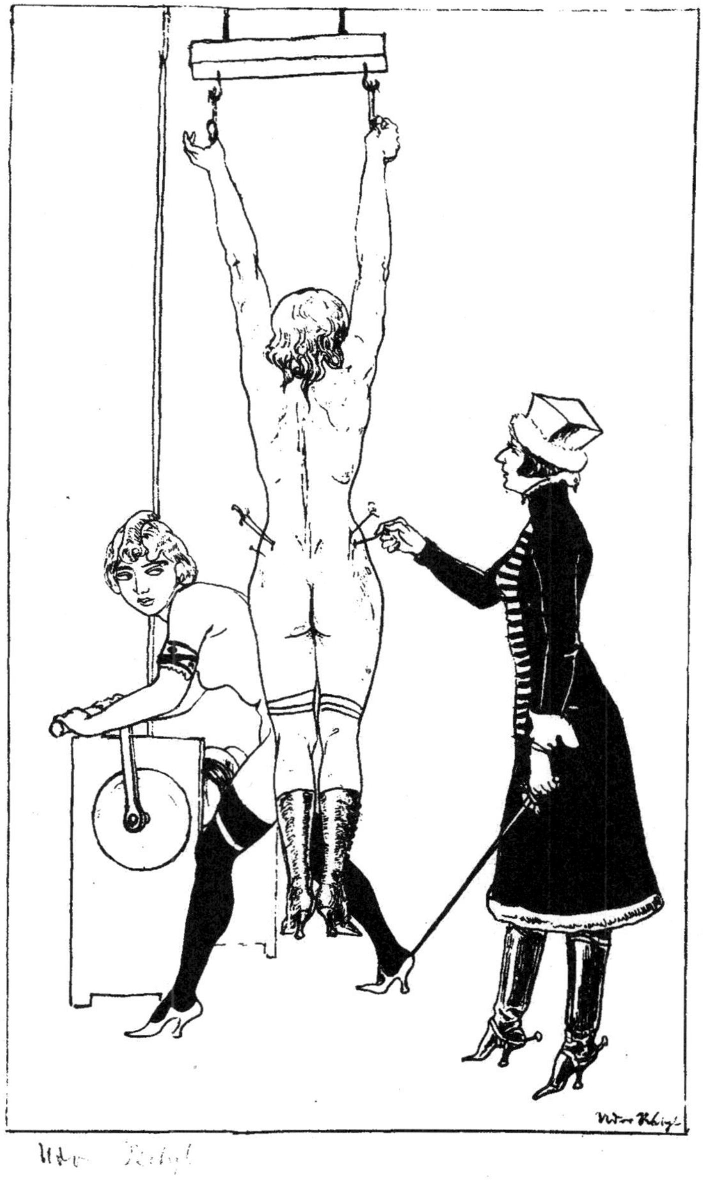

Rudolf Schlichter (under the pseudonym Udor Rétyl), *Die Polin* (The Polish woman), ca. 1913. Lithograph, 27.6 × 16.5 cm. Private collection. © Viola Roehr v. Alvensleben, München.

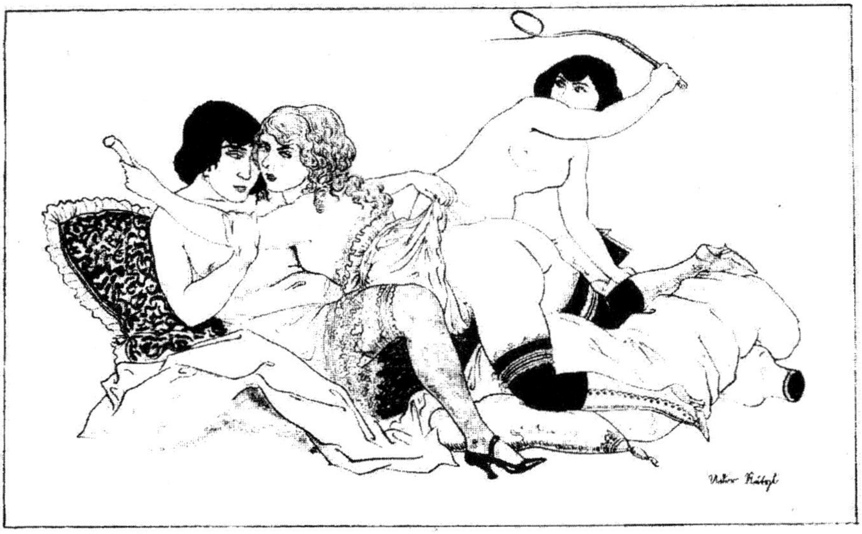

Rudolf Schlichter (under the pseudonym Udor Rétyl), *Drei Frauen (Flagellanten)* (Three women [flagellants]), ca. 1913. Lithograph, 20.0 × 31.6 cm. Private collection. © Viola Roehr v. Alvensleben, München.

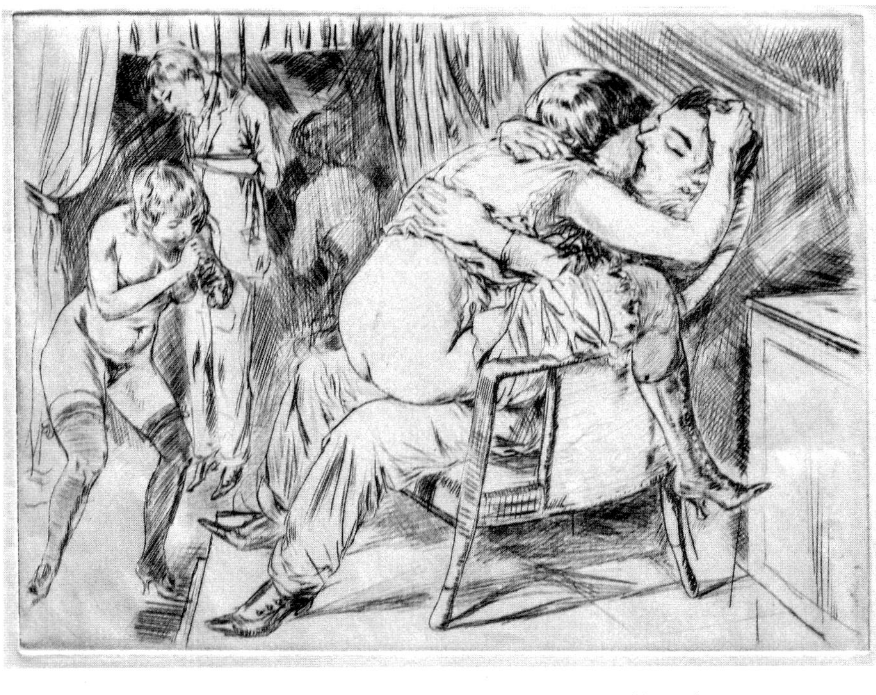

Rudolf Schlichter, from *Liebesvariationen* (Erotic variations), 1922. Etching, 16 × 20.5 cm. Private collection, Offenbach am Main. © Viola Roehr v. Alvensleben, München.

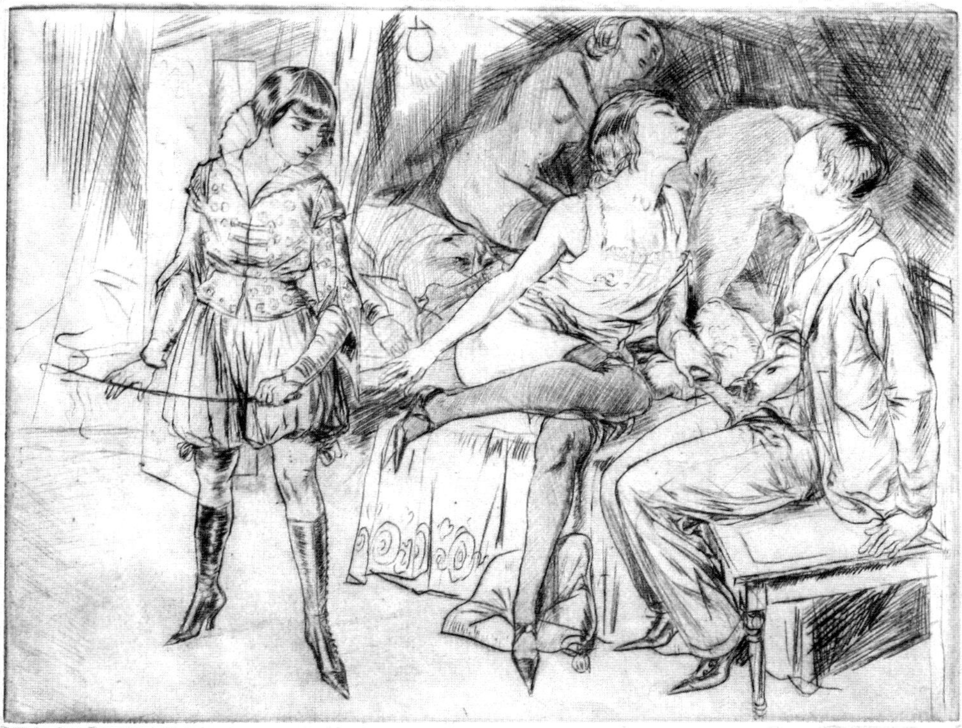

Rudolf Schlichter, from *Liebesvariationen* (Erotic variations), 1922. Etching, 16 × 20.5 cm. Private collection, Offenbach am Main.

> a means of financing my passions ... I lost myself in pedantically drawn descriptions of pornographic proceedings from which I remained emotionally detached, but with which I could satisfy both my own cold need to create a sensation and the demands of my clientele.[11]

Emotional detachment, however, does not characterize most of the large number of works showing "deviant" practices in the 1920s; in both their frequency and their style, they show the signs of private obsessions. Brothel scenes abound—now with a more convincing seediness—as do drawings and watercolors of women at lesbian bars. There are numerous images of strangulation, including a watercolor variation on one of the illustrations from Peter Paul Althaus's *Jack der Aufschlitzer*, showing the artist, now in despair, before the hanging corpses of two women in a bare room.

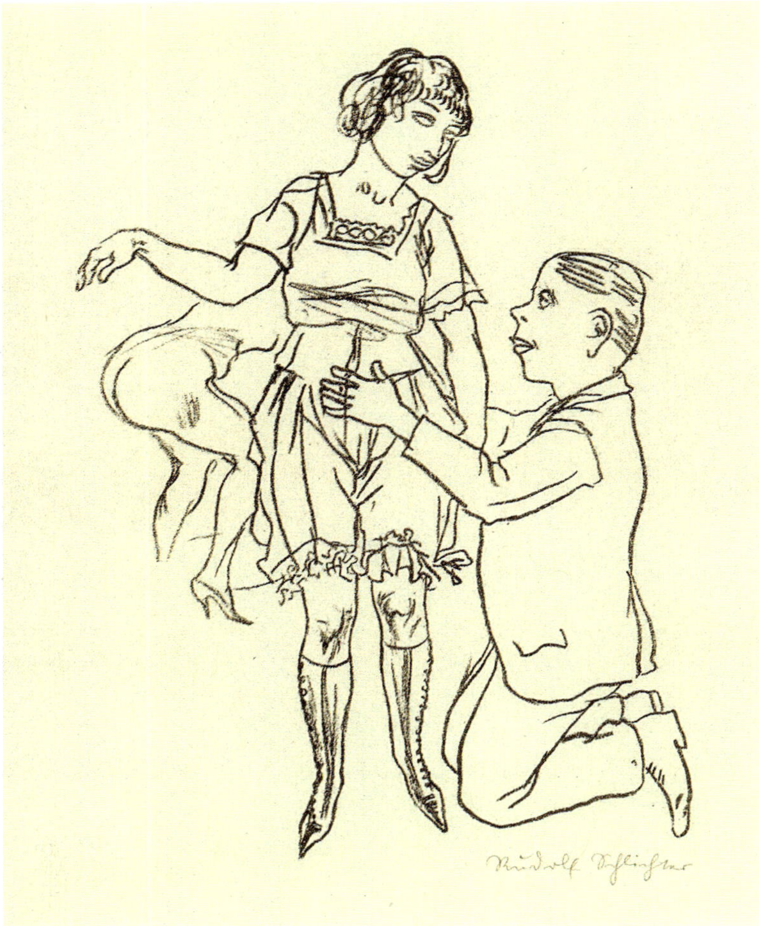

Rudolf Schlichter, *Bräutigam* (Bridegroom), 1922. Lithograph, 41 × 31 cm. Private collection.

There are images of *Lustmord*, several of which also vary scenes from *Jack der Aufschlitzer*, one clearly based on Erich Wulffen's *Der Sexualverbrecher*, another showing a rueful murderer in a tenement courtyard looking at the twisted corpse of a prostitute (see pp. 210, 255). Masochism and humiliation appear as well, both in brothel scenes and in a particularly delicate image of his fiancée Speedy in green negligee, a cigarette in her hand and her booted toe on the head of the despairing artist.[12] Schlichter and Speedy also staged photographs of sadistic practices, much like George

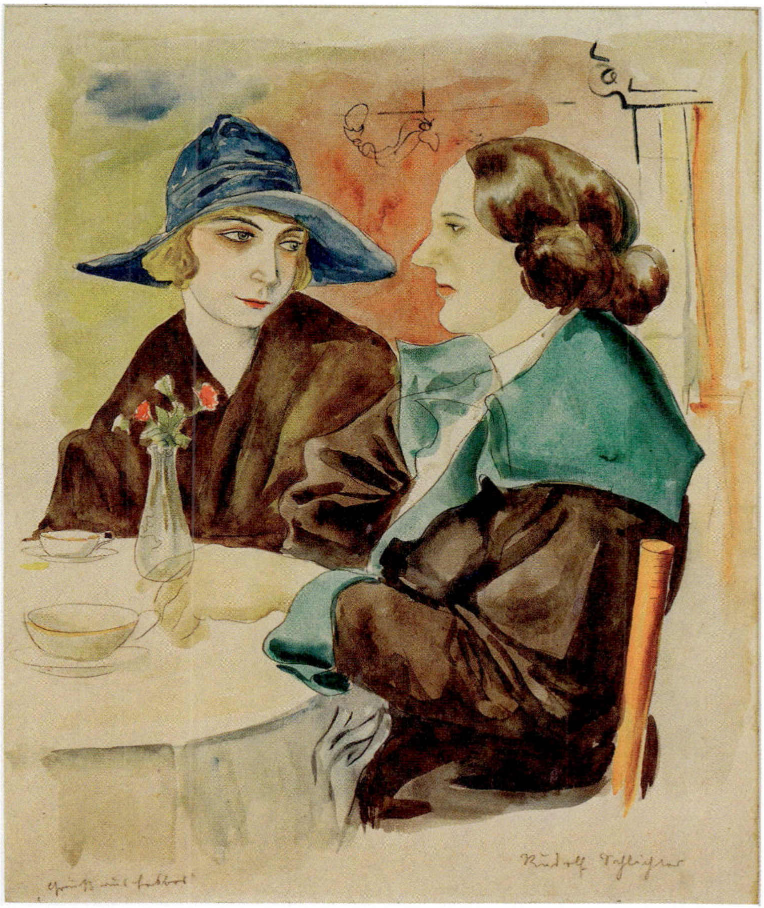

Rudolf Schlichter, *Gruß aus Lesbos* (Greetings from Lesbos), ca. 1923. Watercolor and pencil on paper, 63.7 × 50.1 cm. Kunstmuseum Stuttgart. Photo © akg-images. © Viola Roehr v. Alvensleben, München.

Grosz's famous photograph of himself as Jack the Ripper stalking his wife Eva; and here we recognize the harness suspended from the ceiling. Schlichter's works showing such "deviant" sexual practices are varied in style, from caricature to grim realism, but one constant is the motif of women in the high-heeled button boots of the dominatrix.

Such scenes of sexual deviance and violence were a constant in Schlichter's visual production, and the evidence of friends such as Grosz shows their meaning for the author. It is in his literary works, however, that Schlichter discusses his obsessions in

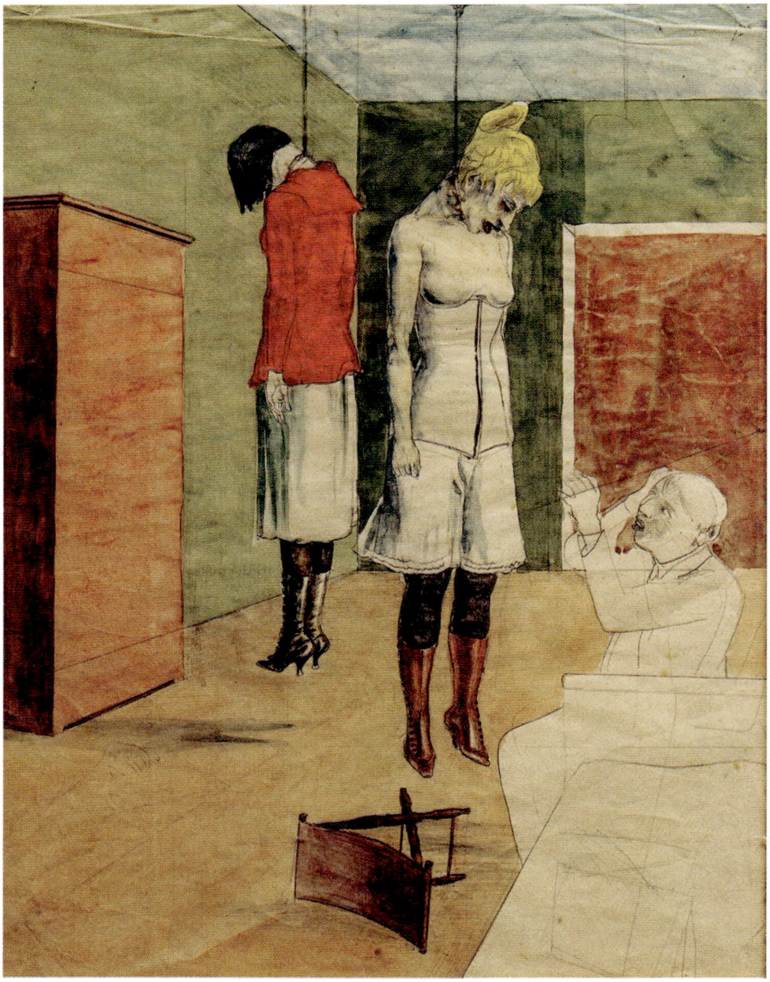

Rudolf Schlichter, *Der Künstler mit zwei erhängten Frauen* (The artist with two hanged women), ca. 1924. Watercolor and pencil on paper, 45.0 × 33.0 cm. Private collection, Karlsruhe. Photo © akg-images. © Viola Roehr v. Alvensleben, München.

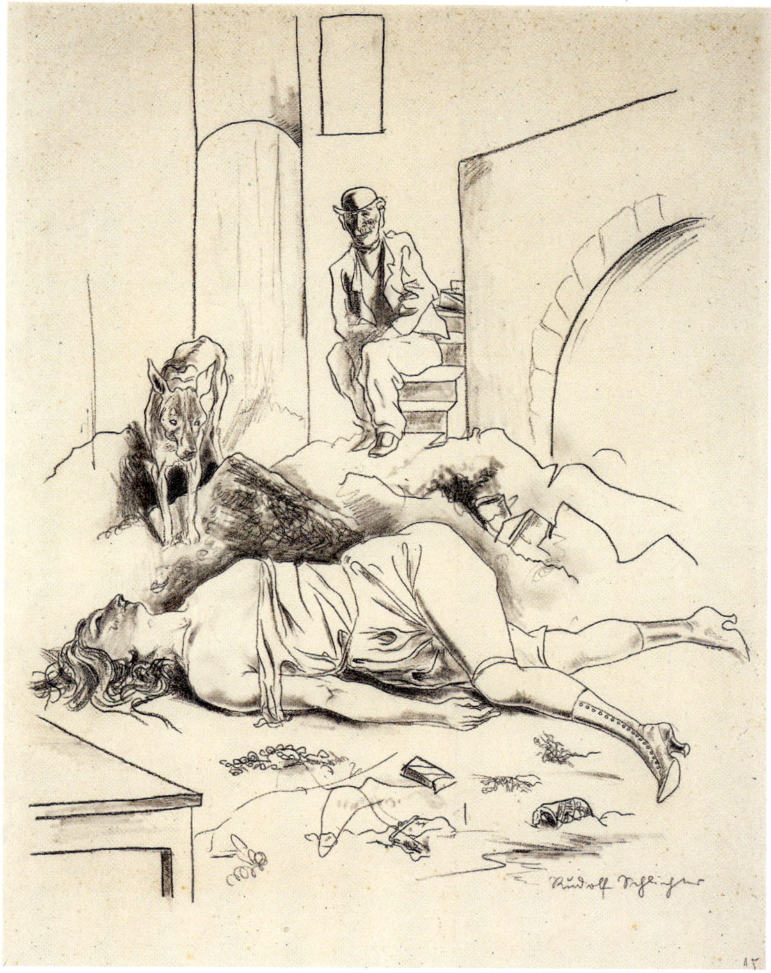

Rudolf Schlichter, *Sexualmord* (Sex murder), ca. 1924. Pencil and charcoal on paper, 58 × 47 cm. Private collection. © Viola Roehr v. Alvensleben, München.

exhaustive, confessional form (indeed, from about 1930 Schlichter considered himself as much a writer as an artist). His first three books are autobiographical, though the first—a novella titled *Zwischenwelt: Ein Intermezzo* (The world in between: an intermezzo) of 1931—is slightly fictionalized.[13] Schlichter describes here how, under the guidance of his beloved, he rejected his dissolute life in the political and criminal underworld of Berlin; it is a story of salvation, a lover's understanding and acceptance of his aberrance,

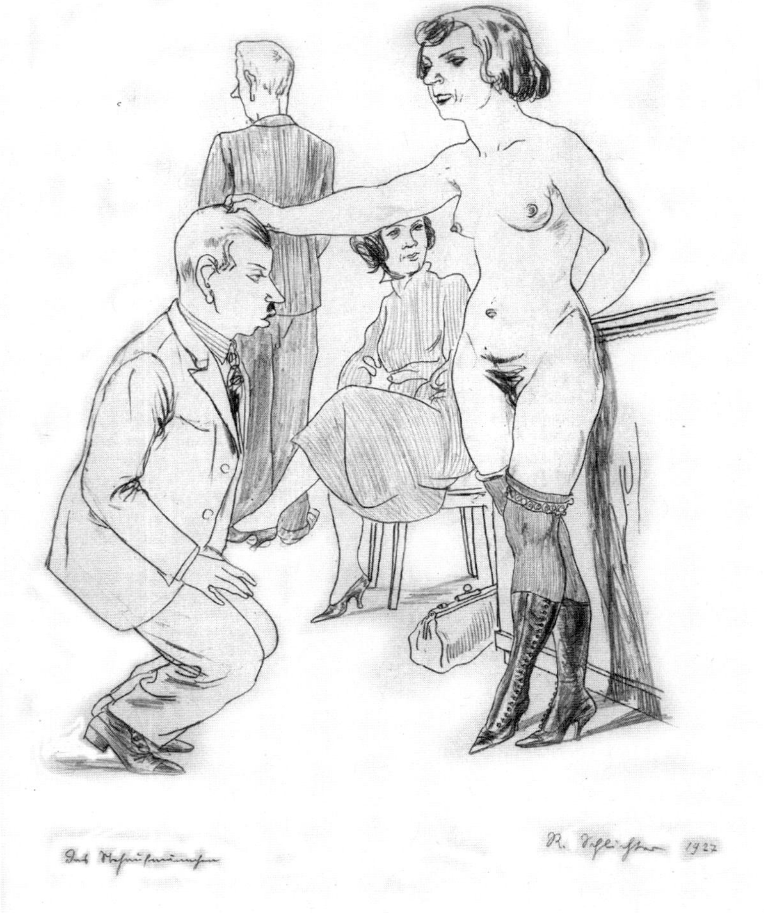

Rudolf Schlichter, *Das Stehaufmännchen* (Jack-in-the-box), 1927. Pencil on paper, 65 × 47.8 cm. Private collection, Offenbach am Main. © Viola Roehr v. Alvensleben, München.

and ultimately of his rejection of Communism and turn to Catholicism. (Schlichter and Speedy married in December 1929; George Grosz served as a witness.) After the more stylized *Zwischenwelt*, the artist embarked on an ambitious autobiographical cycle planned as three volumes, of which only two appeared: *Das widerspenstige Fleisch* (Rebellious flesh) in 1932 and *Tönerne Füße* (Feet of clay) in 1933.[14] The books recount Schlichter's upbringing in

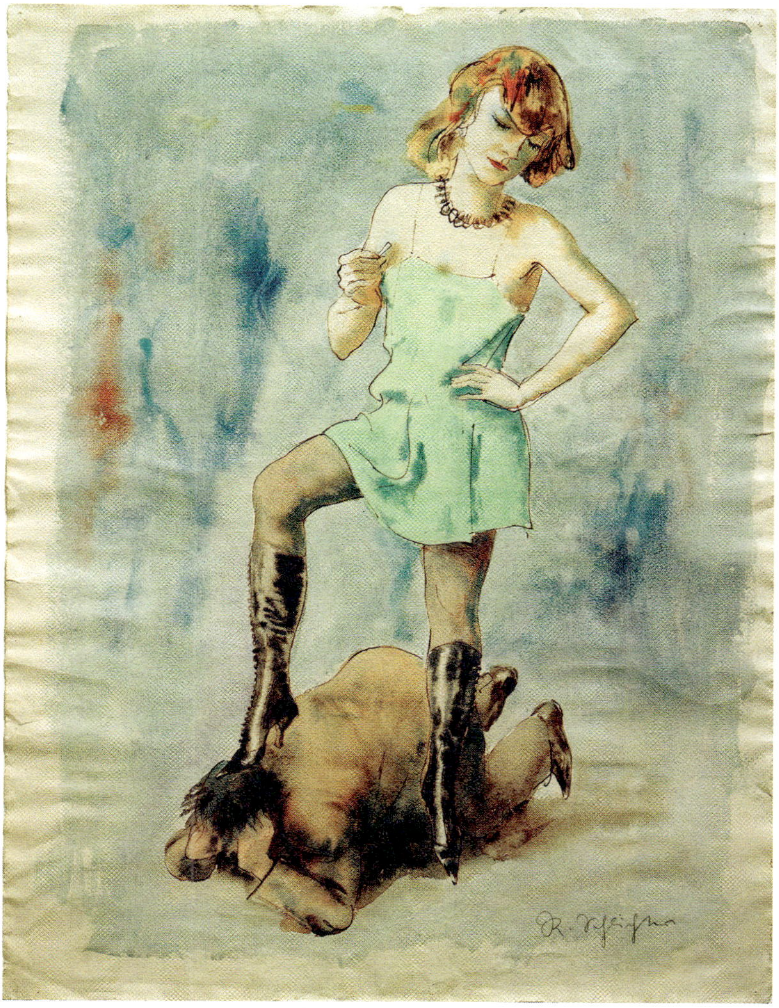

Rudolf Schlichter, *Domina mea*, 1927–28. Watercolor and ink on paper, 72×51 cm. Private collection. Photo © akg-images. © Viola Roehr v. Alvensleben, München.

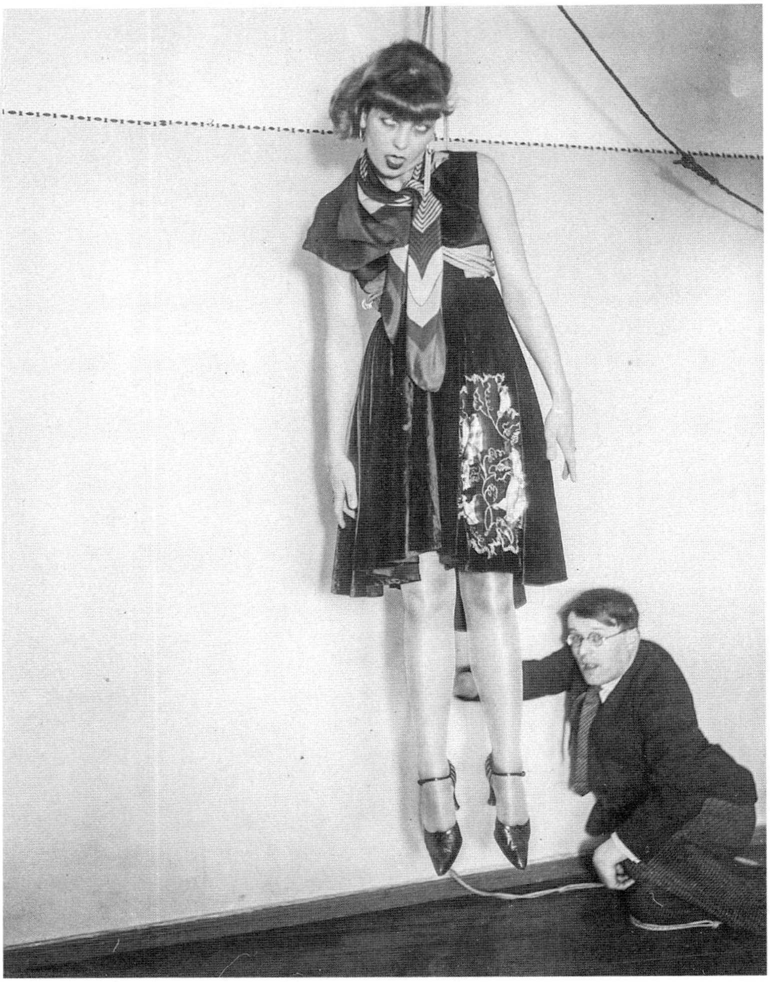

Speedy and Rudolf Schlichter, ca. 1927. Photograph. Rudolf Schlichter Archive, Deutsches Literaturarchiv, Marbach am Neckar. Photo © DLA Marbach. © Viola Roehr v. Alvensleben, München.

provincial Swabia, his apprenticeship in Pforzheim, and student years in Stuttgart and Karlsruhe up to the outbreak of the First World War. Schlichter's difficulties with the Reichskulturkammer during the Third Reich—his work was classed as "perverse-erotic"—prevented him from writing the final volume, though some fragments have been identified by Dirk Heißerer and published in 1995.[15]

We can take Grosz's word that Schlichter knew the literature on sexual deviance—in fact better than did Grosz, who, we saw, confused his authors. Schlichter was a voracious reader and known to friends for his wide learning,[16] and his autobiographical writings show his meticulous construction of the persona of a sexual deviant—by the book, we could say. Indeed, in *Zwischenwelt*, he introduces his object choice with a clear nod to an earlier avant-garde's most famous fetishist, Panizza's "Korsettenfritz": both tell of a provincial, pubescent boy displaced and alone in a nearby city for the first time (for Schlichter it is Strasbourg, then part of Germany) who is overwhelmed by the apparition of the partial, clothed female body in a shop window and is from then on fatefully under its spell.[17] The trope of the shop window was overdetermined: it was the site at which the commodity fetish assumed visibility and a figure through which, in the social and cultural theory of the time, it could be represented; and its display of the isolated and packaged body part merged seamlessly with contemporary accounts of the aberrant erotic synecdoche of sexual fetishism.[18] That it was fictional in Schlichter's novella is clear from his later, more explicitly autobiographical writings, in which his unhealthy obsession emerged earlier in his childhood in an entirely feminine domestic space (Schlichter was raised by his mother in a fatherless household).

But while the literary qualities in Schlichter's written works are central to them—*Zwischenwelt* is a tight and honed novella; the longer autobiographical works comprise a *Bildungsroman* with picaresque elements à la Grimmelshausen—it is with the literature of sexual science that Schlichter's description of erotic obsessions correlates most closely. In *Das widerspenstige Fleisch*, he narrates the emergence of his fetish without the simultaneous framing, isolation, and abruptness that characterize the shop window scene, one tied so closely to a particular moment in the emergence of a culture whose terms are set by the mass market for consumer goods. It is more developmental than sudden, more a dawning realization than a moment of insight, more a matter of family history than, at first, public display:

> I began gradually to discover the charms of the opposite sex, but ... by a circuitous route. It was not the attraction of the female body hidden beneath its covering that excited my

erotic fantasy. ... It was precisely those covers that excited my sensual pleasure, that piqued my desires. Above all else it was of course the footwear, most particularly those button boots made from fine kidskin with toecaps of shining patent-leather; but also long lace stockings, the waist in its narrow corset, clothes with their frills and ribbons and lace, and not least the artistic hairstyles—all were a source of inexhaustible erotic stimulation. Soon I discovered finer distinctions in the choice and form of the objects that excited me; I followed the nuances of these objects of my attraction down to the small details such as clasps, buttons, ribbons, color, and height of the bodice, even the stitches and the weave of the stockings. ... This was particularly clear in the matter of my fetishism for shoes. If boys' laced shoes had previously served as the object of my lust just as much as the button boots ... now my feelings of pleasure became concentrated more distinctly on the button boots. ... It was at first just a shift of emphasis but at the same time an expansion and an amplification of the possibilities of pleasure. I began around this time to discover the charms of thin, high heels. As I have mentioned, I was struck by the beauty of such heels for the first time in the high, yellow shoes of my ominous Aunt Wilhelmine, and the first impression remained indelibly etched in my memory.[19]

Such accounts are legion in the contemporary publications on sexual science. Biographical details vary, but the tone is usually the same, as a passage from a patient's own account in Magnus Hirschfeld's *Die Transvestiten* shows:

I recall my tendency toward women's clothing as far back as the time I began school. I knew nothing about external influences. ... To me, even the mere names of pieces of clothing, such as a woman's gown, pinafore, veil, and slip, had something magical about them. ... Truly twenty to twenty-five years' of fashion journals I bought were looked at page by page.[20]

Schlichter too cultivated considerable expertise from women's fashion magazines.[21]

Though Schlichter regularly wore women's shoes, he did not consider himself a transvestite. But his own account strays into this area:

> At first my longings were concentrated on my sister Gertrud, as she was the closest object of desire. Often I would sit with her for hours on end or help her in the kitchen just to enjoy the sight of her feet covered with dainty button boots. But because this brought no liberation of my burning lust but instead increased my nerve-wracking, enervating turmoil to its limit, it occurred to me to take secretly the objects of my hellish lust to my room to satisfy myself. With trembling hands I tried on the boots, and by devilish coincidence they fit me as if custom-made. I took a few steps back and forth in my room to savor fully the feeling of walking on high heels. Suddenly I felt a strange transformation of my entire being. I felt at once that I was a girl.[22]

Readers of the relevant literature would recognize the trembling fingers, and they would recognize the feeling of transformation. From Hirschfeld's *Die Transvestiten*:

> When I put on a woman's dress my whole relationship to the external world changes. During this metamorphosis ... I have a totally different view into the environment; the outside world affects me differently, finer and gentler, and challenges me to appreciate the delicate and the gentle. ... The total variation of the process in my psyche moves and is dispatched in the demonstrative perception of the feminine in me.[23]

Schlichter's feelings of effeminization, however, are not satisfied with cross-dressing but instead lead directly to masochistic and homosexual fantasies. His account continues as follows:

> I was gripped by a terrible desire for masculine violence; I would have wished to throw myself on a bed, willing to suffer any abuse of my body. I lost myself to the extent that, for a moment, the memory of my earlier state disappeared completely and I sank into a dark sea of perilous,

> all-consuming feminine receptivity. It was as if my entire masculine force of will had sunk into the single wish to suffer violence. Although I had no notion of exactly what happened in the union of the sexes, I was gripped by the terrible fear of losing myself in this ocean of confused desires.[24]

This is thoroughly plausible: scientific writers at the time were united in considering shoe fetishism to be fundamentally a form of masochism. Krafft-Ebing gives a case study of "latent masochism—foot and shoe fetishism" that sounds familiar:

> Case 70. Mr. X., aged twenty-five, parents healthy, never before ill, placed the following autobiography at my disposal. "I began to practice onanism at the age of ten, without ever having any lustful thoughts during the act. Yet at the time—I am sure of this—the sight and touch of girls' elegant boots had a peculiar charm for me; my greatest desire was also to wear such shoes, a wish that was occasionally fulfilled at masquerades. But I was also troubled by a very different thought: *my ideal was to see myself in a position of humiliation; I would gladly have been a slave*, and whipped."[25]

For Schlichter, any arousal was accompanied by deep feelings of guilt, and his litany of fetishistic and masochistic urges is inevitably followed by accounts of torment. One example:

> My condition—a permanent sexual arousal that would never achieve a natural form of satisfaction—brought forth terrible, endless depressions; my excessive sensuality took on grotesque dimensions, turned into a tangled mass of the most absurd wishes and provoked necessarily the desire for the most disgusting debauchery.[26]

In his book on fetishism, Stekel described such feelings well:

> The fetish lover's suffering derives from an almost invincible spirit of expiation and atonement. But, we ask, what does he have to expiate? What is his great sin? The previous analyses have given us the answer: fetishism is a self-inflicted punishment for the individual's cruel attitudes and phantasies. We were also able, in every case, to demonstrate

> the presence of this sadistic component in the fetishistic ideal itself. This compulsion must be marked by unpleasantness, pain, or coercion if it is to fulfil its fetishistic purpose.[27]

And indeed, Schlichter's fetishistic and masochistic acts were always shadowed by sadistic fantasies. They centered on strangulation. In *Das widerspenstige Fleisch*, he recounts how he would spend his Sunday afternoons

> using all sorts of refined and complicated techniques to intensify my lust. Thus I came upon the idea to try out on myself the forms of execution that always made such a strong impression on me and which I could never imagine realistically enough. For these purposes I used the strong iron hook from which the petroleum lamp in our parlor hung, and which was perfectly suited to making a sort of gallows. As soon as my mother left, I took down the lamp, threaded a double knot through the hook, stood on a chair, took then the end of the rope under my arms and tied it across my chest. Then I kicked the stool away (but only so far that I could still reach it with my feet) and hanged in the air. I kept my eyes glued to my feet, which I moved this way and that in convulsions. In this way I sought to create the illusion of an execution. To intensify the gruesomeness of the scene, I imagined myself a depraved criminal who deserved to meet such a shameful end.[28]

Later in life this turned into fantasies of strangling the object of his attractions. From *Zwischenwelt*:

> Into the terrifying fear of losing her was mixed the depraved but lustful urge that he had long harbored: to escape all of his agony by actually stringing her up, to achieve the peak of his satanic lust even at the risk of her sudden death and his eternal damnation.[29]

In this book, Schlichter repeatedly recounts his fantasies of *Lustmord*. One of many examples will suffice:

> He knew that his ultimate goal, the final fulfilment of his most burning wishes, could only be murder. He knew that

> for this he might be prepared to face privation and death. "Kill, kill" he heard from the depths: only when he saw these delicate limbs that he worshiped wringing in the throes of death—only then did he believe in the climax of earthly happiness.[30]

Now these last passages, in their escalation and exaltation, are highly fictionalized; they are from the earlier novella and not the later autobiographies. They cannot be read apart from the fascination with *Lustmord* in the larger culture of the time and they bear the stamp of the general medial fixation on sex and crime. They are, in other words, as much a product as a symptom of the general thematics of violence out of which he wrote and into which his writings fed. They show a writerly voice inserting itself into penny dreadfuls, the black humor of the streets, the Jack the Ripper role; they show the general, tropic intensification of the publicly perverse. But the fascination with and fantasies of violence are also a theme of the later books recounting his youth in painful detail, and there is no reason to doubt the more sober reports of his inner development discussed over nearly seven hundred pages—though they, too, are rehearsals of a more particular genre, the psychiatric study of sexual deviance. In any case, we are left with an image familiar to the psychiatrist. As Stekel writes,

> In all the cases of genuine fetishism we have been able to note a marked admixture of sadism. At first sight, they all look like distinctly masochistic persons. They torture themselves, subject themselves to compulsions, deny themselves the joys of life. But the analysis reveals this masochism as the superstructure founded upon a highly original form of sadism. Guilt feelings and the pangs of conscience are added to make of the fetishist a lamentable picture of humanity.[31]

Perhaps the expression is apt: we would not want to be in Schlichter's shoes. But more interesting here than the pathos and pathology of a singular subject are the feelings, the turns of phrase, the narratives that Schlichter and the objects of sexual science share. For the subjectivity of the "deviant" was the shared product of the nexus of "pervert" and the psychiatrist. The very genre of the autobiographical psychological case history was the data out of which psychiatry generally constructed its deviants. Albert Moll's, Krafft-Ebing's, Hirschfeld's, and Stekel's analyses are based upon case studies, and many of them were provided—often in written form—by the patients themselves.[32] And these accounts produced more patients. We know that readers at a loss with their own non-normative sexualities recognized themselves in the scientific literature at the time and then fed their own accounts straight back into it, the shared project of the construction of the "pervert" as "species" so compellingly described by Foucault in the first volume of his *History of Sexuality*.[33] As the editions of such books accumulated, so too did the number of case studies as the discourse and its objects became increasingly intertwined. One masochist wrote to Krafft-Ebing that "Reading your chapter on this topic made, as you can imagine, an extraordinary impression upon me."[34] He wrote to recount his own experiences, to add nuance to the picture provided by other cases; and thus became his own case, no. 57 in the twelfth edition of *Psychopathia Sexualis*. A fetishist wrote to the psychiatrist Leopold Löwenfeld, interweaving into his account of self such passages as "Dr. Moll's book came into my hands when I was twenty-two, and I might mention that at that time I also visited a prostitute. ... Even on the way there, I felt as if I were going to be impotent and, like the persons in Krafft-Ebing's book, I had no more desire to visit one of them."[35] Schlichter was another informed observer of himself as a case. Here is a final passage from his autobiographical writings, from his student days, about his research into the physiology of sex:

> I fell ever deeper into the jungle of my aberrant drives. A tortured curiosity led me to look for the origins of this perversion in all sorts of books. Then I read about the effect of hanging on the "sexual apparatus." When I read there that ejaculation had been noted in the victims of hangings, and that erections had been observed at the gallows, I was dumbstruck. A terrible shudder went through me. So that was the secret of my lust! That was why I felt such inexplicable excitement at the pictures of executions, the dark origin of which had always been such a sinister mystery. But what shook me most was the disturbing discovery that the development of my sexuality (*Sexus*) had been determined by this terrible fact from childhood on. ... How

> often had I prayed in vain for enlightenment ... how often had I sought, all through the night, to determine the root of this evil.[36]

And, moving from research into the physiology to the psychology of sex, Schlichter voices the words of countless "deviants" who came to understand themselves in the pages of the sexual psychiatry of the time, and found that they were not alone: "For my own peculiar tendencies were just one version of thousands."[37]

Schlichter presented himself to the world as a case, a psychiatric case of sexual "deviance." As was the nature of such diagnoses and classifications, his case emerged from other cases. He writes as a patient suffering from and aware of his own pathology; he rehearses the confessional epistles that comprise so many of the case studies in Stekel, Krafft-Ebing, and similar works. This was a key component of the discourse of classification and control, with advantages on both sides: the suffering are offered a classification, a reason, a prognosis, and the awareness of belonging to a sexual community. In turn the disciplinary discourse gains its data, so often already cut to the cloth of its own generic form, the case study. (In fact Dirk Heißerer has found letters from doctors in Schlichter's archive attesting to the potential importance to science of his literary accounts.[38]) Both sides were engaged in a sort of mimetic assimilation to the other, the clinch in which, for example, the hysteric found herself with her doctor at the end of the nineteenth century, as Foucault has described it.[39] But the process had now gone beyond the hospital and entered into a more public space through its media. This produced perhaps more intense, if less intimate, examples of what Ian Hacking has called "feedback mechanisms" or "looping effects."[40] Schlichter's discourse is part of this phenomenon, one that post-dates the construction of the hysteric. Schlichter shows how the subjectivity of the "deviant" was mediated through the sexological literature of the time. He reproduced it to the letter and produced picture-perfect images of it.

§

I hope it is clear that my intentions are in no way hermeneutic. The literature of sexual science does not tell us what Schlichter, deep down, "was," what he felt, the sources of his desires, or the

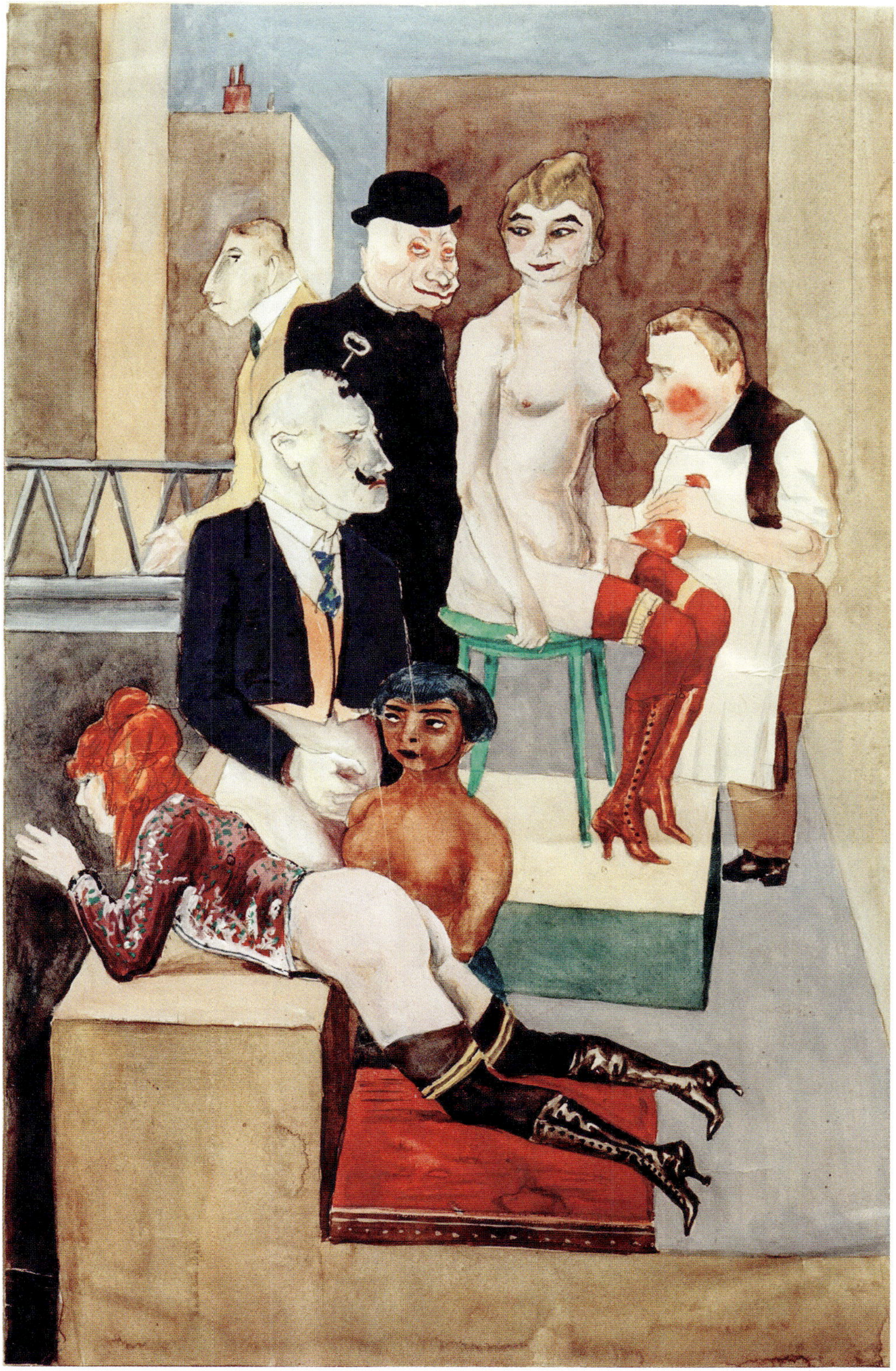

Rudolf Schlichter, *Zusammenkunft von Fetischisten und manischen Flagellanten* (Gathering of fetishists and manic flagellants), ca. 1923. Watercolor on paper, 43.9 × 27.3 cm. Private collection. Photo © akg-images. © Viola Roehr v. Alvensleben, München.

nature of his self. His own writings were literature, however much they were framed as confession. Like all sexuality, his was, to use Judith Butler's term, a performative one. That we have found evidence of a "script" or "scripts" brings us only so far. Our goal cannot be to dig further into the truth of a single subject, for it is, in its fabric, so interwoven with media and performed through them. I am more interested in the way Schlichter used these tools in their medial imbrications than in grasping a subjectivity. And moreover, however much we need to take seriously Schlichter's intense and at some level sincere interaction with discourses by which sexuality was mediated and produced, he shows occasional signs of distance and dissimulation.

Certainly it is hard to take too seriously an image such as *Zusammenkunft von Fetischisten und manischen Flagellanten* (Gathering of fetishists and manic flagellants) of about 1923. It is a late Dada effort, showing figures on a balcony in a city constructed

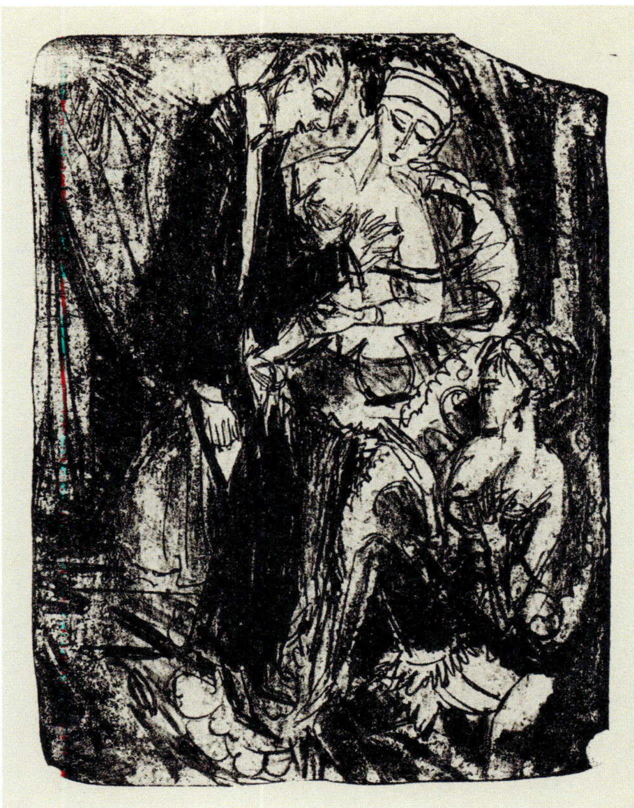

Ernst Ludwig Kirchner, *Der Busenfreier* (The breast fetishist), 1915. Lithograph, 42 × 32 cm. Courtesy Galerie Kornfeld, Bern.

according to the odd but evacuated logic of *pittura metafisica*. We see two voyeurs, one a priest with a swine's features; there are two women in high-heel button shoes, one merely on display, the other prepared for flagellation. A butcher in his rubber apron eyes the surrounding flesh with a more than professional interest.[41] The mix of classes united by wayward desires is indicated by a bourgeois: he is properly dressed above, with facial scars indicating university days spent with the sort of right-wing fraternity for which such *Schmisse* were a badge of honor, and his waxed, upturned moustache is modelled on the recently abdicated Kaiser's. Below he is naked, his hand encircling a blur around his groin, the winding key in his head above alluding to his mechanical movements above the displayed breasts of the dark-skinned woman kneeling before him. It is the fate of masturbation shared by all fetishists, for whom desire is displaced from the whole object and its prescribed genital center.

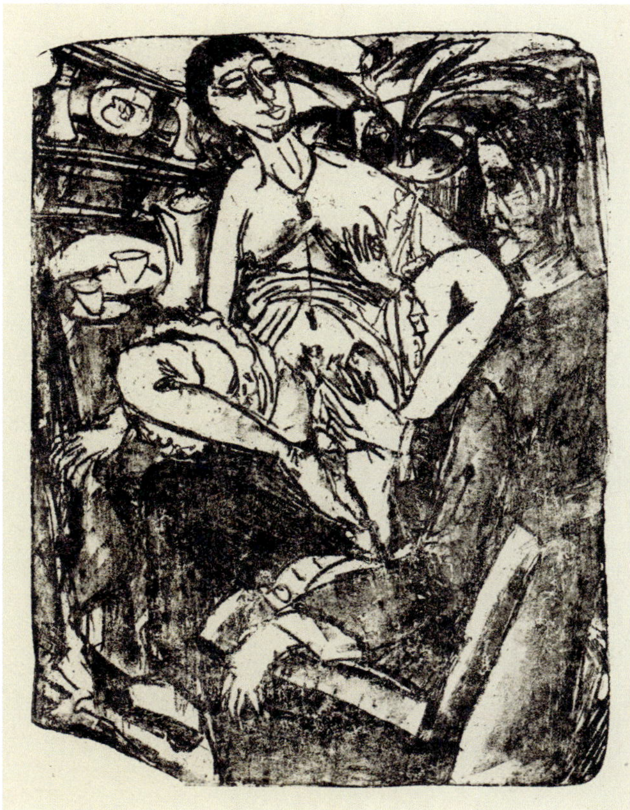

Ernst Ludwig Kirchner, *Der Fußfreier* (The foot fetishist), 1915. Lithograph, 42 × 32 cm. Courtesy Galerie Kornfeld, Bern.

Such catalogs of "perversity" were not unusual at the time. Already in 1915, Ernst Ludwig Kirchner produced a series of eight lithographs titled *Erotika II*, showing brothel scenes: they show a sadist, a masochist, two breast fetishists, a foot fetishist, a glove fetishist, and a urine fetishist.[42] One writer described the picaresque novel *Bordell* (Brothel) by Curt Corrinth as "a translation of Krafft-Ebing's *Psychopathia Sexualis* into Expressionism."[43] The catalog of sexual acts was, as we have seen, a conceit of erotic graphic series at the time; it was standard in novels as well.[44] A series of drawings by Christian Schad shows a similarly playful approach to the literature of sexual science. Such books often contained handwriting samples: "Graphology casts an interesting light on the relation of temperament and characterology to sexuality," one reads.[45] Schad took this complex as his model and merely switched the kind of illustration, the way the body would yield this sort of knowledge. The series is at once explicit and allusive, critical, clever, and exquisitely drawn. In general, contemporaries had an acute awareness of the very public nature of the varieties of sexual desire, neatly classified and packaged for those exploring their longings, for connoisseurs, or simply for curious readers. A drawing in the satirical journal *Simplicissimus* depicts this situation, alluding to the death of Eros (a cupid figure is shown hanged from a tree) in the flood of packaged tastes visible at a kiosk: we see pamphlet and magazine titles such as *Lesbos*, *Ohne Hemd* (Topless), *Mimis Unterhose* (Mimi's underwear), *§175* (alluding to the statute against homosexuality), and *Ein Lustmord*; the journal *Venus* sports a wrapper announcing the journal's reappearance after censorship and another pamphlet advertises that it had earlier been confiscated.[46] The titles themselves were fictitious, but they are of a kind found by the hundreds in the police's *Polunbi* catalogs of publications investigated for obscenity.

Schlichter contributed to this market for images and texts of erotic interest and also to the literature that sought to subject it to scientific knowledge. His work features prominently in one of the many publications that blurred the distinction between these genres, the *Bilder-Lexikon der Erotik*.[47] (Christian Schad, Heinrich Zille, and George Grosz are also well represented.) In the second volume, on literature and art, he is presented as an artist in his own right who makes objects of cultural value from a social-critical stance; a tendency to represent shoes and legs is mentioned. But the account is held carefully within the discourse of

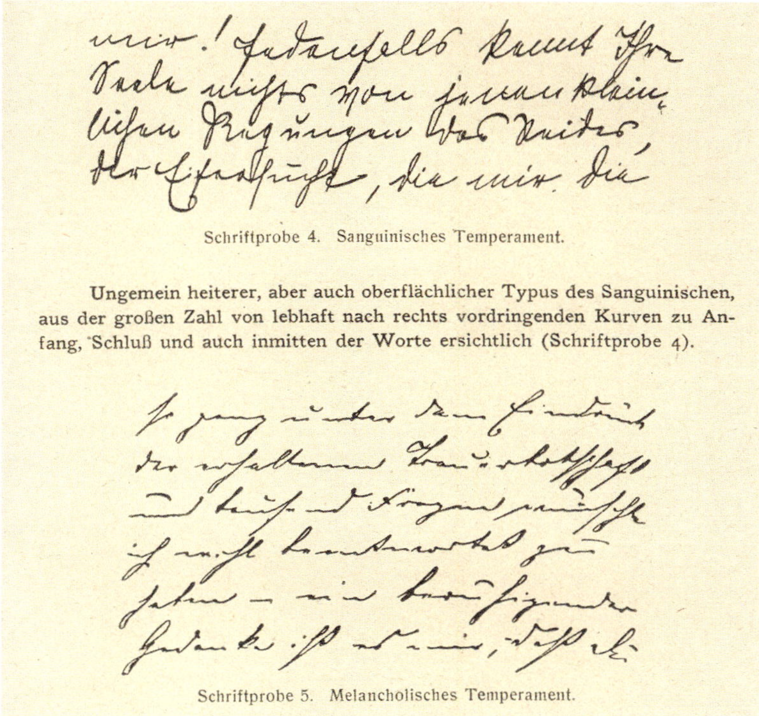

Schriftprobe 4. Sanguinisches Temperament.

Ungemein heiterer, aber auch oberflächlicher Typus des Sanguinischen, aus der großen Zahl von lebhaft nach rechts vordringenden Kurven zu Anfang, Schluß und auch inmitten der Worte ersichtlich (Schriftprobe 4).

Schriftprobe 5. Melancholisches Temperament.

"Writing sample 4: Sanguine temperament; 5: Melancholic temperament." From Erich Wulffen, *Der Sexualverbrecher* (Berlin: Langenscheidt, 1910).

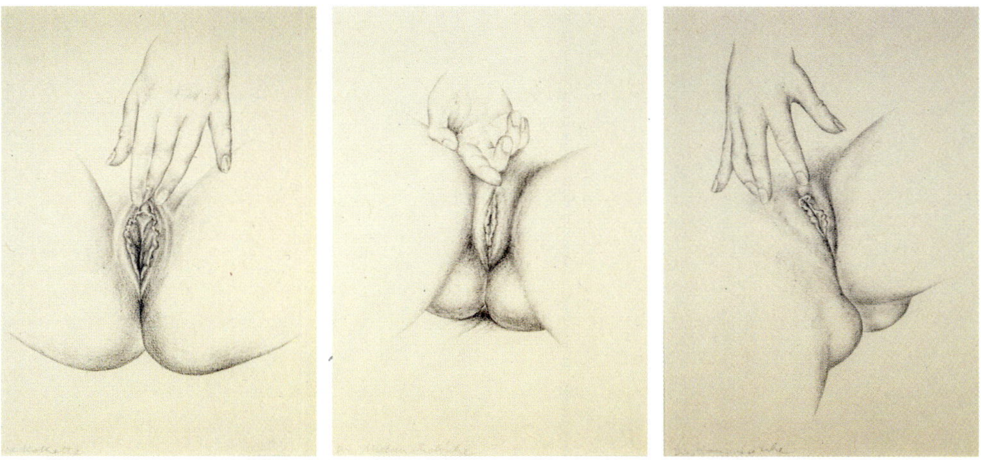

Christian Schad, from *Die fünf Temperamente* (The five humors), 1931. Left to right: *Die Kokette* (The coquette), *Die Melancholische* (The melancholic), *Die Sanguinische* (The sanguine). Lithograph crayon on paper, each 23 × 16.8 cm. The Museums of the City of Aschaffenburg. © Christian Schad Stiftung.

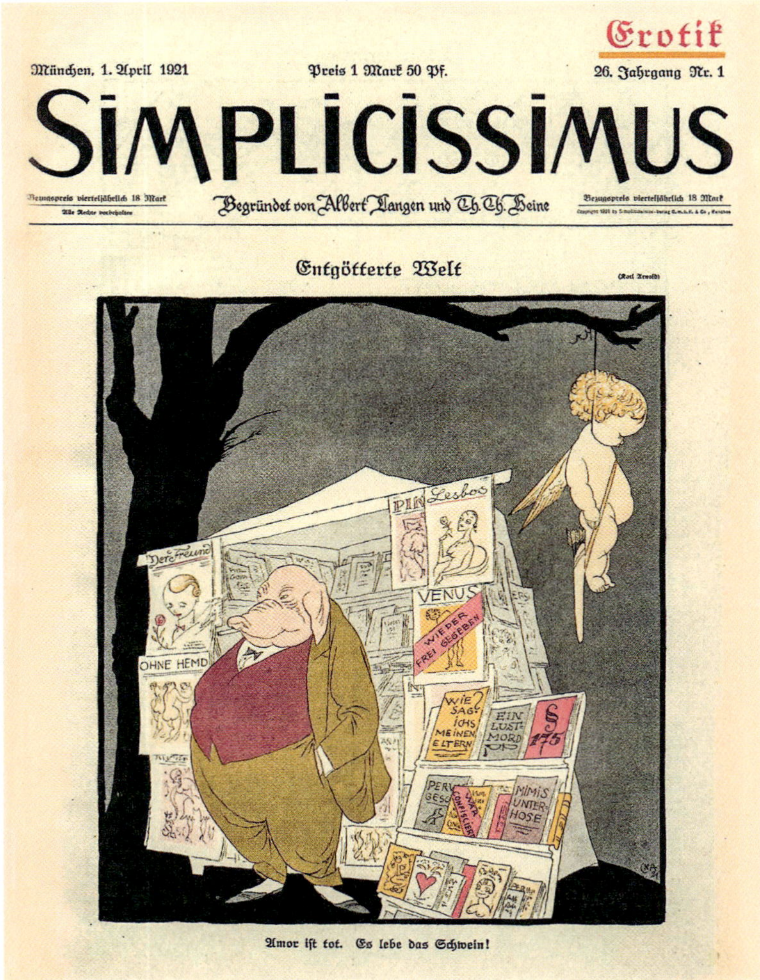

Cover of *Simplicissimus*, vol. 26, no. 1 (April 1, 1921): "A godless world. Amor is dead. Long live the pig!"

art; indeed the language replicates precisely the legal distinction between art and prurient representations: "Many of these sheets are very strongly erotic, but they are neutralized by the artistic seriousness of the depiction."[48] Three of his works are illustrated as art: a drawn nude study (a woman shown from neck down, with button boots), a watercolor scene of *Venal Love*, and the Dada photomontage *Phänomen-Werke* of 1919/20, here titled *Unser Zeitalter* (Our age). But then his work is used to illustrate "perversion," as *evidence* of various forms of sexual deviance, proof of their existence and demonstration of their nature and variety.[49] The third volume, on *Sexualwissenschaft*, is littered with Schlichter's works used in this way. The entry for "Domina" is illustrated by *Domina mea*;[50] the entry on "Fetishism" shows a photograph of Speedy as "Puss in Boots," with the added information that it shows the "wife of the painter R. Schlichter."[51] The entry on "*Hinrichtungsamateure*" (amateurs of execution) is illustrated with an uncredited Schlichter drawing of two women and one man suspended from makeshift nooses in a bare room,[52] while the lengthy article on *Lustmord*, with many photographs from Wulffen's *Der Sexualverbrecher*, shows one of Schlichter's drawings of the subject (indeed one from the confiscated and destroyed *Jack der Aufschlitzer*, now given a new lease of public life in a scientific publication).[53] "*Rétifismus*," another term for shoe fetishism, is illustrated by a full-page watercolor of Speedy, dressed as in *Domina mea*; it is titled *Der Knöpfelstiefel* and captioned "watercolor by Rudolf Schlichter, with an emphatically shoe-fetishistic tendency."[54] The long entry for "Strangulation" is illustrated by two images of Speedy: an oil painting of the artist's wife as corpse called *Tod im Walde* (Death in the woods) and a drawing with the title *Das erhängte Mädchen* (The hanged girl). Both captions note the "fetishistic tendency."[55] In the final supplementary volume, the neat distinction between art and science breaks down. "Foot and shoe fetishism" is illustrated by Grosz's 1929 drawing, here titled "The foot fetishist as painter";[56] the supplement to "Masochism" shows a Schlichter watercolor of the artist kneeling before Speedy in high boots;[57] the supplementary entry on Schlichter, again by Curt Moreck, repeats this image and adds another brothel scene and two brothel images of women with whips.[58] Finally, one of the photographs of Speedy hanging from a noose illustrates the addition to "Strangulation"; it is uncredited and captioned only "Original photograph showing a rare case of strangulation fetishism."[59]

In other words, Schlichter had the sort of distance from his own subject matter and his own professional tools to manage the identity, or the reputation, that he had gained. This is less a cultural logic than a commercial strategy for placing works in a wide array of venues and receiving fees for different, and often contradictory, uses of the images. He was called upon to show the cultural as well as clinical versions of deviance, and he was happy to do so. Schlichter had a living to make, and found that his works could fit into many of the genres, themselves promiscuously mixed, in which sexuality was discussed, whether for the production of knowledge or pleasure, of discipline or self. The result was that Schlichter was able to assert his position profitably as both subject and object of the discourses of sex.

§

There were, however, cases that Schlichter could not control. These arose when the institutions of criminal justice and state security took an interest in his work, a not infrequent occurrence. In the last chapter we saw how Schlichter's *Lustmord* images led to his conviction for publishing works that were deemed obscene. In 1929, in a special issue of the journal *Die neue Bücherschau* on the topic, Schlichter was asked to reflect upon his experiences with censorship.

> In the ten years of the Republic I have been "censored" five times. The first time on the occasion of the Dada exhibition in 1920, because my figure of a Reichswehr officer supposedly insulted the army. That cost two hundred marks. The second time in 1921, when my drawing *The Mother* was confiscated. The third time in 1924, when my drawings for *Jack der Aufschlitzer* were banned and I was given a punishment of two hundred marks for "production of obscene works." The fourth time, one of my drawings apparently insulted Herr Reichspräsident Ebert. The fifth time, my drawing *Filmkarriere* (Film career) was the object of offence and led to a trial. The state prosecutor, it seems, has just lodged an appeal against my recent acquittal. Beyond this, I note in passing, a good dozen of my political drawings have been confiscated and I have myself been threatened, more than once, with the statutes against high treason and other treasonous activities. That's old news.[60]

Schlichter mentions his obscenity conviction for his violent and sexually explicit work, and also his and John Heartfield's trial for insulting the military for their *Preußischer Erzengel* (Prussian archangel), a life-size, stuffed soldier's uniform with a pig's head suspended from the ceiling at the First International Dada Fair of

1920.[61] But we also see that Schlichter ran into trouble with the law over his political activities.

Between 1919 and 1928, Schlichter lived a precarious existence in the petty-criminal underworld and the political underground of Berlin. He was active in various Communist endeavors and devoted his life as much to this cause as to his artistic career. He was an early member of the Arbeitsrat für Kunst and the Novembergruppe, but was more directly involved in political agitation than other artists. Along with John Heartfield and George Grosz, he founded the Rote Gruppe (Red group) of Communist artists in 1924, and he joined the more official Communist Party artists' group ASSO when it was founded in 1928.[62] In addition to exhibiting his works, he was active as an illustrator and published political drawings in journals such as the *Arbeiter-Illustrierte-Zeitung (AIZ)*, *Der Knüppel*, *Die Rote Fahne*, and *Der Gegner* as well as in other Party publications.

We have very little information about his life at the time, as so many of his activities were clandestine and he did not go on to write the third volume of his autobiography, which would have covered the period after 1914. But an outline of what he planned to write survives, and a section he titled "Underworld," with its kaleidoscopic account of the early Weimar *bohème*, is worth reproducing at length:

> My brother Max ... Karl [*sic*] Einstein, George Großz [*sic*], Heartfield, [the Karlsruhe painter] Julius Kasper, [the prostitute] Jenny, the studio, Motzstraße, cocaine clubs, Tauentzien[straße], cocaine, Dr. [Wilhelm] Fränger, Kasper's world ... wandering at night, Kasper goes mad, 3 days of ranting, I visit the studio, Jenny is saved, Kasper goes into the Charité [hospital]. I take over the studio, become an active Communist. First meetings, disillusionment, the narrow-mindedness of the revolutionaries, Dada ... gay clubs [*schwule Dielen*], lesbian bars, dance lessons, fraud ... all sorts of girls and dolls, masks and weasels, Franz Jung, going underground [*Illegalität*], Kapp-Putsch, 1921 March Rebellion, [the Communist bandit] Karl Plättner ... the other expropriations, attacks, the police, home is searched, the hidden rifle ... the money in the oven, speeches about dictatorship, Ukrainian gypsies, the Communist

> mother from Magdeburg, [the Communist and syndicalist revolutionary] August Merges, his theories ... Otto Burchardt [*sic*], art dealer for Dada, the Dada Fair, first trial for insulting the Reichswehr, conviction ... Dada triumphs, Raoul Hausmann, Walter Mehring, Baader, Hülsenbeck, Wieland Herzfelde ... the Dutch anarchist Leo Lobeskordoze ... we make counterfeit money, Max Pulver ... Toppkeller ... cocaine, Cocaine-Ralph, Harry the crook, robbery at the Hotel Exzelsior, home searched, IAH [Internationale Arbeiter-Hilfe]. I become the fall-guy for Valeriu Marku [*recte*: Marcu, friend of Lenin and Trotsky], *Chronik des Faschismus*, theft at Cocaine-Ralph's, again counterfeiting ...[63]

Even without the details, we get a sense of Schlichter's life and work at the time. Like his frequent models Margot and Jenny, the latter mentioned in the outline, his partners during these years were sex workers, and he frequented the locales of the sexual minorities.[64] Drugs and petty crime were part of the milieu; Dada too. But most revealing are the terse references to his political activities and connections. We read that he was involved in the *Märzaktion*, the armed Central German workers' uprising in 1921 that centered on Halle and Leuna and met a bloody end. He was apparently close to Karl Plättner, who, along with Max Hoelz, led a series of armed robberies to finance these activities; indeed, he hid Plättner and his accomplices in his studio when they were the object of a police manhunt.[65] Franz Jung was involved in the *Märzaktion* too, and apparently he figured in Schlichter's world as well. We read of his connections to the IAH (Internationale Arbeiter-Hilfe; International workers' aid), the organization Willi Münzenberg founded to support the Soviet Union abroad and the core of a publishing empire that was behind the *AIZ*, in which most of John Heartfield's works appeared. "Fall-guy for Valeriu Marcu": Schlichter's word is *Sitzredakteur*. This referred to the practice of listing someone as responsible editor—and thus legally accountable—in order to protect those really calling the shots from the frequent prison sentences imposed on editors of the radical press.[66] Was Marcu really behind the short-lived journal *Chronik des Faschismus*, for which Schlichter was listed as editor?[67] So it seems.[68] Schlichter was, in any case, deeply involved in illegal radical activities.

"Threatened, more than once," writes Schlichter, "with the statues against high treason and other treasonous activities."

We have evidence of two such cases, and the episodes happened concurrently.

The pursuit of Schlichter for political crimes took place first at the behest of the Ministry of the Interior. In 1920, the ministry had set up a "Reichskommissariat für Überwachung der öffentlichen Ordnung und Nachrichtensammelstelle" (Reich commission for monitoring public order and intelligence office) to inform the government of threats to the Republic from the left and right.[69] A report from 1924 shows that they were already exercised about the Rote Gruppe; Schlichter was named in the report and thus came under their watchful eye.[70] Within six months, the Reichskommissariat had gathered more information and decided that Schlichter was worth pursuing, less for his artistic work than for other activities. The Reichskommissar wrote to Section IA of the Berlin police, the so-called "political section," "Re: the Communist Rudolf Schlichter":

> I have been confidentially informed of the activities of the painter and engraver Rudolf Schlichter ... Schlichter ... has long played a role in the Communist movement. He was editor of the journal *Chronik des Faschismus* as well as, last year, director of an exhibition of artworks by George Grosz that was organized by the Malik-Verlag. Schlichter belongs to the so-called Rote Gruppe ... I have been informed that Schlichter stands in close and direct contact with Russian Communists and is engaged in the production of stamps for identity documents and passports, as required by the Russian agitators.[71]

A month later, the head of the Berlin political police, Ernst Wündisch, wrote back that Schlichter was indeed well known to them but that there was no sign that he was counterfeiting official stamps. "A discreet search of his studio is not possible," wrote Wündisch, and in his opinion the Reichskommissar's information was not sufficient to obtain a search warrant.[72] Nonetheless, the Reich state prosecutor approved the opening of an investigation into "preparation of high treason," and Schlichter was entered into the "high treason list" (*Hochverratsliste*).[73] The investigation continued for two years; finally, the Reichsgericht—part of the Justice Ministry—decided in April 1927 that the case should be closed "for lack of evidence."[74] A close call indeed—especially as Schlichter wrote in the outline for the third volume of his memoirs that he was in fact repeatedly involved in counterfeiting.

Schlichter's second brush with the law has left a slightly longer paper trail. This time the Justice Ministry opened the investigation for preparation of high treason through the investigating magistrate of the State Court for the Defense of the Republic, and they thought they had the evidence they needed.[75] At issue were political cartoons published in the *AIZ* and in short-lived periodicals aimed at influencing particular groups (here lower-level law enforcement officials) at the end of 1925; these were seen to be directly inciting action against the state. The question concerned Schlichter's authorship, and the ministry sent the police samples of Schlichter's work for comparison. The police reported back that they had searched the premises of the Neuer Deutscher Verlag and Schlichter's studio on December 4, 1925.[76] We know nothing of the details of this latter search, but

> In the Neuer Deutscher Verlag, the director, Willy [*sic*] Münzenberg, declared that he had given the contract for printing the September issue of the *Arbeiter-Illustrierte* to the Firm Selle & Co. ... The material sent to them included the drawing appearing on page 15 of the aforementioned journal ... [Münzenberg said that] the drawing had been prepared by a draughtsman whose name he cannot recall. He said it was not Schlichter.[77]

The police continued to pursue the matter, identifying a number of drawings that were punishable and that they suspected Schlichter of producing. What follows is connoisseurial comedy, though it involved at least two interrogations of the artist. The police enlisted an expert, the Berlin illustrator Fritz Koch-Gotha, who identified a large number of the questionable drawings as Schlichter's work. On August 16, 1926, Schlichter was called to the police and questioned; the verbatim record shows that he identified precisely those he had created and those—most of them—that he claimed not to have produced; he also pointed to aspects of the drawings that showed that his own style might have been imitated, but poorly.[78] Koch-Gotha was then brought in to cross-examine Schlichter; after Schlichter's departure, he declared himself unconvinced. As a way out of the stalemate, the police sought another expert. The prominent artist Emil Orlik declined the request, but they found Dr. Wilhelm [Willy] Kurth, from 1924 curator of the State Museum Print Room, willing. In his opinion, only one drawing was demonstrably by Schlichter, and it was one of the comparative samples.[79]

Though he was brought before the Reichsgericht tribunal in Leipzig,[80] the Chief State Prosecutor dropped the case for lack of evidence on April 9, 1927.[81] It is instructive to see how the wheels of Weimar justice turned, and also how Schlichter was well known to the police and other authorities as one of the usual suspects. Unfortunately the visual material is missing from the Justice Ministry's files, so we cannot compare the images ourselves. But it is interesting to read perhaps the first of Schlichter's longer autobiographical statements—he wrote many—from a minuted interrogation before the investigating magistrate of the Reichsgericht in Berlin on September 29, 1926.[82] The account of his youth tallies with his later autobiographies. His account of time in the military, however, differs from the one he gave after the Second World War in the American military government's questionnaire. There he claimed to have been discharged from the army due to a hunger strike;[83] in 1926 he recounts that he was sent back from the front to duty in Germany because of a heart ailment and goiter. His statements about the specific works reiterate the points from the first interrogation, but there are some interesting details about his political activities:

> Since 1919, with short interruptions, I have been a member of the Communist Party [KPD]; for a while, in 1921, I was a member of the Communist Workers' Party [KAPD]. I do not belong to any specific organization within the party, nor do I belong to the [paramilitary] Roter Frontkämpferbund [Alliance of red front-fighters]; I hold no party office.[84]

By his own admission, Schlichter was a member of the KAPD, which split from the KPD and advocated immediate and direct revolutionary action—the Central German revolt, the spectacular robberies ("expropriations") of Max Hoelz and Karl Plättner, the party of Franz Jung in the early 1920s. His assertion that he belonged to no "specific organization" within the KPD no doubt shows the Rote Gruppe's distance from the party bureaucracy; the ASSO had yet to be founded.

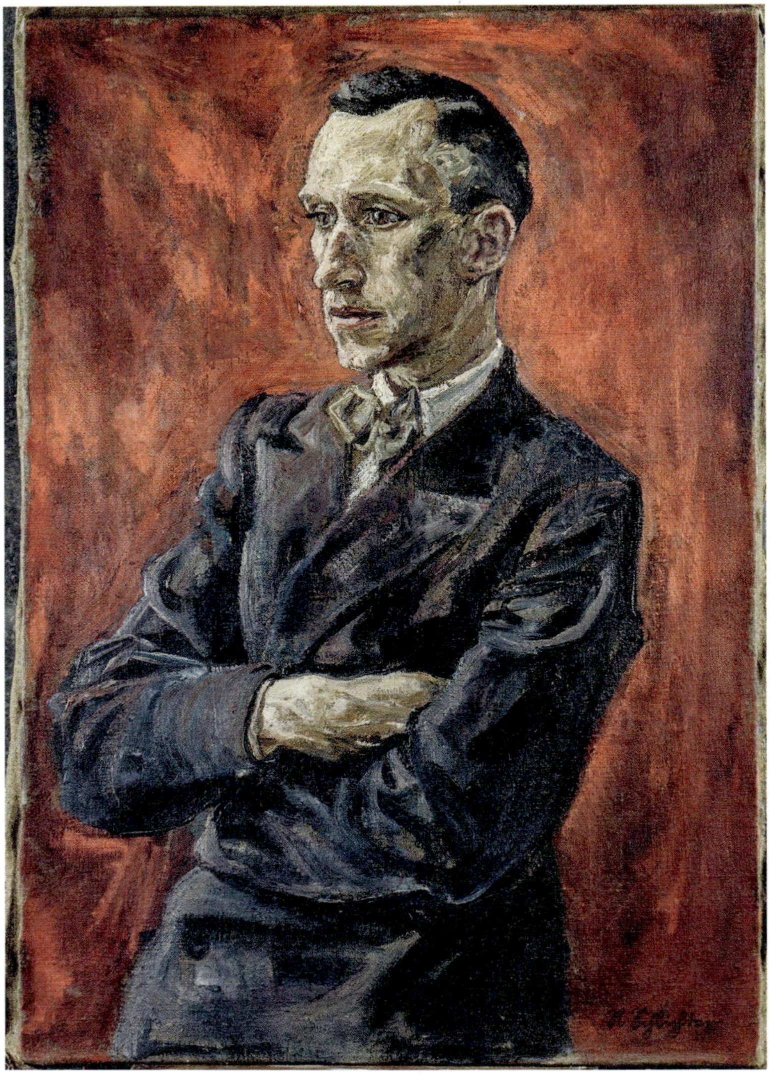

Rudolf Schlichter, *Ernst Jünger*, ca. 1929. Oil on canvas, 94 × 64 cm. Berlin, Nationalgalerie. Photo © bpk/Nationalgalerie, SMB/Bernd Kuhnert. © Viola Roehr v. Alvensleben, München.

§

Schlichter's life, politics, and relation to his own sexuality were transformed by his encounter with Speedy, her acceptance of his predilections, and their subsequent marriage. He broke completely with the Communist Party and life underground, also with his underworld circle of friends. He embraced Catholicism and nationalism, specifically the National Bolshevism of Ernst Niekisch, Ernst Jünger, and Ernst von Salomon; he developed a close relationship with the last two in particular while maintaining his friendships with figures of the left such as Bertolt Brecht and the Marxist economist and sociologist Fritz Sternberg.[85] Indeed, Schlichter served as a conduit, introducing Jünger, Salomon, and Arnolt Bronnen on the right to Brecht, Sternberg, and George Grosz on the left.[86] (Perhaps it was Ernst Rowohlt, who printed the works of Walter Benjamin, Salomon, Bronnen, and later Schlichter, who brought them together.[87]) Schlichter designed the cover for Jünger's 1930 book *Krieg und Krieger* (to which Benjamin devoted an important and devastating review).[88] In a letter of the time, we get a sense of the way Schlichter was thinking:

> I'm keeping close company with the so-called "New Nationalists," particularly Ernst Jünger, whom I have painted; they are surprisingly decent people. I've never encountered on the left the sort of unambiguous candor I find here. *With the exception of the KPD workers, but not with the half-left-leaning intellectual shits* (*Intellekscheißern*).[89]

When Brecht tried to convince Schlichter that everything he heard in this circle was "Scheiße," the artist apparently replied "Yes, but I like this *German* Scheiße."[90]

In 1932, Schlichter and Speedy turned their backs on Berlin and moved to Rottenburg am Neckar, in Swabia; they moved again to Stuttgart in 1936. Schlichter began an intense engagement with landscape painting. His lifestyle, however, remained unconventional: he reported that his marriage with Speedy was a *Josefsehe*, or a celibate marriage. Perhaps masochistically, he tolerated her relationships with other men, and he continued to pursue his own sorts of satisfaction.[91] But the conservative turn and the rejection of his past on the left was real and permanent. He continued to produce and publish works of an erotic and fetishistic nature for a time, but these became rare. This was also the context in which his autobiographical writings—*Zwischenwelt*, *Das widerspenstige Fleisch* and *Törnerne Füße*—were drafted.

Thus Schlichter's *literary* accounts of his tortured sexuality were, in fact, a product of his conservative turn. He is explicit that they should be read allegorically, as a reflection of a godless

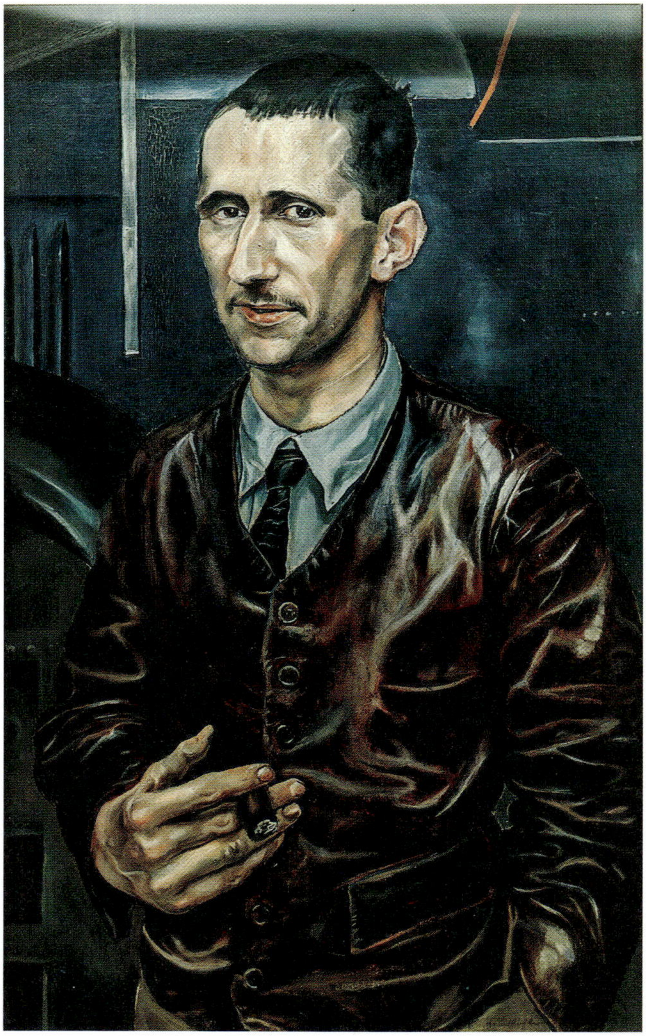

Rudolf Schlichter, *Bert Brecht*, 1926. Oil on canvas, 75.5 × 46 cm. Städtische Galerie im Lenbachhaus, Munich. Photo © akg-images. © Viola Roehr v. Alvensleben, München.

world and godless politics; he took himself and his privations to be emblematic for, and a case study of, everything that was wrong with Germany at the time. Once again, he took a position exterior to his own desires, now not so much for professional reasons as for ideological ones, projecting his "perversion" outward as a symbol of an epoch that had lost its way (and that could find it

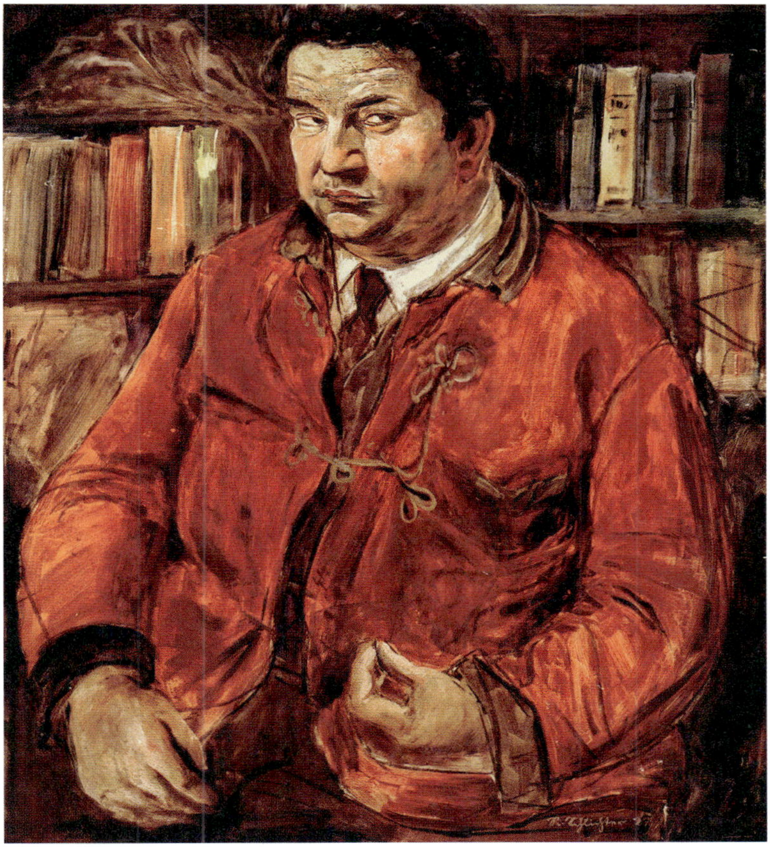

Rudolf Schlichter, *Dr. Sternberg*, 1927. Oil on canvas, 91 × 75 cm. Private collection. Photo © akg-images. © Viola Roehr v. Alvensleben, München.

again in the nation and the Church). He introduces *Das widerspenstige Fleisch* with a note clarifying his purposes:

> This book and its continuation are meant not as a folkloric novel, nor a psychoanalytic, sociological, psychological one, nor as an *Entwicklungsroman* in the sense of German literature ...
>
> This book is a settling of accounts, a damnation (*Vernichtung*) of the epoch portrayed, and this sublates the private existence it recounts. It indicates the path out of the swamp of human errors and excesses, emancipated ideas,

> opinions, and worldviews that have moved this era so deeply, and toward true insight (*Erkenntnis*) into absolute truth.[92]

Now this is, perhaps, not terribly satisfying. But though we certainly need to reconsider Schlichter's motives for laying bare his dark desires, it does not alter the careful construction of a "deviant" sexuality in public—which was after all carried out, before the literary works, primarily by his pictures. In fact, it is only one in a series of ways in which he distanced himself from his own sexuality and deployed it for purposes of various kinds. And this consistent and systematic public exteriorization of sexuality raises the question of the politics of this changing and developing project beyond the explicit political purposes to which it was put after Schlichter's "turn." Schlichter was, after all, always a political animal, and though his positions shifted, he always pursued the sublation of the private in the public form of the case.

What, then, were Schlichter's politics of the case? There was, in fact, a certain party-political context to Schlichter's affiliations and habitus in his Communist years. His outline of the projected third volume of his autobiography puts him in the "gay clubs, lesbian bars" with "all sorts of girls and dolls." And beyond the venues of specific sexual minorities, these were also the places at the center of left-leaning sexual reform, written about by the likes of Magnus Hirschfeld and Curt Moreck.[93] Indeed, Magnus Hirschfeld, though not a Communist, was close to the KPD; and Willi Münzenberg, in whose orbit Schlichter worked, lived for many years in an annex to Hirschfeld's *Institut für Sexualwissenschaft*.[94] In a published satirical drawing, Schlichter depicted Hirschfeld and his circle in a gently mocking way: sitting in a park surrounded by amorous heterosexual couples, Schlichter has Hirschfeld tell his minions "Gentlemen—in spring such regressions nonetheless still occur spontaneously in nature."[95] Karl Plättner too, the Communist bandit whom Schlichter hid in his apartment, moved his left politics in this direction after his imprisonment, embracing the politics of sexual reform in prisons with his book *Eros im Zuchthaus*, published with a photomontage cover by John Heartfield.[96]

But two passages from Schlichter's voluminous writings help us grasp the stakes behind Schlichter's negotiation of his own subjectivity by means of the literature on sex. The first is from

Törnene Füße, and it recounts an encounter he had, at the age of about twenty, with a boy of twelve in Italy:

> And for the first time I had the exhilarating experience of having my affections tenderly reciprocated. The unaccustomed naturalness with which he accepted my caresses, the utter unselfconsciousness in all of his emotions and his words were liberating. How pleasant it was to finally see a boy who showed no trace of the unhealthy repression through which the young soul is tamed north of the Alps. ... The Eros of this young boy had not been beaten out of an abused body nor drummed out of the mind by the dismal lessons of proper, healthy behavior.[97]

The second is the beginning of a poem of 1931 titled *Tabu* (Taboo):

> Over me as a silent threat
> Stands the law forbidding my desires
> For I, yielding to the overpowering greed
> Seek, wickedly, the revelation and submission to the secret.
> The deafening silence never drowned out
> The colorful, ringing bells of discharged lust.[98]

We recognize these texts as examples of a very specific genre: they echo the accounts of both self-discovery and self-reproach of the subject of socially unaccepted sexual desire in the form of popular kitsch.[99] In the sexual subcultural press of the time, one finds these in their thousands. But what is striking about them in the context of Schlichter's work is how utterly rare they are, how foreign these passages are to the cool analysis in *Das widerspenstige Fleisch* and *Tönerne Füße* or to the demonic exaggeration of *Zwischenwelt.* Such texts are utterly exceptional for Schlichter, while they were the very medial vehicles of identification and emancipation for important sexual minorities of the time.

In their rarity, their status as exceptional, these passages make something clear about any potential sexual politics for Schlichter. Despite these two slips when he approached the contemporary discourse of sexual emancipation, his was *not* the project of what has come to be called "sexual citizenship."[100] He kept his distance from sexual reform—not engaging closely with it when he moved in its orbit, and rejecting it completely after he left it. He was harsh, in retrospect, to Karl Plättner, writing an extraordinarily unflattering portrait of him as "Karl, der Terrorist" (Karl the terrorist).[101] He never explicitly took up the left-leaning reformers' offer of acceptance, nor did he actively fight for tolerance. He always rejected the label of the "transvestite," and rarely used the term "fetishism" to describe his erotic investment in women's shoes. Nowhere did he intervene in the space of public representations with the purposes of finding or establishing a community in the way that many autobiographies or articles in the sexual subcultural press did. That was one kind of work that was carried out with the representation of non-normative sexualities in the public sphere, but it did not interest Schlichter. In his contributions to publications such as the *Bilder-Lexikon der Erotik*, he was happy enough to serve such projects, but they were not his own. His politics was not an identity politics.

Schlichter refuses the inclusion offered by the scientific literature on sex and, more importantly, in the popular books and periodical literature of sexual minorities. He rejected both the disciplinary aspects of sexual science, even as he rehearsed its texts; and he rejected the identificatory ones as well, the community such texts generated even as they contributed to classification. He makes his desires unassimilable: he stresses the degraded, the humiliating, the repugnant, the unacceptable face of non-normative sexuality. He is not the misunderstood homosexual nor the transvestite who wants only to live according to his wishes in a non-judgmental environment; instead he fashions himself as the *Lustmörder*, the fetishist in his most unappealingly compulsive form, the masturbator (and in *Zwischenwelt*, the nose-picker and the farter for good measure).[102] *Lustmord* was the pathological limit of sexual desire, and one that could never shake off the label of deviance, the repugnance and disgust of the reader or viewer looking for real signs of identity and desire. And yet the *Lustmörder* was the vanishing point of his account of self.

In Schlichter's work, we see a strange and radical strategy of negation. He turns himself into cases, he inhabits them—the sexual deviant, the Communist, the "German"—but ultimately refuses identification or integration. (Even when embracing the "German," it was still German "Scheiße.") This is unusual in the media and genres of the case. He rejects both the tendency toward discipline and classification, and also the reverse use of such discourses to ground stable narratives of personhood. It is a profoundly negative, disruptive, undermining use of the case, and it lends his oeuvre both its fascination and its deeply unsatisfying quality. His is not the constant reinscription of the madman within the media of madness, nor the happy discovery of sexuality as an identity, nor a clear and consistent politics. He uses the public media of psychiatry and sex precisely to explode these possibilities; even if they offered belonging, they seemed to have represented coercion. The confusion is that there is always an identity at play, but he uses each one to undermine another. Perhaps it is a freedom of negation, one that he establishes by engaging with, and not just rejecting, the space of the representable. In accepting the space of the representable as the space of subjectivities, he seems to show these as unstable, illogical, and unassimilable. He is more interested in the entropic effects of representation, the identity-shattering energy of the public sphere. In inhabiting and personifying cases of sexual and political subversion, he at once establishes identities, rejects them, and is pursued for them. As a compulsive negotiation of subjectivity in public, it offers a compelling analysis of the possibilities of self by rejecting the happier projects of inclusion and identification that were also taking place there.

But whatever his project was, it took place through the media and genres of the case. He shows the inscription in an individual of the shifting criteria of classifications and control; he showed how a life could be lived in and through the space of public representations; and he maintained a tenuous and chaotic control over it. The private, as he wrote, was meaningless unless it was "sublated." And thus if there is anything positive about Schlichter's politics of the case, it is in the potential of the case to be public. His overwhelming instinct was what Maximilian Harden called the "*Flucht in die Öffentlichkeit*"—the rush to the public sphere, the demand for a voice, the risky exposure of self that nonetheless seized the possibility of agency.[103] Schlichter grasped at the form of the case, at the open spaces between the discourses and institutions in which cases were unstably constituted when put in the unruly realm of public representations.

§

Of course, Schlichter's project came at a cost, or would remain productive only in a constant evolution that would ultimately be less a case of negative dialectics than a lesson in bad infinity. His turn to nationalism and faith marked a move away from a series of shifting and unstable assimilations to the forms of the deviant or the illegal, and ultimately to a pathologizing position toward them. From borrowing disciplinary classifications from politics, sex, and crime as unstable subject positions in the complex public field of German culture, he then adopted their exclusionary and minoritizing logic.

The institutions of social control in the Third Reich, however, had little time for such subtleties; they simply could not follow the logic by which Schlichter exteriorized his carefully constructed pathology and turned it into an allegory of a society that he (and indeed they) rejected. In July 1933, the Kampfbund für Deutsche Kultur found *Das widerspenstige Fleisch* to be a "perverse-erotic self-portrait" and placed it on its blacklist for libraries.[104] At about the same time, Schlichter published a drawing titled *Goliath verhöhnt das Volk Israel* (Goliath taunts the people of Israel), which, as Goliath would shortly be slain by David, was misinterpreted as a criticism of the new state; he was temporarily excluded from the Reichskammer für Bildende Künste. On September 10, 1935, he received notice of his exclusion from the Reichsverband deutscher Schriftsteller and the Reichsschrifttumskammer: "*Das widerspenstige Fleisch* and *Törnene Füße* show that he is unreliable and unsuited for the production of German cultural goods."[105] (Intriguingly, the Kulturkammer's file on Schlichter indicates that he might have come to their attention because he had written to the president of the Reichsschrifttumskammer complaining that though he had paid his membership fees and continued to receive bills, he had not received his membership card or lapel pin with the insignia of the Reichsverband.[106]) Schlichter was then imprisoned for three months in 1938; apparently his unusual domestic arrangements had led to a denunciation. At this time, the Reichskammer für Bildende Künste learned of his removal from the writers' organization and excluded him as well. Goebbels, however, approved his reinstatement in the art section "because Schlichter is a gifted painter and displays an artistically unobjectionable stance."[107] The support of Ernst Jünger seems to have been important in obtaining Schlichter's release and permission to continue his artistic work.

§

The research on Schlichter brings us into contact with the media of the case: the police files with their bureaucratic messages instigating and closing investigations, progress reports, signed statements, and transcripts of questioning, the affidavits and court decisions. The archival traces of his professional life in the National Socialist state, however, reveal a relatively new form of gathering information and maintaining control: the questionnaire. This represents a curious flattening of the life that earlier came under scrutiny only in the context of medical or court cases, with their slow and careful attention to specific episodes, their clearly focused questions, their scrupulous separation of competences between the different ministries or medical specializations, prosecutors' offices, police departments, and so on. Though they must have been trying, Schlichter's early encounters with the law went by the book: procedures were followed and the nets of control were largely separate and stayed in their own areas of authority and jurisdiction.

The new form was binary. It sought not to determine if a law had been broken but rather to summarize a life so that yes/no decisions could be made. They were, in that sense, crude. They were meant to establish political credentials and ensure compliance with appropriate institutions. Those who did not do so were simply excluded from the professional and the public sphere. The questionnaire tended toward a simpler form of decision-making in line with the more centralized control of the subject in a totalitarian state. These papers were checked by central authorities who could fairly quickly join up the dots of different offices and authorities. They turned everyone into a bureaucratic and a political case. But they offered a way out: they relied more on the subject's interpretation of the questions than the widely ramified professional knowledges and powers of the legal organs of social control of the *Rechtsstaat*, the constitutional state under the rule of law that the Weimar Republic represented (as did the preceding Kaiserreich).[108] Thus they also opened up ample room for dissimulation.

Two of the questionnaires filled out by Schlichter are notable. One is for his acceptance into the Reichsverband Deutscher Schriftsteller, in which membership was compulsory until it was absorbed into the Reichsschrifttumskammer.[109] When this happened, we saw, authorities shared their information and found he was the author of works not considered "unobjectionable."

The questionnaire shows why it might have taken two years for this to happen (and indeed might not have happened at all had Schlichter not worried about his membership card and lapel pin). Schlichter's answers to two of the questions give pause. First, to the question asking "Who published your books (only for authors of books)," Schlichter lists only the respected Ernst Rowohlt Verlag, publisher of *Das widerspenstige Fleisch* and *Törnerne Füße*, but also of works by figures of the Conservative Revolution. He omitted the Ernst Pollak Verlag, publisher of *Zwischenwelt*—whether because of the more extreme nature of that book or the *ostjüdisch*-sounding name of the press is unknown. And second, to the question of "Previous political affiliations" (after the question of membership in the NSDAP, to which Schlichter did not belong), he wrote, simply and astonishingly, "none."

The second is the notorious American Military Government "Fragebogen," which Schlichter was required to submit as he and Speedy then lived in Munich.[110] This questionnaire was better designed and more complete. Now, however, Schlichter writes of almost all of his cases in order to present himself as a victim of the regime and earlier forces of the right. He denies all involvement in the First World War, writing that he was dismissed from the army after a hunger strike. (In his interrogation over the political drawings, of course, he had spoken of having been sent back from the front with heart trouble and goiter). He writes of his conviction for insulting the military with George Grosz ("now in America"), his pursuit for treasonous activities (which he now defines as "anti-militaristic agitation" and not a call for revolution). And he does not deny the conviction for his illustrations for the "parodic-bawdy verses of Althaus." We learn that his troubles with the authorities in 1938 were for "procuring," presumably for his wife, and "un-National-Socialist lifestyle (*unnationalsozialistische Lebensführung*)." "This," he wrote, "came at the time of the synagogue fires and the series of prosecutions of monastics and lay Catholics under the pretense of immorality. How could I have imagined that I would be charged with such an offence!" And he cites the warnings he had received from Alexander Mitscherlich, of the circle around Ernst Jünger, "who had [at the time] just been released from detention" and now worked for the Department of Health in Rhein-Hessen. Schlichter suffered no sanctions under the Military Government.

The cultural space of the case, so central to Schlichter's career and his life, had become constricted with the disappearance of the state under the rule of law, but after the war, he began to reassert some control. After a new period in the public eye—he published criticism and exhibited his artistic work extensively—Schlichter died in 1955.

5 *Paper, Scissors, Photograph: Bertolt Brecht and the Culture of the Case*

Bertolt Brecht was fascinated by court cases. Legal proceedings of various kinds appear in many of his works—in *Mahagonny* (1930), *Die Maßnahme* (The measures taken, 1930), the film *Kuhle Wampe* (1932), and others. Sergei Tretyakov described him as "obsessed with goings-on at court" and "a skilled and cunning casuist."[1] "In 1932, when Brecht was in Moscow," Tretyakov recounts further,

> he told me of his idea of establishing in Berlin a sort of panopticon-theatre, where he would stage the most interesting trials from the history of mankind. "The theatre must be set up like a courtroom. Two trials every evening, an hour and a quarter each. For example the trial of Socrates. Or a witch trial. The trial against Karl Marx's *Neue Rheinische Zeitung*. George Grosz's blasphemy trial for his caricature *Christ with a Gas Mask*."[2]

We know that artists and writers often had to defend themselves before a court of law—for blasphemy (like Grosz and Carl Einstein), or for obscenity (Grosz, Schlichter, and others). And also, like Marx, for political reasons. The Weimar years saw several trials for the new offence of "literary high treason": as we have seen in chapter 3, Johannes R. Becher's recently published political novel *Levisite* was confiscated by authorities in Berlin and the author charged with this crime in 1926. It was a serious matter until the charges were dropped two years later, but there was a lighter side. Walter Benjamin reported to Siegfried Kracauer in a letter as follows:

> I recently participated in a quite curious private event. The members of the *Schriftstellergruppe 1925* convened a meeting in which Becher's recent book *Levisite* was debated in the form of a court proceeding, with [Alfred] Döblin prosecuting and [Egon Erwin] Kisch as counsel for the defence.[3]

Benjamin tells us no more, but fortunately minutes of the proceedings were taken and circulated to the group. Brecht, it turns out, served as chief judge, with the writers Klabund (Alfred Henschke) and Rudolf Leonhard as jurors and Leonhard Frank as expert witness.[4] Becher was found innocent as he had not "abused" the form of the novel, merely "used it poorly."[5] It is a nice legalistic distinction.

All of this must be borne in mind when considering Brecht's most ambitious engagement with the law: his unsuccessful court action of 1930 against the Nero Film company, with whom he had a contract to supply the screenplay for the film of the *Threepenny Opera* to be directed by G. W. Pabst, and his essay "The *Threepenny* Lawsuit," an analysis of the proceedings.[6] Brecht had negotiated the right to "co-determination" of the final film, and did in fact write a sketch for the screenplay.[7] But he finished this late and never properly delivered it to Nero; he also rewrote the play considerably, giving it a new and sharp political edge. He even gave it a new title: *Die Beule* (The bruise).[8] Not surprisingly, the film company, facing the complete disruption of its production schedule, simply proceeded without Brecht's treatment. While the details of the case are well known, what interests me here is Brecht's claim that the legal action to assert his authorial rights was carried out not for personal gain but as a "sociological experiment," a stratagem by which he could stage a battle between artistic freedom and capital in the public forum of the court of law. The case showed, he wrote, the inevitable result: that laws protecting artists are mere ideology, and that legal contracts concerning artistic rights would, when push came to shove, be found null and void before the power of big business. Beyond discussing the legal judgment per se, Brecht explored the press coverage to show that the case generated conflicting notions in the public sphere about art, business, and capitalism more generally. Using the seemingly public realms of the courts and the press, Brecht sought to show both how these institutions failed in their task of revealing and properly regulating the relations between subjects and larger social institutions, and also how they might after all do so, even as such relations were becoming increasingly opaque.

I would like to put these examples into a larger context, one that I have been calling the "culture of the case." As we have seen, cases of many kinds in the late nineteenth and early twentieth centuries functioned as crucial sites for the public production of knowledge; and focusing on practices of the case in Germany and Austria can do much to illuminate a diverse array of artistic phenomena. In these "cases," a number of elements coalesced: legal process, often medical knowledge, and finally a fragile, volatile public sphere. This confluence has emerged as a consistent reference point for many artists of the time, the site of a set of practices that are themselves not necessarily purely visual or literary, but that nonetheless had a profound effect on how artists of different kinds negotiated their political, economic, and in fact medial contexts. The Brecht case is another literary episode, but it draws on terms from the visual arts, and the visual more generally in modernity, and it casts light on practices of montage, both avant-garde and vernacular. And again, the practices of the case are hard to grasp: they move promiscuously between genres, media, and institutions, all of which have their own histories, and they take place in varying and often incommensurate registers of the social and the cultural. These practices are not consistent or even much theorized—and here Brecht is an exception. Instead I have traced them more as instincts, gestures, even reflexes that crossed lines of discourse, style, ideology, and medium. A look at how some of these practices functioned gives us a better sense of the breadth of issues at stake in the legal action as "experiment."

§

The "*Threepenny* Lawsuit" is usually treated as a critique of the ideology of culture in advanced capitalism or as a founding text of media theory. It is here that Brecht developed his notion of the "apparatus," and it is the source of many quotable insights. One is particularly well known: "The situation has become so complicated," writes Brecht, "because the simple 'reproduction of reality' says less than ever about that reality. A photograph of the Krupp works or the AEG reveals almost nothing about these institutions. Reality as such has slipped into the domain of the functional."[9] Brecht's remarks are usually considered in terms of the necessity of montage, of the *construction* of reality.[10] The point is an important one that emerged out of his discussions with the Marxist economist Fritz Sternberg about the difficulty of *seeing* the social under capitalism.[11] But the "*Threepenny* Lawsuit" addresses another, less frequently noted issue beyond the one about vision and the problems of materialist epistemology; it concerns the relation of knowledge to the spaces of representation in modernity. For any such epistemology must also be social. Brecht later described this in his "Five Difficulties in Writing the Truth" as the necessity of "*cunning* to spread the truth amongst many."[12]

How, then, do you reveal the "functional"? What sort of "cunning" is required? The "case," I think, provides one answer. It was not only a form by which to assemble evidence and construct a context in which isolated or reified instances of modern life could reveal their logic and necessity; as such it was, in fact, quite imperfect. More importantly, the case was a site at which this could be attempted in public. Brecht's "*Threepenny* Lawsuit" needs to be seen as part of a broader and shared project of using law as a medium, of using its procedures and discourses, its authority as well as its spectacularization in the press, as a way of tangibly condensing the complex workings of the social field and bringing them before the public eye. At issue here are not so much the ostensible matters of artistic freedom and authorial control. The real concerns are matters such as the obscure technical and legal structures that might lie behind the making of a film, business practices and their human effects that he then explored in *The Threepenny Novel* (1934),[13] or the invisible social configurations of *The Threepenny Opera*. And most important: the establishment of something like a public sphere—punctual and fleeting—when the traditional spaces for reasoned discussion and debate, for the reliable establishment of consensus or public opinion, were no longer serving these purposes—if, of course, they ever did.

So: a lawsuit as a "sociological experiment." Brecht claims to have known that the case would be decided against him, but that he pursued it in order to reveal the way the institutions of the judiciary worked under conditions of late capitalism. This is hard to take at face value. Certainly victory would have set a valuable precedent for artists, and moreover have yielded substantial damages. But few people without ample funds enter the notoriously unpredictable institutions of legal justice speculatively, and those who did so were both more circumspect and more expert. He might have known his case was weak, but more likely he thought, mistakenly, that his contract was watertight. The lawsuit as experiment was almost certainly an ex post facto rationale, one that could be called upon to justify an otherwise trivial and self-serving case and to provide material for another part of what was turning into his extraordinarily productive *Threepenny* complex. The terminology also situates this in a specific phase of Brecht's interests: claiming it was an "experiment" seeks to turn the spaces of justice into a laboratory in line with his interest in behaviorist psychology and logical positivism, and implies a scientific model for the establishment of social truth.[14] But this invocation of the natural sciences might blind us to the fact that the speculative, "experimental" turn to the courts had many precedents at the time, that it was hardly novel, that it was indeed a commonplace.

Criminal trials, civil lawsuits, and their public reporting were at the center of the German-language press from the turn of the century. It was here, when something went wrong, when someone broke the law or when the law itself turned out to be broken, that matters of general concern could be drawn into public discussion, from miscarriages of justice to laws in need of reform and even to fights over political influence. But this was not Habermas's ideal type of the public sphere. The practices here involved raising the ante in often unpredictable ways, working in public with the very means of spectacle and sensation, the forms of a commodified market for news and images that represented in fact as great a threat to reasoned debate and consensus as did censorship. This culture of the case had its maestros. Maximilian Harden, editor and main author of the Berlin journal *Die Zukunft* from 1892 to 1922, was one of the greatest.[15] At times self-destructively, he drove a series of court actions to combat what he saw as the disastrous policies of Wilhelm II. He flirted with the strictures against *lèse-majesté* and faced trial in 1893, 1898, and 1900. Sometimes he could establish his claims as fact and was acquitted, other times he ended up in prison; his average was about fifty-fifty. To counter the influence of certain circles over the monarch, he maliciously exposed the homosexuality of some of the Kaiser's advisors—the so-called Eulenburg Affair.[16] Harden called such use, or abuse, of the press and courts his "*Flucht in die Öffentlichkeit*," the risky, go-for-broke flight to the public stage.[17] It could go wrong and often did, but it opened up a different sort of maneuvering room in the tactics of any cause. He even developed his own literary form for this kind of *forensis* as a key to political or historical life. The third and final volume of his popular *Köpfe*—a series of extended historical character studies—was titled *Prozesse* (Trials), and included chapters on Carl Hau, the charismatic jurist convicted on circumstantial evidence in 1907 of the so-called Molitor murder; on the private tutor Andreas Dippold, convicted of excessive discipline leading to the death of his charge; even on Pontius Pilate, considered in terms of the legal proceedings leading to the crucifixion of Christ.[18] And of course, Harden's one-time protégé, Karl Kraus, was another master of the case, generating much of the copy of his journal *Die Fackel* with documents of Viennese legal proceedings. The annotated files of Kraus's many court cases have been published and fill four thick volumes.[19]

There was, in other words, a thriving and recognized culture of the case. It had various literary forms as well. Beyond the crime novel, the Pitaval tradition of published criminal cases found a readership in a significant literary public from the beginning of the nineteenth century.[20] In the early twentieth century, Hugo Friedlaender's series *Interessante Kriminal-Prozesse von kulturhistorischer Bedeutung* (Interesting criminal trials of cultural-historical significance) had a wide following.[21] These appeared in the format of colportage, of the penny dreadful or dime novel: cheap paper, orange or red cover, and purchased by mail order or from travelling colporteurs. The tradition was given new life in a particularly ambitious literary project starting in 1924: the series *Außenseiter der Gesellschaft: Die Verbrechen der Gegenwart* (Outsiders of society: crimes of the present) published under the editorship of Rudolf Leonhard, where prominent cases such as that of the Austrian spy Colonel Alfred Redl, the mass murderer Fritz Haarmann, and others were treated.[22] Some of the finest writers of the time contributed to the series: Alfred Döblin, Egon Erwin Kisch, Theodor Lessing, Hermann Unger, and Ernst Weiß. The series ceased publication with the bankruptcy of the press before announced volumes by Arnolt Bronnen, Max Brod, Thomas Mann, Walter Hasenclever, and Joseph Roth appeared. The level was high, despite the deliberate reference to the colportage format in the volumes' bright red covers, and the series has been studied in its contribution to the intersection of literary modernism and the case study. Where the series departs from earlier precedents is in its focus on the courts as the site of an important form of reciprocity: in studying how criminals were subject to the machinery of justice, that system itself was held up for inspection.[23] Not only crimes but the intricacies of their treatment by the criminal justice system were to be brought before the public eye; the justice system was used as a lens through which the problems of the present were to be brought into a new and sharp focus.

The overlap of literature and law was a significant one in the second and third decades of the twentieth century. This was a period of the so-called "crisis of justice," one of many perceived crises in a period of accelerated change. And while the historiographic model of "crisis" has been justifiably challenged in recent years,[24] the problems of judicature were both very public and very real. The legal positivism (attention to the letter of the law and limiting of the discretion of the judge) that had accompanied the formation of the German legal code in the nineteenth century led to an increasing distance between judiciary and public under changing social conditions; combined with the independence of judges from political oversight, the continuity of personnel in the legal bureaucracy from the Kaiserreich into the Weimar years turned what was once a modernizing approach into an increasingly conservative, indeed reactionary political form of justice; and the many incompatibilities between the new Weimar Constitution and the existing legal codes undermined the achievements of the former.[25] The administration of justice was a site at which the various nonsimultaneities of a changing society were seen to be figured. The bestsellers of the time included many "cases" or *Fälle*, fictional and otherwise (Ricarda Huch's *Der Fall Deruga* (1917) and Jakob Wassermann's extraordinary *Der Fall Maurizius* (1928), to name just two). The court was also a *topos* in literary Expressionism. And if important works by Kafka, for example, can be seamlessly subsumed under this phenomenon, we might better think of them as commentaries on it as well—an attempt, among other things, to come to terms with the relationship between the archaic concerns of justice and the bureaucratic and often opaque administration of contemporary law.

It was thus a truism that the law was a sensitive site, a place where the skin of administered modernity wore thin and the pulse of the contemporary could be felt. While court reporting had a history, its practitioners were now celebrities.[26] The most prominent was Paul Schlesinger, who covered the Berlin court at Moabit under the pseudonym "Sling" for the prestigious *Vossische Zeitung*.[27] Court reporting was the *métier* of the famous *rasende Reporter*, the racing reporter Egon Erwin Kisch, who was famous for both his tattoos (with their criminal resonance) and his vast criminological library.[28] Sling's protégée Gabriele Tergit achieved fame as the court reporter for the *Berliner Tageblatt*. She sums up the cliché:

> Better than the work of our authors, poets, and historians, the original sources—the letter, the diary, the notes after a chance conversation—tell us the essence of the era. Beyond the usual formalities, the files of a criminal case consist of these original sources in which we gain insight (*Erkenntnis*) into the typical feelings of an epoch.[29]

The other side of the epistemological potential of the criminal case is, of course, its spectacularization, as legal matters came to be selected, packaged, dramatized, and distributed in a commercial press drawing energies from, and feeding into, a well-supplied public fascination with crime in literature, film, and crime magazines, the commodified forms through which representations of crime circulated. And it is here that the *Außenseiter der Gesellschaft* series was notable. It often drew attention to the intersection of the courts with other institutions. The press was seen as a constituent element of the cases, despite its seemingly subordinate, supplementary status. It was clear in these volumes that the newspapers did not simply report on and react to what happened in court: the press was shown to be the site of an event every bit as "real" as the acts that precipitated the reportage. The focus is shifted from crime scene and the scenography of justice to the site of their mediation. And the books of the series drew attention to wider phenomena in their forensic forms, for example to the natural sciences in the form of criminalistics, and to the rapidly changing and professionalizing field of psychiatry. The books not only reflected but reflected upon the nuts and bolts that held together the edifice of modern justice.

Involved in this series were the likes of Döblin, Kisch, Leonhard: this was the circle of the radical *Gruppe 1925*, in which Brecht was active—indeed as judge in the mock trial of one of its members, Johannes R. Becher. In his "experiment" that turned legal proceedings into a literary text, one with exemplary ambitions of public representation, Brecht was knowingly working within an established model, one of the most prominent and ambitious of the culture of the case.

For cases and their documentation were also the site of exploring the radical possibilities of literary form. In *Die beiden Freundinnen und ihr Giftmord* (The two girlfriends and their murder by poisoning), Döblin wrote an extraordinary book out of the files of a famous murder trial (which he did not attend);[30] in *Berlin Alexanderplatz*, he incorporated medical, legal, and press documents.[31] These were part of his project of "epic" writing: his way of making writing "a public matter,"[32] of achieving a "closeness to everyday communication,"[33] of incorporating documents and pre-existing material into writing. Döblin could, he wrote in 1928, "hardly prevent [himself] from simply transcribing entire documents from files (*Aktenstücke*)."[34] The case was one way of achieving the "*Konnex mit dem Publikum*" he sought.[35] It represented a crucial intersection of daily life with the actual dramas of the present, with the fates of contemporary subjects, however mundane. "Life writes in an unsurpassed way," he wrote, and the case and its documentation was one place to find history writing itself.[36] It was a ground of epic literature.

§

Back to "The *Threepenny* Lawsuit": it is a complex, rich, and rewarding text, but it is also problematic at many levels, and this is no doubt the reason for the strange lack of sustained engagement with it in critical theory, its relegation to the status of a source for a few key passages of media theory and a treasure trove for useful aphorisms. It is worthwhile, I think, to pursue a few of these problems for the light they shed on what is at stake in the lawsuit itself and in the larger culture of the case.

Indeed, the very premise of the text is questionable. Brecht takes for granted that the film company's termination of his contract allowing co-determination of the screenplay for the *Threepenny* film was an "intolerable injustice,"[37] that the fundamental legal battle was not between different positions or sides of a contract but simply a matter of the interests of those with a million marks at stake against a single, isolated artist. The legal victory of the side with greater financial power was "only a question of time"[38] and showed that "intellectual interests can be protected only as long as they are not too expensive. Any further than this and they lose their claim for justice."[39] "When the court decided against us in the suit, it proved the flexibility of the laws, gave the rights to the crude forces of [economic] reality," and was "an all-too-obvious confirmation of the power of capital."[40] The logic is circular: this state of affairs is both starting point and conclusion. And we ignore at our peril the fact that Brecht had a very feeble case. In his invaluable and authoritative study of "The *Threepenny* Lawsuit," Steve Giles has looked into all aspects of the case and shown Brecht's overestimation of the right of "co-determination" he had negotiated, his misunderstanding of the law, his failure to deliver on his obligations, and his frequent displays of bad faith. Brecht also overlooks the fact that at stake was not the huge issue of what rights an artist had in late capitalism, but a single contract. And it was a contract of a kind Brecht had little experience with, although it already had precedents and customary usage. Cases such as these were important, for they concerned the nature of the contracts that govern this kind of economic exchange, what could and could not be assumed in them. The legal models for these relations were crucial for authors whose texts were to be turned into films, for screenwriters, composers, and others whose creative work was part of the machinery of production in the new technical media such as film. Brecht's case on its own, however, could hardly carry the weight and exemplary status he ascribed to it in his polemical account.

Further problems emerge from Brecht's naïve assumptions concerning the rights historically granted to authors in traditional media and genres (fiction, poetry, and drama in print; the visual arts of painting, drawing, and sculpture; musical composition; etc.), as if the law in fact reflected the very fetishized notion of art Brecht himself rejected. He writes as if great privileges were given to these producers of intellectual (*geistige*) goods, setting them apart from "material" or monetary concerns, in line with Enlightenment and Romantic notions of individuality, personality, and genius. Yet the category of "intellectual property" did nothing of the sort. It simply identified products of a specific, non-tangible type whose status as commodity required different rules. Without protections of property of a generally "cultural" kind, the fundamentally economic activity of literary authorship and publishing could not proceed in a consistent and stable way, nor could the production of images be successfully exploited by artists and their publishers. Laws such as copyright were always already about economic exploitation, and the privileges accorded to artists—though inflected by and framed within the bourgeois discourse of autonomous art—existed in order to protect property of different kinds and to allow them to be integrated into the larger economy in which they functioned. The logic of such statutes was not to protect but rather to take something intangible and render it saleable and tradeable nonetheless. As Molly Nesbit and others have shown, new media and production technology were always a problem for the law (indeed, copyright was the result of negotiating the economic conditions created by the printing press).[41] The law was always playing catch-up with such developments, needing to redefine the nature of both labor and saleable commodities (including immaterial ones) in order to keep the wheels of social production turning. In writing that "the court must make production possible," as if that were a development of industrial capitalism, Brecht fails to understand that ensuring the smooth production and distribution of works of art was a legislative and juridical imperative already in the age of artisanal technique.[42] In writing of the assumption that "incorporeal rights must be protected," he neglects to say that this was a matter of *commercial* law;[43] and in writing that "the rights of the individual must be protected," he does not identify the passage in the Civil Code (BGB, *Bürgerliches Gesetzbuch*) he cites; he could not, for it simply is not there;[44] nor could he have explained why that has any bearing on economic activity of a cultural kind. There is a fundamental mismatch between his polemics and the mundane context of the minutiae of commercial law. And when we look at other examples of the culture of the case—court reportage, the *Neue Pitaval*, Egon Erwin Kisch's *Kriminalistisches Reisebuch*, Carl Hau's *Das Todesurteil*, films such as Fritz Lang's *M*—very few indeed address issues of commercial law (unless, of course, business matters took on human interest or precipitated more spectacular crimes).[45]

In the second strand of Brecht's argument, it is not the legal decision per se but the *Vorstellungen*—the ideas or notions about the case, about law and art that prevail in society—that are the object of study. Here Brecht's sources are not the legal arguments, positions, and judgments but less expert examples from the extensive reporting of the case in the German cultural, business, and general press. If the axis defining the first part of the argument separated the artist from capital, the axis around which these texts are now disposed is a different one. On the one side, there are those who recognize the modern conditions under which artists work: the inevitable commodification of the work, its lost autonomy and aura, its separation from the subjectivity and personality of the individual creator, the role of capital in its production, the commercial pressures on taste, the division of labor within the production. Even when such analyses come from those opposed to Brecht in the case, Brecht sides with their clear-sighted recognition of the nature of modern media and their economic conditions. Thus he has nothing but praise for some of the subtle reasoning contained in the legal opinion *against* him; this represents, in its materialist and "dialectical" analysis, a "progressive" position in the analysis of the apparatus of film production and the recognition of the principles organizing it. On the other side are those whom he criticizes as behind the times, who support his *legal* position in the name of justice, out of reverence for the artist, and out of a belief in the autonomy and the sanctity of art.[46] In the cultural press Brecht finds elements of both views combined: the recognition of the "weight of economic facts" and the critical disenchantment with them. In both camps, pro- and contra-Brecht, he finds the "ideological schizophrenia of the petty-bourgeois journalist," which

> manifests itself in the cohabitation in his consciousness of different realms of ideas, in their gradual shifting towards one another. At one and the same time he has at least two ideas about the same thing: he derives one from upper-class idealism, which will impose Individuality, Justice, Freedom, etc. on reality and the other from reality itself, which prevails in all its tendencies against the idealism, deflects it, domesticates it, *but also lets it exist.*[47]

Those whose views emerge from "reality," which Brecht affirms, fail to use this perspective to criticize the bourgeois ideology of art; and those working from this "ideology" refuse to challenge the reality that destroys these ideals. The juxtaposition of different views shows two sides of a false coin, in Barthes's terms a "myth" that holds competing and irreconcilable views in tension. The radically different views—espoused on all sides—are not separate but part of a whole, albeit a false one. The bourgeois press recognizes precisely what is happening in the arena of culture in a society whose production is based on industrial capitalism, but it neither draws (progressive) conclusions about the nature of the work of art under these conditions, nor does it challenge these conditions. It is the situation Peter Sloterdijk has influentially called "cynicism" and has defined as "enlightened false consciousness."[48]

This is a *tour de force*: in pursuing aims he himself ultimately finds untenable, Brecht erects a screen on which he can project a large array of comments, judgments, and analyses to be studied and compared. With this distance, he dismisses critics who supported him (most significant, perhaps, is Siegfried Kracauer[49]) and draws happily for support from those who opposed him. That this also serves to justify, ex post facto, his own disingenuous actions and deflects criticism of those who saw him as compromised by accepting a settlement from the film company to end the case, is only in keeping with the extraordinary potential of the *Threepenny* project, which started with an opera (which itself prompted accusations of plagiarism of its materials, and indeed lawsuits over this[50]) and resulted in an additional film treatment, a novel, and a theoretical monument of his turn to Marx—not to mention a film at Nero's expense that ultimately did little to harm Brecht's popularity.

But when faced with Brecht's text, the legal experts could only have shrugged their shoulders. For Brecht's project is ideology critique, based on the firm bed of what he called "reality" and demonstrating conflicting and contradictory beliefs about it. The law approached things rather differently. Though it could support sophisticated philosophical thinking, in practice its ontologies were more inductive and emerged ad hoc. Its epistemology looked quite different too. There the logic was of determining the facts of the case (the *Tatbestand* that is the start of any legal judgment in German courts) and the *Subsumtion* under the most appropriate law. Though its legal casuistry was the very opposite of dialectics, it was a method that worked well; indeed, the legal acuity in evidence in the attempts to define the nature of cultural contracts in an age of rapidly emergent media is nothing if not impressive (if produced under urgent commercial pressures).

Perhaps this is all beside the point. In the use of the institutions of legal process as a medium of a public sphere, in conjuring a space for debate in an oversaturated print culture, Brecht's "case" is a monument. He understood the inadequacy of the press as the site of necessary and rational debate. "The public had the right to our pursuit of justice," he wrote, perhaps disingenuously. But he recognized that

> the public had not made this claim for quite some time ... We had to furnish the public with a claim which they were no longer in a position to make themselves but were nonetheless still obliged to make. The speculative quality of our suit soon receded behind these possibilities of bringing into view social attitudes (the press, the cinema and the courts), that is, of staging an experiment in collaboration with players who otherwise are difficult to engage.[51]

Brecht grasped the potential for reciprocity inherent in the case, the possibility of bringing into the public eye and putting on trial the very institutions of social order and discipline. In the course of such a case,

> the court becomes the defendant, whose defense is the social order, which then also becomes the defendant. For the court, which in the beginning was permitted to apply the law, is soon forced to state something about the law itself. The legal case becomes unimportant and the case of the law becomes acute.[52]

He translated the instincts, habits, and projects of many other practitioners of the case into a program:

> *The courts, and with them the press, must systematically and on a large scale be drawn into the organization of sociological experiments.* Since the public prosecutor in the bourgeois state in no way represents the interests of the entirety, the interests of the individual injured party being also those of the masses, court lawsuits can be used precisely to bring into the public consciousness the deeper, less noticeable social processes

> that constantly transpire ... Discussion methods are needed that resemble more closely collective thinking processes.[53]

From a case played out in public, an attempt at the public production of knowledge, Brecht leaves us with many conclusions in the conditional tense. He might have had a poor grasp of the law. He might have convinced no one with his text at the time. He might have at first missed his target (the film company Nero) before finding another he could hit (petty-bourgeois ideology). He might have only followed the example of prominent figures such as Alfred Apfel, George Grosz's lawyer, in mobilizing the press as an extension of the courtroom.[54] He probably played very dirty indeed, starting legal action against critical voices who threatened to steal his thunder.[55] He might have extricated himself from his self-inflicted legal difficulties only by the seat of his pants. Like many practices of the case, his was a deeply ambivalent endeavor. But Brecht filled a courtroom and turned it into "an auditorium full of writers listening attentively to the lawyers' words,"[56] he generated public discussion, and he left a text that thoroughly mines the events and their written representations in different genres and discourses for their complex and contested potential for social knowledge.

§

Turning legal proceedings into a medium of *Öffentlichkeit* was, as I have described it, a sort of reflex, an instinct, and as we have seen it had its complexities. Yet there was a logic that connected the practices of the case and its practitioners. It involved opening up a space between three social entities: the institution of the press, the institution of the law, and the new demographic constellation of artists and intellectuals without a secure economic base for their work and for their lives, who started with concerns essentially cultural but tended toward political radicalization (left or right) due to their proletarianization. That constellation was called at the time *geistige Arbeiter* (intellectual workers); we can consider a smaller section of this group and call it the avant-garde. They were not lawyers—though surprisingly many of the writers among them had studied law or otherwise knew its workings intimately, something indicative of the class backgrounds and high level of education of this group.[57] As a radicalized group of intellectuals outside the university and art academies, it produced much of what we consider the important criticism of the time (and included the likes of Benjamin and Kracauer, though neither of them had, in fact, studied law). But we need to separate their work from what Brecht called the "apparatus," here the medial venues of the press which provided the intellectuals of the word with concrete possibilities for publication (to the extent that it could be absorbed into the model of journalism). Or, in Brecht's case, we need to recognize that his work involved, but was not identical with, the theatre, where avant-garde practices could develop in nonsimultaneous, potentially obsolete media due to the fact that their productions were based on limited investment and therefore limited capital risk.[58] Publishing too could sustain this work, having similar corners of insignificant risk. In the interchanges between the precarious social group and the improvised, occasionally incidental institutions that offered concrete supports for it, we might also identify the zone of extra-academic *theory*. And created in this space in between, the invoked, interpellated, artificially created public sphere cannot be equated with pre-existing (if themselves changing) institutions such as the press and its readers alone, nor with the formally public procedures of the courts, nor with the small group that mobilized both. To historians, institutions and venues seem, perhaps, relatively stable, and histories can attach to them. But the practices of the case were more fragile, messy, unpredictable, and contingent than such traditional objects of social and historical study, as was the space in which a public could form; and the practitioners of the case, as "free-floating intellectuals,"[59] were also always in between and improvising. Their work with the press had shown them that despite the lack of pre-publication censorship, this area was not transparent but needed to be activated by practices of publicity (of which the case was one). It thus made sense for Brecht to open this space in between, and it would have resonated with those like him. It was a reflex, and this explains some of the contradictions of Brecht's text: the traces of improvisation, the sense of meddling and gambling, the tendency toward disingenuousness and dissimulation that characterize the "experiment." As a *Flucht in die Öffentlichkeit*, a reckless rush to the public, Brecht's case did not have to be orchestrated as carefully as he claimed: according to the rules of this game, that could happen retrospectively.

In discursive terms, the move involved written interventions that prized open an area between different discourses and genres: between court reporting, legal texts, and the new forms of the proletarianized intellectual turned avant-gardist: the essay, the aphorism, the miniature, or the fragment. Medially, all these involved print, but here too the avant-garde made up its own rules. And here we can identify a crucial distinction between Brecht's "*Threepenny* Lawsuit" and some other examples of the culture of the case. Brecht's use of print media was distinctive: it was the practice of *montage*.

As printed and bound prose, a page from "The *Threepenny* Lawsuit" does not look that different from, say, a published legal decision. Each is read from the first page to the last; each works with quotes. Both have a clear order: the legal case with the judgment (*Urteil*), facts of the case (*Tatbestand*), and the reasons for the decision (*Entscheidungsgründe*); in Brecht's text an ad hoc but logical, intuitive, and clearly indicated set of sections. But Brecht's "case" section differs from the legal "facts of the case," though both call on a mix of authorial voices and inserted documents. Though the *Tatbestand* mixes, like Brecht, different sources—narrative, contracts, letters, precedents, and so on—the point is to create a coherent overview of facts deemed relevant. Brecht's section on the case starts similarly but then changes tack. After a brief introductory narrative and quotations from the contract, followed by the court's decision, the text shifts to a kaleidoscope of extracts from the press, identified by the source periodical but not by date or author, representing contradictory views and divided into sections preceded by short, ironic phrases that mimic headlines or advertisements, rather like the sections of Benjamin's *Einbahnstraße* (One-way street) of 1928. Instead of a clear or ironed-out narrative, we have a cacophony of differing views which do not resolve into a clear image. The case is exploded, reversing the usual labor of legal judgment, and Brecht's work in the following sections becomes that of drawing out the contradictions, pointing up the gaps, stressing not only the heterogeneity of the incorporated documentary material but the confusion of the different positions, the mutual exclusivity of views often expressed in the same text.

Brecht incorporates foreign material, often documentary in nature, highlights its heterogeneity, stresses contradictions, and refuses narrative or logical harmony: this is an avant-garde technique. His working method evokes that of visual artists such as Raoul Hausmann, Hannah Höch, and John Heartfield, and of writers such as Döblin. As Werner Mittenzwei describes it, Brecht

> usually wrote with a typewriter. Corrections were carried out with scissors and paste. After reviewing the manuscript, he cut the text apart and montaged (*montierte*) it anew. He cut out even short sections of a few lines and pasted them on [to the paper], even when rewriting them would have been far more rational. Montaging the sentences was fun and increased his pleasure in the task. He operated here like a cutter or editor (*Schnittmeister*) with a film.[60]

Brecht's use of this technique in the context of the case would have made sense, certainly to his colleagues from the *Gruppe 1925*. As we have seen, for Döblin and others the law looked "epic": it showed how heterogeneous elements of contemporary experience came together, and it was an important source of material for their own use. But how were materials in fact used in the administrative forms of the case? Was the avant-garde instinct a logical response to the sites and practices of judicature? And what of the spectacularization of the "case" in the newspapers, illustrated weeklies, in novels, theatre dramas, and film? It is worth reconsidering "The *Threepenny* Lawsuit" in the light of such questions. Instead of asking how Brecht used the case as a medium, we can ask in reverse: how did he use the media of the case? For the manipulation of texts on paper was central to many aspects of the culture of the case.

§

In writing "The *Threepenny* Lawsuit," Brecht worked with newspaper clippings. Anke te Heesen has described in great detail the function of newspaper clippings in the cultural and knowledge production of the late nineteenth and early twentieth century.[61] The practices drew upon long traditions of both scholarly excerpting by longhand and women's scrapbooking. In the former, practitioners sought to compile and store text data for later use at a time when books were expensive and scarce; in the latter, women sought to select textual and visual evidence of events they found meaningful, drawing from an increasing flood of impersonal news and assembling a set of subjectively meaningful items.[62] The establishment of newspaper clipping agencies commercialized and rationalized the practices of extracting meaningful data. Customers of various kinds could contract out the work of scouring scores of newspapers for items on a single topic. Artists, for example, would subscribe to such a service and receive published reviews or mentions of their exhibitions; scientists could keep abreast of public reports of developments across the world; and those in the public eye kept track of their representation in the press. Subscribers were spared the time and expense of finding these clippings themselves, which was, in any case, impossible for a single person. The clipping services allowed for a universe of print now beyond survey to be scanned by employees with scissors, paste, and instructions to find clippings of a constantly changing set of topics. It was a method of overseeing the daily flood of public texts from newspapers and journals, managing the data and archiving it. In montaging accounts of his own court case, Brecht might well have engaged the services of one or more clipping agencies; and in doing so, he would have been following a thoroughly normal practice of the time.

The newspaper clipping had a past that was scholarly and learned, and a contemporary resonance that was up-to-date, bureaucratically organized, and invoked the latest practices of commerce and industry. And, as te Heesen has explored, it was central to the practices of the avant-garde. But it also continued the scrapbook tradition of the personal management of public representations. Moreover, the use of the newspaper clipping was contemporary with, and embedded in, documentary practices of the culture of the case. Consider a literary genre of the time: the edited diaries, journals, or memoirs of those at the center of cases—legal, medical, or publicistic. There was no shortage of such books. One of the most famous was *Tagebuch einer Verlorenen: Von einer Toten* (Diary of a lost girl: by one now dead) of 1905.[63] It is a diary, the account of a young girl's life from a middle-class upbringing to prostitution and death, told with a remarkable candor, self-awareness, and touching humanity, in an at times awkward and changing style as the girl grows into an adult. Pages were missing, and the central events they apparently recount need to be reconstructed by the reader. The book showed a thoroughly typical case, a fate that could be that of many women. The documentary material was published with an introduction by the popular novelist Margarete Böhme, who writes that she is merely the "editor" and explains how the (incomplete) manuscript has come into her hands. A facsimile of two pages of the original, handwritten diary is included in early editions to vouch for the book's authenticity. But it was in fact a fabrication by Böhme, though she never admitted it.[64] And since practices of the case moved across media with great energy and usually ease, it is no surprise that the bestseller was turned into a theatre drama and adapted as a film three times (the last was the famous film by G. W. Pabst, starring Louise Brooks).[65]

From the medical-psychiatric side, we could point to books such as the anonymous *Tagebuch einer männlichen Braut* (Diary of a male bride), the journal of a hermaphrodite "edited" by one Walter Homann.[66] Or indeed, from the time of the *Threepenny Opera*, the sensational *Vom Leben getötet: Bekenntnisse eines Kindes* (Killed

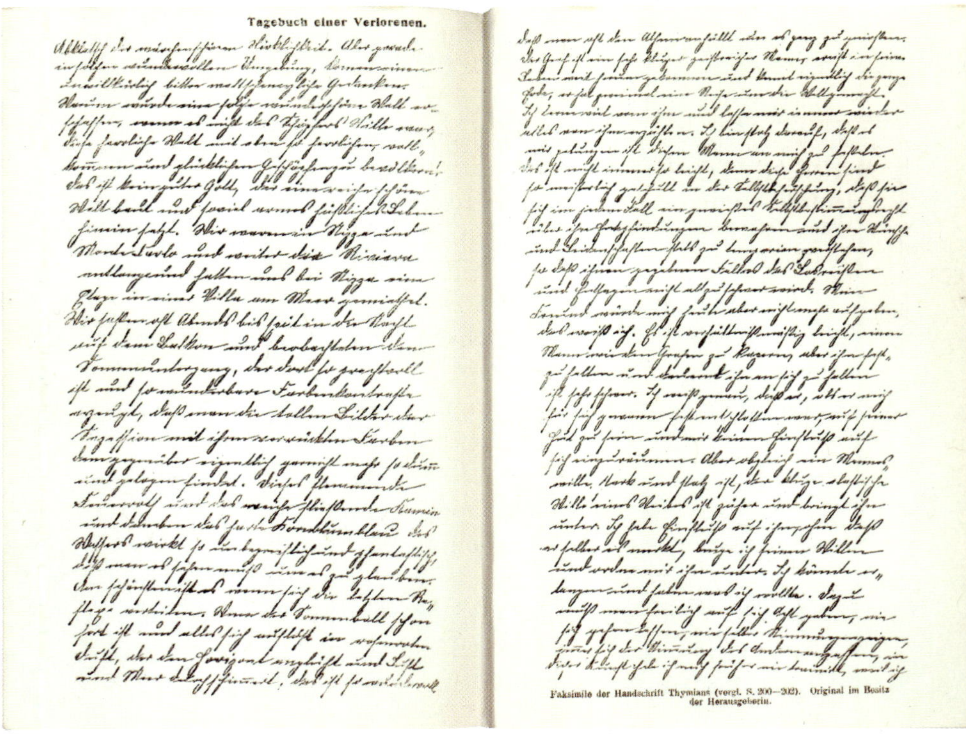

Facsimile of "original" manuscript for Margarete Böhme, *Tagebuch einer Verlorenen*. Photo: author.

by life: confessions of a child), edited by M.I. Breme.[67] It is a complicated case, full of deception; but then, media store and distribute data, not "truth" (though certain forms spoke the rhetoric of documentary authenticity: the facsimile showing the "fallen" girl's handwritten diary). Here the story is of a Bremen girl's two-year descent from innocence to death, and it is a powerful indictment of the hypocrisy of civil authorities in dealing with women suspected of prostitution, and of the inhumane penal and medical treatment to which they were subjected while forcibly separated from family, friends, or legal advice. It is a dated diary in the young girl's own voice. The book was a bestseller: five thousand copies were sold in the first three weeks of its appearance, and it went through many more editions. The case became even more notorious when the victim's mother, Elisabeth Kolomak, was exposed as author, and with that she became the author of a whole series of crimes as well. Procuring was the one for which she stood trial. The shift transformed her from the bereaved to the accused. But it was a typical case in that the publication and trial opened a view into the actions of authorities; the claims of shocking brutality on the part of the Bremen police turned out to be as true as the original authorship was false. It was typical too in that the roles of accuser and accused, victim and offender switched, exposing the problems of youth and of class sexuality, the plight of women, and the institutions of social discipline alike to unwelcome but breathless public scrutiny. The celebrity court reporters of the time were dispatched to Bremen and reported on the steady flow of revelations and competing allegations.

But it is the practice of the case on the side of the *readers* that interests me. One reader turned her copy of the book into an album of newspaper clippings, leaving evidence of (presumably) her close concern with the case and attention to its development and reporting. Photographic portraits from an unidentified illustrated newspaper are pasted in to make a frontispiece; a small notebook glued into the back cover and titled with a clipped headline contains newspaper reports, including the court decision (only the judgment and legal reasoning, as the *Tatbestand* or "facts of the case" were well known). Perhaps it was someone familiar with the conditions described, perhaps someone who knew one of the protagonists. The clipping of the theatre listings from the *Hamburger Fremdenblatt* show how the case crossed media and genres, turning from court case and documentary to spectacle in a melodramatic drama by June 1927 ("age restricted"); by the end of the year it had also been made into a film.[68] The inside back cover expands the scope with an article comparing Frau Kolomak to an eighteen-year-old woman who stood before a court in Duisburg accused of the murder of two children, a court reportage concerning "sensational trials." The object shows both the entropic energy of the case, the new relationships into which it could be brought, and one reader's attempt to draw together paper traces of it and to make sense of the story.

The book, the court case, the clippings, the scrapbook, the theatre play, and the film trace a social, legal, and also a medial narrative. But though a practice of cutting and pasting and an engagement with modern, spectacularized forms of information and entertainment, the scrapbook is a kind of montage very different from Brecht's. It shows not cool observation but emotional investment, not distance but involvement. The insertion of heterogeneous material does not estrange; instead the differences between the documentary texts, the commentary, and the images are played down. Any shocks or jolts come from the human drama contained in the collaged materials, not the physical, spatial

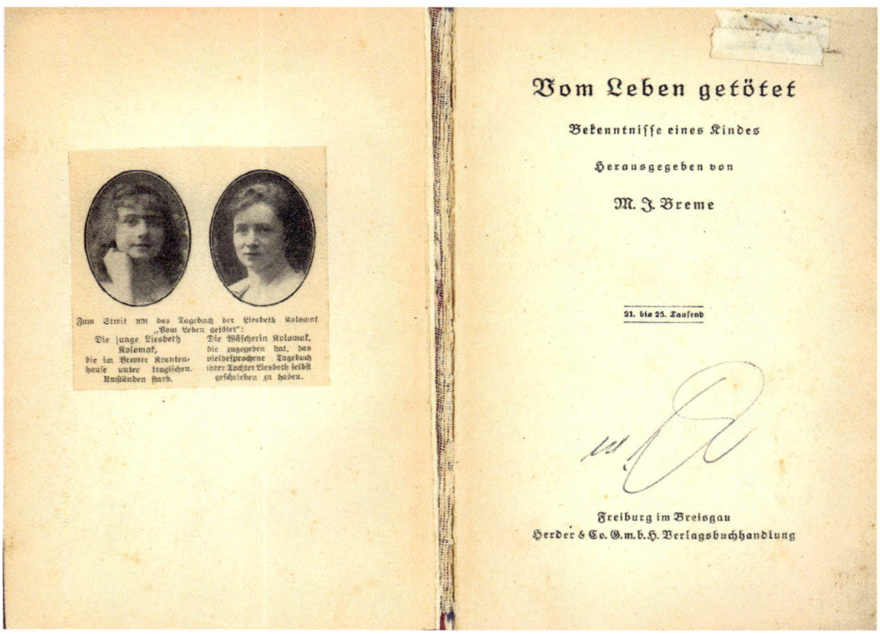

M. I. Breme, *Vom Leben getötet*. Private collection. Photo: author.

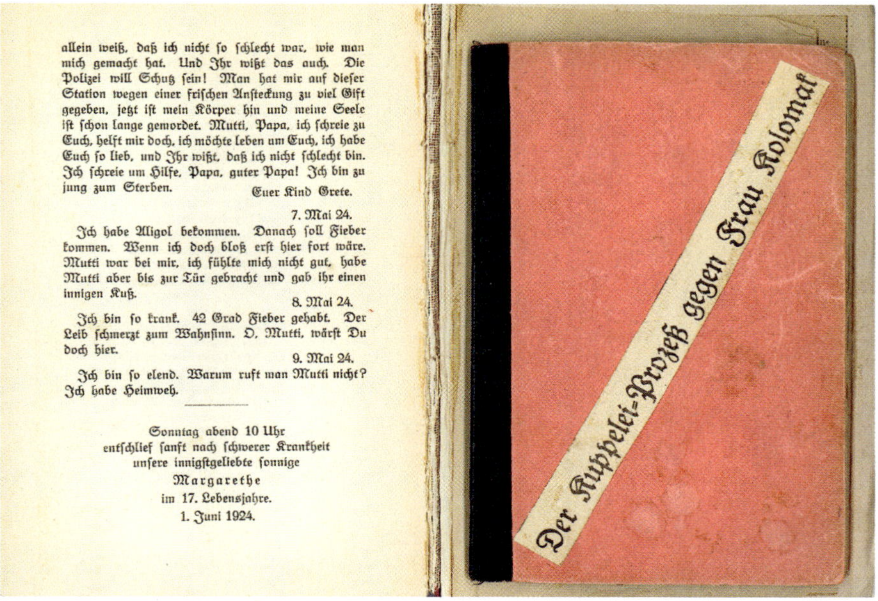

allein weiß, daß ich nicht so schlecht war, wie man mich gemacht hat. Und Ihr wißt das auch. Die Polizei will Schutz sein! Man hat mir auf dieser Station wegen einer frischen Ansteckung zu viel Gift gegeben, jetzt ist mein Körper hin und meine Seele ist schon lange gemordet. Mutti, Papa, ich schreie zu Euch, helft mir doch, ich möchte leben um Euch, ich habe Euch so lieb, und Ihr wißt, daß ich nicht schlecht bin. Ich schreie um Hilfe. Papa, guter Papa! Ich bin zu jung zum Sterben.

Euer Kind Grete.

7. Mai 24.

Ich habe Aligol bekommen. Danach soll Fieber kommen. Wenn ich doch bloß erst hier fort wäre. Mutti war bei mir, ich fühlte mich nicht gut, habe Mutti aber bis zur Tür gebracht und gab ihr einen innigen Kuß.

8. Mai 24.

Ich bin so krank. 42 Grad Fieber gehabt. Der Leib schmerzt zum Wahnsinn. O, Mutti, wärst Du doch hier.

9. Mai 24.

Ich bin so elend. Warum ruft man Mutti nicht? Ich habe Heimweh.

Sonntag abend 10 Uhr
entschlief sanft nach schwerer Krankheit
unsere innigstgeliebte sonnige
Margarethe
im 17. Lebensjahre.
1. Juni 1924.

M. I. Breme, *Vom Leben getötet*. Private collection. Photo: author.

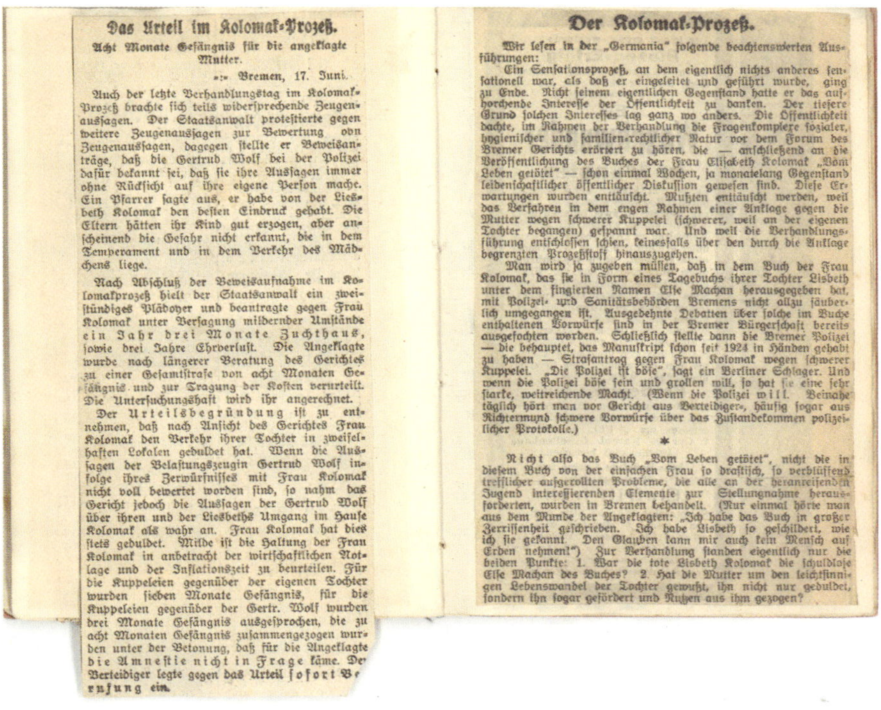

Das Urteil im Kolomak-Prozeß.

Acht Monate Gefängnis für die angeklagte Mutter.

Bremen, 17. Juni.

Auch der letzte Verhandlungstag im Kolomak-Prozeß brachte sich teils widersprechende Zeugenaussagen. Der Staatsanwalt protestierte gegen weitere Zeugenaussagen zur Bewertung ovn Zeugenaussagen, dagegen stellte er Beweisanträge, daß die Gertrud Wolf bei der Polizei dafür bekannt sei, daß sie ihre Aussagen immer ohne Rücksicht auf ihre eigene Person mache. Ein Pfarrer sagte aus, er habe von der Liesbeth Kolomak den besten Eindruck gehabt. Die Eltern hätten ihr Kind gut erzogen, aber anscheinend die Gefahr nicht erkannt, die in dem Temperament und in dem Verkehr des Mädchens liege.

Nach Abschluß der Beweisaufnahme im Kolomakprozeß hielt der Staatsanwalt ein zweistündiges Plädoyer und beantragte gegen Frau Kolomak unter Versagung mildernder Umstände ein Jahr drei Monate Zuchthaus, sowie drei Jahre Ehrverlust. Die Angeklagte wurde nach längerer Beratung des Gerichtes zu einer Gesamtstrafe von acht Monaten Gefängnis und zur Tragung der Kosten verurteilt. Die Untersuchungshaft wird ihr angerechnet.

Der Urteilsbegründung ist zu entnehmen, daß nach Ansicht des Gerichtes Frau Kolomak den Verkehr ihrer Tochter in zweifelhaften Lokalen geduldet hat. Wenn die Aussagen der Belastungszeugin Gertrud Wolf infolge ihres Zerwürfnisses mit Frau Kolomak nicht voll bewertet worden sind, so nahm das Gericht jedoch die Aussagen der Gertrud Wolf über ihren und der Liesbeths Umgang im Hause Kolomak als wahr an. Frau Kolomak hat dies stets geduldet. Milde ist die Haltung der Frau Kolomak in anbetracht der wirtschaftlichen Notlage und der Inflationszeit zu beurteilen. Für die Kuppeleien gegenüber der eigenen Tochter wurden sieben Monate Gefängnis, für die Kuppeleien gegenüber der Gertr. Wolf wurden drei Monate Gefängnis ausgesprochen, die zu acht Monaten Gefängnis zusammengezogen wurden unter der Betonung, daß für die Angeklagte die Amnestie nicht in Frage käme. Der Verteidiger legte gegen das Urteil sofort Berufung ein.

Der Kolomak-Prozeß.

Wir lesen in der „Germania" folgende beachtenswerten Ausführungen:

Ein Sensationsprozeß, an dem eigentlich nichts anderes sensationell war, als daß er eingeleitet und geführt wurde, ging zu Ende. Nicht seinem eigentlichen Gegenstand hatte er das aufhorchende Interesse der Öffentlichkeit zu danken. Der tiefere Grund solchen Interesses lag ganz wo anders. Die Öffentlichkeit dachte, im Rahmen der Verhandlung die Fragenkomplexe sozialer, hygienischer und familien-rechtlicher Natur vor dem Forum des Bremer Gerichts erörtert zu hören, die — anschließend an die Veröffentlichung des Buches der Frau Elisabeth Kolomak „Vom Leben getötet" — schon einmal Wochen, ja monatelang Gegenstand leidenschaftlicher öffentlicher Diskussion gewesen sind. Diese Erwartungen wurden enttäuscht. Mußten enttäuscht werden, weil das Verfahren in dem engen Rahmen einer Anklage gegen die Mutter wegen schwerer Kuppelei (schwerer, weil an der eigenen Tochter begangen) gespannt war. Und weil die Verhandlungsführung entschlossen schien, keinesfalls über den durch die Anklage begrenzten Prozeßstoff hinauszugehen.

Man wird ja zugeben müssen, daß in dem Buch der Frau Kolomak, das sie in Form eines Tagebuchs ihrer Tochter Lisbeth unter dem fingierten Namen Else Machan herausgegeben hat, mit Polizei- und Sanitätsbehörden Bremens nicht allzu säuberlich umgegangen ist. Ausgedehnte Debatten über solche im Buche enthaltenen Vorwürfe sind in der Bremer Bürgerschaft bereits ausgefochten worden. Schließlich stellte dann die Bremer Polizei — die behauptet, das Manuskript schon seit 1924 in Händen gehabt zu haben — Strafantrag gegen Frau Kolomak wegen schwerer Kuppelei. „Die Polizei ist böse", sagt ein Berliner Schlager. Und wenn die Polizei böse sein und grollen will, so hat sie eine sehr starke, weitreichende Macht. (Wenn die Polizei will. Beinahe täglich hört man vor Gericht aus Verteidiger-, häufig sogar aus Richtermund schwere Vorwürfe über das Zustandekommen polizeilicher Protokolle.)

*

Nicht also das Buch „Vom Leben getötet", nicht die in diesem Buch von der einfachen Frau so drastisch, so verblüffend trefflicher aufgerollten Probleme, die alle an der heranreifenden Jugend interessierenden Elemente zur Stellungnahme herausforderten, wurden in Bremen behandelt. (Nur einmal hörte man aus dem Munde der Angeklagten: „Ich habe das Buch in großer Zerrissenheit geschrieben. Ich habe Lisbeth so geschildert, wie ich sie gekannt. Den Glauben kann mir auch kein Mensch auf Erden nehmen!") Zur Verhandlung standen eigentlich nur die beiden Punkte: 1. War die tote Lisbeth Kolomak die schuldlose Else Machan des Buches? 2. Hat die Mutter um den leichtsinnigen Lebenswandel der Tochter gewußt, ihn nicht nur geduldet, sondern ihn sogar gefördert und Nutzen aus ihm gezogen?

M. I. Breme, *Vom Leben getötet*. Private collection. Photo: author.

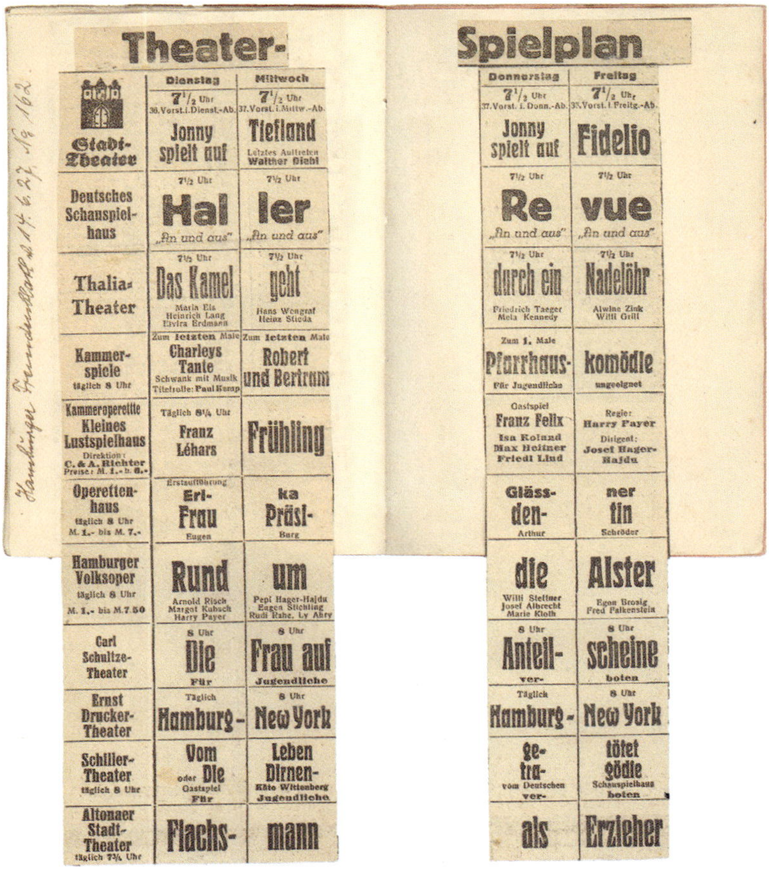

M. I. Breme, *Vom Leben getötet*. Private collection. Photo: author.

juxtaposition of them. It leaves the texts uncommented (beside the editorial acts of their selection and placement) instead of subjecting them to further analysis. While in Döblin's terms the incorporation of the familiar, the everyday, the documentary makes it an "epic" practice, it is not Brecht's form of epic. The collaged book revels in the ambiguity of the case, its twists and turns. It makes of the case not a social-scientific experiment but a melodrama.[69] In the attention to scandal, tragedy, injustice, and their spectacular traces in print culture, however, it too is a practice of the case and a manipulation of its modern media.

Similar practices used to rather different ends from Brecht's emerge from a look at another medium of the case, the

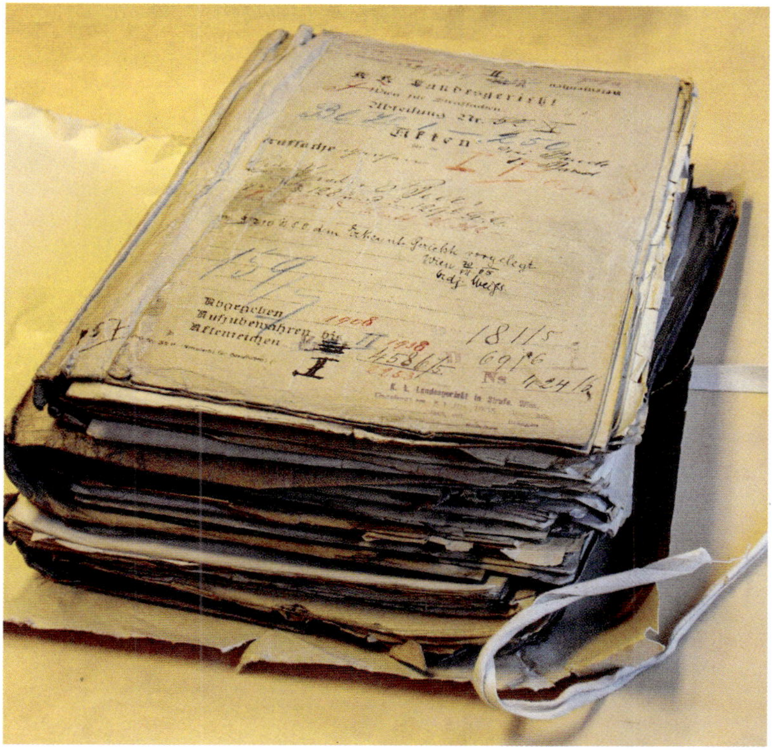

The file of the Theodor Beer case. Photo: author.

administrative-technical form of its documents: the records or "files." These similarly involve paper. Instead of scissors and glue, however, the tools are mostly the hole-punch, staples, string, horizontal stacks of files, or rows of vertical lever-arch files.[70] The files of a criminal case might mix handwritten text, typed pages, and photographs. We can take the file of the Theodor Beer trial from chapter 1 as an example. There we find also the printed and distributed arrest warrant, affidavits from experts of various kinds, letters to the accused and his own letters to others, court transcripts, correspondence with the lawyers, sworn statements, newspaper clippings, and the pre-printed forms that expedited the office work of the machinery of justice.[71]

The volumes of the *Außenseiter der Gesellschaft* series mimic and replicate the legal file's practice of aggregation. There are the authors' narrative and analysis, photographs and biographies of the principals in the case, handwriting samples and expert analyses, transcripts of the court proceedings and the legal judgments, newspaper clippings and reports showing the press coverage, excerpted passages from the expert medico-forensic literature, crime scene maps, and witness lists. Here too we see the physical

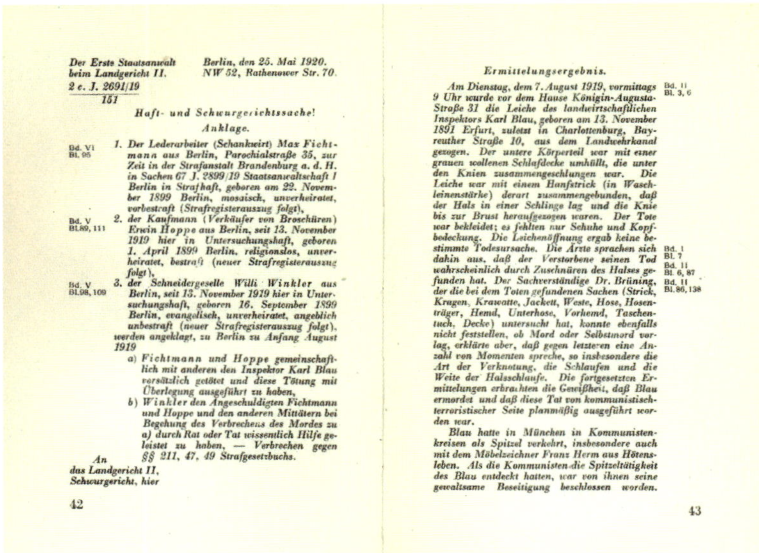

Der Erste Staatsanwalt beim Landgericht II. — *Berlin, den 25. Mai 1920. NW 52, Rathenower Str. 70.*

2 c. J. 2691/19
151

Haft- und Schwurgerichtssache!

Anklage.

Bd. VI Bl. 95 — *1. Der Lederarbeiter (Schankwirt) Max Fichtmann aus Berlin, Parochialstraße 35, zur Zeit in der Strafanstalt Brandenburg a. d. H. in Sachen 67 J. 2899/19 Staatsanwaltschaft I Berlin in Strafhaft, geboren am 22. November 1899 Berlin, mosaisch, unverheiratet, vorbestraft (Strafregisterauszug folgt),*

Bd. V Bl. 89, 111 — *2. der Kaufmann (Verkäufer von Broschüren) Erwin Hoppe aus Berlin, seit 13. November 1919 hier in Untersuchungshaft, geboren 1. April 1899 Berlin, religionslos, unverheiratet, bestraft (neuer Strafregisterauszug folgt),*

Bd. V Bl. 98, 109 — *3. der Schneidergeselle Willi Winkler aus Berlin, seit 13. November 1919 hier in Untersuchungshaft, geboren 16. September 1899 Berlin, evangelisch, unverheiratet, angeblich unbestraft (neuer Strafregisterauszug folgt),*

werden angeklagt, zu Berlin zu Anfang August 1919

a) Fichtmann und Hoppe gemeinschaftlich mit anderen den Inspektor Karl Blau vorsätzlich getötet und diese Tötung mit Überlegung ausgeführt zu haben,

b) Winkler den Angeschuldigten Fichtmann und Hoppe und den anderen Mittätern bei Begehung des Verbrechens des Mordes zu a) durch Rat oder Tat wissentlich Hilfe geleistet zu haben, — Verbrechen gegen §§ 211, 47, 49 Strafgesetzbuchs.

An das Landgericht II, Schwurgericht, hier

42

Ermittelungsergebnis.

Am Dienstag, dem 7. August 1919, vormittags 9 Uhr wurde vor dem Hause Königin-Augusta-Straße 31 die Leiche des landwirtschaftlichen Inspektors Karl Blau, geboren am 13. November 1891 Erfurt, zuletzt in Charlottenburg, Bayreuther Straße 10, aus dem Landwehrkanal gezogen. Der untere Körperteil war mit einer grauen wollenen Schlafdecke umhüllt, die unter den Knien zusammengeschlungen war. Die Leiche war mit einem Hanfstrick (in Waschleinenstärke) derart zusammengebunden, daß der Hals in einer Schlinge lag und die Knie bis zur Brust heraufgezogen waren. Der Tote war bekleidet; es fehlten nur Schuhe und Kopfbedeckung. Die Leichenöffnung ergab keine bestimmte Todesursache. Die Ärzte sprachen sich dahin aus, daß der Verstorbene seinen Tod wahrscheinlich durch Zuschnüren des Halses gefunden hat. Der Sachverständige Dr. Brüning, der die bei dem Toten gefundenen Sachen (Strick, Kragen, Krawatte, Jackett, Weste, Hose, Hosenträger, Hemd, Unterhose, Vorhemd, Taschentuch, Decke) untersucht hat, konnte ebenfalls nicht feststellen, ob Mord oder Selbstmord vorlag, erklärte aber, daß gegen letzteren eine Anzahl von Momenten spreche, so insbesondere die Art der Verknotung, die Schlaufen und die Weite der Halsschlaufe. Die fortgesetzten Ermittelungen erbrachten die Gewißheit, daß Blau ermordet und daß diese Tat von kommunistisch-terroristischer Seite planmäßig ausgeführt worden war. Bd. II Bl. 3, 6; Bd. I Bl. 7; Bd. II Bl. 6, 87; Bd. II Bl. 86, 138

Blau hatte in München in Kommunistenkreisen als Spitzel verkehrt, insbesondere auch mit dem Möbelzeichner Franz Herm aus Hötensleben. Als die Kommunisten die Spitzeltätigkeit des Blau entdeckt hatten, war von ihnen seine gewaltsame Beseitigung beschlossen worden.

43

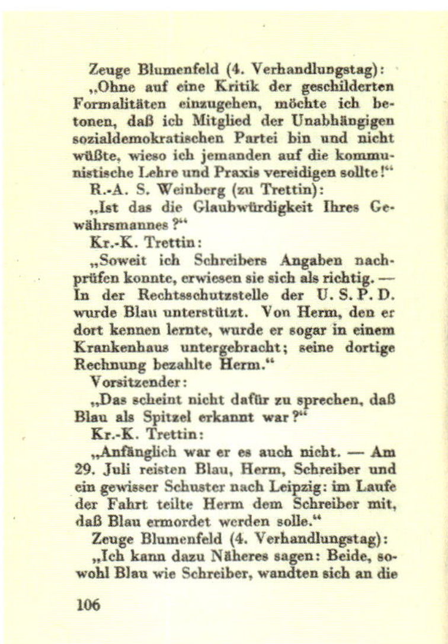

Zeuge Blumenfeld (4. Verhandlungstag):

„Ohne auf eine Kritik der geschilderten Formalitäten einzugehen, möchte ich betonen, daß ich Mitglied der Unabhängigen sozialdemokratischen Partei bin und nicht wüßte, wieso ich jemanden auf die kommunistische Lehre und Praxis vereidigen sollte!"

R.-A. S. Weinberg (zu Trettin):

„Ist das die Glaubwürdigkeit Ihres Gewährsmannes?"

Kr.-K. Trettin:

„Soweit ich Schreibers Angaben nachprüfen konnte, erwiesen sie sich als richtig. — In der Rechtsschutzstelle der U. S. P. D. wurde Blau unterstützt. Von Herm, den er dort kennen lernte, wurde er sogar in einem Krankenhaus untergebracht; seine dortige Rechnung bezahlte Herm."

Vorsitzender:

„Das scheint nicht dafür zu sprechen, daß Blau als Spitzel erkannt war?"

Kr.-K. Trettin:

„Anfänglich war er es auch nicht. — Am 29. Juli reisten Blau, Herm, Schreiber und ein gewisser Schuster nach Leipzig: im Laufe der Fahrt teilte Herm dem Schreiber mit, daß Blau ermordet werden solle."

Zeuge Blumenfeld (4. Verhandlungstag):

„Ich kann dazu Näheres sagen: Beide, sowohl Blau wie Schreiber, wandten sich an die

106

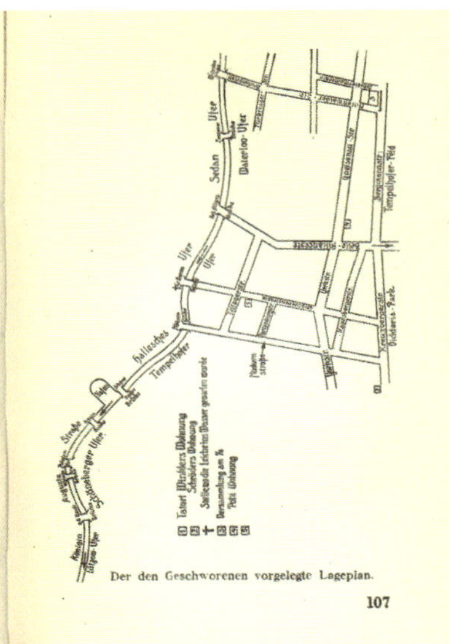

Der den Geschworenen vorgelegte Lageplan.

107

Pages from Eduard Trautner, *Der Mord am Polizeiagenten Blau, Außenseiter der Gesellschaft*, vol. 3 (Berlin: Die Schmiede, 1924).

elements of "The *Threepenny* Lawsuit," but with a very different texture, organization, and phenomenology of production.

In other words, Brecht's lawsuit was about media, but it was also negotiated *through* media. His manipulation of them looks, on the surface, rather like other practices of the case. Foucault would consider these manipulations to be work with the "'dossier,' that is to say, a case, an affair, an event that provided the intersection of discourses that differed in origin, form, organization, and function" that would allow one "to draw a map, so to speak, of those combats, to reconstruct those confrontations and battles, to rediscover the interaction of those discourses as weapons of attack and defense in the relations of power and knowledge."[72] In general, however, I prefer to name these accumulations by the specific media of the case used, not only to point to the space at which various discourses and dispositives meet but to insist upon the materiality and the specific practices they entail. For as we have seen, these practices were not only those of apparatuses of power; their practitioners were not always authorized to enter the dossier; their intersections were material and embodied. Moreover, the differences between Brecht's use of these media, and both popular and administrative uses of them, are significant: they point to a sort of mismatch between Brecht's experiment and the more common texture of the case. Perhaps this might go some way towards explaining the problematic status of Brecht's text, its eccentric position in the culture, its failure to convince as a whole.

Brecht's montage is that of the avant-garde. It is diacritical and dialectical; it works by juxtaposition and surprise; it generates meaning by difference. The cutting, pasting, binding, and archiving in the more widespread medial practices of the case have a different principle. Instead of juxtaposition, they work by *accumulation*. They grow inexorably and organically, and they stop only arbitrarily, not with a conclusion but with the end of proceedings or press coverage, or indeed with the end of interest, perhaps even by the statute of limitations. They have an air of tedium about them, of melancholy and indeed helplessness that contrasts with Brecht's sovereign and playful approach. The usual practices of the case involve immersion, absorption, and the danger of getting utterly lost in the endlessly accumulating documentary material. They are not agile: instead they involve the risks of obsession or compulsion or complete loss of overview and perspective.

The different practices imply different epistemologies. The "experiment" elaborates its methodology, moves its objects around, and exposes contradiction. These lead to conclusions, a tidy taxonomy of attitudes toward media and law that can be classified as progressive or regressive, up-to-date or obsolete, a clear view of reality or ideology. The text is filled with gestures that say "*Q.E.D.*" Scrapbooks and records yield a different kind of knowledge, one a little less secure and satisfying. Evidence is piled upon evidence; expert opinions clarify or fail to clarify any of myriad questions, and then they raise new ones. The facts of the case may be disputed and need to be established, often by fiat. Evidence is laboriously altered in its media: photographs, for example, need to be transposed into words, and written words into oral ones in a criminal trial. The case needs to be pieced together as a narrative, and this story or picture of the world is always incomplete and imperfect. Conclusions emerge on the balance of evidence, from the laborious and often contested determination of relevant laws under which the facts of the case as they have been laid out can be subsumed. Formulations are sober and quick wit is scarce. Decisions emerge by weight and accretion of evidence rather than bolder jumps of reasoning. Meaning is often absent, and the things often signify nothing but themselves. In contrast, Brecht sought to do precisely what most practitioners of the case were trained to avoid. His intention was to generalize; from the beginning, he tried to draw out of the case not a contingent and limited decision but an overall truth.

And the different practices have their own differing temporalities. The shock of juxtaposition, of montage, generates meaning in a flash. Except in rare instances, the spark of illumination is foreign to the cases of the *Außenseiter der Gesellschaft* series or its lower-market, melodramatic contemporaries. Duration and exhaustion are the leitmotifs of contemporary literary accounts of the work of the courts.[73] Court cases are rarely seen to end *correctly*; they simply terminate and form the basis of a contingent form of knowledge that could start an endless series of appeals, brought to a halt only by a court's refusal to review judgments or accept new evidence, or by the decision of a higher instance. And even then, the cases do not necessarily end. The text of Theodor Lessing's account of the crimes and trial of Haarmann, the "werewolf of Hannover," does end with a conclusion: "*Unser aller Schuld*": our own fault. The words were written, he says, in January 1925.[74] But between the delivery of the manuscript and its printing, Lessing added a nearly endless series of notes, epilogues, and accounts of new evidence. It shows the messiness of an open-ended process of publicity and knowledge, a montage with the glue never dry, with conclusions rarely final and seldom trustworthy.

In context, we can see that Brecht's montage has a shadow: not the work of an avant-garde, nor the intersection of apparatuses within the dossier, but a lower-order form of accumulation of paper materials that neither negotiates between institutions nor resolves into secure knowledge. Brecht's text thus involves a complex series of moves. First, Brecht remediates the contemporary practices of the popular interest in the case, the newspaper clippings and scrapbooks. This is, in fact, remediation in reverse: Brecht takes the medial fragments that made up his evidence and smooths them out into a conventionally printable text, turning the occasionally compelling visual interest of the photographs and playlists, of the reader's reengagement with news at discrete moments in time, into a neat set of fifty-seven pages analyzing a general state of affairs.[75] Second, he remediates the legal file, the court records, reorganizes the untidy material of the older culture of the case into a neat series of juxtapositions and analyses. The cutting and pasting make the end product shorter, not longer. Brecht shows a kind of nonsimultaneity of the law in relation to the new media, not only in its judgments on them but in its use, or not, of them, in its forms of utterance, its publicity, its often inadequate staging, its narrow, reifying focus on the *Sache*, matters relevant to the case, and the careful bracketing of *obiter dicta*. And though the older culture of the case, based on orality and the written word, the physical presence of the witnesses, judge, and jury might seem obsolete in the age of new media, its rigid code of court procedure was still in effect and the definitive form of legal process.

§

Readers of "The *Threepenny* Lawsuit" would have recognized its obvious but ambivalent position in the culture of the case, and somehow found it lacking. Those more familiar with legal casuistry than Brecht might simply have shrugged, appalled or amused by Brecht's dilettantism. For his part, Siegfried Kracauer found Brecht's grandstanding a misuse of an overstretched legal system, and a misuse of the sphere of publicity that could surround it:

> Such a transformation from a naïvely instigated suit into a conscious experiment would have been extraordinarily useful if the experiment had disclosed certain social conditions and the ideas conditioned by them that could not have been achieved otherwise. If, however, it only leads to results that could be achieved by other means, and without instigating a lawsuit, then it is at least superfluous. It *is* superfluous. ...
>
> And beyond the fact that "The *Threepenny* Lawsuit" has little meaning as an experiment—in its present stage, reality is so provocative that it hardly needs to be provoked through "experiments." On the contrary, the "sociological experiments" that Brecht suggests be organized are harmful. In their very superfluity they damage what they claim to affirm: the necessary measures in the class struggle. Not only due to their superfluity, but also because they originate in an *individualistic* attitude. They have the willful character of a private sport.[76]

Others may have missed the ambiguity and ambivalence of both the law and human action for which the case provided the stage. For that, Brecht would have had to show how people of the time were exposed to the institutions of modern bureaucracy and the machinery of justice, or insight into how laws might not be fit for purpose. For this, perhaps, he would have had to be an "outsider of society." But he was an insider; he was in a position to bring legal action and not merely find himself exposed to it. Or if not an insider, he adapted himself to the machinery and protocols of social power, even if ironically; while prompted by the downward mobility of the intellectual, his starting point was the outmoded claim of the privilege of the cultural producer. Declassed "cultural workers," *geistige Arbeiter* like Kracauer, did not appreciate his solidarity; and those less politely proletarianized could hardly have recognized it.

But beyond that, I suspect most would have missed a compelling social concern brought to light, an understanding of the human dimension of the case, the access it offered to the daily life of many, their shared experiences and concerns. For the court reporter Gabriele Tergit, the case, its media and genres—"the letter, the diary, the notes after a chance conversation ... the files of a criminal case"—offered knowledge, but it was a kind of "insight (*Erkenntnis*) into the typical *feelings* of an epoch" that had to be found through experience.[77] Brecht, with a leap over experience to a sovereign view of the "functional," the very totality that rendered individual experience an epistemological dead end, would have rejected this. But the public of the time was not so arid and devoid of the human: there had to be a subject to piece together the whole picture, to "reveal [something] about these institutions." The public sphere, the space for the social production of knowledge, was, to quote Oskar Negt and Alexander Kluge, a space for the "organization of experience,"[78] for making sense of what confronted the subject—gendered, embodied, and classed. The solidarity it could produce was, in their terms, a "sensuously tangible" one.[79] Today we would talk in terms of affect, but the sensuous experience was also one of the manipulation of paper and image and the multiple possibilities of recognition and knowledge it could both mediate and produce. Here the widespread and immense archive of the lesser practices of accumulation and montage had their appeal and their use. Brecht manipulated a very familiar set of elements in an ironic, self-reflexive, and virtuosic way, making clean copy and easy conclusions when most readers would have been sensitive to the fragility, disorder, ambiguity, and utter contingency of these public media through which contemporaries sought to make sense of a bewildering and occasionally dangerous world.

§

Brecht, I think, realized this. After the "experiment" or "essay" (*Versuch*), he never again seriously addressed the case in the form of its statutes and its procedures, its reified forms of institutionalized knowledge, bureaucracy, and indeed literary culture. But the case as a cultural form and its epistemological potential continued to haunt him. Even as he wrote "The *Threepenny* Lawsuit," he was exploring other forms of justice, the social production of knowledge, and collective decision-making.

Consider two scenes from Brecht's film *Kuhle Wampe* that show contrasting possibilities for the proceedings of justice.[80] The first concerns the eviction of the Bönicke family from their apartment

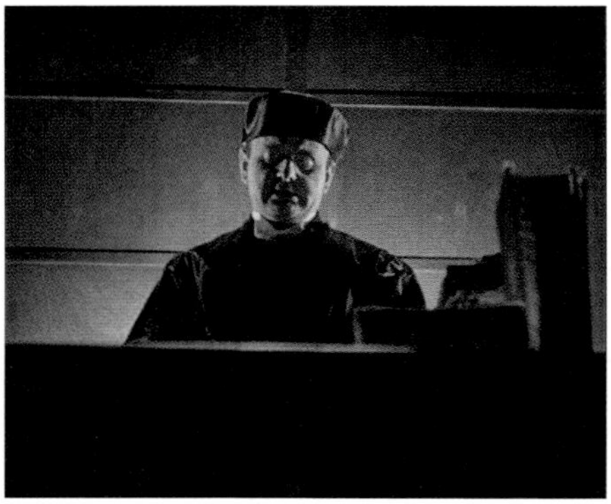

From *Kuhle Wampe*, 1932, dir. Slatan Dudow.

in Berlin; both father and son are unemployed (out of despair, the latter takes his life in the first section of the film), and they are behind with their rent. In a brief sequence, Annie—the daughter of the family and the only one in paid work—takes their case through the legal process of eviction and unsuccessful appeal. In the first sequence, the judge is clearly bored and does not recall the name of the defendants. He reads out the verdict in a quick monotone: "Although the defendant has been for a considerable time unemployed, the [pause] Bönickes should, with a minimum of good will, have been able to pay the overdue rent. Their current hardship must therefore be considered the result of their own actions."[81] In rapid succession, she then visits the officials at the rental affairs office and the welfare authority, then the landlord and the bailiff, who all wordlessly shrug and shake their heads.

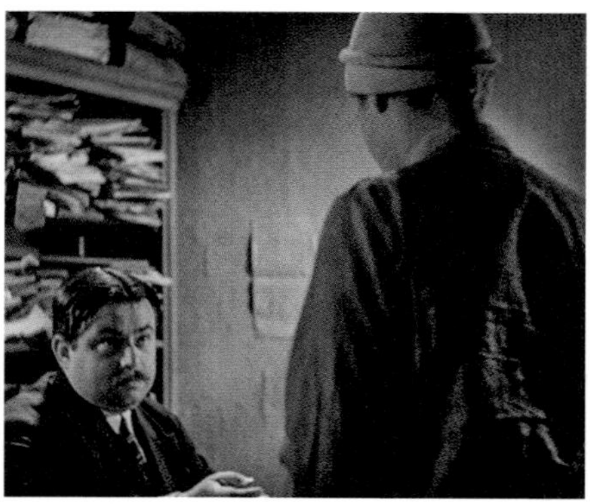

From *Kuhle Wampe*, 1932, dir. Slatan Dudow.

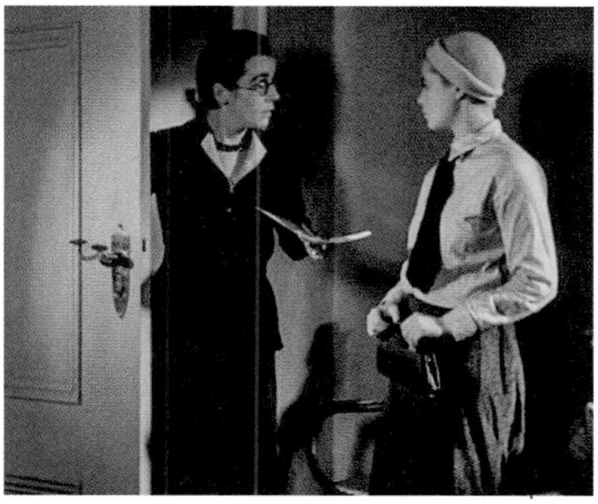

From *Kuhle Wampe*, 1932, dir. Slatan Dudow.

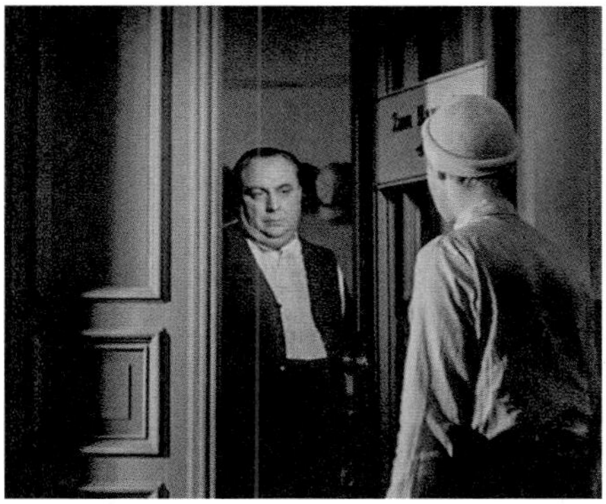

From *Kuhle Wampe*, 1932, dir. Slatan Dudow.

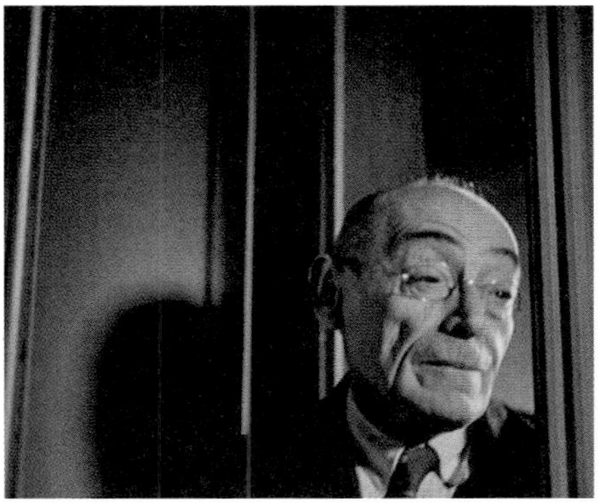

From *Kuhle Wampe*, 1932, dir. Slatan Dudow.

This very scene formed part of the case of the film itself: the censors twice forbade screening of the film before substantial cuts were made, and the courtroom scene was one where cuts were required. We can reconstruct the portions edited out of the film from the records of the censorship proceedings. Originally the Bönickes' case was the third eviction in a row, with the judge's bored and distracted verdict portrayed as a habitually repeated action. This was considered subversive and insulting to the judiciary, an institution of the state.[82]

Three times—"stereotypically"[83]—or just once: the verdict is one the judge knows to be unjust but declares out of mere indifference, habit, and lack of any easy alternative. The landlord, the municipal official, and the bailiff all shrug similarly: it is now a *gestus*. It shows in a momentary, embodied way the comprehension of a complex social situation and the specific way the characters respond to it; it shows cynicism, the uncomfortable enlightenment of false consciousness. In four two-second-long shots, we see the characters' full understanding of social contradictions, even a modicum of sympathy, but the eloquent, if wordless, indication that they have no desire to change the situation.

A later scene replays the event, an eviction, but from the perspective of proletarian justice. The scene is a public performance, at a working-class sporting event, of the Red Megaphone agitprop group, and it proposes a different outcome of the case, a different judgment:

> We are the Red Megaphone,
> Megaphone of the masses we are.
> We say out loud what oppresses you,
> We say out loud what oppresses you.
> We are the Red Megaphone,
> Megaphone of the masses we are.

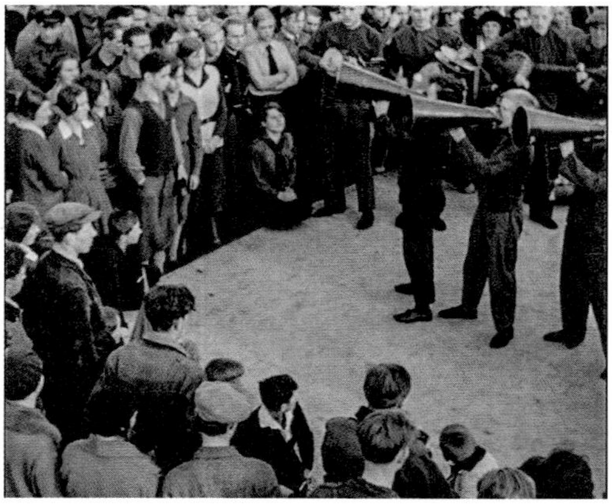

From *Kuhle Wampe*, 1932, dir. Slatan Dudow.

Kösliner Straße, Wedding district, back building.
The landlord throws the old tenant out.
He brings along the removals man:
"Go ahead and load up the junk!"
"But wait a minute. You must've made a mistake.
We've lost our welfare benefits, Mr. Landlord!"
"You're six months behind with your rent.
Lord knows, I've been patient enough!"
Patience, patience, that's a funny thing.
The proletarians, the neighbors, form a ring.
The removals man asks some questions, he talks it through,
Until ... every last one there understands it too.[84]

One provocation made it through the review board: the Red Megaphone troupe sets their fictional scene in Kösliner Straße. This was the site of bloodshed on May 1, 1929, as Communist demonstrators defied the Social Democratic city government's ban on the traditional May Day festivities, an event that can be seen as the last nail in the coffin of cooperation on the left.[85] But again the documents of the censorship proceedings show that another passage was seen as subversive and cut. The verse is quoted as follows:

The neighbors stand, united as one,
Those in charge look around ... but not a word.
The bailiff, the policeman, the landlord,
Faced with resistance, away they run![86]

Whereas the court scene and the march through the bureaucracies afterward show a passive acceptance of the status quo combined with the cynical tendency to blame the victim, the Red Megaphone performance suggests the possibility of social agency and action. In the first, the situation is summed up in the *gestus* of the shrug, the silent confession of complex social understanding and the subjective state of the politically passive. In the second, we see the wide gestures of physical power as the removals man pushes away the landlord, the casual dismissal of traditional authority, and the opening of a space in which people with similar experiences can reach their own conclusions. The solidarity of the working class leads to united and just action that creates a new law. And here the medium is not the courtroom verdict recorded

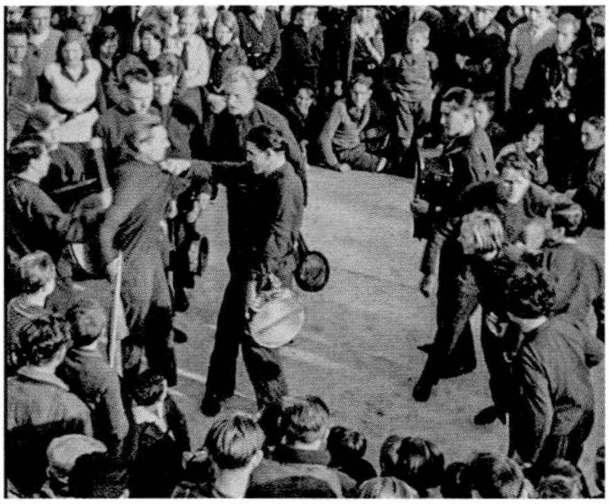

From *Kuhle Wampe*, 1932, dir. Slatan Dudow.

on paper, but the megaphone with its direct, oral address to the street, to the courtyard, to a classed public that can spontaneously convene and enforce its own uncodified justice.

In looking for alternative arenas and protocols of justice, Brecht was exploring a legal form Cornelia Vismann has termed the *tribunal*, and which she contrasts to the traditional court.[87] The form of the court, she writes, is in its origins theatrical. Rules are codified and procedures are familiar to all involved; furthermore, the action takes place in a site permanently devoted to the definitive judgment of a neutral judge or jury solely on the basis of material presented during the proceedings. The action is rigorously isolated from extraprocedural voices, information, or perspectives. With a judge tasked with maintaining the focus on the specific matter at hand and the relevant statutes or precedents, the court works in a centripetal way. The model of the tribunal, in Vismann's typology, is centrifugal. It takes place outside the official spaces of justice, with their specific rules, furniture, and props: it takes place in the world. It is ad hoc; it is addressed not only to specific parties but to a broader public. Rejecting the sanctioned codes of justice, accusations at a tribunal are often formulated in terms of extralegal categories. Its rules and sites are adapted to the specific case; no actor is neutral; and the actors tend to be invested with allegorical significance rather than limited to legal subjects. Thus defendants can be tried as "enemies of the state," to take an example from the typical twentieth-century instance of the show trial, instead of charged with specific infractions or crimes. In Brecht's unsuccessful attempt to tribunalize his *Threepenny* lawsuit, to make it a public showdown, the competing parties are characterized as "artists" and "capital." Everything in the tribunal, Vismann writes,

> is contested, as nothing is predetermined. In the [tribunal] trial, the antagonistic parties are so unfixed that they can, in the contest, be ever configured anew; in the terms of official justice, they can switch their roles between accuser and accused, between plaintiff and defendant. Even the accusation is not predetermined. There is no prior agreement about the very categories by which accusations are made and judgments delivered ... The absent or merely loose correlation with established law allows tribunals a wider scope of action than the courts. They can negotiate anything that should become a matter of public concern.[88]

If the law in some accepted or codified form is the precondition of the court, it is the *public* that is constitutive for the tribunal.

Around 1930, Brecht's project centered on cases, involving a critique of traditional forms of right based on exploitation, and also on developing new models for the public production of knowledge and justice. In that, "The *Threepenny* Lawsuit" was only the most public, most conventional model in its context of institutions of law, and the most closely tied to traditional forms of the culture of the case. But perhaps more significant for Brecht's thinking about the case were his *Lehrstücke*, or learning plays.[89] Thus in *Das Badener Lehrstück vom Einverständnis* (The Baden-Baden lesson on consent, 1929) the crew of a crashed airplane ask the community in which they arrive for help. The people form an assembly to decide whether humans owe assistance to their fellows in need; according to the principle of self-interest, they decide against this. The pilot learns consent, or *Einverständnis*: he realizes that he will die, but that his fate is understandable and meaningful only as a member of a collective. In another of the *Lehrstücke*, *Die Ausnahme und die Regel* (The exception and the rule, 1929/30), a rich merchant shoots his coolie, misinterpreting the servant's helpful actions as a threat; he is brought to trial and found innocent in a clear case of class justice.

But the revolutionary tribunal is the subject of perhaps the most successful of the learning plays of those years, which concern the formation of social consensus and establishment of justice in a world of emergencies. They address states of exception when principles above and beyond the law need to be established, when existing codes—along with inherited notions of innocence, guilt, and just action—need to be renegotiated by a collective.[90] *Der Jasager* (He who says yes, 1929) starts out in the mode of a lesson in consent to the fate of a cause that transcends the individual and his traditional rights. A young boy joins a group undertaking a hazardous journey through the mountains to get medicine for their village, in which an epidemic is raging. He falls ill and puts the crucial mission in peril. The village's "Great Custom," or *Brauch*, states that rather than returning to the village, the one who endangers such a group must be sacrificed for the greater good. But he must always be asked for consent. The young boy agrees to being hurled off the mountainside, finding justice and meaning in his death in the cause of a larger collective. But the negative reaction of early performers—students from a Berlin high school—led Brecht to explore alternative forms of law. He created a pendant to the *Jasager* called *Der Neinsager* (He who says no, 1930), in which the power of a collective to reject old laws and create new ones to account for new conditions is developed. From the same starting point, the young boy withholds his consent. The travelers ask "Why do you not answer in accordance with the Custom? He who says A must also say B,"[91] and the boy replies:

> The answer I gave was wrong, but your question was even more wrong. He who says A need not necessarily say B. He may realize that A was wrong. I wanted to get medicine for my mother, but now I myself have fallen ill, so it is no longer possible. And because of the altered situation I want to turn back at once ... As for the old Great Custom, I see no rhyme or reason in it. What I need is a new Great Custom to be introduced at once, to wit, the Custom of rethinking every new situation.[92]

As in other forms of the case, the law itself can be put on trial, and the ad hoc, extralegal form of the tribunal creates the negotiable conditions for this to happen.

Die Maßnahme (The measures taken, 1930) is Brecht's most sustained reckoning with the justice of the tribunal in the modern state of exception: it concerns illegal, underground work in the service of revolution. Three agitators report to a committee of superiors—the Control Chorus—in Moscow. They had been sent on an undercover mission to China to bring the teachings of the revolution to the exploited of an important city. In the course of their mission they had been put in danger four times by another agitator, whose heart burned for the revolution but who acted impulsively, out of empathy for the workers instead of an analysis of the situation. Finally, they are exposed and on the run; to cover their tracks and avoid capture, they are forced to shoot their impulsive comrade and throw his body into a lime pit. In the interests of the revolution and to spare his fellow agitators, the comrade gives his consent. The play takes the form of the agitators' presentation of their mission and their request for a judgment on their actions, a verdict on whether they had acted responsibly or criminally. The Control Chorus becomes a tribunal: "Describe how it happened and why, and you will hear our verdict."[93] The agitators accept this justice. They underscore the state of emergency and the dangerous, extralegal conditions of revolutionary activity: "We are not yet granted the choice not to kill."[94] The tribunal's verdict: "We agree with you." Here the judges seek not to negotiate a new law but to develop principles for decision-making and responsibility under extremes where there are no laws under which to subsume social conduct:

> ... your report shows us what is
> Needed to change the world:
> Anger and tenacity, knowledge and indignation
> Swift action, deep deliberation
> Cold endurance, unending perseverance
> Comprehension of the individual and comprehension of the whole:
> Taught only by reality can
> Reality be changed.[95]

The developing media of the nineteenth and twentieth centuries opened up new and complex possibilities for tribunalization and for making justice public. Photographs were problematic in forensic contexts but they could arouse emotion and steer public opinion outside of the courts. The press, as we have seen, spectacularized cases in many ways: Maximilian Harden and Karl Kraus used their journals to turn court cases into tribunals, putting the law on trial before a wide reading public; more commercial court reporting gained readers precisely by undermining the judicial imperative of objectivity and by including contextual matters that were not, legally, germane to the case. And of course film and radio served and generated new configurations of a mass public. Brecht's exploration of the possibilities of tribunalization was programmatically informed by the new medial conditions of the time. "The *Threepenny* Lawsuit" crossed the printed press with film, opening to public view the space between the new mode of cinematic production and the developing legislation and legal practices around it. *Kuhle Wampe* used sound film and the means of epic theatre to put the legal justice system in the dock. Of course, these very means—interruption, montage, mixed media—were themselves developed out of an engagement with photography and film.[96] The megaphone could make justice a public matter, a matter of the proletarianized population, and one that poses highly political but fundamentally extralegal questions: To whom does the world belong? Who will change the world?[97]

Brecht followed closely the spectacular development of justice, tribunals, and show trials in the twentieth century. His library contained extensive documentation of them, including the published transcripts of Soviet show trials of the 1930s and beyond, as well as of the Nuremberg Trials of 1945–1946, the Allied military tribunals in which the political, judicial, and military elites of Germany were tried for war crimes.[98] Brecht himself was called to testify at one of these publicly broadcast tribunals, the House Un-American Activities Committee, in 1947 (and more on this below). Of course these postdate Brecht's work discussed here, but the new media nonetheless lay at the core of the earlier learning plays, and specifically in his focus on the so-called *gestus*.

Manfred Wekwerth, who worked with Brecht at the Berliner Ensemble between 1951 and the playwright's death in 1956, recalled the following about the plans to dramatize famous trials, as discussed by Tretyakov:

> Famous trials ... were to be restaged by actors before a public. With just a few carefully chosen *gestic* means, the documents, without the need to create the illusion of a real court, would be presented for judgment. More than the facts—anyone could read the protocols himself—Brecht was interested in the physical attitude (*Haltung*) assumed by the actors and the

> audience: one sits in judgment. Elements of the epic theatre are inherent in every court trial by their very nature.[99]

Gestus and *Haltung*: these are at the core of the program of the learning play, and Brecht found them "inherent in every court trial." The *gestus* was, in Benjamin's words, the "quotable gesture."[100] It was the way complex social states and modes of behavior (*Haltung*) were embedded in the body: adapting certain behaviorist psychological theories as well as Vsevolod Meyerhold's dramatic ideas of "biomechanics," Brecht saw gestures as offering insight into both the emotions and the thought processes of an embodied subject. It is a variant of a widespread concern with bodily forms of communication and knowledge in the early twentieth century that went by many names: *Ausdruckskunde* or the science of expression, physiognomy in film theory, certain forms of Gestalt psychology; it affected post-Saussurian linguistics, underlay the philosophical anthropology of Max Scheler and Helmuth Plessner, the graphology of Ludwig Klages, the art-historical thought of Hans Sedlmayr, and the centrality of the notion of mimesis in the work of Benjamin and Adorno.[101] Brecht reversed the logic of "expression" and adapted it to acting technique: if physical comportment revealed the processes of emotion and cognition, adopting these motions could induce, indeed produce, these very movements of the mind in the subject.[102] Brecht's interest was not in producing a more convincing or lifelike representation on stage. The learning plays were not even meant, primarily, for an audience: through the imitation of gestures and modes of bodily being, the actors themselves would learn the thoughts, feelings, reflexes of other subjects, forms of bodily being, habits, actions, and thoughts that were socially produced, shared, and taught. When the learning play *Der Flug der Lindberghs* (The flight of Lindbergh, 1929) was performed before an audience, the public was asked to recite certain parts, making them part of the action and putting them in the position of acting or speaking gestically. By isolating typical actions, making them strange, and engaging with them corporeally, actors would gain insight not into character or feelings but instead into the situated and conditioned behavior of social subjects.[103] Thus the replaying of assemblies, court proceedings, and tribunals gets to the social core of the testimony that the textual record could not register. Indeed, *Die Maßnahme* thematizes the process of distanced re-enactment: the four agitators not only report to the court, but re-enact the background to their actions in detail, actors playing characters who were playing other characters in the drama within a drama.

The point here about the *gestus* and Brecht's use of it in his exploration of justice is that its conditions were those of the new media: of photography, film, and the recorded voice. The *gestus* is "citable": it can be pointed to like a photograph, replayed like moving images or recorded speech, or both. The *gestus* is discontinuous: it can be cut out of its context and reintroduced into others. It could exist in multiple "takes," played differently, and varied endlessly. It is the repeated short clip that we see in *Kuhle Wampe*: the close-up of the judge, the rental court official, the bailiff, the landlord, and the welfare officer, and the shrugs that tell us what they know and how they think. Or it is the wide gesture, the nonchalant power of the removals man in the Red Megaphone rent tribunal. It is the public face of the proceedings that, as Wekwerth reported, *does not make it into the written protocols* of the trial, which anyone could *read* himself. Photography, film, and recorded sound provided new possibilities of, and indeed models

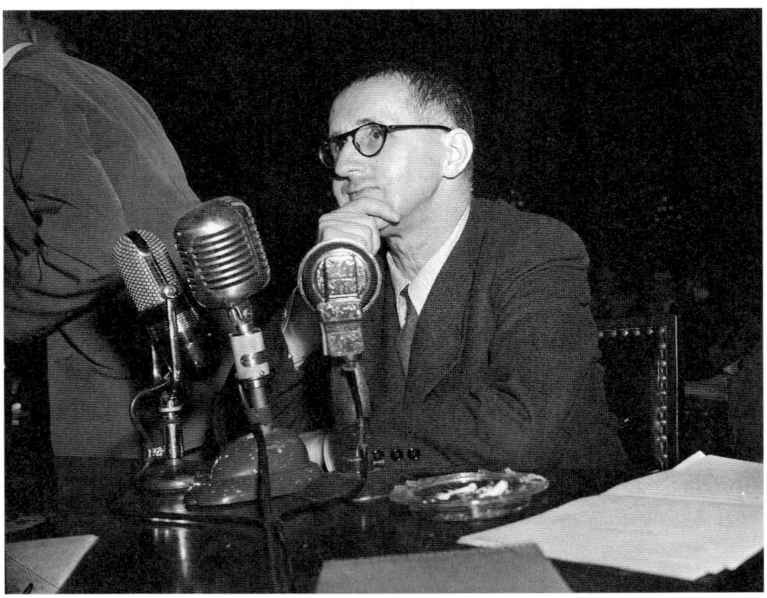

Bertolt Brecht before the House Un-American Activities Committee, October 30, 1947. Photo © ullstein bild/TopFoto.

for, justice beyond the space of the court and the written forms of its depositions, decisions, and records.

§

When Brecht was called to testify before the House Un-American Activities Committee on October 30, 1947, he entered the new, tribunalized spaces of justice. The committee was ad hoc; it was not part of the judiciary at all but put together by a faction of the legislative branch. Its competences were unclear, rather crudely claimed on its own authority, and in fact the activities it prosecuted did not represent the violation of any laws. The committee set its own norm, worked by association instead of establishing illegal acts, fed on the widespread public fear of subversive activity and fed that fear in turn. And yet, in this improvised form the possibility of shifting the roles of accuser and accused was always present. In a shouting match a few days before Brecht's testimony, the writer John Howard Lawson tried that gambit: "This Committee is on trial here before the American people. Let us get that straight."[104] By means of radio and film, the proceedings took place before a vast and new public, which followed it closely.

Brecht understood these conditions well, and he inhabited the new, technically mediated space of justice with aplomb. Asked if his work was based on the works of Marx and Lenin, he showed how crude the question was: "No, I don't think that is quite correct": Marx was a thinker about history, but Brecht wrote historical plays. The two are very different things. Asked about incriminating meetings on specific dates, he could neither affirm nor deny them: who remembers such dates? They were, he allowed, possible. He spent so much time quibbling with the Committee's translations that the content—for the Committee political, for Brecht poetic—could never be discussed. Finally, when faced with an English rendering of his *Solidaritätslied* (Song of solidarity)—pure revolutionary agitation—and asked point-blank "Did you write that Mr. Brecht?" he responded: "No, uh I wrote a German poem, but that is very different [audience laughter] from this thing [audience laughter]." The Committee gave up. He did not deny saying A, but he saw no reason to say B. His answers were the wrong ones, but the questions were even more wrong.

His actions, however, probably had a greater effect than his words—the evasive answers, the quibbling with translations, and the apparently unexpected news that he had never joined a Communist Party. In a space dominated by tense testimony, sharp exchanges, and the battle to be heard—heightened by microphones and camera close-ups—Brecht assumed a *Haltung* of casual openness. He smoked a cigar, the habit of relaxed male authority. (*Life* published a photograph of Brecht behind his "smoke screen" at the hearing.)[105] In the face of inquisitorial questioning that sought to build a crescendo and cut to the chase, he answered slowly, controlling the rhythm and producing comedy by pauses and syncopation. In an atmosphere of cynicism, he answered naïvely. Tightly framed by the camera, he showed the world the actions and voice of an innocent man trying to be helpful but caught in an absurd situation. It was perfectly packaged for broadcast. He listened to himself on the radio that evening, writing in his diary of the newsreel cameras, the two radio stations and eighty reporters covering his testimony,[106] and his friend Lion Feuchtwanger reported that his testimony was replayed repeatedly on radio.[107] Finally, Brecht retrospectively turned his appearance into a cameo by leaving the country the next day, for Zurich and then East Berlin, never to return to the US.

§

Brecht was interested not only in the new media of law, but in the new conditions of law in a world that seemed permanently at war, with front lines moving unstably both within and across shifting national borders. Recent research has explored one of Brecht's most important reference points at the time of *Kuhle Wampe* and the learning plays: the work of the jurist and legal theorist Carl Schmitt.[108] (Indeed, the *Badener Lehrstück vom Einverständnis* contains a clown by the name of Herr Schmitt, and one of the four agitators of *Die Maßnahme* is "Karl Schmitt from Berlin.") Brecht's interest is counterintuitive: Schmitt was no revolutionary, and though the precise political goals of his legal theory and interventions during the crisis of the Weimar Republic have been hard to pin down—whether his purpose was to undermine or preserve the republic—by 1932 he was clearly on the side of the authoritarian right. He became the "crown jurist of the Reich" by defending the national government of Franz von Papen, who had dissolved

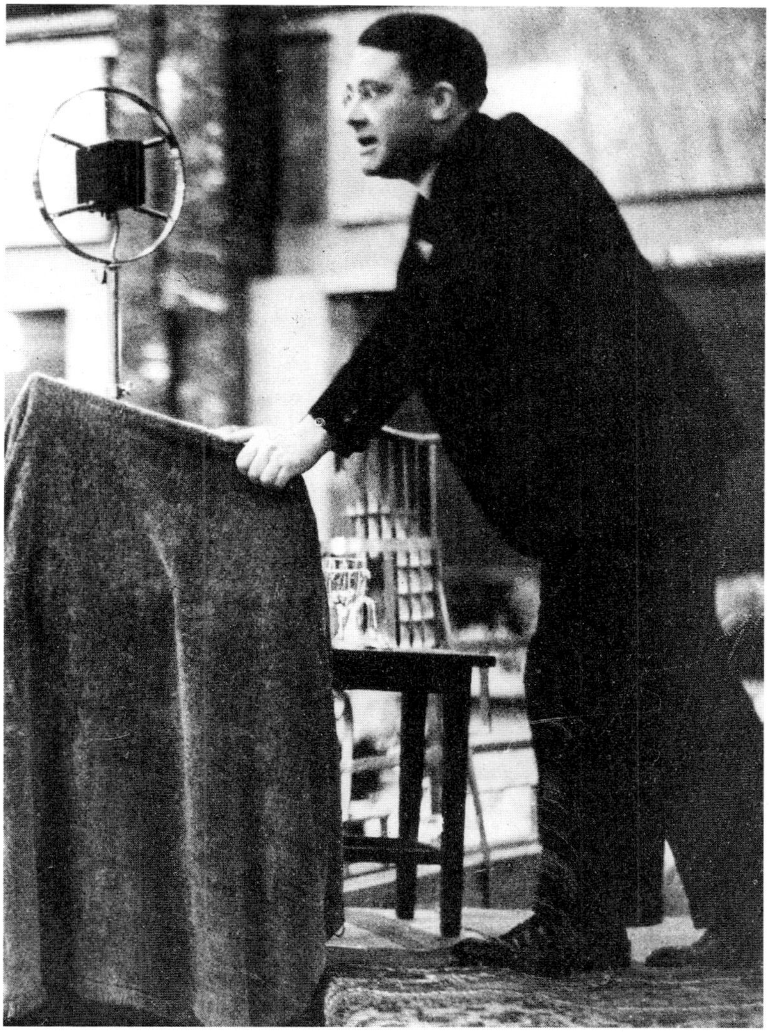

Carl Schmitt in 1930. Photo © Getty Images/ullstein bild.

the Social Democratic government of Prussia in that year and who, as chancellor, assumed direct commissarial control of Germany's largest province. Associated with the National Bolshevist circles of the Conservative Revolution around Ernst Jünger and Ernst Niekisch (which included Rudolf Schlichter, and with which Brecht had contact in those years), Schmitt swiftly accommodated himself to the Third Reich, and, under the protection of Hermann

Göring and the jurist Hans Frank (who went on to serve as head of the *Generalgouvernement* in Poland during the Second World War), his influence in the Nazi government was considerable until his fall from grace in 1936 due to factional infighting. Imprisoned and interrogated by the Allies at various times between 1945 and 1947, Schmitt lost his chair at the university in Berlin but continued to publish and remained influential among younger generations of historians and jurists of the Federal Republic, mostly in conservative circles until a leftwing interest in his work developed from the late 1970s, shortly before his death in 1985.

It was through Walter Benjamin that Brecht came to grapple with Schmitt's political and legal theory. In a note of April 21, 1930, Benjamin summarizes the contents of a conversation with Brecht as follows: "Schmitt / consent hatred suspicion."[109] And Schmitt's work was of fundamental importance to Benjamin in its elaboration of what could be called an epistemology of the extreme. Benjamin's first reference to Schmitt's work is in his *Origins of German Tragic Drama*, in which he cites the definition of sovereignty from Schmitt's *Political Theology* of 1922: "Sovereign is he who decides on the exception"—he, in other words, who could suspend the rule of law.[110] In the hermetic "Epistemo-Critical Prologue" to the *Trauerspiel* book, Benjamin incorporated Schmitt's dictum into his theory of knowledge:

> [T]hose elements which it is the function of the concept to elicit from phenomena are most clearly evident at the extremes ... It is therefore erroneous to understand the most general references which language makes as concepts, instead of recognizing them as ideas. It is absurd to attempt to explain the general as an average. The general is the idea. The empirical, on the other hand, can be all the more profoundly understood the more clearly it is seen as an extreme. The concept has its roots in the extreme.[111]

From the *Trauerspiel* of 1925 to the 1940 theses "On the Concept of History," with their attention to the "moment of danger" and the "state of exception," Schmitt's insights from the political right underlay Benjamin's attempts to develop a new set of concepts and principles of political action from the left in a world of extremes.

Brecht's reliance on Schmittian concepts in the learning plays is manifest. The notion of the *Ausnahme* or exception—the suspension of law that paradoxically underwrites the power of the sovereign—is in the very title of *Die Ausnahme und die Regel*, in which, on a tiny scale, the law is suspended against the perceived threat of the proletariat. *Die Maßnahme* takes up another of Schmitt's key ideas. From his earliest writings, Schmitt focused on the problems of judicature in modernity. The judicial crisis of modernity consisted in the fact that the speed of change in society outstrips the ability of legislative statutes to keep pace. His first solution to this was to reject the legal positivism that saw the role of the judge as merely to subsume an act or state of affairs under the appropriate law: he saw the judge as an instance that is instead *productive* of the law.[112] He asserts the priority of the decision over the statute: when cases ceased to be subsumable under existing codes, the primary role of the court had to be to make a decision anyway, even if, in taking account of new conditions, the judgment violates the original law on which it is based. That a judgment, a decision, is made at all is more important to the rule of law than the contents of law in its codified form. Thus Schmitt's notorious "decisionism" was put in the service of political order instead of abstract, Enlightenment notions of right. (His thinking is based on the absolutist theory of Thomas Hobbes, for whom, writing in the age of civil war, order was the primary necessity.)

Die Maßnahme explores this problem in the context of illegal revolutionary activity. There are no laws when challenging the class rule of the state, and there are no maxims to follow. How, then, to act? Schmitt's answer is to find a point of reference prior to the law in the very nature of the state. "The concept of the state," wrote Schmitt in 1927, "presupposes the concept of the political." The political depends not on a social contract but on the cohesion that is formed by the conditions of existential threat to a polity:

> The distinction of friend and enemy denotes the utmost degree of intensity of a union or separation, of an association or dissociation. It can exist theoretically and practically, without having simultaneously to draw upon all those moral, aesthetic, economic, or other distinctions.[113]

Brecht translates this into the conditions of illegal politics:

> He who fights for Communism must be able to fight and not fight; must tell the truth and not tell the truth; render service and not render service; place himself in danger and avoid danger; be recognizable and be unrecognizable. He who fights for Communism has of all virtues only one: that he fights for Communism.[114]

The very name of the play cites another of Schmitt's categories, developed as his concerns moved from those of the judiciary to those of the executive functions of the state. Again, the problem was the modern condition of judicial nonsimultaneity. At a time when the state itself was under threat, existing statutes might not provide the means to respond effectively. Radically relativizing the Enlightenment concept of the state, he argues that the rule of law as enshrined in liberal constitutionalism served as an effective means of politics and state-formation only in a specific and limited era: the security and prosperity of the bourgeois west from the late eighteenth century to the rise of mass politics, prior to the shift of government to an instance that is meant to balance interests and thus become, in a politicized or neutralizing way, a "total state." Inevitably, in the twentieth century, the existence of the state would require the suspension of the rule of law and the move beyond the realm of "legality" into the decisionistic realm of "legitimacy" outside the law. For Schmitt, this happened through the emergency decrees of a sovereign executive entitled to the suspend the constitution, decrees he termed *Maßnahmen* or "measures," as opposed to laws. Brecht was interested in the distinction. Consider his addition to *Die Maßnahme* in a version of 1934/35, when he was in exile. About the killing of their comrade, the agitators are asked by the control chorus: "'So that was your judgment?' [The four agitators, very loud] 'No! It was a measure!'"[115] In other words, it was not an application of the law but a sovereign, extralegal decision forced upon them by a situation that was new, unprecedented, and not covered by existing law. If Brecht here mixes the sphere of the judiciary with that of the executive, this was, after all, the logic of the tribunalization of justice; moreover, it follows the development of Schmitt's thought. For both Schmitt and Brecht, existential threat to the state or the movement, from within or without, defined the space of the political. Schmitt explored this in legal and constitutional theory; Brecht describes the situation of *Die Maßnahme* from the point of view of the party:

> In times of extreme persecution and the confusion of theory,
> Fighters sketch out the situation
> To gauge action and possibilities.[116]

Schmitt, Benjamin, and Brecht shared the project of thinking through action and knowledge in a state of exception, a moment of danger.[117] They concurred in their conclusion that, in Benjamin's terms, "the 'state of emergency' (*Ausnahmezustand*) in which we live is not the exception but the rule."[118]

There would be much more to say about the uncomfortable relationship of Brecht to Schmitt, or more broadly of the independent intellectual left to the circles of the Conservative Revolution.[119] But I think it is more interesting here to turn the question around and ask what Brecht's reliance on this imposing but deeply problematic figure of the right tells us about the thought of Schmitt himself. For Schmitt recognized the affinity between their political projects. In the *Glossarium*, the book of notes he kept after the war, Schmitt writes of Brecht's *Threepenny Novel* as "an extraordinary and uncanny illustration of my thesis of the distinction between legality and legitimacy"; and in a marginal note to the Italian translation of *Legalität und Legitimität* of 1932, Schmitt wrote "see Bert Brecht, *Die Maßnahme*."[120]

Looking backwards at Schmitt through the lens of Brecht's borrowings from him reveals something worth attending to: that Schmitt too was fascinated by the new media and their relation to law and to the state. In October 1929, when Brecht had just published his *Badener Lehrstück vom Einverständnis* and was beginning his *Der Jasager/Der Neinsager* project, Schmitt gave a lecture at a conference convened at the Barcelona World's Fair.[121] (He apparently saw Ludwig Mies van der Rohe's famous pavilion there, but we have no record of what he thought.[122]) Schmitt sought here to get to grips with the relation of technology and politics:

> The inventions of the fifteenth and sixteenth centuries seemed to promote freedom, individualism, and rebellion; the invention of the printing press led to the freedom of the press. Today, the technological developments are the means

> of a colossal domination of the masses: along with radio comes the monopoly of the radio, along with film comes film censorship.[123]

"The ultimate meaning" of these media, he said, "will only be clear when we see what form of politics is strong enough to seize control of the new technology, and what authentic friend/enemy alignments will grow from this new ground."[124] In 1947, when Brecht was summoned to testify before the House Un-American Activities Committee, Schmitt had just been released from detention in Nuremberg; in an earlier period of arrest in Berlin, he mused in his prison notes about the tribunalization of justice and its legal implications:

> The establishment of revolutionary tribunals and people's courts is not intended to diminish the terror but rather to sharpen it. The public, legal defamations and discriminations, the public or secret blacklists, the acts of declaring individuals enemies of the state, of the people, or of humanity do not mean granting the opponent the legal position of an enemy in the sense of a belligerent party. On the contrary, they are supposed to deprive him even of this last right. They amount to a total disenfranchisement in the name of the law. The enmity becomes so absolute that even the age-old sacral distinction between enemy and criminal dissolves in the paroxysm of self-righteousness.[125]

But it is photography, I think, that provides most insight into the medial conditions of political action in Schmitt's work. He finds the ultimate ground of justice in the moment of decision, of politics in the moment of danger. It calls to mind the work of Ernst Jünger at the time. In his photobook *Der gefährliche Augenblick* of 1930, Jünger describes a Schmittian historical typology: modernity is characterized not, as Max Weber and others described it, as a time of disenchanted predictability, but as an age characterized by permanent danger.[126] With the development of mass politics and a technologized world, the bourgeois era of security was a bygone age. The pictures make his point. He shows scenes of threatening mass demonstrations and of revolt and revolution, the split second of accidents when the victim of a violent death is still alive, the tense instant before an execution by firing squad. For his part, Benjamin found a revolutionary philosophy of history in this space opened up in the split second: "The past can be seized only as an image which flashes up at the instant when it can be recognized and is never seen again."[127] His historical materialist must "seize hold of a memory as it flashes up at a moment of danger."[128] Schmitt too was fascinated by Jünger's thought of the time: seeking contact as the latter was preparing *Der gefährliche Augenblick*, he found a kindred spirit and their friendship would last decades.[129] (And indeed, as the exiled Benjamin was writing his "On the Concept of History," he made notes on Schmitt's published lecture on politics and technology.[130]) The politics, phenomenology, and historical implications were all very different, but at its medial core, this aspect of the thought of Schmitt, Jünger, Brecht, and Benjamin on danger is of a piece. Photography provided them with cognate models of justice at a time of the total state and its enemies, of politics in an age of ever-present danger.

§

Thinking politics and law through the lens of the camera produced a compelling constellation of thought. Yet the media history of the administration of justice tells a different story. In those years of peril, the emblematic technique of social control was far humbler than these new technological media. It circulated on paper but usually disappeared into the files of the courts, tribunals, and state bureaucracies. It was an up-to-date tool of the social sciences, and it served to speed up the passing of important judgments that affected the lives and careers of those it surveyed, but it had none of the spectacle, speed, precision, or immediacy of the new technical media. It was, again, the simple questionnaire.

Developed primarily for use in the field of psychology, the questionnaire arose in tandem with statistical forms of research.[131] Like many modernist techniques, it discouraged narrative and its accumulated details unfolding in sequential time; it also reduced the subject to a type. It was a technique for classifying masses rather than creating individual cases. Yet though it served the rationalization of biographical data, it remained tied to older forms of data registration and storage. And it seeped inexorably into the spaces between biographies and bureaucracies in the

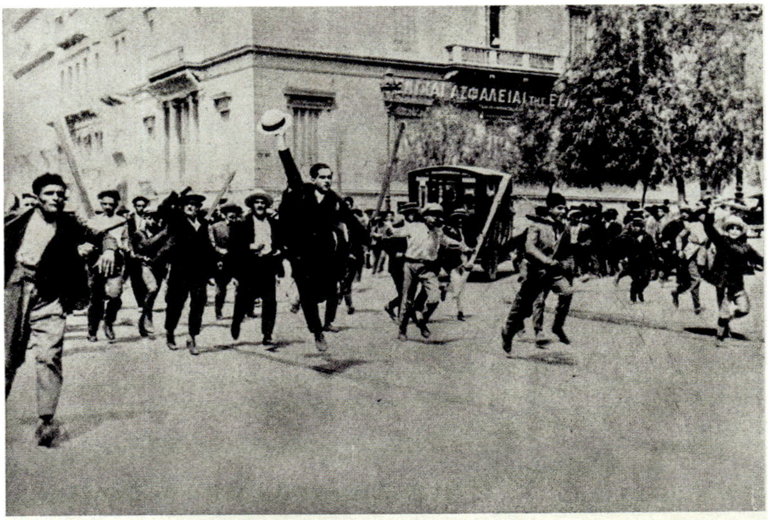

Athen. „Hoch der Volkswille! Nieder mit der Regierung!“

From Ernst Jünger and Ferdinand Bucholtz, *Der gefährliche Augenblick* (1931).

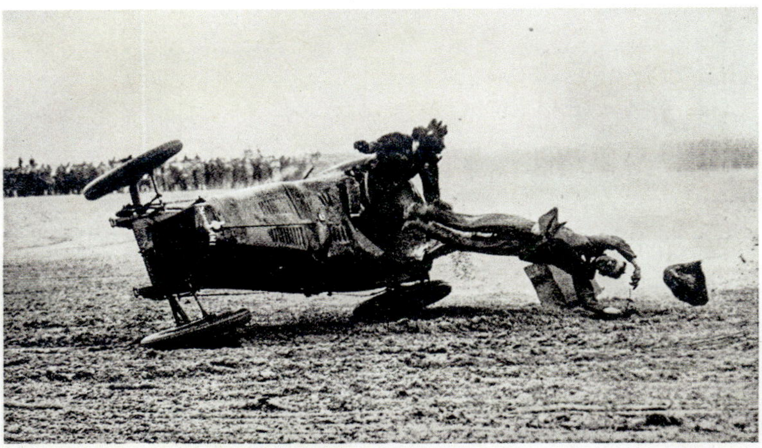

Die letzte Sekunde.

From Ernst Jünger and Ferdinand Bucholtz, *Der gefährliche Augenblick* (1931).

twentieth century. Magnus Hirschfeld derived much of his sexological data not from the traditional medical practice of recording case histories, but by means of questionnaires. Karl Plättner appended a questionnaire to *Eros im Zuchthaus*, his exposé of the

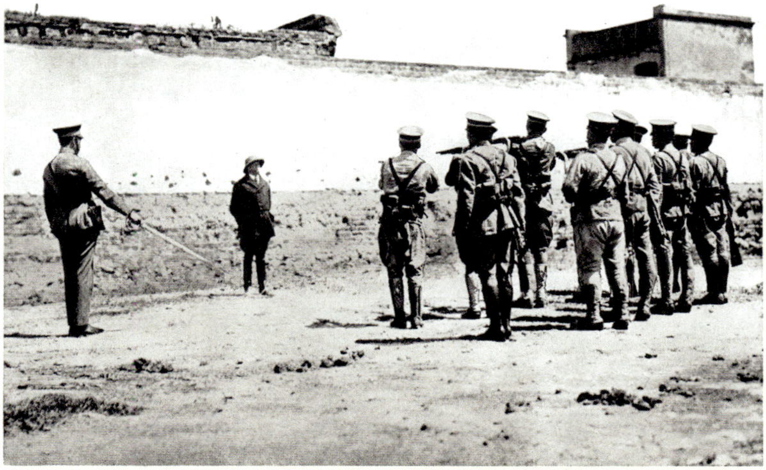

Mexiko. Vor den Mündungen der Gewehre.
Erschießung des Generals Quijano nach einem gescheiterten Revolutionsversuch.

From Ernst Jünger and Ferdinand Bucholtz, *Der gefährliche Augenblick* (1931).

plight of sexuality in the modern prison, casting his net widely to gather information for his project of penal reform.[132] Brecht distributed questionnaires to the audience and performers to gauge the effects of his learning plays and rewrote them according to the responses he received.[133]

It was in Germany that the questionnaire, the *Fragebogen*, came to be most intensively used as a means of political and criminal control.[134] In the case of Rudolf Schlichter, we have seen the two bookends of one of the most important episodes in the history of this paper tool. His answers to the questionnaire of the Reichsverband Deutscher Schriftsteller stand at one end, his answers to the Allied denazification questionnaire at the other. Succeeding the genres of the confession and the medical case history, it also entered into literature as a trope by which to negotiate innocence or guilt. Schmitt's prison memoires open on this note: "Who are you? *Tu quis es?* This is an unfathomable question. I plunged deeply into it at the end of June 1945 as Eduard Spranger, the famous philosopher and teacher, awaited my response to a questionnaire."[135] The most famous literary use of the questionnaire was, without doubt, the conservative revolutionary Ernst von Salomon's *Der Fragebogen* of 1951, in which the Allied questionnaire's sequence of questions is used as the frame for a rambling account of his life during and after the Third Reich.[136] He did so ironically, making much of the crudity of the tool in judging a person's life and politics, and he did so in a particularly disingenuous way. The book was a bestseller, though far too long to translate into English in its entirety; only an abridged version was published as a warning about the unrepentant atmosphere in occupied Germany.[137] Arnolt Bronnen tried something similar three years later in *Arnolt Bronnen gibt zu Protokoll*, organized on the similar conceit of answers to an interrogation.[138] It did not have the same success, perhaps because it lacked the bitter resonance with the experience of the millions of Germans who filled in the questionnaires after the war, and whose further livelihood depended on the answers given and how they were judged. In Germany, at least, the public or secret tribunal was the perilous extreme of extralegal justice, whereas the "merciless catechism of 131 questions" was, as Stig Dagerman wrote, "the ideological equivalent of a tax return"; and in John Dos Passos's words, "Everybody gets fragebogened sooner or later."[139] For several generations of Germans at moments of political danger, the completion of a paper questionnaire, by hand or typewriter, was a shared rite of passage, the means by which they sought to *avoid* becoming a case.

Clearly, the questionnaire could be repurposed and turned against its own logic, but by and large it generated a uniform kind of narrative. As Mikkel Dack and others have pointed out, it produced narratives of victimhood.[140] As we have seen in the cases of Rudolf Schlichter, it encouraged dissimulation, parsimony with the truth, lying, or incomplete responses. If as a bureaucratic form (in every sense) it was asymmetric in terms of power, it granted agency to the users, allowed them the luxury of considered and careful response. It was slow, and the questionnaires were processed at an agonizing pace. Though punishment for untruthful answers was severe, if caught, one had time to weigh up answers and embed them in a larger narrative. If a moment of danger produced a decision likely to be judged harshly by the victors, the questionnaire offered a chance to smooth over the crisis. But unlike the cameo of the tribunal or interrogation, it was not over in an instant: it was saved and put on file; it could haunt the author; it formed part of a biographical paper trail for later scrutiny. It was still on paper that past action was registered and made available to history. And the questionnaire created a generation of victims, the losers of history seeking to better their chances by reweaving the weft of their past through the warp of 131 questions on a pre-printed paper form.

§

I wanted to destroy all castles, to burn all files of documents in all of Bohemia without exception, including all administrative, legal, and governmental papers, and to proclaim all mortgages paid, as well as all other debts ... In short, the revolution I planned was terrible and unprecedented, although directed more against things than against people.

—Mikhail Bakunin[141]

In a side street, not far from the burning Palace of Justice ... stood a man, sharply distinguished from the crowd, flailing his hands in the air and moaning over and over again: "The files are burning! All the files!" "Better files than people!" I told him, but that did not interest him; all he could think of was the files.

—Elias Canetti[142]

Perhaps files, with their paper inscription of history, are not so mundane after all. At various times, it was thought that they could fuel a revolution. One such moment was July 15, 1927, Walter Benjamin's thirty-fifth birthday, in Vienna. In January, rightwing paramilitaries had murdered a war veteran and an eight-year-old boy at a demonstration; in early July, the three militiamen charged with homicide were acquitted. A huge crowd of protesters gathered in front of the Palace of Justice, entered it through broken windows, smashed what they could, and set fire to the files. The building burned until the next morning. Armed police dispersed the crowd, killing eighty-nine demonstrators. The event left a deep mark in the work of Karl Kraus, Elias Canetti, and Heimito von Doderer.[143] In the end, there was no revolution.

We search in vain in Benjamin's work for any response to the event. But perhaps we can find traces of a reflection in "On the Concept of History." Here he describes the "historical materialist" as the modern political subject who can cite all of history at

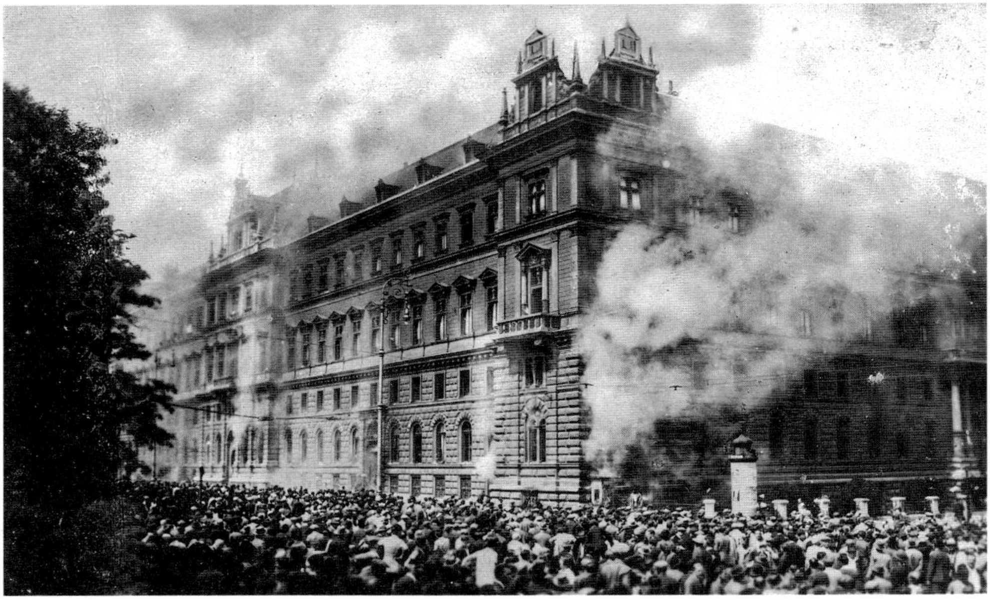

Demonstrators at the burning Palace of Justice, Vienna, July 15, 1927. Postcard.

a moment, who can grasp the revolutionary moments of the past as image, who can see their "time of the now" and blast it out of the "continuum of history."[144] He acts in the moment of danger according to the metaphors and models of photography. The historicist, on the other hand, is faced toward the past and can only witness the wreckage that history hurls before his feet. If the image at the moment of danger was inconceivable without the epistemological figure of the photograph, the pile of debris that grows skyward, we could say, took the medial form of files.

There was, in other words, a sort of nonsimultaneity to which the avant-garde fell prey. Mass politics appropriated the new media, but the protocols of the case clung fatefully to older ones. Certainly Benjamin—scholar, writer, bibliophile, a man of the pen who eschewed the typewriter[145]—knew that the catastrophes of history accumulated in the form of paper. This was the deadweight of history, the rubbish of politics, the longhand of justice.

Brecht might have been less confident before the House Un-American Activities Committee had he known of the extensive files on him produced by FBI surveillance. But no matter: he was in his element before the rolling cameras and flashing bulbs, and the Committee's means were more spectacular than archival. He left the country before anyone could follow the paper trail. But settling in the German Democratic Republic, he entered a new regime that maintained its power using the older media of state control. Those files were not burned, and that is a good thing. That state collapsed before the development of new medial means of control, means that emerged before the battle over the technical media of twentieth-century mass politics was even decided.

Conclusion

I know the megaphones of power and of law,
The amplifiers and meaning distorters of the regime,
The blacklists with many names,
And the card files of the persecutors.

—Carl Schmitt[1]

What, then, is a case? Or, better: what can the cases explored here tell us about the public production of knowledge and of judgments, about the public use of reason and, in Negt and Kluge's terms, the "organization of experience"?[2]

If one of Jürgen Habermas's most important lessons is that publicness is not identical with any single institution, medium, or space and has an uneasy relation to genres, those entities still tell us much about the development of publics. What has emerged in these studies is that the conditions of publicity, though not tied to any one medium, are nonetheless profoundly tied to the specific and changing *conditions* of media in the late nineteenth and twentieth centuries. I have described here how cases tended to arise in the spaces in between: between classes, institutions, and media with their various and shifting genres. And if there is one aspect of the larger history of this period that was a constant, it was the very change in the medial constellations of the moment, changes that had profound effects on other forms of practice, from architecture to literature, painting and photography to the workings of justice. Filmmakers read novels, of course, but Brecht felt it worthwhile to point out that novelists also went to the cinema.[3] We need to attend to the larger implications of this state of affairs. The complex changes in the means and practices of representation were in no way linear, though histories can be, and typically are, written by reifying media and genres and following what might seem to be an internal logic. But developments in the press affected the conditions of both architectural theory and design, and developments in medicine and law left their fault lines in literature. Developments in forensic photography and the book market had effects—surprising ones—on painting and the graphic arts. The attempts to legislate and control the space of the representable led to strange mutations that might seem like inexplicable irruptions; but they have a certain logic when considered in terms of the changing shape of the public sphere and the widespread instinct to look to its borders for reasons of many kinds. And as I have suggested, the spaces between classes, institutions, and media were also (though not only) the spaces in which avant-gardes of various kinds could develop. The very nonsimultaneity in the changes of all of these forces could also subvert their projects.

Carl Schmitt's somewhat hidden but nonetheless heartfelt reflections on media are worth, I think, attending to. That their contexts were either disingenuous or self-delusional, or both, need not concern us too much. What politics, he asked, would be decisive enough to seize the new technology of twentieth-century publicness? He asked this question in the context of his exploration of decisionism, and he did so by pointing to the extremes. The extremes, he reminded us (along with Benjamin and others), were always present, determining the conditions of politics. This was as much a description as a prescription. The extremes also provided the room for action. We can look at media through this lens more programmatically than Schmitt did himself. For if there is one thing that is convincing about the picture of extreme politics that he draws, it is that political stability is at best temporary, limited to historical episodes, and that the twentieth century was not one of those eras. And if there was one thing that was paradigmatically unstable in this period, it was the conditions of media.

Schmitt's concept of both legal judgment and sovereign action has, at its core, a specific temporality. It is that of *urgency* and *catching up*. The legislation of statutes could not keep pace with the conditions that they were meant to order, just as constitutions could not keep pace with the threats posed to them. Molly Nesbit and others have described a similar situation with regard to media.[4] The law was always slow to respond to the new technical and social conditions that media created. The laws concerning the status of texts, architecture, and images, film, video, and the internet, were (and are) always playing catch-up. Those spaces opened up possibilities for action and for politics. And following Benjamin, Schmitt, and Brecht, we can say that those spaces are also dangerous. They are constantly shifting spaces in between, as laws, technologies, publics, and the very conditions of publicness form ever new constellations. If Negt and Kluge write that publics open up in the "ruptures of history," such ruptures were, in fact, often caused by the surprising and unexpected changes in the constellation of media.[5]

These were the ruptures to which the practitioners of the case were drawn. Karl Kraus used the space between the press and the courts to try to negotiate a new and modern relation of public to private. Adolf Loos found himself in the very public space between the beginning of a project and its completion, between the approved plans and the public reaction to the building, and he knew how to use this space as room for maneuver. Oskar Panizza and Otto Gross occupied the interstices between madness and the law and found that the media of the psychiatric case were where these things might be negotiated; George Grosz produced some of his most disturbing and challenging work in precisely this area. Rudolf Schlichter's life was, in fact, lived there, and that life can be seen in the shifting and inconclusive politics of the self that it allowed. And Bertolt Brecht programmatically explored the zones created by the new medial conditions of politics and the law. If for Wittgenstein the world is everything that *is* the case, for the figures here, politics—always opened to a public in the spaces in between institutions and media, genres and their rules—was everything that *could be* a case.

Acknowledgments

This book has developed over so many years that I can hardly remember, let alone thank, all those who contributed to making it happen. But it is a pleasure to try.

For crucial feedback on the chapters here I am grateful to Simon Baker, Peter Chametzky, Steve Edwards, Adrian Forty, Sabine Kriebel, Karen Lang, Maria Loh, Christopher Long, Sven Lütticken, Amos Morris-Reich, Jenny Nachtigall, Nikos Pegioudis, Caitlin Powell, Camilla Smith, Leslie Topp, Michael White, and Tom Wilkinson. Several colleagues in the History of Art Department at University College London engaged closely with this project, and I thank them for their invaluable contributions: Mechthild Fend, Andrew Hemingway, Maria Loh, Rose Marie San Juan, and Richard Taws. But many others there accompanied the long gestation of this project, and they have been crucial to making the department such an extraordinarily supportive environment and at the same time the most exciting and challenging place to think that I have encountered: David Bindman, Diana Dethloff, Natasha Eaton, Briony Fer, Charles Ford, Tamar Garb, Tom Gretton, Bob Mills, Mignon Nixon, Stephanie Schwartz, and Alison Wright, as well as two colleagues I dearly miss: Frances Stracey and Helen Weston. Three people offered their support at critical moments: David Freedberg, Kathleen James-Chakraborty, and Michael Hagner. The Warburg Institute and the Bilderfahrzeuge project there were congenial hosts and sources of inspiration; my thanks to Andreas Bayer, Philipp Ekardt, Hans-Christian Hönes, Eckart Marchand, Stuart Moss, and Johannes von Müller. And for help of many kinds, my thanks to Stina Barchan, Michael Berkowitz, Mark Carrington, Carolin Duttlinger, Paul Fox, Albrecht Götz von Olenhusen, Tag Gronberg, Anke te Heesen, Joan Kee, Markus Kristan, Lynda Nead, Anne Reimers, Carol Scherer, Herbert Stattler, the late Jutta Vinzent, and Vera Wolff. A brief conversation with the late Miriam Bratu Hansen, whose work has been so important to this project, gave me the courage of my convictions.

Research for a book of this kind would be impossible without the generosity and expertise of librarians, archivists, and curators. In London I have been lucky to have had the help of the staff of the British Library and the University College London Library. In Germany my work was made easier by the staffs of the following institutions: the Archive of the Akademie der Künste, Berlin, especially Anna Schultz and Helga Neumann; the Bundesarchiv, where Dr. Stefanie Jost offered much assistance; the Landesarchiv Berlin; the Geheimes Staatsarchiv and the Staatsbibliothek of the Stiftung Preußischer Kulturbesitz; and the Deutsches Literaturarchiv Marbach. In Vienna my thanks to the Graphische Sammlung Albertina, the Wiener Stadt- und Landarchiv; the Handschriftensammlung of the Wienbibliothek, and the Österreichische Nationalbibliothek.

Gillian Malpass offered her encouragement during the early stages of the project. Thomas Weaver's creativity and enthusiasm have made working with MIT Press a pleasure. My thanks as well to Pamela Johnston for her sensitive editing, and to Judith Feldmann, Gabriela Bueno Gibbs, and Hilary Bird for their professionalism and support.

Chapter 1 first appeared in the *Art Bulletin* 94, no. 3 (2012), and it is reprinted here with only minor corrections. An early version of the second half of chapter 3 appeared as "Entzauberte Bilder: Gewalt, Illustration und Neue Sachlichkeit" in *Einwegbilder*, ed. Inge Hinterwaldner, Michael Hagner and Vera Wolff in the series *eikones: Nationaler Forschungsschwerpunkt Bildkritik der Universität Basel* (Munich: Wilhelm Fink, 2016). Parts of chapter 5 were originally published in the article "Brecht's '*Threepenny* Lawsuit' and the Culture of the Case" in the *Oxford Art Journal* 41, no. 2 (2018). My thanks to the editors of those publications for their important input and the permission to reprint that material here.

The book took its final form during a period of research leave generously funded by a Leverhulme Trust Research Fellowship. A grant from the College Art Association's Millard Meiss Publication Fund contributed to the production of the book. Over many years, I have received funding and other support from the Department of History of Art and the Faculty of Social and Historical Sciences at UCL, for which I am most grateful.

Carin Schwartz has read every word of this book many times; she has my thanks as well as my love. So too do Julius and Benjamin, who have lived through the years of research and drafting in other ways. Finally, I'm delighted my sister, Judy Schwartz, could be with me in Vienna when this project began to take form, and saddened that my parents can no longer be with me now that it's finished. This book is dedicated to their memory.

Notes

Introduction

1. Ludwig Wittgenstein, *Tractatus Logico-Philosophicus*, trans. D. F. Pears and B. F. McGuinness (London: Routledge & Kegan Paul, 1961), 7: "Die Welt ist alles, was der Fall ist."

2. Ernst Ottwalt, *Denn sie wissen was sie tun: Ein deutscher Justiz-Roman* (Berlin: Malik-Verlag, 1931). As the book appeared, Ottwalt was writing the screenplay to the film *Kuhle Wampe oder: Wem gehört die Welt?* (Kuhle Wampe, or to whom does the world belong?) with Bertolt Brecht—a film which, as shown in chapter 5, also addresses the contemporary crisis of justice. There is scant literature on Ottwalt (born Ernst Gottwalt Nicolas), though several of his books have recently been republished. The fullest account of his life and work is now Christian Eger's substantial afterword to Ottwalt, *Ruhe und Ordnung: Roman aus dem Leben der nationalgesinnten Jugend* (1929; Halle: Hasenverlag, 2014).

3. Mela Hartwig, "Der phantastische Paragraph," in *Ekstasen: Novellen* (Berlin/Vienna/Leipzig: Paul Zsolnay, 1928), repr. in Hartwig, *Das Verbrechen: Novellen und Erzählungen* (Graz: Droschl, 2004), here 127.

4. Gabriele Tergit, "Die Toten-Klage: Niesebeins Selbstmord und unfreiwilliges Fortlegen," *Berliner Tageblatt*, August 20, 1929, repr. in *Wer schießt aus Liebe? Gerichtsreportagen*, ed. Jens Brüning (Berlin: Das neue Berlin, 1999), 119–121. Unless otherwise indicated, all translations are my own.

5. Jakob Wassermann, *Der Fall Maurizius* (Berlin: S. Fischer, 1928).

6. Ricarda Huch, *Der Fall Deruga* (Berlin: Ullstein, 1918).

7. *Das Todesurteil: Die Geschichte meines Prozesses* and *Lebenslänglich: Erlebtes und Erlittenes* (both Berlin: Ullstein, 1925).

8. There is now a considerable literature on Haarmann, but the fundamental text remains Theodor Lessing, *Haarmann: Die Geschichte eines Werwolfs*, Außenseiter der Gesellschaft, vol. 6 (Berlin: Die Schmiede, 1925; repr. Munich: Rogner & Bernhard, 1973).

9. See *Peter Kürten, genannt der Vampir von Düsseldorf*, ed. Elisabeth Lenk and Katharina Kaever (Frankfurt a.M.: Eichborn, 1997); Matthias Blazek, *Carl Großmann und Friedrich Schumann: Zwei Serienmörder in den zwanziger Jahren* (Stuttgart: ibidem-Verlag, 2009); *Tat ohne Täter: Der Mordfall Fritz Angerstein*, ed. Bernd Stiegler (Konstanz: Konstanz University Press, 2013).

10. On the sensationalization of crime in the decades before the First World War, see Philipp Müller, *Auf der Suche nach dem Täter: Die öffentliche Dramatisierung von Verbrechen im Berlin des Kaiserreichs* (Frankfurt a.M.: Campus, 2005).

11. See Daniel Siemens, *Metropole und Verbrechen: Die Gerichtsreportage in Berlin, Paris und Chicago, 1919–1933* (Stuttgart: Franz Steiner, 2007).

12. Lessing, *Haarmann*.

13. Siegfried Kracauer, "Die Tat ohne Täter: Zum Fall Angerstein" (1925), in Kracauer, *Schriften*, vol. 5, *Aufsätze*, ed. Inke Mülder-Bach (Frankfurt a.M.: Suhrkamp, 1990), pt. 1, 318–321.

14. Daniel Siemens discusses court reporting as an "interdiscourse" between specialized and everyday discourses in *Metropole und Verbrechen*, 25ff. These reporters still have a readership, with editions of their works published and republished: Sling (Paul Schlesinger), *Der Mensch, der schiesst: Berichte aus dem Gerichtssaal*, ed. Axel von Ernst (Düsseldorf: Lilienfeld, 2013); Gabriele Tergit, *Wer schießt aus Liebe?*; Moritz Goldstein, *"George Grosz freigesprochen": Gerichtsreportagen aus der Weimarer Republik*, ed. Manfred Voigts and Till Schickentanz (Hamburg: Philo, 2005); Kurt Tucholsky, *Justitia schwooft! Schriften zum deutschen Justizalltag*, 3rd ed., ed. Richard von Soldenhoff (Frankfurt a.M.: Büchergilde Gutenberg, 1990).

15. The most important general accounts in English are Beth Irwin Lewis, "*Lustmord*: Inside the Windows of the Metropolis," in *Berlin: Culture and Metropolis*, ed. Charles W. Haxthausen and Heidrun Suhr (Minneapolis: University of Minnesota Press, 1990), 111–140; and Maria Tatar, *Lustmord: Sexual Murder in Weimar Germany* (Princeton: Princeton University Press, 1995).

16. In this, they expand upon and historicize the arguments of Klaus Theweleit's groundbreaking *Männerphantasien* of 1977–1978. See Theweleit, *Male Fantasies*, vol. 1, *Women, Floods, Bodies, History*, and vol. 2, *Male Bodies: Psychoanalyzing the White Terror*,

trans. Stephan Conway with Erica Carter and Chris Turner (Minneapolis: University of Minnesota Press, 1987/89).

17. Tatar expands Lewis's chronology, and therefore argument, in *Lustmord*. On the art-historical resonances of these images, see the important contributions of Kathrin Hoffmann-Curtius: "'Wenn Blicke töten könnten': Oder, Der Künstler als Lustmörder," in *Blick-Wechsel: Konstruktionen von Männlichkeit und Weiblichkeit in Kunst und Kunstgeschichte*, ed. Ines Lindner, Sigrid Schade, Silke Wenk, and Gabriele Werner (Berlin: Reimer, 1989), 369–393; *George Grosz: "John, der Frauenmörder"* (Hamburg: Hamburger Kunsthalle, 1993); "Frauenmord als künstlerisches Thema der Moderne," in *Serienmord: Kriminologische und kulturwissenschaftliche Skizzierungen eines ungeheuerlichen Phänomens*, ed. Frank J. Roberts and Alexandra Thomas (Munich: belville, 2004), 269–284; and "Frauenmord als Spektakel: Max Beckmanns 'Martyrium' der Rosa Luxemburg," in *Lustmord: Medialisierungen eines kulturellen Phantasmas um 1900*, ed. Susanne Komfort-Hein and Susanne Scholz (Königstein i.T.: Ulrike Helmer, 2007), 91–113.

18. I discuss Musil's novel briefly in chapter 3, below.

19. 1931, dir. Fritz Lang.

20. "Warte, warte nur ein Weilchen/ Bald kommt der schwarze Mann zu dir/ Mit dem kleinen Hackebeilchen/ Macht er Schabefleisch aus dir": Fritz Lang, *M: Protokoll*, Cinemathek, no. 3, ed. Enno Patalas (Hamburg: Marion von Schröder, 1963), 9.

21. Lang, *M: Protokoll*, 45. On the relation of the film to contemporary cases of serial murder, particular that of Peter Kürten, see Anton Kaes, *M*, rev. ed. (London: BFI Publishing, 2001), 30–35; and Todd Herzog, *Crime Stories: Criminalistic Fantasy and the Culture of Crisis in Weimar Germany* (New York: Berghahn, 2009), 118–133.

22. Among many others: Ernst Engelbrecht, *Fünfzehn Jahre Kriminalkommissar: Ernstes und Heiteres aus meiner kriminalistischen Berufsarbeit* (Berlin: Peter J. Oestergaard, 1928); Engelbrecht and Leo Heller, *Berliner Razzien: Mit 36 Zeichnungen von Conny*, second ed. (Neu-Finkenkrug b. Berlin: Hermann Patel, 1924); Dr. Curt Elwenspoek, *Mord und Totschlag: Polizei greift ein!*, fifth ed. (Stuttgart: Dieck, 1931); Gotthold Lehnerdt, *Mörder: Aus den Erlebnissen eines Berliner Kriminalkommissars. Mit zahlreichen Abbildungen nach authentischen Vorlagen* (Potsdam: Kiepenheuer, 1925). On the legendary detective Ernst Gennat, allegedly the model for Kommissar Lohmann in Lang's *M*, see Regina Stürickow, *Der Kommissar vom Alexanderplatz: Kriminalfälle im historischen Berlin* (Berlin: Aufbau, 2000).

23. Beckert is discussed in relation to the experience of war by Kaes, *M*, 68–69. On *M* and contemporary discussions of capital punishment, see Richard J. Evans, *Rituals of Retribution: Capital Punishment in Germany, 1600–1987* (Oxford: Oxford University Press, 1996), 591–605; and Stephan Jankowski, *Warte, warte nur ein Weilchen ... : Die Diskussion um die Todesstrafe in Fritz Langs Film "M,"* second ed. (Marburg: Tectum, 2000).

24. Six weeks in Tegel represents a short stay in an ordinary prison, perhaps awaiting trial; fifteen years in a maximum-security prison like Brandenburg, where sentences included hard labor, was the maximum prison term for *Totschlag* or unpremeditated murder short of life imprisonment. Premeditated murder carried the death penalty.

25. Todd Herzog, *Crime Stories*. Herzog's fine book overlaps in many ways with this one but takes a very different perspective. Herzog is interested in developments in crime fiction considered in relation to new legal and scientific understandings of criminality; he also seeks to relate these to a traditional notion of the Weimar period as one of crisis. See also other recent treatments of crime and murder in the period: Sace Elder, *Murder Scenes: Normality, Deviance, and Criminal Violence in Weimar Berlin* (Ann Arbor: University of Michigan Press, 2010); Benjamin Carter Hett, *Death in the Tiergarten: Murder and Criminal Justice in the Kaiser's Berlin* (Cambridge, MA: Harvard University Press, 2004); Jay Michael Layne, "Uncanny Collapse: Sexual Violence and Unsettled Rhetoric in German-language *Lustmord* Representations, 1900–1933" (PhD diss., University of Michigan, 2008); and Scott Spector, *Violent Sensations: Sex, Crime, and Utopia in Vienna and Berlin, 1860–1914* (Chicago: University of Chicago Press, 2016).

26. Michel Foucault, *Discipline and Punish: The Birth of the Prison*, trans. Alan Sheridan (1975; New York: Vintage, 1979), 191.

27. Editors' introduction, *Case Studies and the Dissemination of Knowledge*, ed. Joy Damousi, Birgit Lang, and Katie Sutton (New York and London: Routledge, 2015), 1.

28. On critiques of the pathologization paradigm identified with Foucault, see Edward R. Dickinson and Richard Wetzell, "The Historiography of Sexuality in Modern Germany," *German History* 23, no. 3 (2005), 291–305; and Tracie Matysik, "Beyond Freedom: A Return to Subjectivity in the History of Sexuality," in *After The History of Sexuality: German Genealogies with and Beyond Foucault*, ed. Scott Spector, Helmut Puff, and Dagmar Herzog (Oxford: Berghahn, 2012). Others have pointed out that the exclusive focus on discipline and pathologization in fact represents an unnuanced reading of Foucault and a neglect of the development of his thought. See Philippe Weber, *Der Trieb zum Erzählen: Sexualpathologie und Homosexualität, 1852–1914* (Bielefeld: transcript Verlag, 2008); and Scott Spector, "Introduction: After *The History of Sexuality?* Periodicities, Subjectivities, Ethics," in *After The History of Sexuality*.

29. Lauren Berlant, "On the Case," *Critical Inquiry* 33, no. 4 (2007), 663. See also *Critical Inquiry* 34, no. 1 (2007).

30. A recent compilation on this topic is *Making Things Public: Atmospheres of Democracy*, ed. Bruno Latour and Peter Weibel (Karlsruhe: Center for Art and Media/ Cambridge, MA: MIT Press, 2005).

31. Berlant, "On the Case," 664.

32. Foucault discusses the relation between the "dossier" and the case in *I, Pierre Rivière, having slaughtered my mother, my sister, and my brother ... : A Case of Parricide in the 19th Century*, ed. Michel Foucault, trans. Frank Jellinek (New York: Pantheon, 1975), x–xi. See also chapter 5, below.

33. Jürgen Habermas, *The Structural Transformation of the Public Sphere: An Inquiry into a Category of Bourgeois Society*, trans. Thomas Burger and Frederick Lawrence (Cambridge, MA: MIT Press, 1989).

34. Jürgen Habermas, "The Public Sphere: An Encyclopedia Article," trans. S. Lennox and F. Lennox, *New German Critique*, no. 3 (1974), 49.

35. Immanuel Kant, "An Answer to the Question: 'What is Enlightenment?,'" in *Kant: Political Writings*, ed. Hans Reiss, trans. H. B. Nisbet, second ed. (Cambridge: Cambridge University Press, 1991), 54–60.

36. This seems unfair: Habermas argues that the category itself emerged historically and referred to actual developments in bourgeois sociation, yet he is equally clear that the reality of what was called the public sphere both 1) failed to live up to its own ideals; and 2) soon deteriorated as a potential site for the public use of reason—this was its "structural transformation." It is, as a concept, *both* normative and historical: the normative aspect of the (ultimately ideological) claims of an enlightened bourgeoisie thus gives leverage by which to analyze the fate of spaces in which a reasoning public could form. And a look at the context in which Habermas wrote his account of the public sphere and the debates in which he intervened—debates sparked by figures such as Reinhard Koselleck, Hanno Kesting, and Wilhelm Hennis—gives insight into the particular balance between the historical and the normative that he struck. See Frederic J. Schwartz, "Public Sphere," in *Keywords for Marxist Art History Today*, ed. Larne Abse Gogarty and Andrew Hemingway, *Jahrbuch der Guernica-Gesellschaft* 21 (2019), 141–147.

37. Nancy Fraser, "Rethinking the Public Sphere: A Contribution to the Critique of Actually Existing Democracy," in *Habermas and the Public Sphere*, ed. Craig Calhoun (Cambridge, MA: MIT Press, 1992).

38. Oskar Negt and Alexander Kluge, *Öffentlichkeit und Erfahrung: Zur Organisationsanalyse von bürgerlicher und proletarischer Öffentlichkeit* (Frankfurt a.M.: Suhrkamp, 1972), English ed. *Public Sphere and Experience: Toward an Analysis of the Bourgeois and Proletarian Public Sphere*, trans. Peter Labanyi, Jamie Owen Daniel, and Assenka Oksiloff (Minneapolis: University of Minnesota Press, 1993).

39. Guy Debord, *The Society of the Spectacle*, trans. Donald Nicholson-Smith (1967; New York: Zone Books, 1994).

40. Negt and Kluge, *Public Sphere and Experience*, 3.

41. Negt and Kluge, *Public Sphere and Experience*, xliii.

42. "Sinnlich faßbare Solidarität": Negt and Kluge, *Public Sphere and Experience*, 38 (trans. modified).

43. Negt and Kluge, *Public Sphere and Experience*, 297 (trans. modified).

44. Negt and Kluge, *Public Sphere and Experience*, 13 (trans. modified).

45. Oskar Negt and Alexander Kluge, *Geschichte und Eigensinn* (Frankfurt a.M.: Zweitausendeins, 1981). The English translation is considerably abbreviated but also includes new material: Alexander Kluge and Oskar Negt, *History and Obstinacy*, ed. Devin Fore, trans. Richard Langston et al. (New York: Zone Books, 2014).

46. See Michael Warner's important discussion of public sphere as a performative form of "poetic world-making," in *Publics and Counterpublics* (New York: Zone Books, 2002).

47. "The Political Unconscious in Nineteenth-Century Art," ed. Linda Nochlin, *Art Journal* 46, no. 4 (1987).

48. See, for example, Thomas E. Crow, *Painters and Public Life in Eighteenth-Century Paris* (New Haven and London: Yale University Press, 1985) and David H. Solkin, *Painting for Money: The Visual Arts and the Public Sphere in Eighteenth-Century England* (New Haven and London: Yale University Press, 1993). Solkin invokes Habermas's *Structural Transformation* directly; Crow does not.

49. Hansen's English-language publications on Negt and Kluge culminated in her extensive foreword to *Public Sphere and Experience*, ix–xli.

50. Miriam Hansen, "Early Silent Cinema: Whose Public Sphere?," *New German Critique*, no. 29 (1983), 147–184; and Hansen, *Babel and Babylon: Spectatorship in American Silent Film* (Cambridge, MA: Harvard University Press, 1991). Hansen continued her consideration of experience and publicity in her monumental study of German critical theory: *Cinema and Experience: Siegfried Kracauer, Walter Benjamin, and Theodor W. Adorno* (Berkeley and Los Angeles: University of California Press, 2012).

Chapter 1

1. Ferdinand Tönnies, *Kritik der öffentlichen Meinung* (Berlin: Julius Springer, 1922), 178.

2. The dating of this text has long been problematic. It was first published in French in 1913; Loos himself gave the date 1908 when it was republished in Adolf Loos, *Trotzdem* (Innsbruck: Brenner-Verlag, 1931). Burkhardt Rukschcio has identified the first full manuscript, corresponding to a public lecture given by Loos on January 21, 1910: Burkhardt Rukschcio, "Ornament und Mythos," in *Ornament und Askese im Zeitgeist des Wien der Jahrhundertwende*, ed. Alfred Pfabigan (Vienna: Christian Brandstätter, 1985), 57–68. Most recently, Christopher Long has determined that a version of the talk was given in Berlin on November 11, 1909, and that the text in its written form was probably drafted in December 1909 or early January 1910. See Christopher Long, "The Origins and Context of Adolf Loos's 'Ornament and Crime'," *Journal of the Society of Architectural Historians* 68, no. 2 (2009), 201–223.

3. Adolf Loos, "Ornament and Crime," in *The Architecture of Adolf Loos*, exh. cat. (London: Arts Council, 1985), 100; "Ornament und Verbrechen," in Adolf Loos, *Trotzdem*, ed. A. Opel (1931; repr. Vienna: Prachner, 1982), 78.

4. On the sources and context of the lecture, see, most recently and authoritatively, Long, "The Origins and Context of Adolf Loos's 'Ornament and Crime'"; and Jimena Canales and Andrew Herscher, "Criminal Skins: Tattoos and Modern Architecture in the Work of Adolf Loos," *Architectural History* 48 (2005), 235–256. See also Janet Stewart, *Fashioning Vienna: Adolf Loos's Cultural Criticism* (London and New York: Routledge, 2000), passim; and Joseph Masheck, *Adolf Loos: The Art of Architecture* (New York: I. B. Tauris, 2013), 94–115.

5. Sigmund Freud, *The Standard Edition of the Complete Psychological Works of Sigmund Freud*, trans. under the editorship of James Strachey, 24 vols. (London: Hogarth Press and the Institute of Psycho-Analysis, 1953–1974), vol. 3, 191–221, originally presented on April 21, 1896.

6. Sigmund Freud, *Three Essays on the Theory of Sexuality*, trans. and rev. James Strachey (London: Hogarth Press, 1962).

7. See Larry Wolff, *Postcards from the End of the World: An Investigation into the Mind of Fin-de-Siecle Vienna* (London: Collins, 1989), a balanced

discussion of child abuse, its prosecution, and its reporting; and, more polemically, Jeffrey Moussaieff Masson, *The Assault on Truth: Freud's Suppression of the Seduction Theory* (1984; New York: Ballantine, 2003).

8. The best accounts of Loos and the Villa Karma are Vera J. Behalova, "Adolf Loos: Villa Karma," (PhD diss., University of Vienna, 1974); Vera J. Behal, "Die Villa Karma und ihre Architekten Lavanchy/Loos/Ehrlich," in *Adolf Loos*, exh. cat. (Vienna: Graphische Sammlung Albertina, 1989); and Burkhardt Rukschcio and Roland Schachel, *Adolf Loos: Leben und Werk* (Salzburg: Residenz, 1982), 92–104. The information recounted by Loos's second wife, Elsie Altmann-Loos, in her memoirs of life with Loos does not accord with documentary evidence and is clearly marred by failures of memory. See Elsie Altmann-Loos, Lina Loos, and Claire Loos, *Adolf Loos: Der Mensch*, ed. Adolf Opel (Vienna: Prachner, 2002), 69–71. Beer's feuilletons are collected in Theodor Beer, *Aus Natur und Kunst: Gesammelte Feuilletons* (Dresden: Pierson, 1900). These reveal Beer to be, like Loos, an anti-Secessionist and an enthusiast of the Gibson Girls. See "Gibsons Zeichnungen" in *Aus Natur und Kunst*; on Loos and the Gibson Girls, Tag Gronberg, *Vienna: City of Modernity, 1890–1914* (Oxford: Peter Lang, 2007), chap. 2.

9. "Dear Herr Loos, You have probably figured out why you have heard nothing from us for so long. I'm enraged by the impertinence of these accusations ... The work on Karma ... must be interrupted. ... Nonetheless I hope to be able to live in a house designed by you soon." Laura Beer to Adolf Loos, March 6, 1904. "Professor Beer is terribly sorry that the trial has not only interrupted your work, but that Karma might perhaps not be completed. But I know from his own words that, whenever he will establish a home, it will only happen with *your* assistance. Please be patient and trust us. Prof. Beer thinks very highly of you and your taste, which we know so well." Laura Beer to Adolf Loos, May 6, 1904. Graphische Sammlung Albertina, Adolf Loos Archiv, file "Villa Karma," 16, 17.

10. On the case of Theodor Beer, see, besides the works of Karl Kraus discussed below, Florian Mildenberger, "'... als Conträrsexual und als Päderast verleumdet': Der Prozess um den Naturforscher Theodor Beer (1866–1919) im Jahre 1905," *Zeitschrift für Sexualforschung* 18 (2005), 332–351; and Daniel M. Vyleta, *Crime, Jews and News: Vienna, 1895–1914* (New York: Berghahn, 2007), 135–144. There is also valuable information in a biography and documentation of Beer's occasional lover Bertha Eckstein-Diener: Sibylle Mulot-Deri, *Sir Galahad: Porträt einer Verschollenen* (Frankfurt am Main: Fischer Taschenbuch Verlag, 1987). My discussion is based on these accounts as well as material from the Adolf Loos Archiv, Graphische Sammlung Albertina; the Wiener Stadt- und Landesarchiv; the Handschriftensammlung of the Wienbibliothek; and the contemporary press. A brief discussion of both the Beer case and Loos's own later case, based largely on published newspaper reports, appears in Klaralinda Ma, "Der 'Fall' Loos," in *Leben mit Loos*, ed. Inge Podbrecky and Rainald Franz (Vienna: Böhlau, 2008), 161–171.

11. Wiener Stadt- und Landesarchiv, file Landesgericht für Strafsachen, A11 Vr 4586/1905 Fall Beer, Steckbrief Dr. Theodor Beer, K.k. Polizei-Direktion Wien, March 8, 1904.

12. Kraus's coverage of the trial originally appeared in *Die Fackel*; the most important articles are collected in Kraus, *Sittlichkeit und Kriminalität*, vol. 1 of *Schriften*, ed. Christian Wagenknecht, 15 vols. (Frankfurt a.M.: Suhrkamp, 1987); see "Die Kinderfreunde," "Nachträgliches zum Prozeß Beer," and "Der Selbstmord der Themis." I shall cite Kraus's work from their original appearance in *Die Fackel*.

Both Loos and Kraus acknowledged the close connections between their work. Most famously and succinctly, Kraus wrote: "Adolf Loos and I, he literally, I linguistically, have done nothing more than to show that there is a difference between an urn and a chamber pot, and that it is only in this difference that culture has any room to develop. The others, however ... are divided into those who use the urn as a chamber pot, and those who use the chamber pot as an urn." Karl Kraus, "Nachts," *Die Fackel*, nos. 389–390 (1913), 37. The connection is, to a certain extent, a commonplace. For more thoughtful and informative accounts of their relationship, see Allan Janik and Stephen Toulmin, *Wittgenstein's Vienna* (New York: Simon and Schuster, 1973); Dagmar Barnouw, "Loos, Kraus, Wittgenstein and the Problem of Authenticity," in *The Turn of the Century: German Literature and Art, 1890–1915*, ed. Gerald Chapple and Hans H. Schulte (Bonn: Bouvier, 1981); Edward Timms, *Karl Kraus—Apocalyptic Satirist*, vol. 1, *Culture and Catastrophe in Habsburg Vienna* (New Haven and London: Yale University Press, 1986), chap. 6; and Gilbert J. Carr, "The 'Habsburg Myth,' Ornament and Metaphor: Adolf Loos, Karl Kraus and Robert Musil," *Austrian Studies* 15, no. 1 (December 2007), 65–79.

13. The indispensable source on the Austrian press, with valuable information on the affiliations of various newspapers, is Kurt Paupié, *Handbuch der österreichischen Pressegeschichte, 1848–1959*, 2 vols. (Vienna: Wilhelm Braumüller, 1960–1966).

14. *Sittlichkeit und Kriminalität* has been republished in an edition containing helpful essays by Helmut Arntzen and Heinz Müller-Deitz: *Sittlichkeit und Kriminalität* (1908). *Juristische Zeitgeschichte*, ser. 6, vol. 17 (Berlin: Berliner Wissenschafts-Verlag, 2004).

15. The literature on Karl Kraus is immense. I have found the following works most helpful: Timms, *Karl Kraus—Apocalyptic Satirist*, vol. 1; Edward Timms, *Karl Kraus—Apocalyptic Satirist*, vol. 2 *The Post-War Crisis and the Rise of the Swastika* (New Haven and London: Yale University Press, 2005); Reinhard Merkel, *Strafrecht und Satire im Werk von Karl Kraus* (Frankfurt a.M.: Suhrkamp, 1998); Harry Zohn, *Karl Kraus*, trans. Ilse Goesmann (Frankfurt a.M.: Hain, 1990); Helmut Arntzen, *Karl Kraus und die Presse*, Literatur und Presse: Karl-Kraus-Studien, vol. 1 (Munich: Wilhelm Fink, 1975); and Friedrich Pfäfflin, ed., *Karl Kraus*, exh. cat. (Marbach: Deutsches Literaturarchiv/Schiller-Nationalmuseum, 1999).

16. Karl Kraus, "Die Kinderfreunde," *Die Fackel*, no. 187 (1905), 12: "Ein Sittlichkeitsprozeß ist die zielbewußte Entwicklung einer individuellen zur generellen Unsittlichkeit, von deren düsterem Grunde sich die erwiesene Schuld des Angeklagten leuchtend abhebt." I have emended the translation from Karl Kraus, *Dicta and Contradicta*, trans. Jonathan McVity (Urbana: University of Illinois Press, 2001), 26.

17. On the division of competence and labor between the police and the courts, see Merkel, *Strafrecht und Satire*, 97–105.

18. The most important study of Loos in this regard is Beatriz Colomina, *Privacy and Publicity: Modern Architecture as Mass Media* (Cambridge, MA: MIT Press, 1994).

19. Adolf Loos, "Heimatkunst," in *Gesammelte Schriften*, ed. Adolf Opel (Vienna: Lesethek Verlag, 2010), 444.

20. Wiener Stadt- und Landesarchiv, file Landesgericht für Strafsachen, A11 Vr 4586/1905 Fall Beer, Liste der Zeugen und Sachverständigen, October 25, 1905. Loos testified on October 26: *Neue Freie Presse*, October 26, 1905, Abendblatt, 4–5.

21. "In particular, Herr Architekt Adolf Loos, I Giselastrasse 3, can give evidence about the arrangement, the library, and all circumstances of the house [of Beer's parents in Vienna, where the events in question were said to have taken place]. He gained great familiarity with all rooms of the house in the time before its remodeling. Furthermore, the architect Loos is intimately acquainted with the artistic endeavors and the personality and conduct [*dem ganzen Gehaben*] of Herr Professor Beer. We therefore request that Herr Architekt Loos be summoned as a witness and examined in court." Wiener Stadt- und Landesarchiv, A11 Vr 4586/1905 Fall Beer, 426, October 21, 1905.

22. Heinz Lang, son of the women's rights activist Marie Lang and her husband Edmund, had begun an affair with Lina Loos in 1903. When Adolf Loos found out about the relationship, she left Lang. Despondent, Lang turned to their mutual friend Peter Altenberg, who, according to Hugo von Hofmannsthal, gave the following fateful advice: "What *should* you do? Shoot yourself. What will you do? Live on. Cool and composed. Because you're as cowardly as I am, as cowardly as this whole generation, hollow inside, a liar like me. So you'll live on." Near Cambridge, where Lina was supposed to join him, Lang did as he thought he "should" do. It is worth noting that this tragic and scandalous event remained a private incident. To have become a "case," it would have had to be in someone's power and interest

to bring it before a public. The tragedy is discussed in letters from Laura Beer to Adolf Loos in the Adolf Loos Archiv ("Korrespondenz allg. vor 23.8.33," nos. 32, 34, 35); Rukschcio and Schachel, *Adolf Loos*, 75–104 passim; and Lisa Fischer, *Lina Loos, oder Wenn die Muse sich selbst küßt*, second ed. (Vienna: Böhlau, 2007), chap. 3.

23. See Adolf Loos Archiv, file "Korrespondenz allg. vor 23.8.33," nos. 32–36 and file "Villa Karma."

24. Beer presents his side of the case to Loos in an extensive and emotional fifteen-page letter from San Francisco, dated July 1904. Adolf Loos Archiv, file "Villa Karma," 26.

25. The stenographic report of Loos's testimony in the *Neue Freie Presse* reads in its entirety as follows: "At this point architect Adolf Loos was called as a witness. Judge: How long has the witness known the accused? Witness [Loos]: For two years. Judge: Did you meet him socially or professionally? Witness: Professionally; he has commissioned work from me and was to entrust me with the building and furnishing of his villa on Lake Geneva [*wollte mir die Einrichtung seiner Villa am Genfersee anvertrauen*]. I have also visited him there. Judge: On these occasions, were artistic matters also discussed? Witness: Certainly. We became acquainted because Beer, as a purist, a proponent of the simple life, approached me. I am the only architect who has fanatically opposed the use of ornament. Judge: Was photography also discussed? Witness: Certainly. In the evenings I often looked at his pictures and can proclaim that I consider him one of the greatest photographers who has ever lived, and that I have never before seen such an abundance of artistic pictures. I also saw there studies of nudes, namely self-portraits and photographs of boys with naked upper bodies. Judge: Did you also see completely nude photographs [*Nuditäten*]? Witness: Never, and I consider it out of the question that such things would have been shown in the Beer house. Judge: The witness is familiar with the rooms in the villa [of Beer's parents] in the Cottage [neighborhood in Vienna Währing and Döbling]. Can you recall the library, and do you perhaps know if one can enter noiselessly, without being heard? Witness: Since I'm hard of hearing. ... (Laughter.) Judge: Ah, well ... Defense attorney Councilor [Adolf] Bachrach: You have often had long and deep conversations with the Professor. What was at the core of your discussions? Witness: He spoke about the fact that people need to be allowed to live life to the fullest, and that the individuality of every man must come to the fore." *Neue Freie Presse*, October 26, 1905, evening edition, 4–5.

26. This is mentioned in the transcript published in the *Neue Freie Presse*, October 26, 1905, morning edition (Judge: Have you been shown one of these photographs of your son with an unclothed upper body?—Witness [Clementine Freund]: I heard that there was a quite particular photograph of him, and demanded to see it often, but was shown it only a year later.) There is, however, no further discussion or description of the photograph reported. Unlike the other two photographs in the court files (a portrait of Beer (p. 38) and a photograph of a gymnast seen from behind performing a handstand on parallel bars), this is preserved not as a print, but as a negative.

27. Altmann-Loos et al., *Adolf Loos: Der Mensch*, 69–70.

28. Altmann-Loos also reports that Beer's wife Laura prompted and assisted in the prosecution of her husband. All evidence, archival and published, shows that she defended him vigorously.

29. Adolf Loos Archiv, "Villa Karma," 68: "Geehrter Herr Loos! Ich werde morgen (Mittwoch) vor dem Hause Wiedener Hauptstrasse 20 in einem geschlossenen Wagen auf Sie warten morgens (zwischen 9 ¼ und 9 ½ h). Es handelt sich darum die bewusste Action möglichst rasch zu erledigen. Ich rechne sehr auf Ihre Hilfe." As suggested by Leo Lensing, the writer was probably Adolf Bachrach, Beer's lawyer.

30. See Carola Leitner and Kurt Hamtil, *Kaffeehäuser und ihre Besucher: Wien in alten Fotografien* (Vienna: Carl Ueberreuter, 2010), 10–11.

31. On forensic photography, see, from a large literature, John Tagg, "A Means of Surveillance: The Photograph as Evidence in Law," in Tagg, *The Burden of Representation: Essays on Photographies and Histories* (Basingstoke: Macmillan, 1988), 66–102; and

Christine Karallus, "Zwischen Kriminalistik und Justiz: Zur Konjunktur der Fotografie als Evidenzstrategie," *Berichte zur Wissenschaftsgeschichte* 28 (2005), 215–226.

32. Wiener Stadt- und Landesarchiv, A11 Vr 4586/1905 Fall Beer, Urteilsbegründung, 461–464. The Austrian Strafgesetz (penal code) of 1852 defines sexual abuse (*Schändung*, or violation) as follows: "§128. Violation. Whoever sexually abuses a boy or girl under the age of fourteen years, or a person unable to defend himself or in a condition of unconsciousness ... commits the act of violation." Acts of homosexuality were prosecuted as *Unzucht wider die Natur*: "§129. As crimes the following forms of fornication are also punishable: 1. Fornication contrary to nature, i.e. a) with animals; b) with persons of the same sex." The conviction is discussed in Mildenberger, "Der Prozess um den Naturforscher Theodor Beer," passim; and Merkel, *Strafrecht und Satire*, 392–393. On the development of these laws and the changing ways they were enforced, see Friedrich Hartl, *Das Wiener Kriminalgericht: Strafrechtspflege vom Zeitalter der Aufklärung bis zur österreichischen Revolution* (Vienna: Böhlau, 1973), 352–357.

33. Beer refers to "the substantial new book by Friedlaender," presumably Benedict Friedlaender, *Die Renaissance des Eros Uranios: Die physiologische Freundschaft, ein normaler Grundtrieb des Menschen und eine Frage der männlichen Gesellungsfreiheit. In naturwissenschaftlicher, naturrechtlicher, culturgeschichtlicher und sittenkritischer Beleuchtung* (Schmargendorf-Berlin: Renaissance [Otto Lehmann], 1904).

34. Sigmund Freud, quoted in *Die Zeit*, October 27, 1905, quoted in Magnus Hirschfeld, *Die Homosexualität des Mannes und des Weibes* (Berlin: Louis Marcus, 1914), 389–390. Mildenberger, "Der Prozess um den Naturforscher Theodor Beer," 338, surmises, quite reasonably, that Freud and Beer were acquainted. Kraus refers to Freud's statement in "Die Kinderfreunde," *Die Fackel*, no. 187 (1905), 21–22.

35. The move from asylums to university clinics in the treatment of the insane is traced in Eric J. Engstrom, *Clinical Psychiatry in Imperial Germany: A History of Psychiatric Practice* (Ithaca, NY: Cornell University Press, 2004). On psychoanalysis and the move to private practice, see Edward Shorter, *A History of Psychiatry: From the Era of the Asylum to the Age of Prozac* (New York: Wiley, 1997), 145–147, 154.

36. The debates over criminal accountability are discussed in Engstrom, *Clinical Psychiatry in Imperial Germany*, esp. 197–198; psychiatric scandals, the increased public and press scrutiny to which psychiatrists were subject in the late nineteenth century, and the increasing pace of professionalization of the discipline are discussed in ibid., 177–187. On forensic psychiatry and its professionalization in nineteenth- and early twentieth-century Germany, see Richard F. Wetzell, *Inventing the Criminal: A History of German Criminology, 1880–1945* (Chapel Hill: University of North Carolina Press, 2000), chaps. 2 and 3; more generally, Ruth Harris, *Murders and Madness: Medicine, Law, and Society in the fin de siècle* (Oxford: Oxford University Press, 1989); and Roger Smith, *Trial by Medicine: Insanity and Responsibility in Victorian Trials* (Edinburgh: Edinburgh University Press, 1981).

37. On the struggle between jurists and forensic psychiatrists over conflicting legal and medical criteria of responsibility in Germany and Austria around the turn of the century, see Engstrom, *Clinical Psychiatry in Imperial Germany*, 197–198; and Wetzell, *Inventing the Criminal*, 75–96. See also the general discussion of forensic psychiatry and the problem faced by doctors of the "subservience of scientific experts to ends which they do not define" in Roger Smith, "Forensic Pathology, Scientific Expertise, and the Criminal Law," in *Expert Evidence: Interpreting Science in the Law*, ed. Smith and Brian Wynne (London: Routledge, 1989), 56–92, here 57. Smith discusses the risk of "loss of control over the meaning of expert knowledge" in the court context (70).

38. The important and controversial move to a jury system in Germany and Austria in the late nineteenth century is discussed in Merkel, *Strafrecht und Satire*, 53–69, 108–111.

39. Kraus, "Ein Unhold," *Die Fackel*, no. 157 (1904), 1. The sentence was later revised.

40. Among other chapters in Kraus, *Sittlichkeit und Kriminalität*, see "Gerichtspsychiatrie," where Kraus characterizes forensic psychiatry as a "parlor game" of the "tarot players of justice."

Originally published in *Die Fackel*, no. 236 (1907), 15. On the rise of a (proto-) anti-psychiatry movement, see Engstrom, *Clinical Psychiatry in Imperial Germany*, 177–184. Not surprisingly, Kraus and his critique of forensic psychiatry were enlisted in the anti-psychiatry of the postwar period. See Thomas Szasz, *Karl Kraus and the Soul-Doctors: A Pioneer Critic and his Criticism of Psychiatry and Psychoanalysis* (London: Routledge and Kegan Paul, 1977). Szasz's book is useful in drawing attention to Kraus's frequent sparring with the psychiatry of the time, but it is marred by its obvious agenda and polemical tone, its lack of distinction between psychoanalysis and other forms of psychiatry, and its inability to engage with the larger historical issues around psychiatry.

41. Clementine Freund, quoted in the *Neue Freie Presse*, October 26, 1905, morning edition, 10.

42. Mildenberger, "Der Prozess um den Naturforscher Theodor Beer," 8–9. Stern was an expert on the testimony of children: see Clara Stern and William Stern, *Erinnerung, Aussage and Lüge in der ersten Kindheit* (Leipzig: J. A. Barth, 1909). On Stern, who developed the system of the intelligence quotient, see Gerald Bühring, *William Stern oder Streben nach Einheit* (Frankfurt a.M.: P. Lang, 1996).

43. Dr. R. Hennig, "Zeugenaussagen von Kindern," *Die Umschau: Übersicht über die Fortschritte und Bewegungen auf dem Gesamtgebiet der Wissenschaft, Technik, Literatur und Kunst* 9, no. 19 (1905), 376–377; William Stern, "Forderungen für das gerichtliche Verfahren, auf Grund von Ergebnissen der Aussagepsychologie," *Die Umschau* 9, no. 25 (1905), 487–490; and M. Hagenau, "Krankhaftes Lügen," *Die Gartenlaube* 21 (1905), 786–789.

44. *Neue Freie Presse*, October 27, 1905, evening edition, 11; Mildenberger, "Der Prozess um den Naturforscher Theodor Beer," 345–346.

45. Karl Kraus, "Antworten der Herausgeber: Kinderfreund," *Die Fackel*, no. 189 (1905), 22–23; Mildenberger, "Der Prozess um den Naturforscher Theodor Beer," 344.

46. Mildenberger, "Der Prozess um den Naturforscher Theodor Beer," 344.

47. Karl Kraus, "Der Selbstmord der Themis," *Die Fackel*, no. 200 (1906), 4. That Loos assisted her emerges from Theodor Beer's letter of July 1904 from San Francisco (Adolf Loos Archiv, file "Villa Karma," 26, p. 12): "That you helped my wife thrash the main blackmailer ... does me good every time I think of it."

48. Adolf Loos Archiv, file "Villa Karma," 63: "Ich bin wüthend darüber dass Sie ... nicht dass die öffentliche Meinung das grosse Publicum überhaupt erfahren hat unter welchen nichtigen [?] er verhaftet und verurtheilt wurde. ... Hingegen haben Sie es verstanden, die intellectuell hochstehenden Freunde meines Mannes wie Burckhardt, oder Bahr oder Popper oder Kraus von der Verhandlung fernzuhalten. ... Ich werde mich nicht scheuen meine Auffassung die übrigens von unseren engsten Freunden längst getheilt wird in der Öffentlichkeit zur Sprache zu bringen—wenn es sein muss mit einer Gewaltthat. ... Auf den Freispruch kommt es nicht an, *aber zu Wort muessen wir kommen*, es musse für meinen *Mann* die Möglichkeit durchgesetzt werden zum letzten und zum ersten und doch noch zum Wort zu kommen ..."

49. Adolf Loos Archiv, file "Villa Karma," 63: "*Privat nicht zur Publikation*. Bitte bis 13ten IV. 11 h. vormitt. zurück ThB."

50. For his denial of all but the most incidental social contact with Beer, see Kraus, "Antworten des Herausgebers: Kinderfreund," 20–22.

51. Here, in fact, Freud turned to Kraus for publicistic help. Peter Gay, *Freud: A Life for our Time* (New York: W. W. Norton, 1988), 154–156; and Marina Tichy and Sylvia Zwettler-Otte, *Freud in der Presse: Rezeption Sigmund Freuds und der Psychoanalyse in Österreich, 1895–1938* (Vienna: Sonderzahl, 1999), 260–262.

52. Kraus, "Die Kinderfreunde," 4.

53. Wiener Stadt- und Landessarchiv, Bl. 574–583; published in its full length in *Die Fackel*, no. 191 (1905), 14–18.

54. "I did not receive the transcript from Dr. [Adolf] Bachrach [Beer's lawyer], with whom I have nothing to do." Kraus, "Eingeweihter," *Die Fackel*, no. 193 (1906), 21.

55. Kraus, "Die Kinderfreunde," 24.

56. Legal positivism posits the separation of morals and ethics from the law. On the law of the time, see William M. Johnston, *The Austrian Mind: An Intellectual and Social History, 1848–1938* (Berkeley and Los Angeles: University of California Press, 1972), 88–98;

on Kraus's relation to it, see Merkel, *Strafrecht und Satire*; and Timms, *Karl Kraus, Apocalyptic Satirist*, vol. 2, chap. 15, "The Contest for the Law."

57. Documentation for all of Kraus's court cases from 1922 has been published in *Karl Kraus contra ... : Die Prozeßakten der Kanzlei Oskar Samek*, ed. Hermann Böhm, 4 vols. (Vienna: Wiener Stadt- und Landesbibliothek, 1995–1997).

58. Karl Kraus, "Der größte Schuft im ganzen Land ... (Die Akten zum Fall Kerr)," *Die Fackel*, no. 787–794 (1928), 1–208; Timms, *Karl Kraus—Apocalyptic Satirist*, vol. 2, 292, 366; and Pfäfflin, *Karl Kraus*, 97.

59. See Merkel, *Strafrecht und Satire*, esp. 447–462.

60. Walter Benjamin, "Karl Kraus" (1931), in Benjamin, *Selected Writings*, vol. 2, ed. M. W. Jennings et al. (Cambridge, MA: Belknap Press, Harvard University Press, 1999), 443.

61. Bertolt Brecht, "Über Karl Kraus," in Brecht, *Werke: Große kommentierte Berliner und Frankfurter Ausgabe*, vol. 22, ed. Werner Hecht, Jan Knopf, Werner Mittenzwei, and Klaus-Detlef Müller (Berlin and Weimar: Aufbau, and Frankfurt a.M.: Suhrkamp, 1993), 34. The text dates from 1934.

62. Long, "The Origins and Context of Adolf Loos's 'Ornament and Crime,'" has shown that Loos was intent on creating controversy with his lectures, and that when none was forthcoming, he invented it. On Loos's essays and lectures in relation to the Viennese public, see Janet Stewart, *Fashioning Vienna: Adolf Loos's Cultural Criticism* (London: Routledge, 2000); and Bela Kerekgyarto, "Der Architekt und die Öffentlichkeit: Über die Schriften von Adolf Loos," in *Adolf Loos: Die Kultivierung der Architektur*, ed. Akós Moravánszky, Bernhard Langer, and Elli Mosayebi (Zurich: gta Verlag, 2008), 41–59.

63. Rukschcio, "Ornament und Mythos," 58.

64. Long, "The Origins and Context of Adolf Loos's 'Ornament and Crime,'" 207–210, discusses the tone and logic of the lecture and its evaluation in the literature.

65. Loos, "Ornament and Crime," in *The Architecture of Adolf Loos*, 100; "Ornament und Verbrechen," in Loos, *Trotzdem*, 78–79.

66. The "Chinatown Trunk Mystery" and the cover of the *Illustrirte Kronen-Zeitung* are discussed in Daniel M. Vyleta, *Crime, Jews and News*, 162–167; see also Mary Ting Yi Lui, *The Chinatown Trunk Mystery: Murder, Miscegenation, and Other Dangerous Encounters in Turn-of-the-Century New York City* (Princeton: Princeton University Press, 2005). In the United States, the family's name was spelled Sigel; in Austria, either Siegel or Siegl.

67. "Police are concerned that Leon will escape disguised as a Chinese woman, as he earlier appeared in various establishments as a female impersonator": "Der Mädchenmord in Newyork," *Illustrirtes Wiener Extrablatt*, June 24, 1909, evening edition, 2. See also Vyleta, *Crime, Jews and News*, 164.

68. Reinhold Rigale [?], "Das neue Technische Museum für Industrie und Gewerbe," *Illustrirtes Wiener Extrablatt*, June 26, 1909, 6–7, here 7. On Victor Loos, a professor at the Technical Academy in Vienna, see Rukschcio and Schachel, *Adolf Loos*, 684; on the competition entry, 137 and 474. The entries to the (apparently rigged) competition are discussed in Markus Kristan, "Die Ideenkonkurrenz für das Technische Museum für Industrie und Gewerbe in Wien 1909. I. Teil: Die Sieger," and "II. Teil: Die Verlierer," *Architekturjournal Wettbewerbe* 18, nos. 129–130 (1994), 166–70, and nos. 131–132 (1994), 185–89.

69. "Die Ermordung der Elsie Siegel. Die Verhöre mit Tschungfing.—Die Suche nach dem Mörder.—Verfolgte Chinesen." *Illustrirtes Wiener Extrablatt*, June 26, 1909, 7.

70. Karl Kraus, *Die chinesische Mauer* (Munich: Albert Langen, 1910). Loos is identified as designer of the dust-jacket in Kraus, *Schriften*, vol. 2, *Die chinesische Mauer*, 329.

71. Karl Kraus, *Die chinesische Mauer* (Leipzig: Kurt Wolff Verlag, 1914).

72. Karl Kraus, "Die chinesische Mauer," *Die Fackel*, nos. 285–286 (1909), 8.

73. Kraus, "Die chinesische Mauer," 10.

74. Loos, "Ornament and Crime," in *The Architecture of Adolf Loos*, 100; "Ornament und Verbrechen," in Loos, *Trotzdem*, 78.

75. Kraus, "Die chinesische Mauer," 1.

76. On the planning and execution of the Michaelerplatz building, and the controversy surrounding it, the standard account is Hermann Czech and Wolfgang Mistelbauer, *Das Looshaus*, third ed. (Vienna: Löcker, 1984). This has been supplemented and brought up to date in the

equally exhaustive chronology presented in Karlheinz Gruber, Sabine Höller-Alber, and Markus Kristan, *Ernst Epstein, 1881–1938: Der Bauleiter des Looshauses als Architekt*, exh. cat. (Vienna: Jüdisches Museum der Stadt Wien/Holzhausen Verlag, 2002), 17–37. Both of these sources have been incorporated into the up-to-date account in English: Leslie Topp, *Architecture and Truth in Fin-de-Siècle Vienna* (Cambridge: Cambridge University Press, 2004), 138–142. My summary is based on these sources. Since this chapter was first published, two extended studies on the Michaelerplatz building, including the controversy, have appeared: Christopher Long, *The Looshaus* (New Haven and London: Yale University Press, 2011); and Marco Pogacnik, *Adolf Loos und Wien*, exh. cat. (Vienna: Ausstellungszentrum im Ringturm; Salzburg: Müry Salzmann, 2011). The episode is also considered in the context of other artistic scandals in fin-de-siècle Vienna in Tobias G. Natter and Max Hollein, eds., *The Naked Truth: Klimt, Schiele, Kokoschka and Other Scandals*, exh. cat. (Frankfurt a.M.: Schirn Kunsthalle; Munich: Prestel, 2005).

77. The plans were drawn by Ernst Epstein, the executive architect in charge of the construction (*Bauleiter*).

78. Adolf Loos, "Mein Haus am Michaelerplatz," in Loos, *Gesammelte Schriften*, 420.

79. Czech and Mistelbauer, *Das Looshaus*, 25; and Topp, *Architecture and Truth in Fin-de-Siècle Vienna*, 140.

80. For example the unsigned article "Der Neubau auf dem Michaelerplatz: Sistierung des Fassadenbaues," *Wiener Allgemeine Zeitung*, September 29, 1910, cited in Gruber, Höller-Alber, and Kristan, *Ernst Epstein*, 23.

81. "Both I and my client were astonished that the conflict between us and the city building office reached the press. We planned to settle the matter peacefully. We were and remain convinced that we require the approval of the magistrate, but that it does not lie in the power of this body to dictate the sequence of the works ... The decoration of this stucco façade will be an evenly spaced horizontal meander pattern from the cornice to the mezzanine. About the material of this meander decoration we are not yet certain." "Die beanständete Fassade des Baues am Michaelerplatz," *Illustrirtes Wiener Extrablatt*, September 30, 1910, in Loos, *Gesammelte Schriften*, 378. On October 3, 1910, Loos claimed that the halt to the building works represented a "ban on continuing work on the façade." Adolf Loos, "Mein erstes Haus," *Der Morgen*, October 3, 1910, in Loos, *Gesammelte Schriften*, 385.

82. Gruber, Höller-Alber, and Kristan, *Ernst Epstein*, 27.

83. Adolf Loos, "Mein Haus am Michaelerplatz," in Loos, *Gesammelte Schriften*, 426. Loos misspells the name of the councilor, Karl Rykl.

84. In the manuscript published by Adolf Opel, Loos refers to Berger only as "an Outsider." He quotes from Berger's article in the *Neue Freie Presse* and adds: "But only a few months before, he wanted the building to be presented to architects as exemplary, and had congratulated me. I do not wish to discuss publicly what has moved him to misuse the NFP for a petty private matter." "Mein Haus am Michaelerplatz," in Loos, 429–430. Newspaper reports of the time make clear that Berger was named, and the *Tagesbote aus Mähren und Schlesien* reported that Loos showed a slide of Berger's letter (December 23, 1911), quoted in Czech and Mistelbauer, *Das Looshaus*, 40.

85. "Das Haus am Michaelerplatz," *Neues Wiener Tagebblatt*, December 15, 1911.

86. The architects were Ludwig Hoffmann and Martin Dülfer. Loos, "Mein Haus am Michaelerplatz," 428.

87. Gruber et al., *Ernst Epstein*, 17. See also Czech and Mistelbauer, *Das Looshaus*, 41.

88. Gruber et al., *Ernst Epstein*, 34–35. They note further: "It is impossible today to reconstruct the thoughts and motives for this or that action of those involved in the building" (17). Marco Pogacnik has published a large number of newly discovered documents, showing in particular how Loos kept design decisions open. Yet his account remains, in the end, intentionalist: "The design that was realized in May 1912 corresponds, in the end, almost completely to Loos's original conception." Pogacnik, *Adolf Loos und Wien*, 93.

89. Karl Kraus, "Die Zuckerkandl," *Die Fackel*, nos. 334–335 (1911), 22–23. The flower boxes were attached

on October 24: Gruber et al., *Ernst Epstein*, 32.

90. Karl Kraus, "Die Zuckerkandl," 23. On receiving his copy of *Die Fackel*, Loos wrote to Kraus about the Zuckerkandl quote: "Have just received the *Fackel*! What a moving preamble!" Postcard from Adolf Loos to Karl Kraus, November 5, 1911, Wienbibliothek, Handschriftensammlung, I.N. 138.849.

91. See n. 1, above.

92. A transcription of the judgment and sentence is held in the Wienbibliothek, Handschriftensammlung, I.N. 138/870/1–5; a transcription of the court's sentence alone is in the Adolf-Loos-Archiv, Albertina, file "Diverses." Page 3 of the five-page judgment is reproduced in facsimile in Elise Altmann-Loos, *Mein Leben mit Adolf Loos*, ed. Adolf Opel (Frankfurt am Main: Ullstein, 1986), 298. Press reports of the time have long been the main source for information on the case; several are reprinted in Altmann-Loos, *Mein Leben*, 284–300. Information on Loos's arrest and trial can be found in Rukschcio and Schachel, *Adolf Loos*, 339–342; in Elsie Altmann-Loos's affectionate memoirs that, nonetheless, assume Loos's guilt—Elsie Altmann-Loos et al., *Adolf Loos: Der Mensch*, 188–191; a brief and slightly inaccurate summary in Harald Seyrl, *Tatort Wien*, vol. 2, *Die Zeit von 1925–1944* (Vienna-Scharnstein: Edition Seyrl, 2007), 13–14; and responses by Alfred Polgar, Heinrich Eduard Jacob, and Arthur Rundt in the section "Der Prozess," in *Kontroversen: Adolf Loos im Spiegel der Zeitgenossen*, ed. Adolf Opel (Vienna: Prachner, 1985), 117–127. Klarinda Ma, "Der 'Fall' Loos," 161–171, is an informative account of the trial based on published sources.

At the time of completing the original manuscript of this chapter, published in the *Art Bulletin* in 2012, I had been unable to locate the file of the 1928 case in the court archives in the Wiener Stadt- und Landesarchiv; it was considered by the archive to be lost. Since then, however, our knowledge of the case has been broadened considerably. First, the architectural historian Christopher Long published a very complete study of the 1928 Loos case which drew on Ma, "Der 'Fall' Loos," and on the first publication of this chapter in the *Art Bulletin*. Long, however, casts his net much more widely across the press of the time and other sources, and puts Loos's arrest and trial in a broader context: Christopher Long, *Der Fall Loos* (Vienna: Amalthea Verlag, 2015). And second, the entire file of the case has reemerged under somewhat mysterious circumstances. The slightly emended English edition of Long's book takes into account this material and discusses its reappearance: Christopher Long, *Adolf Loos on Trial* (Prague: Kant, 2017). I have left my text as originally published in 2012.

The file—Landesgericht für Strafsachen, A11 Vr 5707/28 Strafsache gegen Adolf Loos Fall Beer, now file 2.3.4.A11.I.5707/1928—has now been published by the Wiener Stadt- und Landesarchiv and can be accessed through the archive search page: https://www.wien.gv.at/actaproweb2/benutzung/search.xhtml.

93. "Der Fall Adolf Loos," *Reichspost*, September 7, 1928.

94. Altmann-Loos's account appears in Elsie Altmann-Loos et al., *Adolf Loos—Der Mensch*, 69–71, 188–191. She claims that the photos in question came from Beer's apartment, but that they were destroyed before the police arrived.

95. "I received the pictures that were found in my home and which have been brought into the context of my current affair from a writer [*Literaten*] fifteen years ago. He was dying and did not wish them to be found among his effects. They were given to me in a sealed package. I want to emphasize that this writer was ... not Peter Altenberg." "Adolf Loos über seine Einstellung zu Künstlern und Kindern: Ein Gespräch mit dem Architekten," *Neue Freie Presse*, September 9, 1928. On Altenberg and his photograph collection, see Leo A. Lensing, "Peter Altenberg's Fabricated Photographs: Literature and Photography in Fin-de-Siècle Vienna," in *Vienna 1900: From Altenberg to Wittgenstein*, ed. Edward Timms and Ritchie Robertson (Edinburgh: Edinburgh University Press, 1990); and Tag Gronberg, *Vienna: City of Modernity, 1890–1914*, chap. 5; on Altenberg's notorious fascination with young girls, see Andrew Barker, *Telegrams from the Soul: Peter Altenberg and the Culture of Fin-de-Siecle Vienna* (Columbia, SC: Camden House, 1996), passim.

96. Austrian Strafgesetz (1852), §133/III: "Solicitation

(*Verführung*), by which someone induces a person entrusted to him for custody, upbringing, or schooling to commit an indecent act or to tolerate such an act." From the judgment: "It has been reliably determined that he [Loos] induced the girls to indecency by causing them to assume certain positions and to be drawn in them. The sketchbook that he used is present, and thus the visual evidence that these positions were, almost without exception, of an obscene nature [*grob unzüchtiger Art*]." Wienbibliothek, Handschriftensammlung, I.N. 138/870/3; see also the facsimile of this page in Altmann-Loos, *Mein Leben*, 298.

97. "The accused denies having abused the girls sexually, and abuse could not be established by the evidence presented. The testimony of the girls is not suitable to do so, as it cannot be ruled out that the girls are reporting the erotic situation in which they found themselves as nude models in a playful or exaggerated way. Moreover, according to the expert opinion of the child psychiatrist and also the testimony of the parents, Fiedler, who seems to be the leader of the others, has a pathological tendency to distort the truth. The accused is therefore acquitted of the charge of abuse." Wienbibliothek, Handschriftensammlung, I.N. 138/870/3.

98. One newspaper termed this "unusual clemency": "Gerichtssaal. Adolf Loos—vier Monate strenger Arrest bedingt," unidentified newspaper clipping in Wienbibliothek, Handschriftensammlung, I.N. 138.870/5.

99. The decision notes the use of the *Gesetz über die bedingte Verurteilung* of July 23, 1920 (*Staatsgesetzblatt für die Republik Österreich*, no. 373).

100. See the notice of sentence and the "Belehrung" outlining the terms of suspension of sentence in Adolf Loos Archiv, file "Diverses."

101. On changes in the Austrian press, see Timms, *Karl Kraus, Apocalyptic Satirist*, vol. 2, 87–104. The changing, and more sensationalistic, reporting on criminal trials is discussed in Franz Karl Hartl, "Kriminal- und Gerichtssaalberichterstattung in der ersten Republik: Untersucht am Beispiel des Mordfalles Katharina Fellner in der 'Neuen Freien Presse' und dem 'Tag'/'Wiener Tag'" (MPhil diss., University of Vienna, 1993).

102. "Der Fall Loos: Der traurige Niederbruch eines großen Talents," *Neue Freie Presse*, September 7, 1928. Oddly, the newspapers made no mention of another case which parallels this one more closely: Egon Schiele's 1912 arrest on suspicion of child abuse in the context of his sketching of children in Neulengbach, near Vienna. He spent twenty-four days in prison. In the end, Schiele was convicted only of the "dissemination of indecent drawings [*Verbreitung unsittlicher Zeichnungen*]." See "Egon Schiele in Prison," in Natter and Hollein, *The Naked Truth*, 126–127; and *Egon Schiele im Gefängnis: Zehn Faksimilieblätter nach Originalen aus dem Besitz der Graphischen Sammlung Albertina*, ed. Christian M. Nebehay and Peter Müller (Graz: Akademische Druck- und Verlagsanstalt, 1990).

103. "Adolf Loos als Mensch und Künstler: Von dem Künstler befreundeter Seite," *Neue Freie Presse*, September 8, 1928.

104. Karl Bühler, "Jugendliche Zeugen vor Gericht," *Neue Freie Presse*, September 9, 1928.

105. "Kinder auf der Modellbörse: Engleskÿpfchen und Elendsfiguren," *Neue Freie Presse*, September 9, 1928.

106. "Gerichtssaal: Adolf Loos—vier Monate strenger Arrest bedingt": unidentified newspaper clipping in Wienbibliothek, Handschriftensammlung, I.N. 138.870/5. On assumptions that Loos was a Jew, see Beatriz Colomina, "Sex, Lies and Decoration: Adolf Loos and Gustav Klimt," *Gustav Klimt: Painting, Design and Modern Life*, ed. Tobias G. Natter and Christopher Grunenberg (London: Tate Publishing, 2008), 42–51, 239, n. 17.

107. "Nachspiel zum Prozeß Loos: Eine Untersuchung gegen die 'Rote Fahne,'" *Neues Wiener Journal*, undated clipping in Wienbibliothek, Handschriftensammlung, I.N. 138.870/4. On Kraus's "crusade" against Schober around the violence involved with the 1927 burning of the Palace of Justice and violence against left-wing demonstrators, see Timms, *Karl Kraus, Apocalyptic Satirist*, vol. 2, 332–347.

108. "Gerichtssaal: Adolf Loos—vier Monate strenger Arrest bedingt," unidentified newspaper clipping in Wienbibliothek, Handschriftensammlung, I.N. 138.870/5.

109. "Adolf Loos vor den Schöffen: Es wird hinter verschlossenen Türen verhandelt," *Das Kleine Blatt*, December 1, 1928.

110. Carlo Ginzburg's seminal essay is "Morelli, Freud and Sherlock Holmes: Clues and Scientific Method," *History Workshop Journal* 9, no. 1 (1980), 5–36.

111. The case of Loos's physician at the time shows this clearly. Fritz Wittels, a young doctor who enjoyed Freud's patronage, was also, briefly, a frequent contributor to *Die Fackel*. One of his essays for *Die Fackel*, "The Child Woman," is a paean to a creature of his and Kraus's fantasy: a sexually precocious, polymorphously perverse girl unfettered by inhibitions, the legitimate underage object of male desire. Wittels, "Das Kindweib," *Die Fackel*, no. 230–231 (1907), 14–33. But the child woman was, apparently, a real one. Edward Timms has excavated the sad story of the actress Irma Karczewska, who seems to have been circulated among the men of the Kraus circle, victim of the sort of male hypocrisy and exploitation they claimed to stand against. Kraus's public fight to keep private matters out of the press had its self-serving side. Soon enough, Wittels broke with Kraus, writing a satire of the satirists' circle. Kraus responded typically: he attacked Wittels personally in print and showed Freud Wittels's private letters, undermining the latter's relationship with his other mentor. See *Freud and the Child Woman: The Memoirs of Fritz Wittels*, ed. Edward Timms (New Haven and London: Yale University Press, 1995).

112. Fritz Wittels, "The *Fackel*-Neurosis," in *Minutes of the Vienna Psychoanalytic Society*, ed. Herman Nunberg and Ernst Federn (New York: International Universities Press, 1962–75), vol. 2, 382–388. On Wittels, Kraus, and Freud, see *Freud and the Child Woman*; and Timms, *Karl Kraus, Apocalyptic Satirist*, vol. 1, 97–103.

113. It is worth noting that Wittels's attacks on Kraus led to Freud severing his own relations with Wittels: Freud tried to prevent Wittels from publishing his satirical novel *Ezechiel der Zugereiste* (Berlin: Egon Fleischel, 1910), a roman à clef about the Kraus circle, fearing the publication would put the psychoanalytic movement in the middle of a press battle while also revealing the closeness of some of its members to the demimonde. Freud's practices of the public case were to *avoid* publicity, to keep the case studies of psychoanalysis of the scientific kind.

114. Michel de Certeau, *The Practice of Everyday Life*, trans. S. Rendall (Berkeley and Los Angeles: University of California Press, 1984), 93.

Chapter 2

1. The painting is also known variously as *Das Leichenbegräbnis* (The funeral) or *Das Begräbnis des Dichters Oskar Panizza* (The funeral of the poet Oskar Panizza). On this work, see Werner Hofmann, "Einschränkende Bermerkungen," in *Zeugnisse der Angst in der modernen Kunst*, exh. cat. (Darmstadt: Mathildenhöhe/Darmstädter Gespräche, 1963), 52–53; Hans Hess, *Georg Grosz* (New Haven and London: Yale University Press, 1985), 53; Joachim Heusinger von Waldegg, "George Grosz 'Leichenbegräbnis. Widmung an Oskar Panizza': Gesellschaftskritische Allegorie als Selbstprojektion," *Pantheon* 44 (1986), 111–125; Peter-Klaus Schuster, ed., *George Grosz: Berlin-New York*, exh. cat. (Berlin: Neue Nationalgalerie/Ars Nicolai, 1994), 328–329; Lothar Fischer and Helen Adkins, *George Grosz: Sein Leben* (Berlin: Bäßler, 2017), 54–57.

2. Letter to Otto Schmalhausen, December 15, 1917, in George Grosz, *Briefe, 1913–1959*, ed. Herbert Knust (Reinbek: Rowohlt, 1979), 56.

3. From notes by Grosz under the heading "Notizen für Prozeß 3. Dez. 1930, Lebenslauf," made for his blasphemy trial of 1930, quoted in Hess, *George Grosz*, 80.

4. From Grosz's notes of 1930, quoted in Hess, *George Grosz*, 80.

5. Grosz, *Briefe*, 57.

6. Undated letter to DuMont, in George Grosz, *Teurer Makkaroni! Briefe an Mark Neven DuMont, 1922–1959*, ed. Karl Riha and Angela Merte (Berlin: Argon, 1992), 106.

7. Letter to Arnold Rönnebeck, February 12, 1944. Grosz, *Briefe*, 329.

8. For a figure often considered "forgotten," there is a substantial literature on Panizza. In English, Peter Jelavich provides perhaps the best overview of Panizza's position within Munich modernism in his *Munich and*

Theatrical Modernism: Politics, Playwriting, and Performance, 1890–1914 (Cambridge, MA: Harvard University Press, 1985), esp. chap. 2; see also Peter D. G. Brown, *Oskar Panizza: His Life and Works* (New York, Frankfurt a.M., Bern: Peter Lang, 1983). In addition, my account relies on the following sources: Michael Bauer, *Oskar Panizza: Ein literarisches Porträt* (Munich: Hanser, 1984); Rolf Düsterberg, *"Die gedrukte Freiheit": Oskar Panizza und die Zürcher Diskußjonen* (Frankfurt a.M.: Peter Lang, 1988); Jürgen Müller, *Der Pazjent als Psychiater: Oskar Panizzas Weg vom Irrenarzt zum Insassen* (Bonn: Psychiatrie-Verlag, 1999); and the material collected in *Der Fall Oskar Panizza: Ein deutscher Dichter im Gefängnis: Eine Dokumentation*, ed. Kurt Boeser (Berlin: Edition Hentrich, 1989).

9. His first publication was *Der Fall Panizza: Eine kritische Betrachtung über Gotteslästerung und künstlerische Dinge vor Schwurgerichten* (Munich: Wohlfart, 1895). Lessing discusses this as the formative moment of his life as a writer in his memoir *Einmal und nie wieder* (1935; repr. Gütersloh: Bertelsmann, 1969), 294–295.

10. See Bauer, *Oskar Panizza*, 29–31.

11. Walter Mehring, *Die verlorene Bibliothek: Autobiographie einer Kultur* (Icking bei München: Kreisselmeier, 1964), 68–76.

12. "Among the few originals whose talent and honesty ... should be mentioned is Oskar Panizza. One of the most adventurous hotheads, who seems to aim for his works to be confiscated, he has recently targeted the popes": *Die Zeit*, December 1, 1894, quoted in Bauer, *Oskar Panizza*, 16.

13. Sigmund Freud, *The Interpretation of Dreams*, trans. James Strachey (New York: Avon Books, 1965), 250; *Die Traumdeutung* (Leipzig and Vienna: Franz Deuticke, 1900), 149.

14. Walter Benjamin, "E. T. A. Hoffmann und Oskar Panizza," March 26, 1930, in Benjamin, *Gesammelte Schriften*, ed. Rolf Tiedemann and Hermann Schweppenhäuser (Frankfurt a.M.: Suhrkamp, 1972–1979), vol. 3, 641–648.

15. Kubin saw *Das Liebeskonzil* in a Munich bookstore and sought out the commission to illustrate a new edition. This was privately published in fifty copies with Kubin's nine pen-and-ink drawings by the Gesellschaft der Münchner Bibliophilen. As a limited edition for members of the organization, the book was not considered available to the public and therefore not subject to the legal ban. *Das Liebeskonzil: Eine Himmelstragödie in fünf Aufzügen von Oskar Panizza. Zeichnungen von Alfred Kubin* (Munich: Gesellschaft der Münchner Bibliophilen, 1913). See the facsimile reprint (Munich: Edition Spangenberg, 1991) and the afterword by Michael Bauer on the edition.

16. He wrote the foreword to the first French edition: *Le Concile d'Amour*, trans. Jean Bréjoux (Utrecht: Coll. Libertés, 1964).

17. In *Der Pazjent als Psychiater*, Jürgen Müller, himself a psychiatrist, discusses Panizza in terms of the psychiatry of the time and its personnel in great detail. Müller summarizes his research in "Oskar Panizza: Psychiatrist, Antipsychiatrist, Patient," *International Journal of Psychiatry in Clinical Practice* 4, no. 4 (2000), 335–338.

18. Two years later, Gudden's own career came to an equally abrupt and inglorious end. He was the most senior of four psychiatrists who wrote a report declaring Bavaria's King Ludwig II legally insane and not competent to handle affairs of state, leading to Ludwig's deposition. The report was considered controversial at the time and ever since. Gudden had apparently not examined Ludwig himself. The day after the deposition, both Gudden, who by then had been made the King's personal physician, and Ludwig were found dead on the shore of the Starnberger See, after they had embarked on a stroll together. One of Panizza's most haunting poems concerns the event. Here Panizza interprets the mysterious events as Ludwig's murder of Gudden by drowning, followed by suicide. See Panizza, "Der König und sein Narrenmeister," repr. in Müller, *Der Pazjent als Psychiater*, 46–47.

19. Panizza's work was known to a larger public in the twentieth century mainly through the only popular edition of his work (discussed below): Oskar Panizza, *Visionen der Dämmerung*, ed. Hanns Heinz Ewers, introduction by Hannes Ruch (pseud. Hans Richard Weinhöppel) (Munich: Georg Müller, 1914).

20. "Das Verbrechen von Tavistock-Square," in Panizza, *Der Korsettenfritz: Gesammelte Erzählungen* (Munich: Matthes & Seitz, 1981). An interesting reading of this story is Joela Jacobs, "'Verbrechen wider die Natur': Oskar Panizza's First Encounter with Censorship," in *Protest and Reform in German Literature and Visual Culture, 1871–1918*, ed. Godela Weiss-Sussex and Charlotte Woodford (Munich: Iudicium, 2015), 125–138.

21. On the Lex Heinze and the debates around it, see R. J. V. Lenman, "Art, Society, and the Law: The Lex Heinze," *Oxford Germany Studies* 8, no. 1 (1973), 86–113; Jelavich, *Munich and Theatrical Modernism*, 139–151; and Gary D. Stark, *Banned in Berlin: Literary Censorship in Imperial Germany, 1871–1918* (New York and Oxford: Berghahn Books, 2009), 21–27. The Heinze murder case itself is explored in Benjamin Carter Hett, *Death in the Tiergarten: Murder and Criminal Justice in the Kaiser's Berlin* (Cambridge, MA: Harvard University Press, 2004), chapter 2.

22. Lenman, "Art, Society and the Law," 94.

23. On the differences in theatrical censorship—laws, procedures, and practices varied considerably in the Reich and were specific to the *Länder* that made up Germany—see Stark, *Banned in Berlin*.

24. A complete account of the *Umsturzvorlage* can be found in Dagmar Kolbe, *Strafbarkeit im Vorfeld und im Umfeld der Teilnahme (§§ 88a, 110, 111, 130a und 140 StGB): Reformdiskussion und Gesetzgebung seit dem 19. Jahrhundert* (Berlin: de Gruyter, 2011), 52–65.

25. Lenman, "Art, Society, and the Law," 97–99.

26. Jelavich, *Munich and Theatrical Modernism*, passim.

27. Panizza, *Der heilige Staatsanwalt: Eine moralische Komödie in fünf Aufzügen* (Leipzig: Friedrich, 1894).

28. Panizza, *Der heilige Staatsanwalt*, 7–8.

29. See Stark, *Banned in Berlin*, 11.

30. These are drawn upon by Jelavich in *Munich and Theatrical Modernism*.

31. Otto Julius Bierbaum, Panizza wrote, suffered "diarrhea" out of fear of the censor: Bauer, *Oskar Panizza*, 124. "Haben Sie schon etwas Konfiszierbares geschrieben?": Müller, *Der Pazjent als Psychiater*, 73.

32. "Bruder Martin O.S.B.," *Die unbefleckte Empfängnis der Päpste. Aus dem Spanischen von Oskar Panizza* (Zurich: Schabelitz, 1893); *Der teutsche Michel und der römische Papst* (Leipzig: Friedrich, 1894).

33. See the very helpful and synthetic account in Jelavich, *Munich and Theatrical Modernism*, chap. 1.

34. The most sympathetic account of the play's literary quality is Bauer's: *Oskar Panizza*, 151–178.

35. On the tradition of the *Lesedrama*, see Amy Kurlander, Stephan S. Wolohojian, and Christopher Wood, "Das erzählte Drama in Bildern: Adolf von Menzel und Max Klinger," in *Der Text des Bildes: Möglichkeiten und Mittel eigenständiger Bilderzählung*, ed. Wolfgang Kemp (Munich: Text + Kritik, 1989), 35–36. Panizza's friend Max Halbe was a particular champion of the form; see Gerhard Schulz, "Theorie des Dramas in deutschen Naturalismus," in *Deutsche Dramentheorien: Beiträge zu einer historischen Poetik des Dramas in Deutschland*, ed. Reinhold Grimm (Wiesbaden: Athenaion, 1981), vol. 2, 104.

36. Bauer, *Oskar Panizza*, 16.

37. Müller, *Der Pazjent als Psychiater*, 76.

38. Panizza then published the text: *Meine Verteidigung in Sachen "Das Liebeskonzil". Nebst dem Sachverständigung-Gutachten des Dr. M. G. Conrad und dem Urteil des k. Landgerichts München I* (Zurich: Schabelitz, 1895), repr. in *Der Fall Oskar Panizza*.

39. The *Fränkische Kurier* noted that "the sentencing of the writer Dr. Panizza in Munich to a year in prison is causing a furor. ... In any case the sentence is a quite strikingly harsh one, one that could not even be higher if we were already under the chains of the *Umsturzgesetz* [subversion law]. For that year in prison, Dr. Panizza could almost have committed manslaughter." Quoted in *Der Fall Oskar Panizza*, 111. Jelavich writes that this was "the harshest sentence meted out to a writer during the Wilhelmine period, inasmuch as several weeks of fortress arrest was the norm for most 'crimes committed in the press.'" *Munich and Theatrical Modernism*, 59.

40. *Das Liebeskonzil*, 74.

41. *Das Liebeskonzil*, 74.

42. Panizza, "Der Corsetten-Fritz," in *Der Korsettenfritz*, 203–222. On the short story, see Sophia Könemann, "Von 'Menschen-Bälgen', 'kostbaren Rassen' und 'Canarienvögeln': Fetischismus in Oskar Panizzas Erzählung Der Corsetten-Fritz," in *Das Geschlecht der*

Anderen: Figuren der Alterität: Kriminologie, Psychiatrie, Ethnologie und Zoologie, ed. Sophie Könemann and Anne Stähr (Bielefeld: Transcript, 2011), 171–186.

43. Panizza, "Der Corsetten-Fritz," 222.

44. On Carl Wernicke's theory of sejunction, see Edward Shorter, *An Historical Dictionary of Psychiatry* (Oxford: Oxford University Press, 2005), 300.

45. Reprinted in *Der Fall Oskar Panizza*, 8–14.

46. Panizza, "Ein scandalöser Fall," in *Der Korsettenfritz*, 230–65. See Auguste Tardieu, *Question médico-légale de l'identité dans ses rapports avec les vices de conformation des organes sexuels* (Paris: J. B. Baillière, 1874), 61–174.

47. *Herculine Barbin: Being the Recently Discovered Memoirs of a Nineteenth-century French Hermaphrodite*, ed. Michel Foucault, trans. Richard McDougall (New York: Pantheon, 1980), xv–xvi.

48. Richard von Krafft-Ebing, *Psychopathia Sexualis*, thirteenth ed. (Stuttgart: Ferdinand Enke, 1903).

49. *Psichopatia Criminalis: Anleitung um die vom Gericht für notwendig erkanten Geisteskrankheiten psichjatrisch zu eruïren und wissenschaftlich festzustellen. Für Ärtzte, Laien, Juristen, Vormünder, Verwaltungsbeamte, Minister, etc.* (Zurich: Verlag der Zürcher Diskussionen, 1898). The title in German shows Panizza's idiosyncratic orthography. My references are to the recent reprint: *Psychopathia Criminalis* (Berlin: Matthes & Seitz, 1985). There is little scholarship on this important work, and the only major essay is very recent: Birgit Lang, "'Writing Back': Literary Satire and Oskar Panizza's *Psichopatia criminalis* (1898)," in *A History of the Case Study: Sexology, Psychoanalysis, Literature*, ed. Birgit Lang, Joy Damousi, and Alison Lewis (Manchester: University of Manchester Press, 2017), 90–118.

50. See, for example, Karl Kraus, "Der Prozeß Odilon" and "Gerichtspsychiatrie," in *Sittlichkeit und Kriminalität* (1908; second ed. Vienna and Leipzig: Verlag "Die Fackel," 1923).

51. The best historical source on the scandals surrounding psychiatry and involuntary institutionalization in the Wilhelmine period is Arthur Kirchenheim and Heinrich Reinartz, *Zur Reform des Irrenrechts: Elf Leitsätze zur Besserung der Irrenfürsorge und Beseitigung des Entmündigungsunfugs* (Barmen: Wiemann, 1895). These controversies and the campaigns for the reform of the laws governing the rights of those with, or attributed with, mental illness are discussed in Ann Goldberg, "The Mellage Trial and the Politics of Insane Asylums in Wilhelmine Germany," *Journal of Modern History* 74, no. 1 (2002), 1–32 and "A Reinvented Public: 'Lunatics' Rights' and Bourgeois Populism in the Kaiserreich," *German History* 21 (2003), 159–182; Karen Nolte, *Gelebte Hysterie: Erfahrung, Eigensinn und psychiatrische Diskurse im Anstaltsalltag um 1900* (Frankfurt a.M.: Campus, 2003); and Dirk Blasius, *Der verwaltete Wahnsinn: Eine Sozialgeschichte des Irrenhauses* (Frankfurt a.M.: Fischer Taschenbuch Verlag, 1980), esp. chaps. 5 and 7.

52. Panizza, *Psychopathia Criminalis*, 43.

53. Panizza, *Psychopathia Criminalis*, 32–33.

54. Panizza, *Psychopathia Criminalis*, 37–38. Tiberius Gracchus was a second-century BCE plebeian tribune who sought reforms favoring the poor. He was murdered by Roman senators.

55. Panizza, *Psychopathia Criminalis*, 35

56. Specifically Rudolf Arndt, *Lehrbuch der Psychiatrie für Ärzte und Studierende* (Vienna and Leipzig: Urban & Schwarzenberg, 1883); Heinrich Schüle, *Handbuch der Geisteskrankheiten*, second ed. (Leipzig: F. C. W. Vogel, 1880); Schüle, *Klinische Psychiatrie: Specielle Pathologie und Therapie der Geisteskrankheiten*, third ed. (Leipzig: F. C. W. Vogel, 886).

57. Panizza, *Psychopathia Criminalis*, 47–48.

58. Panizza, *Psychopathia Criminalis*, 51.

59. Panizza, *Psychopathia Criminalis*, 77.

60. Müller, *Der Pazjent als Psychiater*, 101.

61. Oskar Panizza, *Parisjana: Deutsche Verse aus Paris* (Zurich: Zürcher Diskußjonen, 1899).

62. Müller, *Der Pazjent als Psychiater*, 1.5

63. An analysis of Panizza's philosophical critique of psychiatry is given by Müller in *Der Pazjent als Psychiater*, 61–67, 94–99.

64. Third ed. (Leipzig: J. A. Barth, 1916), 219–224, as identified by Müller, *Der Pazjent als Psychiater*, 41.

65. "eine geist'ge Freistatt": Oskar Panizza, *Düstre Lieder* (Leipzig: Albert Unflad, 1886), 17.

66. Rolf Düsterberg, *"Die gedrukte Freiheit": Oskar Panizza und die* Zürcher Diskußjonen (Frankfurt a.M.: Peter Lang, 1988), 128.

67. Cited in Müller, *Der Pazjent als Psychiater*, 94.

68. For example Kraepelin, *Einführung in die Psychiatrische Klinik*, 220.

69. *Die Fackel*, no. 236 (1907), 15.

70. Grosz was released on April 27 and dismissed on May 26. Barbara McCloskey, *George Grosz and the Communist Party: Art and Radicalism in Crisis, 1918–1936* (Princeton: Princeton University Press, 1997), 36.

71. Quoted in Fritz Mierau, *Das Verschwinden von Franz Jung: Stationen einer Biographie* (Hamburg: Nautilus, 1998), 113.

72. For general accounts of Gross and his ideas, see Emanuel Hurwitz, *Otto Gross: Paradies-Sucher zwischen Freud und Jung: Leben und Werk* (Frankfurt a.M.: Suhrkamp, 1979); Martin Green, *The von Richthofen Sisters: The Triumphant and the Tragic Modes of Love* (New York: Basic Books, 1974), passim; Martin Green, *Mountain of Truth: The Counter Culture Begins, Ascona, 1900–1920* (Hanover, NH and London: Tufts University Press, 1986), passim; Martin Green, *Otto Gross, Freudian Psychoanalyst, 1877–1920: Literature and Ideas* (Lampeter, Wales: Edwin Mellen Press, 1999); Nicolaus Sombart, "Der wahre Feind: Otto Gross," in Sombart, *Die deutschen Männer und ihre Feinde: Carl Schmitt—ein deutsches Schicksal zwischen Männerbund und Matriarchatsmythos* (1991; Frankfurt a.M.: Fischer Taschenbuch Verlag, 1997); Michael Turnheim, "Otto Gross und die deutsche Psychiatrie," Habilitation, Medical Faculty of the University of Vienna, repr. in Turnheim, *Freud und der Rest: Aufsätze zur Geschichte der Psychoanalyse* (Vienna: Turia & Kant, 1993), 71–118; Bernd Nitzschke, "Otto Gross: Ein Psychoanalytiker als Revolutionär," in Nitzschke, *Das Ich als Experiment: Essays über Sigmund Freud und die Psychoanalyse im 20. Jahrhundert* (Göttingen: Vandenhoeck & Ruprecht, 2000), 112–171; and now Gottfried M. Heuer, *Freud's "Outstanding" Colleague/Jung's "Twin Brother": The Suppressed Psychoanalytic and Political Significance of Otto Gross* (London: Routledge, 2017). Since 1999, the Internationale Otto Gross Gesellschaft has organized eight conferences and published the proceedings. These represent invaluable contributions to the research on Gross and are cited separately below where relevant.

73. Perhaps the best account of Gross's work in terms of contemporary psychiatry is in Turnheim, "Otto Gross und die deutsche Psychiatrie."

74. Leipzig: Vogel, 1907.

75. Vienna and Leipzig: Braunmüller, 1909.

76. See Freud's letter to Jung of February 25, 1908: "You really are the only one capable of making an original contribution; except perhaps for O. Gross, but unfortunately his health is poor." *The Freud-Jung Letters: The Correspondence between Sigmund Freud and C. G. Jung*, ed. William McGuire, trans. Ralph Manheim and R. F. C. Hull (London: Hogarth Press, 1974), 126. Freud was also well aware of the importance of alliances with gentiles: his psychoanalytic circle at the time was almost entirely made up of Jews, and he was sensitive to the notion of psychoanalysis as a "Jewish science." See Ernst Falzeder, "Sigmund Freud, Eugen Bleuler, C. G. Jung und das Burghölzli: Die Geschichte einer ambivalenten Beziehung," in *Die Gesetze des Vaters: 4. Internationaler Otto Gross Kongress*, ed. Albrecht Götz von Olenhusen and Gottfried Heuer (Marburg: LiteraturWissenschaft.de, 2005), 129–130.

77. Otto Gross, "Über Konflikt und Beziehung," in *Drei Aufsätze über den inneren Konflikt* (Bonn: Marcus & Weber 1920), 7.

78. Otto Gross, "Zur Ueberwindung der kulturellen Krise," *Die Aktion* 3, no. 14 (1913), 384, trans. in Otto Gross, *Selected Works*, 1901–1920, trans. Lois L. Madison (Hamilton, NY: Mindpiece, 2012), 257.

79. As reported by Gross in "Ludwig Rubiners 'Psychoanalyse,'" *Die Aktion* 3, no. 20 (1914), 506–507.

80. Heuer, *Freud's "Outstanding" Colleague*, 86–105.

81. On Pfemfert and *Die Aktion*, see Douglas Brent McBride, "A Critical Mass for Modernism in Berlin: *Der Sturm* (1910–32); *Die Aktion* (1911–32); and *Sturm-Bühne* (1918–19)," in *The Oxford Critical and Cultural History of Modernism Magazines*, ed. Peter Brooker, Sascha Bru, Andrew Thacker, and Christian Weikop (Oxford: Oxford University Press, 2013), vol.

3, pt. 2, 772–797; Franz Pfemfert, *Ich schneide die Zeit aus: Expressionismus und Politik in Franz Pfemferts 'Aktion,'* ed. Paul Raabe (Munich: dtv, 1964); Franz Pfemfert, *Ich setze diese Zeitschrift wider diese Zeit: Sozialpolitische und literaturkritische Texte*, ed. Wolfgang Haug (Darmstadt and Neuwied: Luchterhand, 1985); *Die Aktion, 1911–1918: Eine Auswahl*, ed. Thomas Rietzschel (Berlin and Weimar: Aufbau, 1986); Seth Taylor, *Left-Wing Nietzscheans: The Politics of German Expressionism, 1910–1920* (Berlin and New York: de Gruyter, 1990), chap. 2; *Pfemfert: Erinnerungen und Abrechnungen, Texte und Briefe*, ed. Lisbeth Exner and Herbert Kapfer (Munich: Belleville, 1999); and Lutz Schulenburg, "Franz Pfemfert: Zur Erinnerung an einen revolutionären Intellektuellen," in *Die Aktion: Zeitschrift für Politik, Literatur, Kunst*, no. 209 (2004), 9–98.

82. The two journals are compared in McBride, "A Critical Mass for Modernism in Berlin."

83. Quoted in *Pfemfert: Erinnerungen und Abrechnungen*, 41.

84. Franz Pfemfert, editorial introduction to Otto Groß [*sic*], "Die Einwirkung der Allgemeinheit auf das Individuum," *Die Aktion* 3, no. 47 (1913), 1091.

85. "La disparition du Dr. Otto Gross," *Mercure de France*, January 16, 1914, 2–3.

86. *Die Zukunft* (February 28, 1914), 306.

87. Franz Jung, *Der Weg nach unten: Aufzeichnungen aus einer großen Zeit* (1961; Leipzig: Reclam, 1991), 89–90.

88. Ludwig Rubiner, "Der Dichter greift in die Politik," *Die Aktion* 2, no. 21 (1912), 645–652 and no. 23 (1912), 709–715; Rubiner, "Maler bauen Barrikaden," *Die Aktion* 4, no. 17 (1914), 353–365.

89. Christina Jung deserves credit for questioning and ultimately disproving the myth of a successful press action: Jung, "'Aber wir wollen Otto Gross wiederhaben': Eine Pressekampagne," in Christina Jung and Thomas Anz, *Der Fall Otto Gross: Eine Pressekampagne deutscher Intellektueller im Winter 1913/1914* (Marburg: LiteraturWissenschaft.de, 2002), 34–68.

90. Jung, *Der Weg nach unten*, 89.

91. See the archival material located by Ralf Rother and reprinted in Jung and Anz, *Der Fall Otto Gross*, 146–155.

92. The untenability of Jung's diagnosis is discussed in detail by Hurwitz, himself a psychiatrist, in his *Otto Gross*, 183–198. Freud too was skeptical; see his letter to Jung of June 21, 1908, in *The Freud-Jung Letters*, 157–160. And as we shall see below, the diagnosis was rejected by Wilhelm Stekel, who treated Gross from 1914.

93. Pfemfert wrote to the critic Arthur Roessler on January 6, 1914, asking him to use his influence at the newspaper to place an article on the matter. The letter is reprinted in "Briefe von Franz Pfemfert an Arthur Roessler," in Peter Sprengel and Gregor Streim, *Berliner und Wiener Moderne: Vermittlungen und Abgrenzungen in Literatur, Theater, Publizistik* (Vienna: Böhlau, 1998), 682. Roessler had been invited to become art critic for the *Arbeiter-Zeitung* by Victor Adler, founder of the newspaper and head of the Austrian Social Democratic Party until his death in 1918: *Egon Schiele & Arthur Roessler—Der Künstler und sein Förderer: Kunst und Networking im frühen 20. Jahrhundert*, exh. cat. (Vienna: Wien Museum; Ostfildern: Hatje Cantz, 2004), 193. Friedrich Austerlitz was the editor-in-chief of the newspaper from 1895 until his death in 1931.

94. See Goldberg, "The Mellage Trial" and "A Reinvented Public." Goldberg describes in detail reformers' effective intervention in the public sphere through publicizing abuses and improper incarcerations. She implies, however, that this is an example of the vigor and transparency, in other words the proper functioning of a public sphere in a Habermasian sense. My sense of the public called into being by "cases" is a different one, in which the mimicry of sensationalism was required to summon a punctual and unstable site of publicity. Goldberg is certainly right about the efforts of the reformers and the strength of certain strains of democratic culture in the *Kaiserreich*, but it must be pointed out that reform attempts here were not successful, and failed not as the result of rational debate and consensus but of a less visible politics of psychiatric professionalization. Goldberg describes compellingly the literature of what she calls the "lunatics' rights" movement in "A Reinvented Public," 167–168.

95. Hans von Weber, "Widerrechtliche Freiheits-Beraubung von Staats wegen?," in *Der Zwiebelfisch* 1

(1914), repr. in Jung and Anz, *Der Fall Otto Gross*, 144–145. A classic account of the *lettres de cachet* is now available in English: Arlette Farge and Michel Foucault, *Disorderly Families: Infamous Letters from the Bastille Archives*, ed. Nancy Luxon, trans. Thomas Scott-Railton (Minneapolis: University of Minnesota Press, 2016).

96. Niklas Luhmann draws this helpful distinction in his discussion of the dynamics of public opinion: Luhmann, "Öffentliche Meinung," in *Demokratische Politik—Analyse und Theorie: Politikwissenschaft in der Bundesrepublik Deutschland*, ed. Wolfgang Seibel, Monika Medick-Krakau, Herfried Münkler, and Michael Th. Greven (Opladen/Wiesbaden: Westdeutscher Verlag, 1997), 35–61, esp. 40–43.

97. Alfred Springer, "Otto Gross als Wissenschaftler," in *Die Rebellion des Otto Gross*, 71.

98. It was apparently titled "Über psychologische Herrschaftsordnung. I. Der Psychologismus seit Nietzsche und Freud": Wolfgang Schwentker, "Passion as a Mode of Life: Max Weber, the Otto Gross Circle and Eroticism," in *Max Weber and His Contemporaries*, ed. Wolfgang J. Mommsen and Jürgen Osterhammel (London: Unwin Hyman, 1987), 496 n. 29.

99. The letter of September 13, 1907 is published, anonymized, in Max Weber, *Selections in Translation*, ed. W. G. Runciman and trans. E. Matthews (Cambridge: Cambridge University Press, 1978), 383–388. The letter is discussed in Horst Jürgen Helle, "Max Weber über Otto Gross: Ein Brief an Else Jaffé vom September 1907," *Zeitschrift für Politik* 41, no. 2 (1994), 214–223. Marianne Weber discusses her and Max's encounter with Gross in Marianne Weber, *Max Weber: A Biography* (New York and London: John Wiley, 1975), esp. 373–380.

100. Heuer, "Otto Gross und der Anarchismus," in *Die Gesetze des Vaters: Problematische Identitätsansprüche—Hans und Otto Gross, Sigmund Freud und Franz Kafka*, ed. Gerhard Dienes and Ralf Rother, exh. cat., Stadtmuseum Graz (Vienna: Böhlau, 2003), 116.

101. There is one exception: Gross's 1914 essay "Über Destruktionssymbolik," which appeared in the *Zentralblatt für Psychoanalyse und Psychotherapie* 4 (1914), 525–534. The journal was published by Wilhelm Stekel, who analyzed Gross in 1914 and had been excluded from the psychoanalytic movement by Freud in 1913.

102. "Ludwig Rubiners 'Psychoanalyse,'" 506–507.

103. The notion of media parasitism is developed in Arndt Niebisch, *Media Parasites in the Early Avant-Garde: On the Abuse of Technology and Communication* (New York: Palgrave Macmillan, 2012).

104. Chapter 14, "Tragödie eines Analytikers," in Wilhelm Stekel, *Sadismus und Masochismus: Für Ärzte und Kriminologen dargestellt* (Berlin and Vienna: Urban und Schwarzenberg, 1925), 487–511; *Sadism and Masochism: The Psychology of Hatred and Cruelty*, trans. Louise Brink (London: Vision Press, 1963), vol. 2, 126–160.

105. Jennifer E. Michaels, *Anarchy and Eros: Otto Gross' Impact on German Expressionist Writers* (New York: Peter Lang, 1983).

106. Mary Gluck, *Popular Bohemia: Modernism and Urban Culture in Nineteenth-Century Paris* (Cambridge, MA: Harvard University Press, 2005), 9.

107. Helmut Kreuzer, *Die Boheme: Beiträge zu ihrer Beschreibung* (Stuttgart: Metzler, 1968), vii.

108. Rolf Schwendter, *Theorie der Subkultur* (Cologne: Kiepenheuer und Witsch, 1973). See also Hubert van den Berg, *Avantgarde und Anarchismus: Dada in Zürich und Berlin* (Heidelberg: Universitätsverlag C. Winter, 1999), esp. 90–107.

109. Rolf Schwendter, "Otto Gross, Subkulturen, soziale Bewegungen," in *Die Rebellion des Otto Gross*, 37–49.

110. Jürgen Gerhards and Friedhelm Neidhardt, "Strukturen und Funktionen moderner Öffentlichkeit: Fragestellungen und Ansätze," in *Öffentlichkeit, Kultur, Massenkommunikation: Beiträge zur Medien- und Kommunikationssoziologie*, ed. Stefan Müller-Doohm and Klaus Neumann-Braun (Oldenburg: Universitätsverlag, 1991), 31–90. The approach of Gerhards and Neidhardt is discussed critically in Jörg Requate, "Öffentlichkeit und Medien als Gegenstände historischer Analyse," *Geschichte und Gesellschaft* 25 (1999), 5–32.

111. Editorial notice by Franz Pfemfert, *Die Aktion* 4, no. 34/35 (1914), 693.

112. Franz Pfemfert, "Ich schneide die Zeit aus," *Die Aktion* 5, no. 18/19 (1915), 214. Pfemfert continued to excerpt objectionable texts and

juxtapose them in a regular section under this title.

113. *Die Aktion* 5, no. 47/48 (1915) and no. 48/49 (1915); *Die Aktion* 6, no. 5/6 (1916) and no. 7/8 (1916) respectively.

114. The author was Theodor Lessing, who had given his review of a play by Hermann Sudermann to Siegfried Jacobsohn for possible publication in *Die Schaubühne*; Jacobsohn then published the text before the actual publication of the play, which might have constituted a breach of copyright. On this minor scandal see Gunther Nickel, *Die Schaubühne—die Weltbühne: Siegfried Jacobsohns Wochenschrift und ihr ästhetisches Programm* (Opladen: Westdeutscher Verlag, 1996), 74–90.

115. On Franz Held, see McCloskey, *George Grosz and the Communist Party*, 19–22; and Franz Held, *Vordadaistische Texte aus Jenesien*, ed. Hans Winkler, Kurt Lanthaler, and Martin Hanni (Bolzano: Edition Raetia, 2012).

116. Pfemfert, "Gewaltsam ins Irrenhaus," *Die Aktion* 2 (1912), 1578.

117. Most comprehensively described and analyzed in Joan Weinstein, *The End of Expressionism: Art and the November Revolution in Germany, 1918–19* (Chicago: University of Chicago Press, 1990).

118. Hugo Ball, "Totenrede (1915)," repr. in Ball, *Der Künstler und die Zeitkrankheit: Ausgewählte Schriften*, ed. Hans Burkhard Schlichting (Frankfurt a.M.: Suhrkamp, 1984), 25. See also Hugo Ball, *Flight Out of Time*, ed. John Elderfield, trans. Ann Raimes (Berkeley and Los Angeles: University of California Press, 1995), 6.

119. Transcript, 1. Strafkammer des Landgerichts Munich I, December 17, 1913, summarized in Hansjörg Viesel, ed., *Der Verleger Heinrich F. S. Bachmair, 1889–1960*, exh. cat. (Berlin: Akademie der Künste, 1989), 34.

120. Jung's Expressionist works are analyzed in Armin Arnold, *Prosa des Expressionismus: Herkunft, Analyse, Inventar* (Stuttgart: Kohlhammer, 1972), 57–95; Arnold Imhof, *Franz Jung: Leben, Werk, Wirkung* (Bonn: Bouvier, 1974), esp. 80–91; Wolfgang Rieger, *Glückstechnik und Lebensnot: Leben und Werk Franz Jungs* (Freiburg i.Br.: Ça-Ira-Verlag, 1987), 58–80; and Jennifer E. Michaels, *Franz Jung: Expressionist, Dadaist, Revolutionary and Outsider* (New York: Peter Lang, 1989), chap. 1.

121. Arnold incorrectly states that the Otto of the story murders Sophie: *Prosa des Expressionismus*, 83.

122. Kurt Pinthus in *Zeitschrift für Bücherfreunde* 6, no. 1 (1914), 21, quoted in Arnold, *Prosa des Expressionismus*, 82.

123. Robert Musil, "Erinnerung an zwei Romane," review of Jung, *Kamaraden ... !*, *Die neue Rundschau* 25 (June 1914), 852.

124. See the concordance of characters and historical figures compiled by Ernst Schürer in Franz Jung, *Werke*, ed. Lutz Schulenburg, vol. 8 (Hamburg: Edition Nautilus, 1986), 367.

125. "In the novel *Kamaraden!* by Franz Jung, a woman summarizes the nature of her internal suffering in these words: 'I hate all women. I should like to be a man and homosexual.' I can add that these works, as in general the story of neurosis in this masterpiece of psychological realism, are taken directly from life." Otto Gross, "Über Destruktionssymbolik," in Otto Gross, *Von geschlechtlicher Not zur sozialen Katastrophe*, ed. Raimund Dehmlow (Hamburg: Edition Nautilus, 2000), 80. The essay was first published in the *Zentralblatt für Psychoanalyse und Psychotherapie* 4 (1914).

126. Jung's text is titled "Von geschlechtlicher Not zur sozialen Katastrophe," and has been published with two different sets of texts by Gross that are intended to reconstruct Jung's planned selection: Gross, *Von geschlechtlicher Not zur sozialen Katastrophe*, ed. Kurt Kreiler (Frankfurt a.M.: Edition Freitag, 1980) and Gross, *Von geschlechtlicher Not zur sozialen Katastrophe*, ed. Raimund Dehmlow (Hamburg: Nautilus, 2000).

127. Cläre Jung, *Paradiesvögel: Erinnerungen* (Hamburg: Nautilus/Nemo Press, 1988), 54.

128. Franz Jung, "Die Telepathen: Eine Novelle," Franz Jung, *Werke*, ed. Lutz Schulenburg, vol. 1, pt. 1 (Hamburg: Edition Nautilus, 1981), 94.

129. Franz Jung, "Akzente II," in *Grosz/Jung/Grosz*, ed. Günter Bose and Erich Brinkmann (Berlin: Brinkmann & Bose, 1980), 242. Jung refers to a "stiff hat" while Groß always wrote of the Seidels' "soft" hats, but Jung wrote these reminiscences sometime between 1953 and 1960, which might explain the error. See also Cläre Jung's reminiscences: at Troppau, Groß "wrote. He filled

page after page of tightly gridded sheets. He named all of his enemies, in blue ink and tiny handwriting. Word after word, line after line, in between drawings of faces and roads." Cläre Jung, *Paradiesvögel*, 55.

130. *Die Aktion* 4, no. 36/37 (1914), 743–749.

131. "Der Fall Groß" first appeared in *Die Erde* 2, no. 1 (January 1920), 29–43 and was published with minor changes as *Der Fall Gross: Novelle* (Hamburg: Konrad Hanf Verlag, 1920). This latter version is reprinted as "Der Fall Gross" in *Grosz/Jung/Grosz*; my citations are from this edition. (There is also a typescript of an expanded version of this text from 1962, the year before Jung's death, repr. in Jung, *Werke*, ed. Lutz Schulenburg, vol. 9, pt. 2 (Hamburg: Edition Nautilus, 1997).) In the publications of 1920 and 1921, Jung refers to the "Groß" of the title—the Austrian Anton Wenzel Groß—alternately as "Groß" and "Gross," though in the printed body of the texts usually as the former (both forms would have been seen as largely interchangeable at the time). I shall follow this usage in my discussion as it both represents the way the name usually appeared, and also allows for a convenient distinction between the other figures with this surname (Otto Gross and George Grosz). Of course, as others have pointed out and I discuss below, the confusion and mobility of the names is certainly intentional on Jung's part.

132. David Bathrick, "Speaking the Other's Silence: Franz Jung's *Der Fall Gross*," in *Modernity and the Text: Revisions of German Modernism*, ed. Andreas Huyssen and David Bathrick (New York: Columbia University Press, 1989), 25. The text is also discussed in Michael White, "The Grosz Case: Paranoia, Self-hatred and Anti-Semitism," *Oxford Art Journal* 30, no. 3 (2007), 431–453; Arnold, *Prosa des Expressionismus*, 95–97; Imhof, *Franz Jung*, 86–91; Rieger, *Glückstechnik und Lebensnot*, 81–98; Mierau, *Das Verschwinden von Franz Jung*, 121–129; and Michaels, *Franz Jung*, 19, 43–44.

133. Bathrick, "Speaking the Other's Silence," 29.

134. Otto Gross, "Beitrag zum Problem des Wahnes," in *Drei Aufsätze über den inneren Konflikt, Abhandlungen aus dem Gebiete der Sexualforschung*, vol. 2 (Bonn: Marcus & Webers, 1920), repr. in Dehmlow, ed., *Von geschlechtlicher Not zur sozialen Katastrophe*. See Wilhelm Stekel, *Sadism and Masochism: The Psychology of Hatred and Cruelty*, trans. Louise Brink (London: Vision, 1953), vol. 2, 159: "I was to hear from him just once more. He sent me the manuscript of a work. It was a work of genius, like all his works, and I arranged for its publication."

135. Hubert van den Berg sees, however, the appearance of Gross's works during the war as "depoliticized" under the influence of Franz Jung. Considering the conditions under which these works were published, it is hard to follow this line of thought. Hubert van den Berg, *Avantgarde und Anarchismus*, 129–133.

136. Pfemfert's rejection of Expressionism appears in his article "Zum Kapitel 'geistige' Karriererevolteure," *Die Aktion* 10 (1920), 158–162.

137. The highpoint of so-called *O Mensch!* Expressionism, with its vague utopian ideals and pathetic rhetoric, is no doubt Kurt Pinthus's anthology *Menschheitsdämmerung: Symphonie jüngster Dichtung* (1919; Berlin: Rowohlt, 1920). Already, of course, Expressionism and its rhetoric were subject to parody. Dada is the most prominent example, but see also the discussion of Curt Corrinth, below, and later classics of satire such as Yvan Goll's *Sodome et Berlin* (Paris: Emile Paul, 1929), and the chapter "Geistige Arbeiter frühstücken" in Alfred Döblin, *Verratenes Volk* (*November 1918*, vol. 2) (1948; Munich: dtv, 1978), 238–241. On late- and postwar Expressionist artists' unsuccessful attempts to ally themselves with revolutionary politics and their relation to Kurt Hiller's *Rat geistiger Arbeiter*, which sought to negotiate a position of power for the artists of this generation, see Weinstein, *The End of Expressionism*.

138. The extant notes are held in the Franz Jung-Archiv in the Akademie der Künste Berlin. See "Aufzeichnungen des Anton Wenzel Groß, Troppau." The preserved typescripts, drawings, and sketches are from October 20 and 23, 1913, April 30 and May 2, 1914; there were apparently many more. Peter Ludewig's transcription of them appears in *Grosz/Jung/Grosz*, 11–71.

139. "Aufzeichnungen," *Grosz/Jung/Grosz*, 13–14.

140. "Aufzeichnungen," *Grosz/Jung/Grosz*, 18–19.

141. Sigmund Freud, "Psychoanalytic Notes on an Autobiographical Account of a Case of Paranoia (Dementia Paranoides)," *Case Histories II*, The Penguin Freud Library, vol. 9 (Harmondsworth: Penguin, 1991), 209.

142. "Aufzeichnungen," *Grosz/Jung/Grosz*, 28.

143. "Aufzeichnungen," *Grosz/Jung/Grosz*, 54–55, 64.

144. "Aufzeichnungen," *Grosz/Jung/Grosz*, 48.

145. "Aufzeichnungen," *Grosz/Jung/Grosz*, 35.

146. "Aufzeichnungen," *Grosz/Jung/Grosz*, 57.

147. "Aufzeichnungen," *Grosz/Jung/Grosz*, 60, 66.

148. Groß's notes from May 2, 1914, begin as a transcription of those from April 30, but then go in a different direction. The editors of *Grosz/Jung/Grosz* have integrated the various versions to avoid duplication and make a more readable text, but this inevitably obscures the role of repetition, transcription, and photomechanical reproduction in the notes.

149. In a brief text Kittler makes this point about Anton Wenzel Groß's head start in the Discourse Network 1900: Azzo [Friedrich] Kittler, "Um A.W.G.," in *Grosz/Jung/Grosz*, 207–215. Kittler addresses the Groß case in terms of the relationship of the medical case history to literature. In my discussion of the mediation of madness, I am drawing a somewhat different arc—from case to public sphere—and am less interested in the internal simulation of insanity in its discourses and media. But I am clearly indebted to this important work, in particular the classic account of language, technology, and insanity in Kittler, *Discourse Networks 1800/1900*, trans. Michael Metteer and Chris Cullens (Stanford: Stanford University Press, 1990), 290–311.

150. Jung, "Der Fall Gross," *Grosz/Jung/Grosz*, 99.

151. While Wieland Herzfelde, late in life, doubted that Jung had written "Der Fall Groß" much before it appeared in 1920, Fritz Mierau has convincingly argued that the text Grosz read was a version of "Der Fall Groß" and not "Die Telepathen": Mierau, *Das Verschwinden von Franz Jung*, 123. In a letter to Grosz of May 12, 1917, Jung implies that his text was ready to "offer" to a publisher and hopes that Grosz's work was advanced enough to show the publisher "a few samples": Jung, *Briefe, 1913–1963*, *Werke*, ed. Sieglinde and Fritz Mierau, vol. 9, pt. 1 (Hamburg: Nautilus, 1996), 13–14.

152. In his essay "The Grosz Case," Michael White has discussed these images and their relation to Franz Jung's text with great insight. My account here is indebted to his sovereign and detailed analysis of this episode in the history of Dada, and I follow much of it here. White's larger argument, however, concerns the relation between paranoia and Jewish identity (often ascribed), whereas I am more interested in the position of this episode in the larger problematics of the case and its medialization in the work of the avant-garde.

153. White identifies the outside figure as George Grosz himself: White, "The Grosz Case," 440.

154. Jung, "Der Fall Gross," *Grosz/Jung/Grosz*, 82–83.

155. *Zum Fall Grosz 1917* (For the Grosz case 1917), pen and ink on cardboard, listed in *George Grosz, 1893–1959*, exh. cat. (Berlin: Akademie der Künste, 1962), no. 164 (not illustrated).

156. "Die Telepathen," in Jung, *Werke*, vol. 1, pt. 1, 99.

157. Gross, "Beitrag zum Problem des Wahnes," 154–155, trans. as "The Problem of Insanity," in Otto Gross, *Selected Works, 1901–1920*, trans. Lois L. Madison (Hamilton, NY: Mindpiece, 2012), 302–303.

158. Jung, "Der Fall Gross," *Grosz/Jung/Grosz*, 81.

159. Panizza, *Psychopathia Criminalis*, 55–56.

160. The painting, whose whereabouts are unknown, appears under the former title in *George Grosz: Berlin-New York*, 332, but was published under the latter title in, for example, Mynona [Salomo Friedlaender], *George Grosz* (Dresden: Rudolf Kaemmerer, 1922), 90.

161. See Beth Irwin Lewis's classic essay "*Lustmord*: Inside the Windows of the Metropolis," in *Berlin: Culture and Metropolis*, ed. Charles W. Haxthausen and Heidrun Suhr (Minneapolis: University of Minnesota Press, 1990), 111–140; Kathrin Hoffmann-Curtius, *George Grosz: John, der Frauenmörder* (Hamburg: Hamburger Kunsthalle, 1993); Maria Tatar, *Lustmord: Sexual Murder in Weimar Germany* (Cambridge, MA: Harvard University Press, 1995); and also Carol Duncan's 1973 essay "Virility and Domination in Early Twentieth-Century Vanguard Painting," repr. in

Duncan, *The Aesthetics of Power: Essays in Critical Art History* (Cambridge: Cambridge University Press, 1993).

162. On these prints see Nadine Löffler, "Verbrechen und Strafe im illustrierten Flugblatt der frühen Neuzeit," in *Spott und Respekt: Die Justiz in der Kritik*, exh. cat. (Wetzlar: Reichskammergerichtsmuseum, 2010), 26–39; Joy Wiltenburg, *Crime and Culture in Early Modern Germany* (Charlottesville: University of Virginia Press, 2012), esp. 9–10; and Franz Mauelshagen, "Was ist glaubwürdig? Fallstudie zum Zusammenspiel von Text und Bild bei der Beglaubigung außergewöhnlicher Nachrichten im illustrierten Flugblatt," in *Wahrnehmungsgeschichte und Wissensdiskurs im illustrierten Flugblatt der frühen Neuzeit (1450–1700)*, ed. Wolfgang Harms und Alfred Messerli (Basel: Schwabe, 2002), 309–338.

163. Grosz discusses his love of penny dreadfuls in Grosz, "Jugenderinnerungen," *Das Kunstblatt* 13, no. 6 (June 1929), 172–173. Reproduced on p. 172 is an "illustration from 'Jack der geheimnisvolle Mädchenmörder,' one of the penny dreadfuls (*Groschenhefte*) that Grosz still has from his youth." The book is Guido von Fels (pseud. Paul Walter), *Jack der geheinmißvolle Mädchenmörder: Sensations-Roman* (Berlin: Berliner Roman-Verlag, 1897). See Günter Kosch and Manfred Nagl, *Der Kolportageroman: Bibliographie, 1850 bis 1960* (Stuttgart: Metzler, 1993), 153 (no. 621). The book was still available but banned in 1918: Wilhelm Fronemann, *Das Erbe Wolgasts: Ein Querschnitt durch die heutige Jugendschriftenfrage* (Langensalza: Julius Beltz, 1927), 219.

164. Krafft-Ebing, *Psychopathia Sexualis*, 73; trans. in Richard von Krafft-Ebing, *Psychopathia Sexualis, with Especial Reference to the Antipathic Sexual Instinct Instinct: A Medico-Forensic Study*, rev. ed., trans. F. J. Rebman (Brooklyn: Physicians and Surgeons Book Co., 1932), 91 (trans. modified).

165. Gisela Steinlechner, *Fallgeschichten: Krafft-Ebing, Panizza, Freud, Tausk* (Vienna: WUV-Universitätsverlag, 1995), 40.

166. As Brigid Doherty points out in "'See: *We Are All Neurosthenics!*' or, The Trauma of Dada Montage," *Critical Inquiry* 24 (Autumn 1997), 104.

167. "Dr. Serner received me in the café wearing a grand fur coat. And that was all: underneath he had only his underwear; he had had to pawn his suit. And this Serner was no doctor and was not even named Serner, but Seligmann. ... Under his full title, Serner wrote a medical report to my new regiment, according to which he had found a soldier of this name and that serial number, in a lamentable state and had referred him immediately to a hospital ... With that I had a head start of a good week for my escape to Austria." Jung, *Der Weg nach unten*, 98. See also Fritz Mierau, "Leben und Schriften des Franz Jung: Eine Chronik," in Franz Jung, *Werke*, vol. 1, part 1, 18; and Andreas Puff-Trojan, *Wien/Berlin/Dada: Reisen mit Dr. Serner* (Vienna: Sonderzahl, 1993), 97.

168. Gross, "Beitrag zum Problem des Wahnes," 155; Gross, "The Problem of Insanity," 303 (trans. modified).

169. Stekel, *Sadism and Masochism*, 139.

170. Stekel, *Sadism and Masochism*, 152–153.

171. Stekel, *Sadism and Masochism*, 155–156.

172. As discussed by Lewis, "Inside the Windows of the Metropolis."

173. Whether Corrinth knew Otto Gross personally is unclear. He became a follower of Gross's ideas, however, through his contact with Franz Jung and Margot Jung. See the unflattering account in Emil Szittya [pseud. Adolf Schenk], *Das Kuriositäten-Kabinett* (Konstanz: See-Verlag, 1923), 153; and also Michaels, *Anarchy and Eros*, 177–179.

174. "Die Maid, bald graziös hingelagert aus dankenswert gestellten Diwan, lüftete brillantblitzende Rechte und winkte gutregissierte Pose: / 'Sie Kühner. Erzählen Sie. / '?' / 'Abenteuer und Nächte–' / 'Um Ihrer einsam feigen Lust neues Selbstbefriedigungswerkzeug zu zimmern?!' / Kein Blitz, zwar, schlug ein. Aber die besterzogene Fassung sank doch in Abgründe. / 'Sie—' / 'Ihnen Prophet spielen: die Brand nie zu flammen mächtig erscheint, trüb nur in Bildern ausbrodelt, was Leben sein will?' / Neues Versinken. Hände vor entsetzensbereitem Antlitz. Aber die Herrliche schaute den Weg. Sah, wie nie befriedigter Körper Kurven wand unter wohltuenden Geißelreden. / Vor ihr hoch: / 'Deinesgleichen: peitschen! Abschaum des Lebens: ihr! Lustverfälschende! Sinnenunterdrückende! Sünderinnen am

Heilgen Geist des Fleichs!' / Schwangere Sekunden, Taten brütend. / Da, aufbiegend, lechzende Stimme: / 'Du—ja——schlage—schlage———' ... / Alalà alalà â! donnerte des Triumphschäumenden jagendes Blut——ruckte die Fäuste, geballt, hoch——/ und paukend schmetterten sie nieder, rasend, über kleine Brüste und krümmenden Schoß, werkten und walkten wuchtigste Tat ... / 'du Starker—oh——oh oh du——' ... / Ah. ... / Leises Winseln nur ... / Aber dann, auf Knien, hinrutschte zu dem Gewaltigen irr verzücktes Gebet, gell schluchzend: / 'Du—du——/ Messias——/ ich erkenne—/ bekenne——.'" Curt Corrinth, *Postdamer Platz, oder die Nächte des neuen Messias: Ekstatische Visionen* (Munich: Georg Müller, 1919), 46–48.

175. Firmin Coar (pseud. Hans Roselieb), review of Corrinth, *Potsdamer Platz*, in *Der Gral: Katholische Monatsschrift für Dichtung und Leben* 15, no. 3/4 (1920), 176, quoted in Uwe Eckardt, "Der Schriftsteller Curt Corrinth (1894–1960), ein Wanderer zwischen den Welten," *Geschichte im Wuppertal*, no. 20 (2011), 113–114.

176. Walther Rilla, review of Curt Corrinth, *Potsdamer Platz*, in *Die Erde* 1, no. 22/23 (1919), 678–679, quoted in Arnold, *Prosa des Expressionismus*, 155.

177. See Arnold, *Prosa des Expressionismus*, 151–155.

178. O. K. Werckmeister discusses the commission in *The Making of Paul Klee's Career, 1914–1920* (Chicago: University of Chicago Press, 1989), 147–155. He gives an analysis of Corrinth's novella in the context of the revolutionary activity of the time but does not note the parody of Otto Gross's ideas and person.

179. Werckmeister argues that Klee modelled the female figure on Grosz's *Der kleine Frauenmörder* of 1918: *The Making of Paul Klee's Career*, 153–154.

180. Mynona, *George Grosz*, 53.

181. Gustav Janouch, *Conversations with Kafka*, trans. Goronwy Rees, second ed. (London: Village Press, 1971), 144–145.

182. See Janko Ferk, "Lauter(e) Urteile. Franz Kafka, sein Lehrer Hans Gross und deren Richter," in *Die Gesetze des Vaters: Problematische Identitätsansprüche—Hans und Otto Gross, Sigmund Freud und Franz Kafka*, 82–93.

183. Thomas Anz, "Die Leiden einer Generation: Kafka und die Psychoanalyse," *literaturkritik.de* 7 (July 2008).

184. This is discussed in Thomas Anz, "Früher Verrat an der expressionistischen Generation: Franz Werfels Diffamierung von Otto Gross in der Novelle 'Nicht der Mörder, der Ermordete ist schuldig,'" in *1. Internationaler Otto Gross Kongress*, ed. Raimund Dehmlow and Gottfried Heuer (Marburg: LiteraturWissenschaft.de and Hannover: Laurentius, 2000), 132–141.

185. On Kafka's encounters with Gross and their importance, see Anz, "Die Leiden einer Generation"; Reiner Stach, *Kafka: The Years of Insight*, trans. Shelly Frisch (Princeton: Princeton University Press, 2013), 173–176, 303–304, 479–480.

186. Letter of June 25, 1920: Franz Kafka, *Briefe an Milena: Erweiterte und neu geordnete Ausgabe*, ed. Jürgen Born and Michael Müller (Frankfurt a.M.: Fischer, 1983), 78–79.

187. George Grosz, *Der Mörder* (The murderer), in *Die Aktion* 5, no. 29/30 (1915), 370.

188. Franz Pfemfert, editorial introduction to Otto Groß [*sic*], "Die Einwirkung der Allgemeinheit auf das Individuum," *Die Aktion* 3, no. 47 (1913), 1091.

189. Pfemfert, "Gewaltsam ins Irrenhaus," *Die Aktion* 2 (1912), 1578.

190. Alfred Bader, "Der 'verdächtige' Staatsbürger," *Die Aktion* 2 (1912), 296.

191. "... wo Dich der Untersuchungsrichter mit Deinem Verbrechen und dem Text *Deines* Paragraphen bekannt macht": Bader, "Der 'verdächtige' Staatsbürger," 297. Alfred Bader was a member of the anarchist Tat-Gruppe in Hamburg and was arrested along with Karl Gustav Kielmeyer for abetting desertion from the army. See "Der geisteskranke Deserteur," *Berliner Tageblatt*, February 16, 1912, evening edition, 1. Beiblatt, 1; "Der geisteskranke Deserteur," *Berliner Tageglatt*, February 17, 1912, 7.

192. Franz Kafka, *Der Prozeß* (Frankfurt a.M.: Fischer Taschenbuch, 1979), 7.

Chapter 3

1. Beth Irwin Lewis, "*Lustmord*: Inside the Windows of the Metropolis," in *Berlin: Culture and Metropolis*, ed. Charles W. Haxthausen and Heidrun Suhr (Minneapolis: University of Minnesota Press, 1990), 114.

2. Lewis, "*Lustmord*," 122, 136.

3. Maria Tatar, *Lustmord: Sexual Murder in Weimar*

Germany (Princeton: Princeton University Press, 1995), 68.

4. Tatar, *Lustmord*, 28.

5. Hania Siebenpfeiffer, *"Böse Lust": Gewaltverbrechen in Diskursen der Weimarer Republik* (Cologne: Böhlau, 2005); also Siebenpfeiffer, "Kreatur und kalter Killer: Der Lustmörder als Paradigma männlicher Gewalt in der Moderne," in *Gewalt und Geschlecht: Bilder, Literatur und Diskurse im 20. Jahrhundert*, ed. Hanno Ehrlicher and Hania Siebenpfeiffer (Cologne: Böhlau, 2002), 109–130.

6. Kathrin Hoffmann-Curtius, "'Wenn Blicke töten könnten': Oder, Der Künstler als Lustmörder," in *Blick-Wechsel: Konstruktionen von Männlichkeit und Weiblichkeit in Kunst und Kunstgeschichte*, ed. Ines Lindner, Sigrid Schade, Silke Wenk, and Gabriele Werner (Berlin: Reimer, 1989), 369–393; Hoffmann-Curtius, *George Grosz: "John, der Frauenmörder"* (Hamburg: Hamburger Kunsthalle, 1993); and Hoffmann-Curtius, "Frauenmord als Spektakel: Max Beckmanns 'Martyrium' der Rosa Luxemburg," in *Lustmord: Medialisierungen eines kulturellen Phantasmas um 1900*, ed. Susanne Komfort-Hein and Susanne Scholz (Königstein i.T.: Ulrike Helmer Verlag, 2007), 91–113. For another art-historical approach, see Rita E. Täuber, *Der häßliche Eros: Darstellungen zur Prostitution in der Malerei und Grafik, 1855–1930* (Berlin: Gebr. Mann, 1997).

7. Hoffmann-Curtius, *George Grosz: "John, der Frauenmörder,"* 11.

8. Mark Seltzer, *Serial Killers: Death and Life in America's Wound Culture* (New York: Routledge, 1998), 6.

9. *Verbrechen—Justiz—Medien: Konstellationen in Deutschland von 1900 bis zur Gegenwart*, ed. Joachim Linder and Claus-Michael Ort (Tübingen: Niemeyer, 1999); *Lustmord: Medialisierungen eines kulturellen Phantasmas um 1900*; Arne Höcker, *Epistemologie des Extremen: Lustmord in Kriminologie und Literatur um 1900* (Munich: Wilhelm Fink, 2012); Joachim Linder, *Wissen über Kriminalität: Zur Medien- und Diskursgeschichte von Verbrechen und Strafjustiz vom 18. bis zum 21. Jahrhundert*, ed. Claus-Michael Ort (Würzburg: ErgonVerlag, 2013).

10. On pulp fiction in late nineteenth-century Germany, see Rudolf Schenda, *Volk ohne Buch: Studien zur Sozialgeschichte der populären Lesestoffe, 1770–1910* (1970; repr. Munich: dtv, 1977), esp. 310–314; Ronald Fullerton, "Creating a Mass Book Market in Germany: The Story of the 'Colporteur Novel,' 1870–1890," *Journal of Social History* 10, no. 3 (1977), 265–283; Fullerton, "Toward a Commercial Popular Culture in Germany: The Development of Pamphlet Fiction, 1871–1914," *Journal of Social History* 12, no. 4 (1979), 489–511; Heinz J. Galle, *Groschenhefte: Die Geschichte der deutschen Trivialliteratur* (Frankfurt a.M. and Berlin: Ullstein, 1988), esp. 14–90; and the very helpful catalog of works now held in the Deutsches Literaturarchiv in Marbach: Günter Kosch and Manfred Nagl, *Der Kolportageroman: Bibliographie, 1850 bis 1960* (Stuttgart: Metzler, 1993).

11. *George Grosz: An Autobiography*, trans. Nora Hodges (New York: Macmillan, 1983), 31.

12. *Reporter: Illustriertes Welt-Blatt* 6, no. 25 (1900), 1. There is little scholarship on such erotic and crime magazines, but see the helpful essay by Hartwig Gebhardt: "'Halb kriminalistisch, halb erotisch': Presse für die 'niederen Instinkte'. Annäherungen an ein unbekanntes Kapitel deutscher Mediengeschichte," in *Schund und Schönheit: Populäre Kultur um 1900*, ed. Kaspar Maase und Wolfgang Kaschuba (Cologne: Böhlau, 2001), 184–217. Very few copies of this journal are extant. I consulted the full set of weekly issues from 1900 in the Staatsbibliothek Preußischer Kulturbesitz in Berlin; there are also two issues from 1897 at the International Institute of Social History in Amsterdam, and one from 1898 in the collection of the Internationales Zeitungsmuseum Aachen.

13. *Reporter* 6, no. 40 (1900), 1.

14. "Ein Massenmörder," *Reporter* 6, no. 40 (1900), 4.

15. See the examples in Mel Gordon, *Voluptuous Panic: The Erotic World of Weimar Berlin* (Los Angeles: Feral House, 2000).

16. Richard von Krafft-Ebing, *Psychopathia Sexualis*, twelfth ed. (Stuttgart: Ferdinand Enke, 1903), 71–78. On Krafft-Ebing and the "invention" of Lustmord, see Siebenpfeiffer, "Kreatur und kalter Killer," 109–111; Siebenpfeiffer, *"Böse Lust": Gewaltverbrechen in Diskursen der Weimarer Republik* (Cologne: Böhlau, 2005), 185–191.

17. Émile Laurent, *Sadismus und Masochismus: Autorisierte deutsche Ausgabe von Dolorosa*, seventh ed. (Berlin:

Barsdorf, 1913). ("Dolorosa" was the pseudonym of Marie Eichhorn, author of a series of erotic novels with a sado-masochistic tendency.) Books such as Dr. Veriphantor [Iwan Bloch], *Der Masochismus: Ein Beitrag zur Sittengeschichte unserer Zeit* (Berlin: M. Lilienthal, 1903) were similar but more scholarly and analytical, though even the respected sexologist Bloch used pseudonyms for his non-clinical publications. See chapter 4, below.

18. Howard Lee McBain and Lindsay Rogers, *The New Constitutions of Europe* (Garden City and New York: Doubleday, Page and Co., 1922), 199.

19. McBain and Rogers, *The New Constitutions of Europe*, 199.

20. McBain and Rogers, *The New Constitutions of Europe*, 203 (trans. modified). The literature on censorship in modern Germany is extensive. I have found the following books particularly helpful, and my discussion is based largely on them: Klaus Petersen, *Literatur und Justiz in der Weimarer Republik* (Stuttgart: Metzler, 1988); Petersen, *Zensur in der Weimarer Republik* (Stuttgart: Metzler, 1995); Gary D. Stark, *Banned in Berlin: Literary Censorship in Imperial Germany, 1871–1918* (New York: Berghahn, 2009). Peter Jelavich, who is currently preparing a book on the topic, has also made important contributions; see his "Metamorphoses of Censorship in Modern Germany," *German Politics and Society*, no. 27 (Fall 1992), 25–35, and *Berlin Alexanderplatz: Radio, Film, and the Death of Weimar Culture* (Berkeley and Los Angeles: University of California Press, 2006).

21. On the debates around this formulation, see Sebastian Ullrich, "Mehr als Schall und Rauch: Der Streit um den Namen der ersten deutschen Demokratie, 1918–1949," in *Die "Krise" der Weimarer Republik: Zur Kritik eines Deutungsmusters*, ed. Moritz Föllmer and Rüdiger Graf (Frankfurt: Campus, 2005), 189–195.

22. On the *Pressgesetz* of 1874, see Petersen, *Zensur*, 33.

23. For the term "subcultural," see Gideon Reuveni, *Reading Germany: Literature and Consumer Culture in Germany before 1933*, trans. Ruth Morris (New York: Berghahn, 2006), 210. The *Gesetz zur Bewahrung der Jugend vor Schund- und Schmutzschriften* was passed, after long debate, in December 1926. There is a large literature on the heated discussions that led to this law; see, for example, Margaret F. Stieg, "The 1926 German Law to Protect Youth against Trash and Dirt: Moral Protectionism in a Democracy," *Central European History* 23, no. 1 (1990), 22–56; and Patrick Major, "'Smut and Trash': Germany's Culture Wars Against Pulp Fiction," in *Mass Media, Culture and Society in Twentieth-Century Germany*, ed. Karl Christian Führer and Corey Ross (Basingstoke: Palgrave Macmillan, 2006), 234–250. It should be noted that despite intellectuals' bitter campaign against this legislation, it had relatively little effect.

24. See *From Liberal Democracy to Fascism: Legal and Political Thought in the Weimar Republic*, ed. Peter C. Caldwell and William E. Scheurman (Boston: Humanities Press, 2000), passim; Peter C. Caldwell, *Popular Sovereignty and the Crisis of German Constitutional Law: The Theory and Practice of Weimar Constitutionalism* (Durham, NC: Duke University Press, 1997), passim; and Petersen, *Literatur und Justiz*, 17–36.

25. I use the translation from Stark, *Banned in Berlin*, 153.

26. Stark, *Banned in Berlin*, 153

27. Carl Einstein, *Die schlimme Botschaft* (Berlin: Rowohlt, 1921). The case is discussed in detail in Heinrich Hubert Houben, *Verbotene Literatur von der klassischen Zeit bis zur Gegenwart* (Berlin: Rowohlt, 1924), 137–174.

28. See Michael White, "Not another Blasphemy Trial! The Prosecution of George Grosz and Political Justice in Weimar Germany," in *The Trials of Art*, ed. Daniel McClean (London: Ridinghouse, 2007), 255–270; Wolfgang Hütt, *Hintergrund: Mit den Unzüchtigkeits- und Gotteslästerungsparagraphen des Strafgesetzbuches gegen Kunst und Künstler, 1900–1933* (Berlin: Henschelverlag, 1990), 60–67 and the documentation on 230–262; and Rosamunde Neugebauer, *George Grosz: Macht und Ohnmacht satirischer Kunst* (Berlin: Gebr. Mann, 1993), 123–174.

29. Johannes R. Becher, *(CHCl=CH)3As (Levisite), oder Der einzig gerechte Krieg* (Vienna and Berlin: Agis-Verlag, 1926).

30. The Justice Ministry's extensive files documenting the pursuit of Becher for preparation of treasonous acts are preserved in the Bundesarchiv Berlin (R 3003/14a J243/25 Bd. 1–14). For the publicity campaign, see Johannes R. Becher et al.,

Der literarische Hochverrat von Joh. R. Becher (Berlin: Mopr-Verlag, 1928); accounts in the contemporary press such as an article by his defense attorney: Alfred Apfel, "Der Fall Becher," *Die Weltbühne*, 1926, vol. 2, 22–23; and the documents in *Aktionen, Bekenntnisse, Perspektiven: Berichte und Dokumente von Kampf um die Freiheit des literarischen Schaffens in der Weimarer Republik*, ed. Friedrich Albrecht (Berlin and Weimar: Aufbau, 1966), 23–127.

31. Petersen, *Zensur*, 72.

32. Decision of February 5, 1927, quoted in Petersen, *Zensur*, 73.

33. Stark, *Banned in Berlin*, 191.

34. Petersen, *Zensur*, 69.

35. Thus wrote the Reichsgericht in 1893 and reaffirmed in 1921: Petersen, *Zensur*, 188 and 321 n. 41.

36. Ludwig Leiss, *Kunst im Konflikt: Kunst und Künstler im Widerstreit mit der "Obrigkeit"* (Berlin: de Gruyter, 1971), 327–330, where the court's decision is reprinted; Peter Jelavich, "Legal Hypocrisy and Artistic Mendacity: The Trials of Corinth, Dix, and Grosz," unpublished paper delivered at the Lovis Corinth Colloquium on German Modernism, Emory University, Atlanta, March 8, 2013. See also the documentation in the files of the Reichsinnenministerium: Geheimes Staatsarchiv Preußischer Kulturbesitz GStA PK, I. HA Rep. 76, Ve, Sekt. 1, Abt. I, Nr. 36, Bd. 2.

37. See the detailed discussion in Neugebauer, *George Grosz: Macht und Ohnmacht satirischer Kunst*, 81–120.

38. On the Zentralpolizeistelle and the Polunbi catalogs, see Petersen, *Zensur*, 89–90, 157–161; and Gotthold Leistner, *Polunbi: "Zentralpolizeistelle zur Bekämpfung unzüchtiger Bilder und Schriften in Berlin." Eine polizeihistorische Studie* (Chemnitz: Gumnior, 2006).

39. Lest they be used as a guide to the very works they were meant to control, the Polunbi catalogs were classified as secret documents, with instructions that they be kept under lock and key. Each copy was numbered and missing volumes were to be reported immediately to the Zentralpolizeistelle. The copies held in the British Library were, in fact, used in this illicit way: they come from the collection of Alfred Rose, who published a two-volume *Registrum Librorum Eroticorum* in 1936 under the pseudonym Rolfe S. Reade. On Rose, see Julie Peakman, *Mighty Lewd Books: The Development of Pornography in Eighteenth-Century England* (Basingstoke: Palgrave Macmillan, 2003), 195. Rose managed to obtain the volumes from the German Embassy in London for scholarly purposes: see the correspondence bound into the British Library's copy (shelfmarks P.C.15.a.15 and P.C.30.e.29).

40. Case files from the lower courts were routinely discarded after a set period of time unless marked "not to be destroyed." Higher courts' records were kept longer, but a large percentage of them was destroyed in the war. Incomplete records occasionally survive in copies and transcripts sent to the Land and Reich justice or interior ministries or in police files.

41. Rechtsanwalt Dr. Willy Hoffmann, "Das Recht am eigenen Bilde," *Die Werkstatt der Kunst* 19, no. 7 (1919), 43–45; Hoffmann, "Das Persönlichkeitsrecht des Künstlers," *Die Werkstatt der Kunst* 19, no. 12 (1919), 77–79.

42. On the trivial nature of many trials for slander or defamation, see, for example, Peter Panter [Kurt Tucholsky], "Der Fall Mischewski contra Pimbusch," *Berliner Illustrirte Zeitung*, October 7, 1928 (no. 41), 1755.

43. Stark, *Banned in Berlin*, 11.

44. The most famous case of successful prosecution under these circumstances is that of the Communist actor Rolf Gärtner: see Petersen, *Literatur und Justiz*, 102–103, 119–124.

45. Ludwig Bäumer, "Dilettanten des Lasters," *Die Aktion* 4, no. 2 (1914), 26–27.

46. Decision of the Reichsgericht, May 14, 1909, quoted in Leiss, *Kunst im Konflikt*, 254. Leiss discusses the "postcard trials" on 245–267; these include decisions declaring as obscene reproductions of works by Rubens (*Judgement of Paris*), Palma Vecchio (*Reclining Venus*), van Dyck (*Danae*), Titian (*Venere corricata, Danae e Amore*), and Ingres (*La Source*).

47. See, most recently, Daniel Siemens, "Die 'Vertrauenskrise der Justiz' in der Weimarer Republik," in *Die "Krise" der Weimarer Republik*, 139–163.

48. Examples include the bestselling novel by Walter Bloem: *Das jüngste Gericht (Der Paragraphenlehrling)* (1907; Berlin-Charlottenburg: Vita

Deutsches Verlagshaus, 1911) and Ernst Ottwalt's *Denn sie wissen was sie tun: Ein deutscher Justiz-Roman* (Berlin: Malik-Verlag, 1931).

49. On *Kuhle Wampe*, see chapter 5, below.

50. Text of the first ruling of the Filmprüfstelle Berlin, Kammer III, no. 31222, March 31, 1932, prohibiting release of the film, repr. in Bertolt Brecht, *Kuhle Wampe: Protokoll des Films und Materialien*, ed. Wolfgang Gersch and Werner Hecht, second ed. (Frankfurt a.M.: Suhrkamp, 1973), 104–105.

51. Jelavich, *Berlin Alexanderplatz*.

52. Compare Karl Plättner, *Eros im Zuchthaus* (Berlin: Mopr-Verlag, 1929) with *Geschlecht in Fesseln* (1928, dir. Wilhelm Dieterle). Plättner criticises the film in *Eros*, 10. On the film, see Tim Gallwitz, "In der Falle von Triebtheorie und repressiver Moral: Geschlecht in Fesseln," in *Geschlecht in Fesseln: Sexualität zwischen Aufklärung und Ausbeutung im Weimarer Kino, 1918–1933*, ed. Malte Hagener (Munich: text + kritik, 2000), 154–165; and Jelavich, *Berlin Alexanderplatz*, 140–141.

53. *Der Film Im Westen nichts Neues in Bildern. Organisationsausgabe der Verlagsgesellschaft des Allgemeinen Deutschen Gewerkschaftsbundes* (Berlin: Ernst Rowohlt, 1931).

54. Heinrich Wandt, *Erotik und Spionage in der Etappe Gent* (Vienna and Berlin: Agis, 1928). There is a duplicate of Jhering's report to the *Zentralpolizeistelle* in the case file from the Landgericht I in Berlin (17 J. 883.28) in the Landesarchiv Berlin, A Pr.Br. Rep. 030–16945.

55. The cover is discussed in Andrés Mario Zervigón, *John Heartfield and the Agitated Image: Photography, Persuasion, and the Rise of Avant-Garde Photomontage* (Chicago: University of Chicago Press, 2012), 227–230 and Anthony Coles, *John Heartfield: Ein politisches Leben* (Cologne: Böhlau, 2014), 117–118.

56. Letter of December 20, 1929, Landgericht I Berlin, 17 J. 883.28, Landesarchiv Berlin, A Pr.Br.Rep. 030–16945.

57. Court judgment of October 1, 1929, Landgericht I Berlin, 17 J. 883.28, Landesarchiv Berlin, A Pr.Br.Rep. 030–16945.

58. Petersen, *Zensur*, 175.

59. For a fine study of the relation of genre to audience, see Patrice Petro, *Joyless Streets: Women and Melodramatic Representation in Weimar Germany* (Princeton: Princeton University Press, 1989).

60. On Wulffen see Birgit Lang, "Influencing Public Knowledge: Erich Wulffen and the Criminal Case of Grete Beier," in *Case Studies and the Dissemination of Knowledge*, ed. Joy Damousi, Birgit Lang, and Katie Sutton (New York and London: Routledge, 2015), 49–65; Lang, "Erich Wulffen and the Case of the Criminal," in *A History of the Case Study: Sexology, Psychoanalysis, Literature*, ed. Birgit Lang, Joy Damousi, and Alison Lewis (Manchester: University of Manchester Press, 2017), 119–155; and the introduction to *Erich Wulffen—Zwischen Kunst und Verbrechen: Kriminalpsychologische Aufsätze und Essays*, ed. Jürgen Seul and Albrecht Götz von Olenhusen (Berlin: Elektrischer Verlag, 2015).

61. Erich Wulffen, *Der Sexualverbrecher: Ein Handbuch für Juristen, Verwaltungsbeamte und Ärzte: Mit zahlreichen kriminalistischen Originalaufnahmen* (Berlin: Langenscheidt, 1910).

62. Lewis, "*Lustmord*," 132; Hoffmann-Curtius, *John, der Frauenmörder*, 18; Olaf Peters, "'Painting, a Medium of Cool Execution': Otto Dix and Lustmord," in Peters, *Otto Dix*, exh. cat. (New York: Neue Galerie/Munich: Prestel, 2010), 101–102. Otto Dix owned the book: Lothar Fischer, *Otto Dix: Ein Malerleben in Deutschland* (Berlin: Nicolai, 1981), 81–82.

63. Wulffen's aesthetic sensibility certainly contributed to this. The caption of one crime-scene photo includes the following sentence: "Note the contrast of the beautiful landscape and the gruesome crime." *Der Sexualverbrecher*, 466.

64. Ernst von Salomon, *Der Fragebogen* (1954; repr. Reinbek bei Hamburg: Rowohlt, 1961), 19.

65. Gerhart Pohl, "Deutsche Kulturchronik V," *Die neue Bücherschau* 4, no. 2 (1926/27), 80. Alfred Hugenberg (1865–1951) was a rightwing politician and owner of the largest media empire in interwar Germany. His huge influence on the press was a major factor in influencing public opinion.

66. *Das Weib als Sexualverbrecherin: Ein Handbuch für Juristen, Verwaltungsbeamte und Ärzte* (Berlin: Langenscheidt, 1923); *Psychologie des Giftmordes* (Vienna: Urania, 1917).

67. *Das Weib als Sexualverbrecherin: Sachbuch* (Flensburg: Orion, 1993); *Woman as a Sexual Criminal: Complete and*

Unexpurgated (North Hollywood: Brandon House, 1967). From the back cover: "The shocking deeds of female sex offenders. *Woman as a Sexual Criminal* is the first book which deals exclusively with the unlawful activities of the weaker sex: it is an alarming documentary of murder, rape, arson, theft, and other heinous crimes—all committed by women! Dr. Erich Wulffen, the leading authority on the subject of criminology in the twentieth century, reveals the fearful truth about the dark side of woman's nature ... With hundreds of authentic case histories, Dr. Wulffen lays bare the little-known facts behind the sex crimes which daily shock the world."

68. The case was popularized in Ernst Weiß, *Der Fall Vukobrankovics*, Außenseiter der Gesellschaft, vol. 4 (Berlin: Die Schmiede, 1924). I discuss Außenseiter der Gesellschaft, an ambitious series covering crimes of the time, in chapter 5 below.

69. *Sexualspiegel von Kunst und Verbrechen: Mit über 100 Tafeln und Abbildungen in Lichtdruck* (Dresden: Paul Aretz, 1928).

70. *Irrwege des Eros: Mit einer Einleitung "Mütter und Töchter"* (Hellerau bei Dresden: Avalun-Verlag, 1929).

71. Magnus Hirschfeld, ed., *Sittengeschichte des Weltkrieges*, 2 vols. (Leipzig: Schneider, 1930). From the mid-1920s, Curt Moreck wrote a series of lengthy *Sittengeschichten*, including a *Sittengeschichte des Kinos* (Dresden: Aretz, 1926) and one on *Geschlechtsleben und Erotik in der Gesellschaft der Gegenwart* (Dresden: Aretz, 1928). See also his notorious *Führer durch das "lasterhafte" Berlin* (Leipzig: Verlag moderner Stadtführer, 1931). The latter is discussed by Camilla Smith in "Challenging Baedeker through the Art of Sexual Science: An Exploration of Homosexuality in Curt Moreck's *Guide to 'Depraved' Berlin* (1931)," *Oxford Art Journal* 36, no. 3 (2013), 231–256.

72. One example: Hirschfeld, along with police officials, doctors, sexual, and penal reformers, contributed to a sober volume with a spectacular title: *Sexual-Katastrophen: Bilder aus dem modernen Geschlechts- und Eheleben*, ed. Ludwig Levy-Lenz (Leipzig: Payne, 1926). The police could not object to the text, but their attention was caught by the advertising poster for the book. The Zentralpolizeistelle pursued the book, and the art critic Paul Fechter provided an expert opinion that the poster could not be considered obscene: it was immune to prurient pleasure due to the "disgusting nature" of the image. (Files of the Innenministerium, Geheimes Staatsarchiv Preußischer Kulturbesitz GStA PK, I. HA Rep. 77/ Tit. 2772 Nr. 5 Bd. 2, 44ff; Fechter's letter (63) is dated June 24, 1926.) True, perhaps, though the poster was clearly aimed at audiences for sensational accounts of sexual matters. In any case, the police dropped their investigation.

73. Hoffmann-Curtius, *George Grosz: John, der Frauenmörder*, 8.

74. *George Grosz: Katalog der 59. Ausstellung der Galerie Neue Kunst—Hans Goltz* (*Der Ararat*, erstes Sonderheft), exh. cat. (Munich: Goltzverlag, 1920), no. 6, illustrated p. 11; *Ausstellung "Neue Sachlichkeit": Deutsche Malerei seit dem Expressionismus*, exh. cat. (Mannheim: Städt. Kunsthalle, 1925), no. 41.

75. Willi Wolfradt, *George Grosz*, *Junge Kunst*, no. 21 (Leipzig: Klinkhardt & Biermann, 1921), pl. 7.

76. The literature on George Grosz often implies that the Zentralpolizeistelle was successful in having the book banned: see Neugebauer, *George Grosz: Macht und Ohnmacht satirischer Kunst*, 112; and Kjeld Bülow, *George Grosz: A Bibliography and Other Check Lists* (Copenhagen: Booktrader, 1993), 73. This is incorrect and is no doubt based on an ambiguous passage in a contribution to a widely read anthology: Ernst Buchholz, "Wann ist Kunst unzüchtig?" in *Sexualität und Verbrechen*, ed. Fritz Bauer et al. (Frankfurt a.M.: Fischer, 1963), 333. The Polunbi catalog of 1926 does indeed list the book—but notes that the book was "frei durch Verfügung einer Staatsanwaltschaft," i.e. a state prosecutor's office had issued a decision that the book would not be pursued. On the earlier confiscation, see Paul Westheim's brief notice in *Das Kunstblatt* 8, no. 1 (January 1924), 32.

77. *Der kleine Frauenmörder* in Mynona [Salomo Friedlaender], *George Grosz* (Dresden: Rudolf Kaemmerer, 1922), 90; and the now lost *John Heartfield, der kleine Frauenmörder* in Carl Einstein, *Die Kunst des 20. Jahrhunderts* (Berlin: Proplyäen, 1926), 464.

78. Jelavich, "Metamorphoses of Censorship," 27.

79. Files of the Reichsinnenministerium: Geheimes Staatsarchiv Preußischer Kulturbesitz GStA PK, I. HA Rep. 76, Ve, Sekt. 1, Abt. I, Nr. 36, Bd. 2, 228ff.

80. Beside the extensive newspaper reports, the most complete contemporary publication on the case is Hugo Friedländer, "Die Ermordung der achtjährigen [*sic*] Lucie Berlin: Ein Beitrag zum Zuhälter- und Dirnenwesen," in Friedländer, *Interessante Kriminalprozesse von Kulturhistorische Bedeutung*, vol. 4 (Berlin: Barsdorf, 1911). See also Peter Fritzsche, "Talk of the Town: The Murder of Lucie Berlin and the Production of Local Knowledge," in *Criminals and their Scientists: The History of Criminology in International Perspective*, ed. Peter Becker and Richard F. Wetzell (Cambridge: Cambridge University Press, 2006), 377–398. Fritzsche works from the contemporary newspaper reports and does not consult Friedländer's widely circulated account; more oddly, he does not discuss the use of the so-called "Uhlenhuth test" to identify human blood, for which the case is still known. For this, see Gunther Geserick, Klaus Vendura, and Ingo Wirth, "Blut und Gene: Der Fall Lucie Berlin," in *Zeitzeuge Tod: Spektakuläre Fälle der Gerichtsmedezin* (Leipzig: Militzke, 2001). For information on and discussions about the Lucie Berlin case, my thanks to Stuart Moss and Gabrielle van der Haegen.

81. Hans Ostwald, *Lieder aus dem Rinnstein*, vol. 3 (Berlin: Harmonie, 1908), 118. On Ostwald, see Peter Fritzsche, "Vagabond in the Fugitive City: Hans Ostwald, Imperial Berlin and the Grossstadt-Dokumente," *Journal of Contemporary History* 29, no. 3 (1994), 385–402; Dorothy Rowe, *Representing Berlin: Sexuality and the City in Imperial and Weimar Germany* (Aldershot: Ashgate, 2003), 90–129; and Ralf Thies, *Ethnograph des dunklen Berlin: Hans Ostwald und die "Großstadt-Dokumente," 1904–1908* (Cologne: Böhlau, 2006). Despite his publications on both Hans Ostwald and the Lucie Berlin case, Fritzsche does not draw attention to the presence of the case in Ostwald's *Lieder aus dem Rinnstein*.

82. See, for example, Zille's *Zwangslose Geschichten* (Berlin: Fritz Gurlitt Verlag, 1919), which was confiscated and found to be obscene; and his even bolder *Hurengespräche*, published by Wolfgang Gurlitt in 1921 under the pseudonym W. Pfeifer and without indication of the publisher. On Wolfgang Gurlitt and his publication of erotica, see Camilla Smith, "Sex Sells! Wolfgang Gurlitt, Erotic Print Culture and Women Artists in the Weimar Republic," *Art History* 42, no. 4 (2019), 780–807.

83. "Wird gesungen nach 'Tief im Böhmerwald'": Ostwald, *Lieder*, 118.

84. On Wedekind's song, see Karl Riha, *Moritat, Bänkelsang, Protestballade: Kabarett-Lyrik und engagiertes Lied in Deutschland* (Königstein i.T.: Athenäum, 1979), 23.

85. Krafft-Ebing discusses the pathology of "sexual dependency" (*geschlechtliche Hörigkeit*) in later editions of *Psychopathia Sexualis*. He coined the term in a publication of 1892: "Bemerkungen über geschlechtliche Hörigkeit und Masochismus," *Jahrbücher für Psychiatrie* 10 (1892), 199–211. See Renate Hauser, "Krafft-Ebing's Psychological Understanding of Sexual Behaviour," in *Sexual Knowledge, Sexual Science: The History of Attitudes to Sexuality*, ed. Roy Porter and Mikulas Teich (Cambridge: Cambridge University Press, 1994), 216–217.

86. [Peter] Paul Althaus, *Jack der Aufschlitzer: Rund zwei Dutzend Lieder* (Berlin: Elena Gottschalk). Page numbers refer to the reprint edited by Herbert Wiesner (Munich: Renner, 1982).

87. Althaus, *Jack der Aufschlitzer*, 24.

88. W. Zadek, "Die tollen Bücher: Eine Sammlung des Elena-Gottschalk-Verlages, Berlin," *Literarische Rundschau, 5. Beiblatt zum Berliner Tageblatt*, August 23, 1925.

89. Althaus, *Jack der Aufschlitzer*, 36.

90. Zadek, "Die tollen Bücher."

91. Althaus, "Dilettanten," *Jack der Aufschlitzer*, 30.

92. "'Jack, der Aufschlitzer' auf der Anklagebank," *Berliner Tageblatt*, October 29, 1925, evening edition, 3.

93. "The court's expert witness, Dr. Max Osborn, explained that while the intentions of the writer were not successfully realized in artistic form, the illustrations had considerable artistic value": "'Jack, der Aufschlitzer' auf der Anklagebank," 3. Max Osborn was a popular art historian and art critic for the *Vossische Zeitung*.

94. Announcing the scheduled proceedings, the *Berliner*

Tageblatt reported that only Gerhart Pohl, editor at the Elena Gottschalk Verlag, and Schlichter faced charges: "Die Freiheit der Kunst," *Berliner Tageblatt*, October 25, 1925, morning edition, 2. The *Vossische Zeitung* reported that Althaus "did not appear for today's court session": "Jack, der Aufschlitzer," *Vossische Zeitung*, October 29, 1925, evening edition, 2.

95. "'Jack, der Aufschlitzer' auf der Anklagebank," *Berliner Tageblatt*, October 29, 1925, evening edition, 3.

96. Polunbi-Katalog, Nachtrag 1, 34.

97. Gerhart Pohl, "Deutsche Kulturchronik III: Der Kultur-Terror der deutschen Justiz," *Die neue Bücherschau* 3, no. 6 (1925), 31.

98. See Linda Nochlin, *The Body in Pieces: The Fragment as a Metaphor of Modernity* (London: Thames and Hudson, 1994), 38–41.

99. Maud Lavin, *Cut with the Kitchen Knife: The Weimar Photomontages of Hannah Höch* (New Haven and London: Yale University Press, 1993), esp. chap. 6.

100. Zadek, "Die tollen Bücher."

101. "Jack, der Aufschlitzer," *Vossische Zeitung*, October 29, 1925, evening edition, 2.

102. Zadek, "Die tollen Bücher."

103. Institut für Sexualforschung in Wien, *Bilder-Lexikon der Erotik* (Vienna: Verlag für Kulturforschung), vol. 1, *Kulturgeschichte* (1928); vol. 2, *Literatur und Kunst* (1929); vol. 3, *Sexualwissenschaft* (1930); vol. 4, *Ergänzungsband* (1931). The subtitles vary, and a reprint edition of 1961 (Hamburg: Verlag für Kulturforschung, 1961) divides each volume into two parts.

104. Schlichter's drawing for the illustration to Althaus's "Die Lotosblume ängstigt sich" appears with the title "Lustmord" in *Bilder-Lexikon*, vol. 3, *Sexualwissenschaft*, repr. 1961, 522 (pl. cxxiii), opposite a photograph from Wulffen, *Der Sexualverbrecher*, on 523.

105. "Strangulation," in *Bilder-Lexikon*, vol. 3, *Sexualwissenschaft*, repr. 1961, 777–784, and an undated drawing, Beilage lxxxii, opp. 784, captioned "'Das erhängte Mädchen'. Zeichnung mit ausgesprochen fetischistischer Tendenz von Rudolf Schlichter" (The hanged girl. Drawing with markedly fetishistic character by Schlichter).

106. *Bilder-Lexikon*, vol. 4, *Ergänzungsband*, repr. 1961, 420–422 and 422–424.

107. Otto Griebel, for example, mentions seeing Otto Dix's *Sex Murderer: Self-Portrait* of 1920 in the latter's studio: Griebel, *Ich war ein Mann der Straße: Lebenserinnerungen eines Dresdner Malers*, ed. Matthias Griebel and Hans-Peter Lühr, second ed. (Altenburg: DAZ Verlag, 1995), 54.

108. This is not to say that there was no "crisis of masculinity" in the early Weimar Republic, but even that interpretative model has been challenged. Birthe Kundrus has recently concluded that "there is considerable evidence that the First World War did not constitute a turning point in gender relations and identity." Birthe Kundrus, "Gender Wars: The First World War and the Construction of Gender Relations in the Weimar Republic," in *Home/Front: The Military, War and Gender in Twentieth-Century Germany*, ed. Karen Hagemann and Stefanie Schüler-Springorum (Oxford: Berg, 2002), 172.

109. See the balanced discussion of trends in violent crime in the early Weimar Republic in Sace Elder, *Murder Scenes: Normality, Deviance, and Criminal Violence in Weimar Berlin* (Ann Arbor: University of Michigan Press, 2010), chapter 1.

110. Hermann Kesten, *Ein ausschweifender Mensch (Das Leben eines Tölpels)* (Berlin: Kiepenheuer, 1929), 77–81.

111. The best sources on Hubbuch are *Karl Hubbuch 1891–1979*, ed. Helmut Goettl, Wolfgang Hartmann, and Michael Schwarz, exh. cat. (Karlsruhe: Badischer Kunstverein/Munich: Prestel, 1981) and *Karl Hubbuch: Retrospektive*, ed. Erika Röder-Diruf, exh. cat. (Karlsruhe: Städtische Galerie im Prinz-Max-Palais, 1993). On the development of Neue Sachlichkeit in Karlsruhe and the developments there generally, see *Kunst in Karlsruhe, 1900–1950*, exh. cat. (Karlsruhe: Staatliche Kunsthalle, 1981) and *Die 20er Jahre in Karlsruhe*, exh. cat. (Karlsruhe: Städtische Galerie, 2005).

112. There is a large literature on history painting, but significantly less on illustration. See, however, J. Hillis Miller, *Illustration* (London: Reaktion, 1992).

113. "*Fruchtbarer Augenblick*": Gotthold Ephraim Lessing, *Laokoon. Oder: Über die Grenzen der Malerei und Poesie. Mit beiläufigen Erläuterungen*

verschiedener Punkte der alten Kunstgeschichte (1766; Stuttgart: Reclam, 1994).

114. On crime-scene photography, see Susanne Regener, "Verbrechen, Schönheit, Tod: Tatortfotografien," *Fotogeschichte*, no. 78 (2000), 27–42; and Christine Karallus, "Zwischen Kriminalistik und Justiz: Zur Konjunktur der Fotografie als Evidenzstrategie," *Berichte zur Wissenschaftsgeschichte*, no. 28 (2005), 215–226.

115. Both are from Wolfgang Kemp's important essay "Death at Work: A Case Study on Constitutive Blanks in Nineteenth-Century Painting," *Representations*, no. 10 (1985), 102–123.

116. See Kemp, "Death at Work." Kemp borrows the notion of "constitutive blanks" from Wolfgang Iser. See Iser, *The Act of Reading: A Theory of Aesthetic Response* (Baltimore: Johns Hopkins University Press, 1978), chap. 7.

117. Rensselaer Lee discusses Lessing's notion of the "pregnant moment" and its necessary expansion in history painting in *Ut Pictura Poesis: The Humanistic Theory of Painting* (New York: Norton, 1967), chap. 9.

118. See Jacques Derrida, "Parergon," in *The Truth in Painting*, trans. Geoff Bennington and Ian McLeod (Chicago: University of Chicago Press, 1987).

119. See the exemplary analysis of Klinger's *Dramen* in Amy Kurlander, Stephan S. Wolohojian, Christopher Wood, "Das erzählte Drama in Bildern: Adolf von Menzel und Max Klinger," in *Der Text des Bildes: Möglichkeiten und Mittel eigenständiger Bilderzählung*, ed. Wolfgang Kemp (Munich: text + kritik, 1989), 35–61. Wolfgang Hartmann suggests that Hubbuch might have been studying Klinger's *Dramen* in the early 1920s. Hartmann, *Karl Hubbuch: Der Zeichner* (Stuttgart: Hatje, 1991), 23.

120. Siegfried Kracauer, *Der Detektiv-Roman: Ein philosophischer Traktat* (Frankfurt a.M.: Suhrkamp, 1979). See, in English, the still important essay by the late David Frisby: "Between the Spheres: Siegfried Kracauer and the Detective Novel," *Theory, Culture and Society* 9 (1992), 1–22.

121. Mynona (Salomo Friedlaender), "Ist Verbrechen denn Liebe?" in *Das Eisenbahnglück oder der Anti-Freud* (Berlin: Elena Gottschalk, 1925, repr. Hamburg: Junius, 1988), 58–62.

122. Hanns Heinz Evers, "Der Lustmord einer Schildkröte," in *Grotesken* (Munich: Georg Müller, 1925), repr. in Evers, *Lustmord einer Schildkröte und weitere Erzählungen*, ed. Marcus Andreas Born and Sven Brömsel (Berlin: Die andere Bibliothek, 2014), 141–148.

123. Ernst Weiß, *Georg Letham: Arzt und Mörder* (1931; Frankfurt a.M.: Suhrkamp, 1980), 232; Weiss, *Georg Letham: Physician and Murderer*, trans. Joel Rotenberg (Brooklyn, NY: Archipelago, 2010), 259–260.

124. Siegfried Kracauer, "Tat ohne Täter" (1925), in Kracauer, *Schriften*, vol. 5, *Aufsätze*, ed. Inke Mülder-Bach (Frankfurt a.M.: Suhrkamp, 1990), pt. 1, 318–321. See now the extensive material, including all of Kracauer's texts on the Angerstein case, in *Tat ohne Täter: Der Mordfall Fritz Angerstein*, ed. Bernd Stiegler (Konstanz: Konstanz University Press, 2013).

125. Kracauer, "Tat ohne Täter," 318.

126. Kracauer, "Tat ohne Täter," 318.

127. Kracauer, "Tat ohne Täter," 321.

128. Kracauer, "Tat ohne Täter," 321.

129. Kracauer, "Tat ohne Täter," 319.

130. Max Weber, *The Protestant Ethic and the Spirit of Capitalism*, trans. Talcott Parsons (1904/05; New York: Scribner's, 1958).

131. Georg Simmel, "The Concept and Tragedy of Culture" (1911), in *Simmel on Culture*, ed. David Frisby and Mike Featherstone (London: Sage, 1997), 55–74; Georg Lukács, "Reification and the Consciousness of the Proletariat" (1923), in *History and Class Consciousness*, trans. Rodney Livingstone (London: Merlin Press, 1971).

132. Max Horkheimer and Theodor W. Adorno, *Dialectic of Enlightenment*, trans. Edmund Jephcott (1944/47; Stanford: Stanford University Press, 2002).

133. Lukács, *History and Class Consciousness*, 89.

134. See Norbert Bolz, *Auszug aus der entzauberten Welt: Philosophischer Extremismus zwischen den Weltkriegen* (Munich: Fink, 1989).

135. Ernst Jünger, "Über die Gefahr," in *Der gefährliche Augenblick: Eine Sammlung von Bildern und Berichten*, ed. Ferdinand Bucholtz (Berlin: Junker & Dünnhaupt, 1931), 11–16, trans. "On Danger," *New German Critique*, no. 59 (1993), 27–32.

136. See Roland März, "Republikanische Automaten: George Grosz und die *Pittura metafisica*," in Peter-Klaus Schuster, ed., *George Grosz: Berlin–New York*, exh. cat. (Berlin: Nationalgalerie, 1994), 147–156.

137. George Grosz, "Zu meinen neuen Bildern," *Das Kunstblatt* 5, no. 1 (1921). Passages are translated in Frank Whitford, ed., *The Berlin of George Grosz: Drawings, Watercolours and Prints, 1912–1930*, exh. cat. (London: Royal Academy of Arts, 1997), 35–36.

138. Ludwig [Lajos] Kassàk and Ladislaus [László] Moholy-Nagy, *Buch neuer Künstler* (Vienna: Buch- und Steindruckerei Elbermühl, 1922), n.p.

139. Anton Kaes, "The Cold Gaze: Notes on Mobilization and Modernity," *New German Critique*, no. 59 (1993), 105–117.

140. Todd Herzog, *Crime Stories: Criminalistic Fantasy and the Culture of Crisis in Weimar Germany* (New York: Berghahn, 2009).

141. Indeed, in *Murder Scenes: Normality, Deviance, and Criminal Violence in Weimar Berlin* (Ann Arbor: University of Michigan Press, 2010), Sace Elder goes so far as to write of murder, and especially *Lustmord*, as "a trope for explaining and describing the crises of Weimar society" (13).

142. In addition to Elder, *Murder Scenes*, see Kerstin Brückweh, *Mordlust: Serienmorde, Gewalt und Emotionen im 20. Jahrhundert* (Frankfurt a.M.: Campus, 2006),

143. Roland Barthes, *Mythologies*, trans. Annette Lavers (1957; New York: Hill and Wang, 1973).

144. Hugo Bettauer, *Der Frauenmörder* (Vienna: Gloriette-Verlag, 1922).

145. Robert Musil, *The Man without Qualities* (1930/1943; New York: Knopf, 1995).

146. Musil's Christian Moosbrugger is based on the Bavarian sexual murderer Christian Voigt, indicted in 1911. See Karl Corino, "Zerstückt und durchdunkelt: Der Sexualmörder Moosbrugger im *Mann ohne Eigenschaften* und sein Modell," *Musil-Forum* 10 (1984), 105–119.

Chapter 4

1. Under his pseudonym, Bloch published *Der Marquis de Sade und seine Zeit: Ein Beitrag zur Kultur- und Sittengeschichte des 18. Jahrhunderts. Mit besonderer Beziehung auf die Lehre von der Psychopathia sexualis* (1899; fourth ed. Berlin: H. Barsdorf, 1906); *Das Geschlechtsleben in England*, 3 vols. (Berlin: Lilienthal, 1901/03); *Neue Forschungen über den Marquis de Sade und seine Zeit. Mit besonderer Berücksichtigung der Sexualphilosophie de Sade's auf Grund des neuentdeckten Original-Manuskripts seines Hauptwerkes "Die 120 Tage von Sodom"* (Berlin: Harrwitz, 1904); and a biography of a famous shoe fetishism: *Rétif de la Bretonne: Der Mensch, der Schriftsteller, der Reformator* (Berlin: Harrwitz, 1906). See Günter Grau, *Iwan Bloch: Hautarzt, Medezinhistoriker, Sexualforscher* (Berlin: Hentrich und Hentrich, 2007). In an otherwise indispensable essay, Dirk Heißerer misidentifies the book and sees instead a reference to the philosopher Karl Eugen Dühring: Heißerer, "Eros und Gewalt: Schlichters 'Liebesvariationen,'" in Götz Adriani, ed., *Rudolf Schlichter: Gemälde, Aquarelle, Zeichnungen*, exh. cat. (Tübingen: Kunsthalle, and Munich: Klinkhardt & Biermann, 1997), 31. Barbara Kemmer has recently suggested the reference to Bloch: Kemmer, "Der Fall Rudi S: Fetisch, Lustmord und Bekenntniszwang im Kontext antibürgerlicher Selbststilisierung," in Matthias von der Bank, Claudia Heitmann, and Sigrid Lange, ed., *Rudolf Schlichter: Eros und Apokalypse*, exh. cat. (Koblenz: Mittelrhein Museum and Petersberg: Michael Imhof, 2015), 24. In addition to these catalogs, see on Schlichter in general *Rudolf Schlichter, 1890–1966*, exh. cat. (Berlin: Kunsthalle, 1984).

2. Émile Laurent, *Sadismus und Masochismus: Autorisierte deutsche Ausgabe von Dolorosa*, seventh ed. (Berlin: Barsdorf, 1913); Albert Eulenburg, *Sadismus und Masochismus* (1902; second ed. Wiesbaden: Bergmann, 1911).

3. "The true fetishist expresses himself in masturbation. There is no fetishism without onanism." Wilhelm Stekel, *Der Fetischismus dargestellt für Ärzte und Kriminologen* (Störungen des Triebs- und Affektlebens (die parapatischen Erkrankungen), vol. 7) (Berlin: Urban & Schwarzenberg, 1923), 25; Stekel, *Sexual Aberrations: The Phenomena of Fetishism in Relation to Sex*, trans. S. Parker (New York: Liveright, 1940), 32.

4. Rosamunde Neugebauer, *George Grosz: Macht und Ohnmacht satirischer Kunst* (Berlin: Gebr. Mann, 1993), 112; and chapter 3, above.

5. Stekel, *Der Fetischismus*, 15, *Sexual Aberrations*, 21.

6. "Um seine Leidenschaft zu befriedigen, ließ er in seinem Atelier eine Art Harnisch anbringen. Er überredete Prostituierte sich daran anzuschnallen. Daraufhin wurde die angeschirrte Dirne an die Decke hochgezogen und dann langsam wieder heruntergelassen. Während ihres Abstiegs konnte Schlichter nun seiner Mariä-Verehrung frönen." Marty Grosz, "Erinnerungen," in Serge Sabarsky, ed., *George Grosz: Die Berliner Jahre*, exh. cat. (Munich: Villa Stuck, 1986), 19.

7. Rudolf Schlichter, *Das widerspenstige Fleisch* (1932; Berlin: Edition Hentrich, 1991), 155. See the drawing and watercolor *Grünfressender Mann (Selbstportrait)* (Man gorging on greens [self-portrait]) of 1925, in Adriani, ed., *Rudolf Schlichter*, 202 (cat. no. 110).

8. For example in Kemmer, "Der Fall Rudi S."

9. Kemmer and Corinne Granof stress this aspect of his persona: see Corinne Granof, "Obstinate Flesh: The Early Career of Rudolf Schlichter" (PhD diss., University of Chicago, 1995). Granof's unpublished dissertation represents the only substantial work on Schlichter in English. In his authoritative writings on Schlichter, which are cited here, Dirk Heißerer shows a less reductive approach that allows the strangeness of Schlichter's life and work to emerge in sharper relief.

10. On this form of sadism, see Richard von Krafft-Ebing, *Psychopathia Sexualis*, twelfth ed. (Stuttgart: Ferdinand Enke, 1903), 378; and Erich Wulffen, *Der Sexualverbrecher: Ein Handbuch für Juristen, Verwaltungsbeamte und Ärzte. Mit zahlreichen kriminalistischen Originalaufnahmen* (Berlin: Langenscheidt, 1910), 334–336.

11. Rudolf Schlichter, *Tönerne Füße* (1933; repr. Berlin: Edition Hentrich, 1992), 176–177. Schlichter's erotic works and scenes of "perverse" practices are discussed in Heißerer, "Eros und Gewalt."

12. Elfriede Elisabeth Koehler (1902–1975), nicknamed "Speedy," was born in Geneva and worked in Berlin as an actor. She had minor roles in G. W. Pabst's *Das Tagebuch einer Verlorenen* (Diary of a lost girl) in 1929 and Ernö Metzner's *Rivalen im Weltrekord* (Rivals for the world's record) in 1930.

13. Rudolf Schlichter, *Zwischenwelt: Ein Intermezzo* (Berlin: Ernst Pollak, 1931).

14. Both were published by Ernst Rowohlt, Berlin. (References, however, are to the reprints as cited above.)

15. Rudolf Schlichter, *Die Verteidigung des Panoptikums: Autobiographische zeit- und kunstkritische Schriften sowie Briefe, 1930–1955*, ed. Dirk Heißerer (Berlin: Edition Hentrich, 1995).

16. "He was one of the most erudite painters, with almost encyclopedic knowledge": *George Grosz: An Autobiography*, trans. Nora Hodges (New York: Macmillan, 1983), 137. See also Schlichter's own statement in the American Military Government questionnaire after the war: "The list of schools I have attended gives an inadequate picture of my general education. Through constant private study I have gained thorough and rich knowledge in the specific areas of history, cultural history, and philosophy." Schlichter, Anlage zum Fragebogen der Militärregierung, Schlichter papers, Deutsches Literaturarchiv Marbach, Dokumente.

17. Schlichter, *Zwischenwelt*, 13–15. Compare Oskar Panizza, "Der Corsetten-Fritz," in *Der Korsettenfritz: Gesammelte Erzählungen* (Munich: Matthes und Seitz, 1981), 205–207.

18. On the display window as a figure for the complex way the consumer commodity could be represented, see Frederic J. Schwartz, *The Werkbund: Design Theory and Mass Culture Before the First World War* (New Haven and London: Yale University Press, 1996), 44–60, 164–176. As a site of the appearance of the sexual fetish, the shop window is regularly invoked by patients at the time, for example in Stekel, *Der Fetischismus*, 6 (case no. 2); *Sexual Aberrations*, 9; or Magnus Hirschfeld, *Transvestites: The Erotic Drive to Cross Dress*, trans. Michael A. Lombardi-Nash (1910; Amherst, NY: Prometheus Books, 1991), 69 (case no. 11).

19. Schlichter, *Das widerspenstige Fleisch*, 168–169.

20. Hirschfeld, *Transvestites*, 64 (case no. 10).

21. Schlichter, *Törnerne Füße*, 205.

22. Schlichter, *Das widerspenstige Fleisch*, 269.

23. Hirschfeld, *Transvestites*, 28 (case no. 3).

24. Schlichter, *Das widerspenstige Fleisch*, 269.

25. Krafft-Ebing, *Psychopathia Sexualis*, 132, here quoted from the English edition: *Psychopathia Sexualis, with Especial Reference to the Antipathic Sexual Instinct: A Medico-Forensic Study*, trans. F. J. Rebman, revised ed. (Brooklyn: Physicians and Surgeons Book Company, 1932), 173–174 (emphasis in original).

26. Schlichter, *Das widerspenstige Fleisch*, 266–269.

27. Stekel, *Der Fetischismus*, 296; *Sexual Aberrations*, vol. 2, 113.

28. Schlichter, *Das widerspenstige Fleisch*, 232–233.

29. Schlichter, *Zwischenwelt*, 92.

30. Schlichter, *Zwischenwelt*, 39.

31. Stekel, *Der Fetischismus*, 296, *Sexual Aberrations*, vol. 2, 113.

32. See Hirschfeld, *Transvestites*, 18–19: "the procedure was such that every case approached me personally or in writing, and then I requested they write detailed autobiographies."

33. Michel Foucault, *The History of Sexuality*, vol. 1, *An Introduction*, trans. Robert Hurley (New York: Pantheon, 1978), 43. There is a growing literature on the symbiotic relation between sexual science and the subjects they studied. See, for example, Harry Oosterhuis, *Stepchildren of Nature: Krafft-Ebing, Psychiatry, and the Making of Modern Sexuality* (Chicago: University of Chicago Press, 2000); and Philipp Weber, *Der Trieb zum Erzählen: Sexualpathologie und Homosexualität, 1852–1914* (Bielefeld: transcript Verlag, 2008).

34. Krafft-Ebing, *Psychopathia Sexualis*, 113.

35. Stekel, *Der Fetischismus*, 239–240 (case no. 45); *Sexual Aberrations*, vol. 1, 292.

36. Schlichter, *Tönerne Füße*, 57.

37. Schlichter, *Tönerne Füße*, 57.

38. "Two letters from doctors in Schlichter's papers confirm that Schlichter 'provides unusual informative material for the researcher.' The Berlin psychiatrist Dr. Placzek even writes: 'For me, the depiction of awakening sexuality, the sexual urges obscure to themselves, the exhibitionist partial attractions, the sadistic supplements, are so valuable that I would like, if at all possible, to evaluate them in the French translation of my textbook *Das Geschlechtsleben des Menschen*.'" Heißerer, "Eros und Gewalt," 29 n. 6. Heißerer refers to a letter from Dr. Siegfried Placzek of November 29, 1933. See Siegfried Placzek, *Das Geschlechtsleben des Menschen: Ein Grundriß für Studierende, Ärzte und Juristen*, second ed. (Leipzig: Thieme, 1926). I have found no record of a French translation of the book.

39. "'Are you mad? Show me your madness! Actualize your madness.' In appealing to the hysteric's stigmata and the regularity of her attacks, the doctor asks her to give him the possibility of performing a strictly medical act, that is to say, a differential diagnoses. However, at the same time—and this is the advantage for the hysteric and why she will give a positive response to the psychiatrist's demands—the hysteric will thereby escape medical extraterritoriality ... [A]s soon as she has been able to provide her symptoms ... the hysteric will cease to be a mad person in the asylum; she will acquire citizenship within a hospital ... Now what is the basis of this right acquired by the hysteric? It is founded on the situation in which the doctor ultimately finds himself dependent upon her ... the doctor depends on the hysteric actually providing him with regular symptoms." Michel Foucault, *Psychiatric Power: Lectures at the Collège de France, 1973–1974*, trans. Graham Burchell (Basingstoke: Palgrave Macmillan, 2006), 310–311.

40. Ian Hacking discusses such effects as well as their social and epistemological implications in *The Social Construction of What?* (Cambridge, MA: Harvard University Press, 1999), chap. 4.

41. On butchers as *Lustmörder*, see Wulffen, *Der Sexualverbrecher*, 489.

42. *Erotika II: Eine Folge von acht Lithographien*, 1915: *Der Sadist* (Gercken 745, Dube L 268); *Der Masochist* (Gercken 746, Dube L 269/II), *Der Busenfreier* (Gercken 747, Dube L 270), *Der Urinfreier* (Gercken 748, Dube L 271), *Onanierszene* (Gercken 749, Dube L 267), *Der andere Busenfreier* (Gercken 750, Dube L 274), *Der Busenfreier* (Gercken 751, Dube L 270), *Der Handschuhfreier* (Gercken 752, Dube L 273). References are to Günter Gercken, *Ernst Ludwig Kirchner: Kritisches Werkverzeichnis der Druckgraphik*, vol. 2 (Bern: Galerie Kornfeld, 2015) and Annemarie und Wolf-Dieter Dube, *E. L. Kirchner. Das graphische Werk*, second ed. (Munich: Prestel, 1980). The term "Freier" refers

to the customer of a prostitute, and this is how "fetishists" were named before this latter term was widely used: see Krafft-Ebing, *Psychopathia Sexualis*, 133. Only one full set of the series exists; it was assembled by Kirchner and given to the Swiss psychiatrist Ludwig Binswanger when the latter was treating him in Kreuzlingen. See Gercken, *Ernst Ludwig Kirchner: Kritisches Verzeichnis*, vol. 2, 230.

43. Manfred Georg, "Der entfesselte Eros," *Literarische Umschau*, no. 185, 1 (fourth supplement to the *Vossische Zeitung*, April 11, 1920).

44. One example: Anonymous, *Frei von allen Fesseln, oder das schamlose Bildnis des Dorian Gray* (ca. 1930; repr. Wolfenbüttel: Melchior Verlag, 2015).

45. Wulffen, *Der Sexualverbrecher*, 148.

46. *Simplicissimus* 26, no. 1 (April 1, 1921), 1.

47. Institut für Sexualforschung in Wien, ed., *Bilder-Lexikon der Erotik* (Vienna: Verlag für Kulturforschung), vol. 1, *Kulturgeschichte* (1928); vol. 2, *Literatur und Kunst* (1929); vol. 3, *Sexualwissenschaft* (1930); vol. 4, *Ergänzungsband* (1931).

48. *Bilder-Lexikon*, vol. 2, 795. The entry is by Curt Moreck (Konrad Haemmerling). On the legal requirement for the "transfiguration" of image by the artistic "curtailment" of sexuality, see chapter 3, above.

49. On fiction (and by extension other artworks) as evidence in sexual science, see Anna Katharina Schaffner, *Modernism and Perversion: Sexual Deviance in Sexology and Literature, 1850–1930* (Basingstoke: Palgrave Macmillan, 2012).

50. Gustav Gugitz, "Domina," *Bilder-Lexikon*, vol. 3, 153; the watercolor is supplementary illustration 16.

51. Georg Buschan, "Fetischismus," *Bilder-Lexikon*, vol. 3, 253–256; the photo, credited to "Binder, Berlin," on 256. (Alexander Binder was a fashion photographer much used by actors and thus would have been known to Speedy.)

52. Gustav Gugitz, "Hinrichtungsamateure," *Bilder-Lexikon*, vol. 3, 387–388.

53. Oskar F. Scheuer, "Lustmord," *Bilder-Lexikon*, vol. 3, 520–524; Schlichter's *Jack der Aufschlitzer* drawing is reproduced full-page on 522, *Das Opfer des Lustmörders* on 524.

54. *Bilder-Lexikon*, supplementary illustration 73; Oskar F. Scheurer, "Rétifismus," *Bilder-Lexikon*, vol. 3, 690.

55. Ernst Ziemke, "Strangulation," *Bilder-Lexikon*, vol. 3, 777–784, illustrations on 780 and supplementary illustration 82.

56. Oskar F. Scheuer, "Fuß- und Schuhfetischismus," *Bilder-Lexikon*, vol. 3, 206; Grosz's drawing 203 (pl. 66).

57. W. Weimann, "Masochismus," *Bilder-Lexikon*, vol. 4, 458–462 (also illustrated by a sample of Leopold von Sacher-Masoch's handwriting); Schlichter's watercolor on 463 (pl. 109).

58. Curt Moreck, "Schlichter, R.," *Bilder-Lexikon*, vol. 4, 710–711; the last two images are the oil painting *In Memoriam Gräfin Strachwitz* and the drawing *Die Gespielinnen* (The playmates).

59. W. Weimann, "Strangulation," *Bilder-Lexikon*, vol. 4, 752–754, photograph on 755 (pl. 179).

60. "Rudolf Schlichter über seine Zensurerfahrungen," *Die neue Bücherschau* 7, no. 5 (May 1929), 243.

61. The figure bore a band across its chest with the words "I come from heaven above" and a sign suspended from it reading "To understand this artwork completely, one should exercise daily for twelve hours with fully packed backpack and in combat gear on the Tempelhof Field." On the *Preußischer Erzengel*, see Michael White, *Generation Dada: The Berlin Avant-Garde and the First World War* (New Haven and London: Yale University Press, 2013), 297–300; on the First International Dada Fair, see Helen Adkins, "Erste Internationale Dada-Messe, Berlin 1920," in *Stationen der Moderne: Die bedeutenden Kunstausstellungen des 20. Jahrhunderts in Deutschland*, exh. cat. (Berlin: Berlinische Galerie, 1988), 156–183.

62. The Rote Gruppe's manifesto of June 13, 1924 was published in *Die Rote Fahne* and is reprinted in Diether Schmidt, ed., *Manifeste Manifeste, 1900–1933* (*Schriften deutscher Künstler des zwanzigsten Jahrhunderts*, vol. 1 (Dresden: Verlag der Kunst, 1965), 318–319. On the group, see Barbara McCloskey, *George Grosz and the Communist Party: Art and Radicalism in Crisis, 1918–1936* (Princeton: Princeton University Press, 1997), 105, 109–112; and W. L. Guttsman, *Art for the Workers: Ideology and the Visual Arts in Weimar Germany* (Manchester: Manchester University Press, 1997), 152–154. The ASSO or Assoziation Revolutionärer

Bildender Künstler Deutschlands, is discussed, in English, in Guttsman, *Art for the Workers*, 127–129, 153–165, 187.

63. Rudolf Schlichter, outline for the third volume of his autobiography for the publisher Ernst Rowohlt, 1931, Schlichter-Nachlaß, Deutsches Literatur-Archiv, Marbach, Box 2. This is also reprinted in the "Biographie in Selbstzeugnissen" in Adriani, ed., *Rudolf Schlichter*, 11–12.

64. These are famously documented in Curt Moreck's *Führer durch das "lasterhafte" Berlin* (Leipzig: Verlag moderner Stadtführer, 1931). On this important publication, see Camilla Smith, "Challenging *Baedeker* through the Art of Sexual Science: An Exploration of Gay and Lesbian Subcultures in Curt Moreck's *Guide to 'Depraved' Berlin* (1931)," *Oxford Art Journal* 36, no. 2 (2013), 231–256.

65. See the fragment from Schlichter's autobiography—probably drafted after the war—titled "Karl, der Terrorist: Portrait eines Berufsrevolutionärs," Schlichter papers, Deutsches Literaturarchiv Marbach, repr. in Schlichter, *Die Verteidigung des Panoptikums*, 49–59. The literature on Max Hoelz is substantial, while that on Karl Plättner is sparse. See, however, the excellent study by Volker Ullrich: *Der ruhelose Rebell: Karl Plättner, 1893–1945. Eine Biographie* (Munich: C. H. Beck, 2000). Ullrich discusses the "March Action" in detail.

66. On the position of *Sitzredakteur*, see Istvan Deak, *Weimar Germany's Left-Wing Intellectuals: A Political History of the Weltbühne and its Circle* (Berkeley and Los Angeles: University of California Press, 1968), 59; and more recently Jörg Requate, *Journalismus als Beruf: Entstehung und Entwicklung des Journalistenberufs im 19. Jahrhundert: Deutschland im internationalen Vergleich* (Göttingen: Vandenhoeck & Ruprecht, 1995), 263.

67. *Chronik des Faschismus* was one of the publications funded by Münzenberg and appeared only from 1923 to 1924: Babette Gross, *Willi Münzenberg: Eine politische Biographie* (Stuttgart: Deutsche Verlags-Anstalt, 1967), 339.

68. "In the summer of 1923 Münzenberg published, for a time, a bulletin with Valeriu Marcu in which Marcu attempted to analyze this new phenomenon, Fascism ... However, such a critique of the workers' parties that included the Communists was out of line with the Comintern, and Münzenberg had to end his collaboration with Marcu." Gross, *Willi Münzenberg*, 161. See also Dirk Heißerer's mention of this passage in *Ernst Jünger—Rudolf Schlichter: Briefwechsel*, ed. Heißerer (Stuttgart: Klett-Cotta, 1997), 346.

69. On this office, see Dirk Emunds, *Vom Republikschutz zum Verfassungsschutz? Der Reichskommissar für Überwachung der öffentlichen Ordnung in der Weimarer Republik* (Hamburg: Dr Kovac, 2017); in relation to the arts, Klaus Petersen, *Zensur in der Weimarer Republik* (Stuttgart: Metzler, 1995), 90–92.

70. Reichskommissar für Überwachung der öffentlichen Ordnung und Nachrichtensammelstelle, report of August 22, 1924, section "KPD und Kunst," Bundesarchiv Berlin, R 1507/2024, 11.

71. Letter of February 16, 1925, Reichskommissariat to the Polizeipräsidium Section IA, Bundesarchiv Berlin, R 1507/704, 1.

72. Letter of March 25, 1925, Enrst Wündisch to the Reichskommissar, Bundesarchiv Berlin, R 1507/704, 3.

73. Letter of May 12, 1925, Oberreichsanwalt to the Reichskommissar, Bundesarchiv Berlin, R 1507/704, 4; letter of May 18, 1925 to the Reichskommissar, R 1507/704.

74. Reichsgericht's decision, 14 a/13 J. 95/1927, X. Tgb 74/27, April 21, 1925; Bundesarchiv Berlin, R 1507/704, 8.

75. Justice Ministry's file on Rudolf Schlichter (17.J.379/25), Bundesarchiv Berlin, R3003 14 a J 95/26AE, 3. In July 1922, after the murder of Walther Rathenau, the Reichstag passed the "Gesetz zum Schutz der Republik," which sought to centralize prosecution of treasonous crimes, taking it over from the Länder. This created the Reichtsgerichtshof zum Schutz der Republik, a so-called *Sondergericht* or special tribunal that heard such cases between 1922 to 1929, and again between 1930 and 1932. See Gotthard Jasper, *Der Schutz der Republik: Studien zur staatlichen Sicherung der Demokratie in der Weimarer Republik, 1922–1930* (Tügingen: J.C.B. Mohr (P. Siebeck), 1963); Petersen, *Zensur*, passim, as well as Klaus Petersen, *Literatur und Justiz in der Weimarer Republik* (Stuttgart: Metzler, 1988), passim.

76. Bundesarchiv Berlin, R3003 14 a J 95/26AE, 4.

77. Bundesarchiv Berlin, R3003 14 a J 95/26AE, 4.

78. Bundesarchiv Berlin, R3003 14 a J 95/26AE, 43–47.

79. Bundesarchiv Berlin, R3003 14 a J 95/26AE, 81–82. Willy Kurth (1881–1963), who had studied under Heinrich Wölfflin, was a supporter of modernist tendencies and acquired many examples for the Berlin Kupferstichkabinett. Later, he was professor at the Humboldt University, Berlin. See Christoph Links, *Wer war wer in der DDR?*, fifth edition (Berlin: Ch. Links, 2010), vol. 1, online at https://www.bundesstiftung-aufarbeitung.de/wer-war-wer-in-der-ddr-%2363;-1424.html?ID=1982, accessed August 9, 2018; also Lee Sorensen, "Kurth, Willy," *Dictionary of Art Historians*, http://www.arthistorians.info/kurthw, accessed August 9, 2018.

80. Schlichter, Anlage zum Fragebogen der Militärregierung, Schlichter Nachlaß, Deutsches Literaturarchiv Marbach, Dokumente.

81. Bundesarchiv Berlin, R3003 14 a J 95/26AE, 90.

82. Bundesarchiv Berlin, R3003 14 a J 95/26AE, 50–52.

83. Schlichter, Anlage zum Fragebogen der Militärregierung, Schlichter Nachlaß, Deutsches Literaturarchiv Marbach, Dokumente.

84. Bundesarchiv Berlin, R3003 14 a J 95/26AE, 51.

85. On National Bolshevism, see Armin Mohler, *Die Konservative Revolution in Deutschland, 1918–1932: Ein Handbuch*, third ed. (Darmstadt: Wissenschaftliche Buchgesellschaft, 1989), 47–53 and passim. Schlichter painted a portrait of von Salomon as well; its present whereabouts are unknown—it was presumably destroyed in the Second World War.

86. Fritz Sternberg recounts how he met Brecht through Schlichter, and also reports how he spent New Year's Eve of 1932 with Brecht, Schlichter, and Salomon, raising a toast with them to "a successful, bloodless rightwing coup": Sternberg, *Der Dichter und die Ratio: Erinnerungen an Bertolt Brecht*, ed. Helga Grebing (Berlin: Suhrkamp, 2014), here 37. On this circle, see the chapter "Grosz, Schlichter, Brecht," in Jan Knopf, *Bertolt Brecht: Lebenskunst in finsteren Zeiten* (Munich: Hanser, 2012), esp. 177–178. Schlichter's friendship with Jünger is documented, with comprehensive annotations by Dirk Heißerer, in *Ernst Jünger—Rudolf Schlichter: Briefe, 1935–1955*.

87. Jünger's recollections of meeting this group at the home of Rowohlt are discussed in Dirk Heißerer's entry on Schlichter's first portrait of Jünger in Adriani, ed., *Rudolf Schlichter*, 274.

88. *Krieg und Krieger*, ed. Ernst Jünger (Berlin: Junker und Dünnhaupt, 1930); Walter Benjamin, "Theories of German Fascism: On the Collection of Essays *War and Warriors*, edited by Ernst Jünger" (1930), in Benjamin, *Selected Writings*, vol. 2, *1927–1934*, ed. Michael W. Jennings, Howard Eiland, and Gary Smith (Cambridge, MA: Belknap/Harvard University Press, 1999), 312–321.

89. Quoted in Gabriele Horn, "Rudolf Schlichter: Eine Biographie," in *Rudolf Schlichter, 1890–1955*, 13a (emphasis in original).

90. The anecdote, often repeated, was recounted by Ernst Jünger to Armin Mohler; see Mohler, *Die Konservative Revolution in Deutschland*, 472.

91. See the particularly graphic passage from Schlichter's entry in his "Geheimes Tagebuch," Schlichter papers, Deutsches Literaturarchiv, quoted in Heißerer, "Eros und Gewalt," 32.

92. Schlichter, *Das widerspenstige Fleisch*, 8.

93. Hirschfeld was perhaps the first to write about this milieu in the broad, popular press: see his contribution to Hans Ostwald's Großstadt-Dokumente series, *Berlins Drittes Geschlecht* (Berlin and Leipzig: Hermann Seemann Nachfolger, 1904). On the complex and often close relations between Hirschfeld's Wissenschaftlich-humanitäre Komitee and the KPD, as well as to social democracy, see Smith, "Challenging *Baedeker* through the Art of Sexual Science."

94. See Gross, *Willi Münzenberg*, 201–202; also Heike Bauer, *The Hirschfeld Archives: Violence, Death, and Modern Queer Culture* (Philadelphia: Temple University Press, 2017), 81–82. Gross writes that Hirschfeld was a Socialist "with a heart for Communists" (201).

95. Described in Walther Kiaulehn, *Berlin: Schicksal einer Weltstadt* (Munich: Biederstein, 1958), 555.

96. Karl Plättner, *Eros im Zuchthaus* (Berlin: Mopr-Verlag, 1929).

97. Schlichter, *Tönerne Füße*, 252–253.

98. "In stummer Drohung über mir/ Steht das Gesetz des Nichtbegehrendürfens,/ Weil ich verfall'n der übermächt'gen Gier/ Sucht frevelnd Bruch und Blösse des Geheimnis'./ Nie übertönt das überlaute Schweigen/ Der lärmend bunte Schellentanz entlass'ner Lust." Schlichter, "Tabu," in *Drohende Katastrophe: Gedichte, 1931–1936*, ed. Dirk Heißerer (Warmbronn: Keicher, 1997), 15.

99. As discussed, for example, in Laurie Marhoefer, "'The Book Was a Revelation, I Recognized Myself in It': Lesbian Sexuality, Censorship, and the Queer Press in Weimar-era Germany," *Journal of Women's History* 27 (2015), 62–86; and Marhoefer, *Sex and the Weimar Republic: German Homosexual Emancipation and the Rise of the Nazis* (Toronto: University of Toronto Press, 2015), passim.

100. On sexual citizenship in Germany, see *Not Straight from Germany: Sexual Publics and Sexual Citizenship since Magnus Hirschfeld*, ed. Michael Thomas Taylor, Annette F. Timm, and Rainer Herrn (Ann Arbor: University of Michigan Press, 2017); and a fine case study by Katie Sutton: "Sexological Cases and the Prehistory of Transgender Identity Politics in Interwar Germany," in *Case Studies and the Dissemination of Knowledge*, ed. Joy Damousi, Birgit Lang, and Katie Sutton (New York and London: Routledge, 2015), 85–103. For a history and critical account of this notion, see Diane Richardson, "Rethinking Sexual Citizenship," *Sociology* 51, no. 2 (2017), 208–224.

101. Schlichter describes Plättner as "loveless, humorless, pitiless, and without humility" and wrote of the "inhuman coldness" that surrounded him: "Karl, der Terrorist," in *Die Verteidigung des Panoptikums*, 58–59. The artist also dismissed Plättner's efforts at sexual reform as mere cynicism: "He was amnestied after seven years. During his imprisonment, he had written a book: *Eros in Prison*. A clever publisher close to the movement caught scent of an opportunity and published the book complete with a gaudy photomontage cover. And in fact, it was a good bit of business. Karl founded an association for marriage reform and free love with the money. The enterprise turned out to be profitable—not only the membership dues but a journal that he published made him a pretty penny. He was never a bad calculator" (58).

102. Schlichter, *Zwischenwelt*, 41–47.

103. On Harden and the "flight to the public," see Harry F. Young, *Maximilian Harden, Censor Germaniae: The Critic in Opposition from Bismarck to the Rise of Nazism* (The Hague: Martinus Nijhoff, 1959), 80.

104. See Schlichter's "Erklärung" of February 27, 1934, presumably to the Reichsschrifttumskammer: "The accusations made against me—that my two books *Das widerspenstige Fleisch* and *Törnerne Füße* manifest obscene tendencies—astonishes me ... The INTENTION of the books is clear from the mottos placed at the beginning. I refer in particular to the introduction to the first book, which clearly states the moral intention of showing aberrations for what they were. In the representation of these experiences, of both intellectual and physical nature, my only criterion has been unconditional adherence to the truth." Schlichter papers, Deutsches Literaturarchiv Marbach.

105. Letter of September 10, 1935 from the President of the Reichsschrifttumskammer to Schlichter, Bundesarchiv Berlin, R9361/ v 34908.

106. Letter of February 19, 1935 from the President of the Reichsschrifttumskammer to the Reichsverband Deutscher Schriftsteller, Bundesarchiv Berlin, R9361/ v 34908.

107. Letter of July 23, 1938 from the President of the Reichskammer der bildenden Künste to the President of the Reichsschrifttumskammer, Bundesarchiv Berlin, R9361/ v 34908.

108. For a convincing argument of the Kaiserreich as a *Rechtsstaat*, see Margaret Lavinia Anderson, *Practicing Democracy: Elections and Political Culture in Imperial Germany* (Princeton: Princeton University Press, 2000).

109. Reichsverband Deutscher Schriftsteller, Fragebogen für Mitglieder, signed by Schlichter December 14, 1933, Bundesarchiv Berlin, R9361/ v 34908.

110. Schlichter, Anlage zum Fragebogen der Militärregierung, Schlichter papers, Deutsches Literaturarchiv Marbach, Dokumente.

Chapter 5

1. Sergej Tretjakow, *Lyrik, Dramatik, Prosa*, ed. and trans. Fritz Mierau (Leipzig:

Reclam, 1972), 333. The only major study of Brecht and judicature is Yasco Horsman, "Brecht on Trial: The Courtroom, the Theater, and *The Measures Taken*," in Horsman, *Theaters of Justice: Judging, Staging, and Working Through in Arendt, Brecht, and Delbo* (Stanford: Stanford University Press, 2011). Horsman, whose subtle account informs my argument here, discusses Tretyakov's comments on pp. 91–93. See also Fredric Jameson, *Brecht and Method* (London: Verso, 1998), 28, 118–122; and Hildegard Emmel, *Das Gericht in der deutschen Literatur des 20. Jahrhunderts* (Bern: Francke, 1963), chap. 3.

2. Tretjakow, *Lyrik, Dramatik, Prosa*, 336. Brecht's ideas for a "*Prozeßtheater*" (trial theatre) are discussed in more detail in Manfred Wekwerth, *Notate: Über die Arbeit des Berliner Ensembles, 1956 bis 1966* (Frankfurt a.M.: Suhrkamp, 1967), 144–147.

3. Letter of November 16, 1926 to Siegfried Kracauer. Walter Benjamin, *Gesammelte Briefe*, ed. Christoph Gödde and Henri Lonitz (Frankfurt a.M.: Suhrkamp, 1995–2000), vol. 3, 214. The *Schriftsteller-gruppe 1925* was a loose union of roughly forty left-leaning authors founded in that year by Rudolf Leonhard; it included, among others, Brecht, Becher, Ernst Bloch, Alfred Döblin, Leonhard Frank, Ernst Toller, and Kurt Tucholsky. The only study of the group is Klaus Petersen, *Die "Gruppe 1925": Geschichte und Soziologie einer Schriftstellervereinigung* (Heidelberg: Carl Winter, 1981).

4. From the circular letter of November 19, 1926 to members of the group (these were written and circulated by Rudolf Leonhard or Alfred Döblin); portions are quoted in Petersen, *Die "Gruppe 1925,"* 168–169. The "literary court" was held on November 8 in the Hotel Kaiserhof, Berlin. Petersen cites a copy of the minutes in the Literaturarchiv, Akademie der Künste, Berlin, Ernst-Toller-Sammlung, but this is missing from its place (Sig. Toller 150); a copy remains in the Handschriftenabteilung of the Zentralbibliothek Zürich, Nachl. A. Turel 28. My thanks to Fr. Helga Neumann of the Literaturarchiv, Akademie der Künste, Berlin, for her help in determining the fate of this document.

5. Petersen, *Die "Gruppe 1925,"* 169.

6. Bertolt Brecht, "Der Dreigroschenprozeß: Ein soziologisches Experiment," in Brecht, *Versuche*, no. 3 (Berlin: Kiepenheuer, 1931 [*recte*: 1932]), 256–306. Citations here are from Brecht, *Werke: Große kommentierte Berliner und Frankfurter Ausgabe*, ed. Werner Hecht, Jan Knopf, Werner Mittenzwei, and Klaus-Detlef Müller (Berlin and Weimar: Aufbau, and Frankfurt a.M.: Suhrkamp, 1988–2000), vol. 21, *Schriften 1*, 448–514; and from the English translation "The *Threepenny* Lawsuit," in *Bertolt Brecht on Film and Radio*, ed. and trans. Marc Silberman (London: Methuen, 2000), 147–199. The best account of the lawsuit and its background is Steve Giles, *Bertolt Brecht and Critical Theory: Marxism, Modernity and the* Threepenny *Lawsuit*, second ed. (Bern: Peter Lang, 1998); see also the editors' notes in Brecht, *Werke*, vol. 21, 769–787; the documents reproduced in *Photo: Casparius* (Berlin: Staatliche Kunsthalle and Stiftung Deutsche Kinemathek, 1978); Burkhardt Lindner, "Der Dreigroschenprozeß," in *Brecht-Handbuch*, ed. Jan Knopf (Stuttgart: Metzler, 2001–2003), vol. 4, *Schriften, Journale, Briefe*, 134–155, as well as the sources in Lindner's bibliography, 154–155. Recently, Albrecht Götz von Olenhusen, a jurist, has discovered new documents and reconsiders the case with impressive legal expertise: Götz von Olenhusen, "Der Zufall, das Glück und der Dreigroschenfilm: Die Dreigroschenprozesse von Bertolt Brecht und Kurt Weill revisited," in *Zufall und Wissenschaft: Interdisziplinäre Perspektiven*, ed. Christian Bachhiesl, Sonja Maria Bachhiesl, Stefan Köchel, and Bernhard Schrettle (Weilerswist-Metternich: Velbrück Wissenschaft 2019), 268–302; see also his essay "Filmkünstler und Filmproduzenten zwischen Urheberrecht und gewerblichem Rechtsschutz: Die Filmurheberrechtsreform in der Zwischenkriegszeit, 1929–1939," in *Vom Reichshofrat zur Reichsfilmkammer: Privilegienpraxis und Urheberrechte an Büchern und Filmen (16.-20. Jahrhundert)*, ed. Thomas Gergen (Berlin: Duncker & Humblot, 2019), 325–401.

7. Brecht's *Mitbestimmungsrecht* is discussed by Giles, *Bertolt Brecht and Critical Theory*, 15, 22–23, and 31–32.

8. Brecht, "Die Beule: Ein Dreigroschenfilm," in Brecht, *Werke*, vol. 19, *Prosa 4*, 307–320; "The Bruise: A

Threepenny Film," in *Bertolt Brecht on Film and Radio*, 131–143.

9. "Der Dreigroschenprozeß," 469; "The *Threepenny* Lawsuit," 164.

10. See for example Martin Brady's discussion in "Brecht and Film," in *The Cambridge Companion to Brecht*, ed. Peter Thomson and Glendyr Sacks, second ed. (Cambridge: Cambridge University Press, 2006), 302–303.

11. Fritz Sternberg, *Der Dichter und die Ratio: Erinnerungen an Bertolt Brecht* (Göttingen: Sachse & Pohl, 1963), 14–15: "Brecht was very critical about many of his own plays, and I said to him that he would have great difficulties, greater than Shakespeare. 'In the time when Shakespeare wrote ... [s]ociety was clearly visible in its sociological character. ... Today, on the other hand,' I tried to explain to Brecht, 'things are different in a decisive point. Today, in a modern, industrial society, one cannot simply see the various social strata with the naked eye. Go to a factory, watch what the businessmen, what the directors, the office staff, the workers do. When you've seen all that, you know nothing. The worker could be well paid or utterly exploited. Vision alone yields no answers, just as little as does intuition. First you need an analysis of today's society that can only be achieved through reason (*Ratio*) and not through intuition.'" Or 47–49: "In antiquity and the middle ages, the fact of exploitation was considered by both sides ... to be self-evident, indisputable, and never to be eliminated. Precisely because both parts were aware of this, the relations of the classes were so clear; precisely because agriculture was the absolutely dominant production sector, one could 'see' the exploitation of the lower classes in all its clarity. I want to emphasize this expressly—it is so important for the later analysis—*one could see this in the literal sense*. ... That is no longer the case for our epoch. ... Thus there arose precisely that phenomenon that I described to Brecht as the 'sociology of repression (*Verdrängung*).' In contrast to the middle ages and antiquity, the fact of an exploitation was no longer recognized, and this 'sociological repression' was made easier in that ... this exploitation could no longer be immediately seen." On Sternberg and Brecht, see the material in the fine new edition of *Der Dichter und die Ratio* edited by Helga Grebing (Berlin: Suhrkamp, 2014).

12. Bertolt Brecht, "Fünf Schwierigkeiten beim Schreiben der Wahrheit," in *Werke*, vol. 22, *Schriften 2*, 81; "Five Difficulties in Writing the Truth," in *Brecht on Art and Politics*, ed. Tom Kuhn and Steve Giles (London: Methuen, 2003), 148 (emphasis added).

13. *Der Dreigroschenroman*, in *Werke*, vol. 16, *Prosa 1*; *The Threepenny Novel*, trans. Desmond I. Vesey and Christopher Isherwood (London: Granada, 1981). This work is discussed insightfully in Devin Fore, "The Time of Capital: Brecht's *Threepenny Novel*," *nonsite.org*, no. 10 (2013).

14. On this aspect of Brecht's thought, see Giles, *Bertolt Brecht and Critical Theory*, chap. 3; and Todd Cronan. "Art and Political Consequence: Brecht and the Problem of Affect," *nonsite.org*, no. 10 (2013).

15. Considering his erstwhile prominence, literature on Harden is scarce. Still useful in English is Harry F. Young, *Maximilian Harden, Censor Germaniae: The Critic in Opposition from Bismarck to the Rise of Nazism* (The Hague: Martinus Nijhoff, 1959).

16. See most recently Norman Domeier, *Der Eulenburg-Skandal: Eine politische Kulturgeschichte des Kaiserreichs* (Frankfurt a.M.: Campus, 2010) and Frank Bösch, *Öffentliche Geheimnisse: Skandale, Politik und Medien in Deutschland und Grossbritannien, 1880–1914* (Munich: Oldenbourg, 2009), 117–154.

17. Young, *Maximilian Harden*, 80.

18. Maximilian Harden, *Prozesse: Köpfe, dritter Teil* (Berlin: Erich Reiss, 1913). The Hau case came to be the subject of two books by the accused (*Das Todesurteil: Die Geschichte meines Prozesses* and *Lebenslänglich: Erlebtes u. Erlittenes*, both Berlin: Ullstein, 1925) and of several films and semi-fictional accounts, most recently Bernd Schroeder, *Hau* (Munich: Hanser, 2006). On the Dippold case, see the exemplary study by Michael Hagner: *Der Hauslehrer: Die Geschichte eines Kriminalfalls. Erziehung, Sexualität und Medien um 1900* (Berlin: Suhrkamp, 2010).

19. Hermann Böhm, ed., *Karl Kraus contra ... : Die Prozeßakten der Kanzlei Oskar Samek in der Wiener Stadt- und Landesbibliothek*, 4 vols. (Vienna: Wiener Stadt- und Landesbibliothek, 1995–97).

20. Joachim Linder, "Deutsche Pitavalgeschichten in der Mitte des 19. Jahrhunderts: Konkurrierende Formen der Wissensvermittlung und der Verbrechensdeutung," in *Erzählte Kriminalität: Zur Typologie und Funktion von narrativen Darstellungen in Strafrechtspflege, Publizistik und Literatur zwischen 1770 und 1920*, ed. Jörg Schönert (Tübingen: Niemeyer, 1991), 313–348; Todd Herzog, *Crime Stories: Criminalistic Fantasy and the Culture of Crisis in Weimar Germany* (New York and Oxford: Berhgahn, 2009), 37–41.

21. Hugo Friedlaender, *Interessante Kriminal-Prozesse von kulturhistorischer Bedeutung: Darstellung merkwürdiger Strafrechtsfälle aus Gegenwart und Jüngstvergangenheit, nach eignenen Erlebnissen*, 12 vols. (Berlin: Hermann Barsdorf Verlag, then Berliner Buchversand, 1911–1921).

22. See Joachim Linder, "Außenseiter der Gesellschaft: Die Verbrechen der Gegenwart: Straftäter und Strafverfahren in einer literarischen Reihe der Weimarer Republik," *Kriminologisches Journal* 26 (1994), 190–227. Todd Herzog uses the series to develop the idea of a "modernist" case history in "Crime Stories: Criminal, Society, and the Modernist Case History," *Representations*, no. 80 (2002), 34–61.

23. The notion of the reciprocity of the case is developed most famously in André Jolles, *Einfache Formen: Legende, Sage, Mythe, Rätsel, Spruch, Kasus, Memorabile, Märchen, Witz* (Halle: Niemeyer, 1930), 171–199; now in English as *Simple Forms*, trans. Peter J. Schwartz (London: Verso, 2017), chap. 6. Interestingly, Jolles explores this reciprocity using an example of the rich popular journalism discussing court cases and criminal law to appear at the time, in this case an article of 1928 by "Balder" (probably the journalist Balder Olden) in the *Berliner Illustrirte Zeitung* (*Einfache Formen*, 173; *Simple Forms*, 139). See also the work of Fredric Jameson, who has long championed Jolles's book, e.g. *Brecht and Method*, 118–122; and Herzog, "Crime Stories," 39–40.

24. Most notably in *Die "Krise" der Weimarer Republik: Zur Kritik eines Deutungsmusters*, ed. Moritz Föllmer and Rüdiger Graf (Frankfurt a.M.: Campus, 2005).

25. On the "crisis of justice" in relation to the culture of the time, see Petersen, *Literatur und Justiz*, 15–75.

26. See Daniel Siemens, *Metropole und Verbrechen: Die Gerichtsreportage in Berlin, Paris und Chicago, 1919–1933* (Stuttgart: Franz Steiner, 2007).

27. After his death in 1928, a popular collection of Schlesinger's articles appeared as Sling, *Richter und Gerichtete* (Berlin: Ullstein, 1929). A more complete edition has recently been published: Sling (Paul Schlesinger), *Der Mensch, der schiesst: Berichte aus dem Gerichtssaal*, ed. Axel von Ernst (Düsseldorf: Lilienfeld, 2013).

28. See, for example, Kisch's collections *Kriminalistisches Reisebuch* (Berlin: Die Schmiede, 1927) and *Prager Pitaval* (Berlin: Erich Reiss, 1931).

29. *Berliner Tageblatt*, March 6, 1931, quoted in Gabriele Tergit, *Wer schießt aus Liebe? Gerichtsreportagen*, ed. Jens Brüning (Berlin: Das Neue Berlin, 1999), 6.

30. Alfred Döblin, *Die beiden Freundinnen und ihr Giftmord*, Außenseiter der Gesellschaft, vol. 1 (Berlin: Die Schmiede, 1924; repr. Düsseldorf: Artemis & Winkler, 2001). This is probably the volume of the series that has received most attention from scholars. See, for example, Walter Müller-Seidel, "Alfred Döblin, *Die beiden Freundinnen und ihr Giftmord*: Psychiatrie, Strafrecht und moderne Literatur," in *Literatur und Recht: Literarische Rechtsfälle von der Antike bis in die Gegenwart*, ed. Ulrich Mölk (Göttingen: Wallstein, 1996), 356–369; Hania Siebenpfeiffer, *"Böse Lust": Gewaltverbrechen in Diskursen der Weimarer Republik* (Cologne: Böhlau, 2005), 117–122; and Devin Fore, "Döblin's Epic: Sense, Document, and the Verbal World Picture," *New German Critique*, no. 99 (2006), 171–207.

31. Jürgen Stenzel, "Mit Kleister und Schere: Zur Handschrift von Berlin Alexanderplatz," *Text und Kritik*, no. 13/14 (1966), and Harald Jähner, *Erzählter, montierter, soufflierter Text: Zur Konstruktion des Romans "Berlin Alexanderplatz" von Alfred Döblin* (Frankfurt a.M.: Peter Lang, 1984).

32. Alfred Döblin, "An Romanautoren und ihre Kritiker (Berliner Programm, 1913)," in Döblin, *Schriften zu Ästhetik, Poetik und Literatur* (Frankfurt a.M.: Fischer, 2013), 119.

33. Alfred Döblin, "Bemerkungen zum Roman (1917)," in *Schriften zu Ästhetik, Poetik und Literatur*, 125.

34. Alfred Döblin, "Der Bau des epischen Werks (1928)," in

Schriften zu Ästhetik, Poetik und Literatur, 226.

35. Döblin, "Der Bau des epischen Werks," 229.

36. Döblin, "Bemerkungen zum Roman," 125.

37. "Der Dreigroschenprozeß," 463; "The *Threepenny* Lawsuit," 160.

38. "Der Dreigroschenprozeß," 460; "The *Threepenny* Lawsuit," 158.

39. "Der Dreigroschenprozeß," 500; "The *Threepenny* Lawsuit," 188 (trans. modified).

40. "Der Dreigroschenprozeß," 462–463; "The *Threepenny* Lawsuit," 159–160 (trans. modified).

41. On this, and copyright law generally, see Nesbit's classic essay "What Was an Author?," *Yale French Studies*, no. 73 (Fall 1987), 229–257, now reprinted in Nesbit, *Midnight—The Tempest Essays* (New York: Inventory Press, 2017). Steve Edwards engages critically with Nesbit's discussion in "'Beard Patentee': Daguerreotype Property and Authorship," *Oxford Art Journal* 36, no. 3 (2013).

42. "Der Dreigroschenprozeß," 503; "The *Threepenny* Lawsuit," 190.

43. "Der Dreigroschenprozeß," 493; "The *Threepenny* Lawsuit," 182.

44. "Der Dreigroschenprozeß," 492; "The *Threepenny* Lawsuit," 182.

45. As in, for example, the *Threepenny Novel*.

46. "Der Dreigroschenprozeß," 500; "The *Threepenny* Lawsuit," 188.

47. "Der Dreigroschenprozeß," 489–490; "The *Threepenny* Lawsuit," 180.

48. Peter Sloterdijk, *Critique of Cynical Reason*, trans. Michael Eldred (Minneapolis: University of Minnesota Press, 1987), 5. A reference to Sloterdijk might seem out of place in an argument situated within the terms of Critical Theory, but it is worth pointing out that his early work addressed issues of the public sphere with reference to the Frankfurt School: beyond the *Critique of Cynical Reason*, see Sloterdijk's first book: *Literatur und Lebenserfahrung: Autobiographien der Zwanziger Jahre* (Munich: Hanser, 1978), esp. 5–13.

49. Kracauer had published an extensive résumé of the trial in the *Frankfurter Zeitung* on November 9, 1930 that was supportive of Brecht's claims for artistic control; Brecht then used Kracauer's writings from a different article against him in the "*Threepenny Lawsuit*." See Kracauer, *Werke*, ed. Inke Mülder-Bach (Frankfurt a.M. and Berlin: Suhrkamp, 2004–2012), vol. 6, *Kleine Schriften zum Film*, pt. 2, 418–423 for Kracauer's résumé; Kracauer, "Asta Nielsen und die Filmbranche: Grundsätzliche Bermerkungen," *Werke*, vol. 6, pt. 2, 482–486 for the text used by Brecht in "Der Dreigroschenprozeß," 467, 459–460; "The *Threepenny* Lawsuit," 163, 165–166.

50. On these accusations and Brecht's self-confessed "fundamental laxness in questions of intellectual property," see, among other accounts, Stephen Parker, *Bertolt Brecht: A Literary Life* (London: Bloomsbury, 2014), 217, 247; and more recently *Laxheit in Fragen geistigen Eigentums: Brecht und Urheberrecht*, ed. Annett Gröschner and Christian Hippe (Berlin: Vebrecher Verlag, 2018).

51. "Der Dreigroschenprozeß," 459; "The *Threepenny* Lawsuit," 157 (trans. modified).

52. "Der Dreigroschenprozeß," 463; "The *Threepenny* Lawsuit," 160 (trans. modified).

53. "Der Dreigroschenprozeß," 513; "The *Threepenny* Lawsuit," 198–199.

54. Alfred Apfel, prominent defender of, among others, George Grosz, Max Hoelz, and Johannes R. Becher, wrote regularly in the *Weltbühne* as a way of influencing public opinion on the cases in which he was involved. See Apfel, *Hinter den Kulissen der deutschen Justiz: Erinnerungen eines deutschen Rechtsanwalts, 1882–1933*, trans. Jan and Ursla Gehlsen (Berlin: Berliner Wissenschaftsverlag, 2013), and the very helpful recent edition of Apfel's writings: *Alfred Apfel: Sein Schriftwerk. Autobiografien, Publikationen*, ed. Heinrich Schwing (Berlin: epubli, 2014).

55. The generally sympathetic critic Ludwig Marcuse had published a parody sketch of the *Threepenny* litigation in Stefan Großmann's journal *Das Tage-Buch* called "Brecht ist Brecht" (Brecht is Brecht), accusing Brecht of mercenary motives. When Brecht's lawyer Paul Casper responded in the journal with a denial, Marcuse published another article titled "Brecht ist doch nicht Brecht" (Brecht isn't Brecht after all). Brecht instigated legal measures against Marcuse, in the course of which the two agreed to drop the matter. See Brecht, *Werke*, vol.

21, *Schriften 1*, 779–780, and Marcuse's own account: "Der arme Bertolt Brecht und der weniger arme," in Marcuse, *Mein zwanzigstes Jahrhundert: Auf dem Wege zu einer Autobiographie* (Zurich: Diogenes, 1975), 132–136.

56. "Der Dreigroschenprozeß," 454; "The *Threepenny* Lawsuit," 153. Press reports confirm this: the *Film-Kurier* reported on October 18, 1930 as follows: "Toward 2.00 p.m. the onslaught of the press and spectators was so great that the lawyers had to request more room to move. A rope was used to separate the spectators from the principals of the trial." Repr. in *Photo: Casparius*, 202.

57. In *Literatur und Justiz*, Klaus Petersen discusses many examples of writers who were lawyers or familiar with legal culture.

58. For an extraordinary contemporary account of artistic labor that stresses the separation of the intellectual or artist from the "apparatus," see Peter Suhrkamp, "Kunst und Künstler," in *Deutsche Berufskunde: Ein Querschnitt durch die Berufe und Arbeitskreise der Gegenwart*, ed. Ottoheinz von der Gablentz and Carl Mennicke (Leipzig: Bibliographisches Institut, 1930). Suhrkamp was working closely with Brecht at the time of this publication, and his ideas there certainly reflect their discussions. The text should also be seen in the context of the well-known "Notes on the Opera *Rise and Fall of the City of Mahagonny*," which Suhrkamp co-wrote with Brecht: "Anmerkungen zur Oper 'Aufstieg und Fall der Stadt Mahagonny,'" Brecht, *Werke*, vol. 24, *Schriften 4*, 74–84; on Suhrkamp's co-authorship, 476; "Notes on the Opera *Rise and Fall of the City of Mahagonny*," *Brecht on Theatre*, third ed., ed. Marc Silberman, Steve Giles, and Tom Kuhn (London: Bloomsbury, 2015), 61–71. On *Deutsche Berufskunde* and the social epistemology of labor developed there, see my *Blind Spots: Critical Theory and the History of Art in Twentieth-Century Germany* (New Haven and London: Yale University Press, 2005), chap. 2, esp. 95–96.

59. The problem of a socially "free-floating intelligentsia" (*freischwebende Intelligenz*) is a crucial subtext in the works of the nineteenth- and twentieth-century avant-gardes. It emerged in the discussions around the "plight of the intellectual workers" (*die Not der geistigen Arbeiter*), the proletarianization of intellectual labor as universities and academies produced more graduates than could be absorbed into the traditional professions and institutions. More than any specific social space ("Bohemia," etc.), this situation unified literature, the arts, and potentially radical politics. For a classic statement of the problem, see Alfred Weber's *Die Not der geistigen Arbeiter* (Munich and Leipzig: Duncker und Humblot, 1923); an excerpt of this appears in translation in *The Weimar Republic Sourcebook*, ed. Anton Kaes, Martin Jay, and Edward Dimendberg (Berkeley and Los Angeles: University of California Press, 1994), 294–295. The idea of the free-floating intelligentsia was most famously taken up by Karl Mannheim, who turned the social contradiction into an epistemological advantage, seeing this group as tending toward immunity to ideologies. His mistake is to see the epistemological potential in isolation from the vacuum of social practice. See Mannheim, *Ideology and Utopia: An Introduction to the Sociology of Knowledge*, trans. Louis Wirth and Edward Shils (1930; New York: Harcourt, Brace & Company, 1936), esp. 136–146. Nikos Pegioudis reconsiders the history of the German avant-garde in the visual arts through the lens of the predicament of intellectual labor in *Artists and Radicalism in Germany, 1890–1933: Reform, Politics and the Paradoxes of the Avant-Garde* (London: Bloomsbury Publishing, forthcoming).

60. Werner Mittenzwei, *Das Leben des Bertolt Brecht, oder Der Umgang mit den Welträtseln*, second ed. (Frankfurt a.M.: Suhrkamp, 1989), vol. 1, 493–494.

61. Anke te Heesen, *The Newspaper Clipping: A Modern Paper Object*, trans. Lori Lantz (Manchester: Manchester University Press, 2014).

62. On the scrapbooking tradition, here in the American context, see Ellen Gruber Garvey, *Writing with Scissors: American Scrapbooks from the Civil War to the Harlem Renaissance* (Oxford: Oxford University Press, 2012).

63. *Tagebuch einer Verlorenen: Von einer Toten*, ed. Margarete Böhme (Berlin: F. Fontane, 1905).

64. The controversy over the book is discussed in Arno Bammé, *Margarete Böhme: Die Erfolgsschriftstellerin aus Husum*

(Munich: Profil Verlag, 1994), 16–36.

65. The theatre production by Wolf von Metz-Schillbach premiered, after difficulties with the censor, in 1907. The screen adaptations were directed by Richard Oswald (1918, with Ema Morena and Conrad Veidt) and Pabst (1929, screenplay by Rudolf Leonhardt (not Leonhard)): Bammé, *Margarete Böhme*, 48. There was apparently an earlier screen version from 1912: see https://de.wikipedia.org/wiki/Tagebuch_einer_Verlorenen_(1929) (accessed February 6, 2018).

66. *Tagebuch einer männlichen Braut: Die Geschichte eines Doppelwesens. Bearbeitet von Walter Homann* (Berlin: D. Dreyer & Co., 1907; repr. Hamburg: Männerschwarm Verlag, 2010). There is an extensive and almost entirely unexplored quasi-documentary literature of such cases, by or about those falsely accused or convicted of crimes, suffering at the hands of the medical profession, or involuntarily committed to insane asylums, and it is central to the culture of the case. The often fictional diaries of the kind discussed here drew upon this larger culture and ultimately became a part of it. The only discussion of the genre I have found focusses specifically on the issue of involuntary psychiatric institutionalization and offers insight into the role of such publications in the public sphere: Anne Goldberg, "A Reinvented Public: 'Lunatics' Rights' and Bourgeois Populism in the Kaiserreich," *German History* 21 (2003), 159–182.

67. *Vom Leben getötet: Bekenntnisse eines Kindes. Herausgegeben von M.I. Breme* (Freiburg i.B.: Herder & Co., 1927). This case was covered extensively be court reporters such as Gabriele Tergit; see Tergit, *Wer Schießt aus Liebe?*, 70–79, 85–90. More recent discussions include Daniel Siemens, "'Vom Leben getötet': Die Gerichtsreportage in der liberaldemokratischen Presse im Berlin der 1920er Jahre," in *Ordnungen in der Krise: Zur politischen Kulturgeschichte Deutschlands 1900–1933*, ed. Wolfgang Hardtwig (Munich: Oldenbourg, 2007), 327–354; and Heidi Sack, *Moderne Jugend vor Gericht: Sensationsprozesse, "Sexualtragödien" und die Krise der Jugend in der Weimarer Republik* (Bielefeld: Transcript, 2016), 325–366.

68. *Vom Leben getötet* (1927, dir. Franz Hofer, with Eva Speyer, Ernst Rückert, and Gerdi Gerdt).

69. On melodrama, the female mass-market audience, and women's modernity in early twentieth-century Germany, see Patrice Petro, *Joyless Streets: Women and Melodramatic Representation in Weimar Germany* (Princeton: Princeton University Press, 1989). Also relevant here is Miriam Hansen, "Early Silent Cinema: Whose Public Sphere?," *New German Critique*, no. 29 (1983), 147–184.

70. See Cornelia Vismann, *Akten: Medientechnik und Recht* (Frankfurt a.M.: Fischer, 2000), and the slightly abridged English edition: *Files: Law and Media Technology*, trans. Geoffrey Winthrop-Young (Stanford: Stanford University Press, 2008).

71. On pre-printed forms, see Lisa Gitelman, *Paper Knowledge: Toward a Media History of Documents* (Durham: Duke University Press, 2014), chap. 1.

72. *I, Pierre Rivière, having slaughtered my mother, my sister, and my brother ... A Case of Parricide in the 19th Century*, ed. Michel Foucault, trans. Frank Jellinek (New York: Pantheon, 1975), x–xi.

73. See, for example, the judge's nervous breakdown in the final chapter of Ernst Ottwalt, *Denn sie wissen, was sie tun: Ein deutscher Justiz-Roman* (Berlin: Malik-Verlag, 1931). For its wide-ranging exploration of German legal culture, famous cases, and the practical and theoretical problems of legal positivism, Klaus Petersen considers the book "the most significant work of contemporary critique of justice in the literature of the Weimar period" and suggests that it represents a fictionalization of another important work: Ernst Fraenkel, *Zur Soziologie der Klassenjustiz* (Berlin: E. Laub, 1927). Petersen, *Literatur und Justiz*, 159–161. Ottwalt (actually Ernst Gottwalt Nicolas) worked closely with Brecht at the time, as one of the authors' collective of the film *Kuhle Wampe* along with Slatan Dudow and Hanns Eisler.

74. Theodor Lessing, *Haarmann: Die Geschichte eines Werwolfs*, Außenseiter der Gesellschaft, vol. 6 (Berlin: Die Schmiede, 1925; repr. Munich: Rogner & Bernhard, 1973), 217.

75. On the notion of "remediation in reverse," see Andreas Huyssen, *Miniature Metropolis: Literature in an Age*

of Photography and Film (Cambridge, MA: Harvard University Press, 2015), esp. 7–10.

76. Sigfried Kracauer, "Ein soziologisches Experiment? Zu Bert Brechts Versuch: Der Dreigroschenprozeß," *Frankfurter Zeitung*, February 28, 1932, repr. in Kracauer, *Werke*, vol. 5, *Essays, Feuilletons, Rezensionen*, pt. 4, 48–49.

77. Tergit, *Wer schießt aus Liebe?*, 6 (emphasis added).

78. Oskar Negt and Alexander Kluge, *Öffentlichkeit und Erfahrung: Zur Organisationsanalyse von bürgerlicher und proletarischer Öffentlichkeit* (Frankfurt a.M.: Suhrkamp, 1972), 20–28; trans. as *Public Sphere and Experience: Toward an Analysis of the Bourgeois and Proletarian Public Sphere*, trans. Peter Labanyi et al. (Minneapolis: University of Minnesota Press, 1993), 1–8.

79. "[S]innlich faßbare Solidarität": *Öffentlichkeit und Erfahrung*, 75; *Public Sphere and Experience*, 38 (trans. modified).

80. *Kuhle Wampe oder Wem gehört die Welt* (1932, dir. Slatan Dudow, screenplay Bertolt Brecht and Ernst Ottwalt, music Hanns Eisler).

81. Bertolt Brecht, *Kuhle Wampe: Protokoll des Films und Materialien*, ed. Wolfgang Gersch and Werner Hecht (Frankfurt a.M.: Suhrkamp, 1969), 23–25 (shots 122–135); "Kuhle Wampe or Who Owns the World?" in *Bertolt Brecht on Film and Radio*, 220–222 (trans. modified).

82. From the first decision: "At the beginning of the third act, a judge appears in close-up. Fully uninterested and mechanically, he delivers three eviction orders against the families of the unemployed in a droning fashion." "The lethargic, mechanical way in which the judge reads out the eviction orders in quick tempo" was seen to make the impression that "the state offers no protection for the unemployed and acts without concern or understanding." *Kuhle Wampe*, 104, 111. The censors' reports found that this represented an "attack on the institutions of justice" and an "insult to the judiciary." *Kuhle Wampe*, 114, 125.

83. *Kuhle Wampe*, 125.

84. *Kuhle Wampe*, 60–61 (shots 400–412); "Kuhle Wampe," 243–244 (trans. modified). On Brecht and the Red Megaphone, see Richard Bodek, *Proletarian Performance in Weimar Berlin: Agitprop, Chorus, and Brecht* (Columbia, SC: Camden House, 1997), chaps. 4 and 5; on the Red Megaphone more generally, the extensive material in *Deutsches Arbeitertheater, 1918–1933: Eine Dokumentation*, ed. Ludwig Hoffmann and Daniel Hoffmann-Ostwald (Berlin: Henschelverlag, 1961).

85. A detailed study in English is Chris Bowlby, "Blutmai 1929: Police, Parties and Proletarians in a Berlin Confrontation," *The Historical Journal* 29, no. 1 (1986), 137–158.

86. From the first decision of March 31, 1932; *Kuhle Wampe*, 109.

87. Cornelia Vismann, *Medien der Rechtsprechung*, ed. Alexandra Kemmerer and Markus Krajewski (Frankfurt a.M.: S. Fischer, 2011).

88. Vismann, *Medien der Rechtsprechung*, 161.

89. On the learning plays, see Reiner Steinweg, *Das Lehrstück: Brechts Theorie einer politisch-ästhetischen Erziehung* (Stuttgart: Metzler, 1972); *Brechts Modell der Lehrstücke: Zeugnisse, Diskussion, Erfahrungen*, ed. Reiner Steinweg (Frankfurt a.M.: Suhrkamp, 1976); in English, Roswitha Mueller, "Learning for a New Society: The *Lehrstück*," in *The Cambridge Companion to Brecht*, 101–117.

90. On the *Lehrstück* as a specific theatrical response to an age of political emergency, see Marie-Luise Knott, "Die Mut barbarisieren: Bertolt Brechts Zeit der Lehrstücke," in Knott, *Dazwischenzeiten: 1930. Wege in der Erschöpfung der Moderne* (Berlin: Matthes & Seitz, 2017).

91. Bertolt Brecht, *Der Neinsager*, in *Werke*, vol. 3, *Stücke 3*, 71; *He who says No*, trans. Wolfgang Sauerlander, in Brecht, *The Measures Taken and other Lehrstücke* (London: Methuen, 1977), 78.

92. *Der Neinsager*, 71; *He who says No*, 78–79.

93. Brecht, *Die Maßnahme*, in *Werke*, vol. 3, *Stücke 3*, 101; *The Measures Taken*, in Brecht, *The Measures Taken and other Lehrstücke*, 9.

94. Brecht, *Die Maßnahme*, 124; *The Measures Taken*, 33 (trans. modified).

95. Brecht, *Die Maßnahme*, 124; *The Measures Taken*, 34 (trans. modified).

96. A good summary account is Roswitha Mueller, *Bertolt Brecht and the Theory of Media* (Lincoln: University of Nebraska Press, 1989).

97. The former question is the subtitle of the film: *Kuhle Wampe, oder Wem gehört die Welt?* The latter is posed in the final scene: "Who will change it [the world]?" (Wer wird sie ändern?) The answer

is "Those who are not satisfied with it!" (Die, denen sie nicht gefällt!).

98. *Die Bibliothek Bertolt Brechts: Ein kommentiertes Verzeichnis*, ed. Erdmut Wizisla et al. (Frankfurt a.M.: Suhrkamp, 2007), 401–404 (nos. 2818, 2821–2824, 2828, 2835).

99. Wekwerth, *Notate*, 144.

100. Walter Benjamin, "What is the Epic Theater? (II)," in Benjamin, *Selected Writings*, vol. 4 (Cambridge, MA: Belknap Press, 2003), 305.

101. On the problematic of *Ausdruck* and its wide ramifications, see my *Blind Spots*, chap. 4, and more recently Matthew Vollgraff's ambitious study: "The Science of Expression: *Ausdruckskunde* and Bodily Knowledge in German Modernist Culture" (PhD diss., Princeton University, 2018).

102. His ideas are perhaps best summed up in an untitled poem from the time of the learning plays: "Working with particular gestures / Can change your character / Change it. / When your feet are higher than your bottom / Then your speech will be different, and the manner of your speech / Will change your thoughts. / A certain vigorous / Movement of the hand, with the back facing downwards and / The upper arm against the body, will convince / Not only others, but also you who make the gesture / Leafing back through when reading, the sketching of a design." *The Collected Poems of Bertolt Brecht*, ed. and trans. Tom Kuhn and David Constantine (New York: Liveright, 2019), 480.

103. This is a necessarily foreshortened summary of a complex aspect of Brecht's theatre. See, among other accounts, "Dialektisches Theater," in Jan Knopf, *Brecht-Handbuch: Theater. Eine Ästhetik der Widersprüche* (Stuttgart: Metzler, 1996), 392–394; Fredric Jameson, *Brecht and Method* (London: Verso, 1998), 89–130; and Brigid Doherty, "Test and *Gestus* in Brecht and Benjamin," *MLN* 115, no. 3 (2000), 442–481.

104. James K. Lyon, *Bertolt Brecht in America* (Princeton: Princeton University Press, 1980), 326–327.

105. *Life*, October 30, 1947, 50: "SMOKE SCREEN is thrown up by cigar of German-born Writer Berthold [*sic*] Brecht, an acquaintance of Communist Gerhard Eisler. His thick accent mystified the committee, which excused him after he denied being a party member."

106. Lyon, *Bertolt Brecht in America*, 334.

107. Werner Hecht, *Brecht Chronik, 1898–1956* (Frankfurt a.M.: Suhrkamp, 1997), 796.

108. Hans-Dietrich Sander, "*Die Maßnahme*, rechtsphilosophisch betrachtet: Carl Schmitt—Karl Korsch—Bertolt Brecht," *Deutsche Studien* 17 (1979), 135–154; Nikolaus Müller-Schöll, "Der Eingriff ins Politische: Bert Brecht, Carl Schmitt und die Diktatur auf der Bühne," *Brecht-Jahrbuch* 23 (1997), 113–117; Müller-Schöll, "'Wichtig zu lernen vor allem ist Einverstandnis': Brecht zwischen Kafka und Carl Schmitt," *MLN* 119 (2004), 506–524; Eva Horn, "Die Regel der Ausnahme: Revolutionäre Souveränität und bloßes Leben in Brechts *Maßnahme*," *Deutsche Vierteljahrsschrift für Literaturwissenschaft und Geistesgeschichte* 75, no. 4 (2001), 680–709.

109. Walter Benjamin, *Gesammelte Schriften*, ed. Rolf Tiedemann and Hermann Schweppenhäuser (Frankfurt a.M.: Suhrkamp, 1972–1979), vol. 2, 1372.

110. Carl Schmitt, *Political Theology: Four Chapters on the Concept of Sovereignty* (1922), trans. George Schwab (Chicago: University of Chicago Press, 2005), 5.

111. Walter Benjamin, *The Origin of German Tragic Drama*, trans. John Osborne (London: New Left Books, 1977), 35.

112. Carl Schmitt, *Gesetz und Urteil: Eine Untersuchung zum Problem der Rechtspraxis* (1912; second ed. Munich: C. H. Beck, 1969).

113. Carl Schmitt, *The Concept of the Political* (1927), trans. George Schwab (Chicago: University of Chicago Press, 1996), 26–27.

114. Brecht, *Die Maßnahme*, 104–105; *The Measures Taken*, 13 (trans. modified).

115. Bertolt Brecht, *Die Maßnahme: Kritische Ausgabe mit einer Spielanleitung*, ed. Reiner Steinweg (Frankfurt a.M.: Suhrkamp, 1971), fifth version of 1934/35, 100.

116. Brecht, *Die Maßnahme*, 95; Brecht, *The Measures Taken*, 31 (trans. modified).

117. The most compelling account of Brecht's *Lehrstücke* as an attempt to learn conduct in a state of exception is Knott, "Die Mut barbarisieren." But see also Horn, "Die Regel der Ausnahme," and Eva Horn, "Actors/Agents: Bertolt Brecht and the Politics of Secrecy," *Grey Room*, no. 24 (2006). Sustained scholarly consideration of Brecht's relation to Schmitt is relatively recent, as the political valences of the learning plays

had long been considered in terms of allegiance to the Communist Party during the 1930s and (somewhat anachronistically) Brecht's ambivalent response to the Moscow show trials. The link to the culture of the case and to the rise of tribunalization is, I am arguing, a somewhat different one with a longer history.

118. Walter Benjamin, "On the Concept of History," in Benjamin, *Selected Writings*, vol. 4, *1938–1940*, ed. Michael W. Jennings (Cambridge, MA: Harvard University Press, 2003), 392.

119. Helmut Lethen has discussed this in relation to Brecht and Jünger in an essay originally published in 1984: "Zwei Barbaren: Über einige Denkmotive von Ernst Jünger und Bertolt Brecht in der Weimarer Republik," in Lethen, *Unheimliche Nachbarschaften: Essays zum Kälte-Kult und der Schlaflosigkeit der Philosophischen Anthropologie im 20. Jahrhundert* (Freiburg i.B.: Rombach Verlag, 2009). But the issue is older and centers on the delayed and problematic attention to Benjamin's closeness to Schmitt and the perceived attempt on the part of Benjamin's editors to play down the importance of an admiring letter to Schmitt of 1930. The first scholar to explore this in depth was Jacob Taubes in the late 1970s, and his correspondence is now available in English: Taubes, *To Carl Schmitt: Letters and Reflections*, trans. Keith Tribe (New York: Columbia University Press, 2013). Since then, this has been addressed by others. See esp. Samuel Weber, "Taking Exception to Decision: Walter Benjamin and Carl Schmitt," *diacritics* 22 (1992), 5–18; Horst Bredekamp, "From Walter Benjamin to Carl Schmitt, via Thomas Hobbes," *Critical Inquiry* 25, no. 2 (1999), 247–266; Bredekamp, "Walter Benjamin's Esteem for Carl Schmitt," in *The Oxford Handbook of Carl Schmitt*, ed. Jens Meierhenrich and Oliver Simons (Oxford: Oxford University Press, 2017).

120. Carl Schmitt, *Glossarium. Aufzeichnungen der Jahre 1947–1951*, ed. Eberhard Freiherr von Medem (Berlin: Duncker & Humblot, 1991), 300 (note of May 5, 1950). For Schmitt's marginal note, see Hans-Dietrich Sander, "*Die Maßnahme*, rechtsphilosophisch betrachtet," 151; and Horn, "Die Regel der Ausnahme," 698.

121. Reinhard Mehring, *Carl Schmitt: A Biography* (Cambridge: Polity, 2014), 219–220.

122. Dietrich Neumann, "The House that Mies Built," *The Berlin Journal* 25 (2013), 15.

123. Carl Schmitt, "Die Zeitalter der Neutralisierungen und Entpolitisierungen" (1929), repr. in Carl Schmitt, *Das Begriff des Politischen*, ninth ed. (Berlin: Duncker & Humblot, 2015), 84.

124. Schmitt, "Die Zeitalter der Neutralisierungen," 86.

125. Carl Schmitt, *Ex Captivitate Salus: Experiences, 1945–47*, ed. Andreas Kalyvas and Federico Finchelstein, trans. Matthew Hannah (Cambridge: Polity, 2017), 48.

126. Ernst Jünger, "Über die Gefahr," in *Der gefährliche Augenblick: Eine Sammlung von Bildern und Berichten mit einer Einleitung von Ernst Jünger*, ed. Ferdinand Bucholtz (Berlin: Junker und Dünnhaupt, 1931), 11–16; trans. by Donald Reneau as "On Danger," *New German Critique*, no. 59 (1993), 27–32.

127. Benjamin, "On the Concept of History," 390.

128. Benjamin, "On the Concept of History," 391.

129. On their initial contact, see Mehring, *Carl Schmitt*, 227–230.

130. Benjamin's notes on Schmitt's essay, which he read in quotations in an essay by Karl Löwith, are reprinted in Benjamin, *Gesammelte Schriften*, vol. 7, 673.

131. On the history of the questionnaire, see Robert H. Gault, "A History of the Questionnaire Method of Research in Psychology," *The Pedagogical Seminary* 14, no. 3 (1907), 366–383.

132. Karl Plättner, *Eros im Zuchthaus* (Berlin: Mopr-Verlag, 1929).

133. A typical question: "Which of the pedagogical tendencies in *Die Maßnahme* do you object to for political reasons?" See Brecht, *Werke*, vol. 3, 441; *Brecht-Handbuch*, vol. 4, 74; Roswitha Mueller, "Learning for a New Society," *Cambridge Companion to Brecht*, second ed., 112; Brecht, *Die Maßnahme: Kritische Ausgabe*, 238.

134. While the literature on denazification is extensive, that on the questionnaire itself is sparse. See now Mikkel Dack, "Questioning the Past: The Fragebogen and Everyday Denazification in Occupied Germany" (PhD diss., University of Calgary, 2016).

135. Schmitt, *Ex Captivitate Salus*, 13. The questionnaire was, in this case, not from the Allied governments but from the University of Berlin. As an early denazification measure,

those who had taught there were required to complete the questionnaire as part of their reapplications for positions held prior to the defeat. Spranger was the first postwar rector of the University. See Mehring, *Carl Schmitt*, 408–409.

136. Ernst von Salomon, *Der Fragebogen* (1951; repr. Reinbek: Rowohlt, 1961).

137. See the preface by Goronwy Rees to von Salomon, *Fragebogen (The Questionnaire)*, trans. Constantine Fitzgibbon (Garden City, NY: Doubleday, 1955).

138. Arnolt Bronnen, *Arnolt Bronnen gibt zu Protokoll: Beiträge zur Geschichte des modernen Schriftstellers* (1954; repr. Kronberg i.T.: Athenäum, 1978).

139. Zelda Popkin, *Small Victory* (1947); Stig Dagerman, *Tysk höst* (1947); and John Dos Passos, "Land of the Fragebogen" (1946), all quoted in Werner Sollors, "'Everybody gets Fragebogened sooner or later': The Denazification Questionnaire as Cultural Text," *German Life and Letters* 71 (2018), 147.

140. Mikkel Dack, "Retreating into Trauma: The Fragebogen, Denazification, and Victimhood in Postwar Germany," in *Traumatic Memories of the Second World War and After*, ed. Peter Leese and Jason Crouthamel (Basingstoke: Palgrave Macmillan, 2016), 143–170; also Gregor Streim, "Germans in the *Lager*: Reports and Narratives about Imprisonment in Post-War Allied Internment Camps," in *A Nation of Victims? Representations of German Wartime Suffering from 1945 to the Present*, ed. Helmut Schmitz, *German Monitor* 67 (2007), 31–49.

141. Mikhail Bakunin, "Confessions to Tsar Nicholas I," *Bakunin on Anarchy: Selected Works by the Activist-Founder of World Anarchism*, ed. and trans. Sam Dolgoff (New York: Vintage Books, 1971), 69. Bakunin wrote this while in prison in 1851. See also Bakunin's letter of 1870 to Albert Richard: "If Paris itself stages a successful uprising, it would then have the obligation and the right to call for solidarity in the complete political, juridical, financial, and administrative liquidation of the State, and of political and privately owned or controlled (but not strictly) personal property; the demolition of all the functions, services, and powers of the State; the public burning of all public and private legal documents and records. Paris will immediately and to the greatest possible extent organize itself in a revolutionary manner." *Bakunin on Anarchy*, 179.

142. Elias Canetti, *The Torch in my Ear*, in *The Memoirs of Elias Canetti*, trans. Joachim Neugroschel (New York: Farrar, Straus and Giroux, 1999), 485.

143. See Gerald Stieg, *Frucht des Feuers: Canetti, Doderer, Kraus und der Justizpalastbrand* (Vienna: Edition Falter, 1990).

144. Benjamin, "On the Concept of History," 395.

145. Howard Eiland and Michael W. Jennings, *Walter Benjamin: A Critical Life* (Cambridge, MA: Belknap Press of Harvard University Press, 2014), 281–282.

Conclusion

1. Carl Schmitt, "Song of the 60-Year-Old," dated June 11, 1948. In Schmitt, *Ex Captivitate Salus: Experiences, 1945–47*, ed. Andreas Kalyvas and Federico Finchelstein, trans. Matthew Hannah (Cambridge: Polity, 2017), 73.

2. Oskar Negt and Alexander Kluge, *Public Sphere and Experience: Toward an Analysis of the Bourgeois and Proletarian Public Sphere*, trans. Peter Labanyi, Jamie Owen Daniel, and Assenka Oksiloff (Minneapolis: University of Minnesota Press, 1993), chap. 1.

3. Bertolt Brecht, *Werke: Große kommentierte Berliner und Frankfurter Ausgabe*, ed. Werner Hecht, Jan Knopf, Werner Mittenzwei, and Klaus-Detlef Müller (Berlin and Weimar: Aufbau, and Frankfurt a.M.: Suhrkamp, 1988–2000), vol. 21, *Schriften 1*, 464; Brecht, "The *Threepenny* Lawsuit," in *Bertolt Brecht on Film and Radio*, ed. and trans. Marc Silberman (London: Methuen, 2000), 161.

4. See Molly Nesbit, "What Was an Author?," *Yale French Studies*, no. 73 (Fall 1987), 229–257, now reprinted in Nesbit, *Midnight—The Tempest Essays* (New York: Inventory Press, 2017). I discuss the development of architecture and design in early twentieth-century Germany in the light of changes in patent, copyright, and trademark law in *The Werkbund: Design Theory and Mass Culture before the First World War* (New Haven and London: Yale University Press, 1996) and "Utopia for Sale: The Bauhaus and Weimar Germany's Consumer Culture," in Kathleen James-Chakraborty, ed., *Bauhaus Culture: From Weimar to the Cold War* (Minneapolis: University of Minnesota Press, 2006).

5. Negt and Kluge, *Public Sphere and Experience*, xliii (trans. modified).

Index

Page numbers in *italics* refer to illustrations.

Publication of this book has been aided by a grant from the Millard Meiss Publication Fund of CAA.

The MIT Press would like to thank the anonymous peer reviewers who provided comments on drafts of this book. The generous work of academic experts is essential for establishing the authority and quality of our publications. We acknowledge with gratitude the contributions of these otherwise uncredited readers.

This book was set in Haultin by Jen Jackowitz. Printed and bound in Canada.

Library of Congress Cataloging-in-Publication Data

Names: Schwartz, Frederic J., 1963– author.
Title: The culture of the case : madness, crime, and justice in modern German art / Frederic J. Schwartz.
Description: Cambridge, Massachusetts : The MIT Press, [2023] | Includes bibliographical references and index.
Identifiers: LCCN 2022017781 | ISBN 9780262047708 (hardcover)
Subjects: LCSH: Art and society—Germany—History—20th century. | Art and society—Austria—History—20th century. | Crime in art. | Art, German--20th century—Themes, motives. | Art, Austrian—20th century—Themes, motives.
Classification: LCC N72.S6 S3425 2023 | DDC 700.943—dc23/eng /20221121
LC record available at https://lccn.loc.gov/2022017781

10 9 8 7 6 5 4 3 2 1

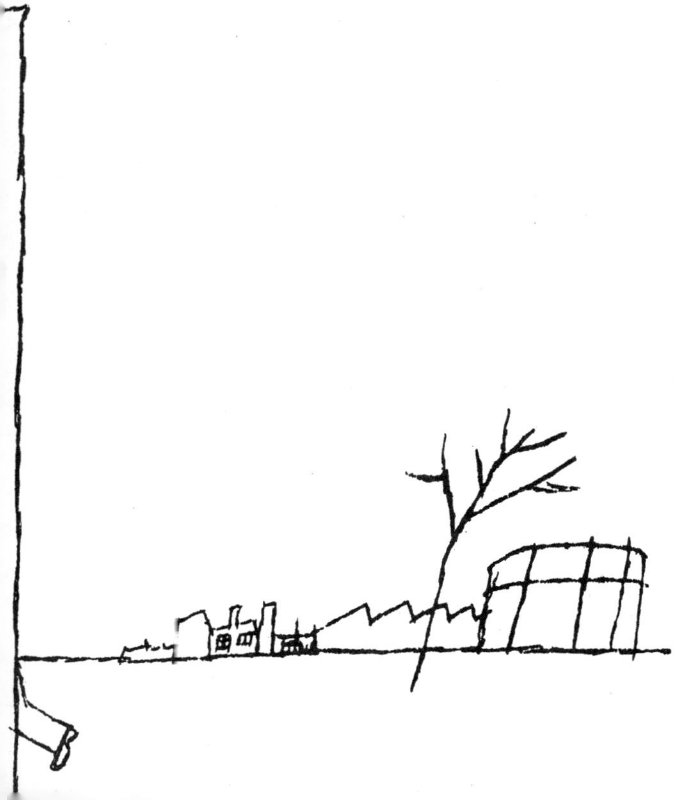